Nelson
MANDELA

The Past is Another Country
The First Dance of Freedom
In the Name of Apartheid
South Africa's New Era

Nelson
MANDELA
A BIOGRAPHY

Martin Meredith

St. Martin's Press ❧ New York

For T

A THOMAS DUNNE BOOK.
An imprint of St. Martin's Press.

NELSON MANDELA: A BIOGRAPHY. Copyright © 1997 by
Martin Meredith. All rights reserved. Printed in the United
States of America. No part of this book may be used or
reproduced in any manner whatsoever without written
permission except in the case of brief quotations embodied
in critical articles or reviews. For information, address
St. Martin's Press, 175 Fifth Avenue, New York, N.Y. 10010.

Grateful acknowledgement is made to Little, Brown & Co.
for permission to reprint extracts from *Long Walk to
Freedom* by Nelson Mandela (copyright © 1994 by Nelson
Rolihlahla Mandela); and to the Alan Paton Trust for
permission to quote an extract from *Cry, the Beloved
Country* by Alan Paton (copyright © 1948 by Alan Paton).

ISBN 0-312-18132-9

First published in Great Britain by the Penguin Group

First U.S. Edition: February 1998

10 9 8 7 6 5 4 3 2 1

CONTENTS

LIST OF ILLUSTRATIONS

ACKNOWLEDGEMENTS

In the years that I have been writing about South Africa, as a journalist and as an author, I have encountered much generosity and goodwill. Many people on many occasions have given me valued help and assistance and shown great hospitality. For all the acts of kindness I have received, I am profoundly grateful. I would like here to record my thanks in particular to Nelson Mandela and to his friends and colleagues who were so forthcoming about him. I am especially grateful to Walter Sisulu, and to Beryl Baker, Fikile Bam, Mary Benson, Hilda Bernstein, Rusty Bernstein, George Bizos, Nat Bregman, Amina Cachalia, Yusuf Cachalia, Ruth Fischer, Bob Hepple, Rica Hodgson, Joel Joffe, Adelaide Joseph, Paul Joseph, Kathy Kathrada, Wolfie Kodesh, Mac Maharaj, Govan Mbeki, Godfrey Pitje, Lazar Sidelsky, Joe Slovo, Ben Turok and Harold Wolpe. My thanks are also due to librarians at the William Cullen Library and Jan Smuts House Library, University of the Witwatersrand, at *The Star*, Johannesburg, and at Queen Elizabeth House, University of Oxford. I am also grateful to Penny Hoare, for her early encouragement of the work; to Christina Hardyment, Heidi Holland, Felicity Bryan, Kate Jones and Antonia Till; and to Rachel Whitehead, for providing the rural retreat where this book was written.

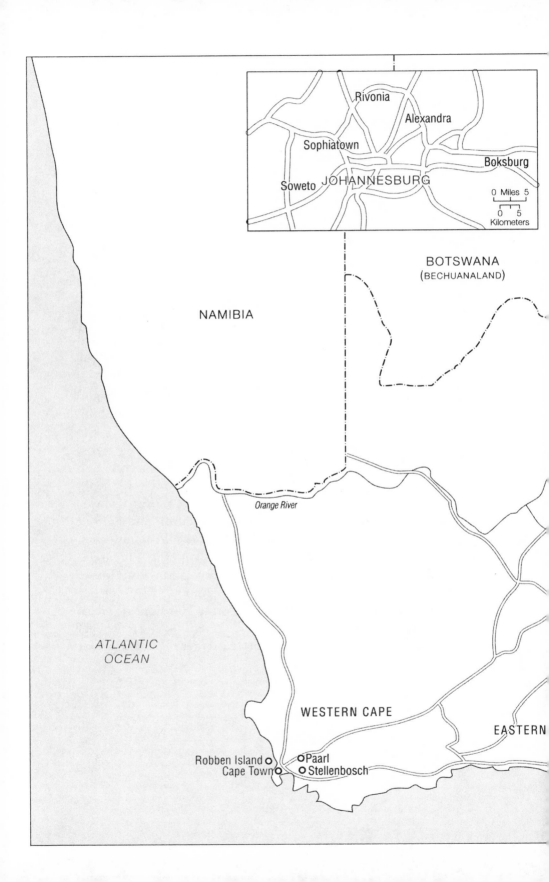

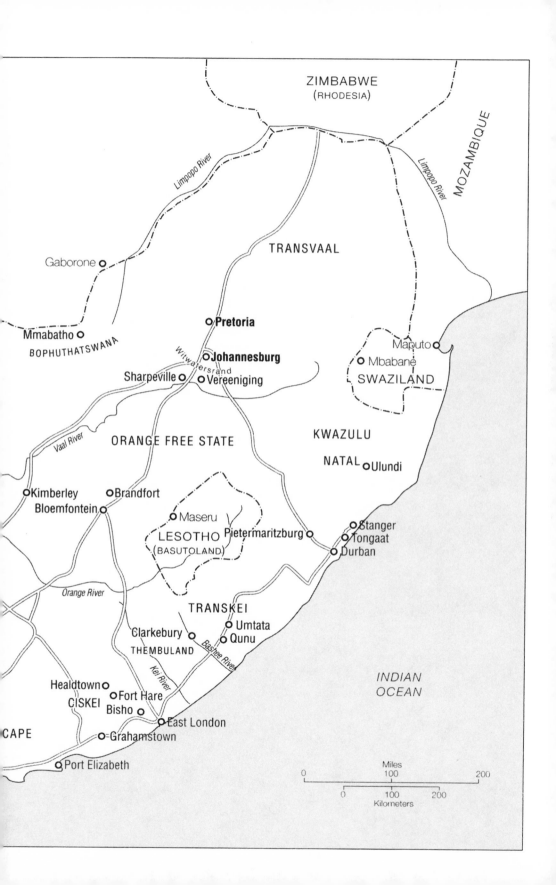

PROLOGUE

During his years of imprisonment, Nelson Mandela often dreamed of returning to the village of Qunu in the Transkei, longing to see again the green rolling hills where he had spent his boyhood. After his release from prison, he decided to build a house in Qunu, intending to retire there once his term of office as president of South Africa had ended. 'It becomes important, the older you get, to return to places where you have wonderful recollections,' he told a visitor after taking one of his customary early-morning walks across the hills. 'This is really home.' The house he built in Qunu stands now on a hillside, a modern red-brick residence making a marked contrast to the thatch-roofed huts of the village around it. But what is most striking about it is the design. It is an exact replica of the prison warder's house in which Mandela spent the last year of his twenty-seven years of imprisonment.

Even to his closest friends, Mandela is at times an enigma. Prison colleagues who were his companions for years on end sometimes felt they did not really know him. He emerged from prison an intensely private person, accustomed to concealing his emotions behind a mask. He confides in few people. He dislikes familiarity. The grip of self-control he acquired in prison rarely leaves him. His habits remain austere. He does not drink or smoke and never swears. At the state residences he occupies, in Cape Town and Pretoria, his housekeepers are well versed in his liking for neatness and order. As president, he has continued to make his own bed.

Yet prison life did not rob him of either his charm or his civility. The radiance of his smile is undiminished. He possesses a natural authority and charisma, evident to all who encounter him. Despite his patrician nature, he retains the common touch. His manners are punctilious, reminiscent of another, more gracious age. He remains courteous and attentive to individuals, whatever their status or age, often stopping to talk with genuine interest to children or youths. He greets workers and tycoons with the same politeness. Indeed, he sometimes seems more at ease with strangers than in the company of friends.

As president, he has managed not only to sustain his popularity among the black population he fought to liberate from white rule but to gain the respect and admiration of the white community which once reviled him. His efforts to overcome the deep racial divisions afflicting South Africa have earned him universal acclaim. Outwardly, few signs of the titanic struggle for possession of South Africa are evident. As a mark of his standing, the name by which he has become affectionately known, by black and white alike, is Madiba, his clan name dating from an eighteenth-century chief. National sporting victories in rugby, soccer and cricket have sometimes been attributed to 'Madiba magic', the effect of his presence among the spectators. Mandela enjoys the fame, but remains unmoved by it and has become increasingly conscious of the gap between his public image and the ordinary man he feels himself to be.

His nature is not always benign. He is feared as well as revered. He tends to be autocratic. At times he has wielded his massive authority unwisely. In his old age he has been known to act as impetuously as in the days of his youth. He is still renowned on occasion for his stubbornness and quick temper. His face sometimes settles into an inscrutable, sphinx-like stare, the lines and furrows on it marking his displeasure.

Despite the ailments of old age, he has brought to his years as president remarkable energy, as if anxious to make up for lost time. Approaching his eightieth year, he usually rises before dawn, relishing the prospect of an early-morning walk, devouring newspapers and telephoning colleagues long before the normal working day has begun. Amid an endless stream of meetings, speeches and official functions, he nevertheless ensures he has time to respond to individual requests, readily accepting invitations from schoolchildren and from ordinary citizens, telephoning strangers when the occasion arises and making himself available for snapshots.

But while enjoying contact with common people, the company to which he is most attracted is that of the rich and famous; status impresses him.

The relentless pace he has set himself has taken its toll. He succumbs occasionally to bouts of exhaustion. Constant plane travel has exacerbated a hearing problem. His ankles are perennially swollen. He walks with an increasingly stiff gait. The eye affliction he acquired from years of working in the harsh glare of the lime quarry on Robben Island gives him chronic trouble. The burdens of office sometimes seem too onerous. 'One gets used to it, but it destroys your family life. I miss children – just being able to be with children at the end of the day and listen to them chatter.'

His private life has been plagued by difficulty and disaster. Upon his release from prison, he had hoped above all else to re-establish a family home. But the wayward conduct of his wife, Winnie, her criminal activities and flagrant infidelity all blighted his late years of freedom. At the height of his popularity and fame, Mandela was a lonely figure, often spending his evenings alone.

Then, in his late seventies, his close friends noticed he had taken on 'a new lease of life'. An attachment he formed with Graca Machel, the widow of a former president of neighbouring Mozambique, a charming and strong-willed political leader with her own revolutionary credentials, blossomed into love. On a spring afternoon in 1996, they declared their affair in public by wandering hand-in-hand through the leafy suburb of Johannesburg where Mandela lives, greeting passers-by and neighbours working in their gardens. Mandela has been characteristically taciturn in public about their relationship, but Graca Machel has been more forthcoming. 'To me it is wonderful that we have found each other after so much pain, and that we can share a life together,' she said. She is equally forthright about her view of Mandela: 'He is really a very simple man. He doesn't have hidden parts of himself. That's what makes him so lovable.'

In his latter years as president, Mandela has become more mellow and more reflective. His official speeches are often interspersed with reminiscences and anecdotes, usually told with self-deprecating humour. One anecdote he particularly enjoys concerns a private visit he made to the Bahamas, shortly before his election victory in 1994. In the street he was approached by a man and his wife who appeared to recognize him. 'Aren't you Nelson Mandela?' the man asked. 'I'm often confused with that chap,' replied Mandela mischievously. The man was not convinced and whispered to his wife about their unexpected find. 'What is he famous for?' his wife inquired in a hushed tone. Not satisfied with her husband's mumbled response, the woman turned to Mandela and asked outright, 'What are you famous for?'

CHAPTER 1
The Mission School Ladder

Mandela was born in the simple surroundings of a peasant village on the banks of the Mbashe river in Thembuland. But for his royal connections, his childhood would have been no different from those of many others there. His great-grandfather Ngubengcuka, however, was a Thembu king, renowned for his skill in bringing stability to diverse Thembu clans in the early nineteenth century. And although Mandela was descended from only a minor branch of the dynasty – the Left-hand House – his link with the Thembu royal family was to have a marked influence on both his character and his fortunes.

His father, Gadla Henry Mphakanyiswa, was the village headman at Mvezo. A tall, respected figure, he presided over local ceremonies and officiated at traditional rites for such occasions as births, marriages, funerals, harvests and initiation ceremonies. Like most of his generation, he had had no formal education; he could not read or write. But he had a keen sense of history and was valued as a counsellor to the royal family. He was also wealthy enough at one time to afford four wives and sired in all thirteen children.

Mandela's mother, Nosekeni Nkedama, was the third of Gadla's wives. She bore four children, the eldest of whom, Mandela, was her only son but the youngest of Gadla's four sons. Like Gadla, she could neither read nor write. While Gadla adhered to the traditional Qaba faith, involving the worship of ancestral spirits, Nosekeni became a devout Christian, taking the name of Fanny.

The Xhosa name given to Mandela at his birth on 18 July 1918 was Rolihlahla, which meant literally 'pulling the branch of a tree', but more colloquially 'troublemaker', and there were friends and relatives who later ascribed to his Xhosa name the troubles he would encounter. But the name by which he became popularly known was an English one, Nelson, given to him by an African teacher on the first day he attended school. For that, there was no ready explanation, only surmise that it was taken from the famous English admiral.

It was shortly after he was born that the Mandela household itself encountered serious trouble. Gadla's position as headman was dependent not only upon tribal lineage but upon the approval of white officials in the Cape colonial administration. After its annexation by Britain in 1885, Thembuland had come under the control of colonial magistrates who maintained a system of indirect rule through village headmen appointed to keep order among the local population as well as to represent their interests. The same system remained in place when Thembuland became part of the Union of South Africa, established in 1910, eight years before Mandela was born.

Well known for his stubbornness, Gadla fell into a minor dispute over cattle with the local magistrate and refused to answer a summons to appear before him. Gadla took the view that the matter was of tribal concern and not part of the magistrate's jurisdiction. He was dismissed for insubordination, losing not only his government stipend but most of his cattle and his land and the revenue that went with them. Facing penury, he sent Nosekeni and her young son to Qunu, a village to the north of Mvezo, about twenty miles from the town of Umtata, where her family could help support her. It was there that Mandela spent his boyhood.

The landscape around Qunu – undulating hills, clear streams and lush pastures grazed by cattle, sheep and goats – made an indelible impression on Mandela. Qunu was the place where he felt his real roots lay. It was a settlement of beehive-shaped huts in a narrow valley where life continued much as it had done for generations past. The population there, numbering no more than a few hundred, consisted predominantly of 'red' people, who dyed their blankets and clothes with red ochre, a colour said to be beloved by ancestral spirits and the colour of their faith. There were few Christians in Qunu and those that there were stood out because of the Western-style clothes they wore.

The Mandela homestead, like most others in Qunu, was simple. Their beehive huts – a cluster of three – were built without windows or chimneys. The floors were made of crusted earth taken from anthills and kept smooth with layers of fresh cow dung. There was no furniture, in the Western sense. Everyone slept on mats, without pillows, resting their heads on their arms. Smoke from the fire filtered through the grass roof. There was no opening other than a low doorway. Their diet was also simple, mainly maize, sorghum, beans and pumpkins grown in fields outside the village and *amasi*, fermented milk stored in calabashes. Only a few wealthy families could afford luxuries like tea, coffee and sugar, bought from the local store.

Having four wives, each living in her own kraal several miles apart, Gadla visited them in turn, spending perhaps one week a month with each one. With his children, he was a strict disciplinarian. Complete obedience was expected, in accordance with Thembu tradition; questions were rarely tolerated. The life that Mandela led as a child was governed by strict codes of custom and taboo, guiding him through each state of adolescence. The number of taboos restricting the course of daily life, for men, boys, girls and especially married women, ran into hundreds. Most were associated with sex, with key passages of life and with food. All were held in superstitious awe. Any transgression could incur the wrath of ancestral spirits, which was to be avoided at all costs.

Along with tribal discipline came the support of an extended family. The Mandela household in Qunu was often full of relatives, taking as much interest in the Mandela children as in their own. In Thembu tradition, as with many other African tribes, uncles and aunts were as responsible for the welfare of children as the children's own parents and were referred to as 'little fathers' and 'little mothers'. The family circle in which Mandela grew up was thus an affectionate one. Even though he remembered his father mainly for his stern countenance, Mandela tried to emulate him by rubbing white ash into his hair in imitation of the tuft of white hair above Gadla's forehead. Like Gadla, he had the distinctive facial features of the Madiba clan, high cheekbones and slanting eyes.

From the age of five, Mandela was set to work as a herdboy, looking after sheep and calves and learning the central role that cattle played in Thembu society. Cattle were not only a source of meat and milk but the main medium of exchange and the measure of a tribesman's wealth. As the price of a bride was paid in cattle, without cattle there could be no marriage. Moreover, the principal means of propitiating ancestral spirits were through the sacrifice of cattle. Significant events like funerals were marked by their slaughter.

Much of Mandela's time was also spent in the open veld in the company of members of his own age group, stick-throwing and fighting, gathering wild honey and fruits, trapping birds and small animals that could be roasted, and swimming in the cold streams – the normal pursuits of young Thembu boys.

What first set him on a different course was the influence of two villagers known as Mfengu. The Mfengu had arrived in Thembuland and neighbouring Xhosaland as refugees fleeing southwards from a series of wars and upheavals called the *mfecane* which accompanied the rise of the Zulu kingdom in the 1820s. Drawn from a number of different clans among the northern Nguni, the refugees, some moving in scattered bands, others in larger groups, were given the name of Mfengu to describe their position as suppliants and were often treated with contempt and animosity. Lacking land and cattle, many formed a servant class for the Thembu and their Xhosa neighbours. But they were also more readily adaptable to serving the interests of white colonists. Mfengu levies fought as combatants on the colonial side in four frontier wars in the Cape Colony, helping to inflict defeats on the Xhosa. They were rewarded with land and cattle. A large area of what had been Xhosa territory was designated as Fingoland. They were also among the first to take advantage of Christian missionary education, acquiring new skills and finding employment as teachers, clerks, policemen and court officials.

Mandela's father did not share the common prejudice against Mfengu. Among his friends were two Mfengu brothers, George and Ben Mbekela, both Christian, one a retired teacher, the other a police sergeant. It was their suggestion that Mandela should be baptized and sent to the local mission-run school. Gadla, recognizing that an education was the only advancement available for his youngest son, accepted the idea.

At the age of seven, Mandela went to the one-room school in

Qunu, crossing the boundary between 'red' people and 'school' people. To mark the occasion, Gadla presented him with a pair of his old trousers, cut off at the knee and fastened around his waist with a piece of string. Hitherto, the only clothing that Mandela had worn had been a blanket, wrapped around one shoulder and pinned at the waist. 'I must have been a comical sight,' he wrote in his autobiography, 'but I have never owned a suit I was prouder to wear than my father's cut-off trousers.'

Two years later, in the Mandela household in Qunu, Gadla died, leaving Nosekeni without the means to continue her son's education. The event changed Mandela's life dramatically. Because of his family ties to the Thembu royal house and to the Madiba clan dating back to an eighteenth-century Thembu chief, the young Mandela was taken up as a ward by Chief Jongintaba Dalindyebo, the acting regent of the Thembu people. Accompanied by his mother, he left the simple idyll of Qunu, walking across the hills westwards to Mqhekezweni, the provisional capital of Thembu-land, where Jongintaba maintained his Great Place, and entered a new world.

The royal residence, consisting of two large rectangular houses with corrugated-iron roofs surrounded by seven thatched rondavels all washed in white lime, was more impressive than anything the young Mandela had ever seen. As he approached, Jongintaba himself arrived in a Ford V8, to be greeted by a group of tribal elders who had been waiting in the shade of eucalyptus trees with the traditional salute, 'Bayete, Jongintaba!' – 'Hail, Jongintaba!'

In accordance with tribal custom, Mandela was accepted by Jongintaba into the Great Place as if he were his own child. He shared a rondavel with his only son, Justice, wore the same kind of clothes and was subject to the same parental discipline. The regent's wife, NoEngland, treated him with equal affection and, once his own mother had returned to Qunu, soon filled her place. Life at Mqhekezweni was too full of excitement for Mandela to miss for long the world he had loved at Qunu. Even the chores seemed more enjoyable. He took particular pride in ironing the creases in the trousers of Jongintaba's suits.

What impressed him above all was the influence of the chief-taincy. Under colonial rule, hereditary chiefs had retained a wide range of powers and functions. They continued to conduct traditional court cases, to collect tributary fees and dues, and to exercise considerable authority over the distribution of land. They constituted a central part of the colonial administrative system, held in high esteem by white officials, while enjoying at the same time the traditional support of the local population.

Watching at close quarters the way in which Jongintaba exercised his power as regent, Mandela became absorbed by the workings of the chieftaincy. At tribal meetings at the Great Place, when high-ranking councillors gathered to discuss both local and national issues, he observed how Jongintaba would take care to hear all opinions, listening in silence to whatever criticism was made, even of himself, before making a summary of what had been said and endeavouring to find a consensus of views. It was a style of leadership which made a profound impression upon him. He learned too of the proceedings of the traditional courts at Mqhe-kezweni, where chiefs and headmen from surrounding districts met to settle disputes and judge cases.

It was from these tribal elders, sitting around the fireside at night, that Mandela first heard stories of Robben Island. It was mentioned often by them when recounting the long history of conflict between white colonists and Xhosa-speaking tribes in the turbulent eastern frontier region of the Cape Colony during the nineteenth century. The name given to it in the Xhosa language was Esiqithini, a word which quite simply meant 'on the island'. Everybody knew which island was referred to and what it meant. For the Xhosa, it was a place of banishment and death.

The first Xhosa leader whom the whites sent to Robben Island was a warrior-prophet called Makana; he was also known by the name of Nxele, meaning the Left-handed. In 1819, in retaliation for a raid by colonial troops into Xhosa territory, Makana had led an army of 10,000 men against the British military outpost at Grahamstown, intending 'to chase the white men from the earth and drive them into the sea'. The attack, in broad daylight, failed. Four months later, after British forces had laid waste to a vast stretch of Xhosa territory, Makana gave himself up at a military camp, hoping to stop the slaughter. 'People say that I have occasioned this war,' he said. 'Let me see whether delivering myself up to the conquerors will restore peace to my country.'

Makana was sentenced to life imprisonment, taken in shackles to Port Elizabeth, put on board the brig *Salisbury* and delivered to Robben Island, 400 miles away, off the coast at Cape Town. It had been used since the seventeenth century as a prison colony for both criminal convicts and political dissidents. Within a year of his imprisonment, Makana, along with other inmates, helped organize an escape, seized a fishing boat and headed for the mainland three miles away. As the boat came into the breakers off Blauberg beach, it capsized. According to the survivors, Makana clung for some time to a rock, shouting encouragement to others to reach the shore, until he was swept off and engulfed by the raging surf.

Makana was never forgotten by his Xhosa followers. Many refused to believe that he was dead and waited for years for his return, giving rise to a new Xhosa expression, '*Kukuzakuka Nxele*', the coming of Nxele, meaning forlorn hope.

The fate of Maqoma, the greatest military commander the Xhosa ever produced, was also well remembered. Expelled from his native valley in 1829, Maqoma engaged in a series of wars against the British in an attempt to regain lost Xhosa lands. During the 1850s, his guerrilla force based in the Amatola mountains held at bay a British army for months on end, inflicting one defeat after another.

Twice Maqoma was shipped off to Robben Island. During his first term of imprisonment, lasting eleven years, he was allowed the company of his youngest wife and a son. But on the second occasion, at the age of seventy-three, he was sent back there alone. No one else on the island spoke any Xhosa. He received no visitors. According to an Anglican chaplain who witnessed his last moments in 1873, he cried bitterly, before dying of old age and dejection, 'at being here alone – no wife, or child, or attendant'.

After nine frontier wars, Xhosa resistance against British colonial rule finally ended. Once an expanding and aggressive nation, the Xhosa had lost great swathes of land to white settlers. In the process, Xhosa leaders squabbled and fought with each other as much as they did with the white colonists. Some chiefs defected to the colonial side. Others were willing enough to collaborate. In the most desperate act of resistance, the Xhosa slaughtered vast herds of their own cattle, believing the prophecy of a teenage girl, Nongqawuse, that it would help 'in driving the English from the land'. It resulted only in mass starvation, in which tens of thousands of Xhosa died, and enabled the authorities to take yet more Xhosa territory for white settlement.

Unlike their Xhosa neighbours to the south-west, the Thembu, a Xhosa-speaking people, managed to avoid most of the frontier conflict and lost little land to white settlement. Yet Thembuland, like all the other independent chiefdoms in the area, eventually succumbed to Cape control and became incorporated into a new region known as the Transkeian Territories. It was the largest area of South Africa not to fall into white hands. But just as much as the Xhosa, the Thembu had lost political control. The authority of their chiefs had become secondary to that of colonial officials, like the magistrates, as Mandela's father had found to his cost.

What stirred the young Mandela's imagination, as he listened to these tales of Xhosa history around the fireside, were the bravery and defiance shown by Xhosa leaders who stood against the whites' advance. The age of the chiefs was seen as a heroic time. The memory of men like Makana and Maqoma was carried down from one generation to the next to ensure that a tradition of resistance survived. They became the heroes of Mandela's youth.

Another profound influence on Mandela at Mqhekezweni, pulling in a different direction, was the Church. The mission station there, centred around a white stucco church, was revered in Mqhekezweni as much as the Great Place itself. It was part of a century of endeavour by Wesleyan Methodist missionaries to carry Christianity to the African peoples of the Eastern Cape which had started when the Reverend William Shaw, a pioneer missionary accompanying a party of British settlers to the Cape frontier region in 1820, decided that a far greater potential for mission work lay in Xhosa territory to the east, 'a country abounding with heathen inhabitants'. Within a few years his chain of mission stations had reached 200 miles into African territory. One of the mission stations, Clarkebury, on the banks of the Mgwali river in the heart of Thembuland, was built on land donated by Mandela's great-grandfather, King Ngubengcuka. Anglican, Presbyterian and Moravian missionaries were also active in the Transkei region.

Before arriving in Mqhekezweni, Mandela had been to church only on one occasion, to be baptized in the Wesleyan chapel in

Qunu as a prelude to attending school there. At Mqhekezweni, church was taken much more seriously. Jongintaba himself was a devout Wesleyan who regularly attended church each Sunday, together with his wife, NoEngland, and Mandela was expected to do the same. Once when Mandela missed Sunday service, preferring to take part in a fight against boys from another village, he was given a hiding by the regent.

The church was always full on Sundays, men dressed in suits, women in long skirts and high-necked blouses – a style favoured by missionaries at the time. The local minister, Reverend Matyolo, was a popular figure whose fire-and-brimstone sermons, seasoned with a dose of African animism, found a ready audience. But what impressed Mandela, even more than the rituals and ceremony, was the impact of missionary education. The African élite of the time – clerks, teachers, interpreters and policemen – were all products of missionary schools.

At the primary school at Mqhekezweni, a one-room building next to the royal residence, Mandela showed no particular flair, but he was a diligent learner and received special attention from his teachers, taking homework back every day to the Great Place, where an aunt would check it. The subjects he studied were standard: English, Xhosa, history and geography. They were taught, in the tradition that missionaries had long established, with a notable British bias, for the missionaries believed in the virtues of the British Empire, British culture and British institutions just as much as they did in the virtues of Christianity.

Thus Mandela grew up a serious boy, respectful of the chieftaincy, the Church and British tradition. At the Great Place, his solemn demeanour earned him the nickname Tatamkhulu, meaning Grandpa. He spent much time in the company of Justice, Jongintaba's son and heir, a student at Clarkebury mission who was four years older, admiring him for his outgoing nature, his achievements in sport and ballroom dancing, and his success with young women, wishing he could be as accomplished.

At the age of sixteen, Mandela underwent the ritual of circumcision. It was an event not just of passing interest among the Thembu and other Xhosa-speaking peoples, but of fundamental significance. The elaborate ceremonies for initiates, lasting several weeks, marked their passage to full manhood. Without circumcision, no Thembu male could marry, set up his own home, inherit his father's wealth or participate in tribal councils. In Thembu tradition, he would remain a boy.

Preparations for the sacred rites of the *abakhwetha*, the groups of youths undergoing circumcision, were made well in advance, involving whole families. To prove that they were ready to accept adult responsibilities, initiates were required to undergo a number of ordeals which had been prescribed for generations. The most important was the act of circumcision itself. It was performed by an *ingcibi*, a surgeon skilled in the use of an assegai blade, who sliced off the foreskin with a single, quick motion. No word was spoken; no sound came from the circle of parents and relatives looking on. No matter how severe the pain, the initiates were instructed not to betray the slightest emotion, not to moan, clench a fist, or even frown or blink. To do so would be to incur shame and ridicule. Without a moment of hesitation, once the cut had been made, their only action was to shout, '*Ndiyindoda!*' – 'I am a man!'

After the ceremony, the initiates were secluded in a specially constructed lodge for weeks on end under the guidance and discipline of an overseer who instructed them on the rules of manhood and ensured that they adhered to strict lodge rules and activities. Their bodies and heads were shaved and covered in white clay until the end of their seclusion. Humbled by the experience of initiation, the *abakhwetha* were welcomed back into everyday tribal life with gifts and songs and feasting.

The occasion of Mandela's circumcision was more important than usual, for the group of initiates – twenty-six in all – included Justice, a royal son, and the ceremony was held at a traditional place for circumcision for Thembu kings at Tyhalarha, on the banks of the Mbashe river. In accordance with Thembu tradition, Justice was both preceded and followed by commoners. Waiting in line, Mandela heard the first boy call out '*Ndiyindoda!*' followed a few seconds later by Justice. Suddenly, the *ingcibi* was before him. 'The pain was so intense that I buried my chin in my chest,' he wrote in his autobiography.

Many seconds seemed to pass before I remembered the cry, and then I recovered and called out '*Ndiyindoda!*' I looked down and saw a perfect cut, clean and round like a ring. But I felt ashamed because the other boys seemed much stronger and firmer than I had been; they had called out more promptly than I had. I was distressed that I had been disabled, however briefly, by the pain, and I did my best to hide my agony. A boy may cry; a man conceals his pain.

Once the period of seclusion was over and the initiates, now daubed in red ochre, had been welcomed back to society as men, Mandela's spirits revived. His gifts included two heifers and four sheep – the first property he had possessed. 'I remember walking differently on that day, straighter, taller, firmer. I was hopeful, and thinking that I might some day have wealth, property and status.'

A succession of speeches followed, delivered by fathers and tribal elders, lengthy discourses on Xhosa customs, beliefs and etiquette, on the host of responsibilities that initiates now faced and on the standard of behaviour expected of them. The speech that stuck in Mandela's mind was one by Chief Meligqili, a brother of Jongintaba. He began with conventional remarks about the importance of tribal tradition, but then became increasingly outspoken about the plight of the Xhosa under white rule. They were, he said, slaves in their own country, with no power or control over their own destiny, performing work for the whites to make them prosperous. The talents and abilities of young Xhosa men, like the initiates present, were meanwhile squandered. Without freedom and independence, the Xhosa nation would die.

Mandela was irritated by the speech and put it down to the ramblings of an old man who did not understand the value of education and the other benefits that white rule had brought.

The career laid out for Mandela at the age of sixteen seemed assured. His guardian, Jongintaba, intended that he should continue his education, climbing steadily up the mission school ladder, until he was fit for service in the Thembu royal household. His destiny, like that of other members of the Left-hand House before him, was to become a counsellor to the Thembu chieftaincy. Mandela readily accepted such an outcome. He saw himself fulfilling a role at the heart of Thembu society, upholding the authority of the chieftaincy and maintaining traditions of which he felt immensely proud.

The alternative, as it applied to the vast majority of young

Thembu men of his age, was for him to seek work far beyond the borders of Thembuland, in the mines or on the farms of white South Africa. There was a certain glamour attached to such journeys. Men returned home after months away in dashing attire – flared trousers, sharp-pointed shoes, striped ties, wide-brimmed hats and coloured handkerchiefs – bearing tales of the excitement of city life, of trams, motor cars and electric lights, and bringing with them new possessions like gramophones. They spoke of the mines as places of daring and courage where men were able to prove their manhood.

But more lay behind the exodus of men from Thembuland and other African 'reserves' than tales of adventure. The reserves were becoming overcrowded, without sufficient grazing land or arable land to support their growing populations. Parts of the Transkeian Territories consistently failed to produce enough food to meet local needs. The burden of taxation, like the poll tax, added to the spur to men to find wage employment, as it was specifically designed to do. The result in the Transkei, once one of the most prosperous African areas in South Africa, was that by the 1920s nearly half of all able-bodied men were absent from their homes at any given moment on long spells of contract labour. In villages like Qunu, where Mandela grew up, the population consisted predominantly of old men, women and children.

However much Mandela was attracted by stories of adventure and money far afield, Jongintaba decided otherwise. Once he had completed his primary education at Mqhekezweni, Mandela was sent to Clarkebury, the mission school which Justice had previously attended. Jongintaba himself drove him there, in his Ford V8, westwards across the Mbashe river, with Mandela wearing his first pair of boots, given to him to mark the occasion.

Clarkebury was the most advanced educational institute in Thembuland. It had been founded in 1875 through the efforts of a Wesleyan minister and with the help of funds donated by Thembus themselves. It served as both a secondary school and a teacher-training college, as well as providing practical training in carpentry, shoemaking, printing and other trades. It was also the centre of a Methodist network of forty-two outstation schools in Thembuland, including the primary schools at Qunu and Mqhekezweni which Mandela had attended. Its buildings were on a far grander scale than anything he had previously encountered.

On arrival, Jongintaba, himself a former pupil, took Mandela to meet the school principal, the Reverend Cecil Harris. Hitherto, Mandela had had few direct dealings with whites. At Qunu, the only whites to be seen, apart from the local magistrate and the local storekeeper, were occasional travellers and policemen. At Mqhekezweni, white government officials and traders had often called at the Great Place to speak to Jongintaba and Mandela had observed them from a distance. But, as Jongintaba explained while they were on their way to Clarkebury, the Reverend Harris was different from all of them. A man renowned for his understanding and affection for the Thembu people, he was regarded by them as a Thembu himself. One day, said Jongintaba, he would be entrusted with the upbringing of the future paramount chief, Sabata Dalindyebo. He was to be treated with as much respect and obedience as the regent himself. In the principal's office, as he was introduced by Jongintaba, Mandela shook Harris's hand, the first time he had shaken hands with a white man.

Mandela soon discovered that the Reverend Harris ruled Clarkebury with an iron rod. His countenance was invariably severe. Punishment was handed out swiftly to anyone who transgressed the rules. Students went in fear of him and the staff, both white and black, tended to adopt a servile manner.

In private, however, Mandela came to see a different figure. Because Jongintaba had asked the principal to take a special interest in Mandela, in view of his likely destiny as a royal counsellor, the Reverend Harris had arranged for him to work in his garden after school hours, instead of participating with other pupils in manual labour elsewhere. There Mandela observed a more gentle man, often lost in thought, taciturn but broad-minded and devoted to the cause of educating young Africans. His wife too made a favourable impression, carrying out to the garden warm scones and passing the time in conversation. The Harris family were the first white family with whom Mandela became familiar.

At the age of nineteen, Mandela moved up the mission school ladder to Healdtown, a Wesleyan foundation sited at the head of a large and fertile valley six miles from the village of Fort Beaufort in Ciskei, an area where many of the frontier wars had been fought. It had been established in 1857, originally for the education of Mfengu as a reward for their loyal service to the British cause, but had since grown into the largest educational establishment for Africans in South Africa, providing a wide range of schooling for boys and girls, from primary education to the end-of-school matriculation examination. Its Christian and liberal arts education founded on English grammar and literature had profoundly influenced generations of students. Most of the staff came from Britain and the English model provided the basis for all teaching. The principal, Dr Arthur Wellington, was a man who liked to boast to pupils of his connection to the Duke of Wellington, the British general who defeated Napoleon at the battle of Waterloo. Mandela recalled, 'We were taught and believed that the best ideas were English ideas, the best government was English government and the best men were Englishmen.'

Healdtown was also renowned for its spartan routines, attributable in part to a shortage of mission funds. Breakfast in the dining hall, overlooked by portraits of George VI and former Healdtown teachers, consisted of a mug of lukewarm water with sugar and a piece of dry bread; anyone who wanted butter had to buy it. Lunch on three days of the week consisted of meat, beans and samp-porridge made from coarsely ground maize; on other days, there was no meat. Supper was the same as breakfast.

Wednesday afternoons were set aside for sport. Friday afternoons were free. Saturdays were spent in competitive sports against other schools. They were also the one day of the week when pupils were given permission to walk to Fort Beaufort, a village which boasted a general grocer's store and a fish and chip shop. On Saturday nights, once a month, there was a film show and, occasionally, a concert given by a local music troupe. On Sundays, boys attended church in their full uniform: grey trousers, white shirts, red-and-yellow-striped ties and blazers with a badge on the pocket and the Latin motto *Alis velut aquilarum surgent* – They soar as if with the wings of eagles.

There were more than 1,000 pupils at Healdtown. They mostly came from Xhosa-speaking districts and, after school hours and at weekends, tended to keep to groups from their own home areas. But some came from further afield in South Africa, as well as from the British protectorates of Basutoland, Bechuanaland and Swaziland. To Mandela, they were mostly strangers. His sense of identity in belonging to the Thembu tribe broadened to include the Xhosa people in general but not yet a wider African community. He felt quite bold at having as a friend a Sotho-speaking African and was amazed to discover a Sotho-speaking teacher there who was married to a Xhosa woman. He had never known of anyone marrying outside his tribe before.

Mandela adapted well to life at Healdtown. He much admired his housemaster, the Reverend Seth Mokitimi, took up long-distance running and boxing, became a prefect and in due course passed matriculation, enabling him to climb to the top of the mission school ladder, the South African Native College at Fort Hare.

Before he left, the Xhosa writer and poet Samuel Mqhayi paid a visit to Healdtown. Mqhayi was renowned for his performances as a *mbongi*, a praise-singer and orator in the flowery court tradition of the Xhosa people. He was often at odds with the educational establishment. He had once taught at Lovedale mission school, but left teaching because he opposed the way African history was presented. His own writing was a major source of inspiration to early African nationalists. In 1927 he had written seven stanzas for the song 'Nkosi Sikelel' iAfrika' – 'God Bless Africa', a song composed by the Xhosa teacher Enoch Sontonga in Johannesburg's Nancefield location in 1897 which African nationalists had decided to use as their anthem.

Gathered in the dining hall, the entire school watched as Mqhayi, dressed in a leopard-skin kaross and hat and carrying a spear in each hand, walked on to the stage from a side door, followed by Dr Wellington. For Mandela, it was an electrifying moment. He listened enthralled as Mqhayi declaimed against the curse of foreign culture, predicting how the forces of African society would eventually overcome it. And when he ended with a well-known praise-poem about the Xhosa people, his school audience rose to their feet clapping and cheering. It was an event, said Mandela, which for him was 'like a comet streaking across the night sky'.

Fort Hare was an educational institute for Africans of unique importance. To reach there, as Mandela did in 1939 at the age of twenty, represented a great achievement. To obtain a degree from there, so few were the number of graduates each year, ensured personal fortune and advancement in any career then open to Africans. No other place in South Africa offered such opportunity.

Like most of the African education system, its origins lay largely in missionary endeavour. Three missionary churches – Anglican, Methodist and Presbyterian – had combined their efforts to establish a centre for higher education where none previously existed. The site they chose, on mission lands belonging to the United Free Church of Scotland, lay within and adjacent to the ramparts of Fort Hare, the largest of all the border forts, built in 1846 and named after a British officer. It stood on a small plateau overlooking the Tyumie river, half a mile from the village of Alice and near to Lovedale mission. Only one of the old fort's buildings, a square blockhouse, was still standing, but the lines and trenches, once manned by British soldiers, were still clearly visible.

There was no imposing building in which the college could start, only a collection of rudimentary bungalows, one of which was adapted for use as a hostel, another as a classroom and a third as a house for the principal. The sanitation was primitive, there was no gas or electricity, and water for bathing had to be drawn from the Tyumie river. At the opening ceremony, in February 1916, the platform for dignitaries was erected under an awning of railway wagon covers on what had once been a parade ground for British troops.

There was also a shortage of African students qualified to enter higher education. Only one school in South Africa at the time, Lovedale mission, provided secondary education for Africans. Of the first intake of students at Fort Hare in 1916, sixteen had to undertake a four-year course in order to pass matriculation. The initial task at Fort Hare, in fact, was to ensure that African students could reach the minimum standard required for university entrance. The first graduation ceremony was not held until 1924.

The eventual success of Fort Hare was due in large part to the efforts of the two original members of staff, both of whom were still active when Mandela arrived in 1939. One was a Scot, Alexander Kerr, educated at Edinburgh University and appointed principal at Fort Hare at the age of thirty. Free of the racial attitudes common to most whites in South Africa, he was devoted to the cause of African education, taught English with a rare passion and maintained firm discipline. The other was an African teacher of legendary talent, Dr Davidson Jabavu. The son of a well-known Mfengu teacher, he had been refused admission as a day scholar to a high school for white boys in King William's Town, so he was sent instead to Wales to complete his secondary education. He had studied at the University of London, graduating with honours in English, obtained a diploma in education from the University of Birmingham, then visited Negro schools in the United States before returning to take up a post at Fort Hare at the age of thirty. He spoke Xhosa, Zulu and Sotho; played the piano and the violin competently; trained and conducted the college choir; and taught Latin, Bantu studies and history with the same enthusiasm and verve he gave to music. He was also active in Church affairs, in journalism, in politics and in founding an agricultural society. At graduation ceremonies at Fort Hare, Jabavu was a favourite subject for the praise-poems of the *mbongi*, Samuel Mqhayi.

Under the guidance of these two teachers, Fort Hare expanded year by year. The first permanent buildings were finished in 1920. New hostels were built, each accommodating students according to their Church denomination. The Methodist hostel, Wesley House, was completed in 1922. No account was taken of tribal affiliations and women were admitted on equal terms. One of the first two graduates in 1924 – the first Africans with a South African university degree – was Z. K. Matthews, who went on to study at Yale University before returning to Fort Hare in 1936 as a lecturer in anthropology and native law. By 1938, the year before Mandela arrived, the number of graduates had risen to seventeen and the number of students to 150. No longer was Fort Hare needed for matriculation purposes, as secondary schools like Healdtown were by then able to provide a sufficient number of qualified entrants.

Mandela arrived, a tall, thin figure, proudly sporting his first suit, a double-breasted grey outfit given to him by Jongintaba to mark the occasion. He was assigned a place in Wesley House in a wooden-floored dormitory of sixteen beds with lockers and cupboards, along with other first-year students. Also resident at Wesley House, in his third year there, was a distant cousin, Kaizer Matanzima. Like Mandela, Matanzima was a descendant of King Ngubengcuka, but he came from the Great House and was destined to become chief of the Emigrant Thembu, part of the tribe that had split away in the nineteenth century. They became close friends. Matanzima took an avuncular interest in Mandela, introduced him to soccer and shared his allowance with him. They attended church services at nearby Lovedale mission together. Mandela admired Matanzima, looking up to him as he had to Justice. He introduced Matanzima to his great wife and stood as best man at their wedding in 1940. But they were later to become political adversaries.

Mandela adapted to the routine at Fort Hare without difficulty. In his first year he studied English, anthropology, politics, native administration and Roman Dutch law. In his second year he opted to take an interpreter's course, thinking that he might settle for a career as an interpreter in a magistrate's court or some other government office – positions of considerable importance for Africans. He joined the Dramatic Society, took part in soccer and cross-country running competitions and spent hours honing his skills as a ballroom dancer to the tunes of Victor Sylvester on a crackly old phonograph. His personal habits changed. He wore pyjamas for the first time, used toothpaste instead of ash to clean his teeth and a toothbrush instead of a toothpick, and used toilet soap instead of blue detergent to wash.

He also joined the Student Christian Association. The tradition at Fort Hare was for students to set out on foot in groups on Sunday mornings to conduct services and Sunday schools in nearby villages, in accordance with a long-established practice inherited from the missionary institutions in which they had been educated. In addition to religious talks and teaching, the students would hold discussions on more mundane matters such as village sanitation and the prevention of disease.

On such occasions Mandela was often accompanied by a serious-minded student named Oliver Tambo. Tambo came from humble origins from the village of Bizana in Pondoland, north-east of Thembuland. The tribal scarification marks on his cheeks were to remain throughout his life. His parents were poor, illiterate peasants but he had been rescued from village life by Anglican missionaries. At Holy Cross mission in Pondoland, he had been so impressed by the workings of the church that he resolved to become a priest himself. 'I arrived there on Easter day, and I shall never forget that moment,' he once told an Anglican priest, Father Trevor Huddleston. 'We entered the great church while the Mass of Easter was being sung. I can still see the red cassocks of the servers, the grey smoke of the incense, the vestments of the priest at the altar.' Having reached the mission's highest class, he was sent to an

Anglican school in Johannesburg, St Peter's, the first school in the Transvaal at which Africans could take matriculation, and from there gained a scholarship to Fort Hare. A resident of the Anglican hostel, Beda Hall, he saw little of Mandela at the time, but the enduring friendship they eventually forged was to become a central part of Mandela's life.

Remote as Fort Hare was from the outside world, it was nevertheless touched by the gathering momentum towards world war. From the warden of Wesley House, students heard of each development abroad and gathered round an old radio to listen to patriotic speeches. When General Smuts, the deputy prime minister, called in at Fort Hare while campaigning for South African support for the British war effort, Mandela cheered him to the hilt.

His own fortunes, however, were soon to suffer a serious setback. An abiding grievance among students at Fort Hare was the monotony of the food. It was an issue which constantly preoccupied the Student Representative Council. The low fees charged at Fort Hare, to ensure that students from poor backgrounds could gain access, meant that there was little room for variation in diet. Towards the end of Mandela's second year, complaints about food reached one of their periodic boiling points. A meeting of students unanimously demanded an increase in the powers of the Student Representative Council to enable it to deal with their grievances. A majority voted to boycott elections due to be held for the six members of the council unless their demands were met. Mandela, nominated to stand as a candidate for one of the six seats, voted in favour of the move. The election was duly boycotted by a majority of students, but a minority of twenty-five went ahead and elected six members, one of whom was Mandela. The six then decided to resign on the grounds that they did not enjoy majority support and sent a letter of resignation to the principal, Dr Kerr.

Dr Kerr accepted the resignations, then arranged for new elections to be held the next day in the dining hall at supper time, when the entire student body would be present. At these new elections the same twenty-five voters supported the same six candidates, but this time Mandela's five colleagues accepted the result. Mandela alone held out, deciding to resign once more. He was summoned by Dr Kerr, who, after calmly reviewing the matter, asked Mandela to reconsider his decision, pointing out that he could not allow students to act irresponsibly and warning that if Mandela insisted on resigning he would be expelled from Fort Hare.

When set against the opportunities that awaited Mandela and the expectations of his family and his guardian, Jongintaba, who had paid for his education and provided him with a home for twelve years, the issue was an utterly trivial one. Mandela well knew that a degree from Fort Hare was a passport to success. Time and again, his teachers – Kerr, Jabavu and Matthews – had stressed the life of privilege and prestige to which graduates could look forward. Mandela himself had dreamed of how he would be able to care properly for his mother and sisters, restoring the family fortunes that had been lost upon his father's dismissal as village headman.

What overcame him was a fit of stubbornness of the kind for which his father had been renowned. When he appeared before Dr Kerr the next morning, he was still largely in a state of indecision, but, confronted with the need to decide, he declared that in good conscience he could not serve on the Student Representative Council. After a moment's thought, Dr Kerr replied that he would allow Mandela to return to Fort Hare for a third year, provided that he joined the Student Representative Council. In the meantime, he would have the summer holiday to consider the matter.

Mandela returned to Mqhekezweni to face the wrath of Jongintaba. Jongintaba brooked no argument about Mandela's behaviour, which he regarded as senseless, and ordered him to obey Dr Kerr's instructions and to return to Fort Hare after the summer holiday to complete his third year.

In all likelihood, Mandela would have returned to Fort Hare, but for an unexpected development. In accordance with Thembu tradition, Jongintaba, in his old age, had begun negotiations to arrange a marriage for both his son, Justice, and his ward, Mandela, without informing either of them, to settle the matter before his death. A few weeks after Mandela's return to Mqhekezweni, Jongintaba summoned them both and told them not only who their brides were to be but that the marriages would take place immediately.

Mandela had had a number of love affairs. He enjoyed the company of women and felt able to relax with them in a way he was unable to do with men; with women, he could admit his weaknesses. He was not short of admirers, being a handsome man, powerfully built, with an engaging laugh, a radiant smile and dark piercing eyes. He was also by nature a romantic, whose education had distanced him from the notion that an arranged marriage was an acceptable fate. The bride whom Jongintaba had chosen for him came from a respectable family; her father was the local Thembu priest. Mandela had also known for many years that Jongintaba might exercise his traditional prerogative to arrange a marriage for him, but the reality of it was more than he could face. He briefly tried to enlist the support of the regent's wife, NoEngland, but Jongintaba remained unmoved. The idea of seeking a solution through tribal intermediaries, as custom allowed, he did not pursue.

Justice was no more enamoured of the prospect than Mandela and together they decided to run away. Justice, always more of a playboy than a serious student, had struggled to complete his secondary education at Healdtown for several years. He had recently returned from Cape Town and, with Jongintaba's consent, had made plans to take up employment as a clerk at a gold mine outside Johannesburg. Johannesburg seemed the obvious destination for both of them.

First, they waited for Jongintaba to depart for a scheduled week-long visit to the Transkei capital, Umtata. Then, needing money for the journey, they deceived a local trader into paying them for two of Jongintaba's prize oxen, implying that they were selling them on his behalf. They then hired a car to take them to the local station, only to find that Jongintaba, suspecting their escapade, had been there before them and instructed the station manager to refuse to sell them tickets should they appear. Considerably shaken by this, they drove off in the hired car to the next station. After taking the train to Queenstown, they disembarked, hoping to be able to arrange travel permits for Johannesburg, without which they risked arrest. By chance, at the house of a relative with whom they stayed, they met Chief Mpondombini, a brother of Jongintaba. Claiming that they were on an errand for the regent, they explained their need of travel documents from the local magistrate. Having no reason to doubt their story, Mpondombini agreed to help and accompanied them to the magistrate's office. After listening to the chief's explanation, the magistrate issued the necessary permits. But before handing them over, he decided to check first on the telephone with the chief magistrate in Umtata. By a remarkable coincidence, Jongintaba happened to be visiting the chief magistrate when the call came through. When told what was happening, he shouted out in anger, 'Arrest those boys!' loud enough for Mandela to hear. Mandela managed to stave off arrest, but left the magistrate's office in humiliation and disgrace, without the travel permits. Some time afterwards, he and Justice succeeded in arranging a lift to Johannesburg in a car driven by an elderly white woman visiting relatives there, but for a sum which took virtually all their remaining money.

Mandela's fall from grace had been swift. One minute he was part of an African élite, attending the most advanced educational institute for Africans in South Africa, assured of prosperity and prestige in whatever field of work he chose and welcomed at home in the ruling circles of the Thembu people. A few weeks later he had fallen foul of the authorities at Fort Hare over a triviality, forsaken the patronage and goodwill of his guardian, Jongintaba, his benefactor for twelve years, and laid a trail of deceit and lies in an escapade arranged in haste and with wanton impatience. Now he was bound, virtually penniless, for a city renowned for its harsh and violent character, without the slightest idea of what lay ahead.

CHAPTER 2
Johannesburg

Johannesburg was known in the vernacular as Egoli – the city of gold. It stood in the centre of the richest goldfield ever discovered, a reef stretching for some forty miles along the line of a rocky ridge named by Afrikaner farmers as the Witwatersrand, the Ridge of White Waters, after the glistening streams that flowed from it. The gold rush there, starting in 1886, had brought hordes of white foreigners to Paul Kruger's ramshackle Transvaal republic and transformed a barren stretch of highveld, 6,000 feet above sea level, into a landscape of mining headgear, battery stamps and ore dumps. From the original tented diggers' camp there had grown a frontier town of corrugated-iron buildings and boarding houses, renowned for drunkenness, debauchery and gambling. 'Monte Carlo superimposed on Sodom and Gomorrah' was one visitor's verdict. A survey in 1895 counted ninety-seven brothels of various nationalities, including thirty-six French, twenty German and five Russian; the brothels in one part of the town were so numerous that it became known as 'Frenchfontein'.

By 1896, after only a decade's existence, Johannesburg's population had reached 100,000. Railways had arrived from the Cape, from Durban and from Delagoa Bay (Maputo). More substantial buildings had appeared: a stock exchange, banks and mining houses. At the newly built Rand Club, the white élite – bankers, financiers, lawyers, engineers and businessmen – gathered to grumble and plot against Kruger's republic. For gold had made the Transvaal the richest state in southern Africa. By 1899 more than a quarter of the world's output of gold came from the Witwatersrand.

All this was too glittering a prize for Britain, then at the peak of its imperial ambitions, to ignore. An attempted *coup d'état*, known as the Jameson Raid, engineered by mining magnates with the connivance of British ministers, failed ignominiously. But, still determined to extend the realms of empire, Britain provoked a war with Kruger's republic in 1899, expecting it to be over within a few months. Much of Johannesburg's population – the immigrant miners, shopkeepers, prostitutes and pimps – fled to the Cape Colony and Natal to await the end; most of the mines closed down. But it was eight months before the British army managed to reach Johannesburg and another two years before the war was finally over.

In the post-war era, Johannesburg acquired a more settled appearance, though its reputation remained much the same. 'It is a city of unbridled squander and unfathomable squalor,' wrote the Australian journalist Ambrose Pratt in 1913. Its population by then had risen to more than a quarter of a million and its boundaries extended to eighty-two square miles. Wealthy whites lived over the crest of the ridge in grand mansions in Parktown, with views stretching away to the Magaliesburg mountains to the north, protected from the noise and dust of the mine workings and ore dumps by northerly winds which blew it all southwards. The middle classes went north and east, to suburbs like Hillbrow, Yeoville and Bellevue. Working-class suburbs sprang up in Jeppe, Troyeville and Belgravia in the east and Fordsburg to the west. And a location for the poorest whites, mainly unskilled Afrikaners driven out of the Transvaal countryside by poverty and war, was specially established in Vrededorp to the west. The city centre itself continued to prosper and expand. At its core was the financial district, Marshallstown, where the City Hall, the Stock Exchange and the Rand Club stood within a few blocks of each other. Johannesburg, above all, was a city of money. But its origins as a mining camp were never far away. The din of stamp batteries crushing gold ore persisted throughout the night in the city centre and on windy days clouds of yellow dust from nearby ore dumps swirled through the streets.

The African population survived in this milieu as best it could. African mineworkers were confined to mine compounds, living in primitive barracks, sleeping on narrow concrete shelves, cut off from family and social life on average for periods of nine to twelve months before returning to their homes at the end of their contracts. Thousands of migrant mineworkers passed through the railway station in Johannesburg each week but were otherwise seldom seen there. The resident African population mainly dwelt in squalid and overcrowded quarters scattered around the town. Johannesburg's municipality made little effort to provide adequate housing, even for its own employees. Many 'locations' like Sophiatown, Martindale and Newclare to the west and Klipspruit ten miles to the south-west were built adjacent to municipal sewage-depositing sites. Klipspruit, Johannesburg's first 'Native location', was the worst. By 1917, it was virtually surrounded by a sewage farm; the mortality rate was appalling. Close by lay Pimville, established in 1904 originally as an emergency camp for refugees evacuated from a city slum after an outbreak of bubonic plague. Most of its buildings had been condemned time and again but were left to stand because of the lack of alternative housing. Part of Pimville consisted of ninety-nine watertanks sliced lengthways down the middle. In 1940, Pimville possessed sixty-three water taps to serve an estimated 15,000 people. Closer to the centre, scattered throughout the western, central and eastern districts of Johannesburg, a network of 'slumyards' proliferated, properties controlled by white landlords who crammed as many tenants as possible into shanties and single rooms at exorbitant rents. Slumyard life revolved around the illicit liquor trade and the 'incessant relentless war' that police fought to suppress it.

In the mid-1930s, in an attempt to make urban segregation more effective, Johannesburg's municipality destroyed many of these slumyards, moving the population to a new location twelve miles to the south-west, in the vicinity of Klipspruit. It was named Orlando, after the chairman of the municipal Native Affairs Committee at that time, Councillor Edwin Orlando Leake. By 1940, nearly 6,000 houses had been built there. Orlando was the prototype for modern-day Soweto: monotonous rows of identical houses stretching across the barren highveld, with few facilities provided other than municipal beer halls. The advantage for the authorities was that it was relatively easy to regulate and administer.

To avoid municipal controls, many Africans preferred to live in the freehold areas of Sophiatown, four miles west of the city centre,

and Alexandra, nine miles to the north, lying just outside the
municipal boundary, where blacks had been allowed to buy and
own land since the early years of the century. Both were densely
populated, full of dilapidated buildings, disease-ridden, rife with
crime, violence and prostitution, but home for an ever-increasing
black community. By 1940, Johannesburg's total African population had risen to a quarter of a million.

The official government attitude towards South Africa's black
urban population was based on the Stallard commission of inquiry
into local government in the Transvaal, published in 1922, which
asserted that 'natives – men, women and children – should only
be permitted within municipal areas in so far and for so long as
their presence is demanded by the wants of the white population'
and 'should depart therefrom when they cease to minister to the
needs of the white man'. The towns were regarded essentially as
white preserves; Africans living there were treated as 'temporary
sojourners', a convenient reservoir of labour for use when required,
but whose real homes were in rural reserves. Hence there was no
need for the authorities to make anything more than the minimum
provision for them. To ensure this policy worked, a system of pass
laws was employed. African men were required to carry passes
recording permission to work and live in an urban area. They
needed passes for travel, for taxes, for curfews, and these were
frequently demanded for inspection by police. Mass police raids
in the locations were regularly organized to ensure that the pass
laws and liquor regulations were being enforced, and, as a police
commission of inquiry noted in 1937, the methods used were often
violent.

For the hundreds of new arrivals who reached Johannesburg
each week, mainly peasants trying to escape poverty in the reserves
and drawn by the prospect of jobs, the city was a bewildering and
hostile place. The tall buildings, the noise, the traffic, the crowds,
the bustle were but a beginning. Everywhere were signs proclaiming
'For Europeans Only', '*Slegs vir Blankes*'. For Africans, there were
no cafés, restaurants or hotels which they could use; public transport was segregated. Life became an immediate struggle to secure
a room, to acquire the right passes, to find a job. Because of
industrial colour-bar legislation, Africans were confined largely to
unskilled, manual work; no skilled work was available. But only

a small percentage of new arrivals could read or write or possessed a trade. What work they could find was invariably low-paid, with long hours and poor conditions. Whites they encountered were often abusive. And on the streets, there was the ever-present danger of *tsotsis*, young gangsters armed with flick knives and sharpened bicycle spokes who left scores of victims maimed and paralysed each week.

Yet the stream of new arrivals grew ever greater. Egoli was the city of gold, of money, of opportunity. 'All roads lead to Johannesburg,' wrote Alan Paton in his novel *Cry, the Beloved Country*: 'If you are white or if you are black they lead to Johannesburg. If the crops fail, there is work in Johannesburg. If there are taxes to be paid, there is work in Johannesburg. If the farm is too small to be divided further, some must go to Johannesburg. If there is a child to be born that must be delivered in secret, it can be delivered in Johannesburg.' So in their thousands they came – Zulus, Swazis, Shangaans, Xhosas, Sothos, Pedis, Pondos and Thembus. And among them, seeking his own fortune, was Nelson Mandela.

Mandela's introduction to Johannesburg in 1941 was a sobering experience. Together with Justice, he made his way south-west of the city through huge mine dumps to the bleak and pockmarked site of Crown Mines. Deafened by the relentless din of mine machinery, they passed lines of African miners tired and dirty from their shifts underground. Justice was expected there: a letter from the regent requesting employment for him as a clerk had arrived some months beforehand. As the son of a Thembu leader, he was accorded special treatment by the mine managers and greeted with gifts on his arrival from Thembu miners. He was also able to persuade the headman, Piliso, to give Mandela a job as a mine policeman, assuring him that another letter from the regent requesting his employment would soon arrive. Out of courtesy to the regent, Piliso invited them both to stay initially with him. Mandela duly started work as a night watchman, armed with a whistle and a knobkerrie, a heavy stick with a knobbed head, guarding the entrance to the mine compound.

It was not long before the regent learned of their whereabouts and sent a telegram with the instruction: 'Send the boys home.'

Piliso, realizing that he had been duped, confronted them angrily and told them arrangements would be made for their journey back to the Transkei. Determined not to return, they continued to use the regent's name, gaining an introduction to a white mining official who issued them with a letter authorizing their employment as clerks at Crown Mines. When Piliso discovered what had happened, he threw them out.

Mandela was without a job, had nowhere to stay and had little money. Worse was to follow. In his suitcase he was carrying an old revolver given to him by his father which he had brought to Johannesburg for protection against gangsters. As he was leaving Crown Mines, his suitcase was searched by a watchman and the gun was found. At a nearby police station, Mandela was charged with possession of the gun and was told to appear in court, but he was not arrested. In court he was given a nominal fine.

From that low ebb, Mandela's fortunes began to change. He found lodgings with a cousin, Garlick Mbekeni, in a house in George Goch township, a few miles east of the city centre, and confided to him his ambition to train as a lawyer. After making inquiries, Mbekeni took him to see 'one of our best people in Johannesburg'. It was a meeting that was to have the most profound effect on Mandela's life.

Walter Sisulu was a man to whom many Africans in Johannesburg turned for help. Only six years older than Mandela, also originally from the Transkei, he had established a reputation as a community leader always ready to take on other people's problems. His office in seedy premises near Market Street on the western edge of the city centre, from where he ran an estate agency for Africans, was often used as a meeting place, particularly by those from the Transkei.

Sisulu came from humble origins and grew up in circumstances far rougher than anything Mandela had ever experienced. He never knew his father, a white foreman who had come to the Engcobo district in Thembuland to supervise black road-workers. Born in 1912, Sisulu had been brought up by his mother, his aunts and an uncle, a village headman. All were devout Anglicans. Prayers were said twice a day at his uncle's house and every Sunday there was a service at the Anglican church hut. The household was often visited by white churchmen. But Sisulu grew up disliking the deferential attitude that his family members invariably assumed in the presence of whites: 'I resented being told how I must behave towards whites.' His own light complexion, setting him apart from his African peers, was a constant source of annoyance. So rude was his behaviour towards white visitors that one of his aunts seriously rebuked him. 'I doubt whether you'll be *allowed* to work for a white man,' she said. 'You won't make a *man*, because you can't serve.' At the local Anglican mission school which he attended, the tales from the Bible that he most relished were those of Moses and David and the struggle of the Jews against foreign rule.

Sisulu followed the path that so many other young men in the Transkei were taking. He left school at the age of sixteen, with little more than a basic education, and headed by train for Johannesburg. Unable to find a job on the mines at first, he worked as a labourer in a dairy for several months, returned home briefly, then signed up for a four-month contract as an underground miner at Rose Deep Mine, hating the work, the living conditions and his white bosses. Moving to Johannesburg with his mother and sister in the 1930s, he took a succession of factory jobs, clashing time and again with white supervisors, becoming ever more embittered and aggressive. One evening, sitting in a train on his way home to Orlando, he watched a white ticket collector confiscate an African passenger's season ticket for no apparent reason. Enraged by this, he intervened, fell into a fight with the ticket collector, was arrested and sent briefly to prison. In his spare time, he developed an intense interest in Xhosa history, joined a Xhosa social group, the Orlando Brotherly Society, and wrote articles on Xhosa heroes for the white-owned *Bantu World*. Then, in 1940, he was introduced to the African National Congress, a small organization attempting to revive African political activity. It became his political home.

The young man who came to see him in his office impressed Sisulu. He explained that he had fallen foul of the Fort Hare authorities, that he intended to study by correspondence course to finish his degree and that he wanted to become a lawyer. His royal connections, his dignified bearing, his evident ambition all seemed promising material. Sisulu quickly recognized his potential: 'I saw a bright young man with high ideals.' Sisulu offered him a job at his estate agency and decided to make inquiries of a white lawyer with whom he had business dealings in the property market to see whether some opening could be found for him.

Lazar Sidelsky was an unusual lawyer. Coming from a modest Jewish family from a rural district in eastern Transvaal, where he was born in 1911, he had found it difficult, after graduating from the University of the Witwatersrand in Johannesburg, to obtain a position with an established law firm and so had set up his own partnership, known as Witkin, Sidelsky and Eidelman, concentrating on the African property market for business. He was regarded in the African community as fair-minded, conscientious and helpful. When African clients visited his office, he allowed them to sit down – something unheard of in other white law firms. He worked in conjunction with a German businessman, Philip Muller, who was involved in constructing houses and rooms for Africans in the few areas of Johannesburg, like Sophiatown and Alexandra, where freehold titles were still available to them. The business was profitable.

When Mandela called at his office on the fourth floor in the Old Mutual Building in Commissioner Street, Sidelsky, remembering his own difficulty in finding an opening in the legal field, was inclined to be sympathetic. Mandela had a pleasing manner, was a member of a royal family and came with a recommendation from Sisulu, a man whose judgement Sidelsky respected. 'I had no difficulty in saying yes,' he recalled. Sidelsky agreed to employ Mandela as a clerk while he completed his university degree by correspondence course with the University of South Africa, studying at night. After that, he could serve his articles with Sidelsky, while studying law, as part of his legal qualification. For a young African to be offered a position as an articled clerk with a white law firm in Johannesburg in the 1940s was extremely rare. What made it even more remarkable was that Sidelsky waived the premium normally paid by articled clerks. From being perilously close to early failure, Mandela, through Sisulu's intervention, had secured a future.

Mandela and Sidelsky developed a high regard for each other. Mandela, joining the firm at the age of twenty-three, was engaged at first in simple tasks but gradually extended the range of his work, handling contracts with African clients, acting as interpreter and dealing with wills and divorces. At each stage, Sidelsky took care to explain the firm's procedures, the reasons for them and the wider purposes of the law. He was also a generous employer, providing Mandela with an old suit and a shirt. In later years, Mandela was to remember Sidelsky as 'a man who trained me to serve our country'. Sidelsky, for his part, found Mandela an agreeable employee: 'It was a pleasure to have him around. He had an intelligent grasp of what was required.'

There was one other African at the firm, Gaur Radebe, ten years older than Mandela. Sidelsky employed Radebe on an occasional basis for a variety of jobs, usually on the property side of the business: salesman, clerk, messenger, interpreter. He was street-wise, smooth-talking and fluent in English, Sotho and Zulu; a short, stocky man, he was well known in the townships. Radebe led a multiple life. At heart a political agitator, he had joined the Communist Party in the 1930s and he was also active in the ANC. As the secretary for mines in the ANC's Transvaal branch, he had played a leading role in launching the African Mineworkers' Union in 1941. He was prominent too in organizing protest against the public transport system from Alexandra township, where he was based. He was often outspoken, particularly on a political platform and occasionally even with Sidelsky. He was also known to be unscrupulous. He was expelled by the Communist Party in 1941 as a result of his moneylending activities in Alexandra. He dabbled in the illicit diamond trade. Usually short of money, he borrowed from Sidelsky without repaying and tended to live off his wife, a hard-working teacher. But he was useful to Sidelsky and Sidelsky regarded him with a certain affection. Their business relationship continued on and off for many years.

Upon Mandela, Radebe exerted a strong influence. They shared an office and Mandela was struck by Radebe's audacious attitude towards whites. He was fond of telling the story of how, on his first day in the office, a white secretary, explaining that there was no colour bar in the firm, told him that, in honour of his arrival, two new teacups had been purchased, one for him and the other for Radebe. These were the ones they were to take from the tray when the teaboy came round. When Mandela relayed the news to Radebe, Radebe responded with a mischievous look. 'Nelson, just do as I do,' he said. When tea arrived, Radebe, with other members of the staff present, ostentatiously avoided the new cups and chose an old one. Mandela, wanting neither to cause offence to the secretaries nor to alienate his new colleague, declined to take any tea at all. He subsequently drank tea on his own.

Radebe's political views also made an impact. Mandela was still untutored in politics. His primary loyalty remained with the Thembu. Radebe, however, stressed the importance of a wider political loyalty, as advocated by the ANC in its campaigns for African rights. His commitment to the African cause made a strong impression on Mandela, but Mandela remained aloof from political involvement. Having had a narrow escape from trouble, his ambition to qualify as a lawyer was all the stronger. He was mindful of warnings from Sidelsky to steer clear of politics, which, his employer stressed, would lead only to ruin.

It was at the firm of Witkin, Sidelsky and Eidelman that Mandela made his first white friend. Nat Bregman, a cousin of Sidelsky, was from a poor Jewish family and had been taken on as an articled clerk, just before Mandela arrived, at the age of eighteen. He was already a member of the Communist Party, but he remained, in his own words, 'a light-hearted communist'. His main interest was in show business. He participated in left-wing shows to raise money for Soviet war charities and went on to perform as a part-time professional comedian at the Plastic Theatre in the white suburb of Northcliff. He introduced Mandela to lectures at the Left Club in Commissioner Street and invited him to multiracial gatherings which Communist Party members organized. For about three years, they shared an office on the fourth floor of the Old Mutual Building, often using the same lift when they were supposed to use separate ones. Bregman remembered Mandela at the time as 'a quiet, studious and reserved person' but with a good sense of humour who could bring a lighter touch to general conversation. Mandela enjoyed Bregman's talent for mimicry and was impressed by his colour-blind attitude to life. Indeed, it was a remarkable stroke of good fortune that Mandela, so soon after his ill-planned arrival in Johannesburg in 1941, should have found himself in the hands of an enlightened white employer, with a radical black activist and an easygoing white youth for company.

Mandela's home life was rudimentary. After staying briefly with his cousin in George Goch township, he found lodgings in Alexandra. It was called 'Dark City', for there were no streetlights or electricity supply. The roads were unpaved, sanitation was primitive, disease was rife and a pall of smoke from coal stoves polluted the air. The streets were roamed by young *tsotsis*. On most mornings, the sight of a corpse lying in a gutter caused no surprise. An ever-increasing population was crammed into this one square mile, many of them 'illegals' arriving from rural areas without proper documents. Plot owners used every available space to build rooms and shacks in their backyards, filling them with as many tenants as possible. Many premises were the haunts of thieves and prostitutes or used by shebeen queens running illegal drinking dens. Police raids in Alexandra were commonplace.

Mandela's lodgings were at 46 Seventh Avenue, the home of the Xhoma family. He occupied a tin-roofed room with a dirt floor at the back of the property. There was no running water, or electricity, or heating. He had no money for comfort. His salary of £2 per week was hardly enough to cover his basic needs, for rent, bus fares, food and candles for studying at night. There was also the cost of his correspondence course with the University of South Africa. Sometimes he walked nine miles to work and back again to save money. Sometimes he had no money even for food. The only reliable hot meal of the week came on Sundays, thanks to the kindness of the Xhoma family. Girlfriends provided the occasional meal and white secretaries in the office also helped him with food, but often Mandela went hungry. The suit that Sidelsky gave him was stitched and patched again and again, year after year.

Despite the poverty and squalor of Alexandra, Mandela developed an affection for the township. It was the first place he regarded as home after Thembuland. He enjoyed its cosmopolitan nature – the mingling of different tribes and languages, the sense of camaraderie that came from belonging to Alexandra. He stayed for only a year, before taking advantage of an offer of free accommodation in a mine compound closer to the city centre, but always looked back to his time there with fondness.

His roots with Thembuland meanwhile steadily loosened. In 1942, his old guardian, Jongintaba, died. Mandela had met him the previous year while he was on a visit to Johannesburg. He had seemed then to be ageing rapidly. They did not speak of the matters that had set them apart, neither Mandela's expulsion from Fort Hare nor his flight from the marriage that Jongintaba had arranged.

Jongintaba was more interested in his current plans. On learning of his death, Mandela travelled to Mqhekezweni, though he arrived there too late to attend the funeral. He found the Great Place unchanged, but realized how much his own ambitions had altered. He was no longer interested in a career as a clerk or an interpreter in the civil service. Nor did he see his future bound up any longer with Thembuland or the Transkei. The new world he had entered seemed to offer far greater possibilities.

At the end of 1942, Mandela passed the final examination for his Bachelor of Arts degree and early the following year returned to Fort Hare for his graduation, proudly wearing a new suit for which Walter Sisulu had provided the funds. Both his mother and Jongintaba's widow, NoEngland, attended the ceremony. It was an occasion which once again reminded him of how distant his old dreams and ambitions now seemed. Although Kaizer Matanzima pressed him to return to Umtata after qualifying as an attorney, he realized he no longer felt any urge to go there.

Back in Johannesburg, Mandela enrolled as a part-time law student at the University of the Witwatersrand, one of four English-speaking universities which permitted blacks to attend specialist courses. The campus was on a hilltop in the district of Braamfontein, north of the city centre. The student body there was almost entirely white. In the law faculty, Mandela was the only African. The experience of dealing with white students was as new to him as dealing with a black student was to them. Some reacted in traditional white fashion, keeping themselves apart. One law teacher, Professor Hahlo, made clear his view that Africans were not sufficiently disciplined to master the subtleties of law. But with others he made lifelong friendships. A part-time law lecturer, Bram Fischer, who came from a prominent Afrikaner family but was also a senior figure in the Communist Party, was to exert the most profound influence on Mandela. Among his fellow students, also studying law, was Harold Wolpe, the son of a poor Jewish immigrant family who had joined the Young Communist League at the age of seventeen. Another left-wing activist at 'Wits' was Ruth First, a brilliant eighteen-year-old social science student, also from a Jewish immigrant family active in Communist Party politics. Mandela's fellow students generally remembered him as being 'a little shy, not assertive in any way'. Harry Schwarz recalled, 'He was very quiet, never a major participant in class debates or discussion.'

Mandela also made his first friends in the Indian community. Ismail Meer was a law student from Natal whose flat on the fourth floor of Kholvad House in Market Street was a regular meeting place for Indian students where Mandela too could often be found. Both Meer and his close friend Jaydew Singh were active in Indian politics and also joined the Communist Party.

It was in the company of Meer, Singh and a third Indian student, Ahmed Bhoda, that Mandela had another brush with the police. Hastening to get from Wits to Kholvad House one day, all four boarded a tram to take them to Market Street. They had not gone far when the white conductor, turning to the Indians, bawled in Afrikaans, 'Hey, you are not allowed to carry a kaffir.' A heated exchange followed. The conductor stopped the tram and called a policeman, who arrested the Indians 'for carrying a kaffir and disturbing the conductor in his duty'. All four were escorted to Marshall Square police station. There Mandela was taken aside and encouraged to make a statement against the three Indians, which he refused to do. Ordered to appear in court the next day, the students sought help from Bram Fischer, who agreed to act as their advocate. In court, the magistrate greeted Fischer warmly, mentioning that he had just returned from the Orange Free State, where he had had the honour to meet Fischer's father, the Judge-President there. The accused were quickly acquitted.

As well as his work at Witkin, Sidelsky and Eidelman and his studies at Wits, Mandela began to take a closer interest in the political world around him, in the web of laws and regulations that kept Africans in a subordinate role and deprived them of a political voice. Under the influence of Walter Sisulu, he was drawn increasingly into the orbit of the ANC. His ambition to qualify as a lawyer did not waver. When Sidelsky gave him an increase in salary, he was pleased to hear, after asking Mandela what he would do with the extra money, Mandela's reply that he would spend it on more candles to help his studies at night. But Mandela's own political ambitions had nevertheless begun to stir. In the office that they shared, Nat Bregman remembered vividly the occasion when Mandela told him, 'One day, I'm going to be prime minister of South Africa.'

*

When Mandela first encountered the ANC, its fortunes were at a low ebb. For thirty years, ANC leaders had tried to gain a hearing from the government for their demands for greater African rights. But every method they had tried – polite petitions, deputations and appeals – had failed. Dissatisfied with the way the old guard of politicians had run the organization, a group of young radicals began meeting in Johannesburg in 1943 to plot a more militant course of action. It was to this small group that Mandela was introduced by Sisulu.

The founders of the ANC were mostly conservative men, schooled in the Christian tradition, respectful of authority and concerned largely with their own position in society. When they gathered on a sweltering day in January 1912 in a community hall in a black location in Bloemfontein, formally dressed in suits, frock coats and top hats and carrying furled umbrellas, their main objectives, to defend African rights and to campaign against racial discrimination, were notably modest. They were members of an African élite, brought up to believe in the inherent value of Western rules and anxious to prove their worth as loyal citizens. What had brought them together was not so much the urge to agitate for advancement as the fear that their existing privileges were under threat.

The tradition that Britain had established for the Cape Colony, on the occasion of granting it representative government in 1853, was to accord equal political rights to all men over the age of twenty-one provided they passed certain property or income quali-fications. Any African was entitled to vote if he qualified. The initial black electorate was small but grew in time to form a significant minority, drawn from the constantly rising number of educated Africans turned out by missionary schools – teachers, priests, clerks, interpreters, journalists and traders.

The African élite put much faith in what they referred to as the 'white sense of fair play' and went to great lengths to demonstrate their suitability to participate in politics, turning themselves into model citizens. They dressed in formal Victorian attire, went regu-larly to church, abstained from alcohol, put portraits of Queen Victoria in their sitting rooms and revered the game of cricket, forming their own teams (which often beat their white opponents). But it was all to little avail.

The first blow to their aspirations came at the end of the Anglo-Boer War in 1902, when Britain took control of the two Boer republics of the Transvaal and the Orange Free State. The African élite had hoped that the political traditions established by Britain in the Cape Colony would now be applied to the two northern territories and also the neighbouring British colony of Natal. Hitherto, no political rights had been accorded to them there. The Transvaal constitution had bluntly stated that 'the people desire to permit no equality between coloured people and the white inhabitants, either in Church or State'. The only relationship tolerated between white and black was that of master and servant. A similar colour bar had operated in the Orange Free State. In Natal the qualification for black voters was so rigorous that only two Africans had obtained the vote.

Britain's main preoccupation at the end of the war was to achieve reconciliation between the Boers and the British, and the Boers were adamantly opposed to the notion of political rights for Africans. Accordingly, the terms of the peace treaty agreed at Vereeniging excluded 'natives' from the franchise in the two former republics until the question was reconsidered 'after the introduction of self-government'. This came as a rude shock to the African élite. One petition submitted by an African group in the Transvaal questioned why the Boers, who had been 'enemies of the King and British principles', should be favourably treated while the interests of Africans, who had shown their loyalty by 'heart and deeds', should be ignored. For years ahead, African spokesmen in all four territories continued to denounce the treaty of Vereeniging as one of the greatest injustices perpetrated against them.

Worse was to follow. Having gained control over four southern African territories, each of which maintained different traditions and different laws affecting the African population, the British authorities were keen to establish 'a common understanding on questions of native policy' in order to facilitate their integration into a new dominion at some future date. The man entrusted with this task, the British High Commissioner Lord Milner, had strong views of his own on the subject. 'A political equality of white and black is impossible,' he said. 'The white man must rule because he is elevated by many, many steps above the black man.' In 1903, he appointed a South African Native Affairs Commission under the chairmanship of Sir Godfrey Lagden, the Commissioner for Native Affairs, to investigate the matter. The Lagden Commission report, issued in 1905, was to have a profound impact on South African thinking on race relations.

Its members were mostly English-speaking and regarded as representing progressive opinion on native matters; in parliament they were described as 'pro-Native men'. Their main recommendation was that whites and blacks should be kept separate in politics and in land occupation and ownership on a permanent basis. In order to avoid an 'intolerable situation' in future whereby white voters might be outnumbered by black voters, a system of separate representation should be established for the black population, though political power, of course, would always remain in white hands. Land should also be demarcated into white and black areas, as the report said, 'with a view to finality'. In urban areas, separate 'locations' should be created for African townsmen. These ideas on the need for segregation between white and black were widely held at the time, by friends of the black population as well as by adversaries. The significance of the Lagden Commission was that it elevated practices of segregation commonly employed throughout South Africa during the nineteenth century to the level of political doctrine. Segregation was used by every leading white politician as a respectable slogan.

Britain's subsequent plans to establish a union between the Cape Colony, Natal, the Orange Free State and the Transvaal galvanized the African élite into national opposition for the first time. The draft constitution for a united South Africa drawn up by white parliamentary representatives from the four colonies and released in 1909 excluded Africans from the franchise in Natal, the Transvaal and the Orange Free State, curbed the right of Cape Africans to sit in parliament, thus making it an all-white institution, and imposed on the Cape African electorate a condition that their right to vote could be removed through a two-thirds majority vote of the upper and lower houses of parliament sitting in joint session. The African view was that the proposed constitution was a sell-out to politicians from the northern territories. 'This is treachery,' remarked Alan Soga, a prominent journalist. 'It is worse. It is a successful betrayal, for the Act has virtually disenfranchised the black man, even before the meeting of the Union Parliament.'

An unprecedented number of protests followed, most couched in suitably respectful terms. A protest meeting of prominent Africans in Waaihoek location in Bloemfontein thanked the authorities for 'giving the delegates the opportunity to hold the meeting and to exercise free speech' and sent expressions of loyalty to the Governor, the High Commissioner and King Edward VII. A delegation was sent to London to make representations. But Britain's House of Commons saw no reason to amend the constitution and it came into effect in 1910 unaltered. From then on, Britain left South Africa to its own devices.

Realizing that further assaults on their position were likely, African leaders resolved to form a national organization to defend their rights. Much of the initiative came from a young Zulu lawyer, Pixley Seme, who had recently returned to South Africa to establish a law practice in Johannesburg, after studying at Columbia University in New York and Jesus College, Oxford. He was adamant about the need for a united front. 'The demon of racialism, the aberrations of the Xhosa–Fingo [Mfengu] feud, the animosity that exists between the Zulus and the Tongas, between the Basuto and every other Native must be buried and forgotten,' he wrote in 1911. 'We are one people. These divisions, these jealousies, are the cause of all our woes and of all our backwardness and ignorance today.'

The following year, at the inaugural conference of the South African Native National Congress, as the ANC was first called, Seme chose the same theme. Giving the keynote address to an audience of several hundred Africans, both delegates and observers, he pointed out that their meeting was the first time 'so many elements representing different tongues and tribes ever attempted to cooperate under one umbrella'. Their purpose was straightforward: 'The white people of this country have formed what is known as the Union of South Africa – a union in which we have no voice in the making of laws and no part in the administration. We have called you, therefore, to this conference so that we can together find ways and means of forming our national union for the purpose of creating national unity and defending our rights and privileges.'

The first challenge was soon upon them. In 1913 the government put forward land legislation prohibiting Africans from purchasing or leasing land outside areas designated as Native reserves, patches of territory scattered throughout South Africa, numbering nearly

300 at the time, which had survived the era of white occupation intact. The reserves varied in size from a few square miles to large districts. In the old Boer republics of the Transvaal and the Orange Free State, only a tiny fraction of land had officially been set aside for Native reserves, while in the Cape Colony and Natal, as a result of the military strength of Nguni chiefdoms like the Xhosa and Zulu, extensive areas remained under African control. The reserves then amounted to no more than about 8 per cent of the country. They were already showing signs of overcrowding, overstocking and land degradation. Acknowledging that the reserves were not large enough to hold their existing populations for long, the government made provision for the 'release' of additional areas for Native purchase at some future date.

The impact of the Natives' Land Act of 1913 was felt most immediately in areas outside the reserves, where nearly a million Africans lived as tenants, sharecroppers and labour tenants on white-owned land. It was particularly severe in the Orange Free State, where sharecroppers, who for years had earned a living by giving half of their produce to white farmers in return for land, were summarily evicted. Some sought refuge in the overcrowded reserves; others were forced, after selling their livestock and implements, to work as labourers for white farmers. The plight of these destitute families driven off the land was described by Sol Plaatje, the ANC secretary-general, in his *Native Life in South Africa*. 'Awakening on Friday morning, 20 June 1913,' he wrote, 'the South African Native found himself not actually a slave, but a pariah in the land of his birth.' Plaatje recorded how, travelling through the Orange Free State by bicycle in the winter of 1913, he found bands of African peasants trudging from one place to the next in search of a farmer who might give them shelter, their women and children shivering with cold in the winter nights, their livestock emaciated and starving: 'It looks as if these people were so many fugitives escaping from a war.' A whole class of prosperous farmers was eventually destroyed.

All the protests and deputations mounted by the ANC against the legislation proved ineffective. The ANC's main argument was based not so much on its opposition to the principle of segregation but on the inequitable distribution of land. The government's pledge to release further areas for African purchase was not forthcoming for another twenty-three years. In 1936, the total amount of land reserved for Africans was increased from 8 to 13 per cent. By then, as official reports warned, the reserves had degenerated towards 'desert conditions': they were 'congested, denuded, overstocked, eroded and for the most part in a deplorable condition'; the 'process of ruination' there threatened 'an appalling problem of Native poverty'.

The same process of segregation was applied to towns and to employment. African entry into urban areas was regulated more strictly through greater use of the pass system. Africans deemed surplus to the labour needs of white households, or those leading 'an idle, dissolute or disorderly life', could be deported to the reserves. Separate 'locations' on the outskirts of white urban and industrial areas were set aside for African occupation. Work opportunities for Africans were severely curtailed. The common tendency had always been to confine Africans to unskilled work in mines, on farms and in domestic service. The Union government now proceeded to enforce an industrial colour bar excluding Africans from skilled employment in the mines, on the railways and in the civil service. By the 1920s, South Africa had developed an economic system allocating skills and high wages to whites and heavy labour and menial tasks to blacks on meagre pay. The ANC's efforts to withstand this onslaught of segregation had a negligible effect.

The ultimate humiliation came in 1936, when African voters were struck from the common roll in the Cape Province, losing a right they had held for more than eighty years. In exchange for the loss of their franchise, they were given a separate roll which allowed them to vote for three white representatives to speak on their behalf in the House of Assembly and four white members of the Senate. They were also entitled to elect twelve members of a new Native Representative Council. But the council was a purely advisory body, without legislative or financial power. The only benefit from this arrangement was that Africans in the northern provinces obtained some form of representation for the first time. The practical effect of the new legislation, the Representation of Natives Act, was limited. By 1935, African voters in the Cape numbered some 10,000, amounting to only 2.5 per cent of the provincial electorate, and only 1.1 per cent of the Union's electorate. But the political significance was crucial. As the historian Cornelis de Kiewiet noted,

'To destroy the Cape native franchise was to destroy the most important bridge between the worlds of two races.'

Contemptuous of the polite methods of protest that ANC leaders had employed to so little effect, the circle of young radicals whom Mandela joined were impatient for confrontation with white authority. They were mostly teachers and other young professional men, with a core group numbering no more than two dozen. Few of them possessed political experience and none had any clear idea of what practical measures to pursue. But they were galvanized by a new vision of an African future inspired largely by the group's leading intellectual, Anton Lembede, a twenty-nine-year-old former teacher who had arrived in Johannesburg in 1943 to train as a lawyer.

When Mandela first met Lembede at Sisulu's house in Orlando in 1943, he was immediately impressed by the breadth of his learning. Born into a family of Zulu farm labourers, Lembede had pursued a life of intense study and regular prayer, driving himself relentlessly in quest of educational and professional achievement. He was fond of discoursing at length about the history of nations from ancient Greece to the modern era. As Mandela noted, Lembede tended to be verbose, but he was nevertheless struck by the boldness of the man's ideas.

Lembede's message was that Africa belonged to Africans. 'Africa is a black man's country,' Lembede argued. 'Africans are the natives of Africa and they have inhabited Africa, their Motherland, from times immemorial. Africa belongs to them.'

At the heart of Lembede's philosophy of 'Africanism', as it came to be called, lay a determination to assert an African identity, to give Africans control of their own future, to use African political power to change South African society. To depend on whites for help was considered a waste of time. No group other than Africans would free them from oppression. Other groups, whether white liberals or communists, would merely seek to subordinate African interests to their own. Africans should unite as one people, regardless of their tribal origins or social status. They should stop emulating white leadership and white culture and develop pride and confidence in their own political culture. They needed a 'nation-building' faith – a faith in their own worth, a pride in their past, a sense of self-reliance and confidence in their ability to determine their own future. This would dispel the sense of inferiority that Africans felt and attract mass support. Mass mobilization in turn would achieve political results.

Compared to the respectful approach long favoured by ANC leaders, with their belief in the value of moral argument and their disdain for mass mobilization, Lembede's ideas offered exciting prospects. Though aware of his own lack of experience and knowledge, Mandela was keen to play a part.

A meeting of young dissidents discontented with the ANC's leadership was soon organized. Among those who attended was Oliver Tambo, Mandela's friend from Fort Hare, who had returned to Johannesburg to take up a teaching post at St Peter's, the Anglican school which he had attended as a student. Popularly known as 'The Christian', he had fallen foul of the college authorities at Fort Hare in 1942, while studying for a postgraduate teaching diploma, over a written pledge they required from students regarding their religious conduct. 'I *knew* I could not sign that pledge,' he later told Father Trevor Huddleston, the Superintendent of St Peter's School. 'It demanded something from me that I could not give. It would have killed my religion stone dead: an agreement with God, written and signed! I could not do it!' So he had been expelled. Hearing of an unexpected vacancy at St Peter's, he had returned there in 1943, at the age of twenty-five, as a mathematics teacher.

By the end of a long evening, the dissidents were convinced of the need to form a youth movement that would steer the ANC towards radical action. They tentatively called themselves the Congress Youth League. But first they had to persuade the ANC hierarchy to give them formal approval. Many of the old guard were hostile to their young critics, seeing them as a threat to their own position. Others, however, were aware that the ANC needed to develop a more aggressive response to reflect the mood of restlessness and discontent growing among the African population.

In the early 1940s, massive numbers of Africans moved to industrial centres on the Witwatersrand, driven by poverty and hunger in the reserves and by harsh conditions on white farms. They were hoping to find work in booming wartime industries, but often met with little but hardship and squalor. The housing shortage reached crisis proportions. The cost of food soared. A sudden rash of industrial action broke out.

In the township of Alexandra, Mandela was given his first taste of protest. In August 1943, when bus fares from Alexandra to central Johannesburg were raised from fourpence to fivepence, causing serious difficulty for factory, office and domestic workers, some 20,000 people boycotted the bus service. Some were given lifts in cars or lorries, often by sympathetic whites, but most of them trudged the nine miles or more to work and back again, day after day, blocking all other traffic for miles along Johannesburg's main northern highway. Prominent among the organizers of the boycott was Gaur Radebe. Mandela joined the stream of marchers with a sense of exhilaration at participating in popular protest and he was duly impressed by the result. After nine days of running empty buses, the bus owners reinstated the old fare.

When a delegation of young dissidents approached the ANC president, Dr Alfred Xuma, hoping to gain his support for founding a Youth League, Xuma was sceptical about their intentions. A distinguished doctor who had qualified at universities in the United States, Britain and Hungary, before returning to Johannesburg in 1927 to establish a medical practice, Xuma had set about trying to infuse the ANC with greater vigour and to reorganize its chaotic administration and finances. He had played a leading role in drawing up a document entitled 'African Claims', which demanded full citizenship rights and an end to all discriminatory laws, in accordance with the Atlantic Charter drawn up by Churchill and Roosevelt in 1941, supporting the right of all peoples to choose their own government. But he was an aloof and authoritarian figure who lacked the common touch, finding it difficult to mix with unsophisticated blacks and preferring a circle of mainly white friends; his vivacious wife, Madie Hall, a black American and a qualified social worker, was socially ambitious. Xuma warned the dissidents that it would be a great mistake to think that Africans could 'march barefoot' against their opponents.

Nevertheless, in December 1943, at the annual conference of the ANC in Bloemfontein, delegates approved the formation of the Congress Youth League. Two months later, bearing a copy of their draft manifesto for him to review, a Youth League deputation led by Lembede called on Xuma at his large house in Sophiatown.

Mandela was present, along with Sisulu and Tambo. While they waited for Xuma to arrive, Madie expounded her own views that the tactics employed by black Americans – patient conduct, education and economic self-help – would eventually pay dividends in South Africa.

Xuma was none too pleased with the draft manifesto. It contained virulent criticism of the old methods of the ANC. Nor did he take kindly to the Youth League's demands for a programme of action, as a record of the meeting showed:

> Dr Xuma replied that the Africans as a group were unorganized and undisciplined, and that a programme of action such as envisaged by the Youth League would be rash at this stage. The ANC lacked people who were concerned about the movement and who knew what they wanted. Action would merely lead to exposure. The masses of the people were unorganized and only committees existed in the ANC ... He felt that what was really wrong with the manifesto was the tone of criticism and the expressions used. The committee should start off without antagonizing anyone.

The Youth League paid little heed. When it appeared in March 1944, the manifesto was still bristling with criticism. It accused the ANC of adopting a policy of yielding to oppression, 'regarding itself as a body of gentlemen with clean hands'. It had come to represent only a privileged few who were out of touch with the needs of the rank and file, was poorly organized and had no proper following. The formation of the Youth League was 'a protest against the lack of discipline and the absence of a clearly defined goal'. It would become the 'brains-trust and power-station' of African nationalism, giving 'force, direction and vigour to the struggle for African National Freedom'.

On Easter Sunday in April 1944, at a meeting of about 200 people at the Bantu Men's Social Centre in Eloff Street in central Johannesburg, the Congress Youth League was formally launched, with a series of rousing speeches. Lembede was elected as president, Tambo as secretary and Sisulu as treasurer. Although Mandela was elected to the executive committee, the role he had played in the formation of the Youth League was a minor one. He was working full-time at Sidelsky's law firm and part-time as a student at the University of the Witwatersrand, leaving him little opportunity for other activities. Compared to the likes of Lembede, he still regarded himself as a novice. In time, however, the Youth League was to become the vehicle for his own political ambition.

The Sisulu home at 7372 Orlando, a small brick house near the railway line in the middle of the township, welcomed a constant stream of friends and visitors. As well as providing a meeting place for the political activists who gathered there, Sisulu was always ready to advise and help with people's problems. His many acts of kindness were renowned in the local community. Also on hand at 7372 Orlando was his mother, Ma Sisulu, long accustomed to providing meals for sudden arrivals. Then, in 1944, Sisulu married a young nurse, Albertina Totiwe. In a speech at the wedding reception, Dr Xuma said to Albertina, 'Let me warn you, you are marrying a man who is already married. He is married to the nation.' Their partnership did indeed have to endure many ordeals; it was also to form the centre of a network of close relationships of which Mandela was a part.

Both Albertina's parents had died by the time she was fifteen, leaving her to look after four brothers and sisters. She swore never to marry but to dedicate her life to bringing them up. Friends at her Catholic school in the Transkei called her the Virgin Mary because she refused to loiter with boys at the train station on the way home. She performed well in school and a priest offered to help her with a bursary for further education. 'I suggested I became a nun, so I could always look after my older brother, who was illiterate, and the youngest, who was only a baby. The priest told me a nun would have to be married to the church. So I became a nurse.' It was while she was training at the Non-European General Hospital in Hillbrow that in 1941 she met a cousin of Sisulu who introduced them. Albertina instilled in Walter a new sense of confidence, making him less sensitive about his light complexion. 'I'm black enough for both of us,' she used to say.

Mandela spent more and more time at the Sisulus' house, regarding it as a home from home. Ma Sisulu took a great liking to him and Walter regarded him as his closest friend. They made an odd couple. Mandela had a tall, athletic figure, a commanding presence and a patrician manner. He was invariably well dressed. 'The beautiful white silk scarf he wore around his neck stands out in my mind to this day,' the writer Ellen Kuzwayo recalled years later. Sisulu was short, stocky and bespectacled. He had a habit at times of nervously biting his lip. His smile revealed a wide gap in his front teeth. At meetings of the Youth League, they tended to sit together, Mandela dressed in a suit and polished shoes, Sisulu usually wearing a lumber jacket and sturdy boots. Mandela was impatient for action; Sisulu was always careful to weigh up the consequences.

It was at the Sisulus' house that Mandela met an attractive twenty-two-year-old nurse named Evelyn Mase. She was indirectly related to Walter's mother and was also a friend of Albertina, training at the same hospital in Hillbrow. Ma Sisulu introduced them, mentioning that Mandela was studying law at the University of the Witwatersrand. 'He was handsome and charming and he made me laugh,' Evelyn remembered of their first meeting. 'He flirted and said he would come to see me at the hospital.'

Evelyn was a 'home girl', born in Engcobo in the Transkei in 1921. Her father, a mineworker, had died when she was an infant and her mother had died when she was twelve years old. She was sent to Johannesburg to attend secondary school and placed in the care of an older brother who was living with the Sisulus in Orlando. When the brother moved to a house in Orlando East, she went with him, but she often returned to visit the Sisulus. She was a quiet, hard-working girl, much loved by them. On the half-day off that she had once a fortnight, her favourite treat was to spend it at the cinema watching Fu Manchu films.

A few days after that first encounter, Mandela duly turned up at the hospital. They began meeting regularly and soon fell in love. Neither of them discussed politics. Within months Mandela proposed and Evelyn accepted. The Sisulus were overjoyed. The couple were married in 1944 at the Native Commissioner's Court in Johannesburg, with Walter and Albertina as witnesses. There was no wedding feast, for they were too poor to afford one.

Their early life was happy but impoverished. Like many other African couples, they found it impossible to find suitable accommodation. At first they went to stay with Evelyn's brother in Orlando East, then with her sister and brother-in-law at City Deep Mines. Early in 1946, they were allocated their own two-room municipal house in Orlando East and finally, a year later, they moved to a three-room house, no. 8115, in Orlando West. Identical to all the other houses around it, which were lined up in one monotonous row after another, it stood on a small plot alongside a dirt road, with a tin roof, a cement floor, a narrow kitchen and a bucket toilet at the back. There were streetlights outside, but in the house paraffin lamps had to be used.

The house was soon full. Mandela's sister, Leabie, joined them from the Transkei to continue her education at Orlando High School. Later his mother came to stay. There were always many visitors, especially from the Transkei. Kaizer Matanzima, now employed as an articled clerk at a law firm in Umtata, regularly called. The Mandelas were always hospitable, making up beds on the floor when too many arrived.

Their first child, a boy, was born in 1945. He was named Madiba Thembekile but known by his nickname, Thembi. Mandela was an attentive father, arriving at Bertrams Nursing Home loaded with clothes for Evelyn and the newborn infant and ensuring that, when they returned to no. 8115, a beautiful cot was ready. At evening time, he enjoyed bathing Thembi, feeding him and putting him to bed with a story. A daughter, Makaziwe, born in 1948, was frail from birth and died nine months later.

Mandela's domestic life was highly organized. He rose at dawn (a routine he has followed all his life), went jogging, ate a light breakfast and occasionally took over the cooking. His home was a place where he enjoyed relaxing and reading. But he was to spend less and less time there.

Completing his three years of articles at Witkin, Sidelsky and Eidelman in early 1947, Mandela decided to study full-time at university to gain an LL B degree, which would enable him to practise on his own as an attorney. Without an income, the financial burden was crippling. He managed to obtain a loan of £150 from the Bantu Welfare Trust at the South African Institute of Race Relations, but he was otherwise dependent on Evelyn's earnings as a nurse.

The work of the Congress Youth League, meanwhile, occupied him more and more. 'We were never really young,' Oliver Tambo recalled. 'There were no dances, hardly a cinema, but meetings, discussions, every night, every weekend.' They were propelled all the more by outbreaks of popular discontent erupting around them, throwing up new movements and new leaders on the political terrain they wanted to capture for themselves.

In March 1944, a mighty exodus began from the overcrowded quarters of Orlando, organized by an eccentric community leader named James Mpanza, a born-again Christian who had spent thirteen years in prison having been convicted of murdering an Indian trader. The first group he led consisted of a few hundred families, living as sub-tenants in municipal housing in Orlando, who moved on to open land belonging to the municipality between the community hall and the railway line, and built themselves shacks from sackcloth, cardboard, scrap metal and corrugated iron. Within weeks, 'Shantytown', as it became known, had grown into a squatter camp of more than 6,000 people and at its height reached 20,000 people, drawing in African families from other overcrowded areas of Johannesburg and the Rand. Mpanza became their unofficial 'mayor'. He liked to compare himself with Jesus Christ, proclaimed himself King of Orlando and organized his camp into a movement called Sofazonke, a Zulu word meaning 'We shall all die'.

Other squatter bosses followed suit, establishing camps on vacant land in the same area in defiance of the municipal authorities. Like Mpanza, they levied rent and other charges on their followers, controlled trading activities and established 'police' and 'courts', developing autonomous enclaves and enriching themselves in the process. No whites could enter except under squatter escort. 'The government is beaten,' said one squatter boss, Oriel Monongoaha. 'The government was like a man who has a cornfield which is invaded by birds. He chases the birds from one part of the field and they alight in another part of the field . . . We squatters are the birds. The government sends its policemen to chase us away and we move off and occupy another spot. We shall see whether it is the farmer or the birds who get tired first.'

It was in 1946 that a maverick white Anglican priest, the Reverend Michael Scott, entered this underworld to investigate conditions there at the request of a group of black ex-servicemen living in a squatter camp named Tobruk, just below Orlando West. Scott was known to Mandela. He had been an occasional visitor to parties at Ismail Meer's flat in Kholvad House. An old-fashioned crusader, he had arrived in South Africa from England in 1943 to work as a priest at a Coloured orphanage near Sophiatown, soon taking up one cause after another. The complaint of the ex-servicemen was about the corrupt regime of the squatter boss who ran Tobruk, Samuel Komo, an ex-serviceman himself, who had named his camp after the North African town where South African forces had fought during the war.

Scott duly set up home in a tent amid a sea of shacks and hovels where 17,000 squatters were living. His headquarters became the Church of Christ, a Congregational outpost made of hessian sacks and wood, which served both as a church and a home for the Reverend Theophilus Dlamini and his family of seven. Their living quarters were separated from the church by a partition of sacking and wood. During divine service, the minister's wife could be heard behind the ragged cloth at the back of the altar, alternately spanking, soothing and dressing her babies.

Scott and the Reverend Theophilus were soon drawn into an ugly conflict with Komo and his gangsters. The church's followers were intimidated into staying away; Scott was attacked and his tent torn down. Finally, armed with sticks and knives, Komo's men assaulted Theophilus and his children one night, ripped the sacking to pieces and burned the church to the ground. Scott, Theophilus, his wife and children sought refuge nearby at Mandela's small house in Orlando West. Mandela remembered Scott as a modest, unassuming guest, but took a dislike to Theophilus, who complained about the food he served.

Over a three-year period, some 90,000 Africans set up home in squatter camps around Johannesburg, surviving in squalor and hardship. So great were the numbers that the municipal authorities abandoned all intention of prosecuting them and launched instead emergency housing schemes, followed by a huge increase in the construction of permanent housing. As the squatters were moved to new sites, officials used what they termed 'culling' measures against all who were unemployed, sending them back to the reserves. The squatter movements were eventually broken. Nevertheless, their actions had provoked government intervention. Years later, Mpanza was remembered in the neighbourhood as 'the man who founded Soweto'. Though activists in the Congress Youth League recognized the potential for gathering mass support over the squatter issue, their efforts to assist Mpanza were negligible. For all the brave talk about the need for action, they had yet to make a beginning. It was from other quarters, from the Indian community and the communists, that the action came.

CHAPTER 3
Friends and Comrades

In 1946, shortly after the squatter exodus from Orlando had begun, two of Mandela's closest friends, Ismail Meer and Jaydew Singh, joined hundreds of other Indian volunteers who were protesting against new legislation restricting Indian rights to land purchase and residence, resulting in their arrest and imprisonment. The protesters included doctors, lawyers, teachers, traders, students and even a seventeen-year-old schoolboy, Ahmed Kathrada, who was to become another of Mandela's close friends. The legislation, denounced by Indians as a 'Ghetto Act' for prohibiting them from owning property outside certain designated areas, had been introduced by the government in response to an increasingly vociferous white clamour against Indian 'penetration' of white areas in Natal and the Transvaal. It was seen as a general attack on the Indian community and provoked a campaign of passive resistance similar to ones that the Indian lawyer Mohandas Gandhi had successfully used in South Africa forty years before. This tradition of civil disobedience in defence of Indian rights was to have a significant influence on both Mandela and the ANC.

Indians had first arrived in Natal in the 1860s to work as indentured labourers for British sugar planters who were unable to secure sufficient labour from among local Africans. By 1911, when their recruitment stopped, some 150,000 Indian contract workers had made the journey, mostly low-caste Hindus from Madras and Calcutta, of whom about half stayed on in Natal after their terms of indenture had expired. Following in their wake came small groups of merchants – 'passengers', as they were known – travelling

56

at their own expense, mainly Muslims from the state of Gujarat, who formed the basis of a prosperous commercial élite. Most of the Indian community stayed in Natal, but several thousand found their way to the Transvaal. In Johannesburg, President Kruger set aside a 'Coolie Location' to the west of the town centre for Asian residents, but they were also allowed to live in other areas there.

When Gandhi first stepped ashore in Durban in 1893, having been hired by a Durban-based Indian merchant company to assist in a law suit against an Indian trader in the Transvaal, he expected no more than a single assignment. But he was swiftly drawn into South Africa's racial vortex, remained for twenty-one years and had a lasting effect on the Indian protest movement there.

He played a leading role in establishing the first permanent Indian political organization, the Natal Indian Congress, in 1894, and the Transvaal Indian Congress in 1904. When the Transvaal government passed a law in 1906 making it compulsory for Indians over the age of eight to carry passes bearing their fingerprints, Gandhi led the first passive resistance campaign in defence of Indian rights. At a mass meeting in the Empire Theatre in Johannesburg, where he took the chair, some 3,000 representatives took an oath pledging to go to prison rather than apply for registration. The pass law was denounced as a 'Black Act' reducing them to the status of pass-bearing Africans. More than 2,000 Indians were eventually jailed or deported. Gandhi himself went to jail several times.

Other campaigns were launched in protest against changes in the status of Indian married women and an Indian poll tax. Gandhi was never concerned with African rights. Indeed, during an African rebellion in Zululand in 1906, out of a 'genuine sense of loyalty to the British Empire', he volunteered to lead an Indian Ambulance Corps to help the authorities, just as six years before he had volunteered his services in ambulance work to the British army during the Anglo-Boer War. Nevertheless, the successes that his passive resistance campaigns achieved in getting pass laws and poll taxes rescinded were long remembered.

Confronted with government proposals to restrict Indian property rights, Indian Congress leaders resolved to use Gandhi's old tactics to try to thwart the move. Passive Resistance Councils were appointed in Natal and in the Transvaal. Mandela's student friend Jaydew Singh served as secretary of the Transvaal Passive Resistance Council, while Ismail Meer edited a weekly journal entitled *Passive Resister*.

The main centre of the campaign was Durban, where the large Indian population was the most seriously affected by the Ghetto Act. In June 1946, the first group of protesters pitched tents on a vacant 'controlled' site at the corner of Umbilo Road and Gale Street. 'Resistance Camp', as it was known, quickly became the target for hostile white gangs, which pulled down the tents, set fire to them and then began to assault the protesters. The protesters were instructed not to retaliate, no matter how brutal the assaults, even if women volunteers were attacked. Day after day, batches of protesters assembled to face renewed assaults. The crusading priest Michael Scott witnessed a night attack.

> Suddenly a whistle blew, and with shouts and catcalls the whole formation charged and bore down upon the little group of resisters who were standing back-to-back so as to face in all directions . . . With their fists they struck the Indians in the face and about the body. No one retaliated but some tried to duck or ward off the blows before falling down. On the ground they were kicked. Some were still, and some groaning.

The protesters also faced arrest and imprisonment. Over the months, some 2,000 protesters, including 300 women, were arrested and imprisoned. Volunteers from Johannesburg, like Meer and Singh, travelled to Durban to play their part. Mandela watched with admiration as the protesters left Johannesburg. Among them was Amina Pahad, whose flat in Orient House near Commissioner Street he often visited for lunch. 'Suddenly, this charming woman put aside her apron and went to jail for her beliefs,' he wrote. 'If I had once questioned the willingness of the Indian community to protest against oppression, I no longer could.'

The campaign lasted until 1948, but failed to move the government. The Ghetto Act remained in force. But the efforts of the protesters were rewarded when their case was taken up by Pandit Nehru's provisional government in Delhi, which proposed that South Africa's treatment of its Indian population should be placed on the agenda of the United Nations General Assembly. For the first time, the South African government found its racial policies under international attack.

Within weeks of the beginning of the Indian passive resistance campaign, an even more potent threat to white authority was launched by African mineworkers. The mineworkers' strike of 1946 was the biggest labour protest in South Africa's history. What lay behind it were not just long-standing grievances about pay and conditions but the influence of a dedicated group of communists with the ability to mobilize workers. Once again, Mandela was left to watch on the sidelines as friends and acquaintances threw themselves into action while the Youth League continued to ponder its ideological position.

The Communist Party in South Africa had a tortuous past. Formed in 1921 by a group consisting mainly of foreign-born British radicals and Eastern European Jews, it found itself the following year supporting an insurrection by white mineworkers on the Witwatersrand determined to protect job segregation and block all African competition. One of its banners, held aloft during a huge demonstration of miners on the streets of Johannesburg, proclaimed: 'Workers of the World, Fight and Unite for a White South Africa.' The interests of white workers rather than black workers remained its preoccupation for several years. At a party congress in 1925, one delegate complained about the activities of a prominent radical, Eddie Roux: 'Comrade Roux should not say at public meetings in Johannesburg that natives should walk on the pavements etcetera. That is what causes trouble at the meetings.'

It was not until the late 1920s that the party began to attract a significant African membership. The night school it ran at its dingy office at 41a Fox Street, in the heart of the Ferreirastown slum in central Johannesburg, became a venue for scores of African workers. Nearby rooms there were occupied by poor white down-and-outs, prostitutes and methylated-spirit drinkers. Lessons were sometimes interrupted by loud stamping from the floor above or by drunkards forcing their way in. But the white volunteer teachers were enthusiastic and the students eager to learn the rudiments of reading, writing and arithmetic.

One of the workers who found his way to the night school soon rose to become a prominent figure in the hierarchy of both the

Communist Party and the ANC. Moses Kotane came from a devout Christian peasant family of Tswana origin from the Rustenburg district in the western Transvaal. Largely self-taught, with little formal education, he became an insatiable reader and could often be found in the back room of Mabuza's butchery on Market Street, where he could read in relative peace and quiet. He joined the ANC in 1928 at the age of twenty-three, but was disappointed by its ineffectiveness. The following year he joined the Communist Party, where his abilities as a diligent and clear-thinking activist, capable of mastering the most abstruse texts, were quickly recognized. In 1931, he became a full-time functionary, unpaid but provided with food and sleeping quarters at the Fox Street office. The following year, he was sent off to study at the Lenin School in Moscow.

The fortunes of the Communist Party had meanwhile slumped. The Communist International, or Comintern, having paid scant attention to its South African offspring since 1921, decided abruptly in 1928 that the true task of the party in South Africa was to work for the establishment of an 'Independent Native Republic' as the first stage 'towards a workers' and peasants' government'. Many white members saw this as racism in reverse and resigned. Others were drawn into a protracted period of purges and internal strife. After four years, most members had deserted; all that was left was a rump of 150 followers, almost all of them white.

Only during the war years did the party's fortunes revive. Once the Soviet Union had joined the war against Germany, communists emerged as enthusiastic supporters of the war effort, organizing a series of patriotic 'Defend South Africa' rallies, which won them hundreds of new members. Speakers who had previously denounced the war as an imperialist enterprise now urged their audiences to 'arm the people' and 'avenge Tobruk'. Pro-Soviet organizations, like the Friends of the Soviet Union and Medical Aid for Russia, gained widespread public support, attracting as patrons respectable figures like the minister of justice, Dr Colin Steyn. Circulation of the pro-communist weekly newspaper, *The Guardian*, reached 50,000. In the 1943 general election, party candidates failed to capture a seat but gained in all some 7,000 votes. The following year, in municipal elections, a party member, Hilda Bernstein, became the first and only communist candidate ever elected to public office by an all-white electorate, winning the Hillbrow seat on the Johannesburg City Council.

A new generation of communists came to the fore. Moses Kotane was chosen as the party's secretary-general and was to exercise a pragmatic influence over party affairs in the years ahead. Also prominent was Edwin Mofutsanyana, editor of the party newspaper, *Inkululeko*, who took to patrolling Orlando's dusty streets in an air-raid warden's uniform.

But while the new membership of the Communist Party was predominantly African, the leadership remained largely in white hands. White communists were accustomed to playing a leading role both as teachers of theory and as organizers in the field. Their financial and professional resources gave them inherent advantages. Mostly they were middle-class activists brought up in an anti-fascist tradition at a time when battles with pro-Nazi groups on the steps of Johannesburg City Hall were a regular event. Many came from Jewish families, descendants of immigrants from Lithuania and Latvia who had arrived in South Africa in a huge influx between 1880 and 1914, escaping from political and racial persecution there as well as economic hardship, and who then faced in South Africa a rising tide of anti-Semitism among Afrikaner nationalists in the 1930s and early 1940s. The reality of white advantage was openly discussed. Writing in the party press in 1942, Moses Kotane observed: 'In a party like ours, where whites and blacks come together, the general tendency of Non-European members is to take back seats and leave the leadership to the Europeans. They feel themselves inferior to the European comrades. The reason for this is to be found in the political, economic and social structure of South Africa.'

What the Communist Party had to offer, to aspiring blacks and Indians in particular, was not just a sense of political purpose, its vision of a socialist future, but an avenue through the racial barriers that shaped South African society. It was the only political organization in South Africa not to practise some form of colour bar. It facilitated friendship across the colour line, giving many people their first glimpse of a multiracial world. The social gatherings organized by the Communist Party, to which Nat Bregman introduced Mandela soon after they first met, drew in a circle far wider than communist sympathizers. Personal contact between white and black was otherwise extremely rare. In the homes of white communists, Africans could sip brandy, away from the liquor laws and the threat of police raids, and enjoy a world of music, painting and discussion normally inaccessible to them.

Despite such efforts, the Communist Party remained an élite group. Its slavish devotion to the Soviet Union in party pronouncements lent weight to the belief that its true allegiance lay there. Lacking mass support, it channelled its energies and abilities into supporting other organizations, seeking to extend its influence by such means. It paid considerable attention to the ailing ANC, where party officials like Kotane served simultaneously in senior ANC posts. An anti-pass campaign initiated by the communists during the war years was in danger of collapse until Xuma agreed to join it. In the joint campaign that followed, there was considerable friction when it appeared that the communists were not prepared to accept anything but token ANC leadership. The communists were frequently impatient with the sluggish pace of ANC activity and dismissive of its capacity to organize mass action. Moreover, their ultimate objectives differed. The communists were intent not simply on fighting for African liberation from white rule, as the ANC was, but on leading South Africa in the direction of a socialist republic. This placed them constantly at odds with African activists, who feared they would try to take over the ANC for their own purposes.

The communists made the greatest impact in the field of trade union organization, notably among African mineworkers. In their first attempt to establish a mineworkers' union during the 1930s, they encountered difficulties over organizing migrant workers and consequently decided to enlist the support of the ANC. The initiative was taken by two prominent communists, Edwin Mofutsanyana, who had trained at the Lenin School in Moscow, and Gaur Radebe; both held posts in the ANC. In 1941, a steering committee to establish an African Mineworkers' Union was elected, headed by J. B. Marks, a former teacher born in 1903 of mixed parentage in Ventersdorp in the western Transvaal. Like Kotane and Mofutsanyana, he had joined the Communist Party in the late 1920s, as well as the ANC, studied at the Lenin School in Moscow in the 1930s and returned to South Africa to become a full-time party and trade union organizer.

The task they faced was formidable. African miners on the

Witwatersrand were rural men with strong tribal allegiances, serving out their contracts in mine compounds, separated from the rest of the black community until they returned home. Their only alternative to compound life was the cheap canteens and shabby concession stores adjacent to the compounds. They were men who understood little of city life or modern politics, whose primary aim was to earn money for their families back home. The compounds, moreover, were closed to union officials. Meetings could be held only clandestinely. Organizers faced dismissal and deportation to rural areas. One of Mandela's tasks as a mine policeman, if he had stayed at Crown Mines, would have been to keep a sharp eye out for such activists.

From the outset, the African Mineworkers' Union pressed wage demands on the Chamber of Mines but received no hearing. In 1943, miners' discontent spilled over into sporadic strikes at individual mines. Seeking to avoid further trouble during wartime, the government appointed a commission of inquiry into the wages and conditions of African miners, giving the Mineworkers' Union the opportunity to organize meetings up and down the Reef to collect and formulate workers' grievances. The commission recommended substantial improvements. But three years later wages in the mines were less than half the minimum amount advocated by the commission, and employers ignored further demands from mineworkers. Sporadic trouble broke out. At Crown Mines, 5,000 miners went on hunger strike.

At a union meeting on 4 August 1946, held in public at the Newtown Market Square, west of Johannesburg's city centre, delegates numbering more than 1,000 voted to call a strike of all Africans employed in the gold mines, starting on 12 August. No previous attempt had been made to organize an industry-wide strike. The union president, J. B. Marks, warned them of the risk of repression. 'You are challenging the basis of the cheap labour system,' he said, 'and must be ready to sacrifice in the struggle.'

The strike brought Mandela into close touch with Marks, beginning another important friendship. Mandela had several relatives working in the mines and visited them during the strike to express support, sometimes in the company of Marks on his own rounds. He was impressed by his 'cool and reasoned leadership' at the height of crisis.

With forty-five mines strung out along fifty miles of the Wit-watersrand, often in isolated areas surrounded by unused scrubland and constantly patrolled by mine police, the strike call far out-stretched the capacity of union organizers. To bolster the strike, Johannesburg's close-knit communists mobilized all their re-sources, providing teams of volunteers, cars, typewriters, dupli-cators and leaflet-writers. The party's district committee met secretly at different venues both by day and by night, directing its members' work. Leaflets were printed and distributed from end to end of the Witwatersrand. Flying squads of communist activists rushed from mine to mine to back up the efforts of the union. A strike bulletin was compiled each evening by Rusty Bernstein, a skilful writer in charge of party propaganda, and dispatched at night to mine compounds by volunteers, sometimes dressed to look like miners.

The strike lasted for five days, drawing in some 70,000 miners, about a quarter of the African labour force. Nine mines came to a standstill and production at ten others was disrupted. An increasingly ugly struggle developed between militant miners and police called in to break the strikes, resulting in the death of twelve miners and injuries to more than 1,200 others. On 16 August, the *Rand Daily Mail* reported how a force of 400 policemen sent 1,000 feet underground at the Nigel gold mine to deal with 1,000 miners staging a sit-down strike 'drove the natives up, stope by stope, level by level, until they reached the surface'.

Police also raided the union's office in Johannesburg and the Communist Party's district office in Commissioner Street, removing caseloads of documents. Determined to show that it could deal with 'the red menace', the government then ordered the arrest of the entire Johannesburg district committee and other strike organizers, a total of fifty-two people, on charges of conspiracy to commit sedition. These were later reduced to a charge of assisting a strike which was illegal in terms of war measures still in force. All the accused pleaded guilty, including Yusuf Dadoo, the communist Indian leader who had been in prison throughout the period serving a sentence for his actions in the passive resistance campaign, and the Afrikaner lawyer Bram Fischer, a district committee member who had been on holiday in a wildlife reserve throughout the strike.

In terms of the objectives that the miners set, the strike was a complete failure. None of their demands was met and their union was virtually destroyed. The communists too now found themselves the target of harassment. Members of the party's central committee were charged anew with sedition. The evidence was flimsy, but the proceedings dragged on for two years. The popular support that the communists had enjoyed during the war evaporated. The more timid or prudent members retired from the fray, leaving behind a committed hardcore.

Nevertheless, the strike produced a considerable shift in the political terrain. Two days after the strike started, members of the Native Representative Council, the advisory body established by the government as compensation for the loss of the African franchise in 1936, assembled in Pretoria for their annual sitting in an angry and defiant mood, appalled by the government's treatment of the mineworkers. Although the council possessed no executive power, it had attracted some of the most able and respected Africans in the country, including Mandela's teacher from Fort Hare, Professor Matthews, an eminent physician, Dr James Moroka, and a distinguished Zulu chief, Albert Luthuli, all of whom were moderate men. During the war years they had become increasingly critical of the government's failure to take their views seriously. Now reports of police brutality against the miners sent them to the brink of rebellion. Their tempers were not improved when they discovered that, on the instructions of the Pretoria City Council, they had been barred from premises they normally used in the Pretoria City Hall and instead given cramped quarters in the Department of Labour, where the lavatories were for whites only. They also found, much to their irritation, that the council's chairman, the Secretary of the Native Affairs Department, had been called away to Johannesburg on strike business and that his place had been taken by a deputy. When the deputy made no mention in his opening address of the miners' strike or police action, the councillors reacted with vigour. Paul Mosaka, a successful Johannesburg businessman, referred to the 'wanton shooting' of miners and went on to launch a blistering attack on the government's neglect of the council's work. 'We have been fooled,' he said. 'We have been asked to cooperate with a toy telephone.'

The following day, the council unanimously passed a resolution which condemned government policy, called for the abolition of all discriminatory legislation and announced that the session would be adjourned. Even government-appointed chiefs voted in favour of the motion. At the end of the debate, a veteran nationalist figure, Selope Thema, turned to the council chairman and warned, 'It may not happen in your day, but it may come about that the black people will stand together against the white people.'

The old style of African politics, of polite requests and suggestions, had finally reached the end of the road. In its place came a growing interest in collaboration between different groups of the government's opponents. To Mandela and to others in the Youth League, this was an unwelcome development.

Mandela's circle of friends and acquaintances in Johannesburg was unusually wide and varied. He established strong friendships with white, black and Indian alike. He enjoyed calling at the International Club in Kort Street, where political radicals of every hue gathered for coffee, social events and lectures. He was as much at ease in the homes of white radicals like Michael Harmel, a leading communist theoretician and writer, as in the homes of black radicals. He developed a liking for Indian cooking and was a welcome guest in many Indian homes. His favourite base in town was Ismail Meer's flat in Kholvad House, where endless discussions and arguments took place and where parties on Saturday nights, with dancing, illicit drink and a selection of curry meals, would go on until the early hours of Sunday mornings. When it was too late to catch the last train for Orlando, Mandela would stay there overnight.

In his political outlook, however, Mandela identified himself with the extreme wing of the Congress Youth League, which was hostile to all suggestion of collaboration with white, Indian or communist groups. As a true disciple of Lembede, he was adamant about the need for African leadership and African control. Lembede's Africanism was essentially a philosophy of racial exclusivity. In an early draft of the Youth League's statement of policy, whites were described as 'foreigners'. The slogans favoured by the more extreme Africanists included 'Africa for the Africans' and 'Hurl the White man to the sea', which they tried to get the ANC's annual conference in Bloemfontein to accept in 1945. Mandela was sympathetic to their views: 'While I was not prepared to hurl the white man into the sea, I would have been perfectly happy if he had climbed aboard his steamships and left the continent of his own volition.'

Above all, Mandela was anti-communist, convinced that the communists were intent on trying to take over the African national-ist movement for their own purposes. The prominent role that white members played in the party and the emphasis that commu-nists placed on class struggle rather than racial oppression all served to confirm his distrust. In 1945, in an overt attempt to rid the ANC of Communist Party members, Lembede, Sisulu, Tambo and Mandela put forward a motion to the ANC's Transvaal branch proposing that members with dual allegiance to other organizations should be expelled from the ANC.

Towards Indian political activists Mandela was only marginally less hostile, fearing that, with their superior education and training, Indians would dominate African initiatives as surely as white communists wanted to. Their interests, moreover, did not coincide with African interests. Africans were preoccupied with issues like pass laws, which did not affect Indians, whereas Indians were pitted against measures like the Ghetto Act, which did not directly affect Africans. The final verdict reached by the Youth League was that Indians would not be regarded as 'intruders or enemies' provided that they did not undermine the African struggle for liberation.

For month after month, members of the Youth League argued over these issues, meeting sometimes in Sisulu's office off Market Street, sometimes in Lembede's office close by, or in each other's homes in Orlando. The core of the group consisted of no more than sixty Africans, with a far smaller number playing an active part in debates. They were preoccupied principally with establishing ideological positions, with constructing a 'nation-building' ideo-logy, rather than planning political action, but they were not short of views on other matters. When King George VI, Queen Elizabeth and the two royal princesses toured South Africa in 1947, the Youth League executive met in Mandela's house in Orlando to consider the question of a boycott. Lembede argued passionately against paying homage to the head of a state that had failed to honour its moral duty to the African people. Mandela, more respectful of royalty than others, cautioned against taking an emotional view, pointing out that the British monarchy was a great and enduring institution; but he was not opposed to a boycott. The Youth League's subsequent call for a boycott, in protest against the 'barbarous policy of the Union Government maintained in the name of His Majesty', infuriated the ANC leader, Dr Xuma.

The main body of the ANC was meanwhile moving in a different direction, seeking new links with other opposition groups. The Africanist attempt at the 1945 annual conference to gain approval for the slogan 'Africa for the Africans and the White Man for the Sea' was rejected as being 'not in accordance with the Congress spirit'. Xuma was also receptive to communist approaches to collaborate, taking part in a communist-organized anti-pass campaign during the war years. In 1946, three veteran communists, Marks, Kotane and Daniel Tloome, were elected to the ANC's national executive committee. Communists within the ANC became articulate critics of the exclusivist position that the Africanists advocated. Attempts by the Youth League to exclude communists from ANC membership, which gained significant support in the Transvaal ANC, failed at a national level.

Cooperation with Indian organizations was also strengthened. In the wake of the Indian passive resistance campaign, the ANC found common cause with the Transvaal Indian Congress and the Natal Indian Congress in opposing discriminatory legislation. In March 1947, all three organizations signed a pact committing them to work together for full franchise rights and the removal of all forms of racial discrimination. One of the first projects they launched was a 'Votes for All' campaign, demanding the extension of the franchise to all South Africans.

It was over the 'Votes for All' issue that Mandela and Sisulu came into sharp disagreement. Sisulu had begun to take a more pragmatic view of opposition to the government. Once a committed member of the Africanist group, as hostile to cooperation with whites, Indians and communists as Lembede, he had come to accept the need for a wider approach if opposition was to succeed. However appealing Lembede's Africanism was at an emotional level, from a strategic point of view it had obvious limitations. Joint campaigns were a practical way forward.

Mandela, however, along with Oliver Tambo, insisted on the need for African leadership of any campaign involving other groups.

68

At a rowdy meeting of the Transvaal ANC called to debate the 'Votes for All' issue, their disagreement burst out into the open. The meeting broke up in disorder. 'Nelson and Oliver were so angry with me that instead of going to the station together to take the train home, as we usually did, we went separate ways,' recalled Sisulu.

What shifted the balance within the Youth League further in the direction of a more moderate stance was the sudden death of Lembede, at the age of thirty-three, in July 1947. Mandela had been visiting Lembede at his office during a lunchbreak when Lembede complained of a pain in his stomach. When the pain grew worse, Lembede was taken to Coronation Hospital, but he died that evening. The Youth League was stunned. Lembede's forceful personality had guided it from the beginning; his ideas on Africanism had become its own creed. However, his obsession with sticking rigidly to Africanist ideals, fending off critics from all sides, had become an obstacle to its advancement.

His successor, Peter Mda, an Orlando teacher with a sharper, more analytical approach, began to move the Youth League away from the extreme positions favoured by Lembede. In place of the term 'Africanism', Mda preferred to use 'African Nationalism'. When the Youth League finally published its 'Basic Policy' in 1948, four years after its formation, Mda was its author.

> It must be noted that there are two streams of African Nationalism. One centres round Marcus Garvey's slogan 'Africa for Africans'. It is based on the 'Quit Africa' slogan and the cry 'Hurl the Whiteman into the sea'. This brand of African nationalism is extreme and ultra-revolutionary. There is another stream of African Nationalism (Africanism) which is moderate, and which the Congress Youth League professes. We of the Youth League take account of the concrete situation in South Africa, and realize that the different racial groups have come to stay. But we insist that a condition for interracial peace and progress is the abandonment of white domination, and such a change in the basic structure of South African society that those relations which breed exploitation and human misery will disappear.

Due warnings were given about 'the need for vigilance against communists and other groups which foster non-African interests

... groups which seek to impose on our struggle cut-and-dried formulas, which so far from clarifying the issues of our struggle, only serve to obscure the fundamental fact that we are oppressed not as a class, but as a people'. The help of white liberals was dismissed as being worthless: 'Their voice is negligible, and in the last analysis counts for nothing. In their struggle for freedom the Africans will be wasting their time and deflecting their forces if they look up to the Europeans either for inspiration or for help.' Indian organizations were given similarly short shrift. What the Youth League essentially wanted was to 'go it alone'. But the extent to which other groups were to be excluded from the African struggle for power was an issue that was left unresolved. Two rival schools of thought developed: the Africanist school, which put African interests above all others, and the Nationalist school, which preferred a more flexible approach towards other groups. This division in African opinion was to be the cause of bitter clashes for years to come.

Mandela remained firmly in the Africanist camp. Yet though he was spending more and more time on political activity, neglecting both his law studies at the University of the Witwatersrand and his family in Orlando, he possessed no clear sense of direction. As a political activist in the 1940s, he made no particular impact. He had a reputation, as he admitted, as 'a gadfly', knowing what he was against rather than what he was for. Whereas Sisulu was developing a strategic outlook about the African struggle for political rights, using the 'Votes for All' campaign as a means to strengthen links with other opposition groups, Mandela was more concerned about tactical issues, worried that the ANC might not gain the credit for the campaign rather than whether the campaign achieved any success. Sisulu, often quiet amid fierce debate going on around him, listened carefully to arguments by veteran communists like Marks and Kotane about the need for collaboration; Mandela, relishing fierce argument, was not so amenable. He was also prone to occasional hotheaded action. Oliver Tambo, in later years, remembered him as 'passionate, emotional, sensitive, quickly stung to bitterness and retaliation by insult and patronage'. Sisulu, recalling their dispute over the 'Votes for All' issue, reflected on the moments of anger that Mandela sometimes showed: 'Essentially, he is a moderate, reasonable man in his approach. That is his general nature. But then there is this contradiction of stubbornness. When it comes to the final point, he can become very stubborn, very arrogant. His anger becomes extreme. It is not in argument that he becomes angry. It is when he suspects people's motives – as he did with the communists.'

So engrossed were members of the Youth League with their own internal debates and meetings that they paid scant attention to political developments in the white community. Nor did they think they were important. It therefore came as a shock to Mandela when, at dawn one day in the streets of Johannesburg, he emerged with Oliver Tambo from an all-night meeting to find newspapers proclaiming that Afrikaner nationalists had taken power in the 1948 election.

CHAPTER 4

The Apartheid Machine

For nearly forty years, since the establishment of the Union in 1910, South Africa had been led by Afrikaner generals – Botha, Hertzog and Smuts – who had fought courageously against the might of the British army in the Anglo-Boer War, but whose main preoccupation in office had been to ensure a stable balance between the Boers and the British that would underpin the Union.

The task had not been an easy one. The Anglo-Boer War had left a legacy of bitterness among the Boers that endured for generations. Faced with guerrilla warfare for which they were ill-prepared, British military commanders devised a scorched-earth strategy in which Boer villages were razed to the ground, thousands of Boer farmsteads destroyed and cattle and sheep slaughtered or carried away on such a scale that by the end of the war the Boers of the Orange Free State had lost half of their herds and those in the Transvaal, three-quarters. Captured burghers were deported overseas in their thousands. Women and children were rounded up and placed in what the British called concentration camps, where conditions were so appalling that some 26,000 died there from disease and malnutrition, most of them under the age of sixteen.

In the aftermath of the war, the British authorities made every effort to re-establish Boer farmers on the land and to resuscitate the shattered economy of their new colonies. Yet the war had destroyed much that reconstruction could never replace, reducing a large part of the Boer community to an impoverished rural people. A growing number drifted to the towns, hoping to find work. But the towns were the citadels of British commerce and culture, where Boers from the *platteland*, possessing no skills or education, found themselves scorned and despised for their poverty, their country ways and their language. Many were forced to live cheek by jowl with Africans in slums on the ragged edges of towns, like the western areas of Johannesburg, and seek work in competition with cheap black labour. Urban poverty became as common as rural poverty.

Even though the Union was launched in 1910 with much goodwill on all sides, with General Botha as prime minister and General Smuts and General Hertzog as members of the cabinet, fear and resentment of British domination ran deep. Many Afrikaners never accepted the idea of being part of the British Empire and mourned the loss of their own republics. Everywhere they were reminded of the presence of British authority. 'God Save the King' became the official anthem. The national flag was a British Red Ensign, with the Union coat of arms in a lower corner. Most civil servants were English-speaking. The British dominated industry, commerce and the mines and controlled banks and finance houses. They also held an almost complete monopoly of industrial skills and training. Moreover, under the 1910 constitution, on questions of war and peace South Africa was not a sovereign independent state but was bound by decisions of the British government. When General Botha took South Africa into the 1914 war with Germany, a group of his old Boer War comrades rose in rebellion.

General Hertzog was prominent among those Afrikaners who feared that the sheer weight of British influence would eventually engulf the Afrikaner people. Dropped from the cabinet in 1913, he formed the National Party in 1914, proposing a 'two-stream' policy for South Africans by which Afrikaners and English would develop separately their own culture and traditions until the Afrikaner stream attained an equal status with the English. As prime minister from 1924, Hertzog achieved many of his goals. South Africa was recognized by Britain as a sovereign independent state and given Dominion status. A new national flag was approved. Afrikaans, a vernacular derived from a mixture of Dutch, Malay, Portuguese creole and Khoisan speech, became an official language for the first time.

But the problem of white poverty continued to grow. In the depression years of 1928–32, the scale of misery affecting poor whites was immense. A Carnegie Commission report estimated that in 1930 nearly half of the white population was living in 'dire poverty'. At least nine out of ten of these poor-white families were said to be Afrikaans-speaking. In rural areas, the commission reported, many families were living in hovels woven from reeds or in mud huts with thatched roofs similar to those used by Africans. One third of these dwellings were said to be 'unsuitable for civilized life'. Many white families lived a narrow and backward existence. More than half of the children did not complete primary education: 'Education was largely looked upon, among the rural population, as something foreign, as a thing that had no bearing on their daily life and needs.'

In an attempt to deal with the problems of poor-white unemployment, Hertzog devised what was known as a 'civilized labour' policy. In practice this meant that, wherever feasible, whites replaced black workers in the public service and state-owned corporations like the railways. Such measures, however, were not sufficient to keep pace with the flood of rural immigrants seeking work in towns. Struggling to cope with the consequences of depression, Hertzog agreed in 1932 to take his National Party into a coalition with Smuts's opposition South Africa Party in what became known as Fusion government. The following year, the two parties merged as the United Party.

It was out of this maelstrom of misery and hardship that a new form of Afrikaner nationalism emerged. It was not simply a return to the old nationalism of the past, of the kind once espoused by Hertzog, aiming to defend Afrikaner traditions and interests. This was a new nationalism, hardened by new ideology and driven by a ruthless determination to achieve Afrikaner domination. In place of the idea of *Suid Afrikaanse volkseenheid*, a unity between all South Africa's whites, which Hertzog now advocated, the new nationalists wanted *Afrikaner volkseenheid*. In the context of the 1930s, the greatest threat to Afrikanerdom was seen to come not from the blacks, as it was at a later stage, but from British imperialism and its allies in the English-speaking population. All the ills facing the Afrikaner people were attributed to the evil designs of British policy, stretching back to the early nineteenth century, when Britain gained control of the Cape and imposed its rule over the Boer inhabitants.

Powerful myths, myths that endured for generations, were used by nationalist politicians and intellectuals to gain popular support.

Afrikaners were portrayed as members of an exclusive *volk* created by the hand of God to fulfil a special mission in South Africa. Their history, their language, their culture, being divinely ordained, were unique. They were an organic unity from which 'foreign elements' like English-speakers were excluded. This vision of the Afrikaners as a chosen people, based on Calvinist ideas, had first been expounded by Paul Kruger, president of the Transvaal republic. Now it became a central part of the nationalist creed. At its core, the new nationalism – Christian Nationalism, as it was called – was essentially a potent mix of the Old Testament and modern politics.

The driving force behind the nationalist revival was a secret, tightly disciplined Afrikaner organization called the Broederbond, which by the mid-1930s had extended its influence to every level of Afrikaner society. Its élite membership, carefully selected and bound together by oath, comprised mainly professional men – teachers, academics, clergymen and civil servants – many of them based in urban areas of the Transvaal. Their objective was made clear by the chairman of the Broederbond, Professor van Rooy, in a private circular issued in 1934: 'Let us keep constantly in view the fact that our chief concern is whether Afrikanerdom will reach its eventual goal of mastery [*baaskap*] in South Africa. Brothers, our solution for South Africa's troubles is . . . that the Afrikaner Broederbond shall rule South Africa.'

When Hertzog agreed to enter the Fusion government and merge the National Party into the new United Party, Afrikaner nationalists led by Dr Daniel Malan, a Dutch Reformed Church *predikant* who had forsaken the pulpit for politics, launched a 'purified' National Party, claiming to stand for the aims and objectives of 'true' Afrikaners, whom, they said, Hertzog had betrayed. The impact they initially made was limited. For several years, Malan's Nationalists remained in the wilderness. Hertzog dismissed them as a group of fanatics merely intent on stirring up discord and hatred.

What provided Malan with a breakthrough was the fierce dissension among Afrikaners that erupted at the outbreak of the Second World War. Hertzog insisted that South Africa should remain neutral, arguing that the war was none of its concern. Smuts, a great admirer of Britain and the Empire and a close friend of Winston Churchill, was adamant that South Africa should stand side by side with Britain. The Fusion government, meeting on 2 September 1939, was split: seven ministers wanted an immediate declaration of war against Germany and six opposed them. The issue went to parliament two days later. By a vote of eighty to sixty-seven, Smuts took South Africa into the war. Hertzog resigned and with his supporters threw in his lot with Malan.

A large part of Afrikanerdom was outraged that South Africa had once again been dragged into another of 'England's wars'. Overnight, Afrikaner republicanism became a potent political force. As Hitler's armies advanced across Europe, the surge of pro-German sentiment grew stronger. Nationalist newspapers cheered each Allied setback. Paramilitary groups supporting Hitler attracted hundreds of thousands of followers. An élite paramilitary corps – Stormjaers – was formed to sabotage the war effort. Attacks were made on railways, power lines and public buildings. The government retaliated by interning thousands of pro-Nazi activists, among them several Nationalist figures who were later to achieve high office. As the tide of war turned against Germany, the heady atmosphere created by early German successes soon dissipated. But the overall effect was to leave Malan's National Party as the main focal point for Afrikaner aspirations.

It was during the war years that Nationalist politicians and intellectuals began to pay increasing attention to 'the Native problem'. The wartime economic boom had drawn massive numbers of Africans into urban areas. More than half a million were added to the urban African population between 1936 and 1946, mostly during the war years. In urban areas, blacks outnumbered whites. On a national basis, as the 1946 census figures showed, the whites were a declining proportion of the population. Since 1910 the white population had increased by little more than a million to 2.4 million, whereas the non-white population had expanded by nearly 4.5 million to 9 million. About 60 per cent of Africans were living in white-designated areas, either in towns or on farms, while only 40 per cent were based in the reserves. By sheer weight of numbers, it seemed to the Nationalists, Africans threatened to swamp the white population. As the problem of white poverty receded, this new threat – *swart gevaar*, the black peril – became their abiding obsession.

As prime minister, Smuts too was obliged to take a closer interest in the mood of militancy spreading among the African population. He had never previously paid much attention to 'the Native problem', preferring to leave it in the hands of the Native Affairs Department. But determined to avoid possible disruption to the war effort, he appointed a commission early in 1942 to investigate the socio-economic, educational and health conditions of urban Africans. The commission pointed out, as previous commissions had done, that a Native policy based essentially on the development of the reserves was an illusion; a large and permanent African urban population was an unavoidable part of South Africa's future. It recommended in particular the abolition of the pass laws, which by then involved the arrest of 350,000 Africans each year: 'The harassing and constant interference with the freedom of movement of Natives gives rise to a burning sense of grievance and injustice which has an unsettling effect on the Native population as a whole.'

Smuts himself spoke eloquently on the matter in 1942: 'A revolutionary change is taking place among the Native peoples of Africa through the movement from the country to the towns – the movement from the old Reserves in the Native areas to the big European centres of population. Segregation tried to stop it. It has, however, not stopped it in the least. The process has been accelerated. You might as well try to sweep the ocean back with a broom.'

Yet though Smuts occasionally expressed liberal sentiments about African rights, he never fulfilled them. His conviction about the virtues of European civilization and government ran too deep. Nor was he able to provide any clear answers to the Native question, believing that for the foreseeable future it was insoluble. He merely hoped, though without much confidence, that in time there might be an improvement in race relations. The impression he gave to an increasingly worried electorate was that his government was beginning to lose control of the black population and, what was worse, lacked the will to restore control.

Malan's Nationalists, meanwhile, put forward a plan which they claimed would provide a permanent solution to the Native problem: apartheid. The word had come into common use in the mid-1930s among a group of Afrikaner intellectuals searching for decisive methods of dealing with the African population. During the war years, Malan began to mention it in speeches in public, but it remained a vague concept. Then, in post-war years, Nationalist intellectuals and theologians defined it more closely.

Apartheid essentially was a simple doctrine. It involved the idea of total racial separation. Every facet of life – residence, amenities, transport, education and politics – would be kept separate, wherever possible. This policy would apply to Coloured and Indian people as well as to the African population. By such means no race group would then threaten any longer the future of any other. The survival of the white race would be assured. The blacks, meanwhile, would be able to preserve their own culture and identity and to develop in their own areas. All this, the Nationalists asserted, was in accordance with Christian principles of right and justice. God had ordained the division of nations and wished them to be kept separate. Texts from the Bible were cited as proof.

These ideas were incorporated into a political manifesto drawn up by a National Party commission under Paul Sauer and issued in 1948, a few months before the general election. The reserves, said the Sauer report, were the proper homelands of the African population. There they would be allowed to develop to their full capacities. Urban Africans, meanwhile, would be treated as 'visitors' and strictly controlled.

> Natives in the urban areas should be regarded as migratory citizens not entitled to political and social rights equal to those of whites. The process of detribalization should be arrested. The entire migration of Natives into and from the cities should be controlled by the state, which will enlist the cooperation of municipal bodies. Migration into and from the Reserves shall likewise be strictly controlled. Surplus Natives in the urban areas should be returned to their original habitat in the country areas [white farms] or the Reserves. Natives from the country areas shall be admitted to the urban areas or towns as temporary employees obliged to return to their homes after the expiry of their employment.

Smuts was thought to be in no particular danger from the Nationalist challenge. With the Allied victory in 1945, his prestige had reached new heights. Abroad, he was hailed as an international statesman, admired by leaders like Churchill and Roosevelt and entrusted with the task of drafting the Preamble to the United Nations Charter, earning widespread applause for the emphasis he placed on fundamental rights. On his return home from the United Nations conference in San Francisco in 1945, he was given a tumultuous welcome. His views about the importance of European rule were common enough at the time, not only in South Africa but throughout the African continent and in the capitals of Europe, from where most of Africa was then ruled. Although South Africa's racial practices were beginning to attract adverse international attention, they tended to differ in detail rather than in essence from the discriminatory policies employed elsewhere in Africa under colonial rule. The platform he put forward in the election was pragmatic. He endorsed a government report which argued that the urbanization of the African could not be reversed and that henceforth blacks should be accepted as a permanent part of the urban population. Although some controls over the movement of blacks to the cities were still needed, the system of migrant labour had become obsolete and wasteful and the idea of territorial separation of the races was 'utterly impractical'.

Not even the Nationalists believed that victory in the 1948 election was within their reach. Their hopes were based on the following election. The ruling United Party, together with its parliamentary allies, went into the election with a majority of more than fifty seats. For the Nationalists to win would require a swing of opinion among the electorate unprecedented in the Union's history. Yet, with relentless propaganda, the Nationalists ensured that the *swart gevaar* issue dominated public debate, using every opportunity to play on the electorate's racial anxieties. The choice for whites, the Nationalists said, was between 'integration and national suicide' on the one hand and 'apartheid' and the protection of a 'pure white race' on the other. The 1948 election, said Malan, would be the most decisive in South Africa's history. One question overshadowed all others: 'Will the European race in the future be able to maintain its rule, its purity, its civilization; or will it float until it vanishes for ever, without honour, in the black sea of South Africa's Non-European population?' Only a National Party government, he said, could provide an effective answer. It would outlaw interracial marriage, control African influx into the cities, protect white workers from African competition and segregate whites and blacks to the maximum extent possible. It would also outlaw the communists and deal effectively with the Indian population. 'Indians are a foreign and outlandish element which is unassimilable,' said Malan. 'They can never become part of the country, and must therefore be treated as an immigrant community.' He would call a halt to immigration and begin repatriation. Two crude slogans used by the National Party summed it all up: '*Die kaffir op sy plek*' – 'The kaffir in his place' – and '*Die koolies uit die land*' – 'The coolies out of the country'.

The National Party, together with its small ally, the Afrikaner Party, won 41 per cent of the vote; the United Party alliance won 51 per cent. But the favourable loading of rural seats gave the Nationalists a decisive advantage. They gained a tenuous majority of five seats.

'Today, South Africa belongs to us once more,' declared Malan in his election victory speech. 'For the first time since Union, South Africa is our own, and may God grant that it will always remain our own.' The age of the generals had ended and the age of apartheid had begun.

Mandela was twenty-nine years old at the time, an impecunious law student struggling unsuccessfully to pass examinations for a law degree and dependent on his wife's earnings to keep his young family afloat. He had developed strong political ambitions, but had so far failed to make his mark as a political activist. The Congress Youth League, the small pressure group which he had helped to launch with the aim of giving 'force, direction and vigour' to the ANC, had spent four years arguing over ideological positions, showing no propensity for political action. The ANC, after thirty-six years of efforts in dealing with governments which professed to be mindful of their 'trusteeship' of the African people, had yet to achieve any significant gains in its campaign for African rights or in its attempts to halt the inexorable march of segregation. Now they faced a government whose explicit objective was to keep '*die kaffir op sy plek*' and which was prepared to use power in a manner which South Africa had never before experienced.

The ruthlessness of the Nationalists became apparent at first in their handling not of the African population but of the English-speaking community. Malan's government was the first in the history of the Union to consist exclusively of Afrikaners. The upper echelons of the civil service, the armed forces, the police and parastatal organizations like the railways were purged of English-speakers and filled with carefully selected Afrikaners, usually members of the Broederbond. The state sector became virtually an Afrikaner preserve. The legal profession eventually faced the same treatment; senior English-speaking members of the bar were systematically overlooked in the appointment of judges. The government also favoured Afrikaner business interests, switching accounts to Afrikaner financial institutions and awarding contracts to Afrikaner companies. The English-speaking community found itself on the defensive at every turn. In an acrimonious debate in parliament, English-speaking members faced accusations of dual allegiance and were questioned on their right to be considered full South Africans. The English would be given equal treatment, said one Nationalist speaker, but 'the country belongs, in the first instance, to those people who opened it up'.

The Nationalists then turned their attention to the Native problem. Malan, in his mid-seventies when he came to office, had never shown much interest in Native policy. His preoccupation had always been to consolidate the Afrikaner community behind his drive for power. He possessed no grand design for the African population of the kind that other Nationalist leaders developed later. His principal aim was to reverse the trend towards interracial integration rather than to devise some final solution to the Native problem.

His first targets, accordingly, were marriage and sex. In 1949 parliament passed the Prohibition of Mixed Marriages Act, outlawing marriages between Europeans and non-Europeans. Few such marriages ever took place – less than 100 a year out of an annual total of 28,000 white marriages – but for the Nationalists it was a blurring of racial lines they were not willing to tolerate. An amendment to the Immorality Act extended a ban on sexual intercourse between Europeans and Natives, in force since 1927, to Europeans and Coloureds. Next came the Population Registration Act, designed eventually to allocate every person to one of three racial groups: White, Coloured or African. 'A national register is the whole basis of apartheid,' declared Malan. Some of the early methods used to determine a person's race were crude in the extreme. Doubtful cases were sometimes resolved by white officials with what became known as the 'pencil in the hair' test. If a pencil stayed in the hair, it meant classification as a Coloured or African; if it fell out it meant classification as a Coloured or white. Small variations in the texture of hair or the shape of the lips could make all the difference in determining where people could live and work. The effect in many borderline cases was to wreck families and ruin careers.

The advent of apartheid prompted Mandela and his radical friends in the Congress Youth League to demand a more aggressive strategy from the ANC. A new document was drawn up calling for civil disobedience, boycotts and 'stay-at-home' strikes on a mass scale.

In December 1949, shortly before the ANC's annual conference was due to be held in Bloemfontein, a Youth League delegation consisting of Mda, Sisulu, Tambo and Mandela called on Dr Xuma at his home in Sophiatown to try to obtain his support for their plan. The ANC, they told him, had become too docile. What was needed was mass action along the lines of Gandhi's passive resistance campaigns and the protests carried out by the Indian community in South Africa in 1946. Like Gandhi, the ANC's leaders had to be prepared to contravene the law and go to prison.

Xuma was dismissive. Such action would be premature, he said, and would merely give the government an excuse to crush the ANC in the name of law and order. Furthermore, he had no intention of going to prison and forsaking his medical practice. The four activists then gave Xuma an ultimatum: unless he supported their plan of action, they would oppose his re-election as president at the forthcoming ANC conference. Xuma reacted furiously to their challenge. 'I don't want your vote,' he said. 'And I won't be dictated to by any clique.'

The ANC's annual conference was duly held in an atmosphere of unusual excitement. Many delegates, alarmed by the government's apartheid programme, wanted to end all trace of collaboration with government institutions and embark on more determined action, as the Youth League proposed. The Youth League's difficulty was in finding a respectable figure to stand as their candidate against Xuma. The first person they approached, Professor Matthews, the distinguished academic, declined the offer.

In the audience as a guest, however, was a man with a remarkable string of credentials. Dr James Moroka came from a wealthy landowning family in the Orange Free State. He was a great-grandson of the Tswana chief Moroka, who in the 1830s had given military protection to groups of *voortrekkers* entering his domain. His father was white, but he had taken his mother's name. After graduating from the University of Edinburgh in medicine in 1918, he had returned to South Africa, one of only two black medical doctors in the country, and established a lucrative practice in Thaba 'Nchu. Local Afrikaners were among his patients. In accordance with South African custom, he provided one waiting room for whites and another for blacks, one entrance for whites, another for blacks. He was also a shrewd businessman, the owner of a large number of farms, shops and other concerns. At his home in Thaba 'Nchu, he lived the life of a country gentleman, highly respected in the local community. He had helped in the building of schools and a hospital for local people and contributed funds to enable needy white students to train as doctors. He had shown no interest in politics until the African franchise was threatened in 1936, when he established a reputation as an outspoken opponent of government policy. As a member of the Native Representative Council, he used it as a platform from which to continue his attacks on the government. The only credential he lacked, in fact, was membership of the ANC; he was involved with another group, the All African Convention.

In the closing stages of the conference, after Moroka had indicated his support for the 'Programme of Action', the Youth League decided to approach him. At first he was reluctant to stand against Xuma but finally he agreed. In the election that followed, the older generation voted for Xuma and the younger for Moroka. Moroka won and the 'Programme of Action' was adopted as ANC policy. The Youth League's coup had succeeded.

Other significant changes occurred at the same time. Believing that the 'Programme of Action' was 'too drastic', the ANC's long-serving secretary-general, the Reverend James Calata, declined to stand for re-election. Walter Sisulu was elected in his place. Sisulu decided henceforth to devote his entire time to building up the ANC, relying on Albertina's wages as a nurse to support him and his family. Five other members of the Youth League were elected to the ANC's national executive committee, including Peter Mda and Oliver Tambo.

Mandela missed all the excitement. Having decided to abandon his studies for a law degree, he had taken a job with the law firm of Terblanche and Brigish, which was not willing to allow him time off to attend the Bloemfontein conference. His employer, Harry Brigish, a left-wing lawyer, regarded Mandela as 'a fine and decent young fellow' but, like Sidelsky before him, disapproved of his political activity.

Mandela's chance to join the national executive committee came two months later, in February 1950, when Dr Xuma, having failed to be re-elected president, decided to resign his seat. At Sisulu's instigation, Mandela was coopted in his place. He viewed his new position with mixed feelings. He had enjoyed his days as a gadfly, attacking the establishment when inclined to do so. Now he was part of the ANC hierarchy, obliged to accept wider responsibilities.

The leadership of the ANC thus passed into the hands of a new generation of political activists. Some members of the old guard, like the Reverend Calata, retained their seats on the national executive committee. But the direction in which the ANC now moved was towards active opposition to the government of the kind advocated in its 'Programme of Action'.

Yet, despite all the efforts of the Youth League, there was still little ideological clarity. Africanists like Mda and Mandela remained vehemently opposed to collaboration with communists. Communists like Kotane and Marks argued in favour of a broader front, trying to balance their loyalty to the cause of African rights with their commitment to socialist revolution. Others, like Professor Matthews, favoured a traditional liberal approach. All factions, however, were agreed on the need for direct action.

The role that Sisulu played as secretary-general, ensconced in new party headquarters down a dingy corridor in New Court Chambers in Commissioner Street, became increasingly important. His aim was to weld the different factions within the ANC into a united organization and to extend its cooperation with other anti-apartheid groups, presenting the government with a more formidable adversary. 'I had gained sufficient confidence that we would survive as a national group,' he said. 'We didn't need to be unnecessarily sensitive about cooperating with other groups.'

The pressure of events came not just from the government but from a massive outbreak of communal violence in Durban in 1949 between Africans and Indians which brought together ANC and Indian Congress leaders in an attempt to defuse the crisis. Tension between the two communities, particularly in the slums around Durban, where both groups struggled to survive, was often close to the surface. Many Indians were as contemptuous of Africans as whites were; Indian traders and landlords were resented in turn as exploiters. In a sudden conflagration, starting from one small incident, Africans burned down Indian homes, clubbed their owners to death, raped wives and daughters and looted stores, killing in all some fifty Indians. Thousands of Indians fled their homes. Nearly ninety Africans died, most of them in the ensuing police action. ANC leaders from Johannesburg joined in the efforts in Durban to calm the strife, recognizing the need for a fuller understanding of each community's problems.

Mandela remained opposed to links with other groups, even when the communists found themselves under direct assault from the government. Almost immediately on assuming power, Malan had set up a committee to investigate the influence of communism in the Union. It reported in 1949 that the Communist Party represented a danger to 'our national life, our democratic institutions and our Western philosophy'. The result the following year was a piece of legislation eventually called the Suppression of Communism Act, which gave powers to the government to suppress not only the Communist Party but other opponents it deemed to be troublesome.

Before the legislation was passed, the communists initiated plans for a one-day strike on May Day 1950, in protest against the government. Support for the plan was forthcoming from the Indian Congress as well as some ANC branches. But it was adamantly opposed by Mandela and other members of the Congress Youth League, who accused the communists of trying to upstage the ANC, which had also called for a one-day strike in its 'Programme of Action' the previous year but had so far failed to organize one. The Youth League's bulletin, *African Lodestar*, attacked communism as a foreign ideology, equating it with movements like fascism.

So hostile were Mandela and his colleagues that they took to breaking up Communist Party meetings canvassing support for the May Day strike, heckling speakers and tearing up placards. At an ANC meeting in Newclare, Mandela pushed the Indian speaker,

Yusuf Cachalia, from the platform. In Commissioner Street, he fell into a heated argument with the young Indian activist Ahmed 'Kathy' Kathrada, who accused him and the Youth League of refusing to work with Indians and Coloureds.

Despite the efforts of Mandela and other members of the Youth League, the May Day strike achieved considerable success. Thousands stayed away from work. But in four places – Alexandra, Sophiatown, Benoni and Orlando – the day ended in violence between police and crowds gathering on the streets in which eighteen people died. In Orlando, trouble broke out as police were escorting home workers who had ignored the strike. Mandela and Sisulu were present at the time, endeavouring to persuade protesters to disperse. When police opened fire, they were forced to take refuge in a nearby nurses' hostel. 'That day,' recalled Mandela, 'was a turning point in my life, both in understanding through first-hand experience the ruthlessness of the police and in being deeply impressed by the support African workers had given to the May Day call.'

Two weeks later, angered by the police action, the ANC's national executive committee decided to call for another day of protest on 26 June, joining forces with the Indian Congress. This time, the Youth League, humbled by the lack of support it had gained on the first occasion, issued a fiery statement in support of the protest, concluding with the words, 'Up, you Mighty Race!'

The Suppression of Communism Act, meanwhile, passed through parliament. It was the first weapon in an arsenal of security measures acquired by the government that over the next four decades would provide it eventually with totalitarian control. So wide was the act's definition of communism that it could be used to silence anyone who opposed government policy simply by 'naming' them. Communism now meant not only Marxist-Leninism but also 'any related form of that doctrine' which sought to bring about 'any political, industrial, social or economic change within the Union by the promotion of disturbance or disorder', or which aimed at 'the encouragement of feelings of hostility between the European and non-European races of the Union'. In effect, the act equated communism with any determined form of opposition to apartheid. The government was empowered to ban any organization, to remove its members from public office, to place them under house arrest, to restrict their movements, to prohibit them from attending public or even social gatherings and to proscribe their writing and their speeches. No reasons had to be given in 'naming' communists; nor was there any right of appeal. Such action could be taken, moreover, against anyone who had ever professed communism.

Meeting in Cape Town in June, before the act took effect, the central committee of the Communist Party debated whether to continue its work underground. Among the seventeen members present were Bram Fischer, Michael Harmel, Yusuf Dadoo, Moses Kotane and J. B. Marks. The difficulties of moving from legal work to illegal work without a pause were known to be considerable. The police were already in possession of membership lists, seized during raids on party offices at the time of the mineworkers' strike in 1946. Attempts to create the skeleton of an underground organization had already failed. The central committee decided, therefore, to disband the party to try to protect its members, announcing its decision on 20 June, four days before the act became law.

Many communists, however, remained politically active. African members, who numbered 1,600 at the time, were able to channel their energies into the ANC; senior figures like Kotane and Marks were already part of the ANC hierarchy. Indian members, who numbered 250, found a similar home in the Indian Congresses. Only the 150 white members lacked an immediate base from which to operate. But it was not long before they were to regroup and continue their work underground.

The day of protest on 26 June 1950 was the ANC's first attempt ever to organize political action on a nationwide basis. Mandela played his part, helping to man party headquarters in New Court Chambers. But the organizers had left themselves with too little time to make a success of it. The response in the Transvaal was poor; only in Port Elizabeth and among Indians in Durban was there a significant result. No further mass action was attempted for another two years.

Even when he was breaking up Communist Party rallies and gaining a reputation as a hotheaded anti-communist, Mandela maintained close friendships with individual communists and their influence

87

began to tell on him. While some communists loudly denounced his activities, his group of communist friends were always ready for discussion. He often visited the home of J. B. Marks, a wise and genial figure with a record of political activity dating back to the 1920s. Moses Kotane, a pragmatic, clear-thinking man, frequently called on Mandela in Orlando, talking late into the night, trying to convince him that his fears about a communist takeover of the ANC were unfounded. Indian communists like Yusuf Dadoo and his old student friend Ismail Meer, both of whom had served prison sentences during the passive-resistance campaign, encouraged him to take a broader view. In no case could Mandela fault their credentials as dedicated opponents of apartheid.

The influence of a number of white communists was also crucial. Among them was Ruth First, a sharply intelligent journalist, whom Mandela had first met as a student at the University of the Witwatersrand in his first term there in 1943. Brought up in Johannesburg in a left-wing Jewish household, she had immersed herself in political work, joining the Communist Party, serving as secretary of the Young Communist League and helping to set up a left-wing club, the Progressive Youth Council, into which she tried unsuccessfully to entice Mandela. Graduating with a social science degree, she worked briefly as a research officer for the Johannesburg City Council and helped to compile a commemorative album for the city's fiftieth jubilee in 1946. She resigned abruptly at the outbreak of the mineworkers' strike to throw herself into strike activity, producing leaflets from duplicating machines set up in her own lodgings and driving African organizers to mine compounds to deliver them to strikers. When police arrested the entire district committee on charges of sedition, First was asked to become temporary secretary of the Johannesburg party office. Six months later she became Johannesburg editor of *The Guardian*, a left-wing weekly newspaper written mainly by white communists. She made her own mark as a journalist in 1947 with an exposé of forced labour practices on white farms in Bethal district in the eastern Transvaal, an investigation she undertook with Michael Scott. 'I really respected that lady,' said Mandela, 'because of her intelligence and her commitment.'

For several years, she had a close relationship with Mandela's Indian friend, Ismail Meer. Then in 1949 she married Joe Slovo, a law student at Wits who was as ardent a communist as she was. The son of a poor Jewish immigrant family from Lithuania, Slovo had left school at the age of fourteen and joined the Communist Party three years later, throwing himself tirelessly into party work 'in the certainty that the revolution was around the corner' – a belief that never really left him. After serving in an army signals unit during the war, he enrolled at Wits to study law. It was during his final year there that he met Mandela, spending hours arguing with him about communist preparations for the May Day strike. After graduating in 1950, Slovo specialized as a defence lawyer in political trials. The Slovo household in Roosevelt Park in the northern suburbs of Johannesburg was to become a regular meeting place for political activists in the 1950s.

Then there was Michael Harmel, another journalist and the party's leading theoretician. Mandela had met Harmel at his first encounter with communists at a social gathering to which Nat Bregman had invited him. Taking care to dress properly for the occasion, with a jacket and tie, as Fort Hare had taught him, Mandela was disconcerted to find that Harmel, whom he had been told held a master's degree, was not wearing a tie. 'I just could not reconcile this discrepancy,' he recalled. Harmel, in fact, possessed few social graces, but it was precisely this dislike of convention that Mandela found so attractive. He led a disorganized, forgetful life, but was admired by his colleagues for his analytical mind and theoretical knowledge. Much of his influence stemmed from his readiness, as a doctrinaire communist, to provide answers and explanations for any issue that arose. Drawn to Marxism while studying economics at Rhodes University, he had joined the Communist Party in 1939 and for nine years served on the central committee, until the party was disbanded in 1950. He was known as a forceful debater and one of the most rigid party men in Johannesburg.

The most remarkable communist of all was Bram Fischer. Not only was he an Afrikaner but he came from the Orange Free State aristocracy. His grandfather had been prime minister of the Orange River Colony during the era of British rule and his father had served as Judge-President of the Orange Free State. A Rhodes scholar at Oxford University, an accomplished sportsman and a successful lawyer, he moved with ease in the highest political and social circles in South Africa, widely admired for his many talents and regarded as having a brilliant career ahead of him.

But Fischer had taken a different road. After graduating in law from the University of Cape Town, he had become involved in adult education courses for Africans in Waaihoek location in Bloemfontein, where he taught reading and writing in a dilapidated building with winter winds blowing dust through the makeshift classroom. It was there, he said later, that he came to understand 'that colour prejudice was a wholly irrational phenomenon and that true human friendship could extend across the colour bar . . . That I think was Lesson Number One on my way to the Communist Party.' He participated in meetings of the Joint Council of Europeans and Africans in Bloemfontein, a liberal institution with branches around South Africa where whites and blacks, usually teachers and clergymen, discussed African conditions; he found his encounters with Africans there a 'real breakthrough'. A visit he made to the Soviet Union in 1933, while on vacation from Oxford, left him deeply impressed by Soviet achievements and he subsequently became a true believer in both communism and the Soviet Union, attracted not so much by ideological considerations as by the humanitarian ideals that underpinned the communist faith.

His life became filled with efforts to assist the African cause. He served along with Dr Xuma on the Alexandra Health Committee, the only form of administration that Alexandra township possessed, he joined the Johannesburg Joint Council and he helped the ANC to draw up a new constitution. He was ready at all times to act in defence of those in difficulty with the police, as on the occasion when he came to the rescue of Mandela's Indian friends.

His wife, Molly Krige, who was related to the Smuts family, shared his ideals, standing as a Communist Party candidate in local elections in Johannesburg in 1945, though without success. On summer weekends their house in Oaklands was open to friends and acquaintances of all races. At the annual dances for *The Guardian* which they held in Beaumont Street, up to 200 guests would come.

The impression that Bram Fischer made on Mandela was profound, as much on a personal level as a political one. But what was especially important in influencing Mandela's own outlook was that Fischer was an Afrikaner. In an age when Afrikaners were coming to be regarded by Africans as the enemy, Mandela had found an Afrikaner friend.

It was by keeping such company that Mandela's hostility towards the communists began to dissipate. Feeling the need to be able to counter their arguments over doctrinal issues, he started to study Marxist literature, finding some of the ideas it contained appealing: 'I found myself strongly drawn to the idea of a classless society which, to my mind, was similar to traditional African culture where life was shared and communal.' He also found aspects of Marxist economic analysis relevant. Above all there was the communist call for revolutionary action, together with the practical example that the Soviet Union set in supporting liberation movements among colonial peoples.

But it was as much the need for allies in facing the onslaught of apartheid legislation that brought Mandela to recognize the value of collaboration with other groups. As one by one the pillars of the apartheid system were erected and ever more draconian measures were introduced to suppress the government's opponents, the idea of Africans 'going it alone' began to look increasingly impractical. Following the Population Registration Act in 1950 came the Group Areas Act, a piece of legislation intended over the years to divide every town and village in South Africa into separate racial zones, even though this would involve uprooting whole communities. Then, in March 1951, Malan turned his attention to the Coloured community, introducing a bill – the Separate Registration of Voters Bill – aimed at removing the Coloureds of the Cape Province from the common roll by which they had been entitled to vote since 1853.

Until Malan came to power, the Coloured community had largely escaped the kind of repressive measures inflicted on the African population by successive white governments. In the Western Cape, where most lived, the Coloureds could reside, work and travel where they chose. In areas of Cape Town, they shared the same streets and sometimes the same houses as whites. They also shared the common roll. In nine Cape constituencies, their voting power was considerable and used mainly in favour of Smuts's United Party in the 1948 election.

In attempting to get rid of the Coloured vote, Malan precipitated both a protracted legal battle by the Coloured community and a wave of political protest. A new organization formed by Coloureds, the Franchise Action Committee, called for strike action and asked for support from other anti-apartheid groups. The support they received came not only from the ANC but also from white protesters. A group of white ex-servicemen calling themselves the Torch Commando organized a series of torch-lit rallies in Cape Town, Port Elizabeth and Johannesburg which drew significant support from the white population. But the Torch Commando soon reached the limits to which traditional liberals in South Africa were then prepared to go. While supporting the campaign for the rights of the Coloured population, it failed to agree over the admission of Coloureds as members, with the result that Coloured ex-servicemen withdrew. Thus ended the first and last major protest by whites against the apartheid system.

Taking stock of all the protest activity under way, by Coloureds, Indians and Africans alike, Walter Sisulu introduced the idea of a coordinated civil-disobedience campaign against the government, involving trained volunteers from all groups who would deliberately court arrest and imprisonment by contravening selected laws and regulations in ways similar to the Indian passive resistance campaign of 1946. If sufficient numbers were arrested, the jails would overflow and the system would begin to break down.

When he first heard the idea, Mandela was enthusiastic, but he wanted the campaign to be exclusively African. Although his resistance to the communists was waning, he remained wary of the influence of Indians in any joint campaign. His Africanist views were still firmly held. In 1950, he had been elected as president of the Youth League, the last stronghold of the Africanist camp. For months, Mandela continued to hold out stubbornly against a joint campaign, even though the tide of opinion in the ANC was running strongly against him. At an ANC national executive meeting in June 1951, when joint action with Indian and Coloured organizations was proposed, his arguments against it were promptly voted down. At the ANC's annual conference in December 1951, when he spoke again in favour of a 'go it alone' strategy, he was given similarly short shrift. Only when faced with an overwhelming vote in favour of joint action did Mandela commit the Youth League to support it.

In January 1952, an ultimatum calling for the repeal of six 'unjust laws', signed by Dr Moroka and Sisulu, was sent to Prime Minister Malan. Among the laws cited were the Suppression of Communism Act, the Group Areas Act, the Separate Registration of Voters Bill and the pass laws, which Malan's government had enforced with ever-greater vigour. Unless the government complied, the signatories warned, a 'Defiance Campaign' would start. Malan's secretary replied that the government had no intention of repealing the laws and warned that it would 'use the full machinery at its disposal to quell any disturbances'. The date then set for the start of the Defiance Campaign was 26 June, the anniversary of the day of protest in 1950. It was a date that was to become a focal point in the calendar of resistance activity for years to come.

The biggest names in the campaign were Moroka and Dadoo. Other key figures included Marks, Sisulu and Yusuf Cachalia, the Indian activist whom Mandela had once pushed from the platform. Mandela too, despite his prolonged opposition to joint action, was given a central role, being appointed national volunteer-in-chief. His main task involved the recruitment, training and coordination of volunteers. Their mission was to flout apartheid laws through acts of defiance such as using railway coaches, waiting rooms and platform seats designated for Europeans only, or by parading on the streets after curfew without permits, or by entering locations without permits. Whenever possible, the authorities were to be forewarned of the intentions of each batch of volunteers; in some cases, full lists of names of the volunteers involved were politely handed in to the police. Following this level of protest would come mass defiance.

Addressing groups of potential volunteers, Mandela warned of the difficulties and dangers they would face from the authorities, who would retaliate with arrests, imprisonment and possibly violence. But whatever happened, he told them, they were to respond to violence with non-violence. Mandela believed that non-violent protest was essential, not on moral grounds, as propounded by Indian campaigners like Manilal Gandhi, the Mahatma's son, but for purely practical reasons: any attempt at violence would be swiftly crushed.

Four days before the campaign was due to start, Mandela addressed a rally in Durban called the Day of the Volunteers, organized jointly by the ANC and the Indian Congress. Some

10,000 Africans and Indians turned out to participate. It was the first occasion that Mandela had addressed a mass audience and he found the experience exhilarating. The Defiance Campaign, he said, would make history. It would be the most powerful action ever undertaken by the masses in South Africa: 'We can now say unity between the non-European people in this country has become a living reality.' For Mandela, the remark had personal as well as political significance in view of his long-held opposition to interracial cooperation.

He displayed a remarkable optimism about what could be achieved by such methods of protest:

> I visualized that if the Defiance Campaign reached the stage of mass defiance, the government would either say to the ANC . . . we will repeal these laws, we will remove discrimination and from now on everybody in this country . . . is entitled to vote for members of parliament . . . or, if the government refused to take this attitude, we would expect the voters, because of the situation, to say, we can't go on with a government like this; we think that the government should make way for a government which is more sensible, more responsible, a government which will change its policy and come to terms with these people; and then they would vote it out of power.

The campaign began in a mood of exuberance. Early in the morning, a group of volunteers in Port Elizabeth marched through the 'Europeans Only' entrance at the railway station, singing freedom songs and accompanied by a cheering crowd of friends and family. They were promptly arrested by police. The same cheerful atmosphere surrounded the next planned event later in the day in Boksburg, east of Johannesburg, when a small group of Africans and Indians, led by Walter Sisulu and a veteran Gandhi supporter, Nana Sita, walked into the African location without entry permits, holding up their thumbs in the Congress salute. Mandela was present, but only as a spectator. He had previously delivered a letter to the Boksburg magistrate, advising him that a group of volunteers would enter the location without permits. All the group were taken off to the police cells. That night, ANC supporters meeting in the Garment Workers' Hall in Anderson Street in Johannesburg left the building after the curfew had started at 11 p.m. and were arrested.

Mandela, who had been attending a meeting of his own with other campaign leaders in a nearby office at the time, was not due to stage his own act of defiance until later in the campaign. But emerging on to the streets at midnight with Yusuf Cachalia, thinking of nothing more than the need for a hot meal and some sleep, he suddenly found himself under arrest. He felt like explaining that it was not his turn to be arrested. But, along with Cachalia, who burst out laughing at the irony of it all, he was taken away in a police truck to the cells in Marshall Square, a gloomy red-brick police station in the city centre, and joined the fifty or so volunteers there.

This was Mandela's first experience of police cells and the treatment meted out there. In the drill yard that night, a young white policeman pushed one of the volunteers so forcefully that he fell down some steps and broke his ankle. Mandela, who had been walking close by at the time, immediately protested, whereupon he was kicked on the shin and told to keep quiet. Eventually a senior policeman was called. When Mandela demanded medical attention, he was told to put in his request the next day. The volunteer spent the night groaning with pain. Mandela stayed in the cells for two days, before being released on bail.

The campaign quickly caught the popular imagination. The slogan 'Mayibuye Afrika!' – 'Let Africa return!' – became a common greeting on the streets. With almost religious fervour, days of prayer, hymn-singing and church services were held throughout the country. During July, more than 1,500 people were arrested for acts of civil disobedience; in September, the peak of the campaign, the number reached 2,500. In five months, nearly 8,000 people went to prison for periods ranging from one to three weeks, most of them charged under the Suppression of Communism Act.

No longer was white help spurned. At a public meeting in November at Darragh Hall in Johannesburg, Walter Sisulu, Oliver Tambo and Yusuf Cachalia urged an audience of 200 whites to join forces by forming 'a parallel white organization' to work in close cooperation with the ANC and the Indian Congress.

> The silence of European democrats to the challenge of the issues involved in the Defiance Campaign is being construed by Non-Europeans as acquiescence in and approval of the government's

policies, thus rapidly creating the belief among large numbers of Non-Europeans that all whites are hostile to them and their aspirations and that the situation is being transformed into a white versus non-white struggle.

In December, in one of the final acts of defiance, when a group of volunteers broke permit regulations in Germiston, their number included seven whites, one of whom, Patrick Duncan, was the son of a former governor-general. Duncan's act of defiance gave the campaign both prestige and respectability. 'It came as a gift from heaven,' remarked Cachalia. 'It stopped the campaign from becoming racial.'

The government, meanwhile, reacted not in the conciliatory manner that Mandela had anticipated but with ruthless determination to crush the campaign. In July, police raided the offices of the ANC and the Indian Congress and the homes of their officials, confiscating documents and papers, and then arrested twenty leaders of the campaign in Johannesburg, including Mandela, Sisulu, Marks, Moroka, Dadoo and Cachalia, charging them with promoting communism. Mandela was arrested in the office of the law firm of H. M. Basner, for which he was working at the time, but, like the others, he was subsequently released on bail.

Their trial in November became the focus of national attention. For the first time, ANC leaders faced the prospect of imprisonment for political protest against the government, an event which distinguished the Defiance Campaign from all previous protests over the past forty years. Crowds of supporters gathered outside the Johannesburg magistrates' court. In a packed courtroom, all were found guilty of what was termed 'statutory communism'. But as the judge in the case, Judge Franz Rumpff, admitted, 'This has nothing to do with communism as it is commonly known.' Furthermore, he accepted that though the accused had planned acts that ranged from 'open non-compliance of laws to something that equals high treason', they had consistently instructed their supporters 'to follow a peaceful course of action and to avoid violence in any shape or form'. They were sentenced to nine months' imprisonment with hard labour, but the sentence was suspended for two years.

But far from being an occasion for demonstrating their solidarity against the government, the trial became the source of considerable acrimony. For Dr Moroka, a pillar of respectability in his community, the idea of being convicted of supporting communism and going to prison for it was too hard to bear. Breaking ranks with the rest of the accused, he decided to employ his own lawyer. Mandela's efforts to get him to change his mind were to no avail. At the trial, he alone took the witness stand to declare his total opposition to communism and entered a separate plea of mitigation that stressed his long friendship with the Afrikaner people and the assistance he had given them. His final assertion was that he did not believe in racial equality. To have the figurehead of the campaign forsake it at its climax was a humiliating blow.

To ensure that not only this campaign was stamped out but that no similar one could ever be started again, the government employed new measures. In December, banning orders were imposed on fifty leaders and organizers, preventing some, like Marks and Dadoo, from participating in any ANC or Indian Congress activity for life and others for lesser periods. Mandela was banned from meetings of all kinds and restricted to the district of Johannesburg for a period of six months. New legislation was then introduced which laid down severe penalties of fines, imprisonment and corporal punishment for anyone inciting others to commit civil-disobedience offences and which empowered the government to declare a state of emergency and use emergency regulations whenever 'the maintenance of public order was endangered'. The effect was to make protest virtually illegal.

The Defiance Campaign of 1952 transformed the ANC from an élite group into a mass movement. The sight of Africans defying the government won it new prestige. The fear of refusing to submit to white authority lost its sting. Its membership rose from 7,000 to perhaps as many as 100,000. The campaign showed, moreover, what could be achieved through African and Indian collaboration. Abroad, the African cause gained international attention for the first time.

But the Defiance Campaign also marked a high point in ANC activity. Never again, during the 1950s, was it able to mount successfully such organized resistance against the government. Deprived of most of its leaders, fearful of reprisal from the government's arsenal of security measures and short of funds, the movement lost much of its momentum. For another two years, no major campaigning was undertaken.

Nevertheless, the sense of achievement among those like Mandela who had participated in it was profound. 'The campaign freed me from any lingering sense of doubt or inferiority I might still have felt,' he said. 'It liberated me from the feeling of being overwhelmed by the power and seeming invincibility of the white man and his institutions.'

But an even more important personal transformation had begun during the course of the campaign. For practical reasons, Mandela had come to accept that a multiracial strategy was necessary in dealing with the government, abandoning the Africanist notions that he had held for so long. In time, his support for a multiracial strategy developed into a unshakeable conviction about the importance of a multiracial approach in striving for non-racial democracy which never wavered, even under the greatest pressure the government could inflict.

What the Defiance Campaign also showed was that Mandela harboured naïve illusions about both the government and the white population – illusions that were to remain with him for many years, with disastrous consequences.

CHAPTER 5

The 'M' Plan

Alongside these political dramas, Mandela's career as a lawyer was slowly taking shape. Although he had abandoned his studies for a law degree, his intention to qualify as an attorney held firm. After working for Terblanche and Brigish for about one year, he joined another liberal firm, Helman and Michel, passing his qualifying exam in 1952. Needing a testimonial to join the Transvaal Law Society, Mandela went to see Lazar Sidelsky, his old employer, with whom he had served his articles. Sidelsky took the opportunity to warn him to stay out of politics. '"You'll end up in jail sooner or later," I said. Mandela replied, "For the benefit of my people I must carry on." I retorted, "You'll do more for your people if you set an example to them. Let your people become educated. Don't worry about politics."' Sidelsky recalled with humour, 'I felt inclined not to give him that testimonial.'

Mandela's next employer, Hyman Basner, the first to hire him as a qualified lawyer, was more accustomed than Sidelsky to the political hurly-burly in which radical lawyers became involved. A former communist who had served as a Natives' representative in the Senate, he was well known for his passionate support of African rights. 'A strike, a boycott, a clash between Africans and the police – where such a thing happened, there would Basner arrive at speed prepared to speak and, as a lawyer, to defend Africans in court,' Eddie Roux, another former communist, wrote of him. It was at the offices of H. M. Basner that Mandela was arrested on charges under the Suppression of Communism Act. Unlike Sidelsky, Basner made no objections to Mandela's political activities, as long as his work for the law firm was handled properly.

He embarked on his first case in court, armed with a battery of legal books and brimming with confidence. The magistrate duly found his client not guilty. 'I started to swell with pride. Then the magistrate said, "Mr Mandela, I have found your client not guilty, not because of you, but in spite of you." He said all the books I had brought had nothing to do with the case, adding, "I hope that, one day, when another poor accused comes to you, you will at least know what books to bring."'

After several months working for Basner, Mandela felt ready to set up his own law practice, opening an office in August 1952. He then persuaded Oliver Tambo, who had given up his teaching post at St Peter's to take up law five years before and who had also just qualified as an attorney, to join him in a partnership.

As partners, as well as political colleagues, they made an interesting contrast. Tambo was by nature quiet and thoughtful, with a cool, logical mind; deeply religious, he was still contemplating the possibility of ordination. At St Peter's, he had been immensely popular with his students and among staff he was highly respected for his principled approach, arguing resolutely against those who criticized his involvement as a teacher in politics. 'Where men cannot help themselves, they must be helped by others who are able,' he said. 'I want to help lead the struggle for African liberation. How can you claim this is not the role of the teacher? I refuse to be diverted from it.'

Mandela was altogether more assertive, more combative and more emotional, quicker to anger and with a liking for action. At the law firm of Kovalsky and Tuch, where Tambo worked before joining Mandela, a white secretary, Betty Shein, accustomed to Tambo's modest demeanour, noticed the contrast with Mandela, who often came round at lunchtime to discuss ANC business with him. Mandela, she recalled, would stride into the reception area, glancing around to see whether anyone was going to greet him; if he encountered only sullen stares, as was customary when blacks entered a white office, he would call out, 'Mr Tambo, please,' and make a point of sitting in a whites-only chair, causing a considerable stir, not least because nobody in the office addressed Tambo as 'Mr'.

Mandela made the same point in magistrates' court, ignoring the segregation rules which applied there, choosing the whites-only entrance and always ready with an answer when challenged. Once, when a supposedly white clerk, whose features clearly suggested mixed parentage, shouted at him, 'What are you doing in here?' Mandela leaned over the counter towards him, staring straight into his eyes, and said quietly, 'What are *you* doing in here?'

The firm of Mandela and Tambo opened for business in December 1952 in Chancellor House, Fox Street, a shabby building across the road from the magistrates' courts, owned by Indians who were prepared to take on African tenants. They were soon inundated with clients. Each morning, queues of Africans crowded into the small waiting room, stretching back into the corridors and down the stairs. Many of them were victims of the apartheid system, caught in the web of pass laws, curfew laws, liquor laws, residence laws and employment laws which made criminals of ordinary people. From Mandela and Tambo they received a sympathetic hearing and a willingness to act.

Mandela was in and out of court all day, using the courts as an opportunity to challenge white authority and gaining a reputation as a bold courtroom performer. In some courts he was treated by officials with courtesy; in others with resentment and hostility. White witnesses often refused to answer his questions directly, speaking only to the magistrate. Police witnesses regarded him with contempt.

One white magistrate in Kempton Park, a village east of Johannesburg, so resented the appearance of Mandela before him that he did his utmost to prevent him from proceeding in court. Acting on behalf of an African clerk accused of fraud, Mandela rose to introduce himself to the magistrate, Willem Dormehl.

MANDELA: I appear for the accused, Your Worship.
MAGISTRATE: And who are you?
MANDELA: My name is Nelson Mandela, Your Worship. I appear for the accused.
MAGISTRATE: How can you appear for the accused? Are you an attorney?
MANDELA: Yes, of course, Your Worship.
MAGISTRATE: Where is your certificate?
MANDELA: I don't usually walk around with my certificate, Your Worship.
MAGISTRATE: How then am I supposed to know that you are an attorney?

MANDELA: I suggest you telephone the registrar of the court in Johannesburg or Pretoria and ask him whether or not my name is still on the roll of attorneys . . .

MAGISTRATE: I am not prepared to do that. This case will be postponed and you can come again with your Certificate of Admission as an attorney.

MANDELA: May I suggest that we proceed with the case? The accused faces a number of charges. The case will not finish today. I can produce my certificate on the subsequent day on which the hearing of the case will be resumed.

MAGISTRATE: It will be quite irregular to do it that way. The case will be postponed. Mr Prosecutor, what date do you suggest?

PROSECUTOR: The 22nd, Your Worship.

MANDELA: (*in an aside to the prosecutor, but within earshot of the magistrate*) I am not available on the 22nd. Can you make it either the 21st or the 23rd?

PROSECUTOR: I would suggest the 23rd, Your Worship.

MAGISTRATE: Mr Prosecutor, you have already suggested the 22nd. I have written it down. I am not going to scratch it out or amend my record. You don't have to agree to a date suggested by a person who has not satisfied me that he is entitled to appear in my court. The case will be postponed to the 22nd.

MANDELA: But . . . !

MAGISTRATE: I have already postponed the matter. I will not hear another word that you have to say in my court. Call the next case, Mr Prosecutor.

Mandela sought the assistance of a young white colleague, George Bizos, a former law student at the University of the Witwatersrand who had recently qualified as an advocate. Born in a rural village in Greece, Bizos had been forced to flee at the age of thirteen, along with his father, to escape the German advance and had arrived in Johannesburg in 1941, the same year as Mandela. They were to form a lifelong friendship. Bizos agreed to take on Mandela's previously arranged case, leaving him free to return to Kempton Park to confront Dormehl. Mandela duly presented his certificate and the case was allowed to proceed. But no sooner had Mandela begun a cross-examination of the first witness than the magistrate made a series of interruptions.

MAGISTRATE: You cannot ask that. The question is not clear to me. The witness doesn't have to answer that question.

MANDELA: Would Your Worship record my question and your ruling that it is not admissible?

MAGISTRATE: You are not here to tell me how to run my court. I will record that which I consider relevant.

MANDELA: The record must be a fair reflection of what transpires in court. If you disallow questions, you are supposed to note the question and the fact that you disallowed it.

MAGISTRATE: I am warning you that you are not here to teach me my job. Ask your next question.

After some fifteen minutes of interruptions, Mandela's patience was wearing thin.

MANDELA: Your Worship makes it very difficult for me . . .

MAGISTRATE: Just one moment. I want to write something down. (*Having done so, Dormehl turned to the accused.*) Your attorney has withdrawn from these proceedings. You have the right to continue . . .

MANDELA: Your Worship . . .

MAGISTRATE: You sit down and keep quiet. (*To the accused*) You have the right to conduct your own defence as a result of your attorney's withdrawal . . .

MANDELA: Your Worship . . .

MAGISTRATE: Sit down or I will commit your for contempt. (*To the accused*) Or you may ask for a postponement in order to get a new attorney to represent you.

MANDELA: I have not withdrawn from this case. I want it recorded that I have not withdrawn. I want it recorded that I merely said that you are making it difficult for me to continue my cross-examination.

MAGISTRATE: I have told you to sit down and keep quiet. You no longer have *locus standi* in my court.

MANDELA: I protest. I am still appearing for the accused.

MAGISTRATE: I will count to three and if you have not sat down by then, I will commit you for contempt and ask the court orderly to take you to the cells. I order you to sit down.

Mandela remained standing while Dormehl counted slowly to three. The magistrate then ordered Mandela to be removed from court. The court orderly, a young constable, moved in his direction. 'You had better not touch me if you don't want any trouble,' Mandela warned. The constable hesitated. Mandela picked up his files and walked out of court with the words 'I'll be back.'

After discussing with Bizos what course of action to take, Mandela decided to get his client to petition the Supreme Court, asking Dormehl to recuse himself on the grounds that he had objected to the client being defended by a black attorney. When the matter came before Judge Quartus de Wet, Dormehl was given short shrift. 'This is the sort of thing that brings the administration of justice into disrepute in our country,' de Wet told Dormehl's lawyer. 'Tell your client that the quicker he recuses himself from this case, the better for all concerned.'

Mandela throve on the racial tension in court, determined to show that blacks did not have to buckle to white pressure. He relished subjecting police witnesses to relentless cross-examination and taking issue with hostile magistrates like Dormehl. One of his articled clerks, Godfrey Pitje, recalled, 'Nelson would walk into court as if it was his own. He sent shivers through some of the officials.'

His court appearances gained a popular following. Hearing of an impending Mandela court case, township residents would fill the public gallery, applauding loudly on occasion, to the fury of court officials. Mandela's showmanship in court duly became part of his reputation. He was fond of telling the story of his defence of an African servant accused of stealing clothes belonging to her 'madam'. Beginning his cross-examination of the 'madam', Mandela walked over to a table where the stolen clothes were on display, studied them and then, with the tip of his pencil, picked up a pair of panties. Turning slowly to the witness box, he asked, 'Madam, are these . . . yours?' Too embarrassed to admit that they were, she replied, 'No.' The case was dismissed.

Outside the courtroom, Mandela's performance was not always so effective. Among the advocates briefed by Mandela was Harold Wolpe, a communist lawyer who had studied with him at the University of the Witwatersrand. Wolpe described Mandela's briefings as 'none too meticulous'. In the office, it was Tambo, with his prodigious capacity for work, who shouldered most of the burden. A young student from St Peter's, Fikile Bam, who went to the offices of Mandela and Tambo on Saturdays, the busiest day of the week, to learn how a law office functioned, noticed how 'Mandela would dash in for two hours then dash out again, while

Tambo put in full hours'. Political activity was Mandela's favourite occupation.

The law practice of Mandela and Tambo, however, was not secure from the tentacles of apartheid. Under the terms of the Urban Areas Act, Africans were not permitted to occupy business premises in the city without ministerial consent. When they applied for consent, it was never granted. Instead they were given a temporary permit under the Group Areas Act. When that expired, the authorities would refuse to renew it, insisting that they should leave the city and practise in an African township miles away from where their clients could reach them during working hours. 'This was tantamount to asking us to abandon our legal practice,' Mandela recalled. So they continued to remain in Chancellor House, but illegally and with the threat of prosecution and eviction hanging over their heads.

A more serious threat came from the Transvaal Law Society, which in April 1954 petitioned the Supreme Court to have Mandela struck off the role of accredited attorneys on the grounds that his political activities, for which he had been convicted under the Suppression of Communism Act, constituted unprofessional and dishonourable conduct. With Bram Fischer's help, Mandela secured the services of a distinguished advocate, Walter Pollack, chairman of the Johannesburg Bar Council, who agreed to appear *pro amico* for Mandela. Judge Ramsbottom, who heard the case, upheld Mandela's position, finding that there was nothing dishonourable in an attorney campaigning for his political beliefs, even if his activities infringed the law.

Despite these hazards, the firm of Mandela and Tambo prospered. For the first time in his life, Mandela became relatively affluent. He purchased a large Oldsmobile, indulged his taste for fine clothes and cut a dashing figure across Johannesburg society, equally at ease at multiracial parties as the back alleys of black townships. His physical presence was striking – he was six feet two inches tall and broad-shouldered – and he exuded confidence and energy. When he first set foot in the Observatory home of two communist friends, Rusty and Hilda Bernstein, one of their children ran into the kitchen shouting excitedly: 'There's a giant in the front room!' After that he was known in the Bernstein family as 'the giant'.

He was able to afford suits from Alfred Kahn, a fashionable tailor favoured by members of the prestigious Rand Club in Loveday Street nearby. George Bizos came across him there on one of his errands as a lawyer's clerk, collecting a list of customers late with their payments; Mandela was there for a final fitting. He frequented Kapitan's, a smart Indian restaurant on Kort Street, as well as cheaper haunts like Moretsele's, a café on Pritchard Street, where the proprietor, Elias Moretsele, a staunch ANC supporter, allowed friends to eat on credit. He was wealthy enough to return favours to people who had once helped him. Lazar Sidelsky remembered how one wet, windy night, as he waited on the street for a bus to take him home, ruing a business failure which had left him financially crippled, Mandela drew up in his Oldsmobile, offered him a lift home and, on the way, mentioned that he had not yet repaid a loan of £75 – a substantial sum. Sidelsky brushed the matter aside, saying it was of no account, and Mandela did not pursue the matter then, but a few days later Sidelsky received in the post a cheque for £75.

Mandela was also a familiar figure in boxing circles. On most weekday evenings, he would drop by for an hour or two of training at a boxing club at an Orlando community centre which he joined in 1950. Like all the other boxing clubs which flourished in Orlando, it was poorly equipped. There was no ring; boxers trained on a cement floor. The club, consisting of both amateur and professional boxers, nevertheless managed to produce several champions. Boxing was the most popular sport among Africans at the time and boxing champions were accorded high status. The greatest hero of all was Jake Tuli, an Orlando boy who became the British Empire flyweight boxing champion. His triumph abroad was all the more significant since at home African boxers were not allowed to box white opponents. Mandela was in the heavyweight division. He enjoyed the tactics of boxing rather than the physical confrontation and his main interest was in the training sessions, which served as an outlet for stress and tension. But it all added to his reputation as a dynamic young leader.

Mandela's political standing, as a result of the Defiance Campaign and his subsequent trial, had never been higher. Before his six-month ban in December 1952, he had become a well-known figure on the platform at public meetings at Freedom Square in

Fordsburg, in Alexandra, in Sophiatown and in Orlando. In October 1952, when the Transvaal ANC was searching for a new president to replace Marks, who had been banned from membership of the ANC for life, Mandela was chosen for the post. His colleagues sometimes noticed about him a certain imperiousness, particularly when giving orders. Both Walter and Albertina Sisulu tried to persuade him to adopt a less lofty manner in public. 'But,' Albertina recalled, 'he was a Xhosa aristocrat and his training from childhood had made him the way he was, aloof and sometimes a bit arrogant. It didn't matter, because the people liked to look up to a leader who was regal and maybe even a bit distant.'

His family life suffered grievously from all this activity. So little time did Mandela spend at home during the 1950 protests that his son, Thembi, then five years old, asked his mother, 'Where does Daddy live?' A second son, Makgatho, was born at this time. Mandela managed to get to the hospital for the birth, but, as he later observed, 'it was only a brief respite'. When the banning order was placed on Mandela's political activities, Evelyn secretly welcomed it.

The marriage soon ran into serious difficulties. Because Evelyn's earnings as a nurse were no longer essential to keep the family afloat, she decided in 1952 to enrol for a course on midwifery at King Edward VII hospital in Durban. While she was away, the two children were cared for in Orlando by Mandela's mother and sister. She returned at the end of 1953 to find Mandela in the thick of an affair with a secretary he employed at his office. To Evelyn's fury, she made free use of the family home, even following Mandela into the bedroom and the bathroom. When Evelyn objected to her presence, Mandela became enraged. Only when Evelyn threatened to throw boiling water over her did the visits to the house stop. But the affair continued.

Another friendship that Mandela made at this time was also the subject of much rumour. Lilian Ngoyi was a vivacious and energetic woman from poor origins who had for years worked as a machinist in a clothing factory in Johannesburg, until the Defiance Campaign inspired her, at the age of forty-one, to throw herself tirelessly into political activity. She rose quickly to become the most prominent woman in the ANC in the 1950s. Her talent as a public speaker, with a direct, emotional style, was admired by all who heard her.

'When she spoke from a platform,' wrote her friend Helen Joseph, 'she could do as she wished with her audience; they laughed with her, wept with her.' In conversation, her face was alive with expression, her hands constantly on the move. Mandela, among many others, found her immensely attractive. Living in Orlando, she often visited Mandela's house, and her work for the ANC, as president of the Women's League, regularly brought them together. Mandela always denied that they were lovers, but the rumours persisted for many years.

Mandela's frequent absences from home became a constant source of argument. Evelyn, knowing of the rumours about his involvement with other women, took to questioning him about his movements, eventually provoking Mandela to respond, 'No policeman asks questions like you.' Evelyn never understood Mandela's deep commitment to political activity, believing his interest to be no more than a youthful aberration which would in time fade away. Nor did she become reconciled to the idea of living permanently in Johannesburg, expecting that they would eventually return to the Transkei to play a prominent role in the community there, as Mandela himself had once talked of doing.

Another source of dispute between them developed soon after the birth of a daughter, Makaziwe, in 1954. Since the death of their first daughter, Evelyn had prayed fervently for another girl. The arrival of Makaziwe she took to be a sign from God. 'It was then that I began my return to my Christian faith,' she said. She became a devout Jehovah's Witness, even attempting to convert Mandela to her belief, arguing that her religious faith was a higher cause than his politics. A tussle between religion and politics soon engulfed the Mandela household, centring on the children. Evelyn would take them to church at every opportunity, read them Watchtower literature and get them to distribute Watchtower pamphlets in Orlando; Mandela would instruct them in politics, earnestly explaining the significance of pictures he had hung on the wall of Churchill, Stalin, Roosevelt, Gandhi and the storming of the Winter Palace in St Petersburg in 1917.

The marriage sank to the level of sullen silence. Mandela became increasingly cold and distant, spending even more time away from home.

*

From 1952, Mandela was never free from the attention of the police Special Branch. His movements, his contacts, his speeches, like those of other prominent political activists, were all recorded in police dossiers. Informers and police agents infiltrated deep into the hierarchy of the ANC as well as the rank and file, creating an atmosphere of suspicion and mistrust. The sudden increase in ANC membership, prompted by the Defiance Campaign, made it especially vulnerable to police infiltration, leading Mandela to warn of 'many shady characters' within its ranks – saboteurs, *agents provocateurs*, informers, splitters and place-seekers: 'Outside appearances are highly deceptive, and we cannot classify these men by looking at their faces or listening to their sweet tongues, or by their vehement speeches demanding immediate action.'

Police raids on ANC offices and the homes of officials became a constant hazard. 'The raids began in the early 1950s,' recalled Sisulu. 'Raids on our homes, raids on the offices. It became impossible to keep any proper records from that time on. You couldn't keep a diary, you couldn't keep minutes, and not having proper records was very frustrating. There was a lot of harassment, which made my job as secretary-general very difficult.'

The Special Branch in time acquired more and more powers, acting without restraint, indifferent to any notion of legal rights and answerable only to ministers. It had started out as a small unit in 1935 in Marshall Square, keeping track of illicit gold and diamond dealings, but had developed a political role during the war, monitoring anti-government organizations like the Broederbond, before switching its attention in post-war years to the Communist Party. The Nationalist government had turned it into a political arm, separate from the rest of the police force, giving it licence to act as it saw fit in dealing with political dissidents. Special Branch detectives regularly invaded political meetings, recording speeches, photographing members of the audience, noting car number plates outside. An attempt to prevent them attending private meetings initially succeeded. A Supreme Court judge ruled that the police were not entitled as of right to be present. 'This is not yet a police state,' he declared. But the government soon overcame this by amending the law, enabling the police to sit in on any meeting they wanted to. The Special Branch tapped phone calls, intercepted mail, bugged meetings, kept activists under constant surveillance and used threats and intimidation with their employers and families. It was directly responsible for making recommendations about banning orders, about banishment to internal exile and other methods of putting dissidents 'out of action'. Its dossiers were never closed.

The activists delighted in trying to outwit Special Branch detectives, regarding most of them as being inept and incompetent. Between the two sides there were many cases of cautious familiarity. Special Branch men tended to address ANC activists by their first names. Occasionally, at the end of the day, the head of the Johannesburg Special Branch, Major At Spengler, a heavy, thick-set Afrikaner detective, would call in at a shebeen in a printing works in Market Street, used by the ANC to produce pamphlets, for a quiet drink with leading activists and black journalists who congregated there.

Compared to the era of torture, solitary confinement, indefinite detention without trial and murder which followed, the 1950s were a relatively benign decade in the annals of the security police. Assaults on political prisoners were extremely rare, lawyers could gain access to arrested activists without difficulty and house searches still required a magisterial warrant. When Head Constable Carl Johannes Dirker, a lugubrious figure who dogged the lives of many activists year after year, once arrived at Michael Harmel's house, he was asked whether he had a warrant. He sheepishly replied that, being in a hurry, he had taken the wrong file, so Harmel's warrant was still in his office. 'What, then, are you looking for?' asked Harmel. 'Politics, man, politics,' he replied.

However inefficient the Special Branch may have been, government repression exacted a heavy toll. Banning orders preventing activists from attending meetings, restricting their movements to specific districts, prohibiting their involvement in political organizations and trade unions had a debilitating effect. Mandela recalled in his autobiography:

> Banning not only confines one physically, it imprisons one's spirit. It induces a kind of psychological claustrophobia that makes one yearn for not only freedom of movement but spiritual escape. Banning was a dangerous game, for one was not shackled or chained behind bars; the bars were laws and regulations that could easily

be violated and often were. One could slip away unseen for short periods of time and have the temporary illusion of freedom. The insidious effect of bans was that at a certain point one began to think that the oppressor was not without but within.

The ANC itself suffered from a similar paralysis. Its attempts to hold public meetings were frequently blocked by the authorities, printers refused to handle ANC pamphlets for fear of prosecution and most newspapers declined to publish ANC statements. 'The old methods of bringing about mass action through public mass meetings, press statements and leaflets calling upon people to go into action have become extremely dangerous and difficult to use effectively,' Mandela warned an ANC meeting in the Transvaal, held in the aftermath of the Defiance Campaign. In an endeavour to circumvent police harassment and to prepare the ANC for the possibility of an outright ban, as had happened to the Communist Party, Mandela drew up a new plan for political action, advocating a radical departure from the methods previously adopted by the ANC.

It was popularly known as the 'M' Plan, named after Mandela but not given his full name to avoid implicating him in ANC activity at a time when he was supposed to be banned. It involved splitting the entire movement into small units – 'cells' at street level, 'zones' and 'wards' covering larger areas of townships – providing a means of communication throughout the organization without the need to call public meetings and issue statements and enabling it to survive government repression. Part of the plan required branch leaders and other officials to organize political lectures for the benefit of local members. The lecturers were often banned members. Mandela himself, despite being banned, frequently gave lectures in the evening to groups in Orlando.

The 'M' Plan, to which the ANC's national executive attached 'the highest importance', according to Mandela, was implemented in only a few places, mostly in towns in the Eastern Cape. It placed a huge burden of work on local officials, far beyond their capacity to carry it out. There were no funds to pay party workers; everything depended on volunteers working in their spare time. 'Most people were so busy with their ordinary work that they could not find time for Congress duties,' a Natal ANC official reported. The plan also ran into resistance from branch leaders with strong local bases opposed to changes which undermined their own influence.

Mandela's frustration at being hemmed in by the government began to boil over into reckless talk about the use of violence. Shortly after his six-month ban expired in June 1953, he addressed a public meeting in Freedom Square in Sophiatown, telling the crowd that the time for passive resistance had ended, that non-violence would never defeat a white minority government bent on retaining power at any cost and that the only weapon that would destroy apartheid was violence, which Africans would have to use in the near future. With the crowd clapping and cheering, Mandela went on to sing a freedom song with the words 'There are the enemies, let us take our weapons and attack them.' The crowd joined in. When it was over, Mandela pointed to the police clustered around the perimeter of Freedom Square and shouted, 'There, there are our enemies.' The crowd cheered and made aggressive gestures at the police. The police looked nervous, Mandela recalled in his autobiography: 'A number of them pointed back at me as if to say, "Mandela, we will get you for this."'

In secret with Walter Sisulu, Mandela went further. Through the assistance of communist friends, Sisulu had received an invitation to attend a student festival in Bucharest in 1953 and he had arranged to extend his journey abroad with visits to China and the Soviet Union. Before leaving, he agreed with Mandela to approach the Chinese about the possibility of their supplying weapons for an armed struggle. The Chinese expressed support for the ANC's political efforts, but warned against armed struggle. The idea was premature, they felt. Sisulu was told, 'Don't play about with it.' On his return, neither of them took the matter further, nor did they disclose to their ANC colleagues what had occurred.

Loose talk about the use of violence appalled other senior figures in the ANC's leadership, in particular its new president, Albert Luthuli, who had been chosen to replace the discredited Dr Moroka at the annual conference in December 1952. Luthuli was a man of great moral authority and dignity who during the 1950s came to personify the ideals of non-racialism and non-violence espoused by the ANC. Unlike his two predecessors, Xuma and Moroka, he was at home in the world of popular politics and mass action, having a genuine insight into the concerns and problems of ordinary people. He also conformed to the image many whites held of the 'Good Native': he was a devout Christian, a Methodist lay preacher and a tribal chief, with a slow and courteous demeanour. For fifteen years he had taught at Adams College in Natal, an American mission high school, and for seventeen years he had served as chief of the Umvoti Mission Reserve in Zululand. But drawn into the world of African politics in the 1940s, he displayed an unexpected determination to fight for African rights. As president of the ANC's Natal region, he had no hesitation in supporting the Defiance Campaign, nor did he see any conflict in doing so with his role as chief.

The government thought otherwise. In October 1952, Luthuli was summoned to Pretoria and given an ultimatum: he was to resign from either the ANC or the chieftaincy. Luthuli refused to make that choice and was duly dismissed as chief.

In a personal statement about his dismissal, entitled 'The Road to Freedom is via the Cross', Luthuli explained his sense of disillusionment about 'the path of moderation' he had followed hitherto:

> Who will deny that thirty years of my life have been spent knocking in vain, patiently, moderately at a closed and barred door? What have been the fruits of my many years of moderation? Has there been any reciprocal tolerance or moderation from the Government, be it Nationalist or United Party? No! On the contrary, the past thirty years have seen the greatest number of laws restricting our rights and progress until today we have reached a stage where we have almost no rights at all . . . in short, we have witnessed in these years an intensification of our subjection to ensure and protect white supremacy.

He went on:

> This stand of mine . . . might seem foolish and disappointing to some liberal and moderate Europeans and non-Europeans with whom I have worked these many years and with whom I still hope to work. This is no parting of the ways but 'a launching further into the deep' . . . I have embraced the non-violent passive-resistance technique in fighting for freedom because I am convinced it is the only non-revolutionary, legitimate and humane way that could be used by people denied, as we are, effective and constitutional means to further aspirations.

Luthuli went to great lengths to try to reassure whites about African political intentions. He spoke of the future in terms of African 'partnership' in government rather than absolute control of it, accepting 'the fact of the multiracial nature of the country'. The ANC's goal, he wrote in his autobiography, 'is not that Congress shall rule South Africa, but that all Africans shall participate in ownership and government'.

He placed great faith in the moral impact on whites of the African struggle and possessed an abiding optimism that whites would sooner or later be compelled to change heart and accept a shared society. It was such thinking which set the tone of ANC policy throughout the 1950s.

Mandela's remarks in Sophiatown about the use of violence consequently earned him a severe reprimand from the ANC's national executive. The Special Branch also exacted its revenge. In September 1953, Mandela was served with an order under the Suppression of Communism Act requiring him to resign from the ANC, restricting him to the Johannesburg district and prohibiting him from attending meetings or gatherings for two years. At the age of thirty-five, Mandela's career as a leading ANC activist was brought abruptly to a halt. Henceforth, his involvement had to be conducted in a clandestine manner. From being at the centre of political activity, Mandela was forced to remain on the sidelines, able to exert little influence over the direction the ANC took.

Other setbacks were to follow.

Sophiatown was one of the most vibrant African communities in South Africa. It was the home of writers, musicians, journalists and politicians like the former ANC leader Dr Xuma. In its narrow, crowded streets were schools, churches, cinemas, shops and night-clubs and the only swimming pool for African children in the whole of Johannesburg. It was famous for its gangsters and its shebeen queens, for its nightly toll of murders and knife fights, and for its passion for jazz and dance parties. Drinking establishments like the Back of the Moon and the Thirty-nine Steps attracted the African élite in business, sports and entertainment from all over Johannesburg. On Sunday afternoons the Odin cinema was a regular venue for well-organized 'jam sessions', featuring popular vocal groups like the Manhattan Brothers quartet and their lead singer, Miriam Makeba, and bringing together white as well as black musicians. Sophiatown produced its own stars, including Wilson's Silgee's Jazz Maniacs and Dolly Rathebe, the blues singer who starred in the 1949 film *Jim Comes to Joburg* and became one of the most sought-after women of the 1950s. It also boasted an all-African female band, the Sophiatown Scottish, who dressed in tartan kilts and white gloves and paraded through the streets on Sundays to the accompaniment of drums and trumpets. Its racy, hard-drinking, exuberant style, influenced by American jazz and gangster movies, set the pace for the rest of black urban South Africa. Black youths referred to it proudly as 'the centre of the metropolis'. The sense of drama and excitement it generated was captured regularly on the pages of the popular monthly magazine *Drum*, whose writers, like Sophiatown's Can Themba, were at the forefront of a new wave of investigative journalism, satire, commentary, fiction and musical criticism and whose readers, as its young English editor, Anthony Sampson, noted, 'thought and spoke in jazz and exclamation marks'. *Drum* used Sophiatown as the yardstick of what readers wanted to read about. Sophiatown's resident community of 60,000 was predominantly African but included substantial minorities of Coloureds, Indians, Chinese and even some whites attracted to its bohemian lifestyle.

As famous as Sophiatown's musicians and writers were its gangs. Two effectively divided Sophiatown into rival zones: the Berliners controlled the territory between Ray Street and Johannes Road, while the Americans held sway between Toby Street and Meyer Street. The Berliners tended to engage in small-scale crime, in particular payroll robberies. The Americans specialized in stealing goods from city shops and railway delivery trucks, recycling them in Sophiatown. 'Sophiatown creaked with stolen property,' recalled Michael Dingake, a former resident. Food, liquor, clothes, cutlery, household appliances and furniture items all sold at a fast pace at give-away prices. Gang leaders liked to see themselves as folk heroes, courageous and clever enough to become wealthy at the expense of whites. They dressed in flashy 'American' clothes, drove American-made cars and copied the style of American cinema gangsters, like Richard Widmark in the film *Street with No Name*. A motto they favoured was taken from Willard Motley's novel about a young American gangster, *Knock on Any Door*, which was popular locally: 'Live fast, die young, and leave a good-looking corpse.'

Amid the noise and bustle of this urban maze stood an Anglican mission, whose church, Christ the King, dominated the skyline. Its priest-in-charge, Trevor Huddleston, was a familiar figure on the dusty streets of Sophiatown, dressed in a white flowing cassock and large black hat and usually surrounded by crowds of grubby urchins calling out 'Fader'. Because of his close-cropped, German-style haircut, he was often referred to in the adult community as 'die Jerry'. Huddleston had arrived in Sophiatown in 1943 at the age of twenty-nine after training in a Yorkshire monastery for a monastic order in the Church of England called the Community of the Resurrection. Like Michael Scott, he had become a political activist, but at a much slower pace. Scott complained, during the Tobruk crisis, that Huddleston had failed to come to his aid; and Huddleston later admitted that it had taken him a long time to 'wake up' to the realities of South Africa. But once aroused, his commitment to the African cause became unshakeable. With immense energy, moral zeal and a flair for publicity, he tackled the authorities over one issue after another, campaigning tirelessly with diplomats, businessmen and officials for support in improving African urban life. With the same gusto, he threw himself into the nationalist fray, developing close friendships with Oliver Tambo and Yusuf Cachalia and earning himself the enmity of the government. 'In the Middle Ages,' said one government minister, Jan de Klerk, 'people like Michael Scott and Huddleston would have been burned at the stake.' After six years in Sophiatown, Huddleston moved to the south side of Johannesburg to take up the post of superintendent of St Peter's School in Rosettenville. But his heart remained in Sophiatown. As prominent churchman Charles Hooper once noted, 'Made in Sophiatown' was branded upon his personality. And it was over Sophiatown that Huddleston was to engage in his most dogged campaign against the government.

What enabled Sophiatown to develop such a distinctive character was no more than an accident of history. In 1897 a speculator called Herman Tobiansky bought 237 acres of land on the slopes of a rocky ridge four miles west of Johannesburg, intending to establish a new white suburb there. He named it after his wife, Sophia, and pegged out streets with the names of his children:

Edith, Gerty, Bertha, Toby and Sol. But his plans went awry when the council decided first to establish a sewerage-disposal site nearby and then a municipal location for Africans called Western Native Township next door. Unable to attract a sufficient number of white buyers, Tobiansky resorted to selling his plots to Africans, Coloureds and Indians, as he was then entitled to do. Sophiatown, along with its two adjoining districts of Martindale and Newclare, thus developed as a 'freehold' township, its houses of all shapes and sizes lining steep streets which climbed the hillside. Unlike municipal locations, there was no fence surrounding it, no super-intendent to allocate houses, no policeman to examine permits at the gate and no restrictions on who came and went. 'The streets of Sophiatown were never deserted, they were always full. There was always life, people going up and down like ants,' recalled one former resident. 'Sophiatown had variety, Sophiatown had difference.'

In reality, much of Sophiatown had degenerated into a slum. Though some impressive houses remained, like Dr Xuma's, most buildings were decaying and decrepit, their yards packed tightly with shacks and hovels in which whole families struggled to survive. Landlords crammed as many tenants as possible into one property, often charging them exorbitant rents; as many as eighty people lived on one stand, sharing a single water tap and a single toilet. Much of the area was a health hazard. Yet despite the squalor, Sophiatown retained a strong sense of community. 'Whatever else Sophiatown was, it was home,' wrote Bloke Modisane. 'We made the desert bloom; made alterations; converted half-verandas into kitchens, decorated the houses and filled them with music. We were house-proud. We took the ugliness of life in a slum and wove a kind of beauty.'

With the growth of Johannesburg, however, Sophiatown became encircled by white suburbs. Only a narrow stretch of open veld separated it from the prim white suburb of Westdene. The residents there soon began to agitate for the removal of this 'black spot'. Bowing to white pressure, in 1944 the Johannesburg municipality approved a scheme for its removal, but then took no action. The Nationalist government, however, saw an opportunity for enforcing its apartheid policy and in June 1953 announced plans to move the entire population to a new site under municipal control called Meadowlands, nine miles from Johannesburg, close to the existing township of Orlando. It cited the need for slum clearance in Sophiatown as the reason, although elsewhere in Johannesburg there were slums under municipal control where conditions were far worse. No freehold ownership was to be allowed in Meadowlands.

The plan ran into a storm of protest. Father Huddleston formed one protest committee and Dr Xuma another. The ANC, stirring itself for the first time since the end of the Defiance Campaign, decided in conjunction with the Indian Congress to organize a joint protest at the Odin cinema. Among the speakers invited were Huddleston, Yusuf Cachalia and Mandela, whose six-month banning order had just expired.

The Odin cinema on that Sunday morning in June 1953 was packed with some 1,200 residents. Huddleston arrived, hotfoot from conducting mass at the Church of Christ the King, and immediately fell into an altercation with Special Branch detectives, questioning their right to attend; the Special Branch men grudgingly withdrew. Shortly after Huddleston had finished his speech, a group of armed police strode in, marched on to the stage and arrested the next speaker, Yusuf Cachalia, dragging him towards the exit. The crowd rose to their feet, shouting and booing. Mandela, fearing an ugly turn of events, jumped on to the stage and began singing a well-known protest song, getting the crowd to join in. Huddleston, pursuing Cachalia through the exit, found himself confronting 100 armed police on the street outside. He remonstrated with the officer in charge and eventually the police withdrew, allowing the meeting to continue. Cachalia was later released without being charged. 'I had seen and felt, in those moments, the terrifying spectre of the police state,' Huddleston wrote in his book *Naught for Your Comfort*. 'There was the fierce breath of totalitarianism and tyranny in every attitude, every movement of the police.'

Protest meetings in Freedom Square in the centre of Sophiatown and in other locations continued week after week. With Special Branch detectives recording every word in their notebooks, speakers vied with each other to impress the crowds with their bravado and fearlessness in denouncing the government. Bloke Modisane recorded, 'Every Sunday morning we assembled at Freedom Square, Morris and Victoria Road, to be stampeded into orgiastic reverberations of resounding slogans by thumb-raising politicians trading on mob passions, and one after another they mounted the platform almost in an effort to outdo the other by the sheer volume of noise.' The crowds responded in kind with shouts of *'Asihambi!'* – 'We will not move!'

Mandela addressed many such meetings, depicting Sophiatown as 'the battle between reactionary forces and the forces of liberation' and raising the spectre of violent opposition, before being silenced by his second banning order in September 1953. His involvement in the campaign nevertheless continued. He was a frequent visitor to the Sophiatown home of Robert Resha, the local ANC leader well known for his militant views. He was also able to act there in his professional capacity as a lawyer, advising and defending residents.

The ANC placed great store on the success of its Sophiatown campaign, believing that it was an issue that would galvanize popular resistance to apartheid elsewhere. Chief Luthuli called for it to become the 'Waterloo of Apartheid'. Resha recruited some 500 volunteers in Sophiatown ready to come to the assistance of any residents threatened with eviction.

Yet the campaign was marked by confusion and disputes. The ANC entirely underestimated the willingness of a large number of tenants to escape their slum conditions and move to better housing at cheaper rents in a new township. Local organizers found themselves accused of acting simply to defend the interests of landlords. When Resha's volunteers appeared in uniform on the streets for the first time, the black newspaper *The World* reported sourly that 'many of the volunteers were the sons and relatives of property owners'. Moreover, neither the volunteers nor the residents wishing to stay were given any clear idea from the ANC about how they should resist or for how long. While urging residents not to move from an area where their homes were to be bulldozed, the ANC was unable to organize anything but temporary accommodation elsewhere.

Even as the day of reckoning approached, there was still no sign of a coherent plan, as Bloke Modisane recorded:

> It began to be rumoured around the protest meetings, in and about Sophiatown, that we would resist, by force if necessary, the will of

the government; a campaign with a top-secret plan was whispered in the wind, the hush-hush M-plan which would be implemented on the night of the day before the first removals; the top-secret plan was of such priority in secrecy that there was found no one who knew any details about it, except that it would spring into effective action on the night before removal day.

The first group of 150 families were warned in December 1954 that they would have to leave their homes by 12 February 1955. Without making any contingency plans, the ANC assumed that the government would not act until 12 February. When the government abruptly announced on 8 February that the removals would take place the following morning, therefore, the ANC was caught unprepared.

A group of young activists meeting that night were in favour of erecting barricades and defying the police with whatever weapons came to hand. But the ANC's leaders, including Mandela, ordered them to stand down, believing that violence would have disastrous consequences.

At dawn on 9 February, a large convoy of trucks and armed police moved into Sophiatown, taking control of every street corner and cordoning off two streets scheduled for removal. Within a few hours, the trucks were on their way, with tenants sitting atop stacks of furniture, stoves and bedding. Some were singing, 'To Meadowlands we will go . . .' Once they had gone, the demolition squads moved in.

There was no resistance, no demonstration, no disruption, just slogans on the walls saying 'We Won't Move!' The ANC had chosen the ground on which to stand and had suffered abject failure. Its campaign had been little more than a propaganda exercise.

Mandela admitted the ANC's shortcomings, but drew other conclusions. 'The lesson I took away from the campaign was that, in the end, we had no alternative to armed and violent resistance,' he wrote in his autobiography. 'Over and over again, we had used all the non-violent weapons in our arsenal – speeches, deputations, threats, marches, strikes, stay-aways, voluntary imprisonment – all to no avail, for whatever we did was met by an iron hand.'

*

The destruction of Sophiatown was but the first of a series of forced removals which tore apart long-established communities in South Africa's towns. Tens of thousands of families were uprooted from their homes under the Group Areas Act, on the pretext of preserving racial harmony. The Indian communities in Johannesburg's western districts of Pageview, Vrededorp and Fordsburg, where they had lived for seventy years, building substantial houses, temples, mosques, schools, clinics, cinemas, libraries, businesses and restaurants, were ordered to quit and move to Lenasia, a 'group area' for Indians twenty miles south-west of the city which the government insisted was to become the sole location for Johannesburg's Indians. Pageview was declared a white area in 1956 even though no whites were living there. A similar fate befell the Indian community in Durban, which once owned a quarter of the total area of the city. In the Transvaal, hundreds of Indian businessmen and traders were expelled from central business districts, to the considerable advantage of white shopkeepers. In Cape Town, District Six, an area close to the city centre occupied by Coloureds since 1834, was razed to the ground, its residents forced to move to a bleak tract of land ten miles away. Compensation was paid to families ordered to leave but usually at derisory rates. White property speculators were able to amass fortunes out of the forced sale of houses. In Sophiatown, the new white suburb which arose from the rubble was named Triomf.

Year by year, the apartheid machine gathered increasing momentum. The driving force behind it was a Dutch-born ideological fanatic, Hendrik Verwoerd, who aspired to create in South Africa a new racial order. Appointed as Minister of Native Affairs in 1950, he had already played a prominent role in shaping Nationalist doctrine and theories both as a professor of sociology at the University of Stellenbosch and as editor of the Nationalist paper *Die Transvaler*. Verwoerd believed that his own rise to prominence was as much a matter of divine inspiration as of the policies he propounded and he allowed nothing to deflect him from his purpose. 'I do not have the nagging doubt of ever wondering whether perhaps I am wrong,' he said.

In 1953, Verwoerd turned his attention to the system of African education. For more than 100 years it had remained largely in the hands of church missions. About 90 per cent of all schools were mission schools, administered by some forty mission bodies. Most were heavily dependent on state assistance for the payment of teachers' salaries and school equipment. In many cases they suffered from low teaching standards, inadequate equipment and over-crowded classes. There was always a shortage of funds. Less than half of all African children of school age attended any school at all. But however poor the education offered, the schools provided a vital lifeline into the world of employment and the chance of an income. The start of each school year was marked by desperate struggles by mothers trying to get their children into schools.

Verwoerd decided that control of African education should be wrested from the churches, explaining his reasons in the long, didactic speeches he was fond of making.

> Racial relations cannot improve if the wrong type of education is given to Natives. They cannot improve if the result of Native education is the creation of a frustrated people who . . . have expectations in life which circumstances in South Africa do not allow to be fulfilled . . . Above all, good racial relations cannot exist when the education is given under the control of people who create wrong expectations on the part of the Native himself, if such people believe in a policy of equality. People who believe in equality are not desirable teachers for Natives. Education must train and teach people in accordance with their opportunities in life, according to the sphere in which they live . . .
>
> Bantu education should stand with both feet in the reserves and have its roots in the spirit and being of Bantu society . . . There is no place for him in the European community above the level of certain forms of labour . . . Until now he has been subject to a school system which drew him away from his own community and misled him by showing him the green pastures of European society in which he is not allowed to graze . . . What is the use of teaching a Bantu child mathematics when it cannot use it in practice? That is absurd.

Under the terms of the Bantu Education Act, which Verwoerd introduced in 1953, church missions were given the choice of turning their schools over to the government or continuing with them as private schools with gradually diminishing subsidies. All schools, whatever their status, would have to be registered by the government. No private schools would be allowed to exist without government approval. Control of schools would pass not to the Department of Education but to the Department of Native Affairs. Introducing the new legislation before parliament, Verwoerd was forthright about its purpose: 'Natives will be taught from childhood to realize that equality with Europeans is not for them.'

Opposition to the Bantu Education Act was widespread, both among churches and within the African community. Verwoerd's blunt explanations left little room for doubt that what was intended, as Mandela noted at the time, was 'an inferior type of education, designed to relegate Africans to a position of perpetual servitude'. The issue was recognized as being of the utmost importance; the whole outlook of African children for generations to come would be affected.

But deciding the best course of action to take caused deep dissension. Some churchmen decided to close their schools rather than submit to the government. The Anglican Bishop of Johannesburg, Ambrose Reeves, shut down all his schools, which had a total enrolment of 10,000 children. Father Huddleston decided to close down St Peter's School. In an article explaining the effect of the act, he wrote:

> There is only one path open to the African: it is the path back to tribal culture and tradition; to ethnic groups; to the reserves; to anywhere other than the privileged places habited by the master race. It is because we cannot accept such principles that we are closing St Peter's ... It has been a decision made in anguish and only after the most careful thought and prayer. For it means the end of forty years of labour and devotion.

Other churchmen argued that however harmful the system of Bantu education might be, the cost of school closures, leaving thousands of children on the streets without any kind of instruction and throwing hundreds of teachers out of work, would be too great to bear. 'A rotten system of education,' said Archbishop Clayton of Cape Town, would be 'better than none'. With the exception of the Johannesburg diocese, the Anglican Church followed his lead, agreeing to hand over its schools to the government. Every other missionary body, except the Roman Catholics and Seventh-Day Adventists, took the same line. Whatever opportunity there was for the churches to take a united stand against the government was lost.

The response of the ANC was far more confused. When members of the national executive committee, including Mandela, met to decide what strategy to adopt, two options were considered: one was to call for an indefinite boycott of schools in an attempt to destroy the Bantu Education Act before it could take root; the other was to call for a temporary boycott. Those in favour of an indefinite boycott argued that popular resentment against the act was so strong that their supporters would not be satisfied with a mere protest. Those in favour of limited action pointed out that the ANC did not have the means to sustain a permanent boycott; it had neither resources nor time enough to organize an alternative to government schools and realistically could offer the public next to nothing in terms of support. Despite his reputation as a firebrand, Mandela spoke in favour of a pragmatic approach. At the end of a heated session, the national executive committee recommended a week's boycott starting on 1 April 1955, the date on which the transfer of schools into government hands was scheduled to take place.

The issue was then put to the ANC's national conference in December 1954. The dilemma facing the African community was summed up by Chief Luthuli: 'The choice before parents is an almost impossible one – they do not want Bantu education and they do not want their children on the streets. They have to choose between two evils and no rule of thumb which is the greater.'

Ignoring the national executive committee's recommendation, the conference voted in favour of an indefinite boycott. Strong doubts remained, however, about the wisdom of the move. 'To imagine that the ANC has the power to bring about such a boycott in a few months would be totally unreal,' declared the left-wing journal *Fighting Talk*. Verwoerd raised the stakes by threatening to ban children involved in boycotts permanently from school education and to close down their schools. In March 1955, the national executive committee, worried by the lack of preparation, announced that the boycott would be deferred.

But some ANC branches, notably those on the East Rand, were determined to carry on the campaign, regardless of the views of the national executive committee. Scattered boycotts began in

April. Attempts were made to provide alternative education at improvised schools known as 'cultural clubs'. But the clubs lacked equipment, qualified teachers and money and were frequently the target of police raids. Father Huddleston described one such cultural club set up in an empty cinema in Benoni: 'Seated at the table was a young African woman trying to demonstrate some game, trying to keep fifty, a hundred children interested, or at least quiet ... There was no blackboard; there were no school books; there were no benches ... Such things as would equip a school would make it illegal.' An African reporter who visited the same club noted how 'the children were unruly and unmanageable'.

The campaign soon collapsed in bitterness and recrimination. Only a small fraction of parents and schoolchildren were ever involved in the boycott. The ANC itself admitted that it had amounted to little more than 'sporadic, unrelated and ineffectual small incidents in various parts of the country'. Critics, like Dr Xuma, claimed that ANC leaders had acted 'for propaganda reasons' and 'aroused vain hopes', in much the same way as had occurred with the Sophiatown campaign. But whereas Sophiatown had been a local issue, African education was a national issue of paramount importance to the African community. By falling at this hurdle, the ANC suffered a far more grievous blow to its reputation.

As the government's opponents had feared, Verwoerd soon moved to reshape African education to his liking. In 1956, new syllabuses were introduced for primary schools, emphasizing obedience, tribal loyalty, rural traditions and use of the vernacular. Vernacular instruction was made compulsory in all African primary schools and later extended to the first class of secondary schools.

More was to come. In 1957, the government introduced legislation to segregate universities. Hitherto, South African universities had been free to choose whom they accepted as students. African students had been allowed to enrol for degree courses at the 'open' universities of Cape Town and the Witwatersrand. They had been admitted to the same lectures and the same student societies as whites. Now separate colleges were to be provided for Coloureds, for Indians and for Africans. In the case of Africans, they were to be tribal in character, sited in isolated rural areas – one in Natal for Zulu students, one in the Transvaal for Sotho, Tsonga and

Venda-speaking students, one in Cape Province for Xhosa students. The university college of Fort Hare, which had achieved such a distinguished record in producing graduates since the 1920s, was to be reduced to the status of a Xhosa tribal college.

In an article in *Liberation*, a left-wing journal run under the auspices of Michael Harmel, Mandela condemned the legislation as 'a step to extend Bantu education to the field of higher education'. Tribal colleges, he said, would be used by the government to enforce its political ideology at a university level: 'They will bear no resemblance whatsoever to modern universities. Not free inquiry but indoctrination is their purpose, and the education they will give will not be directed towards the unleashing of the creative potentialities of the people but towards preparing them for perpetual mental and spiritual servitude to the whites.'

What was needed to fight the government, he said, was not a campaign conducted on the basis of isolated struggles, but 'a broad united front of all the genuine opponents of the racial policies of the government'.

CHAPTER 6

The Freedom Charter

Finding allies in the white community was an exercise fraught with complications. During the Defiance Campaign, the ANC had said that it was 'prepared to work with any white man who accepted the principle of equality'. But while traditional liberals were genuinely appalled by the onslaught of apartheid and the trail of destruction it carved through individual rights and liberties, few were willing to take a determined stand against the government. Mandela developed a particular dislike for their brand of politics.

In May 1953, after Malan's National Party had won a second election victory, white liberals launched the Liberal Party in an attempt to bridge the gap between white and black. By white South African standards, it was a brave endeavour. The Liberal Party opened its membership to all races and advocated the extension of full political rights to non-whites. With the exception of the Communist Party, no political party in South Africa had previously gone so far.

Yet its programme was hedged with reservations. The Liberal Party wanted not full citizenship rights for all but 'equal rights for all civilized people' – in other words, a qualified franchise. Furthermore, it opposed the use of passive resistance, strikes and boycotts, rejecting such tactics as being unconstitutional and insisting that only 'parliamentary methods' should be adopted.

It was also vehemently hostile to having any truck with communists, sharing the intense distrust of communist intentions held throughout the Western world at the time. Indeed, one of the motives of the founders of the Liberal Party was to provide an alternative to the influence of communists among the non-white population. All this came with a heavy dose of paternalism, with liberals expressing 'profound sympathy with the aspirations of all non-European peoples' but urging restraint, caution, compromise and gradualism on their part.

Mandela vented his anger on the liberals in a June 1953 article in *Liberation*. With South Africa divided by racial discrimination into two hostile camps, he wrote, there could be no middle course:

> The fault of the Liberals – and this spells their doom – is to attempt to strike just such a course. They believe in criticizing and condemning the government for its reactionary policies but they are afraid to identify themselves with the people and to assume the task of mobilizing that social force capable of lifting the struggle to higher levels . . .
>
> Talk of democratic and constitutional means can only have a basis in reality for those people who enjoy democratic and constitutional rights . . . The theory that we can sit with folded arms and wait for a future parliament to legislate for 'the essential dignity of every human being irrespective of race, colour or creed' is crass perversion of elementary principles of political struggle. No organization whose interests are identical with those of the toiling masses will advocate conciliation to win its demands . . .
>
> The real question is: in the general struggle for political rights can the oppressed people count on the Liberal Party as an ally? The answer is that the new party gives organizational expression to a tendency which has for many years existed among a section of the white ruling class and in the [opposition] United Party. This section hates and fears the idea of a revolutionary democracy in South Africa, just as much as the Malans and the Oppenheimers [a prominent mining family] do. Rather than attempt the costly, dubious and dangerous task of crushing the non-European mass movement by force, they would seek to divert it with fine words and promises and to divide it by giving concessions and bribes to a privileged minority (the 'suitably qualified' voters perhaps).
>
> It became clear, therefore, that the high-sounding principles enunciated by the Liberal Party, though apparently democratic and progressive in form, are essentially reactionary in content. They stand not for the freedom of the people but for the adoption of more subtle systems of oppression and exploitation. Though they talk of liberty and human dignity they are subordinate henchmen of the ruling circles . . .

Mandela's resentment of white liberals spilled over at a meeting of the ANC's national executive committee attended by Chief Luthuli and Professor Matthews, shortly after they and other ANC officials had held talks in private with a number of white liberals about the formation of the Liberal Party. Mandela recalled the incident in his autobiography. Along with others who had not been present, he had wanted to know what had transpired. When told that the conversations had taken place on a private basis and were therefore privileged, he retorted: 'What kind of leaders are you who can discuss matters with white liberals and then not share that information with your colleagues at the ANC? That's the trouble with you, you are scared and overawed of the white man. You value his company more than that of your African comrades.'

Mandela was quickly rebuked. Matthews, his old teacher from Fort Hare, responded, 'Mandela, what do you know about whites? I taught you whatever you know about whites and you are still ignorant. Even now, you are barely out of your student uniform.' Luthuli replied that if he was being accused of being afraid of the white man, he would have no alternative but to resign. Mandela beat a hasty retreat and apologized.

There were, however, other white opponents of the government willing to identify themselves with the ANC and the cause of African nationalism in a way that white liberals were not prepared to do. In 1953, in conditions of utmost secrecy, a hardcore of communist activists decided to relaunch the Communist Party and to devote its energy to the business of liberation. So secret were the activities of the Communist Party that no word of its existence was heard until 1960, not even by the Special Branch. Its founding conference in 1953 was held at the back of an Indian trader's store in a village on the East Rand to which many delegates were taken in vehicles without knowing their destination. The key working group included Moses Kotane, Yusuf Dadoo, Bram Fischer, Michael Harmel and Rusty Bernstein. Although most members were readily identified as being 'former' communists, their involvement in a well-organized, tightly disciplined, underground version of the Communist Party was never suspected.

They operated mainly in small units of four of five people, meeting clandestinely, often in 'unmarked' cars owned by friends and colleagues. Meetings of the secretariat took place several times each week. National conferences were also held, with delegates attending from towns across South Africa, without attracting the attention of the Special Branch. Among white communists there were a number of notable husband-and-wife teams: Bram and Molly Fischer, Rusty and Hilda Bernstein, Jack and Rica Hodgson, Joe Slovo and Ruth First, Brian and Sonya Bunting, and Ben and Mary Turok. In all, their numbers were small – fewer than 100 members were at the core of Communist Party activity – but the impact they made was remarkable.

They were particularly adept at keeping alive a radical press. When *The Guardian*, run mainly by communists since 1937, was suppressed by the government in 1952, a new paper, *The Clarion*, appeared the following week, using the same staff and the same editor; in Cape Town, a former communist member of parliament, Sam Kahn, managed to sell a copy to the minister of justice outside the House of Assembly, smiling as he did so. When *The Clarion* was suppressed, *People's World* appeared; after that came *Advance* and then *New Age*, at which point the government tired of the game. During the 1950s, Ruth First served as the Johannesburg editor of all five papers, as well as editor of the radical monthly *Fighting Talk*. Another outlet for left-wing views was Michael Harmel's monthly journal *Liberation*, for which Mandela wrote a series of articles in the 1950s. All these papers devoted considerable space to descriptions of Soviet achievements and justifications of Soviet foreign policy.

The main focus of their efforts, however, was a new political organization, the Congress of Democrats. Launched in 1953, largely as a result of communist endeavour, the Congress of Democrats was intended to function as a white counterpart to the ANC and the Indian Congress, in the way that Sisulu and Tambo had advocated at the Darragh Hall meeting in Johannesburg at the end of the Defiance Campaign. Unlike the Liberal Party, it had no qualms about demanding universal franchise.

Its membership was open only to whites. By agreement with the ANC, it confined its recruitment to the white community, to avoid competing with the ANC for black members. But the pool of white sympathizers on which it could draw for support was tiny. Most white opponents of the government were attracted more by the incremental, multiracial approach of the Liberal Party than by the radical vision proposed by the Congress of Democrats. From its inception, therefore, it became little more than an élite organization for whites already committed to the idea of democratic rule in South Africa. Not all its members were communists, but communists played a key role in its foundation and in its leadership ranks. 'But for them, it would not have seen the light of day,' Rusty Bernstein admitted forty years later. 'It was communist pressure which got the ANC to recognize that they had an ally. Communist Party members effectively launched it.'

It was Bernstein who gave the keynote address at the inaugural conference of the Congress of Democrats at the Trades Hall in Kerk Street, Johannesburg, in October 1953, urging white opponents of white supremacy to 'take sides' in the racial confrontation that was coming and fill 'the void in the democratic camp'. A veteran member of the Communist Party, who joined in 1939 while studying architecture at the University of the Witwatersrand, he preferred a backroom role, handling propaganda, but was propelled to prominence by the part he played in launching the Congress of Democrats. Other communists active in the leadership included Bram Fischer, Molly Fischer, Joe Slovo, Ruth First, Michael Harmel and Cecil Williams, a theatre producer. The president, Piet Beyle-veld, a trade unionist, joined the underground Communist Party in 1956, mainly as a result of Bram Fischer's influence. The post of national secretary was also held by communists: first by Jack Hodgson, then, when he was banned, by Yettah Barenblatt and then by Ben Turok.

The presence of so many known 'former' communists in the leadership led to immediate accusations by the Liberal Party that the Congress of Democrats was little more than a communist front. The evidence of communist influence was at times incontrovertible: discussion papers were replete with Marxist theories and concepts, and public pronouncements, notably on foreign affairs, often followed the party line. A war of words between white liberals and members of the Congress of Democrats lasted for years.

The ANC too found itself under attack for its alliance with the Congress of Democrats, not just from white liberals but from its own Africanist wing. Africanists portrayed the Congress of Democrats as a pernicious fifth column, intent on subverting the

African liberation movement for its own purposes. They denounced as 'Eastern functionaries' those ANC members like Walter Sisulu who had accepted invitations to attend a communist-sponsored youth festival in Bucharest in 1953 and subsequently visited Peking and Moscow. When Sisulu returned from his tour of communist countries in 1953, he was greeted by a storm of controversy on all sides. Most whites readily identified him as one of the most dangerous enemies of the state. Africanists nicknamed him 'Mao Tse-tung'.

Chief Luthuli took a more philosophical view of the role of communists. He developed a close personal relationship with Moses Kotane, the Communist Party's general secretary, often seeking his advice. 'He knew Moses was 100 per cent a member of the Communist Party,' remarked Oliver Tambo, 'but he also knew him to be 100 per cent ANC, and this gave Luthuli great confidence in him.' When Luthuli was restricted to his home area by government banning order, he would send for Kotane to discuss ANC issues.

'People ask me why I work with communists and my reply is that I have one enemy, the Nationalist government, and I will not fight on two fronts. I shall work with all who are prepared to stand with me in the struggle for the liberation of our country,' he said. The ANC, he felt, must not be side-tracked by ideological clashes and witch-hunts. The time would come when conservatives and communists within the ranks of the ANC would have to sort out their differences. In the meantime, he would accept help from anyone subscribing to the ANC's aims: 'We leave our differing political theories to one side until the day of liberation.'

Nor was Luthuli unduly concerned about the increasing use the ANC made of anti-colonial rhetoric and its applause of the Soviet Union for its role as an anti-imperial power. The unconditional support it expressed for the anti-apartheid campaign was welcome. Certainly, ANC leaders had 'picked up the language', he said, 'but they learned the language without becoming communists'.

Mandela was later more forthright in explaining his willingness to collaborate with communists:

It is perhaps difficult for white South Africans, with an ingrained prejudice against communism, to understand why experienced

African politicians so readily accept communists as their friends. But to us the reason is obvious. Theoretical differences amongst those fighting against oppression is a luxury we cannot afford at this stage. What is more, for many decades communists were the only political group in South Africa who were prepared to eat with us, talk with us, live with us and work with us. They were the only political group which was prepared to work with the Africans for the attainment of political rights and a stake in society. Because of this, there are many Africans who, today, tend to equate freedom with communism.

Year by year, Mandela was to draw closer to the communists.

In an attempt to revive its flagging fortunes and to restore a sense of purpose to the nationalist movement, the ANC developed the idea of holding a national convention called the Congress of the People to give a vision of the democratic future it wanted. The idea was first proposed by Professor Matthews, president of the ANC's Cape region, at a provincial conference in Cradock in August 1953. What subsequently happened assumed great significance, for not only did the Freedom Charter that was drawn up become a major landmark in the confrontation between the nationalist movement and the government, but the government used it as a pretext to try to crush the nationalist movement by charging its leaders with treason. For more than four years, Mandela's life was overshadowed by the possibility of a death sentence.

Matthews's original proposal was accepted enthusiastically at the ANC's national conference in December 1953 and he was asked to produce a memorandum to bring the idea into sharper focus.

> The main task of the Congress will be to draw up a Freedom Charter for all people and groups in South Africa. From such a Congress ought to come a Declaration which will inspire all the peoples of South Africa with fresh hope for the future, which will turn the minds of the people away from the sterile and negative struggles of the past and the present to a positive programme of freedom in our lifetime. Such a charter properly conceived as a mirror of the future South African society can galvanize the people of South Africa into action and make them go over into the offensive against the reactionary forces at work in this country, instead of being perpetually on the defensive, fighting rearguard actions all the time.

Three other organizations were invited to join in: the Congress of Democrats, the Indian Congress and the newly formed Coloured People's Organization, based in Cape Town. In March 1954, the four organizations, collectively known as the Congress Alliance, formed a National Action Council, on which each organization had equal representation, to prepare for the Congress of the People. Teams of 'freedom volunteers' were recruited to canvass support for the Congress and to collect suggestions for what the Freedom Charter might contain. Thousands of contributions poured in, many written on scraps of paper, pages torn from school exercise books and bits of cardboard, from church groups, women's organizations, sports and cultural clubs. The range of demands was huge, covering everything from the right to vote to the provision of proper toilets.

Members of the Congress of Democrats were notably energetic in the campaign, raising concern in some ANC quarters about the role of their new allies. Africanist suspicions about white participation were voiced anew. Many questioned why the Congress of Democrats, with a membership of no more than a few hundred, had been accorded equal status on the National Action Council with the ANC, with its far higher membership. An even sharper reaction came from the Liberal Party, which refused an invitation to participate in the Congress of the People on account of the prominent involvement of Congress of Democrats members.

Behind the scenes, the influence of Congress of Democrats members was even more crucial. A subcommittee formed to sort out all the bits of paper and to prepare a draft version of the Freedom Charter for debate by delegates to the Congress of the People included Joe Slovo and Rusty Bernstein. It was Bernstein, a member of the Communist Party's central committee and its chief propaganda expert, who undertook most of the burden of writing the draft version of the Freedom Charter.

Only a few weeks had been left at the end of the campaign for the task to be completed before the Congress of the People assembled in June 1955. The thousands of demands, all stored in a trunk, had first to be sorted into categories and topics, like land, employment and housing, before the writing could begin. 'It was one of the most difficult tasks I've done in the political field,' recalled Bernstein. 'Many of the demands were contradictory. Some people, for example, wanted land nationalized; some wanted it redistributed to peasants. It was a process of gradually and unsystematically selecting what made sense, making a précis of them. It was not a scientifically based sample. It was a fairly personal assessment. But I also had to keep my own personal preferences out of it. It was not a process I enjoyed. I was uneasy about some of the formulations. Some of them I formulated against my better judgement. In some cases I would personally have taken a more radical position.'

One clause, later to become the subject of particular controversy, was rewritten at the last minute. In its original version, the general economic clause of the Freedom Charter demanded that 'the land, the forests, the mines of coal, gold and diamonds, the quarries, the factories and workshops, and the railways should be worked for the benefit of the people'. It added, 'The mines should be nationalized.' But a change was engineered by Ben Turok, a prominent COD official and Communist Party member, who had been given responsibility for presenting the economic clause at the Congress of the People. Turok's amended version demanded the nationalization of 'the mineral wealth beneath the soil, the banks and monopoly industry'. It added, 'All other industries and trades should be controlled to assist the well-being of the people.'

The draft version was shown to senior ANC officials, including Mandela, on the eve of the Congress. 'We made few changes, as there was little time and the document was already in good shape,' said Mandela. Neither Chief Luthuli nor Professor Matthews had an opportunity to see it beforehand. Luthuli was not only subject to a banning order restricting him to his home district in Natal but recovering from a stroke; Matthews was preoccupied with university business at Fort Hare.

The Congress of the People duly opened on 25 June 1955 on a rough football field near Kliptown, a ramshackle collection of houses and shacks fifteen miles to the south-west of Johannesburg. Nearly 3,000 delegates attended – lawyers, doctors, clergymen, trade unionists, city workers and peasants – including 320 Indians, 230 Coloureds and 112 whites. It was a multiracial gathering unique in South Africa's history. Those present felt a sense of excitement and festivity. It was also an occasion notable for the number of prominent activists who were absent, forced to stay away by banning orders. Many nevertheless managed to watch the proceedings from a distance. Mandela and Sisulu, both banned at the time, found a safe place on the edge of a crowd of spectators, hidden from the view of Special Branch detectives monitoring the Congress.

The plan had been for delegates to debate each clause of the Freedom Charter and decide what amendments, if any, were needed. But the Congress only started late in the day, because of the delayed arrival of many delegates, and much time was then taken up with prayers, greetings and an awards ceremony for three distinguished activists, Chief Luthuli, Father Trevor Huddleston and the Indian leader Dr Yusuf Dadoo. The following day, when each clause was read out by individual speakers, there was little time left but for their own introductions. Ben Turok, introducing the general economic clause, added his own particular twist. Speaking of the mine owners after liberation, he declared:

> They will not have those lovely big Buicks that they drive around in. The whole system of the big factories and the gold mines in this country are the enemies of the people. When you walk down one of the streets in Johannesburg, you see a very impressive-looking building, and outside you see various banks . . . That money, friends, does not come back to you. It goes to our friends living in Lower Houghton [a wealthy white suburb]. Let the banks come back to the people, let us have a people's committee to run the banks.

Along with everything else that was said from the platform, his words were recorded by Special Branch detectives.

Clause by clause, the Freedom Charter was approved by a show of hands. Only two sections were left by four o'clock in the afternoon, when the proceedings were abruptly interrupted by armed police who surrounded the delegates. Senior officers mounted the platform and presented the chairman, Piet Beyleveld, with a warrant to investigate treason. Beyleveld explained to delegates the reason for the police action, told them he had authorized the removal of all papers and documents and asked if they wished to proceed with the Congress. The crowd roared its assent. While police worked their way up and down the rows of delegates, searching bags, confiscating documents, recording names and addresses, and taking photographs, speakers on the platform resumed reading out the Freedom Charter.

It was a document more notable for its modest content and naïve promises than for any revolutionary intent. The Freedom Charter affirmed the right of all citizens to vote, to hold office and to be equal before the law. It proposed equal status for 'all national groups' and an end to discriminatory legislation. 'South Africa,' it declared, 'belongs to all who live in it, black and white.' It went on to state that the mines, banks and monopoly industry would be transferred to public ownership and that land would be redistributed. Other promises included free compulsory education, minimum wages, free medical care and welfare for the aged. The tone throughout was one of simple idealism. 'Rent and prices shall be lowered, food plentiful and no one shall go hungry,' the Freedom Charter proclaimed. 'Slums shall be demolished and new suburbs built.' No suggestions were put forward as to how all this would be achieved.

In the South African context, however, such sentiments were dangerous. White liberals deplored the 'socialist' character of the Freedom Charter, arguing that left-wing activists in the Congress had clearly got the upper hand, thus justifying their refusal to take part. A prominent African liberal, Jordan Ngubane, who had once played a leading role in the Congress Youth League, claimed that the Freedom Charter's ultimate aim was 'to condition the African people for the purpose of accepting communism via the back door'.

Africanist critics within the ANC were outraged by the clause declaring that South Africa belonged to 'all who live in it, black and white'. In the Africanist view, the only true 'owners' of South Africa were Africans. The Africanists claimed that the ANC, through its willingness to support multiracial objectives, had yielded to the influence of other racial groups like the Congress of Democrats and the Indian Congress. Their journal, *The Africanist*, asserted that the Charter

> did not emanate as a finished document from the ANC. It emanated as such from the vodka cocktail parties of Parktown and Lower Houghton [a number of left-wing intellectuals lived in these white suburbs]. The black masses who met at Kliptown were merely pawns in the game of power politics. The whites who were at Kliptown, apart from the Special Branch, were mainly members of the Congress of Democrats. They are part of the ruling class in South Africa . . . they are in reality concerned with the maintenance of the *status quo*.

What the Africanists wanted, instead of the Freedom Charter, was to return to the era of 'go-it-alone' politics and to revert to the goals of the 1949 Programme of Action, which emphasized 'freedom from white domination'. Nothing could be gained, they insisted, by trying to appease white opinion. The only way by which white domination would be broken was by black force.

In March 1956, at a special ANC conference called to ratify the Freedom Charter, the Africanists kept up a noisy barrage of attacks on the 'Charterists', with shouts of 'Africa for the Africans'. Luthuli had hoped to use the occasion for a thorough debate about the economic clauses of the Freedom Charter, about which he and others had serious reservations. But he was obliged to abandon the idea in order to close ranks against what he called Africanist 'obstructionism'. Those who shared his misgivings, he said, were 'not prepared to split Congress on it'. The Freedom Charter was adopted without any amendment.

Mandela had no such reservations about the Freedom Charter. In an article for *Liberation* in June 1956, he described it as 'a beacon to the Congress movement and an inspiration to the people of South Africa'.

> It is true that in demanding the nationalization of the banks, the gold mines and the land, the Charter strikes a fatal blow at the financial and gold-mining monopolies and farming interests that have for centuries plundered the country and condemned its people to servitude. But such a step is imperative because the realization of the Charter is inconceivable, in fact, impossible, unless and until these monopolies are smashed and the national wealth of the country turned over to the people.

He denied, however, that this would involve a socialist transformation:

> Whilst the Charter proclaims changes of a far-reaching nature, it is by no means a blueprint for a socialist state but a programme for the unification of various classes and groupings amongst the people on a democratic basis. Under socialism the workers hold state power. They and the peasants own the means of production, the land, the factories, and the mills. All production is for use and not for profit. The Charter does not contemplate such profound economic and political changes. Its declaration 'The People Shall Govern' visualizes

the transfer of power not to any single social class but to all the people of this country, be they workers, peasants, professional men or petty-bourgeoisie . . .

The breaking up and democratization of these monopolies will open fresh fields for the development of a prosperous non-European bourgeois class. For the first time in the history of this country the Non-European bourgeoisie will have the opportunity to own in their own name and right mills and factories, and trade and private enterprise will boom and flourish as never before . . . The Charter offers immense opportunities for an overall improvement in the material conditions of all classes and groups.

Mandela was nevertheless clear about the impact it would make: 'The Charter is more than a mere list of demands for democratic reform,' he wrote. 'It is a revolutionary document precisely because the changes it envisages cannot be won without breaking up the economic and political set-up of present South Africa.'

The government thought so too and set out to prove that the Charter's aims could not be achieved without violence.

The knock on the door came just after dawn on 5 December 1956. Armed with a search warrant, Special Branch detectives rifled through every room in Mandela's house in Orlando, seizing documents and papers. They then presented him with a warrant for his arrest. On it Mandela read the words 'Hoogverraad – High Treason'. As his children watched, he was driven away in a police car.

At Marshall Square police station, he found a number of colleagues also under arrest; more arrived during the course of the day. In all, the Special Branch arrested 156 activists around the country in its swoop, including almost all senior ANC leaders, among them Chief Luthuli, Professor Matthews, Sisulu, Tambo and Kotane, as well as prominent white activists like Joe Slovo, Ruth First, Rusty Bernstein, Ben Turok, Jack Hodgson, Piet Beyleveld and a British-born social worker, Helen Joseph. Many of those arrested had expected it to happen. Since the Congress of the People, the police had made more than 1,000 raids on homes and offices of activists in search of evidence, and the government had continued to issue dark warnings about treason.

For two weeks, after being formally charged in the magistrate's court, they were held in the Fort, Johannesburg's main prison, a former Boer fortress built in 1899 on top of a hill near the centre of the city to defend it against the British. The African section there was notorious for its bullying, bribery and harsh treatment of prisoners. Thousands of pass law offenders went through its cells each year, emerging dazed and dumbfounded by the experience.

The African, Coloured and Indian male prisoners – some 120 people – were locked into two communal cells with concrete floors, no furniture and two exposed latrines. They were each given a sisal mat on which to sleep and three thin, lice-ridden blankets. But far from being daunted by their surroundings, Mandela and the others relished the opportunity to make contact with their colleagues after the months of living under bans and restrictions, unable to attend meetings openly. 'Our communal cell became a kind of convention for far-flung freedom-fighters,' wrote Mandela. A committee was formed to organize lectures and entertainment; freedom songs reverberated around the prison walls. Their white colleagues – seventeen men and six women, all members of the Congress of Democrats – were meanwhile placed in more comfortable quarters in a separate wing and provided with mattresses, cushions and newly laundered blankets.

As the accused were too numerous to fit into any courtroom, the authorities converted the army's Drill Hall in Twist Street into a court of justice for the preparatory examination of the case. It was a cheerless barn-like building with a galvanized-iron roof which, during the heat of a summer's day, felt like an oven. At one end of the hall stood the magistrate's table, with other tables for the prosecutors and defence lawyers. In front of the magistrate's table were 156 chairs for the accused, in six long rows. Behind them were placed another 150 seats for the public, divided into two groups, one for whites, one for non-whites.

On the ten-minute journey from the Fort to the Drill Hall for the opening day's session on 19 December, the convoy of police vehicles with the accused on board was greeted with cheering and waving from African onlookers. A huge crowd at the Drill Hall, shouting slogans and bearing placards inscribed 'We Stand by Our Leaders', surrounded the vehicles as they swept into the backyard. 'The trip,' said Mandela, 'became like a triumphal procession.'

The court proceedings quickly degenerated into farce. When the accused were brought in, the spectators' section, though packed, contained not a single African. So many whites had wanted to attend that court officials had simply moved them into chairs intended for black spectators. When defence lawyers drew attention to the matter, the magistrate, Frederick Wessel, was obliged to order that proper arrangements for black spectators be made.

No sooner had the prosecutor, J. C. van Niekerk, begun his opening address than it became clear that hardly anyone could hear a word he was saying. Court officials had forgotten to install loudspeaker equipment. No more than twenty minutes into the case, the court adjourned for lunch. After lunch, just as the prosecutor was about to start again, the magistrate asked whether any interpreters were available for those accused who did not understand English. None was. So, after two minutes, the court adjourned once more. The 156 accused were taken back to the Fort.

When they entered the courtroom the following day, they discovered that a huge wire cage had been erected overnight for them to sit in. They were led inside and seated on benches, surrounded by sixteen armed guards. Defence lawyers, seeking to enter the cage to consult their clients, were told to talk to them through the wire. Some of the accused, more amused than angry at this absurdity, wrote signs saying, 'Dangerous! Do not feed!' and 'No monkey nuts'.

The defence lawyers, however, were furious. Maurice Franks, normally a patient, polite and softly spoken man, could scarcely contain his outrage: 'Your Worship confronts this unprecedented scene which we see before us today, the accused caged, as Your Worship sees, caged, one might almost say – I am most anxious not to allow my indignation to get the better of the language I use – . . . caged like wild beasts . . .' He warned that unless the cage was removed immediately, the entire defence team would walk out of court. The magistrate adjourned the case once more, agreed that the cage should be removed and ordered the front of it to be pulled down forthwith.

Once again, van Niekerk rose to read his opening address. But he had barely begun when there was a new interruption. In the street outside, as crowds of supporters pressed close to the entrance, the police ordered a baton charge to disperse them, causing uproar which overwhelmed the court proceedings. A burst of gunfire was heard. Everyone in court stood up; the magistrate hurried away. The Bishop of Johannesburg, Ambrose Reeves, rushed out of the Drill Hall and ran towards the retreating crowd with his hands in the air, appealing for calm. A score of people were injured in the police shooting. The court adjourned once more.

Over the next two days, van Niekerk completed his reading of the charges. The prosecution's case was that the 156 accused were members of a countrywide conspiracy plotting to overthrow the existing state by revolutionary methods involving violence and to establish a communist state. The Freedom Charter, the Congress of the People and the Defiance Campaign were all cited as key parts of the conspiracy. The penalty for such high treason was death.

Despite the gravity of the charges, the accused were then released on bail that was nominal. The sliding scale fixed for bail was £250 for Europeans, £100 for Indians and £50 for Africans and Coloureds. They were also required to report once a week to the police and prohibited from attending meetings. Mandela and Tambo were back in their office the next day trying to catch up on a backlog of work.

The court resumed in calmer conditions on 9 January, with the accused seated in alphabetical order, all races mixed up, in curious contravention of normal procedure under apartheid. Among their number were clergymen, lawyers, journalists and a member of parliament. Most were clerks, drivers, factory workers and labourers.

The defence response to the charges was made by Vernon Berrangé, an imposing figure, much feared for his rapier-like skills at cross-examination and secretly a senior member of the underground Communist Party. The Freedom Charter, he said, contained ideas and beliefs that were shared by the overwhelming majority of mankind as well as the citizens of South Africa. What was on trial was not just the 156 individuals but the ideas they openly espoused. Not only would the accused defend those ideas; they would show they were 'the victims of political kite-flying' by the government to see how far it could go in stifling free speech. 'This trial has been instituted in an attempt to silence and outlaw the ideas held by the accused and the thousands whom they represent,' he went on. It was no ordinary trial, but a battle of ideas between those who wanted equal opportunities and freedom of thought and expression for all races and those who sought to confine the riches of life to a minority.

After the preliminary exchange, the preparatory examination settled into a routine of numbing monotony. For the first six weeks, the prosecution did nothing else but hand in thousands of documents seized by the police in their frequent raids on homes, offices and meetings. All the newspapers, magazines, books and pamphlets collected over three years were duly produced to the court and numbered one by one. Nothing was left out, not even invitations to dinner and weddings or letters from girlfriends. A notice over the kitchen at the Congress of the People saying 'Soup without meat' was solemnly read, marked as an exhibit and handed in. The next exhibit, logically enough, was 'Soup with meat'. Extracts from the documents were read out, regardless of their relevance. As the prosecution case dragged on, many of the accused began to lose interest. Some took to reading newspapers, tackling crossword puzzles or playing chess; others just dozed. 'The heat beats down in waves,' wrote Alex La Guma, one of the accused. 'Heads nod. Eyelids struggle to keep open. Ears strain to listen.' To break the tedium, Mandela often brought a book to read or a legal brief to work on.

A succession of Special Branch detectives took the witness stand to read out their notes of speeches made at political meetings. Many admitted that ANC speakers had often stressed the importance of non-violence. 'In the past four years, I have attended many meetings of the ANC,' said Detective Wilson Gumisa. 'At all meetings an appeal has been made to conduct the struggle in a non-violent manner. There is also an appeal to cooperate with Europeans. The ANC people say this at almost all meetings.'

Others produced more contentious evidence. An African detective, Jeremiah Mollson, claimed that he had been able to remember verbatim all the speeches made at a five-hour meeting, recording them word for word when he returned home. Under cross-examination from Berrangé, he admitted that he had received only a limited education and that before joining the police in 1953, he had been 'loafing' for fourteen years. A week after his first appearance, he was back in court to give further evidence on speeches. Handed his notes and asked to read them out, Mollson puzzled over them for some time and then said that there was a whole page that he could not decipher. Joe Slovo, conducting his own defence, was quick to pounce:

SLOVO: Do you understand English?

MOLLSON: Not so well.

SLOVO: Do you mean to say that you reported these speeches in English but you don't understand English well?

MOLLSON: Yes, Your Worship.

SLOVO: Do you agree with me that your notes are a lot of rubbish?

MOLLSON: I don't know.

Time and again, defence lawyers were able to demonstrate examples of fabrication by Special Branch detectives. At other times, they had little difficulty in dismissing their evidence as gibberish. Some reports of the speeches caused so much amusement among the accused that the magistrate felt obliged to warn that 'the proceedings are not as funny as they may seem'.

In August 1957, eight months after the proceedings had started, the prosecution announced it would produce evidence linking the ANC directly to planned violence. Into the witness box walked a confident, bespectacled, middle-aged man who said he was a lawyer with a degree from Fort Hare. Solomon Ngubase told the court he was an official of the Port Elizabeth branch of the ANC and a member of the national executive who had been present at a meeting when it had been decided to send Walter Sisulu and David Bopape to the Soviet Union to procure arms for a Mau-Mau type rebellion against whites in South Africa.

Under cross-examination by Berrangé, none of this turned out to be true. Ngubase was not a university graduate, or a member of the ANC, or a lawyer. He had forged his certificate for a university degree, practised fraudulently as an advocate for several years, served four jail terms and was currently facing prosecution on another charge of fraud.

BERRANGÉ: When did you last do an honest day's work?

NGUBASE: I can't remember.

BERRANGÉ: You have lived a life of lies and deception?

NGUBASE: I cannot be able to check that.

'This,' said Berrangé, sitting down, 'is the sort of witness the Crown brings here.'

Another state witness, Andrew Murray, professor of philosophy at the University of Cape Town, had a more distinguished background but also fell foul of Berrangé. Murray was reputedly an expert on communism. After examining various documents like the Freedom Charter and speeches made by the accused, he had no hesitation in describing them as 'communistic'. Berrangé challenged the validity of Murray's opinion and set out to demonstrate how difficult it was to be certain that a particular comment was either communist or bore evidence of communist tendencies. He read out a series of extracts of 'the sort of statement that communists make' and asked Murray to identify them. The first extract concerned the need for worker cooperation. It was communistic, said Murray. Berrangé then disclosed that the author was South Africa's former prime minister, Dr Malan. He read two more extracts, both of which Murray described as communistic. The author of one, said Berrangé, was Woodrow Wilson and the other, Franklin D. Roosevelt, both former presidents of the United States. The climax came when Berrangé read out a passage which Murray again unhesitatingly described as 'communism straight from the shoulder'. The author, said Berrangé, savouring the moment, was Murray himself.

In September 1957, the prosecution completed giving its evidence and the court adjourned. In December, without any explanation, the charges against sixty-one of the accused were dropped. Most were minor figures in the ANC, but among them were Luthuli and Tambo. As the ANC's president, Luthuli was baffled about the reasoning behind his release. 'The truth is I would be happier to see the whole thing through with my comrades,' he said.

When the court reassembled in January 1958, a different atmosphere prevailed. To sharpen up its case, the government brought in a new chief prosecutor, Oswald Pirow, a former justice minister renowned for his pro-Nazi sympathies, his dislike of Jews and his hatred of communism. Pirow, a man who believed that Hitler was 'the greatest man of his age', was also a formidable lawyer. New evidence would be produced, he said, to show the existence of a highly dangerous conspiracy. It would include an inflammatory speech by the ANC's Sophiatown leader, Robert Resha, in which he urged his audience to 'murder, murder'. Later that month, the magistrate found 'sufficient reason' for committing the ninety-five accused to trial in the Transvaal Supreme Court on charges of high treason.

In its preliminary stages, the treason trial served as a rallying point for anti-apartheid activists. The accused became popular heroes. For many blacks, the ANC emerged as a real force capable of challenging the government. White liberals raised their own voice of protest against the trial, fearing that its real purpose was to intimidate the government's opponents of any kind. 'Unless white South Africans defend under all circumstances the democratic values which they cherish,' said Alan Paton, chairman of the Liberal Party, 'the day may soon come when they lose them.' A defence fund launched by prominent whites to assist the accused and their families and to help pay for defence lawyers received widespread support. In London, Canon John Collins established a British defence fund which attracted substantial contributions.

Yet the disruption caused both to the accused and to the ANC itself was severe. Many of the accused lost their livelihoods during the proceedings and suffered much personal hardship. The ANC, deprived of effective leadership, fell into disarray. Disputes and dissension, never far beneath the surface, broke out anew, threatening to wreck the movement from within.

The law practice of Mandela and Tambo, once a thriving concern, was effectively crippled. Mandela and Tambo attempted to keep it going by working in the early morning, in the late afternoon and at weekends. But the practice steadily fell apart, leaving both of them in serious financial difficulties.

Added to all this, Mandela's marriage finally collapsed.

CHAPTER 7

'The Fabulous Decade'

When Mandela was released on bail from the Fort in December 1956, a few days before Christmas, he returned home to Orlando to find that Evelyn had finally moved out. Her leaving did not surprise him. What he found most distressing, in fact, was that she had taken the curtains with her.

The marriage had seemed irreparable for some time. The long sullen silences they endured were broken only by fierce rows. According to Evelyn, after one particular argument, 'Nelson grabbed me by the throat and shook me and shouted at me. Some elderly neighbours heard the noise and came in to break it up.' She went to live at her brother's house in Orlando East for a time but Mandela suggested she should return home: 'I was desperate to save the marriage, even if it meant clutching at a straw,' she said. 'But there was no thawing of the freeze.' She confided in Albertina and Walter Sisulu, both of whom were anxious to help achieve a reconciliation. But when Walter approached Mandela, he was told curtly it was none of his business. The only result was to increase Mandela's anger. 'I don't think Nelson ever forgave me for that,' said Evelyn. He came home less and less, took his laundry to a cousin and started sleeping elsewhere.

The rift between them became common knowledge. In a final attempt to prevent a breakdown, Evelyn asked first her brother and then Kaizer Matanzima to intervene. Mandela's response to both of them was that he no longer loved Evelyn. According to Mandela, he was also presented with an ultimatum from Evelyn: he had to choose between her and the ANC. There was no doubt in his mind where his priorities lay.

After yet another terrible argument, Evelyn left the house to stay in nurses' quarters, hoping that Mandela would come to realize he needed her to keep the family together. But this time Mandela never went to see her, nor did he send any messages. When he was arrested on charges of treason and taken to the Fort, Evelyn visited him only once. It was one of their last meetings. By the time he returned, she had moved in with her brother in Orlando East.

Their children – Thembi, then aged ten years, Makgatho, aged five, and Makaziwe, aged two – were all adversely affected by the collapse of the marriage, but the most deeply wounded was Thembi. According to Evelyn, he 'suffered intensely'. Mandela had taken as much interest in Thembi as he had time to spare. They regularly went jogging together and to the boxing gym. He taught him to drive his Oldsmobile. Mandela was affectionate, but also a strict disciplinarian. A visitor who stayed at the Mandela household, Robert Matji, was shocked by Mandela's severity in dealing with Thembi over an incident involving a school textbook. 'He set about cross-examining his son as if he was standing trial in the Supreme Court,' Matji recalled. 'If we did anything wrong,' said Makgatho, 'we would get a lesson from him that was worse than a beating.' As the marriage disintegrated, Thembi tended to take his mother's side. He lost interest in schoolwork and became quiet and with-drawn. Mandela rarely managed to brighten him up. In time, Thembi would become increasingly alienated from his father.

Mandela first caught sight of Winnie several months later during a recess in the preparatory examination at the Drill Hall. Driving past Baragwanath Hospital, the main black hospital south of Johannesburg, he noticed a young woman waiting at a bus stop and was immediately struck by her beauty.

It was perhaps inevitable that they should have met. Winnie, a social worker at Baragwanath, was a close friend of Adelaide Tsukudu, a nurse at the hospital who was engaged to Oliver Tambo; they both lived at Helping Hand Hostel in Jeppe Street. Winnie had already met Tambo and discovered that they came from the district of Bizana in the Transkei. Several weeks after that first glimpse, Mandela was buying food in a Greek delicatessen in Bree Street in Johannesburg when Tambo arrived with Adelaide and Winnie in tow. Tambo introduced them: 'Winnie from Bizana', he called her.

The next day, Mandela telephoned Winnie at the hospital, inviting her to lunch. 'I cannot say for certain if there is such a thing as love at first sight,' wrote Mandela in his autobiography, 'but I do know that the moment I first glimpsed Winnie Nomzamo, I knew that I wanted her as my wife.'

Winnie had arrived in Johannesburg four years before, a shy, unsophisticated country girl, to enrol at the Jan Hofmeyr School of Social Work, a college for black social workers founded during the war years. Her childhood in Bizana had been marked by rebelliousness, harsh discipline and family discord. Her father, Columbus Madikizela, was a Methodist mission school teacher, a successful farmer and businessman, whose authoritarian manner and fierce temper kept his children in fear of him. When he entered the room, they were made to stand to attention and allowed to sit only with his permission. He showed them no physical affection, never touching or hugging them. The only physical contact he had, in fact, was to beat them for transgressions.

Her mother, Gertrude, was also a teacher, with similar views on the need for discipline. Winnie once described her as a 'religious fanatic'. An ardent Methodist, she made her children pray at least twice a day in a special private corner of a field. Winnie was regularly locked into a room with her mother and forced to pray aloud. Gertrude was also obsessed with physical hygiene and maintained rigid standards of cleanliness and order in the house. Each evening the children lined up for an inspection to ensure that they had washed properly. They had to clean their teeth with ash until the gums bled.

Gertrude's physical appearance, her light complexion, long hair and blue eyes, was a frequent source of family comment. In South African terminology, she was a 'Coloured', of mixed ancestry. Columbus's mother, Seyina, never concealed her dislike of Gertrude for that reason, referring to her disparagingly in front of the children as a *mlungu*, a white person. Columbus sometimes joined in with his own 'teasing'.

Winnie's rebelliousness was evident from an early age. Tall and strong as a child, she preferred the company of boys and took up boyish pursuits. She was often embroiled in fights and gained a reputation among other children as a bully. Arguments usually began when Winnie failed to get her own way. In one memorable quarrel with an older sister, Winnie pulled out a weapon she had fashioned from a baking-powder tin with a nail driven through it and slashed at her sister's face, ripping her lip and tearing into the flesh of her mouth. The beating that Gertrude subsequently gave Winnie she remembered for the rest of her life. Gertrude regarded Winnie as the most wilful and troublesome of her five daughters and regularly beat her.

Gertrude died when Winnie was ten years old, leaving behind a family of nine children. Drawn into caring for the younger children, Winnie began to exhibit a gentler side to her nature. At boarding schools at Emfundisweni and Shawbury, Methodist mission schools, she lost some of her aggression and showed promise as a student. In 1952, at the age of eighteen, she passed her matriculation and gained entrance to the Jan Hofmeyr School of Social Work, arriving there in January 1953. Her home for the next five years was the Helping Hand Hostel.

By the time she graduated in December 1955, Winnie had acquired the outward sophistication of a city girl. Tall and slender, with large, dark, luminous eyes, she possessed a beauty that men found alluring. At college, she proved herself a cheerful and competent student, and was well regarded for her enthusiastic nature and willingness to help others. She took up sporting activities with the same energy, earning herself nicknames like 'The Amazon Queen' and 'Lady Tarzan'. 'I solved problems the simple way, using physical force, as I had done way back in my childhood days,' she explained.

When she was appointed as a social worker at Baragwanath, the popular African press – *Bantu World* and *Drum* – made much of the story of the once barefoot girl from Pondoland who, with brains, beauty and determination, had made her mark in the city of gold. At Baragwanath, she gained a reputation as an effective and dedicated social worker. A young African doctor, Nthatho Motlana, recalled, 'She was an outgoing personality, laughing a great deal, very cheerful and intensely concerned about other people's welfare.'

She was courted for a while by Mandela's kinsman Kaizer Matanzima, who met her while making an official visit to Baragwanath as a chief from Thembuland. By coincidence, Matanzima arranged to use Mandela's house in Orlando and his car to take Winnie for a candlelit dinner. On his return to the Transkei, he wrote passionate letters to her and she replied. But Matanzima appeared to want her for his second wife and Winnie lost interest.

She had known of Nelson Mandela by name for some time, not only because of his political activities but because he was a patron of the Jan Hofmeyr School. She had once seen him in a Johannesburg magistrate's court, representing a colleague of hers who had been assaulted by the police. But her own interest in political activity had been negligible; she took a far greater interest in clothes than in politics. When Mandela telephoned her at Baragwanath asking for help in raising money for the Treason Trial Defence Fund from the Jan Hofmeyr School and suggesting they discuss the matter over lunch, she was overawed. 'I was petrified,' she said. 'I couldn't work for the rest of the day.'

Mandela was thirty-eight years old at the time, sixteen years older than Winnie. He had recently been served with a new banning order, restricting him to Johannesburg for five years and prohibiting him from attending all meetings. He was on trial for treason, a charge which carried the death penalty. His law practice was falling apart. He was in serious financial difficulty. His family life was disintegrating. He rarely had enough time to see his children. To conduct a whirlwind romance with a twenty-two-year-old girl in those circumstances was something of an indulgence.

Their first date set the pattern for their future relationship. It was a Sunday. Mandela was at work in his office. He sent a friend to collect Winnie and together they walked round the corner to an Indian restaurant. Their lunch was constantly interrupted by a stream of people wanting to talk to Mandela. On the street outside, yet others sought his attention. 'Nelson couldn't walk from here to there without having consultations,' she remarked later. They drove south of Johannesburg to a stretch of open veld. Walking through the long grass, Mandela told her of the difficulties he faced with the treason trial and his hopes for the future. On their way back to the car, the strap on Winnie's sandal broke. 'I was walking with difficulty barefoot,' she said, 'so he held my hand as my father would hold a little girl's hand.' When they reached the car, he said, 'It was a lovely day,' and turned and kissed her.

Winnie fitted in to Mandela's activities as best she could: 'He did not even pretend that I would have some special claim to his time.' When he wanted to see her, he would send a car for her or telephone her, telling her to be ready at a certain time. He introduced her to his friends, took her to meetings and arranged for her to meet his colleagues at the Drill Hall. In an aside to Mandela, Moses Kotane remarked, 'Such intimidating and seductive beauty does not go with a revolutionary!'

A striking couple, they delighted in each other's company, holding hands and sitting together intimately whenever they could. Their relationship was extremely physical. On many occasions, Mandela found it difficult to tear himself away. But always there were other demands.

Mandela took it for granted that Winnie would follow whatever he decided and rarely consulted her about his intentions. He never mentioned the matter of his divorce from Evelyn. Nor did he discuss it with Evelyn. He merely placed a notice in a newspaper stating that he intended to institute divorce proceedings. Until then, Evelyn had believed that, though she and Mandela had separated, their marriage would remain nominally in place. 'I had heard that Nelson was going out with a social worker from Baragwanath Hospital,' she said. 'It was just one more woman, I had thought. He would discard her like he had the others.' The children, meanwhile, had commuted amicably between her house in Orlando East and his house in Orlando West, on the occasions that he was there. The news of his intention to divorce her came as a shock not only to Evelyn but to the children and to many of their friends. Winnie was sometimes unfairly accused of breaking up the marriage. Thembi was never reconciled to the divorce.

Averse to any discussion of his private life, Mandela kept the details of his divorce proceedings to himself. Winnie had no idea that the divorce had been finalized until one day he suddenly suggested that she should visit a friend, Ray Harmel, the wife of Michael Harmel, who would make her a wedding dress. 'How many bridesmaids would you like to have?' he inquired, by way of proposing. When Winnie travelled to Bizana to tell her father, Columbus, of the planned marriage, he exclaimed, 'But you are marrying a jailbird!'

The wedding took place in Bizana on 14 June 1958, a year after they had first met. Mandela had to obtain special permission to leave Johannesburg for six days. The ceremony was held at a local church, with Winnie wearing a wedding gown of white satin, made for her by Ray Harmel. At a reception at the Bizana Town Hall, Columbus spoke of his love for his daughter and of Mandela's dangerous career as a politician. He expressed deep foreboding for the future: 'This marriage will be no bed of roses; it is threatened from all sides and only the deepest love will preserve it.' He advised his daughter, 'Be like your husband, become like his people and as one with them. If they be witches, become one with them.'

After all the feasts and dancing at Bizana, there was no time for Mandela and Winnie to travel on to his ancestral home in Thembuland to continue with the celebrations, as custom required. So Winnie wrapped up a piece of the wedding cake and took it back to no. 8115, Orlando West, intending that she and her husband would share it with his family on a later visit when his restrictions were lifted. It was a journey they never made.

The juggernaut of apartheid, meanwhile, rolled on relentlessly. Race laws by now covered every facet of life – housing, education, hospitals, employment, public transport, marriage and sex. In public buildings, on trams and buses, at airports and railway stations, in restaurants, hotels, cinemas and theatres, on the beaches and even in the graveyard 'non-whites', as they were commonly termed, were kept separate wherever possible from the white caste. Signs declaring '*Blanke*' and '*Nie-Blanke*' proliferated on park benches, in elevators, in libraries, in liquor stores and in taxis. New laws were added whenever a gap could be closed. In 1957, legislation was introduced making it a criminal offence for Africans to attend church services in white areas without government permission.

Nothing was allowed to get in the government's way, neither the courts nor the constitution. Thwarted in its initial attempts to remove the right of Coloureds in the Cape to vote by an Appeal Court ruling declaring the legislation invalid, the government introduced a new bill making parliament a High Court, higher in authority than the Appeal Court, with power to give the final judgement on constitutional matters. When the Appeal Court then ruled that the High Court of Parliament itself was invalid, the government changed the Appeal Court – 'six old men in Bloemfontein', as one minister disparagingly described it – by adding five more judges and by passing regulations requiring a full quorum of eleven judges to hear constitutional appeals. It also proceeded to enlarge the Senate from forty-eight to eighty-nine members, elected on a basis which ensured that the government could obtain the two-thirds majority in a joint session of parliament needed to pass constitutional legislation. With the Senate duly packed with its own supporters, in 1956 the government finally succeeded in obtaining legislation removing the Coloured vote and the Appeal Court, filled with new government appointments, formally gave its endorsement.

New regulations were introduced to curb still further African entry into 'white' areas. Under the dreaded Section 10 of the Urban Areas Act of 1952, the only Africans entitled to remain longer than seventy-two hours in a white area were those who could prove either continuous residence in the area since birth or continuous work in the area for the same employer for ten years or continuous lawful residence in the area for at least fifteen years. If an African failed to prove his right to be present in a white area, he was 'endorsed out' – ordered to return to a reserve. In 1956, the pass laws were extended for the first time to women, provoking protests in towns across the country. A crowd of 20,000 women, led by Lilian Ngoyi and Helen Joseph, marched to the prime minister's office in Union Buildings in Pretoria in August 1956 to demonstrate their opposition, singing a song specially rehearsed for the occasion: 'Now you have touched the women, you have struck a rock.' As her initiation into the world of political protest, Winnie Mandela spent two weeks in the Fort in October 1958 after participating in a street protest against the pass laws and consequently lost her job as a social worker at Baragwanath Hospital. None of the protests had any effect on the government.

All this was dwarfed by the scheme that Hendrik Verwoerd had in mind. Elected prime minister by his National Party colleagues in September 1958, after the death of Hans Strijdom, Verwoerd cast himself in the role of a leader chosen by God and proceeded to act accordingly. 'I believe that the will of God was revealed in the ballot,' he said on the day of his election.

Verwoerd's ultimate objective, as he explained it, was total territorial separation between white and black. He acknowledged that this 'ideal' could not be reached for many years. The journey there would be arduous, but it was essential that the goal should be clearly stated. Unless white and black were separated as far as possible, the future would hold nothing but 'rivalry and clashes' between them. The solution lay in giving each race 'mastery' over its own area. Thus the Native reserves would become the homelands of the blacks – or Bantu, as Verwoerd insisted upon calling them – where they would enjoy full social and political rights under a system of government suited to their own tribal background. Those blacks living in white areas would be accorded rights in the home-lands too, which was where their real roots lay, and otherwise treated as 'visitors' and assigned separate locations. For a period of twenty years or so, according to Verwoerd's calculations, the flow of Africans to urban areas would continue to increase. But in the meantime, the reserves would be properly developed, and in white areas the government would endeavour to separate white and black in every sphere of life. The time would then come when the flow would be reversed. At the end of this grand design, Verwoerd confidently expected, South Africa would consist of flourishing black homelands living side by side in peace with an ever-prosperous white territory.

Verwoerd's plans for separate development were far removed from the previous Nationalist strategy of white *baaskap*, but his purpose was essentially the same: to relegate the African population to a permanently inferior status. The key to his policy was tribalism. By reviving tribal authority and by placing greater powers in the hands of tribal chiefs beholden to the government, he intended to establish a new administrative structure for the reserves which could restore traditional customs and practices and keep African advancement in line with what the reserves themselves required. For most of the century, the system of government in the reserves had largely bypassed the chiefs, whose status had long since declined. Verwoerd's objective henceforth was to use the chiefs as the allies of white government, creating small centres of tribally based power on the periphery of South Africa. By emphasizing tribal loyalties, he would keep the black population divided. A central part of Verwoerd's strategy became division of the blacks, which would counter the challenge mounted by African nationalists, destroy the notion of black majority rule and guarantee the supremacy of the whites.

Verwoerd had laid the groundwork for his grand scheme when, as Minister of Native Affairs in 1951, he introduced the Bantu Authorities Act, which was intended to replace the existing European model of administration in the reserves with a structure of tribal authorities staffed by African chiefs and officials appointed and paid by the government. No provision was made for any form of elected representatives. In the case of the Transkei, tribal authorities were installed in place of a partly elected district council system. Chiefs were made responsible for the maintenance of law and order and the implementation of government measures. Those who refused to cooperate were deposed.

The Transkei was crucial to the success of Verwoerd's strategy. Covering an area of 16,000 square miles, it was the only African reserve constituting a coherent piece of territory. Its black population of 1.5 million was enough to give it credibility as a separate entity. What was also important was that Verwoerd had found there a local ally in the business of apartheid: Kaizer Matanzima.

Matanzima saw in apartheid a means both of restoring hegemony for the Xhosa-speaking people of the Transkei and of satisfying his own aspirations for power. Like Verwoerd, he believed in the rule of chiefs. He liked to describe himself as a 'Xhosa nationalist' and was more than willing to forfeit claims in white South Africa if it meant regaining autonomy for Xhosas at home. Mandela spent hours arguing with Matanzima, trying to persuade him to oppose the implementation of the Bantu Authorities Act, but to no avail. In 1955, Matanzima played a vital role in getting the old General Council, or Bunga, in the Transkei, to vote itself out of existence and accept the new system. He was duly rewarded. In 1958, he was appointed Regional Chief of Emigrant Thembuland and was led to expect further promotion. Mandela recalled, 'Something snapped inside me when he went over to the Nats.'

In 1959, consulting only a handful of his closest advisers, Verwoerd unveiled his master plan. South Africa, he announced, would be turned into a 'multi-national state' by fragmenting the African population into separate ethnic groups. The Promotion of Bantu Self-Government Bill provided for the establishment of eight black 'homelands', one for each of the major ethnic groups: North Sotho,

South Sotho, Swazi, Tsonga, Tswana, Venda, Xhosa and Zulu.

No previous attempt had ever been made to implement territorial segregation on this tribal basis. Hitherto the whole emphasis of government policy had been simply to segregate black from white. Now Verwoerd decreed that the African people were not homogeneous but a collection of separate national groups divided by language and culture. Their roots lay in separate homelands; there they would be accorded 'separate freedoms'. This principle applied not only to rural but to urban blacks, regardless of how many generations they had lived in towns; they were all deemed citizens of the new homelands.

Verwoerd's 'new vision', as it was called, was hailed by the National Party as providing a lasting solution for South Africa. The advantages to whites seemed conclusive. The whites maintained unfettered control over their own areas, while claiming to permit blacks equivalent rights in the homelands. The blacks, meanwhile, were divided into separate ethnic groups, inhibiting their ability to act as a single community against outnumbered whites. Because each national group was a minority of the whole, no one 'nation' could claim rights on the basis of numerical strength. Thus the demands for majority rule by African nationalists were irrelevant. The problem of urban blacks was solved by denying them any permanent place in towns. In the long term there was the prospect, according to Verwoerd, that the number of urban Africans might be reduced. On the basis of Verwoerd's calculations, the reverse flow back to the homelands would begin by 1978. All this was to be set in motion in the name of racial harmony, peace and security. 'The development of South Africa on the basis of this bill,' said Verwoerd, 'will create so much friendship, so much gratitude, so many mutual interests . . . that there will arise what I will call a commonwealth, founded on common interests.'

Mandela took a different view. Writing in *Liberation* in its May 1959 issue, he described the bill as 'nothing but a crude, empty fraud' to bluff people that the aim was self-government. 'The Bantustans are not intended to voice aspirations of the African people; they are instruments for their subjection. Under the pretext of giving them self-government the African people are being split up into tribal units in order to retard their growth and development into full nationhood.' The burden would fall on millions of

Africans, born and living in urban areas, who had never seen the reserves, who had no desire to go there and who would now be 'treated as outcasts'. He contrasted the government's aims with the message of the Freedom Charter, which declared that 'South Africa belongs to all who live in it, black and white.'

The new system of administration caused deep dissension in the reserves, splitting apart communities and even families. There was prolonged violence in the Hurutshe Reserve in western Tranvaal, in Sekhukhuneland and in Pondoland. Chiefs and councillors resisting government authority were deposed and deported. Armoured units and aircraft had to be deployed to crush the Pondoland revolt.

The Mandela household was directly affected by these events. Not only did Matanzima throw in his lot with the government but so did Winnie's father, Columbus Madikizela, accepting an appointment to serve on Matanzima's council in the Transkei. Both became the target of attack. Madikizela's house was burned down, his store was burgled and his mother was assaulted. On one occasion, he only narrowly escaped his attackers by climbing through a small back window. ANC supporters were involved in the attacks. To have her father and her husband entrenched in two opposing camps was a difficult experience for Winnie. But life with Mandela was to bring far greater complications.

It was remarkable, in the circumstances, how much optimism about the future survived. Since 1948 the Nationalist government had never shown anything but ruthless determination in pursuit of white supremacy, riding roughshod over all opponents who stood in the way. The white electorate, meanwhile, had demonstrated its appreciation by rewarding the National Party with three successive election victories, with an ever-increasing majority. Yet ANC leaders, convinced that the handful of whites who supported them represented something more than a fringe of white politics, still placed inordinate hope in the notion that eventually enough whites would have a change of heart about apartheid to bring about the downfall of the government.

The optimists included Walter Sisulu, who, despite being forced to resign as secretary-general of the ANC and being subjected to a series of banning orders, managed to play a central role behind the scenes. Writing in the journal *Africa South* in 1957, Sisulu reached this conclusion:

> As far as the Nationalist Party is concerned, any serious analysis will reveal that it has reached its high-water mark. There is no possibility of the Nationalists growing stronger than they are at present ... Already there are signs that the edge of the Nationalist blitzkrieg is blunted in the face of the determined and growing resistance of the people ... In particular, the Europeans of the country are gradually beginning to see that South Africa has no choice but to follow the road to a multi-racial society.

These views were commonly held among the African élite. In his essay on the 1950s which he called 'The Fabulous Decade', the Johannesburg journalist Lewis Nkosi wrote of how the cause of racial justice and intellectual freedom seemed to be gathering strength: 'It was a time of infinite hope and possibility; it seemed not extravagant in the least to predict then that the Nationalist government would soon collapse, if not from the pressure of extra-parliamentary opposition, certainly from the growing volume of unenforceable laws.'

The treason trial had its own effect. Not only was the presence of so many whites on trial seen by many blacks as evidence that whites too were beginning to turn against the government but the swift reaction of white liberals in organizing a defence fund for them suggested a wider concern about government policy. 'The trial has been an inestimable blessing because it forged together diverse men and women of goodwill of all races who rallied to the support of the Treason Trial Fund and to keeping up the morale of the accused,' wrote Chief Luthuli. 'In all humility I can say that if there is one thing which helped push our movement along non-racial lines, away from narrow, separative racialism, it is the treason trial, which showed the depth of the sincerity and the devotion to a noble cause on the white side of the colour line.'

Among the accused themselves, sitting side by side, month after month, there developed an intense camaraderie. It helped that the accused were seated in alphabetical order and not in racial groups. 'The only place in South Africa where there was absolutely no colour bar was in the treason trial,' remarked Bernstein. 'It produced a core at the centre of people who really thought of themselves as a united group. I mean, the treason trial was a sort of family of their own.' Luthuli observed, 'By the time the preparatory examination had drawn to its close, the sense of common purpose among those who reject apartheid was immeasurably deepened.'

It became fashionable during the treason trial for some of the more adventurous white liberals in Johannesburg to invite one or two of the more respectable ANC leaders like Luthuli and Matthews to the northern suburbs for tea or dinner. Bram Fischer was assiduous in organizing dinner parties at Beaumont Street to introduce the ANC leaders on trial to white politicians and businessmen, most of whom had never met Africans on a social basis. On one occasion at Beaumont Street, Mandela encountered the judges who were presiding at his trial. 'We never discussed the trial,' said Mandela, 'but it helped to introduce a particular respect by the judges afterwards.' Luthuli recalled a meeting with the mining magnate Harry Oppenheimer at which he took the ANC to task for the 'extremism' of its demands, such as the demand for votes, which made it difficult for him, he said, to persuade 'liberal-minded people' of the justice of its demands. Luthuli replied that it was better for white South Africa to know the full extent of African demands rather than be introduced to them instalment by instalment and taken by surprise. Mandela met Oppenheimer on another occasion. There was little common ground, but that such meetings took place at all was seen as an example of the rising importance of the ANC in white eyes.

Once he was freed from the treason trial, Luthuli went on a speaking tour of major cities, including Johannesburg and Cape Town, to talk to white audiences, whom he found notably sympathetic. He even received an invitation to address an Afrikaner study group in Pretoria on the subject of African aspirations. The meeting in the Cathedral Hall was interrupted by a group of thirty white thugs, who assaulted Luthuli and began beating up the audience. Lying on the floor of the stage with a chair protecting his head, Luthuli was asked by a concerned white supporter, 'Are you hurt?' 'Oh, I'm used to this,' he replied, scrambling to his feet. Though his head was bruised and his jaw painfully swollen, he continued with his address. 'It was a good and encouraging meeting,' he said. Shortly afterwards, Luthuli received a banning order restricting him to his home district in Natal for five years and prohibiting him from attending all meetings.

There were encouraging signs from other quarters. The Liberal Party, adopting a more radical posture, came out in favour of universal adult suffrage and endorsed the use of tactics like boycotts. On university campuses in Johannesburg and Cape Town, white students demonstrated against new curbs placed on African entrants. Among avant-garde whites, multiracial parties were much in vogue; the more daring went in for illicit affairs.

In the world of music, a new African jazz style known as *kwela* gained a huge following among white teenagers. Played originally on the penny whistle, a cheap, six-hole metal flageolet favoured by African youths in the townships, *kwela-jazz* was developed by African musicians into a fast, colourful and distinctive idiom which became internationally famous. A multiracial Union of Southern African Artists was formed to assist black performers. At Dorkay House in Johannesburg, it initiated a series of talent contests which grew first into small 'festivals' and then into township jazz concerts which attracted enthusiastic white audiences. A performance at City Hall in Johannesburg in 1957 was packed out. The climax of these efforts came in 1959 with the production of *King Kong*, a jazz opera on the life of the heavyweight boxing champion Ezekiel 'King Kong' Dhlamini. With a score by Todd Matshikiza, featuring singers like the Manhattan Brothers and Miriam Makeba and produced and directed by whites, *King Kong* was a success from its opening night in Johannesburg. As Lewis Nkosi wrote:

> The resounding welcome accorded the musical at the University Great Hall that night was not so much for the jazz opera as a finished artistic product as it was applause for an Idea which had been achieved by pooling together resources from both black and white artists in the face of impossible odds. For so long black and white artists had worked in watertight compartments, in complete isolation, with very little contact or cross-fertilization of ideas. Johannesburg seemed at the time to be on the verge of creating a new and exciting Bohemia . . . There was a surge of optimism, very difficult to prove founded or unfounded, that art might yet crack the wall of apartheid.

There was a similar sense of exhilaration about the advance of

African nationalists elsewhere in Africa. Ghana's independence from Britain in 1957 signalled the beginning of the retreat from Africa of Europe's colonial powers and the emergence of new black-run states. As the number of African and Asian members of the United Nations multiplied, so the volume of condemnation of South Africa's racial policies rose. Western governments were also becoming more critical. Foreign support for the anti-apartheid movement was seen to be an increasingly important factor. 'World attention,' said Luthuli, 'is something which we of the resistance need and desire.'

All this seemed to enhance the moral advantage that African nationalists in South Africa perceived they had in their confrontation with the government. Writing in *Africa South* in 1959, Walter Sisulu observed:

> Nothing has brought greater credit to the ANC in the eyes of Africa and the world than its steadfast refusal to respond to the vicious persecution of the Nationalists and their predecessors in the Union Government by a blind and irrational 'anti-Whiteism'. It has shown the African people to be larger-minded than, and morally superior to, their oppressors; it strikingly refutes the ridiculous claims of 'white South Africa' about alleged African 'immaturity' and 'unreadiness for self-government'.

Luthuli also emphasized the moral strength of the ANC's position:

> How easy it would have been in South Africa for the natural feelings of resentment at white domination to have been turned into feelings of hatred and a desire for revenge against the white community. Here, when every day in every aspect of life, every non-white comes up against the ubiquitous sign 'Europeans Only', and the equally ubiquitous policeman to enforce it – here it could well be expected that a racialism equal to that of their oppressors would flourish to counter the white arrogance towards black. That it has not done so is no accident. It is because, deliberately and advisedly, African leadership for the past fifty years, with the inspiration of the African National Congress . . . has set itself steadfastly against racial vaingloriousness. We knew that in doing so we passed up opportunities for an easy demagogic appeal to the natural passions of a people denied freedom and liberty; we discarded the chance of an easy and expedient emotional appeal. Our vision has always been that of a

non-racial democratic South Africa which upholds the rights of all who live in our country to remain as full citizens with equal rights and responsibilities with all others.

The singular achievement of the ANC and its white allies in the 1950s was that they established a multiracial tradition in politics strong enough to withstand all attempts by the government to obliterate it. In the long term this was to have the most profound consequences for South Africa. But at the time, the white audience they reached was minimal and the signs of change they detected were misleading. In power was a government determined to enforce its rule whatever the cost. 'Alas,' Nkosi wrote of the 1950s, 'we didn't realize how small and powerless we were.'

CHAPTER 8

A Trial of Endurance

The treason trial reassembled in August 1958, not in an army drill hall but in a synagogue, with the Star of David hanging high above the judges' rostrum. In order to avoid the spectacle of African crowds milling about in the court precincts, cheering the accused as they came and went, the venue had been changed from Johannesburg to the more staid surroundings of Pretoria, thirty-five miles away, where popular support for the ANC was muted. The Old Synagogue there, a large ornate and empty building long since given up by the Jewish community, was one of the few locations available capable of being converted into a 'Special Criminal Court' dealing with ninety-two accused people.

Since none of the accused lived in Pretoria, the government provided a bus for the journey from the Johannesburg townships where most of them lived. This meant that in addition to the hours they spent in court each day, the accused had to endure four hours of uncomfortable travel to get there and back; on some days they spent as much time in the bus as in court.

To avoid such lumbering journeys, Mandela often travelled to Pretoria with Helen Joseph, whose fast French car was capable of reaching there in an hour. After spending a couple of hours in the early morning working in his law office, Mandela would meet Joseph on the Pretoria road, leaving his car on the roadside for his return in the afternoon, when he would drive back to the office to put in a few more hours of work. For amusement on the way, they picked out houses for themselves for the day when liberation dawned. Joseph described Mandela's choice as 'unpretentious and on the small side'. Mandela thought that Joseph's house, with its well-planned garden and green lawns, was too bourgeois.

The defence team assembled for the trial included some of the most experienced and distinguished lawyers in South Africa. The team was led by Israel Maisels, a former major in the South African Air Force and chairman of the Johannesburg Bar, whose accomplishments as a lawyer were widely admired by the legal profession. In some respects, Maisels was a curious choice. He was not a 'political' advocate; he undertook to lead the defence case on the condition that it was conducted on a legal basis, not a political basis. But whatever misgivings the accused had about his approach were soon overcome. A tall, bespectacled figure, with dark hair receding from a massive forehead, Maisels dominated the proceedings from the outset, cutting a swathe through the prosecution's case.

His second-in-command was Bram Fischer. Fischer's position in the trial was unique. As a member of an eminent Afrikaner family and a distinguished lawyer in his own right, with clients who included the giant mining companies, he was accorded the highest respect by the Afrikaner establishment. He was also known as a staunch friend and ally of the accused, whose home in Beaumont Street was always open to political dissidents and their families and who worked tirelessly in the courts on their behalf. His name occasionally cropped up in the prosecution's evidence. What was not known, except to a few of the accused, like Bernstein, Slovo, First and Kotane, was that he was a senior figure in the underground communist movement. Fischer's quiet demeanour, his courteous nature and his boyish, gentle face gave little clue as to the complex life he led. In court, his manner was equally soft-spoken, almost self-effacing, but he was invariably effective in achieving the results he wanted.

Other members of the defence team included Sydney Kentridge, Tony O'Dowd and Vernon Berrangé. Mandela was elected to a twelve-member liaison committee set up by the accused for consultations with the defence team. Marshalling them all was Michael Parkington, who was an attorney of exceptional ability but who also seemed an unlikely choice: a former Royal Air Force pilot and law lecturer at Cambridge University, he was a renowned conservative and anti-communist.

From the opening moments of the trial, the defence team adopted an aggressive strategy. Their first target was the judges sitting on the rostrum. Three had been appointed: Judge Franz Rumpff, who had been involved in the Defiance Campaign trial; Judge Joe Ludorf, a former National Party official famous for his defence of a Nazi supporter, Robey Leibbrandt, tried for treason during the war; and Judge Alexander Kennedy, a Natal judge who in 1957 had sentenced twenty-two Africans to death in a mass murder trial arising from disturbances following a police raid. Rising to his feet, Maisels asked for the recusal of two of the judges, Rumpff and Ludorf, setting out his reasons why the accused had cause to doubt that they would receive a fair trial at their hands. After an adjournment, Ludorf agreed to withdraw, but Rumpff did not. Ludorf's replacement was Judge Simon Bekker.

Their next target was the indictment. The indictment charged that the accused were guilty of high treason because they had conspired and acted 'in concert and with common purpose' to overthrow the state by violence. It also included two alternative charges of contravening the Suppression of Communism Act. Maisels opened with a devastating assault on the indictment lasting nearly ten hours, arguing that it failed to provide in clear terms exactly what charges the accused had to meet. Fischer followed with a four-hour attack on the two alternative counts under the Suppression of Communism Act, making the same point about the lack of particulars.

The court quashed one of the two alternative charges and ordered the prosecution to supply additional particulars about the other. The court also ordered the prosecution to tell each accused how he or she was affected by the difference between allegations of 'conspiracy' and allegations of 'concert and common purpose'. The prosecution's response was to drop the remaining charge of high treason and to delete the words 'acting in concert and with common purpose', leaving only the allegation of conspiracy. In October, after further protracted argument, the prosecution abandoned the indictment altogether and was forced to start anew.

A huge party was held at the Slovos' house in Roosevelt Park that night to celebrate the event. Towards midnight the house was surrounded by police, who swarmed in through the doors and windows, accompanied by journalists from the Afrikaans press, hoping to find blacks drinking illicit liquor. The blacks were well versed at this game and not a single one was found with so much as a drop of liquor in his or her glass. The newspaper *Die Burger* described the celebration under the headline 'Many colours at party': 'A party at which whites, natives and Indians were present was held in a Johannesburg suburb last night. There were about 200 people present. White and non-white drank, danced, sang and chatted together. The police appeared at 10.30 p.m. In many of the motor cars white women rode with natives.'

In November, when a new indictment was issued, the charges against sixty-one of the ninety-one accused were suspended, leaving only thirty defendants to return to court. This group, the prosecution believed, comprised the most 'dangerous'. They included Mandela, Sisulu, Robert Resha, Lilian Ngoyi, Helen Joseph, Kathy Kathrada and Duma Nokwe, a young advocate recently appointed ANC secretary-general. Those relegated to the 'second division' included Joe Slovo, Ruth First, Rusty Bernstein, Ben Turok, Piet Beyleveld, Moses Kotane and Professor Matthews.

Under the new indictment, the focus of the trial was narrowed considerably. The prosecution's case was limited to proving the intention of the accused to act violently. Specifically, what was at issue was whether or not violence was the policy of the ANC and its allied organizations. At the core of the prosecution's case was the Freedom Charter. To achieve its aims, according to the indictment, 'would necessarily involve the overthrow of the State by violence'.

When the trial reassembled in January 1959, the defence immediately asked for the new indictment to be dismissed as inadequate. The argument over the indictment continued for month after month. But this time the court eventually allowed it to proceed. In May 1959, two and a half years after Mandela and the other accused were arrested, the minister of justice commented: 'This trial will be proceeded with, no matter how many millions of pounds it costs . . . What does it matter how long it takes?'

Mandela's home life, meanwhile, was lived in fragments, as Winnie soon discovered. Not only were there the relentless demands of the treason trial in Pretoria and Mandela's constant struggle to keep his law practice alive in Johannesburg, but he was constantly involved in political meetings and discussions. He spent as little time at home with Winnie as he had with Evelyn, though the enjoyment was far greater. His routine was much the same. He rose before dawn, went for an early-morning run, welcoming the emptiness of the streets at that time, and had a quick breakfast of toast and orange juice before heading for the city. He returned home at night, often in the company of colleagues. 'He would come home from court and say, "Darling, I brought my friends here to taste your lovely cooking," and he would pitch up with ten people and we would have one chop in the fridge,' Winnie recalled. 'I used to be reduced to tears and he would laugh and run around looking for a packet of tinned fish from the local shops.' Money was always tight and much depended on Winnie's earnings as a social worker. Even when they were alone together, there were frequent interruptions from people seeking advice and help. 'There never was any kind of life that I can recall as family life, a young bride's life, where you sit with your husband and dream dreams of what life might have been, even if we knew that it would never be like that.'

Their moments for relaxation were few. Mandela was selective about which parties he went to: 'I wouldn't just go to any party. In fact, I missed most of the parties that were held in Bram's house and in Joe Slovo's house.' On Sunday evenings they sometimes went to Uncle Joe's café in Fordsburg to listen to jazz musicians like Dollar Brand and Kippie Moeketsi. They would occasionally eat at Indian restaurants to indulge Mandela's passion for curry. Mandela also found time to try to teach Winnie how to drive his car, though, inevitably, it ended in a row. On Saturday mornings he would take his three children to a cinema in Fordsburg, leaving them there while he rushed off on another mission.

Life at no. 8115, Orlando West, was nevertheless relatively comfortable. The house possessed electricity, hot water, an indoor bathroom and a telephone. Mandela's small study, partitioned off from the front room and furnished with three cane chairs, a couch, a bookshelf, a display cabinet and a huge picture of Lenin, provided a retreat into which he enjoyed settling. To add to the comfort, Winnie added two rooms, decorated the house in new colours and improved the small garden.

The interruptions, however, never ended. One night, soon after they were married, there was a sudden, violent banging on the front door. 'I was convinced something terrible must have happened,' said Winnie. 'But Nelson, who was wide awake and out of bed in an instant, told me not to be alarmed – it was only a police raid. They were banging with their truncheons, flashing bright torches through the windows, shouting at us to open up and making enough noise to waken the whole neighbourhood.'

She found the experience repugnant as well as frightening:

> There were these coarse Boer policemen thumbing through our personal belongings, pulling books off shelves, turning drawers of clothing upside down, reading our letters, rough-handling our possessions and all the time passing derogatory and derisory remarks about kaffirs. And it was all for nothing. They couldn't find anything incriminating. After they had gone we tidied up the mess and I made coffee before we went back to bed. Nelson warned me I would have to get used to raids like that.

On 4 February 1959, their first daughter, Zenani, was born in Baragwanath Hospital. Mandela was away in Pretoria at the time, attending the treason trial.

In August 1959, the real trial began. The accused were able for the first time to plead not guilty. The chief prosecutor, Oswald Pirow, then set out his case. The essence of the crime of high treason, he said, was 'hostile intent'. Such intent was evident in the demands of the accused for full equality. They knew that to achieve the demands of the Freedom Charter 'in their lifetime' would 'inevitably result in a violent collision with the state resulting in its subversion'. The Congress alliance, he said, was part of an international communist-inspired movement which was 'pledged to overthrow by violence all governments in non-communist countries where sections of the population did not have equal political and economic rights'. The essential element of hostility was to be found in all the facts: 'Insistence upon violence runs through the case in an unbroken thread.' The speeches made by the accused 'bristle with references to the spilling of blood'.

For the next two months, the prosecution, repeating the tedious process adopted at the preparatory examination, submitted more than 4,000 documents – books, pamphlets, magazines, newspapers, letters, bulletins and circulars – seized during the course of 1,000 police raids. Some were read into the record in full, some in part, while the accused sat in a half-doze. Once again, Special Branch detectives gave their evidence and, once again, the defence team pointed out its inaccuracies and unreliability. In all, 150 police witnesses took the stand. The accused complained that they could not properly hear much of the proceedings and used to joke that they could all be hanged 'for what we didn't say, for what we didn't do – and now for what we can't hear!'

Once again, the prosecution produced its expert witness on communism, Professor Andrew Murray, undeterred by the humiliation he had received at the preparatory examination. Murray spent days analysing speeches and documents written by defendants, concluding that they were communist-inspired. But under relentless cross-examination by Maisels, he was eventually obliged to admit that the accused were motivated not by communism but by grievances over apartheid.

> MAISELS: It is clear, is it not, Professor, to summarize this position, that the laws of the white man – and I use that not meaning of this government but of successive South African governments – all these laws in which the black man has, and has had, no say, are such that for a Native and, to a somewhat lesser extent, the Indian and the Coloured – they prescribe, and just listen to this catalogue, where he may live. Correct?
> MURRAY: Yes.
> MAISELS: Where he may work?
> MURRAY: Yes.
> MAISELS: What work he may do?
> MURRAY: Yes.
> MAISELS: What he is to get paid?
> MURRAY: Yes.
> MAISELS: What schools he may go to?
> MURRAY: Yes.
> MAISELS: Where he may travel to in South Africa, in his own country?
> MURRAY: Yes.
> MAISELS: In these circumstances, do you not think that the Native may well regard himself as oppressed and exploited by the white man?
> MURRAY: I think in certain spheres of life, yes.

Murray finally agreed that the Freedom Charter was not a

'communist' document but a natural and understandable reaction to the injustices of white supremacy. Maisels concluded, 'We know, of course, as a fact that no single act of violence was committed over the whole period of this indictment by any [of the accused], notwithstanding all the grievances and the exploitation of grievances. You know that, don't you, Professor?'

'Yes,' Murray replied.

There was, however, one piece of evidence not so easy for the defence team to handle. In January 1960, the prosecution produced a tape-recording of the speech made by Robert Resha to a group of 'freedom volunteers' at a closed meeting at ANC headquarters in Johannesburg, recorded by a microphone hidden in the ceiling, thirteen days before the accused were arrested in December 1956. 'When you are disciplined and you are told by the organization not to be violent, you must not be violent,' Resha had said, but 'if you are a true volunteer and you are called upon to be violent, you must be absolutely violent, you must murder! Murder! That is all.' Here, said the prosecution, was the true and secret face of the ANC, unmasked of its public pretence of non-violence.

On 10 March 1960, the prosecution closed its case. On 14 March 1960, the defence case began. But the defence team had hardly got into their stride when a sudden upheaval occurred that brought the trial proceedings to a halt and shook the country to its core.

The name of Sharpeville was to leave an indelible stain on South Africa. What took place there on 21 March 1960 became a permanent symbol of the brutality of the apartheid regime. The impact was felt around the world. Never before had South Africa faced such universal condemnation.

The events of that day centred not on the ANC but on a rival organization, the Pan-Africanist Congress, which had been launched the previous year by a splinter group of dissident Africanists. Its leader, Robert Sobukwe, a thirty-five-year-old instructor in African languages at the University of the Witwatersrand, was convinced that he would gain a mass following by promising African rule. He rejected the idea of white participation in government, derided 'multiracialism' as a device to keep blacks in subjection and denounced communism and communist influence. He placed great faith in the idea of heroic leadership. Once the masses were given bold, decisive leadership, he believed, then the fires of rebellion could soon be lit. With mass support, African rule, he claimed, could be attained in four years.

Though Mandela had once shared many of the views held by Africanists, he now regarded that as an adolescent phase in his political life. He dismissed PAC policies as 'immature' and 'naïve' and abhorred the crude racist statements made by its more extreme officials. The freedom struggle, he said, required compromise and discipline, not empty rhetoric which ignored the complex realities of South Africa.

Sisulu launched a ferocious public attack on the Africanists, describing their 'inverted racialism' as akin to that of the ruling National Party. But while scorning them as 'armchair revolutionaries', Sisulu was nevertheless mindful of the effect they might have. 'There are men and women amongst them who genuinely believe that the salvation of our people lies in a fanatical African racialism and denunciation of everything that is not African,' he said. 'And such a policy is not without its potential mass appeal.'

From the outset, the PAC, like the ANC, possessed no coherent strategy. It was poorly organized, short of funds and trained leaders and relied on little more than the notion that the time was ripe for militant action. But determined to force the pace and establish the PAC's credentials as the leading nationalist group, Sobukwe devised plans for a campaign of mass protest against the pass laws. The slogans chosen were 'Leaders in Front' and 'No Bail, No Defence, No Fine'. By swamping the prison system, they would make the pass laws unworkable. The campaign, he believed, would disrupt the economy and eventually inspire a popular uprising.

Though few preparations had been made, Sobukwe announced that the campaign would begin on 21 March. On that date, PAC supporters would present themselves at police stations for arrest. They would say, 'We do not have passes. We will not carry passes again. Millions of our people have been arrested under pass laws, so you had better arrest us all now.' They would not return to work until their demands were met. This would be the first step to freedom in 1963.

The PAC's campaign that day was largely a failure. In the early morning, after putting his papers in order and making last-minute arrangements for the welfare of his family, Sobukwe began the three-mile walk from his home to Orlando police station, being joined along the way by small groups of PAC supporters. In all, about 170 volunteers presented themselves for arrest in Johannesburg, an insignificant number. At Pretoria's Hercules police station, six men arrived expecting arrest, only to have their names taken and to be sent away. In Durban, Port Elizabeth and East London there were no demonstrations at all.

But in Sharpeville, a township in southern Transvaal, the response was much greater. From early in the morning, PAC pickets were active on the streets, telling residents they should not go to work. By mid-morning, a crowd of several thousand Africans had gathered outside the police station. Their mood, according to most accounts, was relaxed and amiable. But they showed no signs of dispersing. Police reinforcements were called in. At 1.15 p.m., by which time nearly 300 police were facing a crowd of some 5,000 Africans, a scuffle broke out near one of the gates to the police compound. A police officer was pushed over. The crowd surged forward to see what was happening. According to police witnesses, stones were thrown at them. No order was given to shoot. No warning shots were fired. In a moment of panic, the police opened fire indiscriminately into the crowd. The crowd turned and fled. But still the firing continued. Sixty-seven Africans were killed and 186 wounded. Most were shot in the back.

Later in the day, a similar incident, though on a smaller scale, occurred in Langa, a black township outside Cape Town occupied mainly by migrant workers. Confronted by a crowd of 6,000 Africans, police mounted baton charges to break it up. The crowd retaliated by throwing stones. The police opened fire, killing two Africans and injuring forty-nine others. That night rioting broke out in the township. The Langa protest then turned into a major confrontation with the authorities in Cape Town. A strike which began that day eventually spread until almost all African workers in Cape Town joined it, bringing industry to a standstill.

At the treason trial in Pretoria that day, Chief Luthuli was on the witness stand, giving evidence for the defence about the ANC's policy of non-violence. His banning order restricting him to his home district in Natal had been lifted to enable him to travel to Pretoria, where he was staying at the home of white friends. But he was suffering from high blood pressure and the state of his health was a cause of constant concern.

As the full extent of the shooting at Sharpeville and Langa became clear, a small group consisting of Mandela, Sisulu, Slovo and Duma Nokwe held an all-night meeting in Johannesburg to plan what response to make. There was considerable anger at the PAC's precipitate action in launching its campaign without proper preparation. 'It was a blatant case of opportunism,' said Mandela. 'Their actions were motivated more by a desire to eclipse the ANC than to defeat the enemy.' In just one day, the PAC, hitherto an insignificant splinter group, had captured national and international attention. Yet it had neither the means nor the ability to make any further moves, or manage the surge of black anger that now followed.

The leadership of the crisis thus fell to the ANC. Mandela's group decided to call for a national stay-away on 28 March, to mark it as a day of mourning and to initiate a campaign of pass-burning. Duma Nokwe was sent to Pretoria to gain Luthuli's approval. On 26 March, Luthuli duly announced a day of mourning on 28 March and publicly burned his pass, calling on others to do the same. Mandela burned his pass in Orlando before a crowd of press photographers and several hundred onlookers. The response to the strike call two days later in many large towns was overwhelming. In demonstrations across the country, thousands of Africans burned their pass books. Violence broke out in Johannesburg's black suburbs. In Langa, police brutality in trying to break the week-long strike provoked a mass march by some 30,000 Africans into the centre of Cape Town. Many blacks believed that they were on the verge of liberation.

To much of the white population, it seemed that South Africa had indeed reached a critical turning point. The sight of massed ranks of blacks marching on the centre of a white city suggested that black patience had finally snapped. As fear and alarm about the defiant mood of the black population spread, whites rushed to gunshops in the Transvaal and in Cape Town, clearing out their stocks. House prices and the stock market slumped. Foreign embassies were inundated with inquiries about immigration. Liberal whites were convinced that the government would now have no alternative but to change its policies.

An outburst of international protest against the Sharpeville killings added to the atmosphere of crisis. Photographs of the shooting, published by newspapers around the world, made a sharp impact on millions of people who saw them. In the following days, as reports of demonstrations, marches and police brutality accumulated, the impression gained abroad was of an evil regime in the throws of crisis so severe that it might not survive. Western attitudes towards South Africa became markedly more hostile. A United Nations Security Council resolution blamed South Africa's racial policies for causing 'international friction'. In a General Assembly debate, British delegates, who had previously stuck to the argument that South Africa's racial policies were its own internal affair, now openly attacked apartheid. The United States added its own condemnation. For the first time, the General Assembly approved a resolution not just expressing abhorrence of South African policies but asking for action to be taken. Foreign investors, meanwhile, fearing imminent upheaval, took their own action. A sharp outflow of capital hit the value of the currency and halved its foreign exchange reserves.

To all criticism, both domestic and foreign, Verwoerd remained impervious. Nothing was to shake his faith in apartheid. The British prime minister, Harold Macmillan, who paid a visit to South Africa shortly before Sharpeville in February 1960, held long private discussions with Verwoerd, endeavouring to explain the consequences of 'the wind of change' blowing through Africa but making no headway. As he recalled in his memoirs:

> It was only during these days that I began to realize to the full extent the degree of obstinacy, amounting really to fanaticism, which Dr Verwoerd brought to the consideration of his policies . . . I had the unusual experience of soon noticing that nothing one could say or put forward would have the smallest effect upon the views of this determined man.

Far from being willing to make concessions, Verwoerd ordered a massive crackdown on his opponents. In parliament on 28 March, the government introduced new security legislation, the Unlawful Organizations Act, empowering it to proscribe the ANC, the PAC and any other organizations attempting to further their aims. Government spokesmen claimed that the nationalist parties were determined on the violent overthrow of the government. 'Their aim,' said the minister of justice, François Erasmus, on 29 March, 'is to bring to its knees any white government in South Africa which stands for white supremacy and for white leadership . . . [They] do not want peace and order . . . what they want is our country.' Armed with this new legislation, said Erasmus, the government would be able to protect innocent Africans and bring an end to the ANC–PAC 'reign of terror'.

On 30 March, the government declared a state of emergency and began to round up hundreds of anti-apartheid dissidents. Officials were empowered to arrest suspects without warrants and to detain them indefinitely. Large-scale police raids were conducted in one township after another. In Langa, police units threw a cordon around the township, cut off water and electricity supplies, then staged house-to-house raids, dragging men and women on to the streets and assaulting them with clubs and whips. Four days of continuous brutality eventually broke the strike.

The knock on Mandela's door at no. 8115, Orlando West, came at 1.30 in the morning on 30 March. A posse of armed Special Branch policemen ransacked the house, searching for papers and confiscating everything they found, including transcripts Mandela had recently made of his mother's recollections of family history which he was never to see again. The police possessed no warrant for his arrest, gave him no opportunity to contact a lawyer and refused to tell Winnie where he was being taken. 'I simply nodded at Winnie; it was no time for words of comfort.'

At Newlands police station, close to the old site of Sophiatown, Mandela found a number of colleagues also under arrest, including Sisulu, Resha and Nokwe. A group of about forty men in all were packed into a small, open yard and left standing for the rest of the night without food or blankets. In the morning they were moved into a small cell where the only toilet facility was a single drainage hole in the floor which soon became blocked. The stench was overpowering. Still they were given no food or water.

When the cell door was next opened, the prisoners surged through it into an adjacent courtyard and refused to move until they had been fed. The station commander, called to the scene, berated

Mandela for standing with his hands in his pockets. At 3 p.m., food finally arrived. At 6 p.m., prisoners were given sleeping mats and blankets encrusted with dried vomit and ridden with lice the stench of which was so foul that the prisoners retched in disgust.

The next morning, when the station commander accused him of being 'cheeky', Mandela nearly came to blows with him. 'I was still raving mad with temper when in came Special Branch detective Sergeant Helberg and says, "Hello, Nelson!" in a pleasant way. "I am not Nelson to you, I am Mr Mandela!" I shouted.' By this time tempers all round were running high. Before matters degenerated further, Mandela was told he was to be taken to Pretoria to attend the treason trial. 'Fortunately we were told to get into a truck,' he said.

One week later, the ANC and the PAC were declared illegal organizations. As the government sought to crush all resistance, wave after wave of arrests took place. Few dissidents escaped the dragnet. Oliver Tambo was driven across the border into Bechuanaland (later Botswana) to establish external links for the ANC. The Indian communist leader, Yusuf Dadoo, also went into exile. Ruth First, disguised in a red wig, escaped with her children to Swaziland. A small Communist Party committee, including Michael Harmel, Moses Kotane and Ben Turok, continued to operate underground in Johannesburg, moving from one hide-out to another, evading arrest. But scores of other prominent activists, even Liberal Party members, were incarcerated. The PAC's headquarters in Johannesburg were left in the hands of a student who previously had been working as an office manager. By the beginning of May, the total number of arrests had reached more than 18,000.

But for the shooting at Sharpeville, the day might have marked no more than another abortive episode in the annals of African protest. The poor response to the PAC's call for mass civil disobedience showed how few were ready to seek the confrontation with white power that Sobukwe told them would result in the government's downfall. Not only did Sobukwe misjudge popular reaction to his campaign; he also entirely underestimated the government's real strength and its powers of repression. Though the government was pitched into a political crisis of unprecedented magnitude, it was never in danger of losing control.

But this was not the conclusion that prominent opponents of

the government reached. They saw the Sharpeville crisis, the dramatic fall it produced in white confidence and the torrent of condemnation emanating from around the world as evidence of a regime that was vulnerable at home and abroad. 'The type of despotism we still endure in the Union in this age,' wrote Michael Harmel, the leading theoretician of the Congress alliance, 'is a kind of freak, an anachronism which cannot hope much longer to survive.' With so few avenues left open for political action, Congress activists now began to think in terms of revolutionary strategy to hasten its end.

In the wake of the Sharpeville shooting, the treason trial acquired a new significance. The government maintained that the demonstrations and disorder were all part of a communist-inspired conspiracy to overthrow the state with which the trial was directly linked, even though the indictment related to events before December 1956. The accused took a simpler view of the matter. 'This trial,' said Duma Nokwe, 'is out of date.'

On the day that the state of emergency was declared, the proceedings opened in some confusion. Mandela and seventeen other accused were absent. Those who did attend had yet to be arrested. Also missing from the witness box was Chief Luthuli, who had been in the middle of giving his evidence. When Judge Rumpff asked for an explanation for his absence, he was told that Luthuli had been arrested in the early hours of the morning. Rumpff retorted irritably that he did not see why the state of emergency should stand in the way of the trial and ordered Luthuli to be brought to court.

When Luthuli duly appeared, in frail health, it transpired that he had been assaulted by a white policeman in Pretoria Central police station. 'As we were being marched to our cells in the dim light of early morning,' he recalled, 'I was obliged to slow down to negotiate a flight of steps. I was instantly slapped hard across the face from behind. I stooped to gather my hat, and I was hit again.' He added, 'I was angered, but not surprised. Among Africans, the South African police have long been notorious for this sort of thing.'

The trial soon came to a standstill. The following day, with Mandela and the missing accused now present, Maisels asked the court to adjourn on the grounds that the government, by declaring a state of emergency, had effectively made a judgement on the case. Moreover, defence witnesses would be fearful of giving testimony which might now lead to their prosecution under the terms of the emergency regulations. He questioned the propriety of continuing with the trial. The court was adjourned until 26 April while the judges considered the matter.

Outside the court, as the accused milled about being rearrested, one of them, Wilton Mkwayi, became separated from the others. When he tried to rejoin them, a policeman ordered him to leave. When he pointed out he was one of the accused, he was called a liar, threatened with arrest and once again ordered to leave. Mkwayi shrugged his shoulders, walked away and went underground. Meanwhile, the twenty-nine accused were taken to different prisons in Pretoria.

Mandela's new home, for the next five months, was Pretoria Local. The conditions there were initially as bad as those at Newlands. The prisoners were crammed five to a cell six feet by twelve feet, with a single toilet bucket that was emptied twice a day. The air was foul, the blankets and mats were ridden with lice and bugs and the food, cold and stale, was doled out on rusty dishes. For the first ten days, the prisoners were allowed no exercise; nor did they get a chance to shower.

Mandela became their spokesman, engaged in a constant struggle for improvements. When he first asked for a separate room so that the accused could read and study trial documents in quiet, a senior prison officer retorted, 'Government regulations don't require you prisoners to read books.' But slowly, he gained concessions. The cells were painted and fumigated, new blankets and toilet buckets were issued, exercise periods were allowed and a large cell was provided for consultations and legal books. Over the issue of food, Mandela took the complaint to the court. 'Speaking with the greatest moderation,' he said, addressing Judge Rumpff, 'it is no exaggeration to say that the food which is furnished to us in jail, My Lord, with due respect, is completely unfit for human consumption.' The standard of food duly improved.

When the trial resumed on 26 April, the judges, accepting assurances from the minister of justice of an indemnity for the witnesses, decided that the case could proceed. The accused, however, had agreed on other tactics. To make clear their protest against the conditions under which the trial was being held during the state of emergency, Nokwe announced that they would dispense with their defence lawyers. Maisels duly rose to address the court: 'We have no further mandate and we will consequently not trouble Your Lordships any further.' All the defence lawyers then walked out. For a moment, the court seemed stunned. But Judge Rumpff soon carried on as though nothing had happened. The accused, henceforth, were left to conduct their own defence, with Nokwe acting as advocate and Mandela as attorney.

Luthuli returned to the witness box, looking tired and weary but nevertheless resolute under cross-examination. Because of his poor health, his appearance was limited to two hours a day. After giving testimony, he was taken back each time to the prison hospital, where he lived. His ordeal did not stop there, however, as he was himself charged on 104 counts for burning his pass and inciting others to do the same and faced his own trial. At the treason trial, Judge Rumpff treated him with great consideration, anxious to avoid any undue strain, but the prosecutors gave him no quarter, attacking his honesty and integrity. In all, he appeared in court on twenty-six days and did not finally step down from the witness box until June.

Luthuli spoke of his belief that moral persuasion and economic pressure would eventually lead whites to change their policies. There still remained, he said, goodwill towards the whites, though it was diminishing with each year that passed. He emphasized the ANC's policy of non-violence, pointing out that it could be changed only at a national conference. 'I have heard no suggestion to change that policy, not a whisper,' he said. He would have opposed such a suggestion, firstly on personal grounds and secondly because it would be contrary to the interests of the liberation movement: 'It is not a practical thing.'

As the trial dragged on, week after week, Mandela felt keenly his separation from Winnie, who was pregnant again, and from Zenani, then a year old. He made the most of what few visits they were allowed to make to see him, holding and kissing Zenani if the guards permitted him to do so, but the moments of their departure were always hard to bear. 'As Winnie was saying good-bye, and the guards were ushering them out,' he wrote, 'Zeni would often motion for me to come with them, and I could see from her small puzzled face that she did not understand why I could not.'

Mandela also managed to arrange a few illicit meetings with Winnie during visits to Johannesburg he was permitted to make at weekends to help wind up the affairs of Mandela and Tambo. Accompanied by a Special Branch detective, he would leave Pretoria once the court proceedings had ended, work in his office during the day and spend his nights in a Marshall Square police cell, before returning to Pretoria Local on Sunday. The Special Branch detective, an accommodating man, allowed him to buy items from a nearby café on his own and discreetly turned away when Winnie made an appearance. 'We had a kind of gentleman's code between us: I would not escape and thereby get him into trouble, while he permitted me a degree of freedom.'

On 3 August, with defence lawyers back in court as a result of a relaxation of the emergency regulations, Mandela finally took the witness stand. Winnie was present to watch him. Under the guidance of Sydney Kentridge, he was asked to explain at length about the history of the ANC and its policies, about the Youth League, the Defiance Campaign, the 'M' Plan, the Congress of the People and the Freedom Charter. He was also questioned about his views on communism, capitalism and imperialism, about speeches he had given, articles he had written and books found in his possession. Kentridge's aim was to concentrate on issues that he knew the prosecutors would subsequently try to exploit in their efforts to establish the involvement of the ANC in violence and hence to pre-empt them. Once Mandela had stated his case, the burden would be on the prosecution to prove otherwise. His evidence took up 441 pages of the official record.

Kentridge began by examining Mandela on the Youth League, drawing attention to its anti-communist stand to demonstrate that the ANC's outlook was rooted not in communism but in a broader spectrum of views. Mandela related his own reasons for supporting a resolution to expel communists from the ANC:

> . . . from the little knowledge I had at the time about communists I regarded them as people who were hostile to African nationalism, which I regarded as being extremely important from the point of view of mobilizing the African people as such. I was also under the

view, My Lord, that the communists opposed organizations like the ANC and that they would work to subvert both its policies and its campaigns.

He went on to explain his change of attitude: 'I came to work with them and I discovered that the views I held about communists in the ANC were not justified, both by the outlook and attitude of those persons with whom I worked, as well as by their devotion and loyalty to the policy of the ANC.' Asked if he ever became a communist, he said, 'I don't know if I did become a communist. If by communist you mean a member of the Communist Party and a person who believes in the theory of Marx, Engels, Lenin and Stalin and who adheres strictly to the discipline of the party, I did not become a communist.'

Mandela was in the course of explaining the impact of the Defiance Campaign when Judge Bekker intervened, asking, 'Well, as a matter of fact, isn't your freedom a direct threat to the Europeans?' Mandela replied:

> No, it is not a direct threat to the Europeans, as Europeans. We are not anti-white; we are against white supremacy and in struggling against white supremacy we have the support of some sections of the European population . . . As a matter of fact, My Lord, I think that we in the Congress must take credit for the fact that there is a movement in this country for racial peace. I think in numerous speeches which have been made by leading members of the ANC, some of which have been placed before this court, it is quite clear that the Congress has consistently preached a policy of racial harmony and we have condemned racialism no matter by whom it is professed.

Mandela denied that the Freedom Charter meant eliminating private enterprise.

> MANDELA: Apart from those industries [mines and banks] the Freedom Charter does not call for socialism in this country.
> KENTRIDGE: Have you made any study of socialism?
> MANDELA: I have read some books . . . pro and against.
> KENTRIDGE: And are you interested in socialism?
> MANDELA: I am very much attracted to it.
> KENTRIDGE: Have you read anything about the system in the Soviet Union?
> MANDELA: Very little, My Lords, but I have.

KENTRIDGE: Do you find that system interesting?

MANDELA: I find it very interesting.

KENTRIDGE: As far as you know what the situation is, is there anything about the Soviet Union that impresses you?

MANDELA: Yes. I am impressed by the entire absence of the colour bar . . . Secondly, I am impressed by the fact that the Soviet Union has no colonies in Africa and as far as I know in any other part of the world. I am also impressed by the stand which the Soviet Union has taken on the question of imperialism . . .

KENTRIDGE: Do you hope to introduce the system in the Soviet Union in South Africa?

MANDELA: No, My Lords. All that impresses me is the ideal of a socialist society, but I have no intention of copying anything that has been done in any other country.

Mandela was asked by Kentridge to explain what he meant when, in an article in *Liberation*, he described the Freedom Charter as 'a revolutionary document' which envisaged changes that could not be won 'without breaking up the economic and political set-up of present South Africa'. In reply, Mandela said, 'It doesn't mean that we would do away with parliamentary institutions; they would remain, but the composition would be so radically different that it would be appropriate to say that the political structure has been broken up.'

Judge Bekker asked him to expand on this point.

I accept that the authorities will not of their own free will legislate that we should be given these rights. There will have to be a tremendous amount of pressure put up by the Congress movement . . . We will have to launch defiance campaigns, stay-at-homes, a combination of these, and it will be because of that pressure that we expect the government either to give in to our demands and to say that we have come to the conclusion that we can no longer continue with the present set-up. We will repeal all laws which discriminate against non-Europeans. Either that, or the voters would say that we can't have this mass defiance of the laws, we can't have this situation of uncertainty and insecurity. We call upon the government to resign, and to make way for a government which is going to meet the demands. That is what I have in mind, My Lords, when I say that these demands cannot be attained without breaking up the political and economic set-up in the country. I do visualize the exertion of pressure on a tremendous scale.

In their cross-examination of Mandela, the prosecutors tried time and again to get him to confess on the matter of violence. Phrases like 'revolutionary eruption', 'seizure of power' and 'people's democracy', which he had used in articles and speeches and which other activists had also used, were turned over again and again in the search for violent meaning. The nub of the prosecutor's attack was that in order to achieve the aims of the Freedom Charter the ANC would have to resort to the violent overthrow of the government.

> MANDELA: My own view is that it is not necessary in this country to employ force and violence in order to bring about either the demands set out in the Freedom Charter, or even to bring about socialism. I don't think it's necessary at all to do so . . .
>
> PROSECUTOR: Do you think it's possible to achieve a transformation to a communist state in this country peacefully?
>
> MANDELA: You keep on talking about a communist state; I talk about a socialist state . . .
>
> PROSECUTOR: Is there a possibility that the application of pressure by the Congress movement might result in strong counter-pressure by the government, the ruling class, and that there would be violence?
>
> MANDELA: That possibility is always there . . . but we believe that our policy will bring down the government in spite of its intentions . . . In this country there is a large body of voters who are hostile to the policy of the government, and we believe that because of pressure, both externally and internally . . . the government will be brought to realize that its policy is futile.

Mandela explained that the kind of state he envisaged could not be achieved by 'small concessions' from the government, like having whites representing black interests in parliament: 'You will create that state if the vote is extended to all sections of the population.'

> PROSECUTOR: Do you think that your people's democracy could be achieved by a process of gradual reforms? Suppose, as a result of pressure, the ruling class were to agree next month to a qualified franchise for the Africans, an educational test perhaps – not a stringent one – and next year, as a result of further pressure, a more important concession is made in 1962, and so on over a period of ten or twenty years – do you think that the people's democracy could be achieved in that fashion?

MANDELA: . . . In my own view I would say, 'Yes, let us talk,' and the government would say, 'We think that the Europeans at present are not ready for a type of government where there might be domination by non-Europeans. We think we should give you sixty seats. The African population to elect sixty Africans to represent them in Parliament. We will leave the matter over for five years and we will review it at the end of five years.' In my view, that would be a victory, My Lords; we would have taken a significant step towards the attainment of universal adult suffrage for Africans, and we would then for the five years say, we will suspend civil disobedience; we won't have any stay-at-homes, and we will then devote the intervening period for the purposes of educating the country, the Europeans, to see that these changes can be brought about and that it would bring about better racial understanding, better harmony in the country. I'd say we should accept it, but, of course, I would not abandon the demands for the extension of the franchise to all Africans. That's how I see it, My Lords.

Then, at the end of the five-year period, we will have discussions, and if the government says, 'We will give you again forty more seats,' I might say that that is quite sufficient. Let's accept it, and still demand that the franchise should be extended, but for the agreed period we should suspend civil disobedience, no stay-at-homes. In that way we would eventually be able to get everything we want; we shall have our people's democracy, My Lords . . .

JUDGE KENNEDY: Mandela, assuming you were wrong in your beliefs, do you visualize any future action on behalf of the government, by the government? Because I think the evidence suggests that you could not expect the government to soften in its views. Have you any future plans in that event?

MANDELA: No, My Lords, I don't think that the Congress has ever believed that its policy of pressure would ultimately fail. The Congress, of course, does not expect that one single push to coerce the government to change its policy will succeed; the Congress expects that over a period, as a result of a repetition of these pressures, together with world opinion, that the government, notwithstanding its attitude of ruling Africans with an iron hand, that notwithstanding that, the methods which we are using will bring about a realization of our aspirations.

Mandela said the ANC believed that it would be possible to

achieve its aims through numerical superiority, without resorting to violence.

> We had in mind that in the foreseeable future it will be possible for us to achieve these demands, and we worked on the basis that Europeans themselves, in spite of the wall of prejudice and hostility which we encountered, that they can never remain indifferent indefinitely to our demands, because we are hitting them in the stomach with our policy of economic pressure. It is a method which is well organized. The Europeans dare not look at it with indifference. They would have to respond to it and, indeed, My Lords, they are responding to it.

Mandela's performance under cross-examination allowed the prosecution to make no headway in trying to expose the ANC on the question of violence. But there remained the prosecution's key piece of evidence, the tape-recording of Robert Resha addressing volunteers in ANC headquarters. 'A volunteer is a person who is disciplined,' he had said. 'This is the key of the volunteer – discipline. When you are disciplined and you are told by the organization not to be violent, you must not be violent. If you are a true volunteer and you are called upon to be violent, you must be absolutely violent, you must murder! Murder! That is all!'

Both Luthuli and Mandela were asked to comment on Resha's remarks. Luthuli replied that if a general in the army was at fault, it did not imply he represented a whole policy. 'If Resha as a general departs, he departs as Resha. It has nothing to do with the policy of the African National Congress, definitely.' Mandela's view was similarly straightforward.

> MANDELA: I understand it to mean that when a volunteer is called upon to perform a certain task, he must perform that task, but obviously if that task is contrary to the policy of Congress, we don't expect any volunteer to carry out that task.
> PROSECUTOR: As far as you are concerned, there is nothing in that speech which you find inconsistent with the policy of the ANC?
> MANDELA: If the speech advocates violence, of course it is totally contrary to the policy of Congress.

Resha himself spent days in the witness box under examination and cross-examination. Asked by Bram Fischer how he could reconcile his speech with ANC policy, he replied simply, 'The example I used in that speech cannot be reconciled with the policy of the African National Congress.'

Professor Matthews, the concluding witness for the defence, was also asked about Resha's speech. 'Just words,' said the professor. 'You know,' said the prosecutor, Gustav Hoexter, 'I think you're right.'

In the four years that the treason trial had lasted, Mandela had grown considerably in stature. His skill in handling the defence of the accused, along with Duma Nokwe, when their lawyers withdrew from the proceedings, added to his standing as a lawyer. He appeared confident and at ease in the witness box, holding his own against the attack of the prosecutors, displaying a depth of knowledge and understanding which even they found impressive. As the spokesman for the prisoners in Pretoria, he had shown equal determination in fighting the smaller battles against white authority. He responded instinctively to challenge. When confronted with difficulties, he tackled them undaunted, giving a lead to others, always mindful of the need to keep up their spirits. He had acquired a wider sense of responsibility since his days as a gadfly. Prominent white activists who had once considered him a 'lightweight' came to regard him as 'a man ripe for the moment'. His old mentor, Walter Sisulu, the anchor of the ANC throughout the 1950s, remained as great an influence on him as before. Mandela's first reflex in considering many a problem was to ask, 'What does Walter think?' According to Rusty Bernstein, 'Mandela had good judgement as an arbitrator and a conciliator. He was not so good on individual judgements, but usually he consulted and listened, and usually he consulted Walter.'

That habit would continue for years to come, but by 1960 Mandela had emerged as a leader in his own right.

The state of emergency was lifted on 31 August 1960, enabling Mandela to go home for the first time in five months. 'After one has been in prison,' he wrote, 'it is the small things that one appreciates: being able to take a walk whenever one wants, going into a shop and buying a newspaper, speaking or choosing to remain silent. The simple act of being able to control one's person.'

The problem remained about what to do next. In prison there had been much talk about the use of violence. The banning of the

ANC had closed off the possibility of conventional opposition. Agitation for action against the government was growing among youth groups. The ANC's leaders, however, considered the use of violence to be neither a feasible nor a desirable course of action, on both practical and political grounds. A major concern was the position of Luthuli, who would never have countenanced the idea. But equally important was the ANC's continuing hope that mass action might still shake the government. As Mandela had explained in his testimony at the treason trial, the nationalists believed that they could mount sufficient 'pressure' on the government and on the economy to cause a change of mind among the white population. Though there was scant evidence to support it, they clung to the notion that such a change was already under way. What was decided, therefore, at a secret meeting of the ANC's national executive in September was to reorganize the ANC on an underground basis, resurrecting the old 'M' Plan. A new working committee in Johannesburg was given responsibility for the task; it included Mandela, Sisulu, Nokwe, Marks and Kotane.

While the ANC uneasily pondered its next moves, the communists had no such qualms. Nurtured on theories of revolutionary violence, they read from the trend of events in South Africa a new revolutionary potential and leapt publicly into the fray. On 14 July 1960, after seven years of secret underground activity, the Communist Party distributed leaflets announcing its existence and calling on workers to rally in the struggle against the government. From his hide-outs in Johannesburg, moving between ten different houses in five months, Harmel produced a paper arguing that it was necessary to abandon non-violence as the sole means of struggle and move to armed methods. Harmel's view was, 'No further progress is possible along the traditional paths or by adhering strictly to the non-violence slogan in a situation where every democratic demand or criticism is treated as an act of rebellion or treason.' Such was the respect in which Harmel was held that the idea gained immediate credibility. Some communists, like Ben Turok, regarded him as the 'Lenin of the movement'.

Among those influenced by Harmel was Bram Fischer. Fischer's role in the resistance was becoming ever more extraordinary. During the state of emergency, his wife, Molly, was imprisoned, leaving him on his own to care for his children, one of whom, Paul, suffered from permanent poor health and sometimes hovered close to death. At the treason trial, meanwhile, Fischer's responsibilities included handling Robert Resha, the most difficult of all the accused. At the same time, not only was he providing an important link between the accused and the outside world, even managing to smuggle a radio into Pretoria Central for them, but he was also one of the principal links between the underground party committee, led by Harmel and Kotane, and the outside world, having to avoid police surveillance all the while. On top of all this, he was constantly preoccupied with helping the wives and families of detainees. 'During the emergency,' recalled Bernstein, 'Bram was undertaking everyone else's problems.'

Fischer became a reluctant convert to the idea of armed struggle. He had doubts as to whether an underground movement could mount a campaign of violence as well as survive the repression that would inevitably follow. He was also anxious about taking steps from which there could be no retreat. But ultimately he conceded that every other alternative had been tried, to no avail. Other leading communists, notably Kotane, were also sceptical. Kotane was worried that the resort to violence would undermine the ability of an underground movement to continue with non-violent political work.

The enthusiasts, however, carried the day. They saw themselves in the tradition of Marxist-Leninist revolutionaries determined to strike against a brutal, decaying regime. The armed struggle, they believed, would receive massive support from the oppressed African population. At the forefront of this group was Joe Slovo, a hardline Stalinist with romantic notions about revolutionary warfare. At a secret meeting in December 1960 at a private house in Victoria, a white suburb of Johannesburg, the communists took the decision to establish an armed force consisting of small squads of saboteurs as a prelude to engaging in guerrilla warfare.

Mandela was fully informed of these developments. But though he was as keen as the communists to retaliate against the government, he acknowledged that the ANC, with its broad constituency of interests, was in no position to follow suit. Neither was he himself able to offer any leadership on the matter. For not only was he still preoccupied with the treason trial in Pretoria but he was also subject to a banning order restricting his movements.

His time was also taken up with endeavours to earn a living as a lawyer. Though the firm of Mandela and Tambo had closed down, Mandela was operating on a freelance basis from Kholvad House in the flat in which Ismail Meer had once lived but which had since been taken over by Kathy Kathrada. He was not short of clients. The lounge and the passage outside the flat were often crammed with clients.

All this left Mandela with little enough time to enjoy any kind of family life. Winnie, heavily pregnant, rarely saw him. Even on the birth of their second daughter, Zindziswa, in December 1960, Mandela was diverted from attending by another small crisis. Learning that his son, Makgatho, was ill in the Transkei, where he attended school, Mandela drove through the night to reach him, violating his banning order, bringing him back to Johannesburg for surgery, only to find he had missed the birth.

The treason trial, meanwhile, lumbered on into its concluding stages. The prosecution's closing argument, begun on 7 November 1960, finally ended, after several adjournments, on 6 March 1961. The defence's closing argument followed, with Maisels beginning by refuting all charges of violence. 'We admit that there is a question of non-cooperation and passive resistance,' he said. 'We shall say quite frankly that if non-cooperation and passive resistance constitute high treason, then we are guilty. But these are plainly not encompassed in the law of treason.'

The defence lawyers had expected their closing argument to take up to three months, so complex were many of the issues involved. But after only two weeks, while Bram Fischer was engaged in a lengthy analysis of ANC policies, the judges made a series of interruptions directing him to focus on specific issues. Finally, on 23 March, in a further dramatic intervention, they adjourned the court until 29 March to consider whether they could forgo hearing certain aspects of the defence argument, in the interests of shortening the trial. The clear implication was that they had already made up their minds in favour of acquittal.

This sudden and unexpected turn of events had an immediate impact on Mandela's decisions about his future. His banning order, in place for five years, was due to expire two days hence, on 25 March. He had planned to use the opportunity to travel to Pietermaritzburg at the weekend to address a conference of Congress supporters, called the 'All-in Conference', before returning to Pretoria to resume his place at the treason trial. The purpose of this conference was to issue demands for a national convention for all South Africans to draw up a non-racial constitution.

At a hastily convened meeting of the ANC's working committee in Johannesburg, it was agreed that if on 29 March the accused were acquitted, Mandela should immediately go underground to organize support for the national convention, avoiding any further restrictions on him the government might seek to impose and surfacing in public on carefully planned occasions to achieve a maximum of publicity: 'It was not a proposal that came as a surprise to me, nor was it one I particularly relished, but it was something I knew I had to do.'

Accompanied by Sisulu, Nokwe and one of his new lieutenants, Joe Modise, a tough street-fighter from Alexandra, Mandela went to his house in Orlando to tell Winnie what would now happen. They had never previously discussed the possibility that he might leave home; nor was she even aware that his banning order was due to expire, or that he planned to travel to Pietermaritzburg that weekend. Mandela never confided in Winnie. She was simply told what to do. She recalled:

> They all stood outside in the driveway of the garage and he sent a child to call me. On my arrival he simply said, 'Darling, just pack some of my clothes in a suitcase with my toiletries. I will be going away for a long time. You're not to worry, my friends here will look after you. They'll give you news of me from time to time. Look well after the children. I know you'll have the strength and courage to do so without me. I know you are capable of that.'
>
> I quickly packed his clothes. I was in tears but I had been conditioned in the few months we had together not to ask any questions. I only wished him well before we parted and asked that the gods of Africa take care of him wherever he would be, and that he would have a chance to spare the children and me a few minutes sometime. He scolded me for reminding him of his duties.

Mandela did not enter the house. By the time Winnie had finished packing his bag, he had gone. An hour later, Joe Modise returned to collect it.

Mandela's sudden appearance at the All-in Conference in an

Indian hall in Pietermaritzburg on 25 March had an electrifying effect on the delegates. He had not been seen on a public platform since 1952. He was duly elected to head a National Action Council charged with the task of organizing the campaign for a national convention. The first phase of the campaign was to take the form of a three-day national stay-away, to be carried out if the government failed to respond by 31 May to the demand for a national convention, as everyone expected it to do. Some 1,400 delegates joined enthusiastically in the proceedings, not knowing that this was to be the last large conference organized by African leaders in South Africa for many years. It was also Mandela's last public appearance. Having made a successful impact, he drove back to Pretoria to hear the verdict of the treason trial.

It took Judge Rumpff forty minutes in the Old Synagogue in Pretoria on 29 March 1961 to deliver the court's findings. He reviewed a number of conclusions which the three judges had reached unanimously. The court found, he said, that the ANC and its allies had been working 'to replace the present form of state with a radically and fundamentally different form of state'; that the Programme of Action 'envisaged the use of illegal means' and that illegal means were used during the Defiance Campaign; that some ANC leaders 'made themselves guilty of sporadic speeches of violence which in our opinion amounted to an incitement to violence'; that 'a strong left-wing tendency manifested itself' in the ANC during the indictment period between 1952 and 1956; and that the ANC frequently revealed 'anti-imperialist, anti-West and pro-Soviet' attitudes.

But although there had been some violent speeches by ANC members – 'a minute percentage of the total number of speeches made' – there was no proof of an ANC policy of violent revolution. There was also no proof that the ANC was a communist organization or that it had been infiltrated by communists, or that the Freedom Charter envisaged a communist state.

'The cornerstone of the case', said Rumpff, was the ANC's alleged policy of incitement to violence. The prosecution's failure to prove this policy 'inevitably meant a collapse of the whole case':

On all the evidence presented to this court and on our findings of

192

fact, it is impossible for this court to come to the conclusion that the African National Congress had acquired or adopted a policy to overthrow the state by violence, that is, in the sense that the masses had to be prepared or conditioned to commit direct acts of violence against the state.

In the crowded courtroom, there was not a movement, not a murmur, as Rumpff delivered his final words: 'The accused are accordingly found not guilty and are discharged.'

Once the judges in their scarlet robes had filed out, the spectators' gallery erupted in cheers and the accused hugged one another and waved to the onlookers. In the courtyard outside, Mandela embraced Winnie. As the accused celebrated their release amid a throng of friends and family, laughing, weeping and singing, Maisels and Fischer were hoisted high above their shoulders.

Each of the three judges at the treason trial handed down separate reasons for the conclusions they reached in their joint judgement. In his reasons for judgement, which ran to 168 pages, Rumpff referred to the evidence given both by Luthuli and by Mandela to support his findings that communism had not been adopted by the ANC. In the case of Luthuli, it was because of his openly anti-communist Christian stance; in the case of Mandela, it was because in 1956 he 'foresaw a non-European bourgeois advance under the Freedom Charter'. Rumpff was not convinced, he said, 'that the African National Congress had acquired a policy which caused it to cross the dividing line between non-communism and communism in the spectrum of socialist belief'.

Bekker, giving his reasons for judgement, took issue with the prosecution's contention that the accused planned to set up a communist system of government in South Africa: 'I share the view expressed by Mandela that in order to achieve this state (as envisaged in the Freedom Charter) the present economic and political set-up in South Africa will have to be broken.' But, he went on, he disagreed with the proposition that the only form of state envisaged by the Freedom Charter was a communist one:

> This definition does not in my opinion necessarily imply a one-party system as being put forward since in the classes which remain after the exclusion of the 'few exploiters' as defined, there may very well be room, for instance, for a communist party on the one hand and

a socialist party on the other . . . I am accordingly unable to agree
that the one and only inference to be drawn from the document is
that a dictatorship of the proletariat was being advocated.

The court record of the treason trial ran to nearly 10 million
words bound in 180 volumes of 200 pages each. Yet no single
act of conspiracy or any act of violence was ever alleged by the
prosecution, and many of the claims it made about the 'explosive'
nature of the racial situation in South Africa in 1956 and about
speeches 'bristling with references to the spilling of blood' it never
managed to substantiate. As an attempt to demonstrate that opposition to the government was due principally to the work of communists, the trial was clearly a failure.

The government drew its own conclusions from this outcome.
One of the spectators who went to watch the trial when it was still
in its early stages was John Vorster, an advocate and former Nazi
sympathizer who had been imprisoned without trial during the
Second World War for pro-German activities. Appointed by Verwoerd as his new minister of justice a few months after the treason
trial verdict, with instructions to root out all resistance, Vorster
resolved that if the government's opponents could not be crushed
by the law, then the law would have to be changed and evidence
obtained by other means. Recalling the meeting on the day in
August 1961 that Verwoerd appointed him, he said, 'I remember
saying to Dr Verwoerd that he should let me deal with the threat
of subversion and revolution in my own way. I told him that you
could not fight communism with the Queensbury rules, because if
you did then you would lose. He agreed with me and said that he
would leave me free to do what I had to do – within reason.'

Vorster appointed a new head of the security police, Hendrik
van den Bergh, who had been interned with him during the war
and who shared his views about how to tackle the problem. As
van den Bergh recalled, 'For me the choice was between revolution,
violence and a bloodbath and the so-called rule of law, about which
there was all the noise. I looked at my children and those of others
and said, "To the devil with the rule of law." '

On the night that the accused were discharged, Bram Fischer gave
a party at Beaumont Street to celebrate. As the guests arrived, they

were watched by Special Branch detectives waiting in two cars in the street outside. Mandela did not join them. Nor did he go home. He spent the night in a safe house in Johannesburg, growing accustomed to a life in the underground.

CHAPTER 9
Spear of the Nation

A warrant for Mandela's arrest was soon issued. He was the only member of the National Action Committee, given responsibility for organizing the national strike, who had been publicly identified. The names of other members, like Sisulu, were deliberately not disclosed, since organizing a strike by Africans was a criminal offence. Mandela was therefore certain to face a prison sentence, unless he could successfully evade capture. There was a large contingent of ANC supporters ready to help. But what was even more important was that Mandela had access to the network of Communist Party supporters who had had eight years of experience of working underground undetected and were already proficient in the use of secret communications, safe houses and hidden meetings.

This new style of leadership – operating from an underground headquarters – caused considerable controversy within the ANC. The ANC was accustomed to its leaders standing openly in defiance of the government to demonstrate their willingness to make the same sacrifices they were urging on their supporters. During the Defiance Campaign, prominent officials had lined up to be arrested and had openly sought imprisonment. Imprisonment was seen to be as much a symbol of defiance as the breaking of laws. Mandela's decision, therefore, not to seek arrest or to stand trial in connection with charges arising from his leadership of the strike represented a significant change in how the ANC believed it should conduct the business of liberation; some critics charged it was tantamount to 'running away'.

Mandela's skill in evading capture, however, soon caught the imagination of the press and the public. The press dubbed him the Black Pimpernel, an African version of the Scarlet Pimpernel, a fictional character who evaded capture during the French Revolution. Mandela moved about the country, from Port Elizabeth to Cape Town, to Durban, to Johannesburg, urging support for the strike, meeting journalists and advertising his activities through telephone calls to newspapers. Much of the work he carried out at night, growing used to spending his days in hide-outs. He disguised himself with different outfits, dressing in workmen's overalls or chauffeurs' clothes, growing a beard, wearing round, rimless spectacles, walking and speaking in a manner as unobtrusive as possible. After dark he often appeared as a night watchman, dressed in a large grey overcoat and cap pulled over his eyes and occasionally sporting large earrings.

Police efforts to find him – mounting roadblocks, searching houses – proved fruitless. Mandela was constantly on the move, going from one safe house to another. There were times, however, when he had a narrow escape. An African policeman in Johannesburg recognized him in his chauffeur's uniform, but passed by with a smile. Once while he was waiting in his car at a traffic light, Colonel Spengler, the head of the security police on the Witwatersrand, who had known him for ten years, drew up alongside but did not glance his way.

Mandela adapted to the solitary nature of underground life without difficulty: 'I welcomed the opportunity to be by myself, to plan, to think, to plot.' But he was never able to overcome his longing to see more of Winnie. With Winnie, the discipline by which he was determined to live fell away. 'His meetings with Winnie were foolhardy,' said Rusty Bernstein. 'They were high-risk. This was his Achilles' heel. Otherwise he was extremely cautious.' On one occasion when a scheduled meeting with Winnie fell through, Mandela was so disappointed that he simply drove off to look for her. He eventually managed to see her after getting a friend to telephone her. Winnie recalled:

> I saw him frequently when he was underground. I waited for that sacred knock at the window in the early hours of the morning. I never knew when. I never had an appointment made. At the beginning he used to come home for an hour or so early in the morning, depending

on the political situation. Later, they were watching me twenty-four hours a day and I had to slip out through police cordons to go to him.

Then, someone would come and order me to follow him in my car. We would drive a kilometre or so from the house, we would then meet another car, we would jump from that one into another, and by the time I reached him I had gone through something like ten cars. I never knew where I was. His hide-outs were all over the country. The people who arranged this were, of course, mostly whites.

She never knew the identity of these white couriers. 'I would just find myself at the end of the journey in some white house; in most cases when we got there they were deserted. You could see that arrangements had been made for families to stay away while we were there together.'

The dates chosen for the three-day stay-at-home were 29–31 May, to coincide with the day nominated by the government to proclaim South Africa a republic, 31 May. The establishment of a republic, free from all links with the British crown, had been one of the most cherished objectives of Afrikaner nationalists since Britain's defeat of the old Boer republics of the Transvaal and the Orange Free State in 1902. A referendum among the white electorate in October 1960 had produced a small overall majority in favour of a republic. Verwoerd intended that Republic Day on 31 May would be remembered as a day of celebration.

The ANC's plans for strike action thus became a trial of strength. In April, Mandela wrote a letter to Verwoerd, on behalf of the National Action Committee, requesting him to call a national convention or face a massive strike. 'We have no illusions about the counter-measures your government might take,' he wrote. 'During the last twelve months we have gone through a period of grim dictatorship.' Nevertheless, he added, 'We are not deterred by threats of force and violence.' Verwoerd did not reply.

Mandela appealed for help from the leader of the opposition United Party, Sir de Villiers Graaf. 'Stated bluntly, the alternatives appear to be these: talk it out, or shoot it out,' he wrote. 'It is still not too late to turn the tide against the Nationalist-created crisis. A call for a national convention from you now could well be the turning point.' He did not receive a reply.

In an article in the liberal journal *Contact*, Mandela appealed for support from student leaders and sportsmen. He was optimistic about what could be achieved: 'There are some who are still assailed by doubts and hesitations. We say to them that the times are critical and momentous. We urge them to join in with us and together to deliver the knockout punch.'

The counter-measures ordered by Verwoerd far exceeded anything that Mandela had expected. In the largest mobilization since the war, the government called out army and police reserves. All police leave was cancelled. Armed guards were posted to protect power stations and other essential services. Police raids were conducted night after night in African townships; helicopters were used to train searchlights on houses, yards and unlit areas; police vans broadcast warnings that Africans who went on strike would be sacked and forced out of towns. Employers threatened mass dismissals. All political meetings were banned. A twelve-day detention law was introduced. Troops camped in the heart of Johannesburg, ready for action. It was the biggest show of strength the Nationalist government had ever mounted.

In parliament, Verwoerd issued warnings not only to 'agitators' but also to 'members of the ordinary public', including 'some intellectuals and some pseudo-intellectuals as well as some newspapers' who were 'busy playing with fire' by advocating a multiracial national convention. This proposal, he said, was made by communists and 'everyone who lends support to this proposition, will, whatever his personal aims may be, become jointly responsible for what is their [the communists'] aim'.

Despite this display of might by the government, the strike call on 29 May was answered by thousands of workers in major towns. Scores of industries and factories were disrupted. But the overall result did not match Mandela's expectations. He described the first day of the stay-at-home as 'not the national success I had hoped for'; and on the second day, he called off the campaign.

Later that day, he met foreign journalists in a sparsely furnished flat in Yeoville, north-east of the city centre. He appeared relaxed, dressed in a striped sports shirt and grey trousers, with a side-parting clipped neatly in his hair, laughing easily as he welcomed the visitors. Did he concede, asked one correspondent, that the strike had been a failure? 'In the light of the steps taken by government to suppress the stay-at-home, it was a tremendous success,' he replied. The mobilization of the army as well as the police was 'striking testimony of African strength and a measure of the government's weakness'. As the visitors were taking their leave, he became more sombre: 'If the government reaction is to crush by naked force our non-violent demonstrations, we will have to seriously reconsider our tactics. In my mind we are closing a chapter on this question of non-violent policy.'

The failure of the May strike convinced Mandela that there was nothing further to be gained from continuing with protest action and that the only alternative available was to resort to violence. 'Non-violent passive resistance is effective as long as your opposition adheres to the same rules as you do,' he said. 'But if peaceful protest is met with violence, its efficacy is at an end.' The case for hitting back at the government, he believed, was now overwhelming. Africans had to show that their white rulers were still vulnerable and could be hurt.

Mandela conferred first with Sisulu, who agreed that a change in strategy was inevitable. 'Looking at the situation, I can't see what else could have been done,' said Sisulu. 'There was this dilemma. The government was acting violently. We were leading the movement. People were entitled to know how we were meeting this violence. The time had come for us to make preparations. But this was not the type of issue that we could have taken to the masses. We had to get the leadership committed. We needed a small number of people to start it. With delay, the idea might have fizzled out.'

Mandela and Sisulu both believed that a limited campaign of sabotage would scare off foreign investors, disrupt trade and cause sufficient damage to the economy to force the white electorate and the government to alter course. The government, they assumed, was not strong enough to embark on further repression. 'I didn't think the government could suppress the whole movement,' said Sisulu.

Mandela raised the issue of armed struggle with the ANC's working committee, but ran into a wall of opposition from Moses Kotane. Kotane, in his characteristically blunt manner, accused Mandela of failing to think through his proposal carefully.

Mandela, he said, had been outmanoeuvred and paralysed by the government's actions and now, in desperation, was resorting to revolutionary language. 'There is still room,' he said, 'for the old methods if we are imaginative and determined enough. If we embark on the course Mandela is suggesting, we will be exposing innocent people to massacres by the enemy.' Kotane's argument carried the day.

Shortly afterwards, at a meeting Sisulu had arranged, Mandela and Kotane spent a whole day arguing further over the issue. There was a certain irony about the confrontation. Kotane, a lifelong communist from peasant origins, a graduate of the Lenin School in Moscow, secretary-general of the underground Communist Party, with revolutionary credentials far superior to Mandela's, argued adamantly that the potential for conventional political struggle had by no means been exhausted; it was only because political work had become more difficult that Mandela was seeking the easy way out and trying to escape the responsibilities of political leadership. The time for armed struggle had not yet arrived. An austere, puritanical figure, Kotane was known both for his arrogant and assertive manner and also for his hard-headed realism.

Mandela, a Xhosa aristocrat, a trained lawyer who had just emerged from a marathon trial, the outcome of which had depended on convincing a panel of judges about the ANC's commitment to non-violent methods, responded to Kotane by using arguments fashioned by Kotane's own colleagues in the Communist Party in favour of violence. Castro's recent revolution in Cuba, Mandela said, had shown how it was not necessary for revolutionaries to wait for appropriate conditions, as defined in the textbooks of Lenin and Stalin, to materialize. 'If you wait for textbook conditions, they will never occur.' Militants were already forming their own armed units. The leadership was now falling behind its supporters.

The influence of revolutionary enthusiasts in the Communist Party at this juncture was crucial. The communists had already formed their own specialist units for sabotage activity, some fifteen groups of three to four men each, which had begun trying their hand at cutting telephone and communications links. They also had ready access to the Soviet Union and China, both quartermasters to revolution around the world. Plans had already been made to send recruits outside the country for training.

What further convinced them of the feasibility of guerrilla warfare in South Africa were the heady examples set by Algeria and
Cuba. By mid-1961, Algerian nationalists were on the verge of
victory over French forces seeking to defend the white settler
population. In Cuba, the example was even more potent. A group
of no more than twelve revolutionaries, including Fidel Castro and
Che Guevara, survived a landing on the island's coast in a rickety
old boat and within two years had marched into Havana at the head
of a 10,000-strong victorious guerrilla army. Guevara's 'detonator'
theory of revolution, the idea that armed action on its own would
create a momentum among the population, had a dramatic impact
on the thinking of South African revolutionaries. 'The seminal
work was Che Guevara's *Guerrilla Warfare*. And many of the
errors can be attributed to that fact,' said Ben Turok. 'I remember
the discussions at the time. The point made was, is it wrong to
wait for the objective conditions to develop where violence becomes
naturally part of the struggle, or is the situation such that the
subjective element can create the objective, and that's Che's argument. And we became convinced that the subjective could actually
play an important role.'

The communists' objectives did not stop short at sabotage. Joe
Slovo, the key operational figure in devising the party's military
strategy, believed that sabotage would provide a bridge to popular
armed struggle, drawing in new recruits and conditioning the
population to accept methods of violence, eventually leading to a
broad revolutionary assault on the government. Attaining this
objective was feasible given the mass support enjoyed by the ANC.
What the Communist Party therefore envisaged was 'a united front
of national liberation' which would set out 'to destroy white
domination'. When that goal was reached, the communists would
then work to transform South Africa into a socialist state. These
two stages of the revolution became official Communist Party
policy.

The flaws in this revolutionary strategy tended to be overlooked.
South Africa possessed few heavily wooded areas suitable for
guerrilla bases. It was surrounded by white-run African colonies
which provided no opportunity for rear bases. In rural areas, the
ANC had never been successful in mobilizing support for its
political campaigns; it remained essentially an urban-based organiz-

ation. In urban areas, the black population was subject to a vast array of controls which had already effectively crippled political action. Above all, the government had never shown any signs of losing control. Its security apparatus was formidable, as the crushing of the May strike had just demonstrated.

The communists' enthusiasm for armed struggle had a marked influence on Mandela's own outlook, making it seem more feasible than would otherwise have been the case. 'The communists manoeuvred hard for violence,' remarked Yusuf Cachalia, Mandela's Indian activist friend and himself a member of the Communist Party. 'They certainly influenced Mandela's attitude towards violence.'

At a second meeting of the ANC's working committee in June, it was agreed that the issue of armed struggle should be put to the ANC's national executive committee and that the Congress alliance, comprising the Indian Congress, the Congress of Democrats, the Coloured People's Congress, the South African Congress of Trade Unions and the ANC, should also be consulted. The venue chosen for both meetings, to be held on consecutive days, was Tongaat, a small village surrounded by sugar plantations north of Durban and close to Luthuli's home in the Umvoti Mission Reserve, enabling him to attend. About sixty delegates in all, most of them subject to banning orders, travelled in secret to Tongaat.

The ANC meeting lasted all night. Mandela presented his case vigorously. Violence, he said, had become inevitable, whether or not it was initiated by the ANC. ANC supporters were beginning to lose confidence in the policy of non-violence and would eventually resort to violent methods of protest on their own. If nationalist leaders failed to take decisive action, the undercurrents of hatred rising among the African population would surface in outbreaks of terrorism that would have a disastrous impact on race relations. It was both wrong and unrealistic for African leaders to continue preaching peace and non-violence when the government's only response was to meet their demands with force. It would be far better for the ANC to channel and control the momentum towards violence to ensure that it was directed at proper targets. If the ANC failed to take the lead now, it would be left behind.

Luthuli's commitment to non-violence was well known. He believed that non-violence was the only justifiable course of action on both moral and practical grounds. 'Violence disrupts human life and is destructive to perpetrator and victim alike,' he said in 1961. 'I do not regard peace as a passive thing. The non-violent policy I am advocating is a positive one . . . It demands moral courage and taxes our physical courage.'

Luthuli held firmly to his views, but, after hours of argument, he agreed to a compromise. The ANC would remain committed to non-violence, but it would not stand in the way of members who wanted to establish a separate and independent military organization, nor would it disapprove of 'properly controlled violence'.

The following night, at the Congress alliance meeting, the arguments raged anew. The position was more complex for the ANC's allies, for while the ANC was an illegal organization, the others were still able to conduct political work legally. Within the Indian Congress, the commitment to non-violence was held as determinedly by many members as it was by Luthuli. The Indian Congress leader, Dr Monty Naicker, was adamantly opposed to armed struggle. Jaydew Singh, Mandela's old friend from Kholvad House, declared, 'Non-violence has not failed us; we have failed non-violence.' Yusuf Cachalia argued emphatically that any attempt at armed struggle would end in the government wiping out the entire nationalist movement. 'It was pure adventurism,' he said years later. 'It was impractical. They had not worked out the consequences.' Yet most Indian communists were in favour of armed struggle. The Congress of Democrats, influenced mainly by white communists, also supported the move. By the end of a tumultuous night, Mandela had received the authorization he wanted to establish a military wing.

The new organization rapidly took shape. It was given the name of Umkhonto we Sizwe, meaning the Spear of the Nation, but it became more commonly known by the initials MK. A high command was formed, consisting of Mandela as chairman and Slovo as chief-of-staff; Sisulu acted as a political adviser. Essentially, MK was launched as a joint venture between the ANC and the Communist Party, with access to all the Communist Party's resources and its international connections.

Mandela and Slovo had known each other for more than ten years, but they had never been particularly close. As students at the University of the Witwatersrand, they had argued over the role of the communists in the liberation struggle. They had differed on many occasions since. Slovo was widely known as an urbane and affable character, a witty raconteur with a liking for wine, song and red socks, but he was also a narrow ideologue never deviating from the party line. 'Slovo and Mandela were often at cross-purposes,' noted Mac Maharaj, a Communist Party activist. 'Their relationship was often abrasive. Joe was unable to appreciate what Mandela was saying. He was devious in his arguments, taking contradictory positions. The debate frequently went off the rails.' But over the question of armed struggle they found common ground. 'Slovo was an enthusiast, determined to make an immediate impact,' Maharaj recalled. 'Mandela had a liking for the bold stroke.'

The difficulties they faced were immense. None of the conspirators had any experience of sabotage or guerrilla action. Mandela embarked on the armed struggle knowing literally nothing in practice about what was involved. Slovo's experience had been limited to his role in a signals unit in the closing stages of the Second World War in Italy; he had never taken part in combat. The conspirator with the most military experience was Jack Hodgson, a 'desert rat' who had served in a tank corps in North Africa and also had knowledge of explosives gained while working in the mines. An ardent communist and founding member of the Congress of Democrats, Hodgson became MK's first instructor, teaching recruits the basis of bomb-making. He turned his own flat, on the fourth floor of a block in Hillbrow, into a bomb laboratory and later into a bomb factory. He was a resourceful man, but nevertheless an amateur.

To make up for his own lack of knowledge, Mandela read everything he could lay his hands on about guerrilla warfare and war history: authors like Guevara, Mao Tse-tung, Castro and Clausewitz; books on Algeria, Cuba, Israel, Kenya and the Anglo-Boer War. 'He was particularly impressed by a study of the communist insurrectionary movement in the Philippines,' Bernstein recalled. He spent much of the day studying texts, leaving the nights free for meetings. 'Mandela wanted a theoretical knowledge of guerrilla warfare,' noted Maharaj. 'Slovo was less interested.'

Mandela was provided with a support committee, a small group of activists who arranged everything for him from safe houses

to transport and reading material. Among the group was Kathy
Kathrada, who had been sceptical about the feasibility of armed
struggle but who had nevertheless volunteered his services. Another
member was Wolfie Kodesh, a long-time communist 'foot soldier'
who had seen army service during the Second World War and was
currently a reporter for the radical journal *New Age*. The support
team also included a talented young lawyer, Bob Hepple, whom
Bram Fischer had recruited to the Communist Party. The son of a
former leader of the Labour Party, he was heavily involved in trade
union activity, trying to keep alive the South African Congress of
Trade Unions. Like Fischer and Slovo, he worked from offices in
Innes Chambers in central Johannesburg, a building used by many
advocates, which provided a convenient cover for meetings of the
conspirators.

Mandela's life underground, as leader of MK, became more
settled than it had been when he was trying to organize support
for strike action in May. After staying with a family in Market
Street for a few weeks, he moved into a small bachelor flat in Berea
with Wolfie Kodesh, who rented it under a false name. Mandela
insisted on using a camp bed, letting Kodesh keep the bed, but
Kodesh was considerably 'peeved' to find that it was Mandela's
habit to get up at five each morning to run on the spot. 'It went
on for well over an hour, followed by exercises,' Kodesh recalled.
Mandela told Kodesh that he would have to join in, which he did,
though without much enthusiasm. In daytime, Mandela remained
inside the flat with the blinds drawn, venturing out at night, usually
in his disguise as a chauffeur. After two months in Berea, he moved
briefly to a doctor's residence in Johannesburg, then spent two
weeks on a sugar plantation in Tongaat, before returning to
Johannesburg to a new address. It was here that MK was eventually
to meet its demise.

Lilliesleaf Farm lay in a secluded, wooded hollow in the Rivonia
area, about ten miles north of Johannesburg. It was a smallholding
of roughly twenty-eight acres, reached only by a dirt road or across
the open veld. The farmhouse was spacious, with whitewashed
walls, large curved windows at the front and a high shingle roof,
a desirable residence for a wealthy family. Behind the main building
stood an assortment of outbuildings, storerooms, fuel sheds, work-

rooms and servants' quarters. There was also a large, imposing thatch-roofed cottage.

Lilliesleaf had been bought by the Communist Party in July 1961 for use as its underground headquarters. Michael Harmel, adopting a false name, had handled the transaction with an estate agent and Harold Wolpe, the communist lawyer, had helped set up a dummy company to buy the property. The plan was for Lilliesleaf to be used, by all outward appearances, as a normal white smallholding. The main house would be occupied by a party member, Arthur Goldreich, and his family and the farm worked by African labourers. Goldreich was a little-known activist. By profession an artist and designer, employed by a large department store in Johannesburg, he was a flamboyant personality, charming and talented, who struck many acquaintances as being no more than a dilettante. But in his youth he had joined Palmach, a branch of the underground Jewish army in Palestine, and at heart he was a revolutionary enthusiast.

The buildings at Lilliesleaf were in need of renovation and extension, so before the Goldreichs moved there, a team of African painters and builders was hired to do the job. It was at this stage that Mandela took up residence in the thatched cottage at Lilliesleaf, ostensibly as an employee of the white owner waiting for his arrival. The alias he used was David Motsamayi, the name of one of his former clients. Mandela knew Goldreich quite well; his house in Parktown was one of the secret locations where he met Winnie.

Mandela's routine at Lilliesleaf was much the same as before. He stayed at home during the day and left for meetings at night. 'Mandela had time to read, to think and study at Rivonia,' said Bernstein. 'It was a quiet and peaceful existence. A committee attended to his needs.' He was joined for a while by Michael Harmel, whom he knew as an engaging character but who proved to be a hopeless conspirator. Disorganized and forgetful, he was invariably sloppy about underground work, infuriating colleagues like Bram Fischer with his lapses of security. Mandela returned to Lilliesleaf late one night to find the house lights on, the front door open, the radio at full blast and Harmel fast asleep in bed. When Mandela woke him up, he complained, 'Nel, must you disturb my sleep? Can't this wait until tomorrow?'

Once the renovations were complete and the Goldreichs had

moved into the main house, it was possible for Winnie and the children to spend weekends with Mandela. 'Ironically,' said Mandela, 'we had more privacy at Lilliesleaf than we ever had at home. The children could run about and play, and we were secure, however briefly, in this idyllic bubble.' The older children, Thembi, Makgatho, Makaziwe and Zeni, retained indelible impressions of those times spent with their father, going for walks, playing in the big, rambling house, being carried through the orchard. Zeni imagined Lilliesleaf to be her real house, because it was the only place she could remember where her father played with her. For years afterwards, she would ask Winnie, 'Mummy, when are we going home to see Daddy?'

Meanwhile, the business of organizing armed struggle continued apace. The strategy decided upon by the high command was two-fold. First, a sabotage campaign would be carried out against targets like government buildings and installations, railways, power plants and telecommunications; second, preparations would be made for guerrilla warfare if the sabotage campaign failed to get the government to change its policies. The strict instruction given to all MK members from the start was that on no account were they to kill or injure people in planning or carrying out operations. As Mandela later explained, 'Sabotage did not involve loss of life, and it offered the best hope for race relations. Bitterness would be kept to a minimum and, if the policy bore fruit, democratic government could become a reality.'

The high command, based in Johannesburg, was made responsible for determining tactics and general targets and given charge of training and finance. Regional commands were to be set up in each of the provinces and, below them, local commands and cells. The most readily available source of recruits would be ANC or Communist Party members. An MK constitution was drawn up, devised largely by Mandela, Slovo and Bernstein.

The bomb-making end of the enterprise was also progressing. Hodgson had discovered that permanganate of potash, more commonly used in washing lettuce, mixed with aluminium powder and catalysed by a drop of acid, could make an effective explosion. Sacks of permanganate of potash were duly transported to his fourth-floor flat. 'We spent days with mortars and pestles grinding this substance to a fine powder,' recalled Slovo. 'Permanganate of potash permeated walls, curtains, carpets and every crevice.' Fortunately, Hodgson's wife, Rica, was as ardent a revolutionary as her husband.

Hodgson also constructed timing devices using the thin plastic tubing contained in ballpoint pens. Large quantities were purchased for the purpose: 'Every drawer,' recalled Rica Hodgson, 'seemed to be full of ballpoint pens.' He fashioned an incendiary device by using a small bottle of acid and covering the top with a specific thickness of cardboard or paper. Just before placing the device in the target area, the saboteur had to turn the bottle upside down.

When the time came for the bombs to be tested, Mandela insisted on witnessing the event. The site chosen was a brickworks near Kempton Park, to the east of Johannesburg, owned by Wolfie Kodesh's brother and not in use at the time. Explosions there during the day, to loosen clay, were a normal occurrence. Taking with them a dozen Molotov cocktails and an improvised bomb, Mandela, Hodgson, Kodesh and an obliging chemist who had supplied MK with gunpowder and nitro-glycerine, drove off one morning in a large 1949 Chevrolet to the brickworks to see the results of their handiwork. The site was deserted except for a solitary watchman who was taken to one side by Mandela and persuaded to walk away for a while.

Hodgson first tried out the Molotov cocktails – petrol bombs – on one of the brickworks' buildings and then chose a pit in an open space to test the bomb. He had calculated that the device would explode in fifteen minutes, but after twenty minutes nothing had happened. Hodgson retrieved the bomb from the bottom of the pit, adjusted the charge and put the bomb back. Suddenly, a huge explosion rent the air, throwing up clouds of dust and earth. In an instant the conspirators fled the scene, piling into the Chevrolet and driving helter-skelter out of the brickworks. Mandela was buoyed up by the event. This was the first explosion of the campaign.

The first group of recruits was dispatched to China for training in guerrilla warfare through an arrangement that the Communist Party had already made with their colleagues in Peking. The recruits included Raymond Mhlaba, a trade unionist and Communist Party organizer from Port Elizabeth who had played a prominent role there during the Defiance Campaign; Joe Gqabi, a reporter for *New Age* who had joined one of the first communist sabotage units before MK was formed; and Wilton Mkwayi, another trade unionist and former treason trialist who had escaped into the underground during the trial.

Amid all these preparations, there was a growing sense of urgency. Other armed groups were beginning to surface to challenge the government. Supporters of the banned Pan-Africanist Congress in the Western Cape were in the process of forming a military wing called Poqo, a Xhosa expression meaning 'alone' or 'pure', to emphasize their African origins, still intending to liberate South Africa by 1963. An odd assortment of dissident whites led by Monty Berman, a communist recently expelled from the party who had dreamed up the idea of establishing his own guerrilla outfit while detained in Pretoria prison during the state of emergency, banded together to form the National Committee of Liberation and announced their presence in October by dismantling a pylon carrying power lines in the northern suburbs of Johannesburg, disrupting telephone services and burning down a government office. This was the terrain on which MK wanted to establish its own reputation.

Yet however anxious MK enthusiasts were to get started, they were constrained by an unexpected development. On 23 October 1961, Chief Luthuli was nominated winner of the Nobel Peace Prize in recognition of his determined efforts to gain political rights for Africans through non-violent means. The award was a serious blow for the government, which had endeavoured to portray Luthuli as the head of a dangerous communist conspiracy. But it also came at an awkward time for MK's high command, for to launch the armed struggle just when the ANC's leader had achieved international recognition for his contribution to peace could have resulted in international humiliation for Luthuli. No action could be started at least until the award ceremony in Oslo had taken place on 11 December.

The date finally set for the start of the sabotage campaign was 16 December 1961, a day then known as the Day of the Covenant, on which whites celebrated their victory over the Zulu chief Dingane at the Battle of Blood River in 1838. Leaflets dropped on the streets announced the formation of Umkhonto we Sizwe with the warning, 'The time comes in the life of any nation when there remain only two choices: submit or fight. That time has now come to South Africa.' The leaflets added:

We hope, even at this late hour, that our first actions will awaken everyone to a realization of the disastrous situation to which the Nationalist policy is leading. We hope that we will bring the government and its supporters to their senses before it is too late, so that both the government and its policies can be changed before matters reach the desperate stage of civil war.

Bombs exploded that night at government buildings in Johannesburg, Durban and Port Elizabeth. But not everything went according to plan. Slovo's assignment was to plant one of Hodgson's incendiary devices in the Johannesburg Drill Hall, where the preparatory examination of the treason trial had taken place:

> I had reconnoitred it on more than one occasion and had chosen the spot which would have ignited not only the enormous wooden floor but also the hundreds of wooden chairs which covered it. But when the moment came, I found the military authorities had decided to have their monthly spring-clean. I entered the hall through a side door and found myself in the presence of about fifty black cleaners who were removing the chairs and polishing the floor.

Slovo found another suitable spot, an office with huge wooden cupboards. He turned the bottle of the incendiary device upside down, which gave him fifteen minutes for a getaway, and was about to place the carrier bag behind one of the cupboards when a clipped military voice came from behind him: 'Can I do anything for you, sir?'

Slovo was ready with an excuse about looking for an officer who could deal with an administrative problem about call-up papers for his brother and duly followed the sergeant-major in search of the officer: 'I did so with racing pulse, knowing that the acid in that small bottle had begun to eat away at the flimsy cardboard. Had our kitchen laboratory calculated the fifteen minutes correctly?'

Fortunately, the officer had left the building and Slovo was politely advised by the sergeant-major to come back another day. 'I gave him a sweaty hand and walked briskly away. As soon as I decently could, I opened the tennis-ball cylinder box which housed all the ingredients and snatched the bottle. The three or four minutes which preceded this were perhaps the longest in my life.'

Ben Turok, part of a three-man unit which included Harold

Wolpe, was less fortunate. His assignment was the Native Law Courts, then housed in the same building as the Rissik Street post office. When Hodgson arrived in his car at an agreed spot to deliver an incendiary device to Turok, he was clearly still having trouble with the devices; one of them had caught fire prematurely on the way, leaving the outside wrapping of Turok's parcel charred. Turok rewrapped the device in an old paper packet which he found in the boot of his own car and went on his way to the Native Law Courts. The device briefly caught alight but soon fizzled out due to a lack of oxygen. The police found it virtually intact with fingerprints on the outside wrapping. Five months later, when Turok was arrested in a police raid intended to disrupt an anti-government demonstration, the police found by chance that his fingerprints matched those on the Rissik Street bomb package. He was sentenced to three years' imprisonment. His defence team included Slovo and his co-conspirator, Harold Wolpe.

Another bomb device on 16 December also proved faulty, blowing up prematurely at the municipal office in Dube, an African township south of Johannesburg, killing one saboteur and injuring another. However, the overall result was judged to be successful.

Yet there was a large measure of improvisation to all this which went far beyond the crude home-made bombs that were used in the campaign. In the excitement to strike a blow at the government, armed activity was seen to be the only meaningful form of action worth pursuing; the need for political mobilization, as Kotane had urged, was neglected. Harold Wolpe, Slovo's closest friend, was later scathing in his criticism: 'We weren't prepared at a technical level, or at the level of political strategy. We had no knowledge, no background, we were just naïve.' Turok was equally succinct: 'We threw the first bombs without having an underground.'

Three weeks after MK had initiated its sabotage campaign, Mandela left South Africa to canvass for foreign support for armed struggle. He was taken by car across the border into Bechuanaland, a British protectorate, on 11 January 1962 and did not return for six months. He had never been abroad before and found the experience of being a 'free man' for the first time exhilarating: 'Though I was a fugitive and wanted in my own land, I felt the burden of oppression lifting from my shoulders.'

1. Nelson Mandela at nineteen, in Umtata, Transkei

2. Evelyn Mase, Mandela's first wife, devoted to religion

3. Walter Sisulu, Mandela's mentor and life-long friend

4. At the newly opened offices of Mandela and Tambo in Chancellor House, Fox Street, Johannesburg

5. (Left) Boxing in the heavyweight division

6. (Above) Consulting with colleagues during the Defiance Campaign, 1952

7. Mandela outside court in Pretoria, during the treason trial, 1958

8. After a whirlwind romance, Mandela married Winnie Madikizela in June 1958

9. Addressing the Pietermaritzburg All-in Conference, March 1961, Mandela's last public appearance before going underground

10. Wearing a beaded Thembu necklace, Mandela posed for this photograph while on the run from the police in 1961

11. Communist comrades: Ruth First, Bram Fischer (standing), Joe Slovo and Rusty Bernstein on the podium at a Communist Party meeting in the late 1940s

12. A coterie of communists: (left to right) Joe Slovo, Mary Turok, Ben Turok, Sonya Bunting, Jack Hodgson, Ruth First, Brian Bunting, Rica Hodgson, in the late 1950s

13. With Moses Kotane, secretary-general of the underground Communist Party, during the treason trial in 1958

14. With Oliver Tambo in Addis Ababa, 1962

15. Outside Westminster Abbey during his ten-day visit to London, 1962

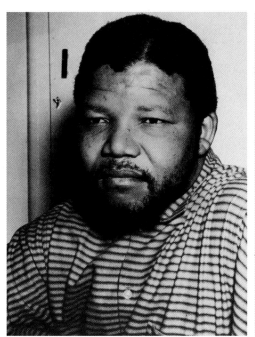

16. In hiding after his return to South Africa from abroad, 1962

17. Sewing clothes in prison in Pretoria, before being sent to Robben Island

18. Crushing stones in the prison yard at Robben Island

19. With Walter Sisulu in the prison yard at Robben Island, 1964

Most of his time was spent in Africa. He travelled from one country to another, seeking financial assistance, political recognition and military training facilities from governments known to be sympathetic to the liberation cause. Much preliminary groundwork had been done by Oliver Tambo, who had set up an exile base in London after his departure from South Africa in 1960 and had since established ANC offices in Tanganyika, Ghana and Egypt.

From the start, however, Mandela found himself competing for attention with the Pan-Africanist Congress, which had also established connections across Africa and had expended considerable effort in denouncing the ANC as a communist-front organization. Time and again, Mandela encountered deep suspicions in African states about the ANC's links with white and Indian communists. 'There is a widespread feeling that the ANC is a communist-dominated organization,' he reported. There was a far wider understanding of the PAC's objectives of African rule in South Africa than the ANC's goal of a multiracial democracy. Since the Sharpeville massacre, the PAC's standing in Africa had risen higher than that of the ANC.

At his first stop in the newly independent state of Tanganyika, Mandela was dismayed to hear President Nyerere suggest that perhaps the armed struggle should be postponed until Robert Sobukwe, the PAC leader then serving a three-year sentence for incitement, came out of prison. 'The PAC has started off with tremendous advantages ideologically, and has skilfully exploited opposition to whites and partnership,' he wrote. 'Sharpeville boosted them up and the stand of their leaders during the trial, and the imprisonment of Sobukwe, fostered the belief that they were more militant than the ANC.'

In Addis Ababa in February, Mandela addressed a conference of the Pan-African Freedom Movement for East, Central and Southern Africa, a joint organization of independent African states and liberation movements. The question was often asked, he said, how strong was the liberation struggle in South Africa?

> The view has been expressed in some quarters outside South Africa that, in the special situation obtaining in our country, our people will never win freedom through their own efforts. Those who hold this view point to the formidable apparatus of force and coercion

in the hands of the government, to the size of its armies, the fierce suppression of civil liberties and the persecution of political opponents of the regime. Consequently, in these quarters, we are urged to look for our salvation beyond our borders. Nothing could be further from the truth.

He acknowledged the importance of outside help, but added, 'We believe it would be fatal to create the illusion that external pressures render it unnecessary for us to tackle the enemy from within. The centre and cornerstone of the struggle for freedom and democracy in South Africa lies inside South Africa itself.'

Before leaving Addis Ababa, Mandela arranged with the Ethiopian military to return later in the year for six months' military training to equip himself as a professional guerrilla leader. 'If there was to be guerrilla warfare,' he said, 'I wanted to be able to stand and fight with my people and to share the hazards of war with them.'

From Ethiopia, he travelled to Egypt, Tunisia, Morocco, Guinea, Sierra Leone, Liberia, Ghana and Senegal. Along the way, he kept notes in meticulous detail of all the ideas, information and offers of help he received. His notes on consultations with Algerian officers based in Morocco in March ran to ninety-four pages. Under a section headed 'Funds', he wrote:

£10,000 from Nigeria
£5,000 in Tunisia
£3,000 in Liberia will be yearly amount
£5,000 in Ethiopia
Definite promises from Senegal and the Sudan
All these monies were sent to O.R [Tambo] in London
Money collecting is a job which requires a lot of time. You must be prepared to wait.
Visit to Socialist countries has become imperative

In June, Mandela visited London for ten days, enjoying the atmosphere of British style and manners which his school education had taught him to regard so highly. He met the Labour Party leader, Hugh Gaitskell, the Liberal Party leader, Jo Grimond, and the editor of the *Observer*, David Astor, whose newspaper took a close interest in African affairs. Accompanied by Tambo and Mary Benson, a South African writer, he went sightseeing to the Houses of Parliament and Westminster Abbey and took a boat ride on the Thames to Chelsea.

Then he returned to Addis Ababa to prepare himself for guerrilla war. He learned how to use an automatic rifle and a pistol, listened to lectures on tactics and strategy, and gained experience of bombs and mortars. Entries in his diary recorded:

> June 29th: First lesson on demolition. Instructor Lt. Befikadu
> June 30th: I have practice in demolition
> July 10th: A demonstration on mortar fire
> July 11th: We spend 4 hours at the shooting range
> July 12th: I spend the day doing fieldcraft drills
> July 13th: Lt. Befikadu and I cover 26 kilometres in fatigue marches. We do it in 3 hours.

But Mandela's training programme was cut short abruptly after three weeks by a message from Sisulu in Johannesburg insisting that he return to South Africa. Sisulu was concerned that Mandela's prolonged absence abroad would give rise to suspicions that he did not intend to return to South Africa, as he had repeatedly committed himself to do. The main purpose of Mandela's trip abroad, as Sisulu understood it, was for him to make connections there, not to get involved in military training. As a farewell gesture, the Ethiopians presented Mandela with an automatic pistol and 200 rounds of ammunition.

During the six months that he had been away, sabotage attacks had continued sporadically. Most of the attempts were clumsy and ineffectual, none causing any lasting damage. The white electorate, on the rare occasions that it was alerted to the danger of sabotage attacks, reacted by demanding tougher measures from the government, not, as Mandela had calculated, by calling for reform.

The government duly responded. In June, Vorster introduced the General Law Amendment Act of 1962, or the 'Sabotage' Act, as it was usually called, which gave new definitions to the meaning of sabotage. Acts of sabotage henceforth included such offences as tampering with property, possessing firearms, hindering essential services, putting up a poster and unlawful entry. The minimum penalty laid down for offences under the Sabotage Act was five years' imprisonment; the maximum was death.

Vorster was further empowered to order the 'house arrest' of anyone he believed to be a threat to security. He could prohibit persons banned or listed under the Suppression of Communism Act from preparing anything for publication, from communicating with each other, from having visitors, from joining organizations, from attending social gatherings.

The security police were also gaining in experience, building up a network of informers and keeping an ever-tighter watch on the movement of activists. Walter Sisulu was arrested by Warrant Officer Dirker six times in 1962. Once, when police were raiding his home, a reporter arrived and asked why they were raiding. 'Just routine,' a police officer told him. 'We just want to see what Sisulu keeps in his house.' But the conspirators, used to treating the Special Branch with contempt, neither anticipated the improvement in their techniques nor paid much attention when they did notice it.

CHAPTER 10

Capture

Mandela crossed the border from Bechuanaland at night in an Austin car belonging to a prominent white activist, the theatre producer and playwright Cecil Williams. Williams, a debonair figure, always immaculately dressed, had played a leading role in the establishment of the Congress of Democrats and had been incarcerated in Pretoria prison during the state of emergency. It was thought safe for him to collect Mandela from Bechuanaland since his car had only recently been purchased and would therefore not be familiar to security police. The guise in which they travelled, Mandela the chauffeur driving his boss home to Johannesburg, was spoilt slightly by Mandela's determination to wear the khaki training uniform he had been using in Ethiopia.

They reached Lilliesleaf at dawn and the following night Mandela held a long meeting with other members of the ANC's working committee, including Sisulu, Kotane, Marks and Nokwe, briefing them on the results of his travels. A major concern was the criticism Mandela had encountered throughout Africa of the ANC's links with communists and its cooperation with whites and Indians. Mandela was convinced that, to circumvent foreign hostility, the ANC needed to distance itself from its Congress allies and assume a leading role of its own, publicly re-establishing its African credentials. He proposed that he should visit Luthuli at his home in Natal to ascertain his views. The working committee approved the idea.

But Kathrada's support committee thought the risks were far too high. 'We worked on the assumption that the police knew he was back in the country,' said Kathrada. 'We thought we should be extra careful, much more careful than we had been before his departure to Africa. We thought we should first send an advance party.' Kathrada himself volunteered to do the advance work, but Mandela opposed the idea. He wanted to leave for Natal as soon as possible. He suggested that he drive down to Durban with Cecil Williams in the Austin car. Kathrada again voiced his objections to the plan – 'Cecil Williams was a marked man' – but he was overruled.

Before leaving, Mandela arranged to meet Winnie. It was, Winnie recalled, 'a hurried meeting . . . our last private moments together'. In Mandela's absence, Winnie had become the target of constant police harassment. She told a newspaper reporter in June:

> The police have been making visits and searched at my house every night for almost three weeks. Whenever my children and I are about to sleep, Security Branch police arrive. They ask me where my husband is and sometimes search the house. Sometimes they joke and at other times they are aggressive, which frightens the children. There are rumours that Nelson is back, but I have not seen or heard from him.

In the company of Williams, Mandela sped off to Durban to sound out two Indian friends, Monty Naicker, the Indian Congress leader, and Ismail Meer, before travelling on to Groutville to meet Luthuli. Both Naicker and Meer were close friends of the chief and Mandela wanted to be able to tell Luthuli that he had already spoken to them about his proposal. Both opposed any move that would unravel the Congress alliance.

In Groutville, Mandela met Luthuli in an Indian-owned house. Luthuli was in the fourth year of a five-year banning order restricting him to his home in the Umvoti Mission Reserve. As president of the banned ANC, known to be in touch with ANC envoys and couriers who visited him from time to time, he was under frequent surveillance by the police. Luthuli listened to Mandela's argument and agreed to think about what he had said.

Mandela returned to Durban for further secret meetings and also found time for a quick rendezvous with one of Winnie's sisters, a nurse. At an Indian house in Reservoir Hills, he met members of the MK regional command, briefing them on his trip abroad and listening to their complaints about the lack of finance and transport. He assured them that help would be forthcoming. One of the members present was Bruno Mtolo, a trade unionist trained in sabotage activity by Jack Hodgson. 'We left Mandela feeling very much heartened and ready to continue the struggle,' he said.

Later that evening, Mandela was given a 'welcome home' party at the home of a photo-journalist, G. R. Naidoo, with whom he was staying. Among the friends who came were the Meers, the Singhs and Monty Naicker. 'Nelson cut a large military figure in khaki, his laugh booming the familiar welcome as he embraced each friend,' wrote Fatima Meer, in her account of the party. 'They drank and ate and discussed politics. They laughed a lot, excited by their intrigue. The police were looking for Nelson and here they were partying with him, virtually under their noses.'

The next afternoon, 5 August, Mandela rejoined Cecil Williams for the journey back to Johannesburg. Along the way, they discussed sabotage plans. Mandela noticed that the main Durban–Johannesburg railway ran parallel to the road for some distance, making it a suitable target for sabotage. As was his habit, he made a note of the idea in a small notebook he invariably carried with him. In the notebook were jottings of ideas he had heard and conversations he had had in the last few days, implicating people whom he had met. Mandela was also carrying a loaded revolver.

At the small town of Cedara near Howick, their car, with Williams at the wheel and Mandela in the passenger seat, was overtaken and stopped by police cars. For a brief moment, Mandela thought of trying to escape up a wooded bank to his left, but decided against it. He quickly hid the gun and the notebook in the gap between the two front seats. A police officer came directly to the window by the passenger's seat and asked who he was. 'David Motsamayi,' replied Mandela, using his alias. The officer asked him other questions about where he was going and where he had come from. Mandela gave him a few perfunctory answers, but the officer soon lost patience: 'Ag, you're Nelson Mandela, and this is Cecil Williams, and you are under arrest!' Mandela and Williams were taken to Pietermaritzburg. The hidden notebook and the revolver were never discovered by the police.

Mandela's arrest caused turmoil among the conspirators. 'There was a great deal of panic,' recalled Sisulu. Wolfie Kodesh was deputed to find Winnie at the offices of the Child Welfare Society in Fox Street in central Johannesburg, where she worked. He came across her as she was about to leave the building. Winnie recalled:

> The way this man looked! He was white like a ghost, his hair was standing on end. I noticed he hadn't shaved and was wearing a dirty shirt and trousers as if he'd just jumped out of bed; you could see something drastic had happened. This was one of the men who used to be along the line when I was taken to see Nelson underground.

'Winnie could see by the expression on my face that something terrible had happened,' said Kodesh. 'She asked, "Is it Nelson?" I said, "Yes. We think he'll be appearing in the Johannesburg court tomorrow."'

Everyone was convinced that Mandela had been betrayed. Suspicion about who the culprit was ran wild. Even Sisulu was suspected in some quarters, for it was he who had insisted that Mandela should return to South Africa.

There were persistent rumours that the United States Central Intelligence Agency was involved. Mandela's links with communists had made him a target for US officials embroiled with the Soviet Union in a murky struggle for influence in a number of newly independent African states and obsessed with the need to contain communist encroachment in Africa. The CIA was active throughout southern Africa, keeping track of the activities of liberation movements there, determined to prevent what it saw as communist-supported armed intervention 'under the guise of African liberation'. It found an ally in the South African government, which was only too willing to collaborate. Intelligence information was exchanged on a regular basis.

The CIA covert-operations section in Johannesburg had expended considerable energy penetrating the ANC. Its chief undercover agent, Millard Shirley, the son of American missionaries who had been born in South Africa, had cultivated contacts at all levels of the organization. A stocky, balding figure, with a reputation as a heavy drinker and a womanizer, he passed himself off as a reporter for an American television news network, readily gaining access to dissident groups. He was known by South African intelligence to possess a high-ranking 'deep throat' – a Durban-based Indian in the ranks of the Communist Party there.

Two pieces of evidence subsequently came to light linking the CIA to Mandela's arrest. The first concerned the local CIA agent in Durban at the time, Don Rickard, a consular officer who, at the end of his tour in South Africa, was heard boasting at a diplomatic party of the role that he had played in Mandela's arrest. The second concerned Paul Eckel, the CIA station chief based at the US Embassy in Pretoria. Eckel, who died in 1986, confided what had happened to another US official and in 1990 that official, then retired, told an American journalist, Joseph Albright, what Eckel had said: 'We turned Mandela over to the South African Security Branch. We gave them every detail, what he would be wearing, the time of day, just where he would be. They picked him up. It was one of our greatest coups.'

Given Mandela's amateurish conduct in the days before his arrest, it was equally possible that the South African police already knew of his whereabouts from their own efforts. Mandela had been carried away by romantic notions of his role as 'Commander-in-Chief', the showman of the law courts now wanting to become the showman of the battlefield, wearing army fatigues and khaki, carrying a gun, though never intending to use it, flaunting his presence at gatherings of the faithful. These were dangerous pretensions at such a time. In all, Mandela survived in the field in South Africa as head of Umkhonto since its launching in December 1961 for no more than five weeks. And in that time, as a result of keeping notebooks, he came close to incriminating a considerable number of other people.

He chastised himself for his own foolhardy behaviour. 'In truth, I had been imprudent about maintaining the secrecy of my movements,' he wrote. 'In retrospect, I realized the authorities could have had a myriad of ways of locating me on my trip to Durban. It was a wonder in fact that I wasn't captured sooner.' When asked in later years about evidence of the CIA's involvement in his arrest, his response was, 'Let bygones be bygones. Let's forget about that, whether it is true or not.'

Whatever suspicions the security police had about Mandela, they possessed no evidence linking him to the sabotage campaign. When he appeared in the magistrates' court in Johannesburg on 8 August, he was charged on two counts: first, inciting workers in essential occupations to act illegally; and second, leaving the country without a valid travel permit. Mandela decided to represent himself, as this gave him the opportunity to turn the trial into an attack on the government, and chose Slovo as his legal adviser.

While Mandela was held in the Fort awaiting trial, Slovo used his access to him as his legal adviser to plot his escape. The conspirators at Rivonia spent hours floating schemes to smuggle him out of the Fort. In the end they decided that the Fort was impregnable, but that the Johannesburg magistrates' court offered better possibilities.

During the lunch break, when court proceedings were adjourned, the accused were taken down steps leading to a basement, where they were locked in individual cells. All that was needed to spring Mandela was a key enabling him to leave the basement, climb the steps to the deserted courtroom above and from there reach the street outside, where a getaway car would be waiting. To ensure that Mandela was not recognized, a disguise would be smuggled in to him – a wig, moustache and beard. Slovo was given the task of obtaining measurements for the disguise during his frequent visits to the Fort. As he and Mandela sat in an interview room, attended by a prison warder, they exchanged written notes and bits of cotton until eventually, after several weeks, all the measurements were gathered. The disguise was duly made by a professional wigmaker and smuggled to Mandela by Winnie sewn in the shoulder padding of his finest suit. He was also given the vital key. Wolfie Kodesh was briefed to provide the getaway car.

Mandela, however, changed his mind about the feasibility of the escape plan, concluding that if it failed it would do fatal damage to the ANC. In a note to Slovo passed across the desk in the interview room, he explained his views, adding at the end, 'Please destroy this after you have finished reading it.' But Slovo decided that the note was interesting enough to be saved as a historical document and it was to reappear in unfortunate circumstances. As it happened, two days before the trial was due to open on 15 October in Johannesburg, the authorities decided to switch the venue to Pretoria.

Congress supporters had meanwhile set up a Free Mandela Committee and organized a series of rallies under the slogan 'Free Mandela'. To prevent further demonstrations, the government prohibited 'any gathering related to Mandela in any place in the Republic of South Africa' for two days at the beginning of his trial.

On 20 October, it banned all gatherings in protest at the arrest or trial of anyone for any offence for a period of six months.

Mandela's appearance in court at the Old Synagogue on 15 October caused a sensation. He entered wearing a traditional Xhosa leopard-skin kaross instead of a suit and tie. In the spectators' gallery, the crowd of his supporters rose to their feet with shouts of '*Amandla!*' – 'Power!' – and '*Ngawethu!*' – 'It is ours!' Winnie was among them, wearing a traditional beaded headdress and a long, embroidered Xhosa skirt. Mandela saluted in acknowledgement, with a clenched first raised high, and turned to smile at Winnie.

On each day that Mandela appeared in court he wore the same kaross. When the prison authorities tried to confiscate it from him, he retorted that they had no jurisdiction over his attire in court and threatened to take the matter as far as the Supreme Court if they interfered. All they managed to do was to prevent him from wearing it on his way to the court from prison and back.

Right from the start, Mandela sought to place the government and its system of justice on trial rather than himself. Given permission to address the court before he was asked to plead, he immediately asked for the recusal of the magistrate, J. van Heerden, on the grounds that he did not consider himself legally or morally bound to obey laws made by a parliament in which he had no representation. Nor did he believe he would receive a fair and proper trial:

> In a political trial such as this one, which involves a clash of the aspirations of the African people and those of whites, the country's courts, as presently constituted, cannot be impartial and fair. In such cases, whites are interested parties. To have a white judicial officer presiding, however high his esteem, and however strong his sense of fairness and justice, is to make whites judges in their own case. It is improper and against the elementary principles of justice to entrust whites with cases involving the denial by them of basic human rights to the African people . . .

No African, he said, enjoyed equality before the law.

> The white man makes all the laws, he drags us before his courts and accuses us, and he sits in judgement over us.
> It is fit and proper to raise the question sharply, what is this rigid

colour bar in the administration of justice? Why is it in this courtroom I face a white magistrate, am confronted by a white prosecutor and escorted in to the dock by a white orderly? Can anyone honestly and seriously suggest that in this type of atmosphere the scales of justice are evenly balanced?

Why is it that no African in the history of this country has ever had the honour of being tried by his own kith and kin, by his own flesh and blood?

I will tell Your Worship why: the real purpose of this rigid colour bar is to ensure that the justice dispensed by the courts should conform to the policy of the country, however much that policy might be in conflict with the norms of justice accepted in judiciaries throughout the civilized world . . .

I hate discrimination most intensely and in all its manifestations. I have fought it all during my life; I fight it now, and will do so until the end of my days. Even although I now happen to be tried by one whose opinion I hold in high esteem, I detest most violently the set-up that surrounds me here. It makes me feel that I am a black man in a white man's court. This should not be.

Mandela concluded by explaining that he had decided to speak frankly because the injustice to which he had referred contained the seeds of 'an extremely dangerous situation for our country and our people'. 'I make no threat when I say that unless these wrongs are remedied without delay, we might well find that even plain talk before the country's courts is too timid a method to draw the attention of the country to air political demands.' His application for the recusal of the magistrate was refused.

The prosecution proceeded to produce some sixty witnesses – policemen, journalists, township superintendents and printers – who gave evidence about the preparations for the three-day strike in May 1961.

On the third day of the trial, Mandela made a surprise application once again for the recusal of the magistrate, van Heerden. His legal adviser, Bob Hepple, who had replaced Slovo after the government refused to lift the banning order restricting Slovo to Johannesburg, had noticed during the previous day's lunch break that van Heerden had left the courtroom in the company of Warrant Officer Dirker of the Special Branch. Dirker had given evidence on the first day of the trial and was due to be cross-examined by Mandela at a later stage. Together with another member of the Special Branch who had been present throughout the trial, assisting the prosecution, they climbed into a blue Volkswagen car and sped off for lunch. It was this incident which prompted Mandela to ask for the magistrate's recusal. But before doing so, in a gesture of remarkable cordiality, he sent van Heerden a private note advising him in advance of the action he was about to take and explaining that there was nothing personal about the matter.

Confronting him in court, Mandela said that the incident had created the impression that the court had associated itself with the state's case: 'I am left with the substantial fear that justice is being administered in a secret manner. It is an elementary rule of justice that a judicial officer should not communicate or associate in any manner whatsoever with a party to these proceedings. I submit that Your Worship should not have acted in this fashion.'

Van Heerden's reply was brief: 'I can only say this, that it is not for me to give you reasons. I can assure you, as I here now do, that I did not communicate with these two gentlemen, and your application is refused.'

On the fourth day of the trial, the prosecution closed its case and Mandela rose to present his defence. He had given the court the impression that he would call a large number of witnesses. But he had long since decided to call none. He knew that the charges were accurate and he had already made the statement about the unfairness of the political and legal system that he wanted to make. Instead of calling witnesses, he said simply, 'Your Worship, I submit that I am guilty of no crimes.'

There was a considerable pause, then the magistrate, clearly taken aback, asked, 'Is that all you have to say?'

'Your Worship, with respect, if I had something more to say, I would have said it.'

The court was adjourned until 7 November, when, in accordance with court procedure, Mandela was to be allowed to address the court with a plea in mitigation before the magistrate gave his sentence.

On 7 November, before the court was called into session, Mandela and Hepple were conferring in an office in the Old Synagogue when the prosecutor, P. J. Bosch, came in and asked for a private meeting with Mandela. He apologized for having to ask the court to send him to prison and reached out to shake his hand. When Bosch walked out of the room, Hepple noticed that he was in tears.

The court was packed again with spectators. Winnie was present, in Xhosa dress, as well as a number of Mandela's relatives from the Transkei. As Mandela took his place in the dock, he turned to the gallery, raising his arm in a clenched-fist salute, and called out 'Amandla!' The crowd rose and responded: 'Ngawethu!'

The magistrate read out his judgement. Mandela, he said, was 'the leader, instigator, figurehead, main mouthpiece and the brain' behind the organization which had called the 1961 strike. 'To incite people to commit a crime by forcing them to protest a law was the same as committing the crime itself,' he continued. Mandela had shown no remorse but seemed proud of his achievements and had stated in no uncertain terms that he would continue his activities whatever the sentence passed on him. 'We are living under abnormal and trying conditions,' the magistrate said, and if law and order were not maintained, anarchy would reign; the court was not concerned with politics but with the maintenance of law and order.

Mandela followed with an hour-long address to the court intended not as a plea in mitigation but as a political testament explaining why he had taken the action which had led to his trial and why he would do it again if necessary:

> The whole life of any thinking African in this country drives him continuously to a conflict between his conscience on the one hand and the law on the other ... The law as it is applied, the law as it has been developed over a long period of history and especially the law as it is written and designed by the Nationalist government is a law which, in our view, is immoral, unjust and intolerable. Our consciences dictate that we must protest against it, that we must oppose it and that we must attempt to alter it ...

Throughout its fifty-year existence the ANC had done everything possible to bring its demands to the attention of successive South African governments. It had sought at all times peaceful solutions for the country's ills and problems. Every attempt had been treated with contempt and met by force. In 1961, as secretary of the Action Council, he had approached the prime minister seeking to gain support for a national convention. But he had not even been treated with the courtesy of an acknowledgement. Instead, the government . . . set out, from the beginning of this campaign, not to treat with us, not to heed us, nor to talk to us, but rather to present us as wild, dangerous revolutionaries, intent on disorder and riot, incapable of being dealt with in any way save by mustering an overwhelming force against us and the implementation of every possible forcible means, legal and illegal, to suppress us. The government behaved in a way no civilized government should dare behave when faced with a peaceful, disciplined, sensible and democratic expression of the views of its own population. It ordered the mobilization of its armed forces to attempt to cow and terrorize our peaceful protest. It arrested people known to be active in African politics and in support of African demands for democratic rights, passed special laws enabling it to hold them without trial for twelve days . . . If there was a danger during this period that violence would result from the situation in the country, then the possibility was of the government's making. They set the scene for violence by relying exclusively on violence with which to answer our people and their demands . . .

He warned of the danger of further violence to come:

Government violence can do only one thing and that is to breed counter-violence. We have warned repeatedly that the government, by resorting continually to violence, will breed, in this country, counter-violence amongst the people, till ultimately, if there is no dawning of sanity on the part of the government – ultimately, the dispute between the government and my people will finish up by being settled in violence and by force. Already there are indications in this country that people, my people, Africans, are turning to deliberate acts of violence and of force against the government in order to persuade the government, in the only language which this government shows, by its own behaviour, that it understands . . .

Perhaps the court will say that despite our human rights to protest, to object, to make ourselves heard, we should stay within the letter of the law. I would say, sir, that it is the government, its administration of the law, which brings the law into such contempt and disrepute that one is no longer concerned in this country to stay within the letter of the law.

His own experience illustrated this: 'The government has used the process of law to handicap me, in my personal life, in my career and in my political work in a way which is calculated, in my opinion, to bring about a contempt for the law' – by restricting him, banning him, harassing him.

> By order of the government, in the name of the law, I found myself restricted and isolated from my fellow men, from people who think like me and believe like me. I found myself trailed by officers of the Security Branch of the police force wherever I went. In short I found myself treated as a criminal – an unconvicted criminal. I was not allowed to pick my company, to frequent the company of men, to participate in their political activities, to join their organizations. I was not free from constant police surveillance. I was made, by the law, a criminal, not because of what I had done, but because of what I stood for, because of what I thought, because of my conscience.
>
> Can it be any wonder to anybody that such conditions make a man an outlaw of society? Can it be wondered that such a man, having been outlawed by the government, should be prepared to lead the life of an outlaw, as I have led for some months, according to the evidence before this court?
>
> It has not been easy for me during that past period to separate myself from my wife and children, to say goodbye to the good old days when, at the end of a strenuous day at an office, I could look forward to joining my family at the dinner table, and instead to take up the life of a man hunted continuously by the police, living separated from those who are closest to me, in my own country, facing continually the hazards of detection and arrest. This has been a life infinitely more difficult than serving a prison sentence. No man in his right senses would voluntarily choose such a life in preference to the one of normal, family, social life which exists in every civilized community.
>
> But there comes a time, as it came in my life, when a man is denied the right to live a normal life, when he can only live the life of an outlaw because the government has so decreed to use the law to impose a state of outlawry upon him.

Mandela concluded with a passionate denunciation of racial discrimination and the system of minority rule in South Africa that went with it:

> I hate the practice of racial discrimination, and in my hatred I am sustained by the fact that the overwhelming majority of mankind hate it equally . . .
>
> Nothing that this court can do to me will change in any way that

hatred in me, which can only be removed by the removal of the injustice and the inhumanity which I have sought to remove from the political, social and economic life of this country.

Whatever sentence Your Worship sees fit to impose upon me for the crime for which I have been convicted before this court, may it rest assured that when my sentence has been completed, I will still be moved, as men are always moved, by their consciences; I will still be moved by my dislike of the race discrimination against my people when I come out from serving my sentence, to take up again, as best I can, the struggle for the removal of those injustices until they are finally abolished once and for all.

Mandela's articulate defence of African rights, his manner and bearing before the court, his skill in dealing with court officials and witnesses alike, marked him out as a leader of distinction. No courtroom in South Africa had ever heard such a powerful indictment of the government. However, the import of his words was largely lost in South Africa at the time. Van Heerden took no more than a ten-minute adjournment after Mandela had finished his address before pronouncing sentence. The press coverage was limited. Mandela was on the list of persons whose statements could not be published and although the government had decreed that reporting of judicial proceedings was permissible 'as long as it is not abused by creating a forum for such persons', newspapers were unsure of the consequences. One of Johannesburg's major newspapers, *The Star*, quoted only a few sentences from his address.

But Mandela's performance, while making little impact in South Africa, had gained worldwide attention. His 1962 trial marked the start of his international reputation. The pleas that he had made for human rights in South Africa were fully understood in Western countries, even if governments there felt little inclination at the time to respond. In the short term, none of this was to make any difference. Mandela's fate was to be sentenced to three years' imprisonment for incitement and two years' imprisonment for travelling abroad without valid documents, five years in all, with no possibility of parole. In the long term, however, the words that Mandela spoke in the Old Synagogue and the reputation he gained there were to be remembered far beyond any term of imprisonment.

The net was meanwhile closing in on other conspirators. Walter

Sisulu was arrested two days after Mandela on similar charges of incitement for his role in organizing the May 1961 strike. He was granted bail by the court, but then placed under twelve-hour house arrest, confined to his house in Orlando between 6.30 p.m. and 6.30 a.m. every day, all weekends and public holidays, required to report to a police station every day and prohibited from receiving any visitors at home. Two weeks later, Sisulu's mother, who lived with him and whom Mandela cherished as much as his own, died in the house. When friends and relatives came to mourn, Albertina tried to explain that Sisulu could not speak to them. He made an urgent application to the chief magistrate in Johannesburg for permission to receive mourners in his home but was turned down. Later that evening, when the visitors had left and the house was in darkness, with the body awaiting removal for the funeral the next day, the police raided the house and arrested Sisulu on charges of violating his house arrest. The charges were later withdrawn.

Like Mandela, Sisulu was found guilty of incitement but the sentence he was given was more severe: six years' imprisonment rather than three. Sisulu decided to appeal and, as the law then required, he was granted bail, pending an appeal. The government responded by placing him under twenty-four-hour house arrest, prohibiting him from setting foot outside at any time. A few weeks later, Sisulu disappeared underground. Albertina was subsequently arrested and held in solitary confinement for three months.

Mandela's bomb-maker, Jack Hodgson, was placed under twenty-four-hour house arrest in his Hillbrow flat for five years and his wife, Rica, under twelve-hour house arrest. As both were banned persons, they needed special ministerial dispensation to communicate with each other. The Hodgsons were eventually to flee the country. Michael Harmel and Moses Kotane were placed under twenty-four-hour house arrest; Kathy Kathrada, Rusty Bernstein and Cecil Williams were placed under twelve-hour house arrest. So too was the civil rights campaigner Helen Joseph. Several leading figures, including Harmel and Kotane, made plans to leave. Others, like Kathrada, went underground.

One by one, the remnants of radical opposition were obliterated. The Congress of Democrats was outlawed in September 1962. All public gatherings on the Johannesburg City Hall steps, a traditional venue for dissidents, were banned, except for divine services. The radical newspaper *New Age* was banned in November 1962. It reappeared the following week under the name *Spark*, but *Spark* was soon forced to close as a result of bans imposed on its editorial staff. Another radical journal, *Fighting Talk*, in which Bernstein had played a prominent role, was closed down three months later. A clause in the Sabotage Act made it illegal to possess any copies of banned newspapers, with a penalty of three years' imprisonment.

Under Verwoerd's rule, white society became increasingly insular and inbred. It was a society which expected conformity and so regarded dissent, however trivial, as a form of treachery. 'Opposing apartheid,' observed a prominent Afrikaner critic, 'is worse than murder to some Afrikaners. You endanger the nation by refusing to conform.'

The national radio network was turned into a propaganda arm of the National Party. Each commentary, each news bulletin conveyed the government's view of the world. Independent views were rarely heard. 'No useful purpose can be served by causing the public distrust of our leaders' policies,' remarked one director-general of the South African Broadcasting Corporation. All attempts to introduce television were blocked because of the 'negative' effects it might have.

The press was exempted from direct controls, but otherwise forced to steer its way through a minefield of legislation. Often unsure of what they could print, editors resorted more and more to self-censorship. Outright attacks on apartheid were rare. The English-language press continued to expose the worst excesses of government policy, but the costs both for newspaper proprietors and for editors and reporters were usually high. Under constant official pressure, they slowly gave way rather than face statutory controls.

An equally tight grip was kept on literature and entertainment. In March 1963, Verwoerd's government set up a Publications Control Board with power to ban any publication, film, record or art show, including the work of South African writers, artists and sculptors. Besides the usual test for obscenity and blasphemy, a publication could be banned if it brought the country into ridicule or contempt; or if it was prejudicial to the safety of the state, the general welfare or peace and good order. Thousands of works were subsequently banned, including those by prominent South African and Western writers. In defending the frequent use of censorship laws, government ministers were given to explain that behind many prohibited works lurked the menace of communism. 'When we think of literature containing filth, then we must think of the communist tactic behind it,' said the minister of education, arts and science, Jan de Klerk, introducing the Publications and Entertainment Bill in 1963. 'It is known to the government that it is a communist tactic throughout the world to use filth to break the backbone of the nation; to use filth to attack a nation on the cultural and social front, to paralyse people and make them an easy prey for communism.'

Through rigorous control of the media, Verwoerd had little difficulty in convincing most whites that the coalition of forces ranged against South Africa – communist states, the Afro-Asian bloc, 'leftists' and 'liberals' in Western countries and revolutionaries from within – was sufficiently threatening to warrant any action the government took to protect the nation. Each new piece of legislation strengthening the government's hand, each inroad made into civil liberties, evoked less and less protest from within the white community. Those advocating concessions or conciliation were simply accused of endangering white survival. Though government action was often taken in the name of defending Western civilization, there was never any doubt about what the ultimate purpose was. 'Our motto,' declared Verwoerd, 'is to maintain white supremacy for all time to come over our own people and our own country, by force if necessary.'

Pretoria Local, a large red-brick building behind a crenellated wall on the western side of the main road leading to Johannesburg, was a familiar place to Mandela. It had been his home for five months during the 1960 state of emergency and also during his trial for incitement. But when he returned there from the Old Synagogue on 7 November, it was to a different regime: he was no longer a prisoner awaiting trial but a convicted criminal, and he was treated accordingly.

Still in a fighting mood, he tried to take on the prison authorities in his customary fashion. Issued with the standard prison uniform for Africans – a pair of short trousers, a khaki shirt, a calico jacket and rubber sandals – Mandela refused to wear the short trousers. When dinner arrived – cold, stiff porridge – he refused to eat it and demanded better food. The solution devised for him by the prison commander, Colonel Jacobs, was to allow him to wear long trousers and to receive better food but to separate him from other prisoners, in solitary confinement. Mandela replied that he had no difficulty with that.

He soon learned differently:

> An hour was like a year. I was locked up in the bare cell, literally with nothing, nothing to read, nothing to write, nothing to do, and no one to talk or turn to. I was guarded by two warders during exercise time. The one was an African. I tried to talk to him. He spurned me, afraid no doubt of his white colleague. I suffered the isolation for two months and finally concluded that nothing was more dehumanizing than isolation from human companionship.

So Mandela exchanged his long trousers and improved rations for the company of fellow prisoners. He was assigned to a small group of political prisoners, a trade unionist, a reporter for *New Age* and several PAC members, including Robert Sobukwe.

Sobukwe by now considered himself a veteran of the prison system. Convicted of incitement for his role in the anti-pass demonstrations of March 1960, he had been moved through a series of prisons – Pretoria Central, Boksburg, Stofberg and Witbank – before reaching Pretoria Local in 1961. He was due for release in May 1963.

Despite their political rivalry, the two men struck up a cordial relationship in prison, choosing to sit next to each other while sewing old mailbags on a concrete ledge in the prison courtyard and addressing each other respectfully by their clan names. Sobukwe advised caution and patience in dealing with the prison system. 'You've got to pull through five years,' he told Mandela. 'There is no point in putting their backs up against you. They can be very vicious.'

The conditions in Pretoria Local were primitive. Mandela was given his own cell, measuring about six by seven feet, complete with toilet bucket. The cold at night was intense. He slept on a thin sisal mat on a cement floor with only two thin blankets for cover. The food was bad and discipline strict. When Mandela and

Sobukwe went together to see Colonel Jacobs to complain about conditions, Jacobs dismissed them curtly. Mandela began to argue, but Sobukwe restrained him: 'Nel, Nel, don't be rash. You've got to live here.'

While Mandela and Sobukwe were sewing mailbags in Pretoria and arguing about whether Shakespeare or George Bernard Shaw was the greatest English writer, South Africa faced a new phenomenon: the underground PAC movement known as Poqo initiated an insurrection against the government which included the murder of whites among its aims. 'The white people shall suffer, the black people will rule,' said a Poqo pamphlet. 'Freedom comes after bloodshed.'

Poqo was poorly organized but inspired a large following, notably in the Western Cape, with visions of an imminent black uprising. Its attacks were random and haphazard, but they created widespread alarm. Poqo supporters were responsible for the killing of African policemen and informers, for an uprising in Paarl in November 1962 in which a mob of 250 men attacked a police station and rampaged through the town killing two whites, and for the murder of five whites, including a woman and two young girls, sleeping at a roadside camp near the Bashee River bridge in the Transkei in February 1963.

In March 1963, plans for a more general uprising were prepared by a group of PAC leaders based in exile in Maseru, the capital of Basutoland, then a British protectorate. Instructions were sent to Poqo supporters to manufacture their own weapons with whatever materials were to hand and to collect food and clothing. On a given date, they were to launch simultaneous attacks on strategic points such as police stations and power installations before turning their attention to massacring whites indiscriminately.

The plan began to go wrong when Potlake Leballo, a volatile figure who had inherited the PAC's leadership from Sobukwe, gave warning of the uprising two weeks before it was due to start at a press conference in Maseru, claiming that 100,000 armed followers were waiting for his signal. As a result of Leballo's impetuous announcement, the colonial authorities in Maseru raided the PAC's premises, seized lists of 10,000 names, arrested PAC officials and closed down their office. In South Africa, police began to round up hundreds of PAC supporters. The date set for the uprising passed by with only a few incidents reported.

The Poqo campaign, together with the sporadic sabotage attacks from Umkhonto, gave Verwoerd's justice minister, John Vorster, the opportunity he needed to acquire virtually unlimited security powers. The General Law Amendment Act introduced on 1 May 1963 empowered the police to arrest without warrant and detain any person suspected of having committed sabotage, or any offences under the Suppression of Communism Act or the Unlawful Organizations Act, and any person suspected of possessing information about such offences. Detainees could be held in solitary confinement, without access to lawyers and family, until they had replied 'satisfactorily' to all questions put by police interrogators. The initial period for which they could be held was ninety days. But the police were entitled to renew the order again and again – 'until this side of eternity', according to Vorster. The act expressly prohibited the courts from ordering the release of a detainee. Scores of men and women now vanished into jails, to be subjected to solitary confinement and prolonged interrogation.

A new breed of police interrogators moved on to the seventh floor of the Grays, an oblong concrete block on Von Weilligh Street used by the security police as their headquarters. They were men prepared to use any method necessary to obtain information from detainees. The most notorious of all was Lieutenant Theunis Swanepoel, a former sergeant previously known for beating confessions out of prisoners, whose ugliness stood out at first sight. A broad-shouldered, heavy-set man with close-cropped ginger hair, he had a bullfrog-like head, tiny eyes and a face that was pockmarked and blotched – features that were to become all too familiar to detainees.

The interrogators soon began to produce results. A favourite method was 'statue' torture. Detainees were forced to stand in a small chalk square for periods which ranged from six hours to sixty hours. If they tried to sit down, they were jerked to their feet again; and if they fainted or lost consciousness, they were revived and forced to stand again. A communist activist, Ivan Schermbrucker, described in a note smuggled out of prison how he was made to stand until exhaustion brought him to the ground after twenty-eight hours of standing: 'I fell twice, had cold water thrown over me and was pulled to my feet . . . I nearly committed bloody suicide by jumping out of the window. This is torture . . . they threatened to keep me standing for four days and nights and even longer.' Other methods included electric shocks and physical assaults.

The General Law Amendment Act of 1963 effectively marked South Africa's transformation into a police state. As the legislation passed through parliament, a lone MP, Helen Suzman, voted against it. One of its first victims was Robert Sobukwe. Due for release on 3 May, having completed his three-year sentence in full, Sobukwe was held under a clause of the act which enabled the minister of justice to keep in prison indefinitely anyone convicted under security laws, even after they had served their sentence.

Sobukwe was taken from Pretoria Local to serve his time on Robben Island. Mandela was soon to follow him there.

CHAPTER 11

Operation Mayibuye

Far from being daunted by the government's increasing use of repression, the conspirators were keen to develop more ambitious plans. Revolutionary enthusiasts like Slovo argued that the phase of limited sabotage had effectively run its course and that the only remaining option was to commit Umkhonto to revolutionary violence. Since the first recruits had been sent out of the country for military training in China in September 1961, some 300 others had followed for training elsewhere in Africa and in Eastern Europe, providing a trained core of activists ready for guerrilla operations. Arthur Goldreich had travelled to China, the Soviet Union and East Germany, seeking military aid for Umkhonto and obtaining information on the manufacture of arms.

Slovo found a powerful ally for his arguments in Govan Mbeki, a talented political organizer from Port Elizabeth who had joined the MK high command at Lilliesleaf Farm after going underground in 1962 to avoid house arrest. A writer and journalist, employed by *New Age* as its Port Elizabeth editor, he had been part of the group in the 1950s which had turned Port Elizabeth and other towns in the Eastern Cape into one of the most successful areas of ANC activity. Detained for five months during the state of emergency in 1960, he had subsequently recruited and run a sabotage unit based in Port Elizabeth until arrested in 1962 under the Explosives Act on a charge of having instructed men in the manufacture of home-made bombs. While being held in prison for five months, three of them in solitary confinement, he had managed to continue work on his study of the Transkei, which was later published as *The Peasants' Revolt*. Unlike other MK activists, he

was a staunch believer in the power of the peasantry to change
South African society and in the importance of rural areas as the
main theatre of resistance. Acquitted of the explosives charge, he
was served with a house-arrest order, but went underground and
based himself at Lilliesleaf. At the age of fifty-two, eight years older
than Mandela, Mbeki was a veteran communist activist, having
first been attracted by communism during his days as a student at
Fort Hare in the 1930s. He was a close friend and collaborator of
Ruth First, Slovo's wife. And like Slovo, he was a hardline, narrow
ideologue, unshakeable in his convictions and certainties.

Slovo and Mbeki began work on a new MK strategy which
they completed by April 1963 and which was given the codename
Operation Mayibuye. The proposals they put forward in their
six-page memorandum were on a scale that no one had previously
contemplated. 'The time for small thinking is over,' they declared.

Part 1 encapsulated their argument for proceeding to guerrilla
warfare:

> The white state has thrown overboard every pretence of rule by
> democratic process. Armed to the teeth, it has presented the people
> with only one choice and that is its overthrow by force and violence.
> It can now be truly said that very little, if any, scope exists for
> the smashing of white supremacy other than by means of mass
> revolutionary action, the main content of which is armed resistance
> leading to victory by military means.
>
> The political events which have occurred in the last few years
> have convinced the overwhelming majority of the people that no
> mass struggle which is not backed up by armed resistance and
> military offensive operations can hope to make a real impact. This
> can be seen from the general mood of the people and their readiness
> to undertake even desperate and suicidal violent campaigns of the
> Leballo type. It can also be gauged by their reluctance to participate
> in orthodox political struggles in which they expose themselves to
> massive retaliation without a prospect of hitting back ... We are
> confident that the masses will respond in overwhelming numbers
> to a lead which holds out a real possibility of successful armed
> struggle ...
>
> The objective military conditions in which the movement finds
> itself make the possibility of a general uprising leading to direct
> military struggle an unlikely one. Rather, as in Cuba, the general
> uprising must be sparked off by organized and well-prepared guer-

rilla operations during the course of which the masses of the people will be drawn in and armed.

After disposing of the arguments against military action, Slovo and Mbeki turned to drawing up detailed plans of operation. Hundreds more activists would leave South Africa for guerrilla training. They would return by sea and by air in trained groups, thirty-strong, armed and equipped to be self-sufficient for at least a month while they linked up with local guerrilla bands: 'Our target is that on arrival the external force should find at least 7,000 men in the four main areas to join the guerrilla army in the initial onslaught.' Lists of targets were drawn up. 'We are convinced that this plan is capable of fulfilment,' they said. 'But only if the whole apparatus of the movement both here and abroad is mobilized for its implementation and if every member now prepares to make unlimited sacrifice for the achievement of our goal.'

Plans were also drawn up to manufacture hand grenades, bombs and other armaments inside South Africa. A new property near Krugersdorp named Travallyn was purchased for use as an arsenal. The man given responsibility for arms manufacture at Travallyn was Denis Goldberg, a thirty-year-old engineer from a well-known communist family, previously president of the Congress of Democrats. The scale of the operation envisaged at Travallyn was considerable. 'Production requirements' were estimated at 48,000 land mines, 210,000 hand grenades and 1,500 time devices for bombs. Goldberg opened negotiations for production equipment from factory owners, wholesale distributors and machinery merchants, using a string of pseudonyms, and obtained quotations for iron castings which matched designs for a hand grenade made by Goldreich. He also approached two firms of timber merchants for wood for 48,000 boxes in which to store all the armaments.

The contents of Operation Mayibuye were debated at length again and again at Lilliesleaf. The revolutionary enthusiasts – Slovo, Mbeki, Goldreich and military figures like Wilton Mkwayi and Joe Gqabi, who had returned from training in China and had joined the high command – wanted its immediate adoption. But others had deep misgivings. 'These people were so involved they lost all objectivity,' recalled Kathrada. 'They were in a hurry, very impatient to get things going. To my mind, it was just impossible.'

Sisulu believed that the plan was 'unrealistic'. Bram Fischer sub-sequently referred to it as 'an entirely unrealistic brainchild of some youthful and adventurous imagination'. The exact status of Operation Mayibuye was a matter of dispute for years to come. Slovo and Mbeki insisted that the document had been properly approved as official policy. Others denied that. In early June, Slovo left South Africa to apprise Oliver Tambo and the ANC's external mission of Operation Mayibuye and to set in motion arrangements for seeking support for it from African governments.

The comings and goings at Lilliesleaf Farm were so frequent as to make it resemble more a business enterprise than the secret headquarters of a revolutionary movement. Slovo often went there, driving from his office in Innes Chambers in town, as many as three times a day; so did Fischer, Bernstein and other leading conspirators. Living there were not only Goldreich and his family, but at times Sisulu, Kathrada and Mbeki, when they needed tempor-ary quarters. Goldberg often drove across from Travallyn. Meetings of the MK high command and of the central committee of the Communist Party took place there. A variety of MK personnel passed through. There were even social events. The farming activi-ties at Lilliesleaf provided some form of cover. But the farm workers themselves were amazed at how careless the conspirators seemed. 'You people are asking for prison if you carry on like this,' the black foreman told Kathrada. Kathrada raised the security issue over and over again. It was generally agreed that further meetings should take place elsewhere. But still the conspirators kept coming back to Lilliesleaf and still they took few precautions.

Yet the risks were becoming manifestly greater by the day. A major police raid on 24 June caught several figures who knew the whereabouts of Lilliesleaf. They included Bartholomew Hlapane, a member of the Communist Party central committee, and Patrick Mthembu, a member of MK's high command, who had been part of the first group trained in China and had since become boastful about his exploits. Another supporter arrested at the same time was Brian Somana, a journalist friendly with Winnie Mandela who had been one of the drivers used to take her to Lilliesleaf.

Two days later the conspirators staged an exercise in bravado with consequences they did not foresee. Using a house in Parktown belonging to Goldreich, they erected a radio transmitter to make

240

an 'Inaugural Broadcast by Radio Liberation'. The taped broadcast was introduced by Mbeki:

> This is the radio of the African National Congress, calling you from underground in South Africa. Our radio talks to you for the first time today, 26 June, but not for the last time . . .
>
> The government imposed a twenty-four-hour house arrest order on Walter Sisulu. We could not accept this . . . Our Congress decided that Walter Sisulu should leave his home . . . Today he continues to lead our organization and the people . . . Here is Walter Sisulu to speak to you from the African National Congress underground headquarters.

A recording from Sisulu followed:

> I speak to you from somewhere in South Africa. I have not left the country. I do not plan to leave. Many of our leaders of the African National Congress have gone underground. This is to keep our organization in action; to preserve the leadership; to keep the freedom fight going. Never has the country, and our people, needed leadership as they do now, in this hour of crisis . . .

Whether anyone other than the conspirators and their friends heard the broadcast was difficult to discover. But a copy of the text was delivered to a South African news agency in the hope of gaining some publicity. The copy quickly found its way into the hands of the security police. They saw it not as an irritating stunt but as a breakthrough in their search for the conspirators. Since 20 April the whereabouts of Sisulu had remained a mystery to them. Some believed he had left the country. Sisulu's broadcast gave them a new target. In questioning detainees in prison, the priority became to locate Sisulu's base.

After spending nearly six months of his five-year sentence in Pretoria Local, Mandela was suddenly ordered one night in late May 1963 to pack his belongings. Taken to the prison's reception office, he found three other prisoners waiting there. The prison commander, Colonel Aucamp, told them curtly that they were to be transferred to another prison. When they asked where, he replied, '*Die Eiland.*'

The journey was 1,000 miles. The prisoners were shackled together and put into the back of a closed van with a single toilet bucket for use on the way. Not until they reached Cape Town on the following afternoon were they allowed out of the vehicle. At the dockyard, still chained together, they boarded the Robben Island ferry, clambering down a steep, narrow ladder into the hold used to accommodate prisoners for the hour-long passage. Mandela caught his first sight of the island from the harbour at Murray's Bay, when he was led back on deck as the light was fading. 'Green and beautiful, it looked at first more like a resort than a prison,' he wrote.

Lying six miles north of Green Point and three miles west of Bloubergstrand, guarding the entrance to Table Bay, Robben Island possessed a reputation as a desolate and forbidding place. Roughly oval in shape, less than three miles long and one mile wide, it was surrounded by the icy currents of the Atlantic Ocean, providing an effective barrier to escape. In summer months, the view of Table Mountain to the south, however magnificent, was a constant reminder to prisoners of another, different world from which they were barred. In winter, north-westerly winds drove dark rain clouds across the mountain, obscuring the view, and kept the island damp and cold. The flat landscape of the island offered little protection against these winter winds and winters there were always colder than on the mainland.

The history of Robben Island had been marked over three centuries largely by misery and misfortune. Named by Dutch mariners after the thousands of seals – *robbe* – that once lived there, it had been used by successive generations as a dumping ground for the miscreants and misfits of society – convicts, political prisoners, lepers, lunatics and paupers. Its quarries had provided the mainland with stone and lime since the seventeenth century. In 1841, convicts had built a small Anglican church there. In 1864, a lighthouse had been constructed on Minto's Hill, the highest point on the island, rising seventy feet above sea level. During the Second World War, the military had taken possession, installing a new harbour at Murray's Bay, on the north-eastern side of the island, an airstrip at its northern end, and gun emplacements, observation towers and residential quarters for its garrison of some 3,000 people. During the 1950s the island was used as a training centre by the South African navy. Then, in 1961, it had been handed over to the prisons department to be used once more as a penal colony for the first time in 100 years.

242

The prison administration set out deliberately to create an establishment feared for its harsh and brutal regime. Prison life for Africans in South Africa was generally grim, but Robben Island attained special notoriety for its violent and vindictive treatment of prisoners. White warders there were given free rein to beat and bully inmates into submission. The daily fare they meted out included assaults, arbitrary punishment and a range of other abuses. Individual warders, like the Kleynhans brothers, became infamous for their cruel and sadistic conduct.

The first groups of prisoners to be sent to Robben Island were hardened criminals, some of whom were considered to be too dangerous to be kept in maximum-security prisons on the mainland, men accustomed to leading lives of violence. 'Most of the prisoners were disfigured,' an ANC arrival recorded, 'their shaven heads covered with scars, their eyes bloodshot, their noses askew, their teeth knocked out, and their bodies full of tattoos, often obscene.' The convicts operated in gangs, which warders used to their own advantage, patronizing some with privileges and employing them to keep others under control. Convicts served warders as enforcers and informers. Murders, assaults and rapes among prisoners were commonplace. When more general forms of discipline were needed, warders organized what was called a 'carry-on', in which they encircled groups of prisoners and continued to beat them with batons, pick-handles and rubber pipes, forcing them to get up once they had fallen so that they could be knocked down once more. 'After about half an hour the command came to stop,' an ANC witness said, describing a carry-on. 'The prisoners staggered away to assemble across the yard and about 200 formed up in front of us. Blood was pouring from their heads; their clothing was torn to ribbons; their faces were unrecognizable. They were barely able to walk; unable to move their arms; moaning; crying.'

The first groups of political prisoners sent to Robben Island were PAC members, many of them arrested as a result of the abortive Poqo uprising in April 1963. Regarded as terrorists and murderers of whites by white warders, political prisoners were treated with an extra measure of contempt. They were mixed in with common-law prisoners. Younger prisoners were often forced to become 'wyfies' to convicts, with the active encouragement of warders as a means of humiliation. The small number of ANC members initially imprisoned on the island had to contend with not only persecution from warders and convicts but open hostility from PAC members, who denounced them as sell-outs to whites and communists. Only a handful were there when Mandela arrived.

On the quayside as Mandela disembarked from the ferry stood a group of white warders shouting taunts that were familiar to all new arrivals, '*Dis die Eiland!*' – 'This is the Island!' – '*Hier julle gaan vrek!*' – 'Here you will die!' The prisoners were told to line up in pairs and jog along the path to the prison compound as their guards screamed, '*Haak! Haak!*', an Afrikaans term used for driving cattle. Determined not to give in to any intimidation, Mandela took the lead with Stephen Tefu, a Communist Party trade unionist, signalling that they should walk slowly and deliberately, not run as commanded. A white warder, one of the Kleynhans brothers, shouted at them, 'This is not Johannesburg, this is not Pretoria, this is Robben Island, and we will not tolerate any insubordination here. *Haak! Haak!*' Mandela and Tefu continued to walk at a leisurely pace. Kleynhans ordered them to halt. 'Look, man, we will kill you, we are not fooling around, your wives and children and mothers and fathers will never know what happened to you. This is the last warning. *Haak! Haak!*' Mandela replied, 'You have your duty and we have ours.'

At the prison compound, the prisoners were told to strip. Each item of clothing was searched and then flung on a wet floor. By the time they put them back on, their clothes were soaking. A belligerent prison officer arrived and started to berate one of the prisoners about the length of his hair. Mandela attempted to intervene. The officer cut him off. 'Never talk to me that way, boy!' he shouted and advanced threateningly, ready to strike. Though frightened, Mandela managed to stand his ground: 'If you so much as lay a hand on me, I will take you to the highest court in the land and when I finish with you, you will be as poor as a church mouse.' Mandela was as surprised by his own bravado as the officer was. The officer asked for his ticket. 'Five years! You are in for five years and you are so arrogant! Do you know what it means to serve five years?' Mandela replied, 'That is my business. I am ready to serve five years but I am not prepared to be bullied. You must act within the law.'

After this initial confrontation, Mandela settled down to a routine which, by Robben Island standards, was relatively benign. He and his three colleagues were given a spacious cell with large windows and its own toilets and showers. The cell, remarked Mandela, was one of the best he had ever seen. Coloured warders stationed on the island at the time were cooperative in supplying them with extra food, tobacco and news. They were kept isolated from all other prisoners. But the manual tasks they were given were far less arduous than the gruelling work in the quarries other prisoners had to undertake.

In July, Mandela was permitted a visit by Winnie, the first time he had seen her since starting his prison sentence eight months before. Their meeting took place in a building at the harbour. They were separated by two sections of wire mesh, about a yard apart, reaching up to the roof, which prevented them from seeing each other properly. There was nowhere for them to sit. To make themselves heard, they had to shout to each other, while white warders stood alongside listening to every word, ready to terminate the meeting if they touched on any forbidden subject. After thirty minutes, their brief encounter was over. 'It was horrible,' Winnie recalled. 'I was so depressed when I came away, but at least I had seen Nelson and he appeared pleased and relieved to see me.'

Mandela's stay on Robben Island ended as abruptly as it had begun. Later in July, without warning, he was transferred back to Pretoria Local and held in solitary confinement. He was given no explanation for the move, but from some fleeting glimpses he had of other prisoners being held there, he began to discern that something had gone seriously wrong.

The meeting of conspirators at Lilliesleaf Farm on 11 July 1963 was intended to be the last time they gathered there for business. The risk of discovery was considered to be too great. Too many people knew of its existence and some of them were currently in the hands of the security police. Bernstein went there only with the greatest reluctance, persuaded to go 'just this once more'. So strong was his sense of foreboding that at the last minute, having at first set out from his home in Observatory carrying a critique he had written of Operation Mayibuye, which was due to be discussed that afternoon, he returned home and hid it instead in his garage.

Others arrived there in disguise. Goldberg brought Sisulu, Mbeki and Mhlaba from Travallyn in his Volkswagen Combi. Sisulu had acquired a lighter complexion, a Chaplinesque moustache and darker hair. Mbeki wore a blue boiler suit and a balaclava, dressed ostensibly as a farm labourer. Goldberg had grown a beard and moustache. Kathrada, who had been staying overnight at Lilliesleaf preparing a radio broadcast, had dyed his hair red, passing himself off as a Portuguese with the name of Pedro Perreira. They were joined by the lawyer Bob Hepple, who came on secretariat business. Goldreich was expected to arrive later in the afternoon for the discussion on Operation Mayibuye.

Even though the conspirators acknowledged the extent of the danger at Lilliesleaf, the old habits of life there died hard. Needing dental treatment, Sisulu had arranged for a white dentist to visit him at Lilliesleaf half an hour before the meeting was due to start at 3 p.m. The dentist duly came and went.

The security police, meanwhile, had begun to move in. The information they had obtained pointed to a house in extensive grounds in the Rivonia area. For several nights, Lieutenant van Wyk drove up and down tracks and byroads in Rivonia, taking with him an informer, searching for landmarks. On the third night they identified Lilliesleaf Farm.

At the Grays, a task force for the raid was assembled, led by van Wyk with Warrant Officer Dirker as second-in-command. The raid was set for 1 p.m., but a senior officer recently seconded to the security police, discovering that no search warrant had been issued, ordered van Wyk to obtain one. So the raid had to be postponed for two hours, to 3 p.m.

As the conspirators settled down around the table in the thatched cottage at Lilliesleaf, a dry-cleaning van belonging to a well-known Johannesburg firm moved slowly down the approach road. In front were two men in white dustcoats; inside were ten more men and a police Alsatian. A farm employee stopped the vehicle, saying there was no one at home. Van Wyk ordered the raid to begin.

They found Sisulu, Mbeki, Kathrada, Bernstein, Hepple and Mhlaba in the thatched cottage. Three of them – Sisulu, Mbeki and Kathrada – tried to escape through a window but were quickly caught outside. They found Goldberg in the main house. Goldreich was captured when he returned to Lilliesleaf later in the day. Subsequently, three more conspirators were arrested: the lawyer

Harold Wolpe; a member of the Johannesburg high command, Andrew Mlangeni; and another communist activist, Elias Motsoaledi.

The importance of the Rivonia raid, however, went far beyond the capture of leading conspirators. For during their search of the premises at Lilliesleaf and later at Travallyn, the police acquired a massive haul of incriminating documents revealing the full extent of the conspiracy and its international connections. The most significant document was Operation Mayibuye, with its grandiose plans for guerrilla warfare, a copy of which had been left in a heating stove standing in a corner of the thatched cottage. But there was a host of other documents relating to revolutionary methods, arms production, guerrilla recruitment and training, and contacts with China, the Soviet Union and East European governments. The Lilliesleaf haul included 106 maps indicating targets like police stations, post offices, government offices, railway lines, telephone lines and power pylons. At Travallyn, the police also found bomb-making equipment and sketches and diagrams for the production of hand grenades.

Mandela was implicated in all this. More than ten documents were in his handwriting. They included his notes on basic and advanced military training and warfare; his diary covering the period from January to June 1962, containing details of his tour of Africa, his discussions with Algerian officials and his military training course in Ethiopia; and monographs he had copied out on such subjects as 'How to be a Good Communist' and 'Dialectical Materialism'. Other items found belonging to Mandela were copies of his press releases and statements, his library of books on warfare, his passport in the name of David Motsamayi, and correspondence and photos. Among them were letters from Winnie beginning 'My dearest love' and a photograph he liked to keep of her.

Nothing illustrated more the amateurism of Mandela's revolutionaries than that one year after his arrest on relatively minor charges they should be caught in a hide-out they knew to be unsafe in possession of useless documents implicating him in offences that could have led to his death by hanging.

CHAPTER 12
The Rivonia Trial

The conspirators were held under the ninety-day detention law, kept in solitary confinement, incommunicado and without access to lawyers. All but two were imprisoned in Pretoria Local. But Arthur Goldreich and Harold Wolpe were detained in police cells at Marshall Square in Johannesburg and from there they fashioned their escape on 11 August by bribing a young Afrikaner prison guard. Out of sheer vindictiveness, the security police then arrested Wolpe's law partner and brother-in-law, James Kantor, a criminal lawyer with a reputation as a playboy but with no political connections. No evidence was ever produced implicating Kantor in the conspiracy.

Meanwhile, the government whipped up a public mood of hysteria and fear. Ministers and police officials openly proclaimed the guilt of the detained men, though none of them had yet been charged with any offence. Their arrests were described by the commissioner of police as 'a major breakthrough in the elimination of subversive organizations'. The head of the security police, Colonel van den Bergh, boasted that the underground was smashed, its leaders apprehended and that nothing remained to be done other than to mop up the remnants. The government was portrayed as being on the verge of victory over all its opponents and critics. 'It was a time when to be a nonconformist, to act offbeat, to speak against the stream, even to think against the stream, was fraught with peril,' said Joel Joffe, a young lawyer witnessing these events.

Like an increasing number of young white professional people, Joffe had made plans to emigrate. He had never been politically

248

active, but he had grown to dislike life in South Africa, with its suffocating atmosphere of paranoia and injustice. He was on the point of leaving for Australia when he was approached by Hilda Bernstein, who had been searching for a lawyer willing to help defend her husband in court in the event of charges being laid against him. Mrs Bernstein had encountered considerable difficulty finding an instructing attorney prepared to undertake the task. The hazards for any lawyer acting on behalf of the Rivonia conspirators were severe, both at a professional and at a social level. Joffe was sceptical about what could be achieved. 'She was asking that I should embark on a case of unknown duration in the defence of people I did not know, whose actions I knew nothing about and on a charge which had not been formulated,' said Joffe. 'I felt that even if I were to agree, it would be a waste of time.' Given all the evidence the government claimed to have, the trial would surely be a mere formality.

Joffe was nevertheless sufficiently appalled by the manner in which his fellow lawyers had shunned Mrs Bernstein – 'I really am too busy' – to decide to take the case. Within the next few weeks, he received other approaches: from Albertina Sisulu, from Annie Goldberg, the frail mother of Denis Goldberg, and, later, from Winnie Mandela.

He had yet to ascertain what charges were to be brought against the conspirators. He went to the Grays to see Colonel George Klindt, the new head of the Johannesburg security police, and Dr Percy Yutar, the deputy attorney-general of the Transvaal, who had been appointed to take charge of any legal proceedings arising from the Rivonia raid and who had set up offices within security police headquarters. Neither was helpful. 'It was all very smooth, all patently false,' said Joffe. 'They were obviously lying and determined to be as unhelpful towards me as they possibly could.'

Joffe also began to assemble a defence team, although there were no funds available to meet their costs. The obvious starting point was Bram Fischer. No one outside a small group of conspirators knew of Fischer's real role in the underground. His public reputation was that of a radical lawyer involved in political cases like the treason trial; he was also known as a skilled advocate appearing on behalf of giant mining companies in some of the most abstruse financial cases in the South African courts. Fischer's political sympathies were evident, but not his involvement in clandestine activity. When Joffe approached Fischer for his help, he had not the slightest inkling of what he was really asking Fischer to do. For Fischer the dilemma was only too clear. The evidence obtained by police at Lilliesleaf was likely to implicate him; his handwriting was on several documents seized there. But what was even more hazardous was that he would be called upon to question witnesses in court who could betray him at any moment. Fischer did not hesitate to offer his help. He was more than willing to assist in the preparation of the case, but, without being able to explain his reasons, he said he was reluctant to be part of the defence team at the trial.

Two other advocates agreed to serve on the defence team. One was Mandela's Greek friend George Bizos, by now well versed in political trials. The other was Arthur Chaskalson, one of the most promising young advocates in the country, who had no political associations but a deep commitment to the defence of people who would otherwise have gone undefended.

Together, Joffe, Bizos and Chaskalson put tremendous pressure on Fischer to agree to lead the defence team. Not knowing of his involvement in the underground movement, they were unable to understand his reluctance to do so. They insisted that no other advocate could put so well the argument that the conspirators had done no more than the Afrikaner rebels who had taken up arms against the government in 1914 and who had received prison sentences rather than the death penalty. Fischer eventually agreed to lead the defence team and persuaded Vernon Berrangé, then living abroad, to join them. The conspirators, however, understood full well the risks that Fischer was taking. When Rusty Bernstein first heard Fischer would be acting on their behalf in the trial, he turned to the others and said, 'He deserves the Victoria Cross.'

Nearly three months had passed since the conspirators' arrest and Joffe could still not obtain any information about who the defendants might be and what charges they might face. Then, on 7 October, without his knowledge, the conspirators were taken from their cells, one at a time, to a prison office. There they were formally charged with offences under three acts of which they were given only the numbers. They were told they would appear in court within forty-eight hours and that they were no longer being held as ninety-day detainees but as awaiting-trial prisoners. Mandela was included on the same charges, but he was to remain in the category of a convicted prisoner.

The same day, hearing rumours on the legal grapevine that the conspirators were due to appear in court the following morning, Joffe phoned Percy Yutar, the prosecutor, and was told that the prisoners would indeed be appearing then in the Supreme Court in Pretoria. Along with Bizos and Chaskalson, Joffe duly travelled to Pretoria the next day, only to find that no one there knew anything about the case. From the attorney-general, Rudolf Rhein, the lawyers eventually ascertained that the prisoners would appear in the Supreme Court on the following day, but they were still not told who the defendants were or what the charges were, merely that they would find the defendants in Pretoria Local.

After a long wait and various arguments about whether white and black prisoners could mix together, the defendants were eventually produced. Mandela's appearance had changed considerably. His large frame had withered; he looked thin and underweight. His face had a sallow complexion, his cheeks were sunken and the skin under his eyes hung in bags. He was dressed in drab prison garb: short trousers, a khaki shirt and sandals. But his mood on seeing his fellow prisoners was buoyant. For the first time in months, he was able to talk to friends, to touch them, to laugh with them.

The sense of reunion was not shared by all the defendants. Of the eleven prisoners present, seven of them – Mandela, Sisulu, Mbeki, Kathrada, Mhlaba, Bernstein and Goldberg – had all played leading roles in the conspiracy. Two others – Elias Motsoaledi and Andrew Mlangeni – had been arrested before the Rivonia raid and were at a lower level of Umkhonto, but both had been involved in sabotage activity; unknown to the police, Mlangeni had been trained in China, as had Mhlaba. But for James Kantor, a flamboyant thirty-six-year-old, on friendly terms with police and criminals alike, who counted Colonel Klindt among his clients, the abrupt change in his fortunes was hard to bear. He was in a state of shock, his face haggard and drawn, his extrovert nature crushed. All the accused knew that he had nothing to do with the conspiracy and urged him to arrange a separate defence.

The predicament of the eleventh prisoner, Bob Hepple, was also acute. Hepple had played an active part in the underground movement, but as a secondary figure, passing messages, providing a conduit between the underground and the outside world, fixing arrangements. His arrest at Lilliesleaf with the others had been more a matter of coincidence than an indication of involvement in MK's military plans. In solitary confinement, his police interrogators, flourishing a copy of Operation Mayibuye, had told him he was certain to be sentenced to death unless he collaborated. 'I didn't want to die for Operation Mayibuye,' he said years later. 'I was going to be hanged for a plan which I thought was crazy and for which I had no responsibility.' To the dismay and consternation of his fellow prisoners, Hepple announced that during his detention he had been 'asked', as he put it, to give evidence against the others. He was still considering what to do, he said. All the excitement of the reunion vanished. As Hepple left the room, the others continued their consultation in a more sombre mood.

The following day, 9 October, the prisoners were driven in a special prison van from Pretoria Local, accompanied by an armed convoy, to the Supreme Court on Church Square, an ornate nineteenth-century building, three storeys high, with columns, marble facings and brass rails, known as the Palace of Justice. On the other side of Church Square stood the Raadsaal, the seat of the old Transvaal Republic government, and, in the centre, a massive bronze statue of President Kruger. Armed policemen were everywhere, both outside and inside the Supreme Court.

From the basement cells, Mandela, the first accused, led the procession of prisoners up the steps into the courtroom, raising a clenched fist as he emerged. This was the first glimpse of him in public for a year. Dressed in shabby prison garb, short trousers, a khaki shirt and sandals, he had lost so much weight and his skin was so pallid from prison life that to friends in the spectators' gallery he seemed almost unrecognizable. But his smile was still full of its old confidence.

The judge assigned to the case was Quartus de Wet, Judge-President of the Transvaal, sixty-five years old, a moody, complex character with a reputation for being self-willed, obstinate and impatient with legal quibbles. He shared the common white view in the virtues of white supremacy. Yet unlike many other judges at the time, he did not owe his position to any allegiance to the National Party. He had been appointed to the bench in 1947, before the Nationalists came to power.

Percy Yutar rose to call 'the case of the state against the National High Command', and, for the first time, produced an indictment, handing one copy to the court and passing another to Bram Fischer. The accused were charged under the Sabotage Act and the Suppression of Communism Act with complicity in more than 200 acts of sabotage aimed at aiding guerrilla warfare and facilitating violent revolution and armed invasion of the country. The Sabotage Act carried the death penalty. In addition to the defendants in court, the indictment listed twenty-four co-conspirators, including Goldreich, Wolpe, Harmel, Slovo, Hodgson, Kotane and Tambo.

Significantly, the accused were not charged under the common law of treason. Prosecution for treason would have required a preparatory examination, useful to the defence, with two witnesses to every overt act, and proof beyond reasonable doubt. Mindful of the abortive treason trial, Yutar decided to proceed under the Sabotage Act, which shifted much of the onus of proof from the prosecution to the defence. But his decision was to have a marked influence on the outcome.

Fischer immediately rose to apply for an adjournment, asking for at least six weeks to allow the defence time to prepare its case against such grave charges and for the accused to recover from their ordeal of solitary confinement. Yutar opposed any postponement. In a high-pitched voice, he spoke of witnesses who had to be called before the end of the month, adding, with a theatrical flourish, 'I fear for their safety.' The judge decided that a three-week pause was quite sufficient and adjourned the court until 29 October.

Immediately after the adjournment, the court reconvened to hear a bail application from Kantor. The case against Kantor was so flimsy that his lawyers were convinced that he should have no difficulty in obtaining bail. After an eloquent address by his lawyer, Harold Nicholas, the judge turned to Yutar and asked simply whether there were any indications that Kantor had been involved in the acts of sabotage alleged against the accused. Yutar assured the judge that there was no doubt whatsoever that Kantor was fully involved. He was denied bail.

The accused and their lawyers were to develop a contempt and hatred for Yutar that lasted far beyond the trial. A small, bald, dapper fifty-two-year-old who held himself ramrod-erect in court, he had ambitions to become the first Jewish attorney-general ever appointed in South Africa. He made no secret of his Jewish origins and seemed determined to prove that Jews could be as loyal as any other subjects of the apartheid state. He harboured a particular dislike for Jewish communists, of whom there were a considerable number, and felt no qualms about ingratiating himself with the security police. When Joel Joffe, himself a Jew, had met Yutar a few weeks beforehand at security police headquarters, Yutar had made a point of praising his police colleagues. 'I have been at the Grays for three weeks now, and in all that time I have not heard a single word of anti-Semitism from any of these people,' he had said. He saw his mission as being to present the accused as violent, vicious, self-interested individuals seeking to overthrow the government for their own aggrandizement. In court, when he thought events were going his way, Yutar resorted to open gloating; when the tide turned against him his voice rose to a high-pitched squeak. He also had a passion for publicity. On the day before the case began, Yutar found time to give interviews to reporters and to hand them advance copies of the indictment, which defence counsel had not yet been able to obtain.

During the three-week adjournment, the accused and their lawyers gathered daily to assess the indictment and to work out their line of defence. Restored to the company of his friends and allowed two half-hour visits a week and one meal a day sent in from outside prison, Mandela's spirits soon revived. But the outlook for the conspirators was bleak. Mandela was convinced that the trial would result in a death sentence and insisted that they had to prepare themselves for that eventuality. He felt a sense of personal responsibility for what had happened. 'He was conscious of obligations over and above others,' Bernstein recalled. 'He had no concern for his own position,' said Joffe. 'His aim was to turn the trial into a showcase against the government.' It was this quality of leadership, of standing firm in adversity, of accepting a greater responsibility for the course of events, of maintaining dignity and confidence in the face of a death sentence, that was to leave its mark on the Rivonia trial.

The accused were determined to use the trial for the purposes not of seeking a lesser punishment but of openly proclaiming their political views and the reasons why they had resorted to violence. They would not deny responsibility for sabotage, nor would they attempt to refute evidence obtained by the prosecution that they knew to be true. They would refuse only to provide further information. The matter of a sentence was less important to them than the need to explain in public the stand they had taken.

Observing the discussions, Joffe noted the influence of Sisulu on Mandela and the others:

> He was a man of deliberation and slow judgement. At no time during the whole of that period did I ever hear Walter make a hasty judgement, or venture an appraisal of anybody or anything without first weighing it carefully, deliberately, generally against his own immediate, instinctive reactions. On every issue, the other prisoners gave the greatest weight to Walter's opinions. It seemed to me throughout the case, neither Nelson nor anyone else made any decision without first seeking Walter's opinion. After a short time, we on the defence team found ourselves behaving the same way.

The immediate concern of the lawyers was the indictment. It contained vague and general allegations, making it impossible to discern precisely what the offence was, by whom the offence had been committed and in what way the accused, either individually or jointly, were alleged to be connected with it. When the lawyers asked the prosecution for further particulars, the replies they were given were curt: either, 'These facts are known' or 'These facts are peculiarly within the knowledge of the accused.' The prosecution, said Joffe, was clearly following a simple precept: 'You are guilty. Therefore you know what you did. Therefore we don't have to tell you.' The lawyers decided to ask the court to dismiss the indictment.

When the accused reappeared in court on 29 October, each in turn emerged from the stairwell, faced the public gallery, gave the ANC's clenched-fist salute and shouted 'Amandla!' to which their supporters in the gallery replied with a loud, 'Ngawethu!' Only Kantor and Hepple did not give the salute, but simply smiled at friends. To prevent further outbursts, the prisoners were subsequently brought into court after the judge had taken his seat and opened the session.

Fischer immediately opened his attack on the indictment, speaking slowly and carefully, weighing up each word, exposing the defects of the indictment one by one. Some of the sabotage acts, he said, had been committed before any Sabotage Act existed in South Africa and therefore could not be offences in terms of the act under which the accused had been charged. He pointed out that Mandela had been charged with having committed 156 acts of sabotage which had taken place while he was in prison. Fischer deplored the lack of particularity and the unsatisfactory, even ludicrous answers given when the defence asked for further particulars. The state, he said, had decided the accused were guilty and therefore the defence was a waste of time. Fischer's crushing exposure of the indictment was followed up with further ridicule from Kantor's counsellor, George Lowen.

The judge then turned to Hepple, who was unrepresented, to ask whether he wished to say anything about the indictment. But before he had time to reply, Yutar, sensing that events were moving against him, sprang to his feet to announce that all charges against Hepple were being withdrawn, adding, in a voice of triumph, that Hepple would be the first witness for the prosecution against the accused. Hepple turned pale, rose to his feet and was accompanied from the dock by Captain Swanepoel down the stairwell to the cells below.

Hepple's defection was a considerable coup for Yutar. His fellow prisoners had been expecting it; Hepple had discussed with them the possibility of inducing Yutar to release him and then skipping the country. However, to the public, it seemed that Yutar had gained a star witness. But he was still left with an indictment virtually in tatters after Fischer and Lowen had finished with it. Ignoring the legal arguments presented by the defence team, Yutar asserted that their application was neither genuine nor sincere, but merely an attempt to harass and embarrass the state. With increasing desperation, he resorted to 'begging' and 'imploring' the court not to reject the indictment, promising to provide whatever further particulars the judge wanted. De Wet replied testily that it was not his responsibility to tell the state what particulars were required to make a good indictment. Yutar continued, 'I would earnestly beg Your Lordship, nay crave Your Lordship, not to squash the indictment, but to order that the state does what it undertakes to do, that is to supply further particulars.'

It was all to no avail. De Wet threw out the indictment. Technically the prisoners were free men. Their friends and relatives and the security police rushed forward. Amid pandemonium, Swanepoel leapt into the dock and struck each of the accused on the shoulder, declaring, 'I am arresting you on a charge of sabotage.' Within a few minutes, the prisoners were herded down to the cells again.

On the same day, bail applications were due to be heard first for Kantor and then for Bernstein. The judge appeared sympathetic to Kantor's case and at one stage asked his defence counsel what he considered would be a reasonable sum for bail. The discussion was nearly at an end when Yutar suddenly intervened to announce that he was in possession of a confidential secret document showing that escape plans had been made for the accused. What had prompted Yutar's latest claim was the discovery among the Rivonia documents of the escape notes which Mandela had exchanged with Slovo in 1962 and which Slovo had decided to preserve for posterity. Kantor's application was rejected; so was Bernstein's.

Back at Pretoria Local, the accused continued with the preparation of their defence in a consulting room on the ground floor specially set aside for them. Assuming that the room was bugged and that everything they said was overheard by the security police, they communicated with each other by using a simple coded language or by writing down messages and then burning them in ashtrays before their daily sessions were over. Prison warders watched this procedure through a door window with some distress. Before long, Captain Swanepoel was seen pacing up and down the corridor, glancing through the window whenever he passed. The prisoners realized how badly Swanepoel wanted to get his hands on their messages and laid a trap for him. On a piece of paper Mbeki wrote, 'It's so nice to have Lieutenant Swanepoel with us again', waited for Swanepoel to pass by and then passed it ostentatiously to Joffe. Joffe studied the message for some time, whispered in a conspiratorial manner to the prisoners and then, placing the message in an ashtray, fumbled for his matches. Swanepoel dashed into the room, seized the ashtray with the message in it and rushed outside. He did not appear outside the door again.

A new indictment was eventually produced. But it was still so badly flawed that the defence lawyers decided to apply again for its dismissal. This time, however, de Wet was in no mood to countenance further delay and he ordered the case to proceed.

But now yet another drama intervened. Yutar's first witness, Bob Hepple, had managed to flee the country and he surfaced in Dar es Salaam, the Tanganyikan capital, stating that he had no intention of testifying against the accused, whom he admired and supported. He spoke of threats and broken promises made by the police, and revealed the mental and physical torture to which detainees under the ninety-day law were subjected. What no one knew at the time was that his escape had been arranged by Bram Fischer, who had met him in secret on three occasions at huge potential risk to himself.

The trial eventually began on 3 December 1963. The accused were asked by the registrar of the court to plead.

> MANDELA: The government should be in the dock, not me. I plead not guilty.

His remark caused some consternation. There was angry muttering among the police.

> SISULU: It is the government which is guilty, not me.
> DE WET: I don't want any political speeches here. You may plead guilty, or not guilty. But nothing else.
> SISULU: It is the government which is responsible for what is happening. I plead not guilty.
> GOLDBERG: I associate myself with the statements of Mr Mandela and Mr Sisulu. I plead not guilty.

And so it went on, except for Kantor, who said simply, 'I am not guilty, My Lord.'

Then Yutar rose to give his opening address. He had spent considerable effort on it. He had also decided to arrange for it to be recorded by the state-controlled radio network; a small black microphone had appeared overnight in front of his desk. Broadcasting court proceedings was unprecedented in South African history. No attempt had been made to consult defence counsel on the matter. No sooner was Yutar on his feet than Fischer rose to demand the removal of the microphones. De Wet looked uncomfortable but ordered them to be dismantled.

The 'cornerstone' of the state's case was Operation Mayibuye, said Yutar. 'The accused deliberately and maliciously plotted and engineered the commission of acts of violence and destruction throughout the country.'

The planned purpose . . . was to bring about in the Republic of South Africa chaos, disorder and turmoil which would be aggravated, according to their plan, by the operation of thousands of trained guerrilla warfare units deployed throughout the country at various vantage points. These would be joined in various areas by local inhabitants as well as specially selected men posted to such areas. Their combined operations were planned to lead to confusion, violent insurrection and rebellion, followed at the appropriate juncture by armed invasion of the country by military units of foreign powers. In the midst of the resulting chaos, turmoil and disorder it was planned by the accused to set up a provisional revolutionary government to take over the administration and control of this country.

Yutar went on to give details of the Rivonia headquarters, the arsenal at Travallyn and the plans for training in sabotage and guerrilla warfare in African states. Documents and witnesses would be produced, he said, to substantiate all this.

The extent of the conspiracy, as Yutar outlined it, left the defence lawyers feeling considerably shaken. 'From that moment on, we saw the case in a very simple light,' said Joffe. 'For most of the accused the only possible verdict was "guilty". The case was therefore, as far as we were concerned, a battle to prevent the death sentence being carried out.'

During the next three months, the prosecution presented 173 witnesses, hundreds of documents, photographs and maps and a whole library of captured books on guerrilla warfare. All Mandela's papers found at Lilliesleaf were produced. 'Nelson felt that he had been let down by that,' Sisulu recalled. Mandela had once asked Sisulu during a chance meeting in Pretoria Local in 1962 to ensure that his documents were removed from Lilliesleaf. Sisulu had raised the matter with Mbeki, but nothing had been done: 'Nelson felt that the fact that he was linked to the whole business was because we were responsible for not taking appropriate steps.'

But prosecution witnesses also inflicted damage. The state's key witness was Bruno Mtolo, a member of MK's Natal regional command, an active saboteur for three years whom Mandela had met on his journey to Durban in August 1962 and who had also visited the Rivonia headquarters in 1963, where he had held discussions with Sisulu and Mbeki. Arrested by the security police in August 1963, Mtolo had decided within hours to defect, claiming he had become disillusioned with MK's leadership and with the extent of communist influence over the ANC, even though he himself was a Communist Party member. Mtolo implicated not only Mandela, Sisulu and Mbeki but a host of other people in MK activities.

Another key witness was Patrick Mthembu, a member of the Johannesburg regional command, who had trained in China and had worked closely with all the conspirators, both during the days when the ANC was a legal organization and during Umkhonto operations. Mthembu had spent two periods in solitary confinement. He was offered indemnity against prosecution in exchange for his testimony.

Just before the Christmas recess, Kantor was finally granted bail. Over the months of the trial he had developed a warm relationship with Mandela. Knowing of Kantor's anguish at being separated from his wife, Barbara, who was pregnant, Mandela had once come over to him and put his arm around his shoulder. 'Tell Barbara I apologize,' said Mandela. 'What for?' asked Kantor. 'Because you are here,' he answered simply.

In January 1964, while sitting in the dock, Kantor wrote a note for Mandela, which was passed along the row of accused. It said, 'Barbara and I have thought about and discussed godfathers at length. We have come to the conclusion that, whether the baby is a girl or boy, we would consider it an honour if you would agree to accept this office as an adjunct to the more disreputable positions you have held in the past.' Mandela's reply took some time to arrive, reaching Kantor just before the tea adjournment: 'I would be more than delighted, and the honour is mine, not the baby's.' As the court rose for the tea break, Mandela hung back as the other accused left, pretending to arrange his papers, and exchanged a quick word with Kantor. 'Now they dare not hang me,' he said, beaming broadly.

In April 1964, soon after the prosecution concluded its case, Judge de Wet found Kantor not guilty and discharged him. He left the court wearing the tie Mandela had offered him in exchange for his own as a token of good luck before the hearing started.

*

During the five-week adjournment allowed to the defence to examine the evidence and prepare their case, the prison authorities at Pretoria Local provided a new consultation room for the conspirators and their lawyers. It was long and narrow and down the middle of it the prison building staff had constructed a wooden counter topped by a heavy metal grating, dividing the room in half. Bar stools had been placed on either side, one side for the lawyers, the other for the conspirators. When the lawyers were first ushered into the new consultation room, the prisoners were already seated on their side of the partition, lined up in a long row like customers at a milk bar. Mandela stood up, smiled politely and said, 'What will it be today, gentlemen? Chocolate or ice-cream soda?' The prison commander, Colonel Aucamp, a malevolent official with whom Mandela had previously clashed, was not amused. The lawyers protested that the arrangements, with nine accused in a single line along the counter on one side and five lawyers sitting on bar stools on the other, made a proper consultation virtually impossible. Exhibits and notes had to be slid through a tiny space under the metal bars. But Colonel Aucamp refused to allow any changes. To add to their difficulties, the lawyers and their clients now had to assume that the new contraption contained listening devices relaying everything that was said to officials outside. They resorted again to passing notes on any issue considered important.

The conspirators were clear about their objective in the trial. They wanted an opportunity to explain to the world their reasons for embarking on a campaign of violence against the government and the circumstances which had forced them to do so. They would admit to initiating the sabotage campaign; they would admit to making contingency plans for guerrilla warfare to be implemented if the sabotage campaign failed to change the government's mind; but they would deny that they had already decided to embark on guerrilla warfare, as the prosecution contended. They therefore needed to clarify the circumstances under which Operation Mayibuye was drawn up. They also wanted to make clear that the sabotage campaign had been carried out with express instructions that under no circumstances should human life be endangered at any time. They would therefore contest prosecution claims of murder and injury. They would also deny that the intervention of foreign forces had been contemplated, as Yutar had further claimed.

The case against individual conspirators, however, was not of equal strength. The evidence against Bernstein was negligible; he had merely been discovered at Lilliesleaf with the others. The evidence against Kathrada and Mhlaba was also limited. The evidence against Mlangeni and Motsoaledi showed mainly that they had been involved in the recruitment and transportation of volunteers for military training abroad, making them lower-level operatives in the conspiracy. Goldberg was identified as a sabotage expert involved in preparations for armaments manufacture. Only Mandela, Sisulu and Mbeki were fully implicated as leading figures in the conspiracy. The solution agreed upon, therefore, was that six of the conspirators would make admissions of guilt on certain charges. The remaining three – Bernstein, Kathrada and Mhlaba – would continue to plead not guilty.

In order to ensure that the court heard a clear and coherent account of their political aims and ideals, the accused decided that Mandela should open the case for the defence by reading a statement from the dock, unhindered by cross-examination or questions from the bench. This procedure also enabled Mandela to avoid any suggestion that he was retracting from the position he had taken at his previous trial in 1962 of refusing to enter the witness box because of the inherent injustice of the legal system. The disadvantage for Mandela was that a statement from the dock was not accorded the same legal weight as ordinary testimony and thus rendered him more vulnerable before the court. But Mandela regarded whatever sentence he received as being of secondary importance to the need for public understanding of the conspirators' beliefs.

Mandela spent about two weeks drafting his speech, working mainly in his cell in the evenings. He showed the draft to his fellow prisoners, who suggested a few changes, and to Bram Fischer. Fischer was worried about the content, about the damage it would do to Mandela's prospects in court, and took it to a highly respected advocate, Harold Hanson, for his opinion. Hanson told Fischer, 'If Mandela reads this in court they will take him straight out to the back of the courthouse and string him up.' Fischer urged Mandela to modify the speech, but to no avail. 'I felt we were likely to hang no matter what we said, so we might as well say what we truly believed,' said Mandela. 'Bram begged me not to read the final paragraph, but I was adamant.'

On 20 April 1964, the conspirators were taken back to the Palace of Justice to commence their defence. Both Winnie and Mandela's mother were present in court. In his opening remarks, made in his customary quiet and calm manner, Fischer announced that certain aspects of the state's evidence would be conceded by the accused, but other parts would be challenged. They would deny that Umkhonto was a section of the ANC – 'the military wing', as the state claimed – but seek to show that the leaders of Umkhonto and the ANC endeavoured to keep these two organizations entirely distinct. 'They did not always succeed in this,' he said, 'but . . . every effort was made to achieve that object.' They would also deny emphatically that the ANC was a 'tool' of the Communist Party, as the state claimed, and that the aims and objectives of the ANC were the aims and objectives of the Communist Party. They would further deny that Umkhonto had adopted Operation Mayibuye and had decided upon guerrilla warfare.

> DE WET: Will that be denied?
> FISCHER: That will be denied. Here the evidence will show that while preparations for guerrilla warfare were being made from as early as 1962, no plan was ever adopted, and the evidence will show why it was hoped throughout such a step could be avoided.

Fischer paused, while the judge finished making notes, and then announced that Mandela would make a statement from the dock. Yutar was caught by surprise. He had been misled into believing that he would have the benefit of cross-examining Mandela. As Mandela rose slowly, adjusting the spectacles which he used for reading, Yutar jumped to his feet, his shrill voice rising in complaint.

> YUTAR: My Lord! My Lord! I think you should warn the accused that what he says from the dock has far less weight than if he submitted himself to cross-examination!
> DE WET: I think, Mr Yutar, that counsel for the defence have sufficient experience to be able to advise their clients without your assistance.

Standing in the dock, Mandela began reading his statement slowly and with calm deliberation, his voice carrying clearly across the courtroom. Gradually, as he spoke, the silence in the courtroom became more profound.

> I must deal immediately and at some length with the question of violence. Some of the things so far told to the court are true and some are untrue. I do not, however, deny that I planned sabotage. I did not plan it in a spirit of recklessness, nor because I have any love of violence. I planned it as a result of a calm and sober assessment of the political situation that had arisen after many years of tyranny, exploitation and oppression of my people by the whites.
>
> I admit immediately that I was one of the persons who helped to form Umkhonto we Sizwe, and that I played a prominent role in its affairs until I was arrested in August 1962.

He went on to explain the reasons behind the formation of Umkhonto:

> Firstly, we believed that as a result of government policy, violence by the African people had become inevitable and that unless responsible leadership was given to canalize and control the feelings of our people, there would be outbreaks of terrorism which would produce an intensity of bitterness and hostility between the various races of this country which is not produced even by war.
>
> Secondly, we felt that without violence there would be no way open to the African people to succeed in their struggle against the principle of white supremacy. All lawful modes of expressing opposition to this principle had been closed by legislation, and we were placed in a position in which we had either to accept a permanent state of inferiority or to defy the government. We chose to defy the law. We first broke the law in a way which avoided any recourse to violence; when this form was legislated against, and then the government resorted to a show of force to crush opposition to its policies, only then did we decide to answer violence with violence.
>
> But the violence which we chose to adopt was not terrorism. We who formed Umkhonto were all members of the African National Congress and had behind us the ANC tradition of non-violence and negotiation as a means of solving political disputes. We believed that South Africa belonged to all the people who lived in it, and not to one group, be it black or white. We did not want an interracial war and tried to avoid it to the last minute.

Mandela referred to the time in mid-1961 when the decision to turn to violence was taken.

For a long time the people had been talking of violence – of the day when they would fight the white man and win back their country – and we, the leaders of the ANC, had nevertheless always prevailed upon them to avoid violence and to pursue peaceful methods. When some of us discussed this in May and June of 1961, it could not be denied that our policy to achieve a non-racial state by non-violence had achieved nothing, and that our followers were beginning to lose confidence in this policy and were developing disturbing ideas of terrorism . . .

After a long and anxious assessment of the South African situation, I, and some colleagues, came to the conclusion that as violence in this country was inevitable, it would be unrealistic and wrong for African leaders to continue preaching peace and non-violence at a time when the government met our peaceful demands with force.

This conclusion was not easily arrived at. It was only when all else had failed, when all channels of peaceful protest had been barred to us, that the decision was made to embark on violent forms of political struggle, and to form Umkhonto we Sizwe. We did so not because we desired such a course, but solely because the government had left us with no other choice.

He outlined what he thought could be achieved by the use of violence.

The initial plan was based on a careful analysis of the political and economic situation of our country. We believed that South Africa depended to a large extent on foreign capital and foreign trade. We felt that planned destruction of power plants and interference with rail and telephone communications would tend to scare away capital from the country, make it more difficult for goods from the industrial areas to reach the seaports on schedule and would in the long run be a heavy drain on the economic life of the country, thus compelling the voters of the country to reconsider their position.

Attacks on the economic lifelines of the country were to be linked with sabotage on government buildings and other symbols of apartheid. These attacks would serve as a source of inspiration to our people. In addition, they would provide an outlet for those people who were urging the adoption of violent methods and would enable us to give concrete proof to our followers that we had adopted a stronger line and were fighting back against government violence.

In addition, if mass action were successfully organized, and mass reprisals taken, we felt that sympathy for our cause would be roused in other countries and that greater pressure would be brought to bear on the South African government.

He dealt with the relationship between the ANC and Umkhonto. The ANC, he said, was a political organization with a political function to fulfil. Its members had joined on the express policy of non-violence. It could not undertake violence without a change in the whole nature of the organization. Nevertheless, it had been prepared to depart from its fifty-year-old policy of non-violence to the extent that it would no longer disapprove of 'properly controlled violence'. Umkhonto remained a small organization, recruiting its members from different races and organizations and trying to achieve its own particular objective of sabotage. Although there had been some 'overlapping of functions' and although the distinction between the two may have become 'blurred', the distinction was still clear: 'The fact that members of Umkhonto were recruited from the ANC, and the fact that persons served both organizations . . . did not, in our view, change the nature of the ANC or give it a policy of violence.'

He also dealt with the relationship between the ANC and the Communist Party: 'It is true that there has often been close cooperation between the ANC and the Communist Party. But cooperation is merely proof of a common goal – in this case the removal of white supremacy – and is not proof of a complete community of interests.' The ANC, unlike the Communist Party, admitted only Africans as members. Its chief goal was for the African people to win unity and full political rights. The Communist Party's main aim, on the other hand, was to remove the capitalists and to replace them with a working-class government. The Communist Party sought to emphasize class distinctions, while the ANC sought to harmonize them. The ANC had never at any period of its history advocated a revolutionary change in the economic structure of the country, nor had it ever condemned capitalist society.

He turned to his own political allegiances. He described himself as 'an African patriot', a socialist influenced by Marxist thought, but not a communist. He was attracted by the idea of a classless society, partly as a result of his reading of Marxist literature, partly as a result of his admiration for early African societies in which the land, then the main means of production, belonged to the tribe. But there were aspects of Marxist thinking with which he fundamentally disagreed:

> From my reading of Marxist literature and from conversations with Marxists, I have gained the impression that communists regard the parliamentary system of the West as undemocratic and reactionary. But, on the contrary, I am an admirer of such a system.
>
> The Magna Carta, the Petition of Rights and the Bill of Rights are documents which are held in veneration by democrats throughout the world.
>
> I have great respect for British political institutions and for the country's system of justice. I regard the British parliament as the most democratic institution in the world, and the independence and impartiality of its judiciary never fail to arouse my admiration.
>
> The American Congress, that country's doctrine of separation of powers, as well as the independence of its judiciary, arouses in me similar sentiments.
>
> I have been influenced in my thinking by both West and East. All this has led me to feel that in my search for a political formula, I should be absolutely impartial and objective. I should tie myself to no particular system of society other than that of socialism. I must leave myself free to borrow the best from the West and from the East.

He went on to outline the conditions in which the African population lived and worked, comparing them to the affluent lifestyle of the white population. Africans were fighting against two features that were the hallmark of African life: poverty and lack of human dignity.

> Africans want a just share in the whole of South Africa, they want a security and a stake in society.
>
> Above all, we want equal political rights, because without them our disabilities will be permanent. I know this sounds revolutionary to the whites in this country, because the majority of voters will be Africans. This makes the white man fear democracy.
>
> But this fear cannot be allowed to stand in the way of the only solution which will guarantee racial harmony and freedom for all. It is not true that the enfranchisement of all will result in racial domination. Political division, based on colour, is entirely artificial and, when it disappears, so will the domination of one colour group

by another. The ANC has spent half a century fighting against racialism. When it triumphs it will not change that policy.

This then is what the ANC is fighting. Their struggle is a truly national one. It is a struggle of the African people, inspired by their own suffering and their own experience. It is a struggle for the right to live.

Mandela stopped reading his statement at this point, put down his papers and turned to face the judge, speaking his final words from memory:

During my lifetime I have dedicated myself to this struggle of the African people. I have fought against white domination, and I have fought against black domination. I have cherished the ideal of a democratic and free society in which all persons live together in harmony and with equal opportunities. It is an ideal which I hope to live for and to achieve. But if needs be, it is an ideal for which I am prepared to die.

In the courtroom there was complete silence as Mandela sat down. For perhaps thirty seconds the silence continued. Then from the public gallery there came a great sigh, like the release of breath, and the crying of women.

Mandela's statement, lasting more than four hours, was followed by the evidence of Walter Sisulu. Sisulu was the key witness for the defence, his knowledge of the ANC and of Umkhonto being greater than anyone else's. Upon him lay the burden of convincing the judge that Operation Mayibuye had been considered as a plan of action but not adopted as a policy, the issue which the defence lawyers considered was the 'hairline' around which the prospect of a death sentence revolved. As Fischer led him through his evidence, Sisulu explained how he had been present when Operation Mayibuye had first been placed before the high command as a plan for consideration. The implications of launching guerrilla warfare were so far-reaching that the high command had sought the views of the ANC and other organizations. Among members of the high command itself, opinion was deeply divided. 'There was a strong argument against the plan,' said Sisulu. Several meetings were held to discuss it further. The last meeting had adjourned without taking a decision. 'My view was that conditions did not exist at that time for Operation Mayibuye.'

Sisulu was subjected to five days of cross-examination, with-standing a barrage of questions, gibes and taunts from Yutar. 'It was a feat of considerable merit, and under extremely difficult conditions,' remarked Joffe. 'For over a week, Sisulu was kept in complete isolation with no human contact at all, day after day in the witness box being hammered by judge and prosecutor.' One by one, the other accused – Kathrada, Mhlaba, Bernstein, Mbeki and Goldberg – took their turn in the witness box to face the same treatment. Motsoaledi and Mlangeni made short statements from the dock, admitting their guilt as minor participants in Umkhonto. Motsoaledi described how he had been assaulted during his period in solitary confinement and how his wife, the mother of seven children, had been detained under the ninety-day law and rearrested when she had completed ninety days. Mlangeni described how he had been assaulted and tortured with electric shocks in police custody.

On 20 May, Yutar arrived in court carrying four volumes contain-ing a summary of evidence which he proceeded to read out as his closing argument. Much of it amounted to a political attack on the accused. 'The deceit of the accused is amazing,' he said. 'Although they represented scarcely more than 1 per cent of the African population [a reference to the ANC's membership] they took it upon themselves to tell the world that the Africans in South Africa are suppressed, oppressed and depressed.' He repeated his assertion that not only had guerrilla warfare been agreed upon but that a date had actually been set.

Then de Wet intervened. 'Mr Yutar,' he said, 'you do concede that you failed to prove guerrilla warfare was ever decided upon, do you not?'

Yutar looked stunned and stammered a submission that prep-arations were being made.

De Wet replied testily, 'Yes, I know that. The defence concedes that. What they say is that preparations were made in case one day they found it necessary to resort to guerrilla warfare. But they say that prior to their arrest they never considered it necessary, and took no decision to engage in guerrilla warfare. I take it that you have no evidence contradicting that, and that you accept it?'

'As Your Lordship pleases,' Yutar replied, in a strangled voice. He then concluded by arguing that the case was one of not only high treason *par excellence* but murder and attempted murder, even though no such charges had been made against the accused.

Arthur Chaskalson rose to refute that the trial had anything to do with murder or attempted murder. He proceeded to demonstrate from the testimony of state witnesses, like Mtolo, that Umkhonto's clear policy was sabotage in circumstances where life was not endangered. The indictment, he pointed out, alleged military training and sabotage. The defence conceded, he said, that Umkhonto recruited men for military training and that members of Umkhonto committed acts of sabotage. The defence denied, however, that they committed all the acts of sabotage they were charged with.

As he began to demonstrate from evidence that there were other organizations committing acts of sabotage at the time, de Wet intervened to say that he already accepted this as a fact. In one stroke, a major part of the state's case – that Umkhonto had been responsible for all acts of sabotage – fell away.

Fischer then rose to deal with the two most serious contentions: first, that the high command had decided to embark on guerrilla warfare; and second, that Umkhonto was the military wing of the ANC – acceptance of which could have made every member of the ANC liable to prosecution for sabotage or treason. Fischer had spent months preparing his submissions on these points, but before he could develop his argument on the first issue de Wet cut him short, saying, 'I thought I had made my attitude clear. I accept no decision or date was fixed upon for guerrilla warfare.' When Fischer moved on to the second issue, de Wet again intervened, saying he accepted that though the two organizations overlapped, they were in fact separate.

All that remained to be determined were the verdict and the sentence. In the case of six accused – Mandela, Sisulu, Mbeki, Goldberg, Motsoaledi and Mlangeni – they had already admitted guilt. The fates of Bernstein, Kathrada and Mhlaba were less certain. But the centre of interest, as it had been throughout the trial, was on whether or not the conspirators would receive the death penalty. During the three-week adjournment before the sentence was announced, Mandela settled down to write a London University law examination, which he was to pass.

As the Rivonia trial reached its climax, the outcome stirred intense interest internationally. Mandela's defiant statement of his beliefs, his testimony declaring his willingness to die for the cause of democracy in South Africa and his bearing before the court had captured worldwide attention. Demonstrations were held in Europe and the United States. Students at the University of London elected Mandela as president of the student's union midway through the trial. On 9 June, two days before the judge was due to give his decision, the United Nations Security Council urged the South African government to end the trial and to grant an amnesty to the defendants and to all others who had been restricted or imprisoned for opposing apartheid; Britain and the United States abstained on the vote. In London, an all-night vigil was held at St Paul's Cathedral.

It took Judge de Wet three minutes on 11 June 1964 to find all the conspirators except Bernstein guilty. He reserved sentence for the following day. Bernstein was immediately surrounded by security police, arrested as he tried to reach the defence counsel's table, hustled down to the cells with the others and charged with new offences.

That evening, the defence lawyers called at Pretoria Local to confer with the prisoners. The lawyers were pessimistic about the sentence they thought likely. Recent sentences imposed by South African courts had established some harsh precedents. An eighteen-year-old youth had been sent to prison for ten years for attempting to leave the country in order to be trained by the ANC as a motor mechanic. Another ANC supporter had received twenty years' hard labour for recruiting a man for military training abroad. Several young men had been sentenced to ten years for attending a single meeting at which sabotage was discussed, even though there was no evidence that the accused had done any more than listen to the discussion.

Yet the lawyers found the prisoners as resolute as ever. Joel Joffe recalled:

> They were calm, living now in the shadow of death. The strain and the tension were becoming almost unbearable, yet the only matter that they wanted to discuss was how they should behave in court if the death sentence was passed.
>
> We told them that the judge would ask the first accused, Nelson Mandela, 'Have you any reason to advance why the death sentence should not be passed?' Nelson decided that he would have a lot to

say. He would tell the court that if they thought by sentencing him to death they would destroy the liberation movement they were wrong; he was prepared to die for his beliefs and knew that his death would be an inspiration to his people.

We pointed out that such an address was hardly designed to facilitate an appeal. Nelson's answer was simple. If sentenced to death he would not appeal.

Mandela, Sisulu and Mbeki had already decided among themselves not to appeal. They believed that an appeal would undermine the moral stand they had taken. It might be interpreted by their supporters as an act of weakness. 'Our message was that no sacrifice was too great in the struggle for freedom,' said Mandela.

That night, after the lawyers had left, dismayed at their decision and hoping they would change their minds, Mandela scribbled a few lines which he intended to use if he were sentenced to death. 'I meant everything I said,' he wrote.

'I was prepared for the death penalty,' Mandela said in his autobiography. 'To be truly prepared for something, one must actually expect it. One cannot be prepared for something while secretly believing it will not happen. We were all prepared, not because we were brave but because we were realistic.'

The following morning, outside the Palace of Justice, a large crowd gathered silently, some carrying banners declaring, 'We are proud of our leaders.' Inside, the courtroom was packed. Winnie and Mandela's mother were once again present.

Before sentence was passed, the court heard two pleas in mitigation. The defendants were at first reluctant to allow anyone to speak on their behalf but then agreed on condition that nothing was said that could be construed as an apology. A number of names were suggested, but most of those approached declined to undertake the task. Bram Fischer finally gained the assistance of two distinguished South Africans: Harold Hanson, a highly respected advocate, and Alan Paton, the writer. As leader of the Liberal Party, a devout believer in non-violence and a known anti-communist, Paton had often been critical of the accused, but when approached for his help Paton asked one simple question: 'Are their lives in danger?' On being told yes, Paton said, 'In that case, there is no question at all. I will give evidence if I am called.' Joel Joffe remarked later, 'He was almost the last of a breed that had become nearly extinct in South Africa – the liberal of principle and courage, who is not afraid to raise his voice against the stream.'

Paton spoke of Mandela, Sisulu and Mbeki as 'men well known for their courage, determination and ability'. He added, 'I have never had any doubt about their sincerity, their deep devotion to the cause of their people and their desire to see that South Africa become a country in which all people participate.' He told the judge that the exercise of clemency in this case was of great importance for the future of the country.

In a move virtually unprecedented in the South African courts, Yutar rose to launch an attack on Paton's character. 'I propose to cross-examine this witness with Your Lordship's leave. And I don't do so in order to aggravate the sentence, but in order to unmask this gentleman and make perfectly clear that his only reason for going into the witness box, in my submission, is to make political propaganda from the witness box.'

Yutar implied that Paton was a fellow-traveller of the Communist Party and that he moved readily in communist circles. He questioned his actions in asking countries abroad to maintain their concern about the injustices of apartheid. As the smears continued, Paton became angry and confused. The security police witnessing the spectacle tittered.

It was left to Harold Hanson to restore some sense of propriety to the proceedings. He spoke eloquently, saying a nation's grievances could not be suppressed, people would always find a way to give voice to those grievances. 'It was not their aims which had been criminal,' said Hanson, 'only the means to which they had resorted.' He reminded the judge that his own Afrikaner people, during their struggle against British imperialism, had conducted armed uprising, rebellion and treason and had appeared for such offences before courts which had decided to show leniency. Two Boer generals, de Wet and Kemp, charged with high treason after leading an armed rebellion against the government in 1914, had been sentenced to no more than six years' imprisonment.

De Wet appeared to pay scant attention to these arguments. He neither looked up nor made notes. When Hanson had finished, he nodded to the accused to rise.

I have heard a great deal during the course of this case about the grievances of the non-European population. The accused have told me and their counsel have told me that the accused, who were all leaders of the non-European population, were motivated entirely by a desire to ameliorate these grievances. I am by no means convinced that the motives of the accused were as altruistic as they wish the court to believe. People who organize a revolution usually take over the government and personal ambition cannot be excluded as a motive.

De Wet paused for a moment, then continued, his voice quieter than before, making it hard for the public gallery to hear what he was saying:

The function of this court, as is the function of the court in any other country, is to enforce law and order and to enforce the laws of the state within which it functions. The crime of which the accused have been convicted, that is the main crime, the crime of conspiracy, is in essence one of high treason. The state has decided not to charge the crime in this form. Bearing this in mind and giving the matter very serious consideration, I have decided not to impose the supreme penalty . . .

There was a gasp of relief, but the judge was continuing:

which in a case like this would usually be the proper penalty for the crime, but consistent with my duty that is the only leniency which I can show. The sentence in the case of all the accused will be one of life imprisonment.

Mandela smiled at his comrades and turned to look for Winnie and his mother in the gallery. But there was consternation among many there who had not heard the sentence. Goldberg's mother cried out in desperation, 'Denis! What is it?' 'Life!' he shouted back, 'Life! To live!' Then they all disappeared out of sight for the last time, down the courtroom steps to the cells below.

Their lawyers stood in silence, then each shook hands silently with Bram Fischer. 'It had been his responsibility in the first place to save their lives,' remarked Joffe, 'and it was his victory in the first place that they would live.'

The outcome of the Rivonia trial made little impact on white public opinion other than to reassure the white population that the government had succeeded in overcoming serious threats to their well-being. The press praised the police, the prosecutor and the judge. Reaction abroad, however, was very different. 'The verdict of history,' prophesied the London *Times*, 'will be that the ultimate guilty party is the government in power – and that already is the verdict of world opinion.' The *New York Times* concurred: 'To most of the world, these men are heroes and freedom fighters. The George Washingtons and Ben Franklins of South Africa.'

From his own lonely outpost in the mission village of Groutville, to which he was restricted, Chief Luthuli, who had remained so adamantly opposed to violence, issued his own verdict:

> In the face of the uncompromising white refusal to abandon a policy which denies the African and other oppressed South Africans their rightful heritage – freedom – no one can blame brave just men for seeking justice by the use of violent methods; nor could they be blamed if they tried to create an organized force in order to ultimately establish peace and racial harmony.
>
> For this, they are sentenced to be shut away for long years in the brutal and degrading prisons of South Africa. With them will be interred this country's hopes for racial cooperation.

His words could not be quoted in South Africa and so went unheard.

In the early hours of 13 June 1964, Mandela and the other African prisoners were taken from their cells in Pretoria Local and put on a military transport aircraft for the flight to Robben Island. As dawn came, they could see below the mountains and forests of the Western Cape. The terrain excited Mandela. He saw it 'not as a tourist but as a strategist, looking for areas where a guerrilla army might hide itself'. Even after being sentenced to life imprisonment for a forlorn and futile campaign of violence against the government, he could still not shake off his ambition to be a guerrilla leader.

In terms of the objectives that Mandela set out in court during the Rivonia trial, Umkhonto's sabotage campaign was a total failure. The impact on the economy was negligible. Foreign investors, far from being frightened away, became more deeply involved. Foreign governments, while vociferous in condemning apartheid, were still content to sit on the sidelines. There was much debate about economic sanctions but little action.

The white electorate remained largely unaffected by the sporadic nature of sabotage attacks and reacted by demanding not reform, as Mandela had anticipated, but tougher action, thus allowing the government to take ever more repressive counter-measures in the name of law and order. At each successive election, the National Party gained higher levels of white support.

By making unlimited use of the ninety-day detention laws, the security police soon broke the back of all underground resistance. Subjected to solitary confinement and prolonged interrogation, allowed no visitors or reading material except the Bible, detainees were constantly taunted with the threat that they could be held in such conditions indefinitely. Their 'cracking point' varied. Writing of her own experience of being held incommunicado for 117 days, Ruth First, a member of the Communist Party's central committee, noted, 'Men holding key positions in the political movement, who had years of hard political experience and sacrifice behind them, cracked like eggshells. Others, with quiet, reticent, self-effacing natures, who had been woolly in making decisions and slow to carry them out, emerged from long spells of isolation shaken but unbroken.' Where interrogation methods failed, torture usually succeeded. 'Under torture,' said Ben Turok, 'many victims found to their regret that they knew too much and that the police knew that they knew.'

In the wake of the Rivonia raid, Umkhonto endeavoured to establish a new high command, whose members included Wilton Mkwayi, a China-trained saboteur, and David Kitson, a young Communist Party instructor who had been due to attend the Lilliesleaf meeting in July 1963 but had fortuitously been confined to bed with influenza. A key figure in setting up the new arrangement was Bram Fischer, who, even during the course of the Rivonia trial, remained actively involved in the underground. Fischer and Kitson would meet in Greek cafés on Nuggett Street in Johannesburg, where Fischer would pass on funds for Umkhonto obtained from abroad and even copies of maps and sabotage targets captured from Lilliesleaf which had been handed to Fischer by the prosecution in the normal course of court proceedings. However ingenious such activities were, they came to naught. Soon after the end of the Rivonia trial, Kitson and Mkwayi were arrested. By mid-1964, Umkhonto was effectively crushed.

276

The same fate befell the other sabotage group, the National Committee of Liberation, or the African Resistance Movement as it eventually became known. The ARM was little more than a collection of white middle-class dissidents, about fifty in number, former communists, Trotskyists and Liberal Party radicals who had set themselves the task of helping to bring about the downfall of apartheid without any clear idea of how this was to be achieved other than by random sabotage strikes. Following the departure abroad of its founder, Monty Berman, the ARM's main organizer became a twenty-four-year-old former student leader based in Cape Town, Adrian Leftwich. Leftwich was a competent administrator who kept detailed records of ARM members and activities in his flat.

Though some members began questioning the wisdom of continuing with sabotage, Leftwich remained an ardent enthusiast. In April 1964, at an ARM meeting in Johannesburg, when a Coloured member, Eddie Daniels, argued that sabotage was a counterproductive strategy that should be abandoned, Leftwich attacked his attitude as cowardly. What he proposed instead was a series of sabotage attacks to coincide with the sentencing of the Rivonia trialists. On 10 June, a number of power pylons were toppled.

The security police responded with a series of raids on the homes and offices of dissidents they had so far neglected. Leftwich's flat, with its large archive of ARM documents, was one of them. Within a few days, Leftwich had 'cracked', supplying his interrogators with all the information on members, addresses and operations they required to roll up the organization. Leftwich went on to compound this betrayal of his friends and colleagues by testifying against them in one trial after another, gaining his own freedom in exile in return.

The end of the sabotage era was marked by an incident which to most whites justified all the security measures the government had enforced. On 24 July, one of the few remaining activists still at large, John Harris, a Liberal Party member, filled a suitcase with explosives and a detonator and left it in the white section of Johannesburg's main railway station. It exploded, killing an elderly woman, maiming a child and injuring a score of other whites. Harris was subsequently hanged, the only white saboteur ever to be executed in South Africa. More than any other episode, the bombing was used by the government to assert the evil nature of all anti-apartheid opponents.

One last defiant stand was taken against the government, a personal stand made by Bram Fischer. For the duration of the Rivonia trial, Fischer had acquired a form of immunity which no one expected to last once the trial was over. He had managed to avoid being identified by farm workers and servants at Lilliesleaf called as witnesses in the trial by making sure he was engaged on other legal business elsewhere when they appeared in court. But his handwriting on documents found at Lilliesleaf provided evidence less easily circumvented. One document identified by a handwriting expert as being written by Harold Wolpe was passed by the prosecutor in court to Fischer, who looked at it without a trace of concern and then passed it to the rest of his team, who, aghast, saw only too clearly that it had been written by Fischer. But the prosecution had other examples of Fischer's handwriting which they chose, for reasons of convenience, not to identify at the time. Percy Yutar would simply say, 'There is a document here, My Lord, which is in somebody else's handwriting . . .'

Fischer's fate, in fact, was already sealed. Unknown to him, the senior ranks of the Communist Party had been penetrated by a police agent, Gerard Ludi, providing the security police with enough information to wipe out its entire structure. What evidence they lacked was subsequently obtained from a senior figure in the Communist Party, Piet Beyleveld, who agreed to testify against his former colleagues, including Fischer, in exchange for his own freedom. A member of the party's central committee, Bartholomew Hlapane, also defected and was used as a state witness in one trial after another.

Not only was Fischer's political world on the verge of disintegration, but his personal life was suddenly afflicted by personal tragedy. On the day after the sentence in the Rivonia trial was given, Fischer and his wife, Molly, left Johannesburg by car for a holiday in the Cape. On the way there, approaching a bridge over a river, Fischer swerved to avoid a motor-cyclist. The car left the road and plunged into a water-hole some thirty feet deep. Fischer managed to escape, but Molly was pinned in the back and drowned.

In September 1964, Fischer and thirteen other white communists were arrested and charged with membership of the illegal Communist Party. Fischer at the time was acting chairman of the central committee, the last survivor of the original 1950s central committee. Released on bail, he was given permission to fly to London to argue an international patents case before the Privy Council, which his client subsequently won. In London, friends tried to persuade him to remain there, but Fischer believed not only that it would be dishonourable to jump bail but that his place was in South Africa. He returned to face trial.

But in January 1965, Fischer decided to go underground in a last act of defiance against the might of the apartheid state. He explained his reasons in a letter to the court:

> What is needed is for white South Africans to shake themselves out of their complacency ... Unless this whole intolerable system is changed radically and rapidly, disaster must follow ... To try to avoid this becomes a supreme duty, particularly for an Afrikaner, because it is largely representatives of my fellow Afrikaners who have been responsible for the worst of these discriminatory laws ... If by my fight I can encourage even some people to think about, to understand and to abandon the policies they now so blindly follow, I shall not regret any punishment I may incur.

He concluded, 'I can no longer serve justice in the way I have attempted to do during the past thirty years. I can do it only in the way I have now chosen.'

Using a variety of disguises. Fischer evaded capture until November 1965. Brought to trial, he was found guilty of conspiring, along with the Rivonia trialists he had defended, to commit sabotage and, at the age of fifty-seven, sentenced to life imprisonment.

Fischer was the last of the conspirators to remain at large in South Africa. By 1965 no active revolutionaries survived there. Those activists who managed to evade arrest soon fled the country, joining a small coterie of exiles based in London. Rusty Bernstein, released on bail after the Rivonia trial, was one of them. Others, like Ruth First and Wolfie Kodesh, accepted the government's offer of a one-way exit permit.

How widespread resistance against the government had been was shown in a series of trials across the country. Nearly 8,000 people were charged with offences linked to political defiance. Most were convicted and imprisoned, some for life, some for fifteen or twenty years, others for lesser periods. Nearly fifty men were sentenced to death. Most of the trials were held in relative obscurity.

In trying to explain the collapse of Umkhonto, Joe Slovo spoke of 'an heroic failure'. The reality, however, was that right from the start the conspirators had made a fatal miscalculation about the power of the government and the ways in which the government was willing to use it. They also underestimated the effectiveness of police techniques. 'Having talked of fascism for a decade or more, the movements were nevertheless caught by surprise when the police behaved like fascists,' noted Ben Turok. All the other mistakes and errors committed by the conspirators – the 'mood of carelessness and bravado' which Slovo admitted had overtaken the conspirators, the neglect of political work among their African constituency that Kotane wanted to continue, the failure to develop a real underground organization of the kind that Mandela had once proposed – all this merely compounded the process of defeat. Whatever reasons were given, what was ultimately proved was that a collection of amateur revolutionaries were no match for the brute strength of the South African state.

The price for this miscalculation was huge. With the nationalist movement destroyed, a silence descended for more than a decade. On Robben Island, Mandela and his colleagues became largely forgotten men.

CHAPTER 13
Prisoner 466/64

The winter of 1964 on Robben Island, when Mandela and six other Rivonia prisoners arrived there, was the coldest that anyone could remember. So fierce were the Atlantic winds sweeping across the island that prisoners working in the quarries were numbed to the bone, hardly able to raise their picks; at night they huddled together in groups, desperate for warmth. On the day that the Dakota aircraft bringing the Rivonia men landed, it was bitterly cold, wet and windy.

In the year since Mandela had left the island, a new maximum-security prison had been constructed, close to Murray's Bay harbour, not far from the old prison buildings. A special section within it, a single-storey rectangular block with a cement courtyard in the centre, had been built at the south-eastern corner of the compound to house prisoners whom the authorities wanted to isolate from the mass of the prison population. This prison within a prison was intended to be the home of the Rivonia group for the rest of their lives.

Mandela's cell, like the others in B Section, was no more than about seven feet square. A barred window looked out on to a cement courtyard and beyond it to a high wall patrolled by guards. The walls of the cell were damp. There was no bed. Mandela was provided with a sisal mat on which to sleep, three flimsy blankets, a toilet bucket and a plastic bottle of water. In the winter months, his cell was so cold he slept fully dressed in prison garb. Outside the cell was fixed a white card giving his name and identification number: 466/64.

As well as the Rivonia group, a number of other political

prisoners were brought to the isolation section, or the *koeloekoetz*, as it was known, from the main communal prison blocks. Among them were Zephenia Mothopeng, a PAC leader; Dennis Brutus, a Coloured poet and writer, once active in campaigning for a sports boycott of South Africa, who had been imprisoned for contravening his banning orders; Neville Alexander and Fikile Bam, both members of an obscure Maoist group known as the Yu Chi Chan Club, which had dabbled with the idea of guerrilla warfare; and Andrew Masondo, a mathematics lecturer from Fort Hare University, who had become an MK saboteur. In the following months this group was joined by other senior MK figures, including Wilton Mkwayi, Joe Gqabi, Mac Maharaj and Michael Dingake. Another arrival was Eddie Daniels, a Coloured member of the ill-fated African Resistance Movement. Together with the Rivonia group, this motley collection of prisoners, numbering in all about thirty, provided Mandela's companions for the years ahead.

Though the prison buildings were new, the regime remained as harsh and as brutal as before. Prisoners in the general section were crowded into large communal cells where few toilets were available. Food rations were meagre. Prisoners reporting sick were often turned away by hospital orderlies, castigated for laziness when they were seriously ill; some gained admission to hospital only when it was too late to save them.

Several incidents had occurred to add to the island's infamous reputation. For work purposes, prisoners were divided up into different teams or *spans*, as they were known. Most were sent to work in the stone quarries; others went to the harbour, the laundry or the stores. The work most dreaded was with the *landbouspan*, the agricultural team run by Piet Kleynhans, one of three Kleynhans brothers then employed on Robben Island. One of the tasks of the *landbouspan* was to push a huge grass roller, seven feet high and weighing several tons, on which Kleynhans would sit perched on the crossbar, shouting and swearing and flicking a leather whip at the prisoners. The roller was so heavy that as many as fifty prisoners were needed to move it, hauling it by a heavy handle and long chains attached to each side and pushing from the back. The work began in the early morning and went on for hour after hour, with guards routinely lashing out at prisoners with canes and hosepipes, cursing them for their laziness.

One morning, Kleynhans singled out for punishment a PAC leader, Johnson Mlambo, whom he had heard complaining about the work. While other prisoners continued hauling the roller round in circles, Kleynhans instructed two convicts to dig a hole deep enough to hold a man and then ordered Mlambo to get into it. The convicts then filled in the hole with soil, leaving only Mlambo's head jutting out above the ground. He remained there for the rest of the morning, his head baking in the sun. At midday, Kleynhans, clearly enjoying himself, went up to Mlambo and asked him, 'Kaffir, soek jy water?' – 'Kaffir, do you want water?' 'Nee ek sal jou nie water gee nie, ek sal hou whisky gee, die beste whisky!' – 'No, I won't give you water, I'll give you whisky, the very best!' As other warders looked on laughing, Kleynhans pulled out his penis and urinated on Mlambo's face. Shortly afterwards, at the lunch break, Mlambo was dug out of the hole and told to join other prisoners for the afternoon work shift on the roller. Mlambo was later to lose an eye; it was gouged out by another PAC prisoner during a fight over food.

In March 1964, the prison authorities ordered a carry-on – a mass assault – involving political prisoners who had complained about work conditions in the stone quarry. One of their main targets was Andrew Masondo, whose arm was severely injured in the beatings that took place. The carry-on was witnessed by Dennis Brutus, who had arrived on Robben Island only the day before: 'We saw dozens of prisoners running wild or crawling vainly under barbed-wire fences while the batons, staves and pick-handles of the warders fell indiscriminately and mercilessly.' Later in the day, Brutus himself, still recovering from a police bullet wound in the stomach, was caught up in the carry-on when he and other prisoners were ordered to wade into the sea to collect seaweed. There, in the water, they were set upon by warders armed with batons and rubber pipes:

> I do not think I will ever be able to erase from my mind the images that day of terror and violence by the sea with the bright water and the bright sunlight, and the men struggling with shiny masses of seaweed and on the sharp slippery rocks . . . and all the time men were beaten and kicked and the batons thwacked.

All attempts at taking legal action against the prison authorities were thwarted.

Prisoners queueing at the dispensary for medical attention were frequently assaulted. One warder named Mostert, a huge ox of a man, made a practice of walking along the queue, punching prisoners as he went, until only the most courageous remained standing. He used to say, to justify his conduct, 'If you don't run away, then you are really sick, you actually need treatment.'

Since Mandela's first incarceration on Robben Island, the prison staff had become exclusively white. No longer were there any Coloured warders to offer a friendly hand. An atmosphere of racial hostility was ever present. White warders regarded themselves as members of a master race and accordingly required prisoners to adopt a servile manner. They insisted on being addressed as '*baas*' and referred contemptuously to prisoners as '*kaffirs*', '*hotnots*' and '*koelies*'. They were used to dealing with hardened criminals, employing only the most brutal methods, and treated political prisoners with similar vindictiveness, handing out punishment at the slightest sign of defiance. Their objective was to destroy the morale of prisoners, to strip them of dignity and self-respect. It was what the system required.

From previous experience, Mandela knew how crushing the effects of prison life could be. The burden to be carried was not just constant abuse from warders and hardship at work, but the sheer tedium of prison routine, stretching for ever into the distance, week after week, month after month, year after year. Mandela's first prison sentence had at least been limited to a fixed term of five years. The Rivonia trial had meanwhile engaged his full attention, keeping him close to lawyers, relatives and friends. But back on Robben Island, the full impact of his new sentence now took its toll. At the age of forty-six, the prospect before him was spending the rest of his life in a cell.

The first weeks were particularly difficult. Prisoners in the isolation section were subjected to rigid control, their every move dictated by a posse of warders ready to pounce on any infringement of the regulations. The routine was deadening. The morning bell rang at 5.30 a.m. Prisoners were required to roll up their mats and blankets and clean their cells, but were not allowed out until 6.45 a.m. Mandela used the time for exercising. In the cramped space of his cell, he found that by standing at an angle he could wave his arms about. At 6.45 a.m., prisoners were let out to clean their toilet buckets in sinks at the end of the corridor, giving them a brief opportunity for a few whispered words if warders were not lingering about there. Back in their cells, breakfast, consisting of maize porridge and what was described as coffee, was delivered to them by convicts from the general section. At inspection after breakfast, prisoners were required to doff their cloth caps to warders as they passed by. If the buttons on their canvas jackets were undone or if they failed to doff their caps, they were punished with either loss of meals or solitary confinement.

They were then taken out to the courtyard, where for hour after hour, sitting cross-legged in four rows, forbidden to talk, they bashed away with five-pound hammers at piles of stones in front of them, crushing them into fine gravel. Not until lunch break at noon were they permitted to rest. Lunch consisted once again of boiled maize and a drink known as *phuzamandla* made from maize and a bit of yeast. In the afternoon, they were allowed to exercise for half an hour under strict supervision, walking in silence around the courtyard in single file, before resuming their places at the rock piles.

Work ended at 4 p.m., when they were given half an hour to clean up using the seawater showers and buckets in a bathroom at the end of the corridor. Supper, consisting of maize porridge with a piece of vegetable or meat gristle added, came at 4.30 p.m., delivered to the cells by convicts. At 8 p.m., the night warder ordered everyone to go to sleep, but each cell's single light bulb remained glowing throughout the night. At weekends, prisoners were kept inside their cells all day, except for half an hour of exercise. No prisoner was allowed to possess a watch or clock. Everyone was ruled by bells and the whistles and shouts of warders.

All political prisoners were automatically given the lowest classification, category D, according them a minimum of privileges. Category D prisoners were allowed to have only one visitor in every six months and to write and receive only one letter in the same period. Sometimes letters were handed over so heavily censored that they made no sense; sometimes they were never handed over at all. No study privileges were permitted. The only way for prisoners to gain a higher classification and hence more privileges was through what the authorities deemed to be good behaviour. Prisoners who eventually won a high classification could be threatened with demotion and hence the loss of privileges – visits, letters and studies – if they were insufficiently compliant.

The only solace in this grim schedule was the company of friends. The courage that each man showed fortified the determination of others to stand firm. Walter Sisulu, in particular, proved a constant source of strength for Mandela and for many other prisoners, always ready to comfort them in moments of anguish and despair, no matter how hard his own burden at the time. 'Even when his own wife and children were put in jail, he was an inspiration,' recalled Kathrada. 'I could always turn to him for help.'

But inmates in the *koeloekoetz* were far from being a harmonious group. The old rivalry between the PAC and the ANC provoked continual bouts of friction. In the general section, hostility between the two groups was an open sore. The reaction of PAC members to the outcome of the Rivonia trial was typical. 'They were very disappointed when none of the Rivonia people were sentenced to death,' recalled an ANC prisoner, Ebrahim Ismail Ebrahim. There was also friction between Neville Alexander and ANC members. Alexander, an intellectual with a doctorate in literature from Germany, initially dismissed ANC prisoners as 'ordinary nationalists inferior to us socialists . . . almost collaborators'. Nor was it long before members of the Rivonia group were embroiled in their own disputes.

Mandela's plan for survival on Robben Island involved challenging the system with a series of complaints aimed at improving prison conditions. Prison life he came to regard as a microcosm of the apartheid system outside, requiring a similar struggle for basic rights. Striving for better conditions gave him both a set of attainable objectives and a sense of purpose otherwise missing in the monotony of prison routine. He hoped to achieve results through negotiation rather than confrontation. This meant according a measure of respect to the prison authorities which several of his own colleagues found difficult to accept. PAC members refused outright to have any dealings with the prison authorities, never lodging complaints of any kind, regarding such contacts as a form of collaboration. Mandela's argument was that not only would each advance raise the morale of prisoners but the process of negotiation itself would require the prison authorities to show a measure of respect for prisoners' interests. It would help break down the walls of prejudice.

The complaints procedure had hitherto been a meaningless ritual. Once a week, prisoners were lined up and asked if they had any complaints or requests. Many complaints were made – about food, about clothes, about blankets, about visits – but no note was ever taken and nothing was ever done. Prisoners who pursued complaints about assaults faced reprisal. No one succeeded in gaining redress.

Mandela's first complaint was about the prison clothes he was given to wear. African prisoners were issued with a pair of short trousers, a coarse collarless khaki shirt, a canvas jacket and a thin jersey. In true apartheid tradition, Indian prisoners, like Kathrada, were allowed long trousers. Mandela objected to wearing short trousers on the grounds that they were demeaning, intended to remind Africans of their position as 'boys'. Though his initial protest was ignored, after two weeks he was given a pair of long trousers. Since no other African prisoner was given long trousers, he declined to accept them and continued to wear short trousers. But he had made a start. When he complained about the dampness of his cell, he was told by a prison official, 'The dampness of the cells will eventually be absorbed by your bodies.'

Along with other political prisoners in the isolation section, he refused to address warders as *baas*. In the general section, any such refusal would incur swift punishment – a beating, a loss of meals or solitary confinement if necessary. But the *koeloekoetz* men stood firm and warders left the issue alone. When the quotas of stone-crushing set for prisoners working in the courtyard were repeatedly raised, they resolved not to meet them. The warders threatened them, but did not succeed in getting their way.

With each case of complaint, Mandela took on the authorities in a polite but resolute manner, in the process gaining not only the attention of warders but the respect of critics within the prisoner community. Neville Alexander, who was serving a ten-year sentence, recalled, 'We were terribly impetuous and would have run ourselves suicidally against the prison walls.' But Mandela and Sisulu had argued that, by adopting a dignified and disciplined approach, 'eventually we would break through'. The impact that both men made on Alexander was considerable: 'Nelson and Walter taught me to respect people, to disagree with them, but to continue to respect them.'

Though prison regulations stipulated that each prisoner was permitted to speak only for himself, not on behalf of others, the prison authorities soon found it expedient to use Mandela as a spokesman for prisoner interests. When an official from the International Red Cross arrived on Robben Island, Mandela was singled out to talk to him and on subsequent occasions he continued to act as the prisoners' representative. Mandela dwelt at length on prisoners' grievances over food, clothing, letters and such matters as the conduct of warders, unsure of whether any worthwhile result might be achieved. Not long afterwards, African prisoners were issued with long trousers.

He became adept at concealing his emotions behind a mask, rarely letting any sign of anger or bitterness emerge and never betraying doubt or despair before others. He built around himself a wall of self-discipline, steeling himself to face whatever ordeal prison might hold. He came to distrust emotion, prizing reason and logic above all else, recognizing that bitterness would bring him no closer to his goal. Time and again, he held back his anger at the taunts and insults from prison staff. Warders enjoyed goading Mandela by letting him know that they were withholding a letter for him – his main lifeline to the outside world. 'It required all my self-discipline not to explode at such times,' he wrote. 'Afterwards, I would protest through the proper channels, and sometimes get it.'

With other prisoners, Mandela exercised the same degree of self-control, never showing any sign of weakness, always conscious of the effect his leadership had on them. Only Sisulu was privy to the inner man. With everyone else, even with old friends like Kathrada, Mandela distanced himself with a measure of aloofness. Kathrada noted his ability in prison to react in a cool manner, no matter how serious the issue was: 'He would return from a meeting with a prison official, having heard of some momentous issue or having had a message of great importance, then come back to the cells, joke with us, talk to us, then relate what had happened very casually.' Kathrada often found it difficult to tell what was in his mind.

His darkest moments, he faced alone. Some of them came during periods of solitary confinement. As he wrote in a manuscript while in prison:

> The worst part of imprisonment is being locked up by yourself. You come face to face with time and there is nothing more terrifying than to be alone with sheer time. Then the ghosts come crowding in. They can be very sinister, very mischievous, raising a thousand doubts in your mind about the people outside, their loyalty. Was your sacrifice worth the trouble? What would your life have been like if you hadn't got involved?

He also had to endure times of great personal anguish, but never betrayed how deeply he had been hurt.

Whatever doubts and despair he suffered, in the company of others he remained steadfast, always seeking to bolster their morale. And he never gave up hope that one day he would emerge from prison a free man. 'I never thought that a life sentence truly meant life and that I would die behind bars,' he said in his autobiography. 'Perhaps I was denying this prospect because it was too unpleasant to contemplate.'

Yet, events in prison were not the only cause of Mandela's concerns. In August 1964, two months after he had been back on the island, Mandela was allowed a visit from Winnie. They met in a cramped cubicle in the visiting room, separated by a partition, able to see each other only through a pane of thick, smudged glass. Their conversation was carried on through holes drilled in the partition. Both had been warned that the only topics permitted were family and personal matters. Warders stood by on either side of the partition, listening carefully to what was said, ready to interrupt if unfamiliar names were mentioned or if the conversation seemed to stray beyond bounds. They were given just thirty minutes together.

Winnie appeared to Mandela to be under tremendous strain. He had known that his imprisonment would leave her exposed to hardship and hazards with few sources of support. In a letter written to her on the eve of his first term of imprisonment, he had tried to offer her every encouragement for the long and lonely road she faced, urging her to act with fortitude and dignity and warning of the traps that would be set for her. It was a letter full of love and inspiration which Winnie cherished, reading it time and again until it was seized by security police during one of their periodic raids on her house in Orlando West.

What worried Mandela most was that Winnie's impetuous and headstrong nature would lead her into ever deeper trouble. In the treacherous world of South African politics, she was a novice, naïve and gullible, and easy prey for the security police. The story often told about her during her early years of marriage was that while Mandela was engaged in serious debate in the front room of their house, Winnie would be found in the back reading a women's magazine. She had joined the ANC Women's League and done a two-week spell in prison for her part in protesting against pass laws, but among political activists she was regarded as being a lightweight.

Once Mandela was in prison, however, Winnie became more ambitious. She saw herself as Mandela's heir, capable of acting on his behalf. Towards other activists, she adopted a superior manner, making herself unpopular with them. 'Winnie always acted on her own,' recalled Rusty Bernstein. 'She wouldn't cooperate with anyone. She refused to take advice. She was an individual piece of militancy, a rogue element.'

She also had a propensity for becoming involved with shady characters. She maintained a long friendship with Maude Katzellen-bogen, the partner of a corrupt Indian businessman, Moosa Dinath, convicted of fraud, who had once tried to inveigle her into a reckless scheme to free Mandela from prison in Johannesburg, even though she knew he had dubious connections with the government.

She also developed a close relationship with Brian Somana, a journalist who had acted as her driver on journeys to see Mandela at Lilliesleaf Farm. Somana had been arrested in June 1963, shortly before the police raid on Lilliesleaf took place. In activist circles, he was widely suspected of being a police informer, possibly the source of their information on Lilliesleaf.

On Robben Island, Mandela was aware of both Somana's role as a police informer and Winnie's involvement with him. One of his own colleagues in the isolation section, Fikile Bam, had encountered them while he was on the run from the police in August 1963. A graduate of the University of Cape Town, he had known Winnie since his youth in the Transkei; his sister had been her close friend. While a student at St Peter's in Johannesburg, he had been befriended by Oliver Tambo, who had enabled him to gain experience of the workings of the law by arranging for him to help out at the firm of Mandela and Tambo on Saturdays. He subsequently became involved with Neville Alexander's Maoist group in Cape Town.

Wanted by the police for distributing literature on guerrilla warfare in Cape Town, he fled to Johannesburg, where Winnie, hearing of his predicament, offered to arrange his escape to neighbouring Bechuanaland and turned to Somana for help. On the day arranged for his escape, Somana turned up driving Winnie's car, with Mandela's two daughters in the back. They had travelled only a short distance when they ran straight into a roadblock manned by police, who had clearly been expecting them. Bam was to spend ten years on Robben Island.

Word soon spread that Winnie was not to be trusted, making her more isolated and vulnerable than before. Bram Fischer warned her about Somana and tried to persuade her to leave South Africa to get her out of the way, but she refused to heed him. In London, Oliver Tambo told colleagues that they should no longer take Winnie into their confidence.

Despite all this, Winnie and Somana remained close. According to Somana's wife, they lived together in Winnie's Orlando house from May 1964, when the Rivonia trial was still under way, until December 1964. On one occasion, Somana was arrested in Winnie's house during a 5 a.m. police raid. Winnie was subsequently cited in Somana's divorce case, though she flatly denied adultery. She also became involved with Somana in a business enterprise which he was able to finance from a sudden and unexplained flow of funds. According to Winnie's testimony in a subsequent court case, concerning an arson attack on her garage, their business partnership foundered 'because of rumours that it was financed out of reward money offered by the police for the capture of Walter Sisulu'.

There was nothing that Mandela could do from Robben Island to curb Winnie's wayward conduct. He blamed himself for being unable to offer her the protection she evidently needed, and his sense of guilt and frustration mounted as the security police instigated a campaign of persecution against Winnie which continued year after year.

The first banning order on Winnie, issued in 1963, restricted her movements to the Johannesburg area and prohibited her from attending meetings and social gatherings. Only by obtaining official permission was she allowed to travel to Pretoria to attend the Rivonia trial or to Cape Town to visit Mandela in prison on Robben Island. A second banning order, in 1965, restricted her movements further, forcing her to leave her job as a social worker with the Child Welfare Society in Johannesburg, a position she cherished. She took a succession of other jobs, working in a furniture shop, a dry-cleaning shop and a shoe-repair shop, but at each place she was fired after security police paid a visit to her employers. She was charged on several occasions with violating her banning order, often for no more than trivial infringements, usually ending up with a suspended sentence or a fine.

Her house was often raided. In her autobiography, she recalled an incident in which a white police sergeant walked into her bedroom without knocking while she was half-dressed and put his hand on her shoulder: 'All I remember is grabbing him, and throwing him on the floor, which is what he deserved. I remember seeing his legs up in the air and him screaming, and the whole dressing-stand falling on him. That is how he broke his neck (he did recover).'

In the subsequent court case, Winnie was defended by George Bizos. She wrote:

> I would listen to him as I would listen to my father. He treats me in the same way as Nelson does. He weighs the same authority with us. So he says to me outside court, 'I want you to behave like a lady in front of the magistrate and not like an Amazon!' Nelson always says to me – 'Zami, you are completely and utterly undisciplined! You need a great deal of taming!' I don't think I'm undisciplined. But you have to use the language they understand: to have peace, you must be violent.

Winnie won the case.

As well as harassing Winnie, the security police turned their attention to her two daughters, Zeni and Zindzi. The terms of Winnie's banning order prohibited her from entering any educational establishment, so she was always obliged to depend on relatives or friends to help with the children at school. The first nursery school which Zeni attended asked her to leave after a few days, according to Winnie, on instructions from the security police. Both Zeni and Zindzi were later expelled from a Coloured primary school after the police intervened. Eventually, they were taken to schools in Swaziland, where Mandela's other three children were being educated.

The anguish that Mandela suffered on learning of these events was acute. 'To see your family, your children, being persecuted when you are absolutely helpless in jail, that is one of the most bitter experiences, most painful experiences I have had,' he recalled.

After six months of pounding stones in the prison courtyard, Mandela and his colleagues in the isolation section were sent to work in the lime quarry. Each morning they set out on a twenty-minute march towards the centre of the island where the quarry was sited. Warders made sure they were kept well away from all other groups of prisoners, isolating them like lepers. On the way, they passed near the small house where the PAC leader, Robert Sobukwe, was being held in relative comfort but confined to a solitary existence, with no one to talk to other than warders and the occasional visitor he was permitted. He complained to one visitor that he was forgetting how to speak. Occasionally the *koeloekoetz* group caught a glimpse of him in his garden.

The lime quarry was a huge crater carved out of a hillside, blindingly white in the sunlight. There was no shade other than a few tin sheds at the base. The heat in summer was stifling; in winter, it became bitterly cold. All day long, with only a break for lunch, the prisoners toiled away with picks and shovels, digging out seams of lime from the rock, their faces and bodies covered in white dust, their eyes aching from the dazzling glare. In the late afternoon, they trudged back to the prison cells, exhausted.

The glare, in particular, caused them severe problems. 'The reflection from the lime catches the sunlight and throws it back on to you and it can be extremely sharp and scorching,' said Maharaj, who spent twelve years on the island. To protect their eyes, the lime quarry prisoners repeatedly put in requests for sunglasses. It took three years before permission was granted and even then the prison authorities made the prisoners pay for the sunglasses themselves.

For all the hardship that working in the lime quarry involved, it also provided the prisoners with an opportunity to engage in day-long discussion and debate. Working in small groups of four or five, they talked endlessly about the politics and history of the African struggle for rights, analysing the past in terms of what successes and failures had occurred. They had time too to dwell on a whole range of other issues, some serious, some trivial. They debated the merits of circumcision, argued over beauty competitions and spent days trying to sort out whether tigers were indigenous to Africa. Discussions in the quarry became the main event of the day. 'The lime quarry was, even at the worst of times, a site for intellectual stimulation,' recalled Michael Dingake.

Mandela gained the reputation of being a hard taskmaster in these discussions. He gave short shrift to anyone putting up flimsy arguments. Some prisoners regarded him as being dogmatic and overbearing. 'He can be harsh with colleagues,' agreed Sisulu, 'even with me.' Writing about his experiences on Robben Island, Dingake referred to Mandela's 'direct, fiercely candid approach' and recalled arguments with him from which he emerged 'bloodied' and 'humiliated'. 'In argument against someone with insubstantial facts, Nelson can be vicious,' he wrote. 'Very few people like to be cross-examined and exposed in their vagueness and ignorance.'

Mandela had no time, added Dingake, for idle chat or gossip. 'Every day, but every day,' he wrote, 'he had numerous appointments with individuals, always on his own initiative, to discuss inter-organizational relations, prisoners' complaints, joint strategies against prison authorities and general topics.'

Not all the discussions were amicable. A serious rift developed between Mandela and Govan Mbeki which resulted in a direct challenge to Mandela's leadership. Mbeki was even more inclined to be dogmatic in argument than Mandela. A hard, uncompromising communist, intolerant of contrary opinion, he clashed with Mandela over the issue of Operation Mayibuye. Mbeki was adamant that the plan had been officially approved. Mandela disagreed. The feud between them opened up a fault line within the small ANC community in the isolation section. Mbeki was supported by other hardline communists, including Raymond Mhlaba, Joe Gqabi and Andrew Masondo. A fierce row flared up in the quarry between Mandela and Gqabi, who considered himself, after six months' training in China, to be better qualified on guerrilla warfare tactics than Mandela. On one issue after another, the rift widened. An acrimonious dispute developed over the relationship between the ANC and the Communist Party, with Mbeki insisting that they were one and the same and Mandela maintaining they were separate entities with the same objectives. At times the feud degenerated into accusation and counter-accusation. Some inmates were accused of being ready to abandon the armed struggle; others of fomenting racial hostility. A memorandum smuggled out of prison to ANC officials in exile spoke of 'extreme tension and bitterness' between Mandela and Mbeki. For several years they were hardly on speaking terms. Eventually the feud was brought formally to an end and Mandela's leadership reaffirmed, but the fault line remained. 'It resurfaced time after time again,' said Maharaj.

The warders in charge of the lime quarry *span* differed in deciding how much discussion to allow prisoners. One warder, known to them as 'Mazithulele' – 'the quiet one' – for his soft-spoken and tolerant manner, usually positioned himself at some distance from the group and took a lenient view of how much work they did. He was there on the first day that Michael Dingake worked in the lime quarry, shortly after his arrival on Robben Island in 1966. 'The whole morning I did nothing but give a report to Mandela and Sisulu,' he wrote. 'Three of us had our right feet on our spades and conversed. Mazithulele sat under a bush and never interfered.'

His replacement, however, a warder named van Rensburg, who sported a swastika tattoo on his wrist, enforced much harsher discipline. He stood close to the prisoners, constantly shouting at them to work harder and accusing anyone he considered was not exerting himself of 'malingering'. All this was accompanied by a stream of racial abuse. Van Rensburg issued so many charges against prisoners that they responded by forming a legal committee, consisting of Mandela, Bam and Maharaj, to advise them on how to defend themselves before the prison's administrative court. Mandela's advice was always the same: ask the court for 'further particulars', a tactic which often had van Rensburg stumped.

Even under van Rensburg's supervision, the prisoners managed to keep up their discussions and the work songs that lightened their day. But the risk of punishment was never far away. One day, the long-running debate over the question of tigers in Africa took on political overtones. As tempers ran high, everyone stopped working and ignored calls from the warders to get back to work. Finally, van Rensburg marched over and bellowed in English, 'You talk much, but you work too few!' At which point, the prisoners collapsed in laughter. The upshot was that Mandela and Masondo were taken away in handcuffs for a spell of solitary confinement on a spare diet of rice water.

When they were first taken to the lime quarry, the prisoners were told that their work there would last six months. Officials of the International Committee of the Red Cross were given regular assurances by the prison authorities that digging at the lime quarry had stopped, but Mandela and other members of the Rivonia group were to spend thirteen years there.

During a tour of inspection of Robben Island in 1965, the Commissioner of Prisons, General Steyn, questioned Mandela, in his role as spokesman for the isolation section, about prisoners' requests for study privileges. 'What is it you want about things like studies?' he asked. 'What is it you want?' Mandela at the time was the only prisoner on Robben Island entitled to study; soon after entering prison in 1962, he had gained permission to complete his law degree with London University and he had pursued his studies intermittently ever since. His colleagues in the isolation section hoped to gain the same right, even though they were category D prisoners. Replying to the general, Mandela said, 'You should let the atmosphere of a university prevail here on the island.'

The following year, the prison authorities granted permission to prisoners to study. They were allowed to register with the University of South Africa for a degree or with the Rapid Results College for secondary school education. Those who had yet to reach secondary-level education were helped by inmate teachers like Neville Alexander. Most prisoners took to the task with enthusiasm, even though it came at the end of a hard day's work at the quarry. 'At night, our cell block seemed more like a study hall than a prison,' recorded Mandela.

The conditions in which prisoners began their studies were primitive. Their cells were permanently damp and in winter bitterly cold. They were given neither desks nor chairs. After complaints, the prison authorities installed in each cell a wooden board attached to walls at chest-height to serve as a makeshift stand-up desk. It took six months of more complaints before they were willing to provide wooden stools and to lower the stand-up desks.

Strict rules were imposed on study activities. Books and periodicals deemed unsuitable were banned. In Mandela's case, study material prescribed by the University of London fell victim to the prison censors, making it difficult for him to meet examination standards. Students were not allowed either to lend books to those who were not students or even to exchange books with prisoners studying the same subject. Students able to afford books they needed were thus unable to help those too poor to buy them. Applications for library books were always carefully scrutinized. Warders were often deliberately obstructive, delaying the delivery of mail and books. Students who failed to abide by study conditions risked losing the privilege altogether.

While working at the lime quarry, prisoners formed their own study groups. 'Our economics class was a very lively class,' wrote Dingake. 'Not even van Rensburg managed to curb the animation of its members. The "laymen" in economics stood and watched as we argued noisily over our supply and demand curves and drew them on the ground to demonstrate their gradients and elasticity.' Mandela and Fikile Bam often worked alongside each other in the quarry, discussing law.

Mandela also took up the study of Afrikaans and encouraged others to do the same. To those colleagues who argued that Afrikaans was the language of their oppressor, Mandela replied that it was a vital means of understanding the mind of their oppressor, useful in the longer term as well as in prison. It was long-term possibilities that Mandela always managed to keep in sight.

With the help of the International Committee of the Red Cross, graduate prisoners were given permission to teach literacy courses to other prisoners. As Govan Mbeki recalled:

> We took people from the lowest level, who came to the island illiterate. I remember one group I had. I started with them when they were illiterate, started them up. And by the time they left Robben Island they were able to write letters home – they didn't require

anybody to write letters for them and to address their envelopes. And they spoke English.

Upon completing each stage of their courses, students were issued with certificates headed 'The University of Robben Island'.

In addition to these approved activities, the *koeloekoetz* men began to develop their own political education courses. The courses grew out of a series of informal talks on ANC history given at the lime quarry by Sisulu, who was renowned for his encyclopedic knowledge of the organization. Other lectures were added. Kathrada talked about the Indian struggle for political rights, Maharaj expounded on Marxism and Mandela taught a course in political economy. The lectures became part of a course of study known as Syllabus A, which was spread over two years. When prisoners in the general section heard of the lectures, they asked to become involved. Copies of the lectures were smuggled out to them.

University activity became the only real source of stimulation that prisoners enjoyed. Many attributed their ability to endure Robben Island to their study privileges. 'It is one single thing that really keeps you together,' said Dikgang Moseneke, who graduated with a school-leaving certificate and then went on to obtain a degree in political science and English.

However, just as much as study privileges were prized by inmates, so they became a weapon in the hands of the prison administration, subject to the whims of prison officials.

The kitchens on Robben Island were notorious not just for turning out food that was barely edible but for corruption. They were manned by common-law convicts who ensured that the tastiest foods were kept back for themselves, their friends and the warders who supervised them. The official rations allowed to prisoners were meagre enough, but what emerged from the kitchens was even less adequate. 'Lunch and supper, especially the supper of African prisoners, were sometimes so full of sand and miscellaneous kinds of dirt and insects that even the strong stomachs of the most hard-bitten would somersault,' said Neville Alexander. 'Hungry people would sometimes leave food uneaten.' Complaints about food were commonplace, but nothing was ever done to improve the system.

298

A particular grievance of political prisoners was the discrimination the authorities applied between food for Africans and food for Coloureds and Indians. African prisoners received what was termed an 'F diet'; Coloureds and Indians were placed higher on the scale with 'D diet'. Both diets were based largely on maize, but D-diet prisoners were given bread and extra helpings of meat, vegetables and coffee. The regulations were quite specific. D-diet prisoners, for example, were allowed one and a half ounces of sugar a day; F-diet prisoners, two ounces. Sharing food with prisoners with different diets was forbidden and resulted in punishment.

It was a shortage of food which in 1966 precipitated the island's first major act of defiance. At the stone quarry, where about 600 prisoners from the general section were working, food for lunch arrived as usual in half-drums transported on two wheeled trolleys. When the bell for lunch rang, the prisoners formed queues, with Coloured and Indian prisoners in front and Africans behind, waiting patiently while a common-law convict doled out food on plates set out in long rows, starting with Coloured and Indian plates and moving on to the African ones. No one was allowed to take a plate until all the food had been laid out.

The food ran out. About 100 plates stood empty. The usual routine when this happened was for warders to send prisoners back to the kitchens for more food, but on this occasion the warder in charge of the quarry *span*, a large red-faced man named Delport, universally hated as a 'slave-driver', gave the order to reduce the F-diet rations already doled out. When two prisoners stepped forward to protest, Delport told them, 'You either take your food or leave it.' Though D-diet prisoners at the front of the queue were not affected, they decided to refuse their food. One by one, prisoners filed past the plates without taking them.

In the afternoon, they resumed work in the quarry having had nothing to eat, then trudged back to the prison and again refused their food. In hurried discussions, ANC, PAC and other prisoners agreed to continue the hunger strike for as long as possible in protest not just against food rations but against all the other grievances they had raised – over working conditions, arbitrary punishment, beatings and other malicious treatment meted out by warders. There were fears that the prison authorities might retaliate by ordering mass assaults. No one was sure what the outcome would be, but the prevailing view among prisoners in the general section was that the time had come to take a stand. The warders, meanwhile, remained confident that the strike would soon collapse.

It was not until the second day of the strike that Mandela and others in the isolation section heard of what was happening. A note wrapped in plastic telling them a hunger strike was under way arrived in their food drum but gave no details. Mandela was sceptical about the value of hunger strikes, arguing that they tended to harm prisoners more than the authorities. He favoured work strikes or go-slow action instead. But on hearing the news, he and others readily agreed to join. When prisoners in the general section in turn learned of Mandela's involvement, their spirits revived.

Each day, the prison authorities produced ever more appetizing food, steaming hot, laced with vegetables and soaked in fat. But still the resolve of prisoners, in both the general and the isolation sections, held firm. Even the sick and elderly insisted on taking part. Patients in hospital who refused food were turned out of their beds and told they would have to work in the quarry. In a pathetic straggle, they stumbled along the road, some in bandages, some crawling, accompanied by a warder shouting, 'No food – no medicine.'

By the fifth day of the strike, the prisoners were beginning to flag. The journey to the quarry, normally half an hour, took an hour. The hospital group hobbled along several hours later. Work in the quarry tailed off. Prisoners started to collapse. In the afternoon, the hospital group was taken back to the prison compound in a van.

On the sixth day, prisoners sat around listlessly in the quarry, not even pretending to work. Nobody had the energy even to speak. Those who collapsed were carted away in wheelbarrows. But just when it seemed to the survivors that they could endure no more, a senior officer arrived and, after a few taunts, asked what their complaints were. Everyone began to shout at once. A deputation of prisoners was organized to present their case at a meeting with prison officials. The officials duly promised to investigate all the complaints the prisoners raised.

For a few days, a more lenient regime prevailed on Robben Island. The food improved, the warders were more restrained and there were fewer beatings. It was not long, however, before the prison administration took its revenge. Some sixteen prisoners deemed to be ringleaders of the strike were sentenced to an extra six months' imprisonment. The improvements turned out to be temporary as the old methods soon returned. Yet the atmosphere on the island was never quite the same as it had been before. The prisoners regarded the strike as a success. They had defied the administration and survived.

As the number of ANC prisoners on Robben Island rose month by month, reaching about 1,000 by 1966, Mandela and his colleagues devised ways and means of setting up their own forms of organization to maintain internal discipline and control, and to circumvent the authorities. An elaborate network of committees was established – disciplinary, political, educational, literary, recreational – to deal with every aspect of prisoners' lives and to keep open channels of communication between different sections. At the apex was a committee known as the High Organ, consisting of four members of the old national executive: Mandela, Sisulu, Mbeki and Mhlaba. Mandela served as its head.

Every opportunity was used to keep the leaders in the isolation section in touch with the mass of prisoners in the general section. Messages were hidden in drums of food, in toilets, which the warders rarely searched, or in matchboxes discarded by warders on their way to the quarries and surreptitiously picked up by prisoners. The prison hospital was a regular contact point to exchange information. The penalties for being caught in possession of messages or any illicit piece of paper were severe: messengers risked a prolonged spell in solitary confinement or the loss of study privileges. The danger from searches carried out by warders or from tip-offs by informers was ever-present. But despite the hazards, the communications system functioned effectively enough.

A perpetual war was also conducted over the possession of newspapers. Prisoners were always desperate for news of the outside world. 'Newspapers are more valuable to political prisoners than gold or diamonds, more hungered for than food or tobacco,' wrote Mandela. 'They were the most precious contraband on Robben Island.' The prison authorities equally relentlessly endeavoured to prevent prisoners gaining access to newspapers. Raids in search of newspapers were commonplace.

Despite the risks, prisoners stole newspapers from careless warders, bribed corrupt ones, retrieved them from rubbish dumps and took them surreptitiously from visiting doctors and priests. Every scrap of newspaper, whether it had been used to wrap warders' sandwiches or for toilet purposes, was seized upon. Old newspapers were as valued as recent ones. Each item, however trivial, was memorized or copied, passed on and talked about for days. The disposal of newspapers, torn into minute shreds and flushed down toilets, took hours. Some cuttings ended up being eaten.

In the isolation section, Kathrada was given the task of organizing communications and newspaper distribution. To minimize the risk, he first took cuttings, then handed them on to other prisoners to make short summaries which were then passed down the line. But there were frequent casualties. Mandela was once caught in his cell reading a newspaper which a warder had inadvertently left lying on a bench at the end of the corridor and which had so engrossed him he failed to hear the footsteps of an approaching officer. It cost him three days in isolation on a diet of rice water.

Prisoners also had some success in managing to talk individual warders into adopting a more tolerant regime. As a matter of policy, the ANC's High Organ took the view that warders who accorded fair treatment to prisoners should be respected in return and that others should be encouraged to act similarly. The results were usually worthwhile. Mandela recalled:

> We soon became aware that in terms of our daily lives a warder in our section, an ordinary warder, not a sergeant, could be more important to us than the commissioner of prisons or even the minister of justice. If you went to the commissioner of prisons or even the minister of justice and said, 'Sir, it's very cold, I want four blankets,' he would look at the regulations and say, 'You can only have three blankets . . . more would be a violation of the regulations and if I give you four blankets I'll have to give others four blankets.' If you went to a warder in your section and said, 'Look, I want an extra blanket,' and if you treated him with respect, he'd just go to the storeroom, give you an extra blanket and that's the end of it. If you said, 'Can I have some gravy today from the kitchen,' he just went to the kitchen and got you gravy.

Mandela developed cordial relationships with a number of individual warders. 'With junior officers who knew their position, Nelson was charming and fatherly,' Dingake recalled. 'Many young warders were friendly to him, occasionally soliciting advice from him in connection with their jobs or social problems.' With senior officers, with whom he was frequently at odds over prison practices, his relationship was far more abrasive.

Prisoners were particularly effective in encouraging warders, often poorly educated, to study, like them, hoping it would bring a more enlightened approach to their prison duties. More and more warders turned to graduate prisoners to help them with their courses. 'Eventually, we ended up teaching them subjects like history, maths, English and even Afrikaans,' said Neville Alexander.

On occasion, they resorted to blackmail. An elderly warder on night duty in the isolation section whom Maharaj had befriended asked him one night for help with writing an essay for a newspaper competition he wanted to enter. Maharaj agreed. Two weeks later the warder asked for more help; he had reached the final round, needed to produce another essay and offered Maharaj a cooked chicken in return. After consulting Mandela and Sisulu, Maharaj agreed to write the essay in exchange for a packet of cigarettes. The warder duly handed one over. Once Maharaj had the packet of cigarettes with the warder's fingerprints on it, he threatened to expose him to the prison authorities unless he allowed him to borrow his newspaper each night. The warder, fearful of losing his job and pension, duly obliged. For three hours every night, Maharaj transcribed items from the newspaper, handing it back before the warders changed shift, and then passed his work on to other prisoners to copy so that nothing could be traced back to him. This nightly transaction went on for six months until the warder was transferred.

The struggle for improvements in conditions, meanwhile, slowly began to show results. In 1967, the authorities allowed prisoners in the general section to start playing football on Saturday mornings. Football and other outdoor sports like rugby and cricket became the mainstay of long, dreary weekends when prisoners were otherwise kept locked up in cells. Within months, the Makana Football Association on Robben Island boasted some twenty-six sides in three divisions. Training was carried out in

303

cells during weekdays. 'Sport was very important on the island,' said Steve Tshwete, an ANC prisoner. 'It relieved the tension and anxiety about family, about home and about survival in prison itself.'

Prisoners in the isolation section were excluded from participating in general-section sports; nor were they permitted to attend as spectators. For a time they managed to get a view of football matches by peering through the tops of windows in the isolation section facing the pitch. Mandela's voice could be heard booming out, 'Good move, well played!' But the authorities soon put a stop to that by painting over the windows. The only relief to the monotony of weekends in the early years, apart from brief exercise periods, came from the visits of priests on Sundays. For the first two years, prisoners were confined to their cells while the priest preached from the head of the corridor, but during the third year services were conducted in the courtyard outside, allowing inmates to bask in the sun.

A notable boost to morale was provided by a visit in 1967 by Helen Suzman, the only member of parliament to take an interest in the welfare of political prisoners. Before her arrival, the warders moved Mandela out of his customary cell, no. 4, which was close to the entrance of the corridor, to no. 18, at the end of it, in the hope that by the time Suzman reached him, she might have little time left to speak to him. But this ploy was quickly thwarted when Suzman stopped at the first cell and was told by Eddie Daniels not to waste time talking to him but to go straight to the end of the corridor to talk to Mandela.

Mandela put his hand through the bars of the cell door and said, 'How do you do, Mrs Suzman, I'm very pleased to meet you.' Suzman was struck by his remarkable degree of self-assurance. With both the commissioner of prisons and the commanding officer of Robben Island standing close by, Mandela proceeded to list grievances over food, clothing, study facilities, labour conditions and the harsh treatment meted out by warders, singling out by name van Rensburg, the warder with the swastika tattoo, for whom he harboured an abiding hatred. Suzman promised to take up all these issues with the minister of justice.

In a subsequent meeting with the minister, when she threatened to expose van Rensburg's conduct in parliament, the minister hastily agreed to his removal. The prisoners had struck back and won. But it was to be another seven years before Suzman was given permission to return to Robben Island.

CHAPTER 14

A Double Ordeal

However much Mandela looked forward to visits from his family, they were occasions tinged as much by sadness as by joy. In 1968, a family group of four visited him: his mother, Nosekeni, his son Makgatho, his daughter Makaziwe and his favourite sister, Mabel. He had not seen the children for more than five years; they were now teenagers and had grown up without him. His mother he had last seen across the courtroom in Pretoria on the day in 1964 that he was sentenced to life imprisonment. Because they had all travelled such a distance, his mother coming from the Transkei, the prison authorities extended the visiting time allowed from thirty to forty-five minutes.

His oldest son, Thembi, did not join them, even though he was living nearby in Cape Town at the time. Thembi never visited his father on Robben Island. The bitterness that he felt at the break-up of his parents' marriage never left him. As a boy of ten, he had become withdrawn and silent. Sisulu, who took an avuncular interest in him, once remarked to Mandela, 'Man, that chap is quiet.' At school in Swaziland, he had fallen in love with a young girl, Thoko, who became pregnant and was obliged to return to her home in Cape Town. Thembi followed her there, finding a job as a clerk. Their first child, a daughter, was followed by a second daughter – Mandela's first grandchildren. But though Robben Island could be seen across the water from Cape Town, Thembi made no effort to go there.

Mandela's mother appeared to him to have aged considerably. She had lost much weight. 'When she left I looked at her walking out and I had the feeling I had seen her for the last time,' he recalled.

Several weeks later, after he had returned from a gruelling day in the lime quarry, a warder with whom he had become friendly, James Gregory, handed him a telegram. It was from Makgatho, telling him that his mother had died of a heart attack. He sought permission from the authorities to attend her funeral in the Transkei, but was refused.

In the following months, he pondered much over the life of his mother, an unschooled woman, widowed at an early age and bewildered by his commitment to politics rather than his family. He felt troubled by how little he had done to help her. 'Her difficulties, her poverty, made me question once again whether I had taken the right path,' he wrote in his autobiography. 'That was always the conundrum: had I made the right choice in putting the people's welfare even before that of my own family?'

An even more painful blow came the following year when another telegram arrived from Makgatho, this time saying that Thembi had been killed in a car accident. The news was again conveyed by James Gregory, who recalled the moment in his autobiography:

> In his eyes I could see the sternness I was to recognize when he struggled to maintain self-control. It was a distancing from me and from others, and in some ways his face receded into a fixed expression, tight lines around his mouth. Those lines always went deeper the more worried, sad or angry he became. At that time, he simply said, 'Thank you, Mr Gregory,' and walked away.

Mandela was devastated. He returned to his cell and stood before the barred window looking out. He did not emerge for dinner. Eventually Sisulu went to see him, and stayed with him, holding his hand. A night warder reported that throughout the night he stood before the window, staring out, not moving. The next morning, he wrote a request asking to be allowed to attend the funeral. His request was denied.

Mandela's anguish over the persecution of Winnie also intensified at this time. In May 1969, in the middle of the night, the security police arrested Winnie at her home in Orlando, detaining her under the new Terrorism Act, which enabled them to imprison her without charge and without any access to legal representation, in solitary confinement, indefinitely. The two Mandela daughters, Zenani, aged ten, and Zindzi, aged nine, were at home at the time, on holiday from school in Swaziland, and watched as their mother was taken away. They were sent to stay with one of Winnie's sisters. On Robben Island, the prison authorities made sure that Mandela knew of Winnie's arrest by leaving newspaper cuttings in his cell.

Winnie's arrest was part of a round-up of several hundred dissidents whom the security police wanted out of the way. In an amateurish fashion, Winnie had tried her hand at underground political activity, exposing both herself and others to considerable risk. She acquired a duplicating machine on which to run off ANC pamphlets and newsletters sent from abroad and accepted an offer from her friend Maude Katzellenbogen to keep it in a room in her house, safe from police raids, not suspecting Katzellenbogen's motives. She also used Katzellenbogen's address as a mail drop for letters from abroad sent to cover names. She was later to discover that the police had detailed information about the pamphlets and the cover names.

Winnie also became increasingly involved with an employee of the United States Information Agency, Mohale Mahanyele, asking him first to act as her driver, then introducing him to clandestine ANC meetings and eventually persuading him to allow her to use USIA offices for reproducing ANC pamphlets on duplicating machines at weekends and as an address for overseas mail. She talked to Mahanyele endlessly about the need for black liberation, but whenever he asked what steps needed to be taken, her reply was always the same: force, she would say, the overthrow of the government. So much time did Mahanyele spend with Winnie that his irate wife threatened to tell everything to the police. Meanwhile, Mahanyele's employers had become suspicious about the amount of foreign mail he was receiving.

Winnie's imprisonment had a marked effect on her character. She was taken to Pretoria Central Prison and placed in a solitary confinement cell, five feet wide and ten feet long. The bedding she was given consisted of a sisal mat and three blankets filthy from months of use without being washed. The only other items she was allowed were a toilet bucket, a plastic bottle of water and a mug. The smell from the toilet bucket was terrible. A single light bulb burned all night long. The only time she was allowed out of the cell was for brief exercise periods. She had no access to a bath or shower.

After two weeks, she was taken to be interrogated. Her chief interrogator was Swanepoel, now a major, notorious for his brutal methods. For five days and nights she was questioned over and over again, one interrogator following another. Their purpose was not so much to find out what she knew, for, as Winnie soon realized, they were already well informed about her meetings, her pamphlets and her address lists. What they wanted to do was to break her spirit, to turn her into a collaborator. They presented her with statements from men who said they had slept with her. They told her of how other prisoners under interrogation had betrayed her. They offered to release her if she cooperated. On the sixth day, utterly exhausted and suffering from fainting fits and heart palpitations, she capitulated, confessing to everything her interrogators demanded.

Back in her cell, Winnie was then subjected to months of solitary confinement. The only contact she had was with white warders, who treated her maliciously. Every day she was required to strip off her clothes for inspection. She was given a Bible to read, but otherwise there was nothing to occupy her. She started to talk to herself. She spent hours unthreading a blanket, then weaving it into threads. The food she was given was so foul she began to suffer from malnutrition. Two months after her arrest, Swanepoel walked into her cell and asked her who Thembi Mandela was. When she replied that he was her stepson, Swanepoel told her curtly, 'Well, he is dead. He was killed in a car accident', and then left. Winnie broke down and wept. There were times in solitary confinement when she hovered on the borders of insanity.

It was not until after she had spent nearly six months in prison that the government produced any charges against her. In October 1969, she was one of a group of twenty-two defendants accused of offences under the Suppression of Communism Act. The others included four women who had also been held in solitary confinement, one of whom, Rita Nzanga, had been savagely assaulted during interrogation.

On the first day of their appearance in the Pretoria magistrates' court, there was some confusion about who was to act as their legal representative. When Winnie was arrested in May, her relatives had turned for help to Joel Carlson, a civil rights lawyer well known to Mandela and highly respected by political activists. But for several months, the security police had been engaged in an elaborate ploy to ensure that Winnie was not represented by Carlson. Maude Katzellenbogen was used to spread rumours discrediting him. Her partner, Moosa Dinath, who had been involved in the scheme to free Mandela from Johannesburg's Fort prison, was sent to Robben Island in July to try to persuade Mandela to let another lawyer, Mendel Levin, represent Winnie instead of Carlson. Mandela turned down the suggestion. But Winnie, in solitary confinement, fell for it, agreeing not only to give Levin a power of attorney but to write a letter to political colleagues in London saying that Carlson was not to be trusted.

Both Levin and Carlson appeared in court, Levin announcing that he was acting as Winnie's legal representative, Carlson admitting that he was not clear of his status but determined if possible not to let the security police win the day. The matter was decided when the magistrate agreed to adjourn the case to give the defendants an opportunity to consult with their relatives. Winnie's sisters, who were in court, had received a message from Mandela on Robben Island insisting that no one other than Carlson should be allowed to represent Winnie and were now able to advise her of the fact. Levin was duly obliged to withdraw.

The indictments against Winnie and the other accused, several of them trade unionists, were largely of a minor nature. They were accused of attempting to revive the ANC by organizing meetings, distributing banned literature, recruiting members and staging funeral rallies. Mohale Mahanyele was produced as a chief witness. The government had hoped to portray their activities as part of a dangerous communist conspiracy against the state and, with the help of a compliant defence lawyer, gain a notable victory in court. But the defence team assembled by Carlson, which included George Bizos and Arthur Chaskalson, soon turned the trial to their own advantage by winkling out the fact that no less than five state witnesses had agreed to give evidence only after they had been subjected to police torture. To avoid further embarrassment, the government abruptly announced in February 1970 that it was withdrawing the charges.

Winnie's ordeal, however, was not over. Along with other

defendants, she was immediately redetained and taken back into solitary confinement, in the hands once again of vengeful white warders. In June, the government brought new charges against her and the others, this time under the Terrorism Act. Winnie did not attend the court hearing, as she was in the prison hospital suffering from malnutrition. When the trial opened in September, their defence counsel, Sydney Kentridge, called for an acquittal, pointing out that the charges the accused faced under the Terrorism Act were virtually identical to the ones they had faced under the Suppression of Communism Act which had resulted in their acquittal. The judge duly acquitted them.

After 491 days in prison, Winnie was finally free to go home. But within two weeks, she was served with a new five-year banning order, restricting her to Orlando West, prohibiting her from receiving visitors at home and placing her under house arrest each night and during weekends. The restriction order was lifted briefly in November, when she was allowed to visit Mandela on Robben Island for the first time in two years – for thirty minutes.

Mandela had been tormented by Winnie's imprisonment. He later described it as a desperately distressing experience, more difficult to contend with than anything else he had known in prison. He spent sleepless nights worrying about her plight, worrying too about who was looking after his daughters, who was paying the bills at home.

The impact on Winnie herself, by the time she emerged from prison, was indelible. Recalling the experience some twenty years later, she remarked, 'It is in fact what changed me; what brutalized me so much that I knew what it is to hate.'

The atmosphere on Robben Island deteriorated markedly in 1970. A new prison commander, Colonel Piet Badenhorst, was appointed at the end of the year to enforce a tougher regime and to stamp out all signs of prisoner resistance. He had a reputation for being one of the most ruthless and authoritarian officers in the prison service, feared alike by prisoners and by warders. Renowned for his incessant use of foul and abusive language, he brought with him a team of hand-picked warders eager to do his bidding, one of whom became known as 'The Devil'. Badenhorst himself was given the name Kid Ruction.

Mandela had made a practice of asking for an interview with all new prison commanders, but Badenhorst ignored him. Two weeks after he arrived on the island, Badenhorst put in an appearance at the lime quarry to find little work under way there. A group of *koeloekoetz* men were standing about trying to explain to one of the new warders the work norms that prevailed at the quarry. Badenhorst singled out Mandela: '*Mandela, jy moet jou vinger uit jou gat trek*,' he shouted – 'Mandela, pull your finger out of your arse.' Then he drove away.

Within minutes, a truck was sent to pick up the prisoners. They were taken back to the isolation section and paraded before Badenhorst. Swearing profusely, he accused sixteen prisoners of refusing to work and summarily demoted all of them to the next lowest grade of classification, so that those who had reached C grade and gained study privileges were demoted to D grade and instantly lost their ability to study. The effect on prisoners was devastating, but their protests were to no avail.

The prison's legal procedures, which prisoners had been able to exploit to their advantage, were suspended. Every decision, every punishment, now came at the whim of warders without explanation or recourse to prison courts. 'For every imaginable triviality, real or pretended, the prisoner would be marched off to the office by a warder who would give a verbal "report", duly distorted or invented, and the prisoner would be marched back to his cell, usually without being asked to explain his "conduct" or to comment on the "report",' recorded Neville Alexander. This arbitrary system of dispensing punishments caused massive resentment. 'Except for the brutality of assaults,' wrote Alexander, 'no other facet of life and experience on Robben Island caused so much bitterness.' Some prisoners were sent to the 'segregation section' – in effect, into solitary confinement – for periods lasting as long as six months.

Cell raids and body searches in the cells became more frequent and more aggressive. Increasingly rigorous censorship was applied to reading material and to letters. Outgoing letters were confiscated, recreation facilities were drastically curtailed and food rations were cut.

In May 1971, in response to a hunger strike started by some Namibian prisoners which other prisoners joined, Badenhorst let loose his warders on a night rampage through the prison. Several

Namibians were savagely beaten. The isolation section was raided by warders armed with batons, screaming and shouting. On a bitterly cold winter's night, prisoners were kept standing naked for an hour while their cells were searched. 'They stripped me and told me to put my hands against the wall,' recalled Sisulu. 'I was worried because I had flu. I thought that their plan might be that I become ill and eventually die.' Mbeki, who was also ill, suffered severe chest pains and collapsed. All complaints were ignored.

The following year, when three judges made a tour of Robben Island, accompanied both by the commissioner of prisons, General Steyn, and by Badenhorst, Mandela was asked to act as a spokesman for the prisoners. The judges suggested that he might prefer to speak to them in private, but Mandela replied that he would rather speak in front of the prison officials so that they could have an opportunity to respond to his criticisms. He related the incident of the beatings that had taken place in the general section and how the matter had subsequently been covered up. When he had finished, Badenhorst intervened to ask aggressively whether he had witnessed the beatings. Mandela replied that he had not, but trusted the account that had been given to him. Wagging his finger in Mandela's face, Badenhorst retorted, 'Be careful, Mandela. If you talk about things you haven't seen, you will get yourself into trouble. You know what I mean?'

Ignoring Badenhorst, Mandela turned to the judges and said, 'Gentlemen, you can see for yourself the type of man we are dealing with as commanding officer. If he can threaten me here, in your presence, you can imagine what he does when you are not here.'

Three months later, Badenhorst was transferred from Robben Island.

A more benign regime followed Badenhorst's departure. In 1973, prisoners regained the right to legal representation. By court order, they could no longer be arbitrarily demoted or deprived of meals or placed in solitary confinement. Study privileges were restored, though many obstacles to study remained. Their living conditions also improved. From 1973, prisoners' bedding consisted of two sisal mats, a felt mat and five blankets. They were entitled to two sets of clothing and given underwear for the first time. Hot water was provided. Political prisoners gained access to the kitchens for the first time, ensuring a fairer distribution of food. Though food for African prisoners was still graded differently, prisoners were allowed to pool their food. Medical treatment improved. Prisoners were permitted to travel to the mainland for dental visits or for specialist hospital treatment. The numbers of letters and visitors allowed to prisoners were increased. Category D prisoners, restricted to one letter and one visit every six months in 1964, were now permitted one letter and one visit every month. Photos of family members and friends, once banned, were now allowed. Both letters and photos were shared with fellow prisoners and often circulated for several months before being returned to their owners. The censors, however, still acted with a heavy hand, sometimes reducing a letter to a mere greeting – 'Darling husband' – and sometimes withholding it altogether. Photos were subject to censorship. Mandela asked Winnie to send him a photo of Oliver Tambo, but it was prohibited.

Recreational facilities were extended. Tennis courts were built for prisoners in the general section. In the isolation section, part of the courtyard was turned into a volleyball court. Table tennis was the most popular pastime in prison. Indoor games, like draughts, chess and bridge, also flourished. Films were shown once a fortnight. Musical instruments were allowed. Records were played over the intercom system for three hours every morning and at weekends. In the general section, prisoners formed a band, consisting of saxophone, trumpet, clarinet, flutes, harmonicas, guitars and penny whistles. Choral singing was performed to such a high standard that even warders were known to listen.

At Christmas time, the prison authorities allowed prisoners to stage a concert and a play and to hold competitions. The food remained the same, but prisoners were given an extra mug of coffee for supper and entitled to purchase a small quantity of sweets. It was the one day of the year, said Mandela, when the prison authorities showed any goodwill towards men.

Mandela's routine, after ten years of his life sentence, was as disciplined and purposeful as he could make it. He woke early, often long before the first bell was sounded at 5.30 a.m. He started the day with a burst of physical exercise, running on the spot for up to forty-five minutes and performing as many as 100 fingertip push-ups, 200 sit-ups and fifty deep knee-bends. Once his cell door was opened at 6.45 a.m. and he had dispensed with the tasks of tidying his cell and cleaning his toilet bucket, he jogged around the cement courtyard, clad in shorts, T-shirt and running shoes, before heading to an exercise hall for some skipping and shadow-boxing. He also took his turn scrubbing and polishing the floors and cleaning the toilets of B Section along with everyone else. Vigorous exercise he always found helpful to reduce tension. When a flu epidemic hit the isolation section in 1974, Mandela, who was spared the outbreak, made the rounds each morning collecting the toilet buckets of his sick colleagues, emptying them, cleaning them and then returning them to the cells.

After breakfast, eaten sitting at a long communal bench with other prisoners, he fell in for the journey to the lime quarry, passing through the prison gates, taking off his cap at each one on the order to do so. The regime at the quarry was relatively lenient. Much of Mandela's time was spent in giving lectures, participating in debates and listening to the discussions of fellow inmates. Though he was sometimes harsh and dogmatic in debate, he was also acknowledged to be a good listener, always eager to draw his colleagues into discussion and quick to understand the points they were making. He preferred to examine issues by hearing differing viewpoints, then reaching a conclusion, in a manner that he had first witnessed as a boy at the Great Place at Mqhekezweni. His grasp of detail and his memory for it were put to good use. 'His capacity to retain what he hears made him an excellent reporter after interviews with authorities,' wrote Dingake. 'He could be detailed not only in the substance of the point made, but in reporting expressions and innuendoes of the participants.'

The lime quarry routine was changed in 1973 when the *koeloek-oetz* group were given alternative work occasionally collecting seaweed, wading into the sea, lining it up in strips on the beach and loading it into the back of a truck for use eventually as fertilizer. In winter, it was bitterly cold work, but Mandela much preferred it. From the shore, he could see the skyscrapers of Cape Town in the distance and watch the shipping move to and fro from the harbour. Seaweed duties also gave prisoners the opportunity to cook themselves delicious seafood stews for lunch and to collect shells and pieces of coral to decorate their cells.

315

Returning to the prison at 4 p.m. for a shower and supper, Mandela was locked up in his cell for the rest of the night by 5 p.m. He used the time for study and writing letters. He also surreptitiously undertook legal work for prisoners in the general section who wanted help preparing judicial appeals. As an A-grade prisoner, he was entitled to three outgoing and three incoming letters each month, as well as two half-hour visits of two people at a time each month.

His cell, seven feet square, had taken on a more homely appearance. As a result of high blood pressure, from which he had suffered for more than ten years, in 1973 Mandela was provided with a bed; and because of back problems, he was given a chair instead of a bench. On a bookshelf stood a picture of Winnie which he would dust affectionately each day, rubbing his nose against hers.

Weekends were spent either in the confines of the courtyard or in the cells. Mandela devoted considerable time to trying to improve relations between the ANC and the PAC, seeking out PAC leaders in the isolation section, believing that if the two organizations could settle their differences on Robben Island, that might provide a basis for national reconciliation. Both the ANC and PAC participated in a prisoners' committee known as Ulundi which represented all groups in the isolation section. But every other attempt at producing a united front proved fruitless.

On Sundays, Mandela attended church services of whatever denomination had been chosen for the day, listening with equal attention to the sermons by Catholic, Hindu, Muslim and Dutch Reformed Church priests who visited the island. Though brought up in the Methodist Church and still regarding himself as a staunch member, he favoured a broad attitude towards religion. The priest whom Mandela most appreciated and who always gained the largest congregation was an Anglican minister named Father Hughes, a burly Welshman who endeavoured to lace his sermons with titbits of news and words of encouragement. One of his favourite quotations was: 'I groused and groused because I had no shoes until I saw a man who had no feet.' Father Hughes brought with him a portable organ with which he accompanied the prisoners, praising them for their singing. During Kid Ruction's regime, the portable organ was prohibited. Mandela took holy communion on a regular basis: 'The sacrament gave me a sense of inner quiet and calm.' But he spoke of himself as not being particularly religious or spiritual: 'I am just an ordinary person interested in trying to make sense of the mysteries of life.'

For relaxation, Mandela enjoyed playing draughts, competing each year in the draughts competition and occasionally winning it. His style of play was slow and deliberate, with each move considered carefully. Once a fortnight he watched a film show in the isolation section, though he tended to become bored with the mediocre selection of films on offer.

His favourite occupation, though, was gardening. He had acquired a love of gardening and growing vegetables during his schooldays at Clarkebury, working in the garden belonging to the principal, Reverend Harris. Soon after arriving on Robben Island, he had asked the authorities for permission to start a garden in the courtyard, but it had taken years for them to agree. Given a narrow patch of earth alongside a perimeter wall, he worked assiduously to nurture plants in the dry, stony soil, studying horticultural techniques from library books, and he took immense satisfaction in the resulting tomatoes and onions he produced.

The highlight of Mandela's routine was the arrival of a letter or a visitor from his family, especially Winnie. She was the focus of his emotions. Without a letter from Winnie, he said, he felt as dry as the desert. A letter from her was like the coming of the summer rains. His own letters in return were full of love and affection and a deep longing for her presence. He constantly referred to memories of their time together, of touching her hand, hugging her, tasting the delicious dishes she cooked, and of the hours they had spent in the bedroom.

On the occasions when they met in the visiting room, separated by a panel of thick glass, Winnie was always careful to dress with flair, knowing that he would cherish the details for weeks to come. Each time, he said, he felt like lingering in the room after she had gone to savour the moment a little longer but forced himself to leave lest emotion overtook him. His next letter would be full of compliments about her dress and about the effect her beauty had on him.

Winnie was also the focus of his main concern. There seemed to be no respite from the harassment the security police meted out to her, nor to her propensity for becoming entangled with police informers and other dubious characters. In 1970, she was charged with violating her banning order when her sister, Beauty, came to her house with her husband, two children and brother-in-law to pick up a shopping list. She was sentenced to six months' imprisonment, but on appeal the sentence was suspended and the conviction was eventually overturned. In 1971, she was again charged with violating her banning order, this time after a family friend, the photographer Peter Magubane, also a banned person, was found by police hiding under her bed. She was sentenced to twelve months' imprisonment, but once again on appeal the sentence and conviction were set aside. Interspersed with all this, Winnie faced random police raids, some mysterious gunshots and a night when she awoke to find three intruders in her house.

Then, in 1973, she was again accused of violating her banning order, this time when Peter Magubane brought her daughters, Zeni and Zindzi, who were on holiday from school in Swaziland, to meet her for lunch near her place of work. Sentenced to one year's imprisonment, she appealed but won only a reduction in her sentence to six months. In September 1974, therefore, she was back in prison, serving her time in Kroonstad in the company of two other political prisoners.

News about Winnie that reached Mandela on Robben Island always seemed to involve controversy and trouble. In 1975, one month after her last visit to Robben Island, Winnie sent Mandela a message saying that her request for another visit had been turned down on the grounds that Mandela himself did not want to see her. Mandela immediately made an appointment to see the head of prison, Lieutenant Prins, to lodge a protest. After Mandela had explained the matter, Prins responded rudely, 'Ag, Mandela, your wife is only seeking publicity.' He then went on to make a remark so offensive about Winnie that Mandela lost his temper, shook his fists and let loose a torrent of abuse. It was one of the rare occasions on Robben Island when Mandela lost his self-control. When charges were brought against him, Mandela prepared counter-charges. The case was subsequently dropped.

Mandela was also concerned about his children. Makgatho had turned into a feckless character. Expelled from school for involvement in a student strike, he had left without passing matriculation and failed subsequent attempts to do so. He had since married and fathered a son. Once or twice a year he went to Robben Island to see Mandela, on one occasion arriving there drunk. Mandela constantly urged him to return to his studies and Makgatho made promises, but he never fulfilled them.

Makaziwe had shown greater aptitude at school, becoming the first of Mandela's children to pass matriculation, but to his deep disappointment, instead of proceeding to university, she had decided to get married. Mandela tried to persuade her to postpone marriage until after she graduated, but she would not listen. She had two children in quick succession, then the marriage failed.

Mandela's other two daughters, Zeni and Zindzi, had been tossed about in the turmoil of Winnie's own life. Both had been deeply affected by the succession of raids, arrests, imprisonments and dark dramas that beset their mother. Only school in Swaziland and the help of good friends in Johannesburg had provided a source of stability. Of the two, Zindzi had adapted most readily to the hurly-burly surrounding Winnie. At the age of twelve, after witnessing police break down the door of their house in Orlando West during the 1972 Christmas holidays, she wrote an appeal to the United Nations Special Committee on Apartheid, asking for help in providing protection for Winnie:

> Hardly a month goes by without the newspapers reporting some incident concerning Mummy, and her friends and family feel that the public is being conditioned to expect something terrible to happen to her. I know my father, who is imprisoned for life on Robben Island, is extremely concerned about my mother's safety, and has done everything in his power to appeal to the government to give her protection, but without success.

Because of prison regulations, Mandela never set eyes on either of his daughters until 1975, when Zeni was sixteen and Zindzi was fifteen. He was by then virtually unknown to them, a man familiar only through old photographs. For their first visits, he took particular care with his appearance, anxious to create a favourable impression. It was a nervous moment for all of them. Trying to put the girls at ease, Mandela gestured towards the warders surrounding him in the cubicle, saying, 'Have you met my guard of honour?' Zindzi recalled:

> I had heard so much about my father that I was rather apprehensive

about seeing him for the first time. He was more a great figure than a father. But when we met, even through the glass partition and speaking on telephones, I found it very easy. He is so versatile and charismatic that in just a few minutes he seemed to change the whole atmosphere. The warders were breathing down our necks all the time, but he put me at my ease at once, recalling little incidents from the time when I was a baby.

That same year, Mandela embarked upon the writing of his memoirs, hoping that they might be published to coincide with his sixtieth birthday in 1978. He worked mainly at night, sleeping during the day, having informed the prison authorities that he was unwell and would not be going to the quarry. Each bit of work was passed on to Sisulu and Kathrada for comments, which they jotted down in the margins. The manuscript was then handed to another colleague, Laloo Chiba, who produced a copy of it in microscopic shorthand. The plan was for Mac Maharaj to smuggle the copy out of prison when his twelve-year sentence came to an end in 1976. The original manuscript, meanwhile, would be buried at a spot in the courtyard, to be dug up and destroyed once Maharaj's copy was safely out of the country.

In four months, Mandela completed 500 pages. Because it was too bulky to bury in one spot, the manuscript was divided into three, each part wrapped in plastic, placed in a tin container and then hidden in a separate hole in the ground at one end of the courtyard.

But the plan went awry a few weeks later when, unexpectedly, a team of prison labourers arrived in the isolation section to dig a trench for the foundations for a new wall in the same area of the courtyard. Mandela managed to retrieve two of the packages and to destroy them, but the third was discovered. The punishment for Mandela, and for Sisulu and Kathrada, whose handwriting was also on the manuscript, was severe. All three were stripped of their study privileges for four years.

The routine on Robben Island, meanwhile, continued relentlessly, week after week, month after month. Then, in June 1976, the atmosphere deteriorated dramatically. Returning to the prison compound, tired and dirty after a day collecting seaweed in bitterly cold conditions, the prisoners rushed to the showers to find that there was no hot water. On following days, even when the rain and the cold made work almost impossible, they were forced outside again. Attempts to negotiate with the authorities proved fruitless. There was a rare disagreement between Mandela and Sisulu about what form their response should take. What neither knew at the time was that an eruption of political violence had occurred in South Africa, sending tremors across the country, with effects that reached even the sequestered world of Robben Island.

CHAPTER 15

Soweto

White society, during the fourteen years that Mandela had spent in prison, had become increasingly prosperous and secure. Throughout the 1960s, South Africa experienced one of the highest rates of economic growth in the world, second only to that of Japan. Foreign trade with Western countries rose by leaps and bounds. Foreign investors from the United States, Britain, France and Germany competed vigorously for positions in new industries. The annual net flow of foreign capital into the country in 1970 rose to a level six times higher than that of the pre-Sharpeville era. The economic boom also brought to South Africa a flood of white immigrants, mainly from Europe: between 1960 and 1970 there was a net gain of some 250,000. All this gave white South Africans a growing sense of confidence about the future. Black resistance had been crushed and the security apparatus seemed capable of meeting any contingency. Many whites believed the apartheid system to be invincible.

The benefits of National Party rule were noticeable particularly among the Afrikaner community. With government assistance, a new class of Afrikaner financiers, businessmen and managers had moved into commanding positions in industry, commerce and banking, areas once the preserve of English-speaking whites. State enterprises like railways, harbours, steel production, electric power generation and heavy engineering were manned at a senior level almost exclusively by Afrikaners and used as training fields for Afrikaner scientists and business leaders. Government contracts and concessions were frequently steered towards Afrikaner companies. The civil service was virtually an Afrikaner preserve.

322

Afrikaner farmers, consisting of three-quarters of the total number, also fared well under National Party rule, assisted by subsidies, research funds, modernization programmes and favourable prices fixed by state marketing boards.

The Afrikaner working class prospered as never before. By 1970, more than 80 per cent of the Afrikaner population were living in towns and cities. White jobs were given whatever protection was needed from black competition. Almost every skilled trade and craft was reserved for white workers. When unskilled whites felt threatened by black competition, the government made use of legislation it had introduced in the 1950s, enabling it to reserve any occupation for whites only. Some orders applied to entire industries, like production jobs for the clothing, building, metallurgical and mining industries. Others affected only small, specific areas protecting a handful of employees, like the jobs of traffic policemen in Cape Town and passenger-lift operators in Johannesburg. At a more general level, white workers were protected by two cardinal principles the government used to determine its labour policy: first, no white worker could be replaced by a black worker in the same job, and second, no white worker could work under a black.

The English-speaking community, of course, shared in the prosperity; few other communities in the world possessed such a high standard of living. The northern suburbs of Johannesburg, where many English-speakers congregated, were said to have the greatest concentration of swimming pools outside Beverly Hills. Whatever reservations English speakers might have held about the nature of National Party rule, the success it enjoyed made them compliant citizens.

The system seemed strong enough to withstand any shock. When Hendrik Verwoerd, the driving force behind grand apartheid, was assassinated in the National Assembly by a deranged parliamentary messenger in 1966, the white community took the prime minister's death in its stride. No shift in policy was considered necessary. Verwoerd's successor, chosen by the National Party, was John Vorster, who, as minister of justice, had made such a success of smashing black opposition. Immediately upon being elected, Vorster declared, 'My role is to walk further along the road set by Hendrik Verwoerd.'

The impact of grand apartheid on the African population was

felt with dramatic force during the 1960s as the government worked systematically to stem the flow of Africans from rural to urban areas and to destroy all notion that urban Africans could have a permanent place in 'white' towns. With remorseless vigour, the government strove to reduce the urban African population wherever possible, stripping urban Africans of what few rights they possessed and ridding white rural areas of vast numbers of blacks. A government circular in 1967 stated: 'No stone is to be left unturned to achieve the settlement in the homelands of non-productive Bantu at present residing in the European areas.' Among those whom the circular defined as 'non-productive' were 'the aged, the unfit, widows and women with dependent children'. A government minister estimated that of 6 million Africans in white areas, 4 million were 'surplus appendages' suitable for deportation to black homelands.

As the policy took effect, the number of prosecutions under pass laws rose sharply, reaching 700,000 in 1968. Countless thousands found themselves 'endorsed out' of urban areas. In the Transvaal and the Orange Free State, massive urban relocation programmes were carried out. African townships considered to be within commuting distance of a homeland were 'deproclaimed' and their residents moved to new rural townships built in the homelands. In some cases, the entire African population was moved, as happened at Nelspruit and Lichtenburg. In other cases, government officials concentrated on removing the unemployed, the elderly and disabled, women and children, leaving behind African workers to live in all-male hostels and visit their families on a weekly or monthly basis.

In place of a stable, urban population, what the government wanted was a workforce composed principally of migrant labour. With migrant workers circulating continuously between black homelands and white-owned enterprises in urban areas, the government saw a means of reconciling the white need for labour with its own determination to prevent permanent black urbanization. African workers could be turned into commuters if they lived in homelands close enough to urban areas, or weekly migrants if the distance was too far. Alternatively, African workers could be engaged in the traditional manner on annual contracts, housed in all-male compounds and released to visit their families in the homelands at the end of the year. In 1970, it was estimated that more than 2 million men spent their lives circulating as migrants between their homes and urban employment. Many of them were deprived of all normal family and social life, confined for months on end to a bleak and barren existence in overcrowded barracks that were notorious for high rates of drunkenness and violence. Others spent hours each day travelling long distances to work in packed buses and trains, rising before dawn and returning home late into the night.

Black townships were deliberately kept as unattractive as possible. Few urban amenities were ever provided. Black businessmen were prevented by government restrictions from expanding their enterprises there. No African was allowed to carry on more than one business. Businesses were confined to providing 'daily essential necessities', like wood, coal, milk and vegetables. There could be no banks or clothing stores or supermarkets. Restrictions were even placed on dry-cleaners, garages and petrol stations. Nor were Africans allowed to establish companies or partnerships in urban areas, or to construct their own buildings. These had to be built and leased from the local authority.

The largest urban area in the country, Johannesburg's South Western Townships, which included Mandela's home district of Orlando, was typical of the bleak urban landscape enforced by the government. Known from 1963 as Soweto, it consisted mainly of row upon row of identical four-room brick 'matchbox' houses with hardly any public facilities. Only a small proportion of houses had electricity or adequate plumbing. There were few paved roads or proper pavements, no modern shopping centres or office blocks, and not a single pharmacy or bakery. Because of restrictions placed on African trading rights, three-quarters of the groceries consumed by Sowetans were purchased in white shops in Johannesburg. More than 1 million people lived there in circumstances which became increasingly cramped. From the mid-1960s, the construction of family housing in all urban areas virtually came to a halt. Priority was given instead to building housing in the homelands and hostels in urban areas for migrant labour. By 1970, the average number of people living in each house in Soweto had risen to thirteen. By 1972, the housing backlog was even greater than it had been in the 1940s.

The effect of apartheid in rural areas was equally severe. Leaving 'no stone unturned' in its drive for racial separation, the government began to excise scores of African settlements surrounded by white farming areas where Africans had lived in relative peace and quiet for generations. In the government's terminology, these settlements were known as 'black spots', small fragments of land in what was deemed to be 'white' South Africa which stood out as irritating blemishes on the apartheid map. Some land was held by title deed, purchased by African farmers in the nineteenth and early twentieth centuries; some was mission land scheduled for African use under the Natives Land Act of 1913, small African reserves which had survived intact the era of white occupation but which were now considered to be 'badly situated'. In all, there were an estimated 300 black spots.

The elimination of black spots began in earnest in the 1960s. Whole communities were uprooted and forced to leave their homes. Many were dumped in areas often unsuitable for cultivation, lacking water supplies, far from main roads and out of reach of hospitals or clinics. Any sign of resistance was dealt with by armed police. A Franciscan priest, Father Cosmas Desmond, who made a journey the length and breadth of South Africa to ascertain the full extent of the forced removals policy in 1969, later described how he found a 'labyrinth of broken communities, broken families and broken lives'. Between 1960 and 1970, nearly 100,000 Africans lost their homes during the elimination of black spots. Many more were to follow.

In white farming areas, where the white population was constantly preoccupied with *die beswarting van die platteland* – the blackening of the white countryside – the government acted with similar vigour to reduce the black population. White farmers were encouraged to adopt more mechanized production methods and to replace permanent black workers with casual employees and single migrant workers. An estimated half a million full-time black workers lost their employment on white farms during the 1960s. Thousands of African labour tenants – 'squatters' – were also turned off white land. The only Africans whom the government wanted in white farming areas were hired labourers, preferably migrants.

The impact of all these changes in 'white' South Africa on black homelands was devastating. Already overcrowded and impoverished, homelands had to cope with an endless flow of displaced

Africans – labour tenants, squatters, redundant farm labourers, urban dwellers – 'superfluous' people, as they were described, all scrabbling for survival. During the 1960s, the homeland population nearly doubled. Once in the homelands, most African men had no alternative but to offer themselves up to the migrant labour treadmill. The government, for its part, pronounced itself well pleased with the results of its policy. 'The elimination of the redundant non-economically active Bantu' in white areas, said a government minister in 1969, was 'a tremendous achievement'.

For ten years, while the apartheid system bit ever deeper into the lives of the African population, little sign of protest emerged. The repression used to crush Umkhonto we Sizwe had made an impact too deep to be forgotten easily. Even traditionally militant areas like the townships of the Eastern Cape were cowed into silence.

But in the early 1970s, a new generation of black activists arose from the ranks of the student population. It was a generation which drew its inspiration not from the concept of multiracial struggle that the ANC had championed but from a sense of black assertiveness more in line with the Africanist tradition of black politics. The black consciousness movement of the 1970s filled the vacuum left by the collapse of the ANC and the PAC. It found an articulate spokesman in Steve Biko, a medical student from the Eastern Cape, who argued that 'group power' would achieve black liberation. Biko was contemptuous of the cowed and submissive attitude of the black population. 'The type of black man we have today has lost his manhood,' he wrote in a student newsletter in 1970. 'Reduced to an obliging shell, he looks with awe at the white power structure and accepts what he regards as the "inevitable position".' What was needed, said Biko, was a massive effort to reverse the negative image that blacks held of themselves and to replace it with a more positive identity. Black oppression was first and foremost a psychological problem. It could be countered by promoting black awareness, black pride, black capabilities and black achievement. The term 'black' was used to include Coloureds and Indians equally with Africans as victims of racial oppression. No help was wanted from white liberals or any other white sympathizers. The slogan used was: 'Black man, you are on your own.'

As the black consciousness movement gathered momentum, it

found outlets in literature, poetry, music, theology and in local community projects promoting education, health and welfare. A host of youth clubs, discussion groups and cultural organizations sprang into existence.

The stirring of black discontent eventually prompted the government to take reprisals. In 1973 it issued banning orders on Biko and seven other leaders of the movement. But its actions failed to prevent the spread of black consciousness. A dramatic boost to black morale occurred in 1974, when Portuguese rule in Mozambique and Angola collapsed, paving the way for African liberation movements there to take control. When South African troops were obliged to withdraw from Angola in early 1976, having failed to prevent a Marxist guerrilla organization from gaining power there, black students again celebrated the defeat of white power.

The issue that finally ignited student anger was the system of Bantu education designed by Verwoerd to limit African education to the needs of the white economy. It had produced a legacy of inferior schooling, poorly trained teachers, overcrowded classrooms and inadequate equipment. Government expenditure had been kept to a minimum: in the early 1970s it spent sixteen times more on white education per pupil than on black education. Because of deliberate restrictions on places in middle and higher schools, hundreds of thousands of children – 'push-outs', as they were known – left school with no greater prospects than menial work or unemployment. Those who managed to complete secondary school were faced with a whole range of apartheid restrictions affecting the kind of employment for which they could apply.

Into this potentially explosive atmosphere the government stumbled with yet another regulation. In 1974, it decided that an old ruling, originally made in 1958, that half of the subjects in secondary schools not taught in the African vernacular had to be taught in Afrikaans and the other half in English should be enforced the following year. Because of the practical difficulties involved, the ruling had hitherto been ignored. African teachers in training college continued to receive their instructions almost exclusively in English. Many teachers were unable even to converse in Afrikaans. In one protest after another, teachers' organizations, school boards, principals and parents sought to persuade the government to change its mind, but the government remained adamant.

The epicentre of the resistance was Soweto. Students, denouncing Afrikaans as the language of the 'oppressor', began to boycott classes in Afrikaans, organized school strikes and then planned a mass demonstration. On 16 June 1976, a dozen columns of students marched through Soweto carrying placards, chanting slogans and singing freedom songs. They were met by armed police who opened fire, killing a thirteen-year-old schoolboy. As news of the shooting spread, students went on the rampage, attacking government buildings, beer halls, bottle stores, vehicles and buses. Two whites were killed. For three days, Soweto was the scene of running battles between groups of students and riot police in armoured convoys, often firing indiscriminately. Clashes spread to other townships in the Transvaal. At least 150 people were killed during the first week of the Soweto revolt, most of them black schoolchildren.

In July, the government retreated on the Afrikaans issue. But by then the students had set their sights on bringing down the whole Bantu education system. Some believed that the government itself could be toppled. Time and again they returned to the streets, showing remarkable resilience in the face of police firepower and displaying a level of defiance and hatred of the apartheid system rarely seen before. As soon as one set of student leaders was detained or disappeared into exile, others stepped forward, ready to take their place.

Yet for all the courage shown, the student revolt lacked any sense of direction. Marches, demonstrations and arson attacks produced little discernible result other than an endless series of police raids and a high cost in casualties – at least 600 dead and 4,000 wounded. From September onwards the momentum of the revolt began to ebb. By December it had virtually died out.

The prison population on Robben Island had undergone several changes over the years. When Mandela was first sent there in 1963 it consisted mainly of hardened criminals divided into rival gangs which constantly fought each other for ascendancy. Murder, assault and sodomy were commonplace. There followed an influx of PAC prisoners, many on short sentences of two or three years. ANC prisoners, at first a small minority, eventually outnumbered them. In the early 1970s, the criminal population was steadily reduced. The number of political prisoners also fell as those on short sentences departed. By the mid-1970s, political prisoners numbered only 400, many of them middle-aged or growing old, long accustomed to a prison routine which they themselves had done much to shape.

The arrival in 1976 of young, unruly black consciousness activists, as determined to confront the prison system as they had been to confront the apartheid system outside, shook the prison to its core. They regarded the settled habits of the older inmates, in particular their willingness to conform to prison regulations, with contempt, as being little different from the submissive attitude to authority shown by their parents and teachers for so many years. Normal rules like standing up in the presence of prison officers and taking off their caps were simply ignored.

Such conduct came as a shock to the older generation of prisoners. In his autobiography, Mandela described an incident he witnessed in which a prison officer told a newly arrived prisoner to take off his cap. 'What for?' retorted the prisoner. Mandela recalled, 'I could hardly believe what I had heard.' The young militants were prepared neither to submit to prison discipline nor to heed the advice of old stalwarts on how best to handle the prison authorities. They considered conditions on Robben Island to be barbaric and cared nothing for explanations about how much they had improved as a result of the efforts of the first political prisoners to arrive there.

Most of the 1976 intake were placed in a new part of the prison known as Section E. But several prominent activists, including two Indians, Strini Moodley and Saths Cooper, were sent to the isolation section. Mandela made a point of catching up with the ideas behind black consciousness. But the gulf in attitude remained. After watching a documentary on an American motorcycle gang known as Hell's Angels which depicted them as being reckless and violent, while portraying the police as being decent and trustworthy, the ANC prisoners were all harshly critical of the bikers for their lawlessness. But Moodley compared their rebelliousness to the rebelliousness of the Soweto students and accused the ANC men of being elderly middle-class intellectuals who favoured right-wing authority.

Both the ANC and the PAC expended considerable energy in trying to recruit black-consciousness supporters to their side. The friction this caused lasted for several years and resulted in serious bouts of violence. In 1977, Patrick Lekota, a black-consciousness leader who decided to join the ANC, was attacked with a garden fork by former comrades. After leaving Robben Island, Saths Cooper observed caustically, 'When the sordidness of prison behaviour is examined, there is little difference between common-law and political prisoners generally. Where the former are often organized into deadly rival gangs, the latter are organized into often warring political groupings.' It was a struggle in which the ANC's older generation of prisoners was largely successful in winning over black-consciousness activists.

Meanwhile, the tempo of life on Robben Island changed in other ways. In 1977, the authorities ended hard labour in the quarries, which had been Mandela's principal occupation for thirteen years. From 1978, political prisoners were allowed to listen to censored newscasts broadcast over an intercom system. From 1980, they could buy newspapers and periodicals, albeit heavily censored beforehand by prison staff. A tennis court was constructed in the courtyard.

Mandela's days were now spent largely at leisure. Most of the time he occupied by reading. 'He would read for hour after hour in unbroken concentration,' recalled Kathrada. Because of the four-year ban on his studies, the books he read were mainly novels obtained from the prison library. He subscribed to a wide range of newspapers and periodicals, including Afrikaans publications. He kept up his correspondence as regularly as he was permitted, worked diligently on legal briefs for fellow prisoners, played tennis and tended his garden patch.

For all the new comforts of prison life, Mandela worried that it was leaving him further and further behind as the outside world moved on. The arrival of the 1976 activists was a reminder not just of how much he was out of touch with political developments, with new ideas and thinking, but of how much time had passed. Most of the new prisoners had been mere infants at the time his prison life had begun.

The departure of close friends added to his sense of being stranded. Fikile Bam and Neville Alexander had gone in 1974 after serving ten years. Mac Maharaj left in 1976, taking with him Mandela's manuscript. Eddie Daniels went in 1979 and Michael

Dingake in 1981. The Rivonia group remained, with not the slightest sign that they would ever be released.

Each year brought news of the death of old colleagues. Albert Luthuli, in poor health and with failing eyesight, had died in 1967, struck by a train while taking a walk near his home in Natal. In 1968, Z. K. Matthews, Mandela's old professor, had died in the United States. J. B. Marks died in Moscow in 1972, Robert Resha in London in 1973, Moses Kotane in Moscow in 1974 and Michael Harmel in Prague in 1974. Bram Fischer died in 1975, suffering from cancer and released from Pretoria prison for only the last few weeks of his life. Robert Sobukwe, who had been released from solitary confinement after six years on Robben Island, died in Kimberley in 1978. In a letter of condolence to Robert Resha's widow, Mandela remarked, 'It seems that the old and stable world we knew so well is beginning to crumble down, leaving us with nothing but painful memories.'

As a resident of Soweto, Winnie was drawn swiftly into the tumult of the student uprising. She played a leading role in the Black Parents Association, formed by a group of local leaders to act as intermediaries between the students and the authorities. The BPA helped organize funerals and raised money for medical and burial expenses. Winnie herself renewed her reputation for militant behaviour when she went to a local police station in the company of an African bishop and ended up by shouting and throwing objects at the police, accusing them of murder. 'There was the usual flare-up,' she said. 'I don't think Bishop Buthelezi had ever seen anything like that in his life. I wanted to restrain myself because of him but it was difficult.' One of her BPA colleagues, Dr Nthatho Motlana, a close friend of the Mandelas who acted as guardian to Zeni and to Zindzi, recalled how Winnie's conduct would scare them: 'Often I would say, you are bloody foolhardy, you are going to get us all locked up, and when they threatened to lock her up she just said, "Do it, man!"'

In August 1976, Winnie and ten other women were detained under the Internal Security Act and taken to the Fort. She remained there, without being charged, for five months. During the school holidays, Zeni and Zindzi went to stay in Johannesburg with the banned activist Helen Joseph and visited their mother each week, taking fruit, clothes and newspapers. Released at Christmas, Winnie was once more issued with strict banning orders, confining her to her house in Orlando between 6 p.m. and 6 a.m. each day.

As the first anniversary of the student uprising drew near, the government devised yet another form of punishment for Winnie: banishment. In May 1977, without warning, armed police arrived at her home in the early morning, took her to a local police station and piled all her furniture and belongings into a truck. She was then driven 300 miles to a barren township on the edge of a small *platteland* dorp in the Orange Free State called Brandfort and prohibited from travelling outside the locality. Zindzi went with her.

The house she was given – no. 802 – possessed neither water nor electricity. It consisted of three tiny rooms, far too small for all her possessions, most of which had to be taken away to be stored at the local police station. When she arrived, the floors were covered with mounds of earth left behind by local builders. The local population had been told that Winnie was a dangerous criminal and instructed to avoid her. She spoke neither of the two languages used locally, Sesotho and Afrikaans. Under the terms of her banning order, she was confined to the house every night and allowed no visitors; during the day, she was forbidden to be in the company of more than one person at a time. Her movements were constantly watched. Her neighbours on both sides were policemen. Every day a security policeman kept her under surveillance, spending most of his time in a car parked on a low hill nearby and using binoculars.

Friends in Johannesburg were quick to help, driving down to Brandfort with supplies of groceries, cosmetics and household items. But they too were subjected to police harassment. After four white women friends were given prison sentences for refusing to make statements to police about their visits to Winnie, the number of visitors from Johannesburg declined sharply.

At shops in the white section of Brandfort, Winnie faced open hostility from staff. Brandfort was a typical rural settlement, with a few shops on either side of the road, a petrol station, a post office, a railway station, two small hotels, two churches, two banks, an Afrikaans school and a police station, and had been long accustomed to a quiet routine and an orderly existence. Blacks who came to shop in Brandfort were usually dealt with by being served through separate small windows. When Winnie took Zindzi to a clothes shop to buy her a black mourning dress to mark the first anniversary of the Soweto revolt in June, she was confronted by an angry white shop assistant who tried to prevent her from entering. The common practice was for blacks to stand outside the shop and point to the clothes that interested them. Winnie's altercation with the shop assistant eventually required the police to break it up. At other shops, when staff complained about her presence or asked her to go to the non-white section, she exploded, shouting and swearing at them.

The persistent attention of the police affected not only Winnie but Zindzi too. Friends who visited her were questioned aggressively about their meetings. Sometimes they were prevented from meeting her at all. Only sixteen years old, she fell into a deep depression, weeping continuously and unable to sleep. From Robben Island, Mandela brought an urgent application for an interdict against the security police to restrain them from intimidating or harassing Zindzi. In a statement to the court, Zindzi described how the police had burst into the house while she was in the company of her teenage friends, demanding names and addresses, issuing threats and evicting everyone present, then calling on them in their homes and detaining them for questioning. As a result, she said, her friends were terrified of visiting her. The court ruled that Zindzi was entitled to receive visitors in peace, even though Winnie was subject to a banning order.

The atmosphere in Brandfort remained grim, but Winnie was loath to let Zindzi go back to Johannesburg. 'I literally couldn't let her out of my clutches, clinging to perhaps the last semblance of a family unit,' she said in her autobiography. When, after two years in Brandfort, Zindzi did return to Johannesburg, to stay with Helen Joseph, Winnie described in a letter to a friend how her daughter's company had helped cushion her from the pain of exile and spoke of the loneliness that followed her departure: 'The empty long days drag on, one like the other . . . The solitude is deadly.'

Mandela found Winnie's plight all the more difficult to bear since he knew nothing about Brandfort or the surroundings in which she found herself. Apart from brief glimpses through blurred glass in the visitor's room and letters carefully written to avoid censorship, his connection with Winnie's life, which he cherished so much, was based above all on shared memories of people and places that were once familiar to him. However bleak the circumstances, he could always picture Winnie at their house in Orlando, cooking in the kitchen, reading in the lounge or waking up in the bedroom. But house no. 802, the Location, Brandfort, was as alien to him as it was to Winnie. It was two years before he saw a photograph of it.

Amid the gloom about Winnie, there were some more cheerful items of family news. In 1978 a collection of poetry which Zindzi had written as a young teenager, long before her days in Brandfort, was published in the United States, together with photographs by Peter Magubane. Zindzi dedicated the book to her parents. She also wrote an article for the magazine *True Love*. Mandela was highly impressed by her abilities and hoped writing might become her profession.

But it was Zeni who occasioned one of the most memorable days of Mandela's prison life. In 1977, at the age of eighteen and eight months pregnant, Zeni had married Prince Thumbumuzi, a son of King Sobhuza of Swaziland whom she had met while at school there. Neither Mandela nor Winnie was in favour of the marriage at first. Both considered Zeni far too young and wanted her first to complete her secondary education and preferably to obtain a university degree before settling down to marriage. Mandela asked George Bizos, his friend and legal adviser, to interview the prince on his behalf. Bizos reported favourably and the marriage duly proceeded.

The following year, a few weeks before Mandela's sixtieth birthday, Zeni brought her husband and her baby daughter to Robben Island. Because she was a member of the royal family of Swaziland, with diplomatic status, she was accorded the privilege of meeting Mandela in a room usually used for legal consultations. As Zeni entered the room, she gave the child to her husband and rushed to Mandela, hugging him tightly. Then Mandela took the baby and sat holding her for the rest of the visit. It was his first experience of normal human contact with his family since his imprisonment.

Whatever signs of black discontent there were, the government pressed on with its policies of grand apartheid as determinedly as before and found willing accomplices among the black population to make them work. The key figure was Mandela's kinsman, Kaizer Matanzima. Since the 1950s, Matanzima had proved to be apartheid's most dependable ally, steering the Transkei towards self-government, overcoming whatever opposition stood in his way and laying the foundations for a personal dictatorship which ministers in Pretoria were only too content to support.

The Transkei's first general election in 1962, in which Matanzima stood as a champion of separate development while his opponents advocated a multiracial future both for the Transkei and for South Africa, resulted in a clear rejection of apartheid. Three out of every four candidates elected favoured a multiracial solution. But by relying on the support of chiefs, whom he had previously ensured were entrenched as a permanent majority in the legislative assembly, Matanzima succeeded in obtaining his own election as chief minister. He then proceeded to claim that he had a mandate to implement separate development policies. 'The people of the Transkei,' he told the assembly, 'have, through the ballot box, expressed their uncompromising rejection of the policy of multiracialism.' One of the ministers in his new government was Winnie's father, Columbus Madikizela.

After thirteen years of controlling public resources and patronage, using his chiefly connections and in the last resort locking up his leading opponents, Matanzima succeeded at his fourth election in 1976 in capturing seventy-one of seventy-five seats. He then used his election victory to claim that it constituted a mandate to launch Transkei as an independent state. Independence for the homelands had become the ultimate goal of apartheid's architects, the final solution for the African population. By bestowing independence on all ten homelands, the government would finally remove all claim that the African population had to South African citizenship. It would also provide proof to the international community, so officials in Pretoria believed, that the South African government had fulfilled its obligations to provide full rights to the African population.

In October 1976, the Transkei was duly pronounced to be an independent state. Overnight, 1.6 million Xhosas living there and 1.3 million Xhosas living in 'white' areas lost their South African citizenship. Ministers in Pretoria announced that South Africa was henceforth a country of 22 million people, as opposed to 26 million beforehand.

Other homelands followed suit. In 1977, Bophuthatswana, the homeland of the Tswana people, consisting of nineteen major pieces of land spread across three of South Africa's provinces, was made independent, despite evident opposition; in all some 1.8 million Tswana lost their South African citizenship. In 1979, Venda opted for independence, even though the chief minister had lost an election on the issue. In 1981, Ciskei's leader decided to accept Pretoria's offer, ignoring the advice of a distinguished panel of experts and an adverse opinion survey. Foreign governments took the view that independence for the homelands was nothing more than a device to perpetuate white supremacy and withheld all recognition. Pretoria was nevertheless jubilant. 'If our policy is taken to its full logical conclusion as far as the black people are concerned, there will not be one black man with South African citizenship,' declared a government minister.

For an élite group of African politicians, chiefs, civil servants and traders, self-government and independence brought substantial rewards. Cabinet ministers, members of legislative assemblies and civil servants gained increasingly from high salaries, loans, land and housing, as the South African authorities sought to establish a prosperous middle class which would underpin the homelands system.

The Pretoria government tried to entice Mandela into the process. In 1973, the minister of prisons, James Kruger, arranged to meet Mandela on Robben Island and offered to remit his life sentence on condition that he recognized the Transkei authorities and agreed to settle there as a Transkei citizen. Several subsequent offers were made, but Mandela turned them all down.

Matanzima also made attempts to see Mandela on Robben Island, but his approaches too were rejected. Yet though they remained political adversaries, family business continued. Matanzima played a prominent role in the arrangements leading up to Zeni's wedding and he was instrumental in persuading the South African authorities to allow Winnie to attend. He also helped Mandela's first wife, Evelyn, take over a trading store in Cofimvaba in the Transkei from departing whites.

The independence process began to falter when Chief Mangosuthu Buthelezi, political leader of some 5 million Zulus, the largest ethnic group in the country, decided to have no truck with it. Buthelezi's role in the apartheid system was a complex one. In his youth he was marked down by the authorities as a troublemaker. While studying at Fort Hare he had joined the ANC's Youth League and in his final year he had been expelled for taking part in political protest; among those whom he openly admired were Chief Luthuli and Mandela. Buthelezi was nevertheless prepared to work within the apartheid system. Elected as chief minister of KwaZulu in 1976, he developed the art of opposing Pretoria's homelands policy while at the same time playing a leading role in it. Cooperation was justified, he argued, on pragmatic grounds. The homelands policy enabled Zulus to acquire vital administrative experience which they would be able to use to good effect in a multiracial South Africa in the future and it provided them too with a platform from which to oppose apartheid.

Using his position as a member of the Zulu royal family, Buthelezi built up a powerful cultural and political movement, Inkatha ye Nkululeko we Sizwe (Freedom of the Nation), which gained support not only in KwaZulu but in urban areas as well. Within a few years, Inkatha claimed to have 350,000 paid-up members, making it the largest black political organization allowed to function in South Africa's history. Buthelezi himself, according to some opinion polls, was regarded by many Africans as a more important national leader than Mandela. In 1978, he won the first election in KwaZulu with nearly a clean sweep of the seats. As head of the KwaZulu government he possessed considerable powers of patronage and control and used them ruthlessly. In many respects he resembled a tribal potentate, intolerant of criticism, brooking no opposition, given to making interminable speeches and constantly reminiscing about the past exploits of the Zulu people. In sum, he seemed an ideal partner for the government. But having lent the homelands system greater credibility than any other homeland leader, he then delivered it a crippling blow by refusing independence.

The apartheid system was in trouble in other ways. The economic boom of the 1960s, together with the increasing use of advanced production techniques, had resulted in such a serious shortage of skilled labour that further economic growth was hampered. The reservoir of white skills had simply run out and white immigration was not sufficient to fill the gap. White businessmen, for reasons of self-interest, argued that the only solution was to scrap the job reservation system giving whites a monopoly of skilled work and to allow blacks to move upwards in the labour market. They were critical of the government's vast system of labour controls which treated millions of workers who passed through it as 'an undifferentiated mass'. What they wanted was a black labour force that was better educated, more highly skilled and stable. They also favoured legal recognition of black trade unions, which would allow them to conduct industrial relations on an orderly basis. A rash of strikes in 1973 pointed to the urgent need for improved labour conditions. The Soweto uprising in 1976 intensified all these arguments and added new ones. What employers now feared was the emergence of a new generation of radical activists who, in their hatred of apartheid, might turn against the free-enterprise system as well.

Foreign criticism of apartheid also flared up in the wake of Soweto. The spectacle of armed police shooting schoolchildren in the streets brought worldwide condemnation. International opinion was again outraged the following year by the death of the black-consciousness leader Steve Biko, in particular the manner in which he died. After five days of brutal interrogation at security police headquarters in Port Elizabeth, during which he suffered severe head injuries, Biko was put naked into the back of a police truck, close to collapse, provided with nothing more than a blanket and a bottle of water, and driven for 700 miles to a prison hospital in Pretoria, where he died a few hours after arriving, lying on a mat on a stone floor. He was the forty-sixth detainee to die in police custody. News of his death unleashed a new wave of fury and violence on the streets which the government eventually brought to a halt by outlawing virtually every black-consciousness organization in the country and detaining dozens of black leaders, as well as a number of white critics.

In Washington and Westminster, there were demands for economic boycotts and sanctions against South Africa. At the United Nations Security Council, members voted for a mandatory ban on arms sales to South Africa. Representatives from thirteen Western governments attended Biko's funeral to mark their own form of protest. Far more damaging was the reaction of foreign investors, who no longer looked at South Africa as such a stable or profitable haven. Foreign capital, which had been a vital factor in helping South Africa to achieve high rates of economic growth, began to flow out. Several prominent American and British banks terminated their South African business. Multinational companies with subsidiaries in South Africa faced intense criticism from anti-apartheid groups, some demanding their withdrawal. For the first time, the costs of sustaining apartheid began to affect white interests.

CHAPTER 16
Free Mandela!

Apart from members of his family and his lawyers, few outsiders had been permitted to see Mandela since his imprisonment in 1964. The only regular outsiders he met were officials from the International Committee of the Red Cross, who in public maintained a discreet silence about their visits. Other outsiders were allowed visits only if it suited the interests of the government. A reporter and photographer from the London *Daily Telegraph* were admitted to Robben Island in 1964. Photographs taken on this occasion showing Mandela and Sisulu talking together in the courtyard while prisoners worked on piles of stones behind them were the only photographs ever taken of Mandela on Robben Island and were used in the foreign press time after time; in South Africa itself, their publication was banned. A visit by a representative of the American Bar Association was discussed by prisoners for many months for the manner in which the American lawyer, perspiring heavily and somewhat inebriated, began to argue with Mandela about conditions on Robben Island, comparing them favourably to prison conditions he had observed in the United States.

In 1970, a former British defence minister, Denis Healey, who had previously met Mandela during his visit to London in 1962, was given an hour to talk to him in the presence of prison officials. 'I was relieved to find that intellectually, morally and physically, he was fighting fit,' Healey reported. 'He wasn't in any way cast down by his experiences of the last eight years.' In 1973, an Australian journalist, David MacNicoll, described Mandela wearing 'well-fitting fawn moleskin coat and trousers, comfortable soft brown leather shoes, and red-and-blue striped woollen socks'. His eyes, he noted, were alert and humorous.

Public interest in Mandela's fate during these years hardly stirred and he remained a largely forgotten figure. During the early 1970s, he wrote, when there was no sign of any break in the apartheid system, the Rivonia prisoners had to force themselves not to give in to despair. But in the wake of the Soweto uprising and the repression that followed it, as anti-apartheid protest both at home and abroad gathered momentum, Mandela in prison became a potent symbol of opposition to the government. In March 1980, the Soweto newspaper *The Post* started a campaign demanding his release with the banner headline FREE MANDELA! Neither his photograph nor his words could be published. To many people he seemed linked more to a distant past than of any relevance to the future. But the campaign caught the public imagination, attracting support from white university students and liberal politicians, as well as a host of black organizations. A growing number of whites were becoming openly disenchanted with the apartheid system. They included not just a large part of the English-speaking community but the Afrikaner élite – businessmen, academics, professionals and journalists – more affluent and broad-minded than before, and more susceptible to foreign opinion about the iniquities of racial discrimination. At a white election in 1977, the opposition Progressive Federal Party, which advocated the removal of racial discrimination and an extension of the franchise to all blacks, had attracted some 17 per cent of the vote. Afrikaans-language newspapers were as outspoken as English-language newspapers in suggesting that the government needed to negotiate with radical black leaders as well as traditional ones.

On the eve of the twentieth anniversary of Sharpeville, in March 1980, Zindzi Mandela addressed a huge gathering organized by white students at the University of the Witwatersrand supporting the call for Mandela's release. 'I have not joined you as a daughter calling for the release of her father. I have joined as part of my generation who have never known what a normal life is,' she said. 'I've seen the suffering of my people escalating to boiling point. I've seen the thunderous eruption of the Soweto volcano when my generation could take it no longer.' Mandela, when he was free, had offered solutions to South Africa's problems. 'The call for

Mandela's release is merely to say there is an alternative to the inevitable bloodbath.'

The campaign to release Mandela was taken up around the world. Millions of people who supported the campaign had little precise idea of who he was. Virtually nothing had been heard of him for fifteen years. But the tide of foreign hostility towards apartheid was now running strong, making him one of the most famous prisoners in the world. Mandela's presence on Robben Island soon reached mythic proportions. Awards by foreign governments, universities and cities were showered upon him; streets were named after him; songs were written about him. In 1981 he was nominated as a candidate for the post of chancellor at the University of London and received some 7,200 votes, losing only to Princess Anne.

Winnie shared in some of the limelight. The story of her banishment to a remote, impoverished township after so many years of persecution was reported around the world. Foreign journalists and diplomats regularly made the journey to Brandfort to talk to her. With characteristic energy, she had set about trying to make life at Brandfort more tolerable. She organized home improvements, established a garden and studied for a social science degree by correspondence. She acquired a companion, a young Rastafarian artist called 'M. K.' Malefane, who was introduced by Zindzi and subsequently moved into her house. Her grandchildren came to stay with her.

She was also largely successful in overcoming the suspicions and hostility of township residents, organizing a series of welfare projects for the local community. She started a day-care centre, a soup kitchen, a mobile clinic and a sewing group, obtaining donations from relief organizations, foreign embassies and private individuals. As news of her work spread abroad, foreign funds for her projects flowed in. Letters of support arrived from church organizations, trade unions and academic institutions.

The attention that Winnie received in Brandfort added to her sense of her own importance. She enjoyed being known as 'Mother of the Nation', a title the press began to repeat endlessly. Her behaviour became increasingly imperious. She came to see the struggle against apartheid more and more in personal terms. The darker side of her character surfaced. She took to drinking heavily, running up huge accounts at the local liquor store for champagne, Cinzano and spirits. In some households in the neighbourhood, she was feared for her temper rather than admired. The mother of a nine-year-old boy complained that Winnie had assaulted him with her belt buckle. While denying the charge, Winnie asserted she had the right to discipline children who played on her premises. She was acquitted. In another incident, she was convicted of assaulting a woman with a bottle and a shoe. Winnie's propensity for settling matters through physical force became more marked.

As the clamour for Mandela's release continued, the government decided to move him from Robben Island to a prison on the mainland near Cape Town called Pollsmoor. Robben Island itself had become a part of the legend the government was anxious to destroy. Without warning, one night at the end of March 1982, Mandela was told he was to be transferred immediately from the island, along with Sisulu, Mhlaba and Mlangeni. Kathrada joined them a few months later.

Leaving Robben Island after eighteen years was an unsettling experience for Mandela. He had become accustomed to its routine. It was a place where he felt comfortable. But above all, it had become a focal point of resistance to apartheid. All the hardships that had been endured, all the campaigns for improvements that had been fought, all the efforts made to turn the island into a university had become part of a powerful tradition which he had helped to shape and to lead. Prisoners leaving Robben Island often did so with a sense of achievement rather than of loss. The prison community there was remembered as a valued part of their lives. The bonds of friendship and loyalty forged were greater than anything experienced outside. One of Mandela's companions, Mac Maharaj, reflecting years later on the decades of struggle against apartheid, remarked, 'Paradoxically, some of the happiest times in that whole long struggle were in the company of my comrades on Robben Island.'

Mandela was now cut off from all this. His abrupt departure meant that he had no time even to say farewell properly to friends with whom he had shared so many ordeals. Nor was there the slightest prospect that he would ever be released. Responding to the campaign for his release, the prime minister, P. W. Botha, denounced him as an 'arch-Marxist' committed to violent revolution who would have to serve the sentence of life imprisonment imposed on him by a court of law.

Botha first made a name for himself in politics as a roughneck breaking up his opponents' meetings. He climbed through the ranks of the National Party to reach the post of defence minister, and then emerged unexpectedly as prime minister in 1978 as the result of a vicious struggle for power between two rival camps within the party, the *verkrampte* wing, the name given to its more narrow-minded, reactionary members, and the *verligte* wing, the name given to its more open-minded, enlightened ones. Like Verwoerd and Vorster, Botha was an authoritarian figure, single-minded, ruthless and intolerant of opposition. His commitment to the cause of white supremacy was no less tenacious that theirs, but he preferred a pragmatic approach to the conduct of government rather than an ideological one. His objective was to modernize apartheid, to rid it of its more impractical encumbrances, to make it function more effectively. This was an objective supported by Afrikaner businessmen, increasingly frustrated by the costs of apartheid, and by the military establishment, which had become openly critical about the lack of urgency shown by the government in tackling the fundamental issues thrown up by the Soweto revolt. As defence minister for twelve years, Botha was close to the military's way of thinking. What the military wanted above all were defensible political goals.

Botha began his term of office by emphasizing the need for change. 'We are moving in a changing world,' he said. 'We must adapt, otherwise we shall die.' In one speech after another, he repeated the same message across the country: 'A white monopoly of power is untenable in the Africa of today ... A meaningful division of power is needed between all race groups ... Apartheid is a recipe for permanent conflict.'

The air was thick with the promises of reform. Botha declared himself to be in favour of removing 'hurtful unnecessary discrimination' and suggested that laws banning interracial marriage and sex should no longer be regarded as 'holy cows'. Petty apartheid, once a key government objective, aimed at keeping blacks apart from whites in the use of public amenities such a park benches, post office windows, museums and libraries, began to fray at the edges. White officials, accustomed to abusing blacks at will, were now told to handle them with respect.

Proceeding with extreme caution, Botha also initiated moves to improve conditions in black urban areas. After thirty years of harsh legislation designed to prevent the African population from putting down roots in white areas, the government finally recognized their right to live there permanently, according them property rights. Restrictions on African, Coloured and Indian businessmen were eased. New housing programmes were started. An electrification project for Soweto was put in hand. Plans to remove Alexandra, the black ghetto north of Johannesburg surrounded by affluent white suburbs, which Verwoerd had condemned as a 'black spot' and marked down for destruction, were abandoned. A similar reprieve was given to the Crossroads squatter settlement outside Cape Town, whose inhabitants had achieved international fame by defying the government's forceful efforts to expel them and raze the settlement to the ground. Botha made his personal contribution towards trying to establish better relations with the black community by paying a visit to Soweto, the first prime minister ever to set foot in a black township, proclaiming as he did so, 'We are all South Africans.'

Labour conditions also improved. African workers were permitted to join registered unions. Most job reservation laws were scrapped. In the field of education, the government committed itself to the goal of providing equal, though separate, education for all population groups, while emphasizing that 'the historical backlog cannot be overcome overnight'. By 1983 only seven times as much was spent on white children per capita as on African children, compared to the sixteen times of 1968. The government's purpose henceforth was to create stable black urban communities with a vested interest in the free-enterprise system.

Alongside this programme of reform, Botha began to develop a national security system designed to overcome any challenge mounted against the government either internally or externally. He was convinced that South Africa was the target of an internationally organized communist strategy to overthrow the government and replace it with a Marxist regime beholden to the Soviet Union. Botha had a fixed and simple view of world politics, believing that they revolved around a struggle between communist and anti-communist forces, with South Africa and its vast mineral resources and maritime facilities the glittering prize. Whatever ills befell South Africa, whether it was domestic unrest, international pressure or regional threats, he attributed ultimately to Moscow's grand design. Every adversity was seen as part of a 'total onslaught' that South Africa faced. In this scheme of things the ANC was to figure prominently.

In its years of exile since 1960, the ANC had met with mixed fortunes. Oliver Tambo had travelled the world seeking to build support in as many different quarters as possible and gaining widespread respect for his skill at diplomacy in the process. The Soviet Union had given most support, providing funds, equipment and training. But assistance had also been forthcoming from Sweden, Denmark, Norway and Holland and a host of political parties, trade unions, student groups and church organizations across the Western world. At the United Nations, the ANC had been granted observer status since 1974 and allowed access to international agencies from which the South African government had been banned. The number of ANC 'embassies' around the world surpassed the number maintained by the South African government.

But as for its main task of confronting the regime at home, the ANC had little to show. At a conference in 1969 at its military headquarters in Morogoro in Tanzania, where guerrilla training camps had been established four years earlier, the ANC formed a revolutionary council with responsibility for conducting guerrilla warfare and expressed its strategy for the first time in revolutionary terms. Among the members of the revolutionary council were Tambo, the ANC's president since the death of Chief Luthuli in 1967, Yusuf Dadoo, the Indian communist leader, and Joe Slovo, still the chief of staff of Umkhonto we Sizwe. For the first time, too, the ANC opened its membership to whites, Coloureds and Indians.

Yet for all the enthusiasm shown for revolutionary ideas, the ANC's years in exile were marked more by internal dissension and disputes than by any headway made in implementing them. Located 1,000 miles away from the borders of South Africa, unable to find a way through the surrounding white buffer states of Angola,

347

Rhodesia and Mozambique, the guerrillas in Tanzania succumbed to boredom, frustration and inertia. In the leadership, splits developed over the decision to allow whites to join the ANC's ranks and over the role of members of the Communist Party. Attempts made to infiltrate agents into South Africa were often amateurish, detected well in advance by Pretoria's spies, who penetrated deep into the organization.

The change in the ANC's fortunes came when Angola and Mozambique were taken over by nationalist guerrilla movements in 1975 and the Soweto revolt the following year brought an army of eager recruits. In the wake of the uprising, some 14,000 youths left South Africa, most of them joining the ANC. Many went to military camps established in northern Angola under the control of ANC instructors. The more promising recruits were sent for training in the Soviet Union and East Germany. The capital of Mozambique, Maputo, less than fifty miles from the South African border, became a key operational centre, to where much of Umkhonto's command structure was transferred. Joe Slovo moved there in 1977, with his wife, Ruth First. ANC groups were also set up in Botswana, Swaziland and Lesotho to help establish an internal network and to supervise the flow of recruits.

From 1977, Umkhonto began a low-level sabotage campaign, selecting targets mainly with a high propaganda value, intending more to re-establish a political following among the black population and to raise its morale than to threaten the economy or white security. Its targets included police stations in black residential areas, administrative buildings, railway lines and electricity substations. A number of informers, security policemen and state witnesses were assassinated. From 1980 more ambitious targets were selected. That year, ANC guerrillas attacked industrial plants in Sasolburg and Secunda, destroying fuel storage tanks; in 1981, rockets were fired at the Voortrekkerhoogte military base; in 1982, bombs exploded in the Koeberg nuclear power station near Cape Town, damaging one of the reactors and two transformers; in 1983, a car-bomb attack was made outside a military building in Pretoria, killing sixteen people and injuring more than 200 – the most serious sabotage incident in South Africa's history.

The government retaliated against neighbouring states with a combination of military might and economic coercion intended to force them into submission and to expel the ANC. Its main target was Mozambique. From bases in the Transvaal, the South African military trained, armed and directed a rebel group whose purpose was to create havoc in Mozambique, attacking bridges, railways, road transport, schools and clinics. Direct military raids were made on ANC targets in Maputo. In 1982, a parcel bomb sent to the Eduardo Mondlane University in Maputo killed Ruth First. Mozambique was also subjected to economic pressure. Similar methods were used against Angola, Lesotho and Swaziland. Assassination squads were used at home and abroad.

Unable to withstand the pressure, South Africa's neighbours capitulated, one by one, to its demands. In 1984, Mozambique expelled some 800 ANC members, allowing only a mission of ten to remain. Deprived of its most important forward positions, the ANC was forced to operate from headquarters in Lusaka, Zambia, hundreds of miles away from the front line.

Botha, meanwhile, proceeded with a plan for constitutional change, which he confidently expected would become the centrepiece of his reform programme. He intended to expand the political base of the white population by incorporating the Coloured and Indian communities into the white political system, providing them with political rights while ensuring that political power remained securely in the hands of the whites. The terminology he used for describing this exercise was 'a healthy form of power sharing'. Much emphasis was placed on the importance of 'group rights', a term which, according to the government, meant that each race group was allowed to govern itself without interference or domination by any other group, but which in practice added up to little more than the old system of racial separation run by whites. Parliament was to be divided into three chambers: a House of Assembly for whites, a House of Representatives for Coloureds and a House of Delegates for Indians. Each chamber was to be given responsibility for its 'own' affairs, such as education, health and housing, leaving other major portfolios, such as law and order and finance, in the hands of the government. A new office of state president was to be established, giving the head of government greatly increased powers. No representation was accorded to the black population. Botha's view was that blacks had been given sufficient political representation through the homelands system. All that he was prepared to concede to urban blacks were elected local councils.

Botha's proposals, as he had expected, caused uproar in the *verkrampte* wing of the National Party, which regarded any attempt to tamper with Verwoerd's doctrine of total separation as heresy. A group of Nationalist MPs broke away to form the Conservative Party, advocating a return to absolute apartheid, a geographical separation of the races, with homelands for Coloureds and Indians as well as Africans. New extremist groups sprang up competing for the loyalty of the *volk*. But Botha was vindicated by the results of a white referendum in November 1983 in which two-thirds of the white electorate voted in favour of the new constitution.

What Botha did not anticipate was the extent of opposition to the new constitution organized by anti-apartheid groups. In August 1983, delegates representing more than 300 organizations, including trade unions, youth groups, student bodies and community associations, met in Mitchell's Plains, a Coloured township near Cape Town, to launch the United Democratic Front to coordinate protest against the new constitution in the broadest display of public opposition to apartheid in nearly thirty years. The UDF was a conscious effort to revive the style of nationalist politics adopted by the Congress movement of the 1950s. It functioned as a popular front rather than as a political organization. It set out only the broadest aims – to create a united democratic South Africa free from homelands and group areas and based on the will of the people – leaving its affiliates to decide their own activities. Its purpose was to draw together as wide a range of opposition forces as possible, cutting across lines of class and colour. White organizations, such as the National Union of South African Students, were welcomed into its fold and soon some 600 organizations were members. Among the leaders were veterans from the 1950s Congress campaigns, including Archie Gumede, a Durban lawyer who served as chairman of the Release Mandela Committee, Helen Joseph, the veteran civil rights activist, and Albertina Sisulu. Like Winnie Mandela, Albertina Sisulu had endured years of imprisonment, solitary confinement, house arrest and harassment, and was greatly admired and respected by anti-apartheid activists. At the time, she was being held in prison, in solitary confinement, without charge. One of the patrons chosen by the UDF was Nelson Mandela.

Mandela was kept informed of these events. In his new abode in Pollsmoor Prison, he was allowed to receive a wide range of newspapers and magazines, including *Time* magazine and the *Guardian Weekly* from London, reading every edition from cover to cover. He was also able to listen to local radio stations. Overall, living conditions in Pollsmoor for Mandela and his colleagues were a considerable improvement on Robben Island. They were allocated a spacious room on the top floor of a prison wing, with an adjacent section containing toilets and showers. They were given proper beds with sheets. They were served meals with meat and vegetables and allowed to buy special provisions each month. They were provided with two rooms for use as a library and for study purposes and a wide variety of books and films. They also had access to a large roof-top terrace for exercise; tennis matches on the roof were taken very seriously. They were free to get up when they wanted.

Despite these improvements, however, they all hankered for the life on Robben Island. They missed their comrades there, the openness of the island, the views across the sea to the mountains on the mainland beyond, the sounds of the birds, the roar of the surf, the flowers and wildlife. Pollsmoor, by contrast, was a modern concrete building, where the only view was of the concrete walls which surrounded them. Their terrace, though half the size of a football pitch, was covered in black rubberized matting and contained by high concrete walls, painted white, which during the summer became unbearably hot. The only glimpse of the outside world they had was a partial sight of the ridges of the nearby Steenberg mountain; all the rest was sky. As Mandela later told a visitor, he came to know what Oscar Wilde meant by 'the little tent of blue that prisoners call the sky'. They made repeated requests to be transferred back to Robben Island, but to no avail.

To compensate for their drab surroundings, Mandela constructed a large garden on the terrace using thirty-two oil drums sliced in half and filled with rich, loamy soil taken from the prison grounds. Mandela's garden became a centre of interest not only for his colleagues, who helped with the work, but also for the prison commander, Brigadier Munro, a gardening enthusiast, and prison staff, who provided him with seeds and manure. Each morning, after his normal round of exercises, Mandela put on an old straw hat and gardening gloves and tended his plants for two hours. The size of the garden steadily grew. At one stage, there were 900 plants – onions, aubergines, cabbages, cauliflowers, beans, spinach, carrots, cucumbers, broccoli, beetroots, lettuces, tomatoes, peppers, strawberries and a variety of herbs. The produce went both to common-law prisoners and to warders.

The visiting arrangements at Pollsmoor were also much improved. Instead of the dingy, cramped, box-like compartments on Robben Island, Pollsmoor had spacious cubicles fitted with large glass partitions through which visitors and prisoners could see each other clearly from the waist up and with modern microphones which enabled them to hear properly.

For Mandela, a moment of pure joy came in March 1984 when he was allowed his first 'contact' with Winnie. The government conceded contact visits only after prolonged pressure from the International Committee of the Red Cross. For the occasion, Mandela was taken to a room separate from the main visiting area which his personal warder, James Gregory, had endeavoured to make more pleasant with some comfortable furniture. Winnie arrived at the prison in the company of Zindzi and Zindzi's youngest son, Gadaffi, not knowing how different this visit would be. Accompanied by Gregory, she was shown into the room, where Mandela was sitting in a large, easy chair. He stood up as Winnie rushed across the room towards him, squealing with delight. They hugged and kissed, laughing with pleasure. It was a moment of which Mandela had long dreamed, the first time he had touched Winnie in nearly twenty years. Then he embraced Zindzi, whom he had last held as a baby. For the rest of the visit, Mandela held Gadaffi in his arms. The following day, Winnie, Zindzi and Gadaffi returned for a two-hour visit. In two days, Mandela used up his entire quota of visits for the month.

But, as always with members of his family, trouble was never far away. In June 1984, Zindzi was attacked by her boyfriend, Patrick Moshidi, the father of Gadaffi, who punched, kicked and stabbed her in the hand and head, leaving her for dead unconscious on a hillside. She was found and taken to hospital, where she spent several days in intensive care. In August 1984, while Winnie was visiting doctors in Johannesburg, her house in Brandfort and the adjacent clinic were wrecked by petrol bombs. While waiting for repairs to be completed, Winnie remained in her house in Orlando West, technically in defiance of her banning order.

Mandela's relationship with Makgatho and Makaziwe was also uneasy. Makgatho stopped visiting his father in 1983, hating the constant goading about his failure to improve his education. Makaziwe also seemed to disappoint him. After she had succeeded in obtaining a degree from Fort Hare, Mandela made clear his view that she should study for a higher degree abroad. When she took a job as a social worker instead, he wrote her a scathing rebuke, condemning her lack of ambition. She subsequently went on to study abroad, but became largely estranged from her father.

Throughout 1984, a mood of tension was spreading among the black population. An economic recession, more severe than anything South Africa had known for fifty years, cast thousands into unemployment. The inflation rate climbed, causing a squeeze on black living standards. Rural areas were hit by a devastating drought. Student groups were active once more, protesting at low educational standards. The elections for Coloured and Indian representatives to the new tricameral parliament in August raised the temperature still further. A low turn-out of voters – less than one in five Coloureds and Indians thought there was any point in voting – suggested massive disapproval of the new constitution. African resentment at being excluded from parliament reached new heights. The new system of local government for African townships, introduced in 1983, also provoked widespread opposition. Rent increases imposed to help finance new councils brought sharp protests. Local councillors, elected in poorly attended polls, were denounced as 'stooges' and 'collaborators'.

In September, outbreaks of violence began. They were sporadic at first, ignited by local grievances, flaring up with great intensity, shifting from one area to the next and gradually drawing in more and more of an urban population that was alienated and hostile. At the forefront were groups of black youths – 'comrades', as they came to be known – determined to destroy 'the system' and ready to defy armed police and soldiers in the dusty and decrepit streets of the townships with stones, catapults and petrol bombs. Many saw themselves as the shock troops of revolution and believed that it was within their reach. Students joined the fray, forsaking their classrooms once more. 'Liberation before Education' became their slogan. The townships' revolt, however, was not solely a 'children's war', as it had been in 1976. This time the revolt was part of a popular movement involving entire communities – parents, teachers, workers, churchmen and women. Nor were the aims of the black activists confined to resolving particular grievances. This time the objective was to overthrow apartheid.

Urged on by the ANC in exile to mount 'a people's war' and make the townships ungovernable, young comrades enforced consumer boycotts, organized rent strikes, attacked government buildings, set up 'people's courts' and hunted down 'collaborators' – township councillors, local policemen and others deemed to support 'the system'. Their trademark became 'the necklace' method of killing – a tyre filled with petrol thrown over a victim and set on fire.

The government responded with a show of military might intended to demonstrate to the white electorate as well as to the truculent black population that it was fully in command. A combined forced of paramilitary police and troops moved into the townships around the industrial centres in southern Transvaal, the epicentre of the first cycle of violence. Opposition groups replied with their own show of strength, calling for a two-day stay-away, demanding the withdrawal of the army and the police from the townships. As well as student groups and local UDF affiliates, labour unions undertook to support the stay-away, lending their weight for the first time to a mass protest over political grievances. The stay-away was the most successful of its kind in nearly thirty-five years. Convinced that forceful action would curb the 'unrest', the government ordered the detention of union and community leaders.

White business leaders were appalled both at the mayhem and at the government's lack of any clear strategy for dealing with black grievances other than repression, and joined in open criticism of government policy. Abroad, there was mounting anti-apartheid activity. From late 1984, the anti-apartheid movement in the United States gained significant momentum for the first time, attracting support for campaigns aimed at getting US corporations to withdraw from South Africa.

Confronted by a rising clamour for major reform at home and

354

abroad, Botha had only a limited stock of ideas upon which to draw. He was prepared to make modifications to the apartheid system but only where they did not diminish white power and privilege. He accepted the need to allow Africans in urban areas greater status, promised to open central business districts to all races, agreed to suspend the forced removals policy, repealed laws prohibiting sex and marriage across the colour line and talked of possible changes to influx controls.

Botha also came up with what he believed was a subtle solution to the Mandela problem. Demands for Mandela's release were by now universal. Western governments saw this as an essential prelude to a negotiated settlement between the government and the black population. Botha's plan was to offer to release Mandela on condition that he publicly renounced the use of violence. If he refused, then the international community would understand why the government could not release him and the blame for his imprisonment would rest with Mandela himself and not the government.

Addressing the House of Assembly on 31 January 1985, Botha declared:

> The government is willing to consider Mr Mandela's release in the Republic of South Africa on condition that Mr Mandela gives a full commitment that he will not make himself guilty of planning, instigating or committing acts of violence for the furtherance of political objectives, but will conduct himself in such a way that he will not again have to be arrested. It is therefore not the South African government which now stands in the way of Mr Mandela's freedom. It is himself. The choice is his. All that is required of him now is that he should unconditionally reject violence as a political instrument. This is, after all, a norm which is respected in all civilized countries of the world.

Mandela's reply was forthright. It was read out in public by Zindzi on 10 February at a mass rally at a stadium in Soweto called by the UDF to celebrate the award of the Nobel Peace Prize to the anti-apartheid activist Bishop Desmond Tutu.

> I am surprised at the conditions that the government wants to impose on me. I am not a violent man. My colleagues and I wrote in 1952 to Malan asking for a round-table conference to find a solution to the problems of our country, but that was ignored. When

355

Strijdom was in power, we made the same offer. Again it was ignored. When Verwoerd was in power, we asked for a national convention for all the people in South Africa to decide on their future. This, too, was in vain.

It was only then, when all other forms of resistance were no longer open to us, that we turned to armed struggle. Let Botha show that he is different than Malan, Strijdom and Verwoerd. Let him renounce violence. Let him say that he will dismantle apartheid. Let him unban the people's organization, the African National Congress. Let him free all who have been imprisoned, banished or exiled for their opposition to apartheid. Let him guarantee free political activity so that people may decide who will govern them.

I cherish my own freedom dearly, but I care even more for your freedom. Too many have died since I went to prison. Too many have suffered for the love of freedom. I owe it to their widows, to their orphans, to their mothers and to their fathers who have grieved and wept for them. Not only I have suffered during these long, lonely, wasted years. I am not less life-loving than you are. But I cannot sell my birthright, nor am I prepared to sell the birthright of the people to be free. I am in prison as the representative of the people and of your organization, the African National Congress, which was banned.

What freedom am I being offered while the organization of the people remains banned? What freedom am I being offered when I may be arrested on a pass offence? What freedom am I being offered to live my life as a family with my dear wife who remains in banishment in Brandfort? What freedom am I being offered when I need a stamp in my pass to seek work? What freedom am I being offered when my very South African citizenship is not respected?

Only free men can negotiate. Prisoners cannot enter into contracts . . . I cannot and will not give any undertaking at a time when I and you, the people, are not free.

These were the first words heard from Mandela in public since his final address in the Supreme Court in Pretoria more than twenty years before. The crowd erupted in a wild display of cheering and chanting.

CHAPTER 17

Talking with the Enemy

The amount of attention focused upon Mandela made the government acutely concerned about his conditions in prison. There was a constant worry that he might die, setting off an avalanche of condemnation and protest. Rumours of his ill-health and ill-treatment frequently circulated, sometimes started deliberately by Winnie. During one visit she paid to Mandela in 1983, he complained he had been issued with a new pair of shoes which were a size too small and pinched his toe. He said he would return them and get another pair, and was subsequently treated in hospital for a sore toenail. But as Winnie reported the matter, Mandela had been forced to wear shoes that were too small for him and as a result had had to have a toe amputated. Articles in the foreign press referred to such ill-treatment and suggested the prison authorities in Pollsmoor were trying to break his spirit. When the veteran opposition MP Helen Suzman visited Mandela to ascertain the truth, she asked how his foot was after the operation. Mandela at first looked blank and then said, 'Oh, you mean the toenail that was removed. That's fine. It was my fault really, as I ordered the wrong size shoe.' He took off his sock, held his bare foot up to the glass partition and wiggled his toes.

To demonstrate that Mandela was in good health and being well treated, the government allowed a number of foreign visitors to interview him. Just before Christmas in 1984, Nicholas Bethell, a member of the British House of Lords and of the European Parliament, met him in the prison commander's office. His account of the meeting appeared in a British newspaper in January 1985.

Mandela entered the room in the company of two senior prison officers – 'a six-foot-tall, lean figure, with silvery hair, an impeccable olive-green shirt and well-creased navy blue trousers'. His manner was self-assured. He was anxious to put Bethell at his ease and invited him to sit down at the commander's desk, where he could take notes. He confirmed that he was in good health: it was not true, he said, that he had cancer or that he had had a toe amputated. He was complimentary about the helpful attitude of senior officers. He listed a number of complaints – a damp patch on the wall of his room, the lack of contact with other political prisoners, the need for more family visits – but mentioned nothing to cause Bethell undue concern. 'The problem is, therefore, not one of brutal prison conditions,' said Bethell. 'It is that Mandela and his friends are in prison at all.'

Mandela explained his position about the armed struggle:

> The armed struggle was forced on us by the government. And if they want us now to give it up, the ball is in their court. They must legalize us, treat us as a political party and negotiate with us. Until they do, we will have to live with the armed struggle . . . Of course, if there were to be talks along these lines, we in the ANC would declare a truce.

When the interview ended, Brigadier Munro invited Bethell to visit Mandela's quarters.

> We walked in slow procession up flights of stairs and around corners, with Mandela leading the way as if showing me around his home. He did not open doors for me; this was done by sergeants with heavy keys after much saluting and clanking. Always, though, Mandela was the one who showed the way, inviting me to go first through every door and plying me with questions on Britain and the world . . .

Mandela introduced Bethell to his cellmates and proudly showed him his vegetable garden before saying goodbye. As a sergeant opened the grey, heavy steel door, Mandela shook hands, saying, 'Well, Lord Bethell, this is my frontier, and this is where I must leave you.'

A few weeks later, Samuel Dash, a professor of law at Georgetown University, met Mandela and he too testified to his commanding personality. He described him as looking younger than his sixty-six years. 'He appeared vigorous and healthy with a calm, confident manner and dignified bearing that seemed incongruous in our prison surroundings. Indeed, throughout our meeting I felt that I was in the presence not of a guerrilla fighter or radical ideologue, but a head of state.'

Dash asked him if he took any encouragement from suggestions that the government might repeal laws banning interracial marriage and ease influx controls. Mandela smiled. 'You are speaking about pinpricks,' he replied. 'Frankly, it is not my ambition to marry a white woman or to swim in a white pool. The central issue is political equality.'

Mandela outlined three basic principles for a future South Africa: a unitary state without homelands; non-racial elections for parliament; and one-person one-vote. Dash asked how this programme would affect the white population, many of whom feared that political equality would mean subjugation at the hands of an embittered black majority. Mandela stressed that this was a fundamental concern of the ANC's leadership. 'Unlike white people anywhere else in Africa, whites in South Africa belong here – this is their home,' Mandela said. 'We want them to live here with us and to share power with us.'

But, Dash asked, how could he reconcile such moderate positions with the ANC's avowed goal of overthrowing the regime by force? Mandela replied that he wished the changes he sought for South Africa could be achieved peacefully. And he conceded that blacks would suffer most if they resorted to violence. 'However,' he said, 'if white leaders do not act in good faith towards us, if they will not meet with us to discuss political equality, and if, in effect, they tell us that we must remain subjugated by the whites, then there is really no alternative for us other than violence. And, I assure you, we will prevail.' Because of the military power of the South African government, blacks could not defeat the white regime in direct combat, but, over time, 'we can make life most miserable for them'.

A second cycle of violence, more intense and more prolonged, began in March 1985, centred on the townships of the Eastern Cape. Army units were sent in to quell the violence but their efforts made little impact. In June, the focus of 'unrest' shifted to the mining towns of the East Rand. In July, Soweto erupted. As well as the daily chronicle of violence, there was an upsurge of boycotts, stay-aways, rent strikes, marches and demonstrations. Funeral services were turned into political rallies where ANC flags and banners were openly flaunted, all adding to the climate of insurrection.

In July, Botha declared a state of emergency in thirty-six magisterial districts in the Eastern Cape, the East Rand, the Vaal Triangle and Johannesburg, giving the police and the army virtually unlimited powers to deal with the local population. Security forces arrested hundreds of community leaders, student activists, church workers and union officials, hoping to break the back of local opposition. Assassination squads were once more at work.

The daily spectacle of violent protest and government repression, shown on television screens around the world, provoked a chorus of international condemnation and calls for action against Botha's government to force him to undertake major reforms and open negotiations with black leaders, including Mandela. Foreign investors, taking fright at the continuing violence and the possibility of international action, began unloading their South African shares. American banks decided to stop rolling over loans to South African borrowers, starting a chain reaction which pitched South Africa into a major financial crisis.

In an attempt to restore foreign confidence, government officials promised that major reforms were imminent and pointed to an address that Botha was due to make at the opening of a National Party conference in Durban on 15 August as a likely occasion on which they would be unveiled. The foreign minister, Pik Botha, travelled to Western capitals bearing the glad tidings and pledging that a formula would be found that would permit the unconditional release of Mandela. International interest in what Botha would say was intense.

But Botha never reacted well to pressure, either from the international community or from cabinet ministers anxious to proceed faster with reform. In a truculent performance that was watched on television around the world, Botha, wagging his finger, contemptuously dismissed demands for more change. 'I am not prepared to lead white South Africa and other minority groups on a road to abdication and suicide,' he said. He offered not a single new reform, blamed violence in the townships on 'communist agitators' and the foreign media, and castigated his critics at home and abroad, warning, 'Don't push us too far.'

It was a display of intransigence which worked well with Afrikaner audiences but made South Africa a leper in the world's financial markets. Foreign investors deserted South Africa in droves. The value of the rand plunged. The government was forced to suspend trading on the foreign exchange market, to close the Johannesburg stock exchange for five days and to impose a unilateral moratorium on the repayment of foreign debt.

The tide of opinion against South Africa was so strong that even conservative Western leaders like Ronald Reagan and Margaret Thatcher, previously outspoken in their opposition to sanctions as a means of dealing with South Africa, were obliged to agree to a package of measures. Though the action taken in Washington and London was of largely token significance, it was a sign of the strength of hostility towards South Africa that it was taken at all. At a Commonwealth conference in October, Thatcher joined other Commonwealth leaders in calling on Botha to dismantle apartheid, end the state of emergency, lift the ban on the ANC and release Mandela.

White business leaders, appalled by the unending cycle of black anger, government ineptitude, disinvestment, financial mayhem and international sanctions, lined up to condemn the government's failure to introduce meaningful reforms, and demanded urgent action, including the release of Mandela and moves to establish a new political system involving 'genuine power sharing'. In September, a small group of businessmen, led by the chairman of the Anglo-American Corporation, Gavin Relly, took the audacious step of flying to Zambia for talks with Oliver Tambo and other ANC leaders. The meeting took place at a lodge in a wildlife park, with the ANC members dressed impeccably in suits and ties and the businessmen wearing more casual attire, looking almost unkempt by comparison. 'What we are concerned with,' Relly told Tambo, 'is not so much whether the following generation will be governed by white or black people, but that [South Africa] will be a viable country and that it will not be destroyed by violence and strife.' Tambo replied that he personally abhorred violence – 'I even take insects out of the bath' – but warned that the conflict was bound to escalate unless apartheid was dismantled. At the end of the meeting, the participants all declared their satisfaction with the outcome. 'It was one of the nicest days I've ever spent,' said Relly. 'A picnic among South Africans talking about their future together.' Botha denounced the businessmen for their 'disloyalty' and for showing 'signs of weakness towards the enemies of South Africa'.

From Pollsmoor, Mandela took his own initiative, writing to the minister of justice, police and prisons, Kobie Coetsee, pressing him for a meeting to discuss talks between the ANC and the government. He received no reply.

By the end of 1985, now anxious to improve South Africa's standing with foreign banks and foreign governments and to head off the possibility of another debt crisis and a more punishing round of sanctions, Botha was ready to move ahead with further reforms. Apartheid, he declared in January 1986, was 'an outdated concept'. Finally conceding the inevitability of African urbaniz-ation, he agreed to scrap the pass laws and influx controls that were once considered vital protection for the white population and had for much of the century constituted a crippling burden for the African population. He pledged his commitment to 'power sharing' and proposed to establish a new national forum to represent African interests which he hoped would appeal to moderate African leaders. He talked of a 'single South Africa' with 'one citizenship' for all South Africans, shedding all further notion of turning South Africa into a country of separate homelands, as Verwoerd had planned. He also agreed to allow a Commonwealth negotiating team, the Eminent Persons Group, to visit South Africa as part of a mission to promote a dialogue between the government and black political leaders, including Mandela and ANC officials in exile.

The circumstances of Mandela's imprisonment now began to change. In November 1985, he had been admitted to the Volks Hospital in Cape Town for surgery on an enlarged prostate gland. While recuperating from the operation, in a tightly guarded section of the hospital, he had received an unexpected visitor: the prisons minister, Kobie Coetsee. By chance, on the day before the operation, Coetsee had boarded the same flight from Johannesburg to Cape Town as Winnie, who was on her way to see Mandela in hospital.

Coetsee had stopped by her seat in the economy section to assure her of the government's concern for her husband's health and later, during the flight, Winnie had marched through to the first-class section to talk to him. As a result of this encounter, Coetsee decided to pay Mandela a visit.

Mandela was amazed by the visit, but immediately took command of the situation, introducing Coetsee and the commissioner of prisons, General Johan Willemse, who was with him, to his nurses, inviting them to sit down, making sure they were comfortable and engaging in pleasantries. Coetsee was struck by his natural dignity and ease of manner. Mandela, for his part, sensed a change of atmosphere from previous meetings with government officials. Coetsee was altogether more gracious and cordial. Little of substance was discussed, but Coetsee hinted that he was looking for a way to put Mandela 'in a situation between prison and freedom'.

Upon leaving hospital in December, Mandela was told that he would not be rejoining his colleagues on the top floor at Pollsmoor but given separate quarters on the ground floor of a separate wing. His new quarters consisted of a large main room, comfortably furnished, with a private bathroom next door, and two other rooms, one for exercise and the other for study. Mandela was not happy to be separated from his colleagues. To meet with them henceforth, he had to put in an official request. But he realized that his new circumstances facilitated the possibility of discussions with the government, an objective he had always held. He also realized that his ANC colleagues would fear that, in isolation, he might be tricked into making a deal with the government which they could not support. He therefore asked George Bizos, his lawyer and friend, to fly to Lusaka to assure Tambo he would take no decisions without their approval. He wrote twice to Coetsee proposing talks, but was disheartened to receive no reply. He spent his days listening avidly to radio news broadcasts, devouring newspapers, exercising hard and continuing his studies, waiting for some signal from the outside world.

The opportunity for talks came not from the government but from the Commonwealth Eminent Persons Group. In early 1986, the Commonwealth negotiators, led by General Obasanjo, a former military leader of Nigeria, and Malcolm Fraser, a former Australian prime minister, began shuttling around southern Africa, endeavouring to find a common basis for negotiation between the South African government and the ANC. After some hesitation, Botha agreed to let Obasanjo meet Mandela in February and then for the group of seven to see him in March and then in May.

The prison authorities made sure that Mandela was well turned out for the occasion. A tailor was summoned to take his measurements for a new pin-stripe suit. He was also given a shirt, tie, underwear, shoes and socks. The prison commander, Brigadier Munro, inspected the result. 'Mandela,' he said, 'you look more like a prime minister now, not a prisoner.'

When they met him at Pollsmoor's guest house, the Commonwealth team were equally impressed. 'We were first struck by his physical authority – by his immaculate appearance, his apparent good health, and his commanding presence,' they reported. 'In his manner he exuded authority and received the respect of all around him, including his jailers.'

At the start of their second meeting, both Coetsee and Willemse put in an appearance. Mandela urged them to stay to listen to the discussion. He had nothing to hide from them, he said. If only the government and the ANC could sit down and talk, some of the differences between them which arose solely through a lack of contact could be eliminated. The fact of talking was essential in the building of mutual confidence. But the two men went away.

Mandela expounded at length on his hopes for a multiracial democracy in South Africa. He acknowledged the fears that whites held about majority rule and stressed the importance of providing minority groups with a real sense of security. He emphasized that he was a nationalist, not a communist, whose principles were unchanged from those to which he subscribed when the Freedom Charter was drawn up in 1955.

He was questioned extensively on the issue of violence. Mandela explained that he was not yet in a position to renounce violence, but stressed that violence could never provide an ultimate solution to South Africa's problems; only negotiations could. The Commonwealth team found him 'reasonable and conciliatory'. They planned one further meeting with him before concluding their assignment.

Botha, however, was becoming impatient with the whole process. During the course of their endeavours, the Commonwealth team had drawn up a 'possible negotiating concept' which went far beyond anything he was willing to contemplate. In exchange for a commitment from the ANC to suspend violence and enter into negotiation, the South African government would have to release Mandela and other political prisoners and detainees, withdraw the military from the townships, lift the ban on the ANC and the PAC, suspend detention without trial and permit normal political activity. Botha had held back from terminating the whole exercise only because of the threat of further sanctions.

Yet Botha was also faced with signs of a growing white backlash. Opinion polls and parliamentary by-elections showed a clear resurgence of support for extreme right-wing parties which accused the government of dealing leniently with township unrest for fear of offending foreign opinion. Added to fears about black unrest and the government's failure to suppress it, there was deep alarm about how far the government was prepared to go with its reform programme. A chance remark by the *verligte* foreign minister, Pik Botha, that he could foresee circumstances in which South Africa might one day have a black president, sent a shockwave through the white community. Botha denied any such notion, but the damage was done. National Party officials reported mass defections to right-wing parties.

Black activists meanwhile, convinced that they had the government on the run, were becoming ever more defiant. Black leaders predicted the government's downfall. The ANC in exile declared 1986 to be the 'Year of Umkhonto we Sizwe' and talked of 'turning every corner of our country into a battlefield'. In scores of townships across the country, the tide of black militancy was thought to be unstoppable. On May Day, workers and students staged a nationwide strike, the largest anti-apartheid protest in South Africa's history. An even larger three-day general strike was planned for 16 June to mark the tenth anniversary of the Soweto uprising.

Under pressure from every quarter, Botha reacted impetuously with a display of belligerence and ill-temper that brought upon him universal condemnation. On 19 May, the day the Commonwealth Eminent Persons Group was due to meet cabinet ministers, Botha ordered air strikes against targets in three neighbouring capital cities, Lusaka, Harare and Gaborone, claiming that they were ANC bases. In parliament subsequently he bragged that the raids were just a 'first instalment' and that they showed 'South Africa has the capacity and the will to break the ANC'. The Commonwealth team immediately cut short its mission.

Next Botha ordered outright repression of all black opposition. Under a nationwide state of emergency declared on 12 June, the security forces set out to decapitate all black resistance through mass arrests and tight control of township activity. The army surrounded whole townships and moved into schools. Prisons were soon filled with community leaders, trade unionists, church workers, students and other anti-apartheid activists. Strict censorship was imposed on the media, prohibiting all but official information on security force activities and black resistance. Defending his proclamation of a state of emergency, Botha claimed he faced a choice akin to that 'between war and a dishonourable, fearful peace'. He acknowledged that there would be a price to pay in terms of sanctions. But he declared that South Africa would not 'crawl before anyone' to avert the threat of sanctions and was quite prepared to 'go it alone'.

Despite the repression, Mandela was determined to find a way out of the deadlock. Soon after the state of emergency was declared, he wrote a note to General Willemse saying he wanted to see him on a matter of national importance. Willemse responded by arranging to meet Mandela in his residence in the grounds of Pollsmoor a few days later. When they met, Mandela told Willemse he wanted to see Kobie Coetsee to raise the question of talks between the government and the ANC. Then and there, Willemse telephoned Coetsee at his official residence in Cape Town and was told to bring Mandela around immediately for a meeting. Within minutes Mandela was on his way to Savernake, Coetsee's residence, eight miles away. Coetsee welcomed him with a glass of sherry and apologized that he had not been given a chance to change out of his prison clothes. To Mandela, the sherry, his first drink in twenty-four years, was like nectar.

Their discussion lasted for three hours. Mandela found Coetsee both knowledgeable about the central issues involved and willing to listen. He asked Mandela under what circumstances the ANC would be willing to suspend its armed struggle and whether he envisioned constitutional guarantees for minorities in a future South Africa. The two men, both lawyers, formed a liking for each other which was to endure for many years. Towards the end of their discussion, Coetsee asked what the next step was. Mandela replied that he wanted a meeting with Botha. Coetsee made a note of this and said he would send his request through the appropriate channels. They parted on good terms.

Mandela told no one of this encounter, neither his colleagues in Pollsmoor nor those in exile in Lusaka. He wanted the talks process to gain some momentum before disclosing that it was under way. But, to his frustration, he heard nothing more for months from Coetsee. He wrote him a letter but received no reply.

The difficulty was President Botha. He had been informed about Coetsee's discussion with Mandela and was willing to allow Coetsee to stay in touch with him. But his interest in Mandela was limited to finding ways and means of releasing him from prison, and he had no intention of engaging in talks about political change. Botha had reached the limits of his reform programme. He believed that the reforms he had introduced to South Africa were of major importance and yet had earned him little credit, either at home or abroad. He certainly had no intention of contemplating the idea of talks with the ANC. In his view the ANC was an organization under communist control, bent on destroying white civilization. It was at the centre of the 'total onslaught' the country was facing. Its links with the Soviet Union and other communist states, the support it received from Marxist regimes in Mozambique and Angola, and, above all, its alliance with the South African Communist Party were all cited by Botha as evidence of the ANC's true nature. The only answer to this 'total onslaught' was 'total strategy' and with this the government was already succeeding.

For the rest of his term of office, Botha concentrated more and more power in the hands of his security officials. A complex web of committees was constructed to give the State Security Council direct control over a vast range of government activity. The security network covered the entire country, reaching down to every level of society and designed to meet any contingency. Specialist teams were set to work on every subject, from manpower and transport to cultural affairs and community services. The underlying belief was that economic welfare and social improvements would win the hearts and minds of the local population. As the defence minister, Magnus Malan, caustically remarked, once blacks had toilets, they would not want democracy. To ensure more effective control of the townships, the government coopted allies in the black community – councillors, policemen, businessmen, traders and vigilante groups – providing them with the means necessary to defend their position against radical activists. In the war against 'enemies of the state', all methods, including assassination, were considered by security officials to be legitimate. At a meeting of the State Security Council in February 1986, Botha, impressed by a magazine article he had read about a 'third force' operating against the Mafia in Italy, suggested the need for a similar 'third force' in South Africa 'to combat terrorism and unrest'.

The state of emergency, meanwhile, effectively crippled organized black opposition. With thousands of activists in detention, opposition groups fell into disarray. Youth organizations, once at the forefront of the township revolt, lost all vigour. The UDF was reduced to a mere shadow of its former self. After two years of bitter conflict, the black opposition movement had proved to be no match for a government armed with totalitarian powers and prepared to use them.

Botha's tough, aggressive posture on security found ready support from the white electorate. In the 1987 election, he succeeded in holding on to his two-thirds majority in parliament. But what the result also showed was a massive lurch to the right. The extreme right wing picked up nearly 30 per cent of the vote. In all, more than 80 per cent of the white electorate voted for right-wing or extreme right-wing parties which rejected all notion of fundamental change to the apartheid system. Liberal opposition parties fared badly. Political debate henceforth was conducted more in terms of right-wing demands to curb reform than liberal demands to increase it. All this served to reinforce Botha's determination to hold firm.

Yet even within the heart of the Afrikaner establishment, there were critics of Botha's *kragdadigheid* approach who believed that it had no long-term future. One of them was Pieter de Lange, chairman of the Broederbond, which had played a highly influential role in Afrikaner nationalist politics since the 1920s. De Lange embarked on a personal campaign to convince Afrikaners of the need for fundamental changes conceding political rights to the black population and established his own contacts with ANC officials in exile in 1986. Other groups too – opposition politicians, churchmen and academics – found their way to Lusaka and Harare for meetings with the ANC. Botha, meanwhile, denounced all such contacts and did his best to obstruct them. A group of respected Dutch Reformed Church clergymen who wanted to talk to the ANC he branded as 'naïve' and 'childish' and threatened to confiscate their passports.

Even though Mandela heard nothing from Coetsee for months on end, there were signs that the government was planning a different role for him. On Christmas Eve in 1986, he was given his first taste of freedom outside prison in twenty-four years. After breakfast, the deputy commander of Pollsmoor, Lieutenant-Colonel Gawie Marx, called by his cell to ask whether he would like to see something of Cape Town. Together they drove along the coast road to Cape Town and meandered in the car through its streets. Mandela was riveted, watching the ordinary activities of people out shopping, walking their dogs, sitting in the sun: 'I felt like a curious tourist in a strange land.' On the way back to the prison, Marx asked Mandela if he would like a cold drink and stopped the car at a café: 'He just left me there, sitting alone in the car with the keys in the ignition.' As he waited for Marx to return, Mandela became more and more agitated and intense, wondering whether he should try to make a run for it, and was greatly relieved when Marx reappeared.

Other trips were arranged for him. He was taken to coastal resorts and fishing villages, to the mountains and inland to the edge of the Great Karoo. He walked on beaches, took tea in cafés and ate fish and chips. Once he visited the home of one of his warders, meeting his wife and children. Only a handful of trusted prison staff and guards knew of these secret journeys. No word of them leaked out. Nor was he ever recognized in public. No photograph of him had been allowed to be published in South Africa since his imprisonment. The last photographs taken of him in the 1960s, for anyone who could remember, showed a heavily built middle-aged man. Now he was a lean, grey-haired, elderly figure, with creases and furrows etched on his face and a slightly fragile air.

He also spent hours whiling away the time in vegetable gardens at the southern edge of the prison grounds in the company of his warder, James Gregory. Together they would sit in the lush, long grass on the banks of a small reservoir, watching the flights of wild geese and ducks and reminiscing about their childhoods and their families. Mandela took a close interest in Gregory's family. 'It was not merely politeness but genuine interest,' said Gregory. 'He was genuinely concerned for people, all people, and when he asked about their welfare, he took time to listen. It was not just a polite refrain.' When Gregory's son, Brent, joined the staff at Pollsmoor, he was astonished when Mandela greeted him as a friend, saying he had known all about him since his schooldays. 'It was like meeting an uncle for the first time,' said Brent.

In 1987, Coetsee resumed his secret discussions with Mandela, seeking a formula that would enable the government to grant him an 'honourable release'. By publicly requiring Mandela to renounce violence, Botha had made the task more difficult. Having taken such a firm stand, he would only appear weak if he subsequently released Mandela unconditionally, and Botha was a man obsessed by the need to appear tough and in control. 'He wanted this thing to be done. He knew it had to be done,' recalled Coetsee, 'but he didn't want to appear weak.'

Mandela, however, had no interest in negotiating his own release unless it was part of a package of measures including the lifting of the ban on the ANC. As he had made clear when first rejecting Botha's conditional offer of release, there was no point in being freed if he was not then free to engage in political activity. He continued to press for a meeting with Botha. He was also concerned to secure the release of his older colleagues, including Sisulu, who was seventy-five, and Mbeki, who was seventy-seven, and asked for Coetsee's help in this matter.

By 1988, the government had decided to take the discussions with Mandela a stage further. A secret committee was formed to explore the political issues that Mandela had long wanted to raise. It was headed by Coetsee and included two senior officials in the prisons department, General Willemse, the commissioner, and Fanie van der Merwe, the director-general, providing the meetings with the ostensible cover, if any word leaked out, that they were concerned with no more than discussions about prison conditions.

The presence of the fourth member of the committee, Niel Barnard, however, signified their true importance. Barnard, a thirty-seven-year-old former academic, was the head of Botha's National Intelligence Service, a member of the inner circle of his advisers. He was an ardent Afrikaner nationalist and a committed supporter of the 'total onslaught' school, but he took a pragmatic view of the government's options. Along with other senior government officials, he believed that splits could be found within the ANC between nationalists and communists which the government would be able to exploit to its advantage, opening the possibility of an accommodation with moderate nationalists. As well as the 'Mandela initiative', Barnard was monitoring secret talks which had begun in England in December 1987 between a number of prominent Afrikaners and ANC officials in exile.

Before agreeing to attend the first meeting of the committee, Mandela decided to consult his colleagues on the third floor. He was less than frank in what he told them. Meeting them one by one, at the insistence of the prison authorities, he gave them no idea of the extent of his talks with Coetsee which had begun two years previously. Nor did he reveal that the government had set up a special committee to handle the talks which included Botha's intelligence chief.

Sisulu, his oldest friend and mentor, was highly sceptical about the idea of talks. 'I was not against negotiations in principle,' he recalled. 'But I would have preferred the government to take the initiative to talk to us rather than our initiating talks with them.' Mandela retorted that if he was not against the principle of negotiations, it did not matter who took the initiative. Realizing that Mandela had already made up his mind, he did not try to stand in his way. Years later Sisulu acknowledged, 'I would have hesitated. I would have wanted certain things done. I might have lost the chance.' Kathrada was even more adamant in his opposition. By initiating talks, he said, it would appear that they were capitulating. Only Mhlaba and Mlangeni were in favour.

Mandela was no more forthcoming with Tambo. When Tambo asked, in a message conveyed by Bizos, what it was that he was talking to the government about, Mandela sent only a terse reply, giving no detail. His colleagues, meanwhile, feared that in isolation from the other prisoners, he would misjudge events and compromise the struggle. Many of them were averse to any idea of dialogue. 'I knew it would be opposed by our own people as well as those on the government side,' Mandela said. What he wanted was to present his ANC colleagues with the *fait accompli* of a dialogue before any of them could disrupt it.

The first meeting of the committee was held in May 1988 in the office of the prison commander at Pollsmoor. It was a tense occasion, with much suspicion on both sides. Mandela had never met Barnard before. Barnard was conscious of the fact that in Mandela's eyes he was 'a youngster', half Mandela's age. The second meeting, which took place at Willemse's house, over sherry and supper, was more relaxed. To put Barnard at ease, Mandela always greeted him in Afrikaans and allowed him to conduct his side of the talks in Afrikaans. Subsequent meetings occurred regularly, almost every week.

Once the preliminary discussions were over, the talks centred on three main issues: the armed struggle, the ANC's alliance with the Communist Party and the question of majority rule. The government representatives insisted that the ANC would have to renounce violence before the government would agree to negotiations and before Mandela would be allowed to meet Botha. The government's position had always been clear: it would not negotiate with any organization involved in violence. To change its position now would involve a loss of credibility. Mandela's reply was that if the government adopted peaceful methods, so would the ANC.

They were equally adamant that the ANC would have to sever its link with the Communist Party before negotiations could begin. The Communist Party, they maintained, dominated and controlled the ANC. No progress could be made until the link was broken. Mandela explained at length the reason behind the alliance. They had similar aims in overthrowing apartheid, but different long-term interests. No move would be made to break the alliance merely because the government wanted it to end.

The government side was also sceptical about the fate of the white minority under majority rule. Their interests, they suggested, would be trampled on. They questioned Mandela on what protection for minorities the ANC would offer. Mandela referred them to the Freedom Charter, which stated that South Africa belonged to all who lived in it, black and white, and tried to reassure them that in any future dispensation the majority would depend heavily on the skills and experience of the whites.

20. Winnie, with Zindzi, on her way to banishment in Brandfort in 1977

21. A moment of liberation experienced around the world: Mandela, with Winnie, on his release from Victor Verster prison in February 1990

22. (Above) After the first round of official talks between the ANC and the government at Groote Schuur in May 1990. Mandela and de Klerk address the press, with Joe Slovo standing behind

23. (Left) Walter Sisulu

24. (Top) With his children, Zindzi, Zenani, Makaziwe and Makgatho

25. (Above) With his great-granddaughter

30. With Queen Elizabeth during a state visit to Britain in July 1996

31. With Percy Yutar, the Rivonia prosecutor, whom he invited to lunch

32. Madiba magic: wearing a Springbok cap and jersey, Mandela celebrating with rugby captain François Pienaar after South Africa's victory in the 1995 Rugby World Cup

33. Odd bedfellows: Mandela, with Chief Buthelezi and F. W. de Klerk, shortly before dismissing Winnie Mandela as a member of his government in 1995

34. A new lease of life: Mandela with Graca Machel

35 & 36. Revisiting Robben Island: the lime quarry; his prison cell for eighteen years

Mandela's grasp of the issues and, in particular, his knowledge and understanding of the Afrikaner people greatly impressed those present. Mandela knew 'more about the Afrikaners' history than many Afrikaners themselves,' recalled Coetsee. Yet the questions, and the answers, soon became repetitive. As Mandela's seventieth birthday passed by in July – marked by a huge festival concert in London but by no particular celebration in Pollsmoor – he became increasingly restless. 'You don't have the power,' he told Barnard. 'I want to talk to the man with the power, and that is P. W. Botha. I want to talk to him.'

On the basis of these secret sessions, Coetsee and Barnard succeeded in persuading Botha to agree to a meeting. 'I spent an hour with him telling him there was no way he could lose out if he saw Mandela,' Barnard recalled. ' "If the meeting goes wrong and jumps the tracks and all that," I said, "you will still be remembered as the one who tried to keep things moving forward to a solution. But if it goes well it will be the beginning of South Africa's settlement politics, and history will acknowledge you for that." ' The meeting was arranged for the end of August 1988.

Yet to Mandela's immense frustration, he fell ill. A persistent cough had troubled him for some weeks. Just before a meeting with one of his lawyers, Ismail Ayob, at the end of July, he began to vomit. At first, doctors diagnosed flu, aggravated by dampness in his ground-floor rooms, but Mandela continued to feel sick. On 12 August, he was taken to Tygerberg Hospital near Cape Town, where he was found to have tuberculosis. He immediately underwent an operation to remove fluid from his lungs. Because the tuberculosis had been arrested at an early stage, no long-term damage was likely and Mandela recovered more quickly than expected. But the prized meeting with Botha, for which he had striven for more than two years, had to be postponed.

In September, he was moved to a luxury private clinic, the Constantiaberg, near Pollsmoor, the first black patient ever to stay there. His meetings with Coetsee and the secret committee resumed. Then in December he was taken to a new location, the Victor Verster prison-farm near Paarl, in the heartland of the Cape wine-growing district, thirty-five miles from Cape Town – a place intended to be half-way between prison and freedom.

The house he was given was the most spacious and comfortable home in which he had ever lived. A whitewashed single-storey residence, it stood in an isolated part of the farm, at the end of a winding dirt road, shaded by tall fir trees and surrounded by fields and a wood. It contained a large lounge and four bedrooms, with a garden full of flowers and fruit trees and a swimming pool, all enclosed behind a high wall.

The keys were left in the doors for Mandela to use as he chose. The cupboards were stocked with provisions, wines and spirits, courtesy of the government. On hand to greet him was the prison commander, Brigadier Keulder, who told him that if he needed anything, he just had to ask. The following day, Coetsee arrived with a crate of wine as a housewarming gift. The prison staff assigned to him included James Gregory, whom he had known for twenty-two years and whom he regarded as a friend, and Jack Swart, a warrant officer who served as his personal chef, providing him with whatever meals and delicacies he fancied. Mandela particularly enjoyed Swart's home-made ginger beer. Gregory's son, Brent, was also a member of the staff.

Mandela soon settled into a comfortable routine. Each morning, he was examined by a doctor. He toured the garden, taking a proprietorial interest in the plants. He tried out the swimming pool. Ignoring protests from his household staff, he insisted on making his own bed and on doing his share of washing the dishes. He finally succeeded in passing his law degree. He watched television. He entertained his lawyers and members of his family in style. His four comrades from Pollsmoor paid him a visit, Sisulu marvelling at his 'five-star hotel' conditions 'complete with room service'. On Christmas Day in 1988, Winnie, Zindzi and Zindzi's two children came for the day, the first proper family gathering Mandela had enjoyed in twenty-six years.

But as for his main immediate objective of opening a dialogue with Botha, he made no further progress. In January, the seventy-three-year-old president suffered a stroke and once again, the meeting had to be rescheduled. And then the sense of tranquillity he had just begun to experience was disrupted by a massive scandal involving Winnie with which he had to contend.

CHAPTER 18

The Football Club

After a series of altercations with police, arrests and court appearances, Winnie eventually succeeded in 1986 in re-establishing her right to live in Soweto, nearly nine years after her banishment to Brandfort. Her battle to stay in Johannesburg, in defiance of government banning orders, attracted worldwide attention. As the result of one arrest, in December 1985, when she was dragged from her Orlando home 'kicking and screaming', according to eyewitnesses, governments in Britain, the United States and France issued strong protests. A posse of journalists and television crews followed her about, waiting for the next encounter. Winnie relished the attention she received.

With the township revolt then in full swing, she endeavoured to play a leading role as a militant activist. She attended funeral rallies, making speeches which became ever more extreme, gaining for herself a loyal following among black youths. A speech she made at a rally in Munsieville in April 1986 which endorsed the necklace method of killing, by which several hundred victims had died, brought her lasting notoriety. 'We have no guns, we have only stones, boxes of matches and petrol,' she said. 'Together, hand in hand, with our boxes of matches and our necklaces we shall liberate this country.'

The damage that Winnie did to the African nationalist cause by those words was considerable. Necklace murders had become a symbol to much of the world of the anarchic black-on-black violence afflicting the townships which the government was eager to claim was all that lay behind the black revolt. The clear implication of Winnie's speech was that she not only supported such methods but also advocated that whites too should be burnt.

The ANC in exile, anxious to prove to Western governments that it was not a 'terrorist' organization, as leaders like Britain's Margaret Thatcher maintained, were appalled. Messages were sent to Winnie telling her to refrain from any more speech-making. In Pollsmoor, Mandela was furious and summoned her for an angry reprimand. But Winnie was not inclined to take orders from anyone and her activities became even more rash and ruthless.

She gathered around her a group of township youths who became known as the Mandela United Football Club. Forming football teams in the name of popular political leaders was a fashionable pursuit at the time; a Sisulu Football Club already existed in Orlando. Winnie allowed them to stay in rooms at the back of her Orlando house and provided them with track suits and money. She acquired a 'coach', a thirty-eight-year-old local man named Jerry Richardson, a skilled football player but someone with limited intelligence, a meagre education and a reputation as a police informer. Like other members of the group, he became dependent on Winnie, calling her 'Mummy' and functioning as her henchman. Zindzi too was involved in Mandela United, some-times playing the role of 'mascot'; two of her boyfriends were leading members.

From its origins as a football club, Mandela United rapidly descended into a world of brutal crime. Winnie used it initially as a personal bodyguard, to accompany her to rallies and funerals and to guard her house. Its members were subject to her own strict rules. They were required to return home by a certain time each night, signing in and out of the house in a special register. Failure to sign the register meant a whipping, from Winnie as well as from other youths. Looking for more recruits, club members roamed the township, accusing those who did not want to join them of being police informers or 'sell-outs'. Many who were coerced into joining subsequently found it difficult to leave. No one could resign voluntarily from the club. Stories began to circulate of youths being taken to Winnie's house and never seen again.

Mandela United soon began operating as a vigilante gang. Vic-tims accused of theft and other crimes or of being police informers were brought to Winnie's house for interrogation by a 'disciplinary committee' and for whatever punishment it decided to order. The head of the disciplinary committee for some time was Sizwe Sithole, the father of one of Zindzi's children. Punishment varied according to the offence, but included kicking, punching, whipping and beating. A favourite form of punishment was known as 'break-down', in which victims were thrown high into the air and left to hit the floor. Other forms of torture were also used.

In May 1987, a teenage youth, Peter Makanda, was abducted, along with his brother, by members of Mandela United, who accused them of being informers. They were taken to Winnie's house and savagely beaten. Makanda was hung by the neck with a plastic rope from a rafter until it broke; his head was placed in a plastic bag and his face was pushed into a bucket of water. Both brothers were then tortured with knives. A large 'M' for Mandela was carved on Makanda's chest and the words 'Viva ANC' sliced down the length of one of his thighs. Battery acid was smeared into the wounds. The brothers claimed that Winnie put in an appearance soon after they were first beaten, returning a few hours afterwards. They later managed to escape from a garage, but others were not so fortunate. Subsequent evidence linked Mandela United to sixteen known murders of local residents, mostly teenagers.

The activities of Mandela United were an evil mess that no one was anxious to deal with. The fear of reprisal deterred many families from making complaints. Parents who suspected that Mandela United were responsible for the disappearance of their children never had any proof as no bodies were ever found. The police were not keen to be seen persecuting Winnie any more. The activities of her gang of vigilantes were no different from those of scores of others which had sprung up during the township revolt. Kangaroo courts, like the one she was running at no. 8115, Orlando West, were relatively common.

When the Makanda brothers reported their ordeal to the police, three members of Mandela United were arrested. But Winnie herself was never charged in connection with the crime; nor was she called as a witness or even questioned. Black political leaders were no keener to confront the problem of Winnie's criminal behaviour. She thus enjoyed a kind of immunity which not only induced greater fear of her but increased her sense of her own power. She seemed untouchable.

Only murmurs of these events reached Mandela in Pollsmoor.

Neither the local nor the foreign press delved into Winnie's increasingly wayward activities for fear that their reports would be used
by the government for propaganda purposes and serve only to
discredit the anti-apartheid struggle. They were also concerned
that rumours about Winnie and Mandela United might have been
manufactured by the government in the first place. Friends and
lawyers visiting Mandela were careful not to draw attention to
Winnie's conduct or to her heavy drinking to avoid alarming him.

But other embarrassments involving Winnie surfaced. Within a
year of returning to Soweto, she ordered the construction of a
mansion in an exclusive area known as Beverly Hills, where a
black élite of businessmen, lawyers and doctors lived. By Soweto
standards, the house, containing fifteen rooms, was vast. Known
as 'Winnie's Palace', it attracted hostile criticism from the local
community. It hardly fitted the revolutionary image that Winnie
was attempting to establish. Where the money came from was
something of a mystery. While spending large sums on clothes,
cars and her bodyguard, Winnie always pleaded poverty.

Some funds came as a result of a business relationship struck up
with a black American entrepreneur, Robert Brown, which led to
yet another scandal. Brown was a former civil rights campaigner
who switched his attention to South Africa and began to raise
substantial funds in the United States for the anti-apartheid cause.
He soon realized that there was a fortune to be made from the
Mandela family. In collaboration with Winnie, he proposed to
copyright and market the Mandela name and prevent others from
cashing in on it. Their negotiations had just reached an amicable
conclusion when an incident involving Mandela United suddenly
erupted, focusing public attention on its activities.

On 28 July 1988, a crowd of teenage pupils from the Daliwonga
High School marched on Winnie's house, smashed the doors and
windows and then set fire to it. The attack was part of a running
feud between them and Mandela United, made in revenge for the
detention of a group of Daliwonga students who had been accused
of rape, found guilty and then beaten up in the back rooms of
Winnie's house.

All the Mandela family records, their photographs, letters and
gifts, and even the slice of wedding cake that Winnie had been
saving for Mandela's release, were destroyed in the fire. As local

residents gathered in the street, none of them ventured to help. They watched in silence as the house burned down.

Winnie appeared to be devastated by the attack. With the street full of people, she drove slowly towards the burning house, saw what had happened and went away. At her office in Soweto, friends found her in a state of shock. Robert Brown was there, full of self-importance, trying to dictate who would be allowed to see her. Members of Mandela United had barricaded the building. To her old friend Amina Cachalia, Winnie said, 'I don't know what is happening to my life.'

Accompanied by Brown, Winnie flew to Cape Town shortly afterwards to see Mandela, both to tell him of the arson attack and to get his approval for the deal with Brown. Mandela had been forewarned by his lawyer, Ismail Ayob, about Brown's attempt to control the Mandela name and he had been outraged. He told Winnie that he would have nothing to do with the scheme and authorized a statement disclaiming any connection with Brown. 'If the family name needed protection it could be protected by the African National Congress,' his statement said.

He also told Winnie to disband her 'football team' and decided not to press charges against the Daliwonga students. To limit further damage, he asked a group of influential community leaders, including the Reverend Frank Chikane of the South African Council of Churches, Cyril Ramaphosa, a prominent trade unionist, and Aubrey Mokoena of the Release Mandela Committee, to form a 'crisis committee' to take control of the matter. The burden of these events added to the exhaustion that Mandela was already feeling as a result of his tuberculosis, which had still to be diagnosed. Shortly afterwards, he collapsed and was taken to Tygerberg Hospital.

But Winnie refused to disband Mandela United. While the house in Orlando was being rebuilt, she moved into a house in Diepkloof Extension in another part of Soweto, taking members of Mandela United with her. It was not long before they resumed their murderous activities.

Two incidents became notorious. In November 1988, a gunfight erupted between police and two MK guerrillas who were hiding in Jerry Richardson's house in Soweto. Richardson had been asked by Winnie to give them temporary shelter. Just before the shooting started, Richardson, who was in the garden, raised his arms in the air and surrendered to the police. The two guerrillas were killed. Richardson was detained for two weeks but then released. He was already suspected in the local community of being a police informer, having often been seen in the company of white men. The shooting of the two guerrillas further increased local suspicion.

Members of Mandela United singled out for retribution a twenty-one-year-old local youth, Lolo Sono, who had been friendly with the guerrillas. Four days after the gunfight, a minibus containing Winnie and members of Mandela United drew up outside the Sono household. According to Sono's father, Winnie accused the youth of being a sell-out. Sono's father denied it and asked where his son was. Winnie told him he was in the back of the minibus. The father saw his son there, battered and bleeding, his eyes swollen. He pleaded with Winnie to let the boy go, but she refused, repeating the claim that he was a sell-out before driving away. Sono was not seen again. The police were informed of the incident, but took no action.

But the second incident, the death of a fourteen-year-old boy named 'Stompie' Moeketsi Seipei, finally ensnared Winnie. This time, by chance, a body was found and witnesses eventually came forward.

Stompie was an obstreperous and boastful youth who had gained a reputation for being both a fervent activist, able to cite the Freedom Charter by heart, and a police informer who had 'cracked' in detention. Along with other homeless youths, he had found lodgings in a church manse in Orlando East run by a white Methodist minister, Paul Verryn, who was highly respected in the neighbourhood for his commitment in helping the local community. The manse, with only three bedrooms, was always overcrowded; on some nights as many as forty people stayed there.

On 29 December 1988, four days after Winnie's Christmas visit to Mandela in Victor Verster prison, she ordered the abduction of four occupants of the Methodist manse, including Stompie, after being told by another occupant, Xoliswa Falati, a troublesome thirty-five-year-old woman who had quarrelled with Stompie and with Verryn, that Verryn had engaged in homosexual practices at the manse. The victims were brought to Winnie's house at Diep-kloof Extension and there, according to the three survivors, Falati repeated her accusations about homosexuality and claimed that Stompie was an informer. All four were then interrogated and beaten mercilessly to extract confessions. Winnie, who had been drinking and who was in a foul mood, was accused of leading the assaults, punching and slapping each of the victims. 'You are not fit to be alive,' she told them. Members of Mandela United joined in, throwing their victims into the air, shouting 'breakdown' as they did. Winnie, according to one of the victims, Kenny Kgase, watched 'with a look of satisfaction'. She called for sjamboks – rawhide whips – to be brought and, humming a freedom song, lashed the victims. Stompie, deemed to be a 'sell-out', came in for specially brutal treatment and eventually he confessed to being a police informer. The following day, he was beaten again and again. On 1 January, he was taken away.

News of the abductions quickly spread around Soweto. On 4 January, a member of the crisis committee, Aubrey Mokoena, questioned Winnie about them, but she denied that any of the youths were at her home. On 6 January, when Dr Nthatho Motlana, an old friend of the Mandela family, went to see Winnie, she admitted that they were at her home, but refused to allow him to see them.

Then, on 7 January, one of the kidnap victims, Kenny Kgase, managed to escape. He immediately alerted Methodist Church elders to what had happened to him and the three others. Led by Bishop Peter Storey, the Methodist Church now became central in trying to free the missing youths, coordinating its efforts with the crisis committee but avoiding contact with the police to minimize complications.

On 11 January, four members of the crisis committee went to Winnie's house. This time she claimed that she was protecting the youths from Verryn and that they were staying at her house at their own request. On the following day, when the committee members were finally allowed to see the two remaining kidnap victims, Pelo Mekgwe and Thabiso Mono, both of whom had clear injuries, they claimed at first that they were staying at Winnie's house of their own free will. Subsequently, however, one of them, when alone with the committee, admitted they were being held captive. The crisis committee obtained further evidence of what had happened from another witness, Katiza Cebekhulu, who had participated in the beatings but had subsequently decided to confess his involvement. Cebekhulu also told the committee that he believed that Stompie was dead.

To help resolve the issue, the Methodist Church and the crisis committee sought assistance from Oliver Tambo in Lusaka and from Mandela in Victor Verster. A human rights lawyer, Fink Haysom, was commissioned to fly to Lusaka to brief Tambo. As he listened to Haysom's account, Tambo, appalled, threw up his hands and covered his face. 'What must I do?' he exclaimed. 'We can't control her. The ANC can't control her. We tried to control her, that's why we formed the crisis committee. You must tell the crisis committee they must do more!'

In Victor Verster, after being informed of the details by Ismail Ayob on 14 January, Mandela issued an instruction that the two youths should be released. After further prevarication from Winnie, they were set free on 16 January and handed over to Bishop Storey. There was, however, still no word of the whereabouts of Stompie.

Having collected a considerable amount of evidence, the crisis committee decided to call a meeting of community and church leaders in Soweto. This was duly held on the night of 16 January, shortly after Mekgwe and Mono had been released. Both of them attended, as did Kgase and Cebekhulu. Bishop Storey was also there, together with Paul Verryn. In all, there were about 150 participants. The meeting heard from Mekgwe and Mono how they had been abducted, taken to Winnie's house and beaten, first by her and then by club members. Cebekhulu confirmed their account of the beatings. When asked whether Stompie was dead, Cebekhulu replied, 'Yes', but was unable to say where his body might be found. Storey asked the meeting at large if anyone knew of any misconduct on the part of Verryn. About a dozen residents from the manse were present, but no one spoke against him.

Another victim of Mandela United, Lerotodi Ikaneng, a former member of the club who had decided to quit despite being accused by Zindzi of being a 'sell-out', described how, on 3 January, Jerry Richardson and other members of the gang had tried to murder him using a pair of garden shears, leaving him for dead; the wound across his neck was still raw.

On the basis of the evidence it possessed, the crisis committee resolved that Winnie should be ostracized. It proposed that 'all

progressive organizations should no longer give her a platform';
that she should 'desist from creating an impression that she speaks
on behalf of the people'; that all 'progressive lawyers' should refrain
from helping her any longer; and that she should be ordered
immediately to dismantle her football club. A report sent to Tambo
in Lusaka confirmed that Winnie had participated in the beatings
at her house. It spoke of 'this new ghastly situation that is developing
before our eyes', and added, 'She seems to think that she is above
the community. She shows utter contempt for both the crisis
committee and the community.'

The crisis was to spread further. On 27 January, a popular
Indian doctor, Abu-Baker Asvat, was murdered in his surgery in
Soweto. Asvat had been a close friend of Winnie, always ready to
respond to her requests for help. He was a prominent political
activist involved not with pro-ANC organizations but with the
black consciousness movement. Members of his family had noticed
in recent weeks that he had become increasingly troubled and
anxious. Their first reaction to the murder was to assume that he
had been killed for political reasons. But other possibilities soon
emerged. The crisis committee knew that Asvat had been called to
Winnie's house on 31 December to examine Stompie, whom he
found to be brain-damaged. Asvat had subsequently reported his
findings to the crisis committee. He was therefore a key witness to
the circumstances surrounding Stompie's disappearance. Asvat had
also been involved in the case as a result of a visit that Winnie had
paid to his surgery, bringing with her Cebekhulu, who, after joining
in the assaults of the four kidnap victims, had become distraught.
Winnie's explanation was that he had been sexually abused by
Verryn. Asvat examined Cebekhulu, found no evidence of sexual
abuse, but noted on his medical record that he was mentally
confused and occasionally hysterical. According to the record book
and the medical card completed in Asvat's surgery, Winnie brought
Cebekhulu to see him on 30 December, the day after the abduction
took place. The date in the record book was written by Asvat's
nurse, Albertina Sisulu; the date on the card was stamped with a
date stamp. This evidence of Winnie's whereabouts on 30 December
was to assume considerable significance at a later stage.

On 26 January, the day before Asvat's murder, as press inquiries
about the activities of Mandela United began to mount, he was

visited in his surgery by a new patient, Jerry Richardson. Richardson said he had been referred by Winnie and complained of an abscess. Asvat made a note in red on Richardson's patient card: 'Sent by Winnie'. He found little wrong with Richardson, but told him to return the next morning for a penicillin injection. Friends and family who met Asvat later that day described him as being tense and frightened. Richardson duly returned the next morning. In the afternoon, two youths arrived at the surgery, shot Asvat dead and escaped.

Winnie's conduct following the murder was strange. Late that night, she arrived at Asvat's house, in the company of Richardson and Zindzi, went straight up to Asvat's widow, Zhora, and asked: 'Who do you think did this?' Then she sat silently on the floor. The following day she gave a press interview claiming that Asvat had been murdered because he possessed evidence of Verryn's sexual misconduct, drawing attention for the first time to a possible link between the kidnapping at the Methodist manse and Asvat's murder. The implication was that the Methodist Church was involved in Asvat's murder. In a subsequent television interview, she referred to 'a gigantic cover-up by the Church'.

Even now, with public and press attention gathering pace, the activities of Mandela United still continued. On 11 February, as a court subsequently heard, a club member known as Dodo rushed to tell a local community activist, Dudu Chili, who had been involved in a long-standing feud with Winnie, that Winnie had just finished chairing a meeting at which it had been decided that Chili's son, Sibusiso, and Lerotodi Ikaneng, whom Richardson had once tried to murder, should be killed. According to Dodo, Winnie had said, 'They have become too problematic.' On 13 February, Sibusiso Chili was intercepted by two Mandela United members, but the alarm was raised and, in the ensuing fracas, it was one of the club members, Maxwell Madondo, who died.

The end of Mandela United, however, was nigh. On 15 February, two forensic pathologists, alerted by press reports about Stompie's disappearance, identified his body in the mortuary at Diepkloof. The body, with knife wounds, had been found lying on an open stretch of wasteland on 6 January by a local woman and had been in the mortuary unidentified ever since.

Now that they had a body, the police began to round up suspects, acting on information from the three kidnap victims, Kgase, Mono and Mekgwe. Richardson and other members of the club were arrested. Winnie's house in Diepkloof Extension was raided. In one of the rooms there, police found a handwritten hit-list with eleven names on it, including those of three Chili brothers, Lerotodi Ikaneng and two of Albertina Sisulu's sons. Police also arrested two illiterate youths in connection with the murder of Dr Asvat.

Winnie herself remained curiously immune from police interrogation. She was questioned about the sjamboks found on her premises but denied any knowledge of them. She was not required to make a statement in connection with either Stompie's death or Asvat's murder. A statement made by one of the two youths charged with Asvat's murder clearly implicated her. He claimed that his accomplice had said, 'Look, I've been bought by Winnie Mandela and I must go and shoot Dr Asvat dead.' But the statement was never produced in court. The official motive for the murder was said to be robbery.

The verdict of the black political establishment about Winnie, however, was far more direct. On 16 February, the day after Stompie's body had been identified, Murphy Morobe, a prominent political leader, read out a statement issued in the name of the Mass Democratic Movement, an umbrella organization representing a huge array of community associations and trade unions, censuring her for criminal activity. He began:

> We have now reached the state where we have no option but to speak publicly on what is a very sensitive and painful matter. In recent years, Mrs Mandela's actions have increasingly led her into conflict with various sections of the oppressed people and with the Mass Democratic Movement as a whole. The recent conflict in the community has centred largely around the conduct of her so-called football club, which has been widely condemned by the community. In particular, we are outraged by the reign of terror that the team has been associated with. Not only is Mrs Mandela associated with the team, in fact it is her creation.

Morobe then directly linked Winnie to Stompie's death. 'We are outraged at Mrs Mandela's obvious complicity in the recent abductions. Had Stompie and his colleagues not been abducted by Mrs Mandela's "football team", he would have been alive today.'

He went on, 'We are not prepared to remain silent where those who are violating human rights claim to be doing so in the name of the struggle against apartheid.' Winnie had 'abused the trust and confidence' of the community. Because of her conduct, he said, 'the Mass Democratic Movement hereby distances itself from Mrs Mandela and her actions'.

The press which had once devoted considerable space to eulogizing Winnie now spoke of her as a 'fallen idol'. An article by Nomavenda Mathiane reflected the particular anger and contempt felt for her in Soweto. 'Headlines like "Fallen Idol" create the impression that blacks had revered the "Mother of the Nation". The fact is that this title is a mystery, and many black people have never known where it came from,' she wrote. 'The title was made popular in the eyes of the outside world, which shows that if a small group of people set out with a determination to create a lie they can succeed.'

In his remote prison cottage at Victor Verster, Mandela was unable to grasp the full extent of the problem. He was well aware of Winnie's wayward nature, but he believed that she had committed no more than 'errors of judgement' in becoming involved with rough elements in Soweto. He wanted the matter to be dealt with internally by the nationalist movement, not through the kind of public denunciation by the Mass Democratic Movement, which was bound to have the effect of undermining the anti-apartheid struggle and bolstering the government's credibility.

On her visits to Mandela, Winnie always maintained that she had done nothing wrong. A passage of conversation recorded by Mandela's warder, James Gregory, in his autobiography gives some idea of the course of their discussions. When Mandela asked Winnie about a newspaper report that she had whipped the kidnap victims with a sjambok, she laughed and said, 'Why would I do a thing like that?'

Mandela replied, 'That is not an answer to my question.'

'You of all people should know that you cannot trust what you read in the newspapers. You know how they twist and bend each and every little fact. How can you sit there and look me in the eyes and tell me you believe the newspaper and not me? How can you?'

'Just get rid of these people around you. They are bad for you, this is poor judgement to have them near you, to surround yourself with them. You must get rid of them.'

'No, these are people, young boys, who have been rescued from the streets. They need help and I am providing it. I cannot abandon them. They have already been abandoned once in their lives.'

The brief glimpses of Winnie that Mandela had enjoyed during prison visits over the years had given him little understanding of the changes in her character that had occurred. In Mandela's company, Winnie was warm and vivacious, full of laughter, dressed to dazzle. He remained deeply in love with her, hoping that one day, when he was set free, he could resolve all the difficulties that had accumulated during his years in prison and pick up the threads of a happy married existence.

CHAPTER 19

Botha's Tea Party

As the furore over Mandela United subsided, Mandela concentrated his attention on preparing for the meeting he sought with Botha. To clarify the issues, he drew up a ten-page memorandum which he sent in March 1989, after Botha had recovered from his stroke. 'The deepening political crisis in our country has been a matter of grave concern to me for quite some time,' he began, 'and I now consider it necessary in the national interest for the African National Congress and the government to meet urgently to negotiate an effective political settlement.'

His task, he said, was a limited one – namely, to bring the country's two major political bodies to the negotiating table. An early meeting between the government and the ANC would constitute the first major step towards lasting peace.

> Two central issues will have to be addressed at such a meeting: firstly, the demand for majority rule in a unitary state; secondly, the concern of white South Africa over this demand, as well as the insistence of whites on structural guarantees that majority rule will not mean domination of the white minority by blacks. The most crucial task which will face the government and the ANC will be to reconcile these two positions.

Mandela addressed the obstacles that stood in the way of talks, in particular the government's demands, elaborated by the secret committee, that the ANC should first renounce violence, break its alliance with the Communist Party and abandon its demand for majority rule.

> The position of the ANC on the question of violence is very simple.

The organization has no vested interest in violence. It abhors any action which may cause loss of life, destruction of property and misery to the people. It has worked long and patiently for a South Africa of common values and for an undivided and peaceful non-racial state. But we consider the armed struggle a legitimate form of self-defence against a morally repugnant system of government which will not allow even peaceful forms of protest ...

It is perfectly clear on the facts that the refusal of the ANC to renounce violence is not the real problem facing the government. The truth is that the government is not yet ready for negotiation and for the sharing of political power with blacks. It is still committed to white domination and, for that reason, it will only tolerate those blacks who are willing to serve on its apartheid structures. Its policy is to remove from the political scene blacks who refuse to conform, who reject white supremacy and its apartheid structures and who insist on equal rights with whites. This is the real reason for the government's refusal to talk to us, and for its demand that we should disarm ourselves, while it continues to use violence against our people.

As he had done countless times with members of the secret committee, Mandela defended the ANC's alliance with the Communist Party:

Cooperation between the ANC and the South African Communist Party goes back to the early twenties and has always been, and still is, strictly limited to the struggle against racial oppression and for a just society. At no time has the organization ever adopted or cooperated with communism itself. Apart from the question of cooperation between the two organizations, members of the SACP have always been free to join the ANC. But once they do, they become fully bound by the policy of the organization set out in the Freedom Charter. As members of the ANC engaged in the anti-apartheid struggle, their Marxist ideology is not directly relevant. The SACP has throughout the years accepted the leading role of the ANC, a position which is respected by the SACP members who join the ANC.

He firmly dismissed any suggestion for an end to the alliance:

No self-respecting freedom fighter will take orders from the government on how to wage the freedom struggle against that same government and on who his allies in the freedom struggle should be . . . No dedicated ANC member will ever heed a call to break with the SACP. We regard such a demand as a purely divisive government strategy.

It is in fact a call on us to commit suicide. Which man of honour will ever desert a lifelong friend at the insistence of a common opponent and still retain a measure of credibility among his people? Which opponent will ever trust such a treacherous freedom fighter? Yet this is what the government is, in effect, asking us to do – to desert our faithful allies. We will not fall into that trap.

Mandela was equally dismissive of the government's rejection of majority rule. The principle of majority rule was a pillar of democracy around the world. It was a principle which was fully accepted in the white politics of South Africa. It was a principle that would have to be accepted in the future if a peaceful settlement was to be reached:

Majority rule and internal peace are like the two sides of a single coin, and white South Africa simply has to accept that there will never be peace and stability in this country until the principle is fully applied. It is precisely because of its denial that the government has become the enemy of practically every black man. It is that denial that has sparked off the current civil strife.

Mandela concluded by saying that the move he had taken in approaching the government provided Botha with an opportunity to overcome the political deadlock in South Africa.

I hope you will seize it without delay. I believe that the overwhelming majority of South Africans, black and white, hope to see the ANC and the government working closely together to lay the foundations for a new era in our country, in which racial discrimination and prejudice, coercion and confrontation, death and destruction, will be forgotten.

While waiting for the date of the meeting to be fixed, Mandela invited many old friends to visit him at Victor Verster. His memory for detail with regard to people and places from the distant past was astonishing. He was assiduous in bringing himself up to date with all that had happened to his visitors, with births and marriages and divorces and deaths, remembering the details long into the future. He made a particular effort to track down his old employer Lazar Sidelsky, who had helped him forty years before in starting his career as a lawyer. They joked about the suit that Sidelsky had given him. Mandela said later that it was one of the most memorable visits in prison he had ever had. A steady stream of political activists also came to Victor Verster and to them Mandela paid the same courteous attention. Though Winnie was told she could remain at Mandela's cottage whenever she wished, she never stayed overnight, claiming that it would not be appropriate while other ANC people languished in prison cells.

The meeting with Botha was finally set for 5 July 1989. Mandela was provided with a new suit, tie, shirt and shoes. His blood group was checked in case of emergency. He prepared himself by reading every newspaper and magazine he could lay his hands on, reviewed his memorandum and checked his notes. The officials who went with him were anxious that he should make a good impression; one of them retied his tie for him before he set out from Victor Verster.

Mandela approached the meeting with some trepidation. Since Botha's stroke in January, his temper was said to be even more ferocious than before. His own colleagues found him increasingly irascible; he refused to listen to advice and harboured resentments against them. Mandela resolved that if Botha resorted to his finger-wagging habit, he would interrupt to say he found Botha's behaviour unacceptable and leave.

Arrangements for the meeting were carried out in the utmost secrecy. Mandela was driven to a basement garage beneath Tuynhuys, the Cape Dutch mansion alongside parliament in the centre of Cape Town which served as the president's official residence. Accompanied by prison officials, he took a lift to the ground floor and stepped out into a wood-panelled lobby in front of the president's office, where he met Coetsee and Barnard. Both were worried that Botha's temper might erupt during the encounter. Barnard noticed that Mandela's shoelaces were not properly tied and quickly knelt down to retie them. 'I realized just how nervous they were,' said Mandela, 'and that did not make me any calmer.'

As Mandela entered the president's office, Botha walked towards him from the opposite side of the room, his hand outstretched, smiling broadly. Instead of the grim, cantankerous figure he had expected to meet, Mandela found Botha 'a charming man indeed', unfailingly courteous and friendly. 'The thing that impressed was that he poured the tea.'

Their conversation amounted to little more than a polite discourse on South African history and culture. Mandela mentioned that he had recently read an article in an Afrikaans magazine about the 1914 Afrikaner rebellion and drew parallels between their rival nationalisms. The African nationalist struggle, he said, was not unlike the 1914 Afrikaner rebellion: the one pitted Afrikaner brother against brother; the other was a struggle 'between brothers who happened to be different colours'. No policy matters were discussed and no negotiations took place. Towards the end of the half-hour meeting, Mandela asked for the unconditional release of all political prisoners. Botha replied that he was afraid he could not do that. They parted amicably, Botha saying what a pleasure the meeting had been and Mandela concurring.

When news of the meeting leaked out a few days later, the meeting was described, fairly accurately, as 'a courtesy call'. The symbolic importance of Botha sitting down with a prisoner whom he had hitherto denounced as a 'communist terrorist' was real enough. But Botha was still no nearer to addressing the central issue of political reform that Mandela had raised in his memorandum. It was a matter he never seriously contemplated.

Six weeks later, on 14 August, after months of friction with his cabinet colleagues, Botha announced his resignation as president in a long, rambling television address. The man who succeeded him, Frederik Willem de Klerk, was chosen because of his solid conservative credentials.

CHAPTER 20

A Step to Freedom

De Klerk had been a dedicated disciple of the apartheid system throughout his political career. He came from a prominent Afrikaner family at the heart of the political establishment which had ruled South Africa since 1948. His father, Jan, had served as a cabinet minister under three prime ministers, including Verwoerd. His uncle by marriage, Hans Strijdom, was a former prime minister outspoken in his support of white supremacy. His grandfather, a friend of Paul Kruger, leader of the old Transvaal republic, had also made his mark as an activist in the Afrikaner cause. The household in which the young de Klerk grew up, therefore, was steeped in the traditions of Afrikaner politics and history.

His own rise within the National Party was rapid. After establishing a successful law practice in the Transvaal town of Vereeniging, he entered parliament in 1972 and in 1978, at the age of forty-two, became the youngest member of John Vorster's cabinet. What was notable about his political record, in seventeen years as a member of parliament and cabinet minister, was his rigid loyalty to the National Party and all that it stood for. He conformed faithfully to every party policy of the time. Over the years, he had spoken out adamantly against integrated sport, mixed marriages, trade union rights for blacks and black demands for permanent residence in white South Africa. Above all, he was a forceful proponent of the National Party's commitment to 'group rights' – keeping apart, wherever possible, South Africa's four main racial groups. In Botha's government, he was given control of the white 'own affairs' portfolio and distinguished himself as a zealous advocate of white interests. Whites, he said in 1989, must be guaranteed a 'community life, their own living areas, schools, institutions and systems'. Each group should have its own power base, he said, and make its own decisions about community issues.

In cabinet, de Klerk was noted for constantly throwing up obstacles to reform. As minister of education, he fought to keep blacks out of white universities. He also sponsored a bill that would have enabled him to use financial pressure to force universities to crack down on anti-apartheid agitators on campus – a measure that the Supreme Court subsequently ruled to be invalid. At a public meeting in 1987, he urged whites to report people of other racial groups living in segregated white areas, even though the authorities by then tended to ignore informal integration. When the *verligte* foreign minister, Pik Botha, suggested in 1986 that South Africa might one day have a black president, it was de Klerk, rather than P. W. Botha, who insisted that he should publicly retract his statement. In his eleven years in cabinet, there was not a single piece of reform with which de Klerk had been associated.

When the time came to choose a new head of the National Party after Botha's sudden and unexpected resignation from the post in February 1989, de Klerk was the favoured candidate of the *verkrampte* camp, which wanted to stand fast against further reform and believed that he was the man to do it. The *verligte* camp, meanwhile, put forward three candidates, split the vote and enabled de Klerk to be elected. As head of the National Party, he was in line to succeed Botha as president.

Examining his record, the press considered it unlikely that de Klerk would get to grips with the fundamental issues facing South Africa any more than Botha had. De Klerk had never shown any particular flair or talent. He was amiable, shrewd and polished but without charisma or vision. Above all else, he was a party man. His main difference from Botha was that he appeared to be more open and communicative. It was noted that his wife, Marike, was an arch-conservative. In a speech she gave at an old-age home, she had referred contemptuously to Coloureds as 'a negative group' of 'non-persons' who were South Africa's historic 'leftovers'.

His older brother, a prominent *verligte* and newspaper editor, had no great expectations of him. 'He is too strongly convinced that racial grouping is the only truth, way and life,' Willem de Klerk wrote in a magazine article published in March 1989. 'He is too dismissive of a more radical style.' He predicted that his brother would follow a cautious, centrist path, holding 'the middle ground by means of clever footwork, small compromises, drawn-out studies and planned processes, effective diplomacy and growing authority through balanced leadership and control'. That, Willem wrote, 'is his style, his nature, his talent and his conviction'. So, there would be no leap of faith in a liberal direction.

From the vantage point of the president's office, however, de Klerk began a reassessment of South Africa's prospects. Forty years of National Party rule had left the white population powerful and prosperous; the Afrikaner community, in particular, had fared well, fulfilling its long-held ambition of acquiring wealth, skills and economic strength. The government's ability to defend the apartheid system was still formidable. Its powers of repression had hardly been tested. Its security forces were more than a match for any threat from either township activists or trained guerrillas. It possessed enough allies within the black community – homeland leaders, urban politicians, vigilante groups – to make the system work. At a regional level, its hegemony over southern Africa remained unchallenged. At an international level, despite the world-wide opprobrium that South Africa aroused, it faced no serious threat; sanctions were a costly rather than a damaging imposition.

What struck de Klerk, in assessing the government's options, was the lack of any viable political strategy. The whole emphasis of Botha's policy in recent years had been security management. South Africa was, in effect, being ruled by security managers with enormous powers at their disposal. All Botha's efforts to lure 'moderate' African leaders into a dialogue with the government, offering them a 'national forum' in which to make their views known, had came to naught. Not a single reputable African politician had stepped forward to support it. Even conservative leaders like KwaZulu's Chief Buthelezi demanded far more from Botha, including the release of Mandela and the lifting of the ban on the ANC, before they were willing to enter negotiations.

De Klerk had long been mindful of the need to find a political accommodation with the black population. While acting zealously to protect white interests, he acknowledged that blacks too had an equal right to run their own institutions. 'We must provide for urban blacks own political institutions, own political power bases, own legislatures, own executives, so that they can get the same degree of self-determination as the "homeland" blacks, as the whites have within the House of Assembly and as the Coloureds have in their own Chamber,' he said in 1987. 'When that is attained, every South African will elect leaders with important and visible powers.'

The advice he received in 1989 from several quarters, from senior figures in the Broederbond, from the National Intelligence Service, from *verligte* politicians in the cabinet and from other prominent Afrikaner intellectuals and journalists, was that the modernized form of apartheid he envisaged would no longer work. If the whites were to preserve the power and privileges they had enjoyed for so long, a more fundamental change was needed. While the government faced no immediate difficulty, the longer political reform was delayed, the weaker its position would become. Without reform, the cycle of black opposition would become increasingly widespread and violent. The fate of neighbouring Rhodesia, where the white-minority leader, Ian Smith, had turned down one favourable deal after another, only to find himself embroiled in a seven-year-long guerrilla war and negotiating a belated settlement which led to the advent of a Marxist government, provided a potent example. 'When the opportunity was there for real constructive negotiation, it was not grasped,' concluded de Klerk. 'We must not make that mistake.' A phrase that Pieter de Lange, the Broederbond chairman, used in a memorandum advocating reform, became embedded in de Klerk's thinking: 'The greatest risk is not to take any risk.' De Klerk later remarked, 'We had to escape from a corner where everything had stagnated into confrontation.'

De Klerk's dilemma, however, once he had accepted the argument that a new political dispensation was necessary, was that there was no way of embarking on negotiations for one without the inclusion of the ANC. No credible African leader would participate until Mandela had been released and the ban on the ANC was lifted. But the risks for de Klerk in doing so were considerable. The government had devoted years of propaganda to telling South Africa's whites that the ANC was a bunch of communist terrorists. It had repeatedly committed itself not to negotiate with any leader or organization engaged in violence. By abandoning this position, it would be conceding a significant victory to the ANC. The result might be further violence as black radicals took to the streets to push the revolution forwards. Moreover, any concession to the ANC was bound to undermine his support within the white community and boost the threat from his right-wing opponents which he constantly feared.

On the other hand, the timing for a new initiative seemed propitious. The collapse of socialist governments in Eastern Europe in 1989 not only deprived the ANC of one of its main sources of financial, logistical and military support but also undermined its sense of ideological direction. The Soviet Union, meanwhile, had made clear its intention of disentangling itself from regional conflicts. A deal in 1989 over the independence of neighbouring Namibia, which South Africa controlled, required the withdrawal of Cuban troops from Angola, once seen as part of the communist threat to South Africa. In a matter of months, the spectre of 'total onslaught', which had dominated government thinking during the Botha era, receded. The fear that the ANC could be used as 'a Trojan horse' by the Soviet Union fell away. De Klerk's principal strategist, Gerrit Viljoen, a former head of the Broederbond, recalled, 'We recognized it as a unique opportunity in the course of history, a God-given opportunity – we thought of it very much in Christian terms – to ensure that conflict in South Africa could be resolved.'

De Klerk quickly grasped the importance of these strategic openings. He was not a man driven by any sense of moral imperative about the need to bring apartheid to an end. The church to which he belonged, the Gereformeerde Kerk, the strictest of the three Dutch Reformed Churches, had spent decades justifying the apartheid system on biblical and moral grounds. De Klerk himself believed firmly that apartheid had been an 'honourable' attempt to assist the separate development of black tribal groups as well as whites. It was only 'wrong', he once said, because it had become 'unworkable'. He also carried with him none of the ideological baggage which had so influenced previous National Party leaders. He was essentially a pragmatist, determined above all else to protect Afrikaner interests. Groups rights remained his lodestar and he was confident of securing them in any new political dispensation.

De Klerk found that considerable preparatory work had already been undertaken. Mandela's persistent efforts since 1986 to establish a dialogue with the government had done much to foster a climate conducive to negotiations. Both Kobie Coetsee and Niel Barnard were convinced that Mandela was a man with whom the government could do business. By inviting Mandela to tea at Tuynhuys, whatever his motives, Botha had already accorded him a measure of respectability that belied years of government propaganda.

Other reports that de Klerk received were also promising. A group of prominent Afrikaners regularly meeting ANC officials in secret at a country mansion in England were impressed by the ANC's willingness to enter realistic discussions. Among the group was Willem de Klerk, who, after each meeting he attended, wrote a frank assessment of ANC intentions which he passed on to his brother. He spoke of the meetings as 'a bridge-building exercise' notable for producing a degree of understanding between the two sides.

In August 1989, the ANC set out publicly for the first time its proposals on how to proceed towards a negotiated settlement. 'A conjuncture of circumstances exists which, if there is a demonstrable readiness on the part of the Pretoria regime to engage in negotiations genuinely and seriously, could create the possibility to end apartheid through negotiation,' said the ANC's Harare Declaration. It listed five preconditions for negotiations: lifting the state of emergency; ending restrictions on political activity; legalizing all political organizations; releasing all political prisoners; and stopping all political executions. In exchange, the ANC would suspend all armed violence, enabling constitutional discussions to proceed.

On his journeys abroad, de Klerk was readily assured by Western governments of support if he changed course. From one capital to the next, the advice he was given was the same: lift the ban on the ANC, release political prisoners and start talks. He was left in no doubt that any initiative he took which excluded the ANC would be dismissed by Western governments as worthless.

The mood of much of the white population favoured change. A new generation of white South Africans disliked being treated as pariahs by the rest of the world, subjected to sports boycotts, travel bans, trade sanctions and hostile comments. Businessmen were adamant about the need for a more stable political system that would encourage economic growth and rid South Africa of the cost of sanctions. Economic prosperity was becoming more important to white South Africa than racial division.

A general election in September 1989 provided some clue as to where the white population stood. De Klerk, fearing the threat from extreme right-wing parties vehemently opposed to reform, campaigned on a right-wing platform, denouncing as traitors white liberal opponents who had been in contact with the ANC and standing firm in defence of group rights. He made no mention of any political initiative. The result gave the National Party a thin margin of victory. Only 48 per cent of 2.2 million whites voted for the National Party, the first time in thirty years it had received less than an absolute majority. The extreme right-wing Conservative Party gained about 30 per cent of the vote. The liberal Democratic Party took 21 per cent. In the months ahead, de Klerk was to argue that two-thirds of the white electorate – the National Party vote plus the Democratic Party vote – had given him a mandate for reform.

The first sign of change came one week after the election when de Klerk, against the advice of his own security managers, gave permission for a demonstration against police brutality to proceed through the streets of Cape Town, an event that during the Botha era would have resulted in outright repression. The shock for many whites of seeing on the television news the spectacle of tens of thousands of anti-apartheid demonstrators swarming through Cape Town was considerable. De Klerk reasoned that if he did not permit orderly demonstrations, then he would soon face disorderly ones.

His next step signalled far more radical change ahead. In October, Walter Sisulu, Ahmed Kathrada and four other ANC life prisoners were set free after twenty-five years' imprisonment. Sisulu was dropped off at his small, red-bricked house in Soweto in a police van. His homecoming, at the age of seventy-seven, was marked by one of the greatest celebrations that Soweto had ever experienced. At home to welcome him was his beloved Albertina, whose own ordeal during his years in prison had matched that of Winnie Mandela. As well as her own spells of imprisonment, solitary confinement and house arrest, one of Albertina's sons had been banned and detained, another had served a prison sentence for resistance activity and yet another son and daughter had gone into exile. Yet through it all, Albertina had been a rock of stability. The Sisulus settled down to a 'second' marriage better, they said, than the first: this time there were no restrictions, no banning orders, no police raids, no prison.

Mandela was the last of the Rivonia group to remain in prison. Mbeki had left in 1987 and now the others had gone. Mandela had negotiated their release during the secret sessions of Coetsee's committee and he expected his own to follow soon. His discussions with the committee, meanwhile, continued to range widely over political issues, taking on greater significance with the addition of Gerrit Viljoen, de Klerk's principal strategist, to the team.

On 12 December, Mandela was taken to the president's office in Cape Town, to the same room where he had sipped tea with Botha. The encounter was amicable and businesslike. 'He met me on the basis of equality and discussed issues objectively,' Mandela recalled. Mandela was impressed by de Klerk's willingness to listen. Mandela made clear his opposition to the idea of 'group rights', which he saw as a means of perpetuating white domination. De Klerk replied that group rights were intended to deal with the problem of white fears of black domination, an issue which Mandela himself acknowledged needed to be addressed. Mandela's response was that the idea of group rights did more to increase black suspicions than to allay white fears, at which De Klerk rejoined, 'We will have to change it, then.'

Mandela raised the question of his own release. There was no point in his leaving prison unless the ban on the ANC was also lifted, since he would then be working for an illegal organization and face arrest once more. The best way forward, he said, was to unban all illegal organizations, release all political prisoners and lift the state of emergency, as the ANC had demanded. De Klerk listened carefully. By the end of the meeting, Mandela had concluded that de Klerk was a man with whom he could do business.

De Klerk had yet to decide how far to take his reforms. The issues were thrashed out at a special bush conference, or *bosberaad*, in north-western Transvaal in December, attended by the entire cabinet and some fifty officials and advisers. There was heated debate about lifting the ban on political organizations, in particular the Communist Party. The defence minister, Magnus Malan, a leading figure in the 'total onslaught' school, argued vehemently against unbanning the Communist Party. Others pointed out that if any opposition group remained unbanned, its allies would launch vociferous campaigns in its support, undermining the credit the government would otherwise gain.

De Klerk believed that there would be considerable advantage in seizing the initiative and capturing the 'moral high ground'. The government was acting from a position of strength and would continue to do so. Its ability to remain firmly in control was not in doubt. The chances were that the ANC, poorly organized and ill-prepared for peace, would fall into disarray, leaving the government to forge ahead in a new alliance with conservative black leaders like Buthelezi and moderate black organizations.

Only a handful of trusted advisers were privy in advance to the decisions de Klerk announced to parliament in Cape Town on 2 February 1990. He did not inform the National Party's parliamentary caucus. He did not even tell his wife. No one expected such sweeping measures.

In a calm, confident manner, de Klerk announced that he was lifting the ban on the whole spectrum of liberation organizations: the African National Congress, Umkhonto we Sizwe, the South African Communist Party and the Pan-Africanist Congress. He further announced that emergency regulations would be eased; media restrictions would be abolished; political prisoners would be released; exiles would be allowed to return home; capital punishment would be suspended; and apartheid laws like the Separate Amenities Act would be repealed. 'It is time for us to break out of the cycle of violence and break through to peace and reconciliation,' he declared, outlining new aims towards which the government would work. These included a new democratic constitution, universal franchise and the protection of minorities as well as of individual rights. He asked black leaders to join him. 'Walk through the door and take your place at the negotiating table together with the government,' he said. 'The time for negotiations has come.'

De Klerk left his announcement about Mandela's release for his grande finale. Mandela, he said, 'could play an important part' in negotiations for a peaceful settlement. He would be released 'unconditionally' and 'without delay'.

The boldness of de Klerk's reforms set South Africa on an entirely new course. In effect, he had pronounced the death sentence of apartheid. The central issue had always been political power. None of the reforms hitherto implemented by National Party leaders had come close to addressing that issue. Now, in a stroke, de Klerk had conceded one-person one-vote and opened the way for its attainment. But the route there was to be marked by greater turmoil than anything South Africa had previously experienced.

The arrangements for Mandela's release were soon enmeshed in argument. On 9 February, seven days after de Klerk's announcement, Mandela was taken to Tuynhuys, where de Klerk informed him that he would be released in Johannesburg the following day. Mandela was intensely annoyed at de Klerk's decision to free him without consultation and without warning. He told de Klerk that he needed a week's notice so that proper preparations could be made both by his family and by party officials; otherwise the result would be chaos. He wanted to be able to walk out of the gates of Victor Verster to visit nearby Paarl to thank the people there for their kindness during his stay there, and then to address a public meeting in Cape Town. Cape Town had been his home for nearly three decades. He would make his own way back to Johannesburg in his own time, he said.

Negotiations over the exact time and place of his release continued for five hours. Mandela remembered the experience as 'a conflict between my blood and my brains', wanting to leave prison as soon as possible but recognizing the risks in doing so. The difficulty for de Klerk was that the government had already told the foreign press of Mandela's imminent release and could not afford delay. The compromise eventually reached was that Mandela would be released from Victor Verster prison at precisely 3 p.m. on Sunday 11 February. De Klerk poured glasses of whisky to mark the occasion. Mandela, disliking strong spirits, pretended to drink. He left the meeting in a thoroughly bad mood.

On the morning of 11 February, Mandela rose at dawn and went through a shortened version of his exercise routine. The prison doctor called by to give him a brief examination. Mandela joked, 'It's a bit late to find something wrong.' Members of his reception committee arrived to discuss the day's schedule. They dismissed Mandela's idea of making his first speech to the citizens of Paarl.

They wanted him instead to drive, as planned, straight to the Grand Parade in Cape Town to address a mass rally of supporters from the balcony of City Hall. A crowd of thousands had been gathering there since the early morning. The details of Mandela's speech had been worked over for hours. Many ANC officials were worried by the rumours circulating about his secret talks with the government which had created the suspicion that he had done a deal with them. They felt it important that Mandela should make clear his loyalty to the ANC and to the party line.

The house was soon full of dozens of people. Amid all the excitement and activity, Mandela took time to say warm farewells to the prison staff who had become his friends. To Warrant Officer Gregory, who had known him for twenty-three years, he wrote a short note: 'The wonderful hours we spent together during the last two decades end today. But you will always be in my thoughts.' The two men shook hands and embraced. 'We will see each other again,' said Mandela.

The schedule for his release soon began to go awry. Winnie's party, flying in from Johannesburg, arrived late. The final meal was delayed. It was 4 p.m. before the cavalcade of cars taking him to Cape Town was ready to leave. As Mandela was driven through the prison grounds, the families of prison guards, all of them white, stood in their gardens and waved goodbye.

Within sight of the prison gates, Mandela alighted and, with a slightly fragile air, walked the last few yards, hand in hand with Winnie, towards a waiting crowd of supporters and the ranks of the world's media. It was a moment of liberation experienced around the world.

The size of the crowd, plus the hundreds of photographers, television crews and reporters gathered to witness the occasion, astounded him. He had expected no more than a few dozen people. 'Only when I saw the crowd did I realize that I had not thought carefully enough about the events of the day,' he said later. As everyone pressed to get nearer, Mandela and Winnie were hustled back into their car and driven away through the throng.

On his way to Cape Town, passing through the vineyards and orchards of some of the richest Afrikaner farms in the country, Mandela remarked on the number of whites he saw standing by the side of the road to catch a glimpse of him. Some even saluted as he drove by. He was to mention it again and again over the next few days. The numbers were, in fact, relatively small, but that they were there at all impressed him. At one point, he stopped the car to thank a white family for their support.

The mood of the crowds awaiting Mandela in Grand Parade had meanwhile become increasingly restless. By mid-afternoon, some 50,000 people had assembled in front of the City Hall, where a huge banner had been draped over the upper balcony saying, 'Nelson Mandela, the nation welcomes you home.' On the edge of the square, groups of youths began breaking into shops and looting them. The police retaliated with shotguns and pistols. An emergency aid post was soon filled with scores of wounded victims. When ANC officials appealed for calm and discipline, they were rewarded with jeers, whistles and slow handclaps. Skirmishes between youths and police continued for hours while the crowd waited for Mandela's arrival. Much of the blame for the disorder on Grand Parade that day was attributed to the ANC's poor organization.

When Mandela's car eventually reached Grand Parade, the driver, instead of taking him to the rear of the City Hall as planned, tried to find a way through the crowd at the front. The car was soon engulfed by a sea of people pressing close, hammering on the windows, the bonnet, the boot. For more than an hour, Mandela was trapped by his own supporters while ANC officials struggled to secure an exit route for the car. Once freed, the driver, instead of heading for the rear entrance, sped away from the City Hall just to avoid the crowds. To calm him down, Mandela gave him the directions to the house of his attorney, Dullah Omar. He had been there for only a few minutes when an agitated telephone call came through from Archbishop Desmond Tutu at the City Hall telling him that unless he arrived soon there might be serious disturbances.

By the time Mandela finally reached City Hall, it was almost dark. Most of the crowd had dispersed and the 10,000 or so who remained found it difficult to see him. Mandela also discovered at the last moment, as he reached for his speech, that he had left his reading spectacles behind at Victor Verster. Fortunately, he was able to use a pair belonging to Winnie, but they were ill-fitting and kept slipping from his nose.

The speech that Mandela made that evening, the first public

speech he had made since the Rivonia trial, was broadcast around the world. It was a crude, partisan speech, reflecting the narrow, parochial interests of ANC officials who had had a hand in drafting it at Victor Verster. There was no sense of vision or wider purpose, no call for national reconciliation. It consisted mainly of messages that party officials wanted to transmit to their own constituency.

Mandela went to great lengths to allay suspicions that he had done a secret deal with the government. He was, he said, 'a loyal and disciplined' member of the ANC. 'My talks with the government have been aimed at normalizing the political situation in the country,' he said. 'I wish to stress that I myself have at no time entered into negotiations about the future of the country, except to insist on a meeting between the ANC and the government . . . Negotiations cannot take place above the heads or behind the backs of our people.'

The armed struggle would continue, he said, until the conditions were right for negotiations to start. The government had yet to fulfil the ANC's demands for lifting the state of emergency and releasing political prisoners. This was not the time for the ANC to relax its efforts: 'Now is the time to intensify the struggle on all fronts.'

He paid tribute to a long list of organizations for their contribution to the struggle and made the point of singling out for special praise his old friend Joe Slovo, the Communist Party's general secretary – 'one of our finest patriots'.

Mixed in with the party rhetoric were a few conciliatory remarks: 'We express the hope that a climate conducive to a negotiated settlement would be created soon so that there may no longer be the need for the armed struggle.' De Klerk, he said, had gone further than any other National Party leader in taking 'real steps to normalize the situation'. In words that would come to haunt him, he described de Klerk as 'a man of integrity'. But the overall tone was uncompromising.

It was a speech which raised doubts about the quality of Mandela's leadership. Was he a man who would inspire his people to make peace and achieve national reconciliation or would he stir up anew black militancy against whites? To whites, his speech seemed needlessly militant. To many blacks, it seemed ambiguous, calling them to arms at one moment and suggesting negotiations the next.

Mandela spent his first night of freedom at Bishopscourt, the elegant residence of the Anglican archbishop, Desmond Tutu, in an affluent suburb on the slopes of Devil's Peak. Tutu himself had long been a prominent anti-apartheid activist, receiving the Nobel Peace Prize in 1984.

The next morning, in the gardens at Bishopscourt, Mandela faced the world's media, presenting a very different image from the night before. He exuded an inner calm and confidence, displaying a spirit of generosity entirely missing from his Grand Parade address. His charm of manner captivated journalists. He answered questions with an agility and ease that they found all the more remarkable because of his years of isolation from the modern world. He graciously paid tribute to the press for remembering him and his colleagues during their long ordeal, and when he recognized the names of questioners familiar to him from his endless reading of newspapers, he greeted them in personal terms. Most remarkable of all was the absence of any trace of bitterness about his long years of imprisonment.

His message now was full of hope and conciliation. He recognized, he said, that whites were concerned about the demand for one-person one-vote and wanted structural guarantees to ensure that they were not dominated by blacks: 'We understand that fear. The whites are fellow South Africans. We want them to feel safe.' He appealed to them to help build a new South Africa: 'We appreciate the contribution they made towards the development of this country.'

He referred again to de Klerk as 'a man of integrity'. In his discussions with him, de Klerk had proved to be very flexible:

> As an organization, of course, we are concerned not so much with the personal virtues of an individual. Our policy and strategies are determined by the harsh reality of the fact that the National Party has a policy which is not progressive. And that is what determines our attitude. But I am confident that, if Mr de Klerk is able to carry the National Party with him in the new line he has taken, he himself wants to normalize the situation as soon as possible. Therefore I think that very soon obstacles to negotiation will be removed and it will be possible for us to sit down and talk.

It was a masterly performance. At the end of the conference, the journalists present, some 300 in all, broke all professional rules and burst into applause, something most of them had never done before. The press that morning had been highly critical of the previous day's mayhem on Grand Parade and of the tenor of his speech from the balcony. In a matter of fifty minutes, Mandela had won them over.

From Cape Town, Mandela and Winnie then flew to Johannesburg. Mandela was determined to live in their house in Orlando West, no. 8115, which held so many memories for him, even though it was now too small for his needs. Since the fire in 1988, it had been solidly rebuilt, but it still consisted of only four rooms. He rejected suggestions that he should move to Winnie's mansion in Beverly Hills, considering it both too ostentatious and too remote from the community. But on arriving in Johannesburg, he was told that the house in Orlando was surrounded by a throng of supporters, so he was obliged to stay at a friend's in the northern suburbs.

The following day, he was given a tumultuous welcome at a football stadium in Soweto packed to capacity and surrounded by even greater crowds outside. It was only then, after the rally had ended, that Mandela finally returned home, after twenty-seven years.

Mandela was asked once how different was the man who emerged from prison after twenty-seven years from the one who went in. He replied, with characteristic brevity, 'I came out mature.' Mandela disliked talking about himself and allowed few glimpses of his personal thoughts or emotions. The years of his imprisonment had turned him into an intensely private person. Even with his closest friends, his true feelings remained hidden. He was anxious never to betray the slightest sign of weakness either to them or to prison staff, determined to stifle the anger that lay within. Self-control became an abiding habit. On his release, he was articulate and fluent in discussing political matters, but uneasy and reticent when asked about himself. At his Bishopscourt press conference, he was asked to describe his emotions as he came out of prison. 'I must confess that I am unable to describe my emotions,' he replied. 'I was completely overwhelmed by the enthusiasm. It is something I did not expect. I would be merely rationalizing if I told you that I am able to describe my own feelings. It was breathtaking, that's all I can say.' His close friend Amina Cachalia, who had known him for forty years, observed, 'He had to learn how to communicate again.'

He preferred to discuss his role as a member of a team of colleagues than his position as an individual: 'I find it difficult to personalize the collective experience of prison.' The comradeship of his fellow prisoners, their strength in adversity, was one of his favourite themes.

But there were other themes that were unexpected. Mandela did not regard his years in prison as wasted. 'One of the advantages was the ability to sit down and to think,' he said. 'We had the opportunity of reflecting on past mistakes and planning how we would handle problems when we were released from prison. It was a rewarding experience.'

Not once did Mandela express bitterness towards the white community for his ordeal, only against the system they imposed. The cause of non-racial democracy, he knew, could only be impeded by hatred and resentment of the white community. It was the knowledge that the cause for which he had been imprisoned was morally right that had done so much to fortify him there: 'It was not so much the inner strength of any individual that enabled us to go through some of the harshest experiences you can imagine, but that we stood for a good cause.' That cause would only be undermined by any expression of racial animosity.

He often felt anger about whites, he said, but not hatred. His hatred was directed at the system. His anger was directed at individuals, never against whites as a group: 'I have felt anger, especially at the police, who have subjected my wife and family to harassment while I was in prison. But anger is a temporary feeling. You soon forget it, particularly if you are involved in positive activities and attitudes.'

Though warders in prison were part of a repressive system, he judged them individually and formed friendships with some: 'We had many friends amongst warders who tried as much as possible to make our conditions as comfortable as possible.' He cited the example of James Gregory: 'Even though Gregory was a warder and had to carry out unpopular and even repressive policies, as an individual he was a gentleman and we became great friends.' It was the attitude of such men that 'wiped out any bitterness which a man could have' about losing twenty-seven years of his life.

While the outside world had expected Mandela to dwell on the suffering he and his colleagues had endured in prison, he himself was more interested in explaining what they had learned there, the understanding they had gained, the reasons for their lack of bitterness, the strength of their commitment to democracy which had sustained them. The example he set was of profound importance. For, if after twenty-seven years in prison, Mandela could emerge insisting on reconciliation, it undermined the demands of those seeking revenge and retribution.

Only on one issue, the persecution of Winnie and their two daughters, was Mandela forthcoming about his own personal feelings. He spoke of the pain and guilt he felt at knowing that his family was exposed to harassment and insecurity without him there to protect them: 'It is not a nice feeling for a man to see his family struggling, without security, without the dignity of the head of the family.' Their suffering, he said, was greater than his own. Mandela made it clear that he felt he owed Winnie a huge debt for what she had endured on his behalf. It was a debt, he said, that he intended to pay off now that he was free. In the coming months Winnie was to exploit to the full his sense of guilt for her own benefit.

Old friends remarked on how much his appearance and his manner had changed. Hilda Bernstein, whose family used to know him as 'the giant', noted, after her first meeting with him:

> Nelson has changed a lot. He is still so upright, bearing himself with dignity, but he is thin, his face, once round and full-cheeked, has narrowed; his eyes, the voice, the smile are the same, but the prison years have robbed him of his air of fun and gaiety. He is sober, immensely dignified, conscious of the expectations arising from the role into which he has been cast.

Reporters watching him descend the stone steps in the gardens at Bishopscourt observed how he walked with the stiff gait of an elderly gentleman. Despite his aristocratic bearing, he seemed at times almost frail. There was much speculation about the state of his health, about whether, at the age of seventy-one, he would stand up to the stresses and strains of leadership in the days that lay ahead. The years in prison had taken their toll. He had suffered from high blood pressure, from tuberculosis and from back pains. He was also afflicted by an eye ailment acquired as a result of working in the lime quarry; his eyes were sensitive to sharp light. Mandela himself admitted 'there are signs of old age, wear and tear, which we must expect'. But he described his health as 'reasonably good' and pointed out that each day he continued with the same set of rigorous exercises he had carried out in prison over the years. Concern about his health was to mount in coming months as he put himself through a punishing schedule of rallies, meetings, press conference, interviews and long trips abroad.

In prison, Mandela's dream of what he would do when he was set free was to take a leisurely drive to the Transkei, to visit the village of Qunu where he grew up and to wander in the hills and valleys where he played as a boy. Yet so great were the demands upon him that it was to be several months before he managed to get to Qunu.

What he craved for most of all was to resume the settled family life that he had forsaken when he went underground in 1961. Yet that too was to be denied him. For Winnie, the focus of all his longing in prison, showed no interest in sharing the intimacies of married life with him. She had found a new lover, half her age, and she made it clear that she had no intention of giving him up.

Thus Mandela's homecoming did not bring the joy and happiness for which he had yearned so long. But as with all the other suffering he had endured, he hid the pain and humiliation behind the mask which he had become accustomed to wearing.

The task facing Mandela was daunting. The ANC had been plunged into deep disarray by the unexpected change in government policy. Its entire strategy for more than twenty years had been based on plans for a revolutionary seizure of power, not on the possibility of peaceful negotiations. Trained guerrillas, brought up on songs about how Umkhonto would march across the Limpopo to take Pretoria by storm, hankered for action. Many activists in the townships were equally reluctant to forgo the prospect of revolution. Distrust of the government's intentions was intense. Many were convinced that de Klerk's reforms were no more than a device to subvert the armed struggle. Within the ANC's hierarchy in exile, there had been long disagreement between a small group amenable to the idea of negotiations and a far larger group committed to armed struggle outright. The Harare Declaration in August 1989 setting out a host of preconditions to negotiation had aroused fierce controversy which remained unresolved. This division between those who wanted to seize power and those who advocated a negotiated compromise was to afflict the ANC for years to come.

Mandela himself was distrusted. Rumours of his involvement in secret talks with the government had led many to conclude that he had gone soft. 'The word was,' said Mac Maharaj, 'that Madiba was wearing a three-piece suit, drinking wine, you name it, he was a sell-out.' Prominent activists inside South Africa questioned his right to leadership and pointedly referred to him as 'an ordinary ANC member'.

The disarray within the ANC was compounded by the illness of Oliver Tambo. In August 1989, after presiding over the drafting of the Harare Declaration, he had suffered a stroke, leaving him partially paralysed and depriving the ANC of a guiding hand at a critical time. The vacuum in leadership still had to be filled.

New tensions emerged between the external wing of the ANC and its internal surrogate, the United Democratic Front. In exile, the ANC had been used to acting as a secretive, autocratic organization. Decisions had been taken by a revolutionary council and passed down the chain of command. The covert nature of operations meant that there had been little room for dissent. Those who opposed the party line were more than likely to be accused of being collaborators. Its headquarters were a cramped, single-storey building off an alleyway in downtown Lusaka, where it had gained a reputation for chronic inefficiency. Its guerrilla army was notably unsuccessful. The casualty rate for MK guerrillas entering South Africa was high; many of those who were captured were turned into informers and used to assassinate colleagues. A senior defence force official, General Constand Viljoen, described MK as 'the weakest of enemies', while an internal ANC document produced in early 1990 admitted, 'We do not have the capacity within our country to intensify the armed struggle in a meaningful way.' Yet the idea of revolution, of being a revolutionary organization, still held immense appeal. The standing of Umkhonto within the liberation movement remained high. And the secretive, tightly knit clique which had made all the ANC's decisions for more than twenty years had no intention of letting their authority slip away.

However, the internal leaders of the UDF, which had borne the brunt of the struggle against the government during the 1980s, were as determined as the ANC's 'old guard' to maintain their own spheres of influence. As a coalition of more than 600 groups, community organizations, youth groups and trade union affiliates, the UDF had evolved a tradition of politics that was highly democratic and decentralized, based on constant contact and discussion between officials and supporters and collective decision-making – a style that was entirely alien to the Lusaka exiles. Scores of local and regional leaders were used to operating from independent power bases of their own and were hostile to the idea of taking orders from a national executive.

There were tensions too as different generations of leadership asserted themselves: the elderly veterans of the 1950s, like Mandela, emerging from years of imprisonment; the Soweto generation of the 1970s, who in exile had served as guerrilla commissars; and the radical young leaders of the 1980s' internal revolt, with their trade union allies, who had provided much of the backbone of anti-government protest.

Mandela's task, after first re-establishing his own leadership credentials, was to weld this massive, disorganized and restless constituency into a coherent political force capable of negotiating a transfer of power from a government possessing huge advantages and determined to secure for itself all the power it felt was needed to protect white interests.

Two weeks after his release, Mandela flew to Lusaka to give the ANC's hierarchy a full account of his dealings with the government and to convince them that the time was right to pursue negotiations. There remained strong distrust of the government's intentions, but Mandela succeeded in removing doubts about his own role and in overcoming some of the resistance to the idea of negotiations. Of crucial importance, Mandela managed to win over Umkhonto's chief of staff, Chris Hani, a hardline guerrilla commander well known for supporting attacks on white civilian targets. 'I think we're going to learn from him that we need to be better South Africans,' said Hani, 'to forgive and forget and to look forward to building a new South Africa.'

Mandela quickly became close to the ANC's old guard. He was nominated to join the thirty-five members of the national executive committee based in Lusaka and given the rank of deputy president. He felt more at ease in their company than in the rumbustious world of the UDF, where his freedom of leadership was constantly challenged. He possessed a strong authoritarian streak and a preference for taking action on his own responsibility, for dealing directly with other leaders rather than waiting for consultations to be completed. His independent style of leadership frequently brought him into conflict with party officials inside South Africa, who insisted upon consultation and set out to curb his autonomy of action. Outwardly, at press conferences and public rallies, Mandela appeared to speak with undisputed authority. In reality, he had to struggle to assert his authority and was often outmanoeuvred.

Among the intrigues surrounding Mandela's leadership, Winnie was hard at work with her own agenda, seeking to control access to her husband. She swiftly took revenge on the group of prominent activists who had publicly condemned her involvement in the criminal activities of the Mandela Football Club, endeavouring to exclude them from the inner circle. Several people received threatening telephone calls. 'Stay away from Mandela,' Winnie told one prominent activist, Azhur Cachalia. 'If you don't, you'll see what will happen.'

Winnie also enlisted Mandela's help to further her own ambitions for high office within the ANC. Her drive for party posts was unrelenting. She began by seeking election as head of the ANC branch and the Women's League in Orlando West to give her a local power base. Mandela dutifully went from door to door, calling on residents to vote for her. She then set her sights on regional and national posts. Mandela indulged her, seemingly oblivious of her true nature and also of the risks to his own reputation in doing so. The full horror of Mandela United was soon to be played out in public during the trials of its members for murder.

Mandela also succumbed to pressure to move out of his 'matchbox' house in Orlando into Winnie's fifteen-room mansion in Diepkloof Extension which had hitherto remained empty. It was more appropriate to his needs, but he felt uneasy there and it was never a place he came to regard as home.

Much of the time during his first months of freedom he travelled the world, to Africa, Europe and North America, urging foreign governments to maintain the pressure of sanctions, seeking funds for the ANC and thanking anti-apartheid groups for their support over the years. Everywhere he went he was acclaimed a popular hero. In an age largely bereft of political morality, he was seen as a man of great moral authority, whose quarter-century of imprisonment for defying an evil system of government and for holding firm to the principles of democracy gave him a status no other politician could match. Western leaders – President Bush in Washington, Prime Minister Thatcher in London, President Mitterrand in Paris, Chancellor Kohl in Bonn, the Pope in Rome – all accorded him a warm welcome. He became the first private black citizen to address a joint session of the United States Congress. Politicians and show-business personalities alike vied to be seen in his company. Special events were organized to celebrate his visits – a ticker-tape parade in New York, a pop concert in London, a grand ceremony on the *terrasse* of the Trocadéro in Paris.

The only time Mandela stumbled on his triumphal progress was when he decided to air his views on international affairs. In the United States, he spoke admiringly of the Cuban leader, Fidel Castro, and the Libyan leader, Colonel Gaddafi, the foremost bogymen of the United States administration. Both ran dictatorial regimes notable for human rights abuses, but both had given support to the ANC, so Mandela singled them out for praise: 'There is no reason whatsoever why we should have any hesitation hailing their commitment to human rights.' When questioned on television about the morality of ignoring human rights violations in countries like Cuba and Libya, he replied, 'We are a liberation movement, which is fully involved in a struggle to emancipate our people from one of the worst racist tyrannies the world has seen. We have no time to be looking into the internal affairs of other countries.' The effect of these remarks on Mandela's reputation was instantaneous. 'You could positively hear his Q-factor – the attractiveness quotient with which America rates its celebrities – crashing through the floor,' reported one correspondent.

The controversy soon passed, but it showed Mandela to be both naïve and perverse. His principal purpose in visiting the United States was to gain the support of the Bush administration in maintaining sanctions against South Africa, an issue which was of crucial importance to the ANC in its confrontation with de Klerk's government. In speech after speech he stressed the need for sanctions to remain in place. But he swiftly undercut his own efforts by praising regimes regarded by the United States administration as its enemies and damaged his moral authority by implying that human rights abuses in countries which supported him were none of his concern.

His travels also took him, finally, to Qunu. It had remained much as it had always been, a scattered collection of circular thatched huts on a hillside close to the main road leading to Umtata. There was still no electricity, no shops, no roads, just grass tracks linking the homesteads, and a cemetery where many of Mandela's relatives were buried. Most of the inhabitants were old men, women and children, just as they had been during Mandela's childhood. But the poor soil had since eroded and there was an unkempt air about the village.

Mandela had not seen it for thirty-four years. Many of his relatives there had never set eyes on him or only dimly remembered him as a child. He arrived with Winnie in a black Mercedes, dressed impeccably in a dark blue suit, blue shirt and blue and yellow tie. The villagers lined up to greet him in their threadbare Sunday suits, old-fashioned dresses and battered, mud-caked shoes. Before taking part in a traditional homecoming feast, Mandela visited the simple grave of his mother, marked only by upturned bricks and stones in an open field below the site where the family rondavel had once stood. It had been demolished after the death of his mother in 1969, as there had been no one to pay for its upkeep. Mandela was struck by the poverty of the village: 'The poverty that was here when I last visited this place, that poverty is still there. My heart is very sore indeed on account of the poverty staring me in the face.'

In the hope that one day he might come and live among them, the village community awarded him a plot of land. Mandela welcomed the invitation and duly built a country house based on the design of his prison cottage at Victor Verster. When friends expressed surprise, Mandela explained that the Victor Verster house was the first spacious and comfortable home in which he had lived, he had liked it and had become accustomed to it.

*

Meanwhile, preparations for a preliminary meeting between the ANC and the government made hesitant progress. Each side was distrustful of the other. When the ANC presented its list of delegates to the meeting, de Klerk was horrified to find that it included Joe Slovo, general secretary of the Communist Party, whom the government had regarded for years as the evil genius behind the ANC's terror campaign. In the government's eyes, he was 'Moscow's man', the chief link between the Soviet Union and the ANC, the gatekeeper for Soviet arms, money and training. De Klerk insisted that Slovo should be excluded. Mandela refused to give way, adamant that the government would have no say in determining the ANC's representatives.

But when in May 1990 the two sides finally sat down together at Groote Schuur, the gabled mansion at the foot of Table Mountain in Cape Town which South Africa's prime ministers and presidents used as their official residence, the atmosphere was unexpectedly cordial. The government's delegation consisted entirely of Afrikaners. The ANC's delegation comprised seven blacks, two whites, one Coloured and one Indian; among them was Slovo, silver-haired, portly and looking more like a benign grandfather than a terrorist mastermind. 'Within a matter of minutes,' said a senior ANC official, 'everybody understood that there was nobody in the room with horns.' Much was made of the personal 'chemistry' between de Klerk and Mandela. Though they came from different backgrounds and from different generations – Mandela was seventy-one, de Klerk was fifty-three – Mandela respected de Klerk's credentials as an Afrikaner leader: de Klerk came from a powerful lineage, a matter to which Mandela attached considerable importance. 'I find him to be an honest person, very capable and a strong leader,' remarked Mandela about de Klerk. 'He is sincere in his efforts to bring about fundamental political changes in the country.'

It was a promising beginning. Both sides emerged with a clear understanding of the obstacles that lay in the way of negotiations. The ANC wanted the government first to lift the state of emergency, to allow political exiles to return home and to release all political prisoners. The government wanted the ANC to declare an end to its armed struggle.

In June, de Klerk lifted the state of emergency. But further progress was impeded by disputes over the return of exiles and the release of prisoners and by the discovery by security police of an underground MK operation named Operation Vula, which had been kept secret from Mandela. When Mandela returned from an overseas trip in July, he was determined to push the peace process forward. Political violence was on the increase; right-wing extremists were gathering momentum. There was a clear danger of the process faltering altogether.

Slovo had reached a similar conclusion. Though he was known more as a revolutionary enthusiast than a pragmatic thinker, after long years in exile he had come to recognize the advantage of using compromise to attain his objectives. He believed that in order to create the right climate for negotiations, it was necessary for the ANC to suspend the armed struggle unilaterally. De Klerk, he reasoned, needed to demonstrate some benefits from his reforms to appease his critics, otherwise he would stall.

When Slovo approached Mandela with the idea of suspending the armed struggle, Mandela's first reaction was negative. But he soon realized that it would provide him with the opportunity of seizing the initiative from de Klerk. If the proposal came from Slovo it would carry far greater authority with the ANC than if it came from him. He was already under suspicion of having 'gone soft', but Slovo's revolutionary credentials were beyond reproach and he would carry the day.

At a meeting of the ANC's national executive committee in July, Slovo made his proposal and Mandela supported him. There were fierce objections, but after several hours their view prevailed. On 6 August, at a meeting in Pretoria, the ANC signed an agreement suspending the armed struggle launched nearly thirty years before.

The practical effect of the Pretoria Minute, as it was known, was negligible. Umkhonto had long since halted guerrilla operations. But the rhetoric of revolution was deeply rooted among the mass of ANC supporters. Many looked upon themselves as soldiers of the revolution. By abandoning the armed struggle, Mandela provoked a furore within the movement. Slovo calculated that 90 per cent of ANC supporters considered the decision to be a 'sell-out'. Militants attacked Mandela's liking for 'personal diplomacy' with de Klerk and set out to curb his room for manoeuvre.

But even as the row was under way, it was overshadowed by a far greater crisis emerging from the green rolling hills of Natal, where a vicious struggle for power had developed centred on the controversial leader of the KwaZulu homeland, Mangosuthu Buthelezi.

CHAPTER 21

The Third Man

In the early days, Buthelezi remained on good terms with the exiled leaders of the ANC. When he launched the Inkatha movement in 1975, they regarded it as a useful ally in the anti-apartheid campaign. They also approved his election in 1976 as KwaZulu's chief minister, confident that he would prove to be a stumbling block to the government's drive to establish 'independent' homelands. But the relationship turned sour in 1979, after Buthelezi met Oliver Tambo in London, with the ANC accusing Buthelezi of building Inkatha into 'a personal power base' and Buthelezi accusing the ANC of trying to hijack Inkatha for its own ends.

During the 1980s, the feud became increasingly acrimonious. From the government's standpoint, Buthelezi was no moderate. His demands for the release of Mandela and other political prisoners, for the lifting of the ban on the ANC, for the abolition of all apartheid measures and for negotiations for a new constitution were no different from those made by radical groups like the UDF. But, to the fury of radical activists, he vociferously opposed the armed struggle, sanctions and disinvestment and praised the free-enterprise system. The ANC and UDF dismissed him as a traitor to the nationalist cause. Buthelezi, for his part, resented any challenge to his authority. In a letter to Oliver Tambo in 1984, he wrote: 'In this part of South Africa, we come from warrior stock and there is a resilient determination in KwaZulu and in Inkatha which even the full might of the state will never be able to flatten. Do your colleagues really think they can flatten us on the way to their envisaged victory?' As the townships' revolt got under way, the level of rhetoric reached new heights. From Lusaka, the ANC denounced Buthelezi as 'a counter-revolutionary', 'a puppet' and 'a snake poisoning the people of South Africa [which] needs to be hit on the head'.

Once regarded as the most popular African politician in the country, Buthelezi showed signs of losing his support. One opinion poll concluded that between 1977 and 1988 Inkatha's support in the Witwatersrand region, the industrial heartland of South Africa, declined from more than 30 to less than 5 per cent. Even more serious for Buthelezi, there were clear indications that Inkatha's support in its home base of KwaZulu-Natal was rapidly eroding, notably among urban blacks. Pro-ANC youth groups and trade unions were becoming increasingly active. In 1987, Inkatha embarked on a recruitment drive.

The ugly contest that followed engulfed KwaZulu and Natal in spasms of violence for years to come. Buthelezi possessed considerable advantages. Since the 1970s, he had run KwaZulu from his capital at Ulundi as a one-party state, controlling its parliament, its police and its civil service. As a member of the Zulu royal family, he could rely on the support of a powerful network of Zulu traditional chiefs – *amakhosi* – whom he in turn rewarded with power and privilege. The Zulu system of loyalty and obedience to its hierarchy assured Buthelezi of bedrock support among more traditionally minded communities, particularly those in the deep rural areas of KwaZulu. Migrant workers on the Witwatersrand, coming from those rural areas, bore him the same allegiance. His party, Inkatha, was a well-organized political movement with a clear hierarchy and chain of command, able to hold regular meetings and rallies. It drew support from the Zulu establishment, from chiefs, councillors, legislative assembly members, indunas, businessmen, civil servants and other government employees. In 1985, it established a trade union wing, the United Workers' Union of South Africa, Uwusa, in an endeavour to compete with the pro-ANC Congress of South African Trade Unions, Cosatu. Above all, it could count on the support of the KwaZulu police, which had been established in 1980 and which Buthelezi, as minister of police, had turned into a formidable paramilitary force. In addition to regular policemen, special *kitkonstabels* were recruited, mainly from the ranks of Inkatha, some with criminal records. They were given limited training, then sent back to their communities, armed with pump-action shotguns. 'We must prepare ourselves not only to defend property and life, but to go beyond that and prepare ourselves to hit back with devastating force at those who destroy our property and kill us,' Buthelezi told the KwaZulu legislative assembly in 1984.

In meeting the challenge posed by pro-ANC activists in the 1980s, Buthelezi and the government found themselves making common cause. Buthelezi was given every encouragement to deal forcefully with the threat. In 1986, he secretly arranged for army training in the Caprivi Strip for a covert paramilitary force of 200 men able to undertake offensive operations against pro-ANC activists. When pro-ANC groups began to make headway in the Natal Midlands in 1987, heavy police reinforcements were deployed to help curb them. At a police ceremony in the provincial capital, Pietermaritzburg, in 1988, the minister of law and order, Adriaan Vlok, declared, 'The police intend to face the future with moderates and fight against radical groups . . . Radicals, who are trying to destroy South Africa, will not be tolerated. We will fight them. We have put our foot in that direction, and we will eventually win the Pietermaritzburg area.'

Buthelezi's strategy was to appeal to Zulu pride and sense of martial tradition, and to assert the notion that the Zulu people and Inkatha were synonymous. Zulus, he said, were a 'mighty nation' with a 'glorious heritage' who needed to stand together in the face of enemies who did not want 'the Zulu nation to unite'. He liked to recount how he had learned politics at his mother's knee, listening to tales of Zulu resistance to British settlers in the nineteenth century and how his great-grandfather, Cetshwayo, had routed the British army at the battle of Isandhlwana in 1879. In public, he frequently appeared in traditional Zulu dress, draping a leopard skin across his shoulders and holding a shield, a stick and a gleaming spear in his hand.

His opponents in Natal were Zulus from the ranks of urban blacks, from community groups, the landless, the unemployed and, above all, the youth, all struggling for survival in crowded shack settlements and townships and resentful of the power and patronage enjoyed by the Zulu establishment. The numbers of this constituency were forever swelling. Between 1979 and 1989, the population of greater Durban more than trebled from under 1 million to 3 million.

The ANC's main organizer in this Zulu civil war was its Natal Midlands boss, Harry Gwala, a modern-day Stalinist and former Robben Island prisoner who had clashed with Mandela there. A diminutive man in his late sixties and suffering from motor neurone disease, which left him partially paralysed, with arms hanging limply from his sides, he was driven by a hatred for Buthelezi and all that he stood for. Gwala wanted a military victory over Buthelezi and harboured dreams of marching on Ulundi to occupy his head-quarters. His uncompromising militancy made him the hero of the ANC's youth in the region.

The conflict became essentially territorial. Inkatha leaders, usu-ally known as 'warlords', formed armed groups – 'impis' – to drive out their opponents. Radical pro-ANC groups responded in kind. Gwala publicly declared that Inkatha warlords should be killed. Hit squads operating in his area, some of them belonging to Umkhonto, succeeded in wiping out scores of middle-ranking Inkatha officials. Police were frequently accused of collusion in Inkatha attacks, of harassing radical groups but failing to deal with the activities of warlords and known killers and of standing by while the impis went to work. Attackers were sometimes transported, heavily armed, in buses in broad daylight. Assassinations were commonplace; massacres were carried out. Many areas became 'no-go' areas for one side or the other. Mixed in with this political rivalry were the activities of criminal gangs and violent disputes over land, water and housing. By 1990, more than 3,000 people had been killed.

In prison, Mandela had been confident of being able to settle the conflict once he was set free. He knew of Buthelezi's difficult nature. Everyone who had had dealings with Buthelezi found him to be a prickly personality, volatile, unpredictable, hyper-sensitive and at times paranoid. But Mandela believed that a personal meeting would enable them to resolve their differences. He was careful to keep in touch with him, writing respectful letters. When he left prison, Buthelezi was one of the first people whom he phoned, to thank him for his long campaign to secure his release. At his first press conference, he steered clear of the usual ANC rhetoric:

We have differences with Dr Buthelezi. Firstly, on the question of violence. Secondly, on the attitude towards government structures. And thirdly, on the question of sanctions. These are fundamental differences, but nevertheless, he is a figure with a following. It may not be as big and may not command as much resources as we command, but he has a following and it seems to me correct to try and settle problems in which he is involved amicably.

Within days of his release, Mandela proposed that they should meet. But he ran straight into vehement opposition from the ANC's national executive committee. Mandela said he thought they would 'throttle' him for suggesting it.

Determined to make contact nevertheless, Mandela urged Walter Sisulu to take up an invitation to visit the Zulu king, Goodwill Zwelethini, who was also Buthelezi's nephew. 'Mandela believed that we needed Buthelezi, we needed the king, we needed the Zulus,' Sisulu recalled. But an immediate dispute broke out over the venue of the meeting. Zwelethini had invited Sisulu to meet him at Ulundi, but the ANC was wary of according any hint of recognition to the KwaZulu homeland by visiting the capital. Sisulu proposed instead a meeting at the king's palace at Nongoma, but Zwelethini saw no reason to agree to the change. And so another opportunity for peace was lost. Sisulu subsequently conceded that it had probably been a mistake for him to refuse to go to Ulundi. Buthelezi's supporters, meanwhile, considered that the king had been snubbed, resulting in another bout of violence.

Mandela's efforts at exerting leadership over the crisis came to nothing. Two weeks after his release, he addressed a huge rally of ANC supporters in Durban, urging an end to the fighting. South Africa, he said, stood on the threshold of a new era but Natal was in flames, 'brother fighting brother in wars of vengeance and retaliation'. He made a dramatic appeal to all Zulus to lay down their arms: 'Take your guns, your knives and your pangas [machetes] and throw them into the sea. Close down the death factories. End this war.'

But no one paid much attention. Gwala argued publicly that the quickest way to establish peace throughout Natal was to win the war against Inkatha. He cited as examples of a 'peaceful solution' several Midlands areas that had become totally peaceful after his supporters had killed or chased away all Inkatha members.

After another round of slaughter in March, Mandela and Buthelezi agreed to meet outside Pietermaritzburg at a rural settlement called Taylor's Halt, an Inkatha stronghold in the KwaZulu homeland. Announcing his decision, Mandela said that when people were dying there was no time to stand on ceremony. 'We must unite,' he said. But Gwala and other ANC leaders in Natal were enraged by the announcement, all the more so as they had not been consulted beforehand. Early the next morning, they confronted Mandela at his Soweto home, warning him that if he went ahead with the Taylor's Halt meeting, it would result only in boosting Buthelezi's prestige and in convincing him that violence paid political dividends. Mandela made his planned trip to Pietermaritzburg, but never went to Taylor's Halt and never met Buthelezi. Instead, Gwala's men took him to a local township to see the charred remains of an ANC supporter and to meet distraught families of the latest victims.

The snub to Buthelezi was fatal. 'It was important for Buthelezi to feel welcomed, embraced and part of the process,' reflected Jacob Zuma, the ANC's intelligence chief, himself a Zulu. If Mandela had embraced him right at the beginning, he believed, the conflict could have been overcome. By allowing Gwala to dictate terms, Mandela lost a crucial opportunity for reconciliation. Buthelezi drew his own conclusions. 'They think they are going to marginalize me,' he said. 'They say Inkatha must be smashed and finished . . . It is not possible.'

The conflict now spread beyond Natal. In protest against the continuing violence in the region, the ANC and its trade union ally, Cosatu, organized an 'isolate Buthelezi' campaign which, on 2 July, brought 3 million workers out on a 'stay-away', closing most factories in Natal. Inkatha was proclaimed 'an enemy of the people'. In the Transvaal townships, the houses of many Inkatha officials, notably township councillors, were petrol-bombed.

On 14 July, Buthelezi took the initiative. He turned Inkatha into a fully fledged political party, the Inkatha Freedom Party, opened its membership to all races and launched a recruitment campaign in the Transvaal, concentrating on township hostels along the Reef. What followed became known as the Reef township war, which brought a level of violence to South Africa that had never been witnessed before.

The hostels were a natural recruiting ground for Inkatha. More than fifty hostels in townships in the East Rand and West Rand were occupied mainly by Zulu-speaking workers from rural areas of KwaZulu and Natal who had come to the Reef in search of work. The conditions in which they lived were appalling. The hostels were generally overcrowded, squalid and insanitary blocks providing only rudimentary facilities. Township residents tended to sneer at people who lived there. But for the occupants they offered a vital base from which to earn a living. Coming mostly from a traditional rural background, they tended to resent the undisciplined behaviour of township youths. They were notably hostile to the coercive tactics used by radical groups in the townships to enforce boycotts, stay-aways and other forms of anti-apartheid protest. The only reason hostel dwellers endured such grim places was to work and earn money for their families in rural areas, for most homesteads in rural Zululand were dependent on remittances from migrants in Johannesburg. Their fears about the ANC were aggravated by demands made by local ANC leaders at public rallies that hostel dwellers should vacate hostels to make way for returning exiles who needed a home, and by suggestions that hostels should be upgraded to family units, which might also have led to single migrants being thrown out. Inkatha officials exploited these fears, warning hostel residents that they were in danger of losing their 'homes' as a means of gaining support. To complicate matters further, there was the ethnic factor. For years, permanent residents and hostel dwellers, whether of Zulu, Xhosa or mixed origin, had lived together peaceably. But Inkatha now used Zulu allegiance as the basis of its recruitment campaign. Its adversaries in the squatter settlements surrounding hostels were often Xhosas supporting the ANC. Ethnic tensions rapidly mounted. Rumours abounded of imminent attack by Zulu or by Xhosa fighters.

On 22 July, the Reef township war broke out. It started in Sebokeng, a township thirty-five miles south of Johannesburg, in a battle between residents and hostel dwellers which flared up shortly after an Inkatha rally was held there. The ANC had forewarning that Inkatha attacks were planned. ANC lawyers had written both to the minister of law and order, Adriaan Vlok, and to local police commanders, urging them to ban the rally, but to no avail. In the morning, busloads of Inkatha supporters arrived from Johannesburg hostels armed with what were known as 'traditional weapons' – spears, clubs, axes and iron bars. In the violence that followed, some thirty people were killed, mostly ANC supporters.

The next day, Mandela went to the Sebokeng morgue and then visited the hospital to express his solidarity with the survivors. His anger about what had happened was directed not so much against Inkatha and Buthelezi as against de Klerk. At a meeting with the president on 24 July, Mandela demanded an explanation: 'I said, "You were warned beforehand. You did nothing about it. Why? Why is it there have been no arrests? In any other country, where thirty-two people had been slaughtered in this way, the head of state would come out condemning the matter and giving his sympathies to the next of kin. Why have you not done so?"' According to Mandela, de Klerk could offer no proper response, nor did he provide him with any explanation.

The violence spread rapidly from one township to another as hostel dwellers launched attacks on nearby squatter settlements and residential areas, setting off endless cycles of revenge and retaliation. Within days several hundred were dead. Zulu hostel dwellers expelled Xhosa-speakers and other non-Zulus from hostels, turning them into Zulu fortresses. Zulu families in surrounding areas, facing persecution, sought protection there. As communities split, Zulus came to be identified as Inkatha supporters and Xhosas as ANC supporters, regardless of their real allegiances. Many Zulu-speakers living near hostels were forced to align themselves with hostel dwellers as their only means of defence against revenge attacks by township residents. Thousands abandoned their shacks and homes to escape the violence. Some townships became divided into rival territories, with large 'no-go' areas of wrecked and deserted houses separating them. In August, 500 people died over an eleven-day period.

The role of the police, as in Natal, became increasingly controversial. Police refused to disarm Zulu impis of their spears, axes, knives, sticks and iron bars, on the grounds that these were traditional weapons that Zulus were entitled to carry. They were also accused of standing by while hostel dwellers launched their murderous raids into surrounding territory or of actually assisting them. There had been a long history of brutal conflict between

426

police and radical groups in the townships. The two sides had, in effect, been at war since the Soweto revolt of 1976. To many in the police, the ANC was still 'the enemy' and a justifiable target for Inkatha supporters.

But the suspicion soon grew that something more sinister was happening. In September, twenty-six people died and more than 100 were injured when a six-man gang ran through a Johannesburg commuter train shooting passengers at random; a second gang, lying in wait on a station platform, attacked survivors trying to escape from the train. The attack had all the hallmarks of the kind of terrorist activity carried out for years in Mozambique by rebels trained and supported by South African military intelligence.

All this coincided with a wave of public disclosures about dirty-tricks operations conducted by police and army units in the 1970s and 1980s in their campaign against the ANC and other government opponents. In October 1989, a black policeman, under sentence of death for the murder of a white farmer, earned a stay of execution by claiming that he had been a member of a security police assassination squad set up to eliminate government opponents. He identified its commander as Captain Dirk Coetzee. The following month, Coetzee, having fled the country, admitted his involvement with assassination squads during the 1970s and 1980s. He had commanded a special counter-insurgency unit based at a secluded police farm called Vlakplaas, west of Pretoria, where hit squads comprised of ANC defectors and Mozambique rebels were trained and used in neighbouring states and inside South Africa for clandestine operations, including murder, abduction and bomb attacks. He claimed that assassination squads were still at work. In March 1990, an official inquiry into the conduct of the security forces, the Harms Commission, which de Klerk eventually agreed to set up with limited terms of reference, was told of similar activities at home and abroad carried out by a defence force covert unit known as the Civil Cooperation Bureau, established during the 1980s. The unit was still active, with an annual budget of 28 million rands. The verdict of the inquiry was that the CCB operated as a law unto itself and had its own political agenda. Its actions had 'contaminated the whole security arm of the state'. In July 1990, the government announced that the unit would be disbanded.

With all this evidence of security force involvement in murder and dirty tricks at hand, it seemed all the more plausible, in the wake of several train massacres and attacks on squatter settlements, to suspect a conspiracy of right-wing elements in the military and the police bent on wrecking the negotiation process. Mandela raised the question of a 'third force' with de Klerk in private in August. In September, he voiced his concern publicly, suggesting that renegades in the security forces were trying to disrupt negotiations.

De Klerk's predicament was considerable. He was an outsider to the security establishment. During the decade of total strategy, when defence and security officials were given a free hand to run guerrilla operations in Mozambique and Angola and mount whatever dirty tricks they considered necessary inside South Africa, de Klerk was preoccupied with domestic issues like education. When he became president, he had never held a security portfolio. Unlike Botha, he had no inside knowledge of how the security establishment worked, nor did he share the sense of camaraderie that prevailed there. Along with a large section of the National Party, he disliked the way in which the security establishment had tended to usurp the role of parliament and the National Party itself. Soon after taking office, he had dispensed with the elaborate system of national security management which Botha had constructed as part of his total strategy. But key personnel wedded to that strategy were still in place, not only within the security establishment but also within his own cabinet, including the minister of defence, Magnus Malan, and the minister of law and order, Adriaan Vlok. They believed the 'enemy' was still the ANC and its communist allies and acted accordingly. Security bosses had also become accustomed to operating autonomously. As the Harms inquiry noted, the CCB had ignored requests from the president, the minister of defence and the chief of the defence force: 'Requests by parliament, the auditor-general and the commission were treated with contempt.' At cabinet meetings, when de Klerk raised questions about the third force, Malan and Vlok were quick to dismiss it as propaganda. De Klerk had no interest in pursuing the matter. He depended heavily on the security establishment to keep tight control of the turbulence churned up by his reforms and feared antagonizing them. All he was prepared to admit was that 'a few rogue individuals' might be involved. Otherwise, he stuck to the standard government explanation for the violence that it was all caused by 'black-on-black' rivalry.

Mandela was unable to believe that de Klerk did not possess the power to clean up the security forces and to put a stop to the violence. But initially he was willing to attribute his failure to do so to de Klerk's 'problems with his own constituency'. In November 1990, after a massive Inkatha attack on a squatter camp known as Zonkizizwe, outside Germiston on the East Rand, which resulted in a rout of all residents and its occupation by Inkatha supporters, Mandela went to see de Klerk and Vlok to ask why the police had taken no action to restore the shacks to their original owners. De Klerk, according to Mandela, seemed totally unaware of the incident. But Vlok's response was to ask rudely, 'Who owned the land anyway on which your people were living?' The land, in fact, belonged to the local authority, which had made it available for squatters generally. De Klerk promised to investigate the matter, but though Mandela repeatedly brought up the issue of Zonkizizwe with de Klerk in the following months, he never received any response.

Their relationship nevertheless remained in good working order. In a press interview in December 1990, Mandela said:

> I still regard de Klerk as a man of integrity, and I think he feels the same about me. We have developed enormous respect for each other. I can call him at any time. I can get him out of bed or out of cabinet meetings. I believe he and perhaps the majority of his cabinet are still as committed to the peace process as we are. But he has problems with elements inside his government – especially his security establishment, which is riddled with right-wingers who are not with him at all – and he is not being frank with me about that.

For month after month the clashes continued, with varying degrees of intensity. Police action to stamp out the violence merely curbed it temporarily. Not only had it become endemic but there were signs that it was escalating out of control.

Since the 1970s, a culture of violence had developed among successive generations of black youths. They had been at the forefront of the Soweto uprising of the 1970s and the township revolt of the 1980s. At each stage the use of violence had become

more widespread and more extreme. For over a decade their schooling had been disrupted by boycotts, protests and street battles.
They had become known as 'the lost generation'. But they were
also a generation which had experienced raw power.

Now, in the political struggles of the 1990s, the same atmosphere
of revolutionary violence prevailed. Mandela himself had helped
stoke up the mood of defiance, declaring, in his first public address
after his release from prison, the need for the armed struggle to
continue. For months on end, as the ANC endeavoured to bolster
its standing in confronting the government, it flaunted the rhetoric
of armed struggle, giving township activists licence to pursue
opponents at will. Their targets were often township councillors
supporting Inkatha and local police. In the first seven months of
1990, more than 400 attacks on black councillors and police were
recorded. Necklace executions once again became commonplace.
Guns, in particular AK-47s, were now readily available, smuggled
in mainly from Mozambique and Angola. The townships were hit
not just by political violence but by a soaring crime rate.

The Reef war added a new dimension. In response to the ferocious
attacks organized by hostel dwellers, young comrades in surrounding residential areas and squatter camps set up self-defence units
with the help of Umkhonto. Some SDUs succeeded in offering
protection for local communities, but others waged an often indiscriminate war of retribution on hostel dwellers, widening the cycle
of violence. Some broke up into factions and engaged in their own
form of territorial warfare; others were taken over by criminal
gangs, becoming notorious for extortion, rape and murder, and
adding to the soaring level of violent crime. All lacked political
control. At the base of this anarchic activity was a vast underclass
of youths roaming the streets – unskilled, unemployed, undisciplined, fed on revolutionary slogans, but now angry and resentful
of how little the revolution had brought them.

Mandela endeavoured to address some of these issues at his
public rallies. 'I must make it clear that the level of crime in our
country must be eliminated,' he said on his homecoming to Soweto.
'All students must return to school and learn.' But such simple
exhortations were lost in the maelstrom.

Mandela's belated efforts to reach an accommodation with
Buthelezi were no more successful. After hundreds of deaths, the

ANC's national executive committee agreed in September 1990 to a summit meeting between Mandela and Buthelezi. But it was not until the end of January 1991, after hundreds more deaths, that it finally took place, at Durban's Royal Hotel.

Buthelezi was in a truculent mood. Before arriving in Durban, he had collected together statements made by ANC officials vilifying him from the previous five years and he proceeded to read them out, page by page, to the assembled delegates and the media. He then catalogued all the political differences separating Inkatha and the ANC.

Mandela chose not to respond in kind. In his own speech, he went out of his way to appease Buthelezi, thanking him for his efforts to secure his release from prison and emphasizing the common goals of their two organizations. The summit ended with the signing of what was supposed to be a peace agreement setting out a code of conduct for dealing with each other. But neither side possessed the will to make it work. Within weeks, hundreds more had died.

The government blamed the ANC and Inkatha. The ANC blamed the government. Inkatha and the ANC each blamed the police for supporting the opposing faction. The police still refused to disarm Zulus carrying traditional weapons. And so the killing went on.

But Mandela's attitude towards de Klerk changed. He began to suspect that de Klerk was pursuing a 'double agenda' – talking to the ANC while at the same time supporting the violent activities of its opponents. Every plea he made to de Klerk for help in protecting ANC victims, like the Zonkizizwe squatters, failed to get any response. Time and again, de Klerk would promise to 'investigate' but did nothing. Mandela's own standing among his supporters was being undermined as a result. He began to fear that he had put too much trust in de Klerk, as his critics in the ANC had argued all along.

In March 1991, Inkatha launched attacks in Alexandra township, north of Johannesburg, and succeeded in gaining control of the Madala Hostel, a massive building standing on a hill overlooking the township, which had formerly been occupied by migrant workers from mixed ethnic groups. In three days of fighting, forty-five people were killed. The government belatedly sent in police and army reinforcements and declared Alexandra to be an 'unrest area' subject to emergency control. Despite this, one week later, Inkatha was allowed to hold a political rally there. Busloads of supporters, many armed with traditional weapons, arrived from other areas. Six more people died that day. One week later, at Daveytown, east of Johannesburg, police opened fire on an ANC demonstration, causing at least twelve deaths.

The ANC was besieged with pleas for help, yet still Mandela could not get a response from de Klerk. At a private symposium in Cape Town on 3 April organized for visiting members of the United States Congress, Mandela launched into a tirade against de Klerk, accusing him of connivance in the violence. He had betrayed his trust, he said, and ignored his requests for help. The following day, at a meeting of the ANC's national executive committee, Mandela apologized for the misjudgement he had made of de Klerk. His critics, he said, had been right all along.

Mandela never regained his trust of de Klerk. Their personal relationship henceforth was marked more by abrasive encounters than signs of cooperation. Mandela now joined others on the national executive committee in advocating a tougher line. In an open letter to the government, the ANC warned that talks would be suspended in May unless the government agreed to seven demands. These included the dismissal of Malan and Vlok; the dismantling of all army counter-insurgency units; the banning of the carrying of traditional weapons in public; the phasing out of migrant-worker hostels; and the appointment of an independent commission to investigate complaints of police misconduct.

De Klerk's response was to call a multiparty conference on violence in May. But the ANC boycotted it on the grounds that the government already knew what to do to bring the violence to an end. De Klerk in turn accused the ANC of 'playing politics' while parts of the country were left 'ankle-deep in blood'.

The evidence of security force involvement in the mayhem, meanwhile, steadily mounted. Press investigations revealed the fact that 200 Inkatha hit-men had been trained secretly by South African military intelligence in the Caprivi Strip in 1986, before being deployed in Natal and the Transvaal. Buthelezi confirmed the training, but said the men had been attached to KwaZulu officials to act as bodyguards. A former army sergeant alleged that a special forces unit had been involved in train massacres and a string of other incidents. In June 1991, a former military intelligence officer claimed that the army was fully involved in the funding and supply of weapons to Inkatha with the aim of fanning violence. A defence force spokesman dismissed the allegations as 'ridiculous', but in July 1991, in what became known as Inkathagate, the government was forced to admit that it had secretly channelled funds to Inkatha and its affiliated trade union, Uwusa. Government funding for Uwusa had been going on since its establishment six years previously. In the case of Inkatha, the security police had given funds to help it organize two political rallies, one in November 1989 and the other in March 1990, to shore up support for Buthelezi. In an internal police memorandum, Major Louis Botha, head of the Durban security police, reported that Buthelezi had thanked him profusely for the funds and signed a receipt for them.

De Klerk's reputation at home and abroad was irreparably damaged by the disclosures. No longer did his denials that he was pursuing a 'double agenda' carry much weight. The worldwide acclaim he had received for launching his reforms now seemed to belong to another era.

Buthelezi's reputation suffered as well. For all his claims of independent leadership, he was shown up to be dependent on hand-outs from Pretoria. Inkatha, claimed Mandela, had 'permitted itself to become an extension of the Pretoria regime, its instrument and surrogate'.

For Mandela too, the disclosures caused considerable embarrassment, providing ammunition for radical critics who questioned his judgement. He was deeply shocked by the cavalier way in which de Klerk tried to gloss over the scandal and continued to dismiss his complaints about security force involvement in 'third force' activity. 'We believed,' he said, 'that President de Klerk was a man of integrity. But subsequent events have shown that perhaps we were hasty and that there was a little bit of naïvety on our part because he has turned out to be a totally different man from what he was initially.'

CHAPTER 22
Winnie's Trial

The drama of the Mandela Football Club was meanwhile being played out in the courts. Winnie's name figured prominently in one trial after another, but the government was wary of taking action against her, anxious to avoid any embarrassment that could damage the fragile peace process. 'We are proceeding carefully, so as not to give any indication that we are acting vindictively against Mrs Mandela,' said the minister of law and order, Adriaan Vlok. 'It is also very difficult for the police to find witnesses prepared to testify against her. In the past, such witnesses have either suddenly changed their minds or just disappeared.'

A serious difficulty arose in January 1990, two weeks before Mandela's release, when Sizwe Sithole, the head of the 'disciplinary committee' based at Winnie's house and the father of Zindzi's three-month-old son, was found dead in a police shower room. Arrested on an arms charge, Sithole had spent nearly four hours telling police at Protea station about a number of serious crimes he said involved Winnie and Zindzi. A commission of inquiry under Judge Richard Goldstone which the government swiftly set up to investigate Sithole's death found that he had committed suicide, a verdict that no one disputed. One of the main reasons Goldstone gave for Sithole's suicide was that he had been overcome by remorse for having implicated Winnie and Zindzi. The police went to considerable lengths to keep Winnie's name out of the affair and took no action on the evidence they had been given.

The main body of evidence against Winnie emerged during the trial of the football club's coach, Jerry Richardson, for the murder of Stompie Moeketsi Seipei. The trial had originally been due to start in February 1990, the day after Mandela's release from prison, but it was postponed until May 1990. Richardson was the only person accused of the murder, but six others were charged on four counts of kidnapping and four counts of assault with intent to cause grievous bodily harm. The state prosecutors planned to bring charges against Winnie if the case against Richardson resulted in a conviction.

Winnie did not appear in court. She had declined to testify as a witness, ignoring requests from Richardson's attorney to take the stand on his behalf. But even in her absence, she overshadowed the proceedings. In their evidence, the three kidnap victims – Kenny Kgase, Thabiso Mono and Pelo Mekgwe – related how Winnie had told them they were not fit to be alive; how she accused Stompie of being a sell-out; how she beat them using her fists and then whips; and how members of the football team joined in afterwards.

Richardson, for his part, denied killing Stompie. He also denied that Winnie had been present on 29 December 1988, when Stompie and the other kidnap victims were brought to her house. But his testimony was riddled with lies. When his defence counsel, Henti Joubert, came to sum up, he admitted Richardson had lied to protect Winnie and to prevent her from being involved in the affair: 'He is protecting himself from others because if he mentions their names his life won't be worth much.' Joubert portrayed Richardson as a poorly educated and somewhat retarded man who had been easily exploited by the likes of Mrs Mandela.

The question of whether or not Winnie had been present during the beatings at her house was obviously crucial. Eighteen months after the event, having previously made no mention of it to anyone, she now chose to claim that she had been on a visit to Brandfort at the time. Both the defence and the prosecution in the Richardson murder trial asked the court to make a finding on the matter.

On 24 May 1990, in the Rand Supreme Court, Justice O'Donovan found Richardson guilty of the murder of Stompie and guilty on other counts of kidnapping, assault and attempted murder. He was subsequently sentenced to death. The judge also ruled on the question of Winnie's involvement: 'The court finding on this issue is that Mrs Mandela was present on 29 December for at least part of the time.'

Winnie was also implicated in other trials involving members of

Mandela United Football Club. In August 1990, Charles Zwane was brought to trial, charged with nine counts of murder, eight counts of attempted murder, one count of arson and the unlawful possession of firearms. One of the crimes with which Zwane was charged was a firebomb attack in February 1989 on the home of Dudu Chili, a well-respected community leader and friend of Albertina Sisulu, with whom Winnie had been engaged in a long-running feud over the activities of Mandela United. Chili's eleven-year-old niece had died in the attack.

Zwane's defence counsel, S. Jacobs, argued, as Richardson's counsel had done, that Zwane had fallen under the influence of Mrs Mandela. He asked Dudu Chili to give her assessment of Winnie's influence.

> JACOBS: Did Winnie Mandela really have the power of life and death over these people? If she made a decision to kill, would the people kill?
> CHILI: I believe so.
> JACOBS: Say, for example, she took a decision that Mr X should be killed – a notional person – and she ordered Mr Y to do it, if Mr Y did not carry out his orders, did you think Mr Y would be in danger himself?
> CHILI: I should think so, because they seem to fear her so much.

Zwane was sentenced to death nine times for the murders.

The most incriminating piece of evidence against Winnie came during the trial of Sibusiso Chili, Dudu Chili's son. Along with five others, Sibusiso Chili had been charged with the murder of a member of Mandela United, Maxwell Madondo, who himself had been sent on a mission to kill him. Chili was convicted of Madondo's murder but was sentenced to only one year's imprisonment. The reason for such leniency was a statement agreed upon by the prosecution and the defence that was placed on the court record: 'The admission the state will make is that the deceased, Maxwell Madondo, was a member of the Mandela Football Club and that a decision was made by Mrs Winnie Mandela and the football club to kill accused number one, Chili, and accused number six, Ikaneng.'

On 17 September 1990, the attorney-general, Klaus von Lieres, announced that Winnie would be charged with four counts of kidnapping and four charges of assault with intent to cause grievous bodily harm, making her the eighth accused in the Stompie murder case.

None of these events stopped Winnie seeking positions of political power within the ANC or Mandela from assisting her at every opportunity. Winnie portrayed the government's decision to prosecute her as part of its political campaign to discredit the Mandelas and the ANC. Mandela took the same view. Shortly after his release from prison, he was asked in a television interview whether he saw the Richardson trial as another government set-up. 'Well, I have no doubt that it is,' he replied. 'The way the South African police have conducted themselves in the investigation of the so-called offence has been totally disgraceful. And it is clear that their intention was not to investigate the commission of any crime, but it was partly to destroy the image of the family.'

Regardless of what evidence was produced against Winnie, Mandela never changed his line of reasoning. He threw his full weight into getting the ANC to declare publicly its support for her. He seemed besotted by Winnie, immune to wiser counsel, determined at whatever cost to foster her ambition and prepared to endure in silence her affair with the lawyer Dali Mpofu. Senior ANC officials referred to Winnie as 'Nelson's blind spot'. Despite considerable opposition from within the ANC, Mandela succeeded in securing her election to the Johannesburg regional executive committee, her position as head of the regional Women's League and her appointment in August 1990 as head of the ANC's social affairs department. Her appointment as head of social welfare brought letters of complaint from more than 100 ANC branches around the country.

As well as obtaining Mandela's support, Winnie cultivated her own power base among party militants and youth activists, preaching belligerence, exhorting the masses to fight. This won her support from revolutionary enthusiasts but set her at odds with Mandela's own efforts towards a negotiated settlement. On tour with Mandela in the United States in 1990, she struck a sour note in Harlem with talk of going 'back to the bush to fight the white man'. Two days after the ANC agreed to suspend armed struggle in August 1990, Winnie described the agreement as merely a strategy. She enjoyed dressing up in designer battle fatigues to address party rallies and took to wearing a Communist Party pin. She projected herself as a champion of the poor and downtrodden, spending much time visiting squatter camps around Johannesburg and helping the victims of violence. She became renowned for her strong-arm methods of obtaining votes in her election campaigns, openly issuing threats to anyone she thought might not support her. Her ambition appeared insatiable.

Winnie's trial opened on 4 February 1991 in Johannesburg's Rand Supreme Court amid much political fanfare. The ANC's secretary-general, Alfred Nzo, an 'old guard' exile doggedly loyal to the Mandelas, declared the trial to be part of a 'continuing campaign of political harassment'. Members of the regional branch of the ANC's Women's League, which Winnie chaired, were on hand outside the court to cheer her: 'Mother of the Nation, we are with you.' Winnie had also organized a Winnie Mandela Support Ad Hoc Committee composed of friends and admirers. The opening session of the trial was attended by prominent activists like Joe Slovo, Chris Hani and Alfred Nzo, who arrived, at Mandela's personal request, to show solidarity with Winnie. Her defence team was led by the Mandelas' old friend George Bizos. It was also notable for including her lover, Dali Mpofu.

From the start, the trial was marked by one drama after another. Four of the eight accused jumped bail and failed to appear. One of the three key state witnesses, Pelo Mekgwe, also went missing. At first it was thought he had been abducted, but he subsequently surfaced in Lusaka, saying that he had left South Africa with the help of ANC officials and alleging that he had been bribed by Winnie not to testify. Mekgwe's disappearance so frightened the two remaining key witnesses, Kenny Kgase and Thabiso Mono, that they refused to testify. Without their testimony, the trial would inevitably have collapsed. After a spell in the police cells, Kgase and Mono changed their mind. The trial proceeded.

The state prosecutor, Jan Swanepoel, began the trial by disclosing that he would introduce two other kidnapping cases in which Winnie had taken part as similar-fact evidence, thus demonstrating that the Stompie incident was not an isolated case. One involved the kidnapping of two people in September 1988 and their subsequent assault, during which Winnie was present. The other involved the abduction in November 1988 of the Sowetan youth Lolo Sono, whose father had pleaded with Winnie to release him just before he disappeared.

In March, Kgase and Mono took the stand, repeating the evidence they had given during the Richardson trial, testifying how Winnie had led the assault on them and how Stompie had been so badly beaten that he could barely walk. Despite relentless cross-examination from Bizos, they remained steadfast in their main version of the events.

By the time Winnie took the stand in April, the ANC had decided to distance itself from the trial and from Mandela's adamant defence of Winnie. Winnie was told by senior ANC officials that the trial concerned her and not the ANC. Apart from Mandela, no senior figures attended court sessions any more.

Winnie's defence was to deny everything. She claimed that the Mandela United Football Club had ceased to exist by the time of the incident. She knew nothing about any of the 'boys in the back' living on her premises. Nor had she met any of the four kidnap victims there.

Winnie claimed that on the evening of 29 December 1988, hours before Jerry Richardson, Xoliswa Falati and her driver, John Morgan, had gone to fetch the four victims from the Methodist manse, she had left Soweto for Brandfort, arriving there sometime after ten. She produced two witnesses to corroborate her stay. One of them, Thabo Motau, a seventeen-year-old youth who lived opposite the Mandela house in Orlando West, testified that he had driven Winnie to Brandfort on 29 December. The other, Norah Moahloli, a schoolteacher who lived in Brandfort, testified that Winnie had stayed with her there. Winnie claimed that she had remained in Brandfort until 31 December, returning to Soweto in the evening. But no witnesses other than Moahloli were produced to corroborate her claim.

At least two pieces of evidence directly contradicted Winnie's version. One was a statement made to the police in February 1989 by John Morgan, who was one of her co-defendants. Morgan had told police that on 29 December he had seen Winnie slap Stompie, accusing him of having had sex with the Methodist minister Paul Verryn. Later that night, he said, he had used Winnie's vehicle to take Falati and her daughter back to the Methodist manse. The next day he had driven the vehicle back to Winnie's house, where he washed it. Winnie was at home that day and had told him to drive her to her office in Commerce House. Zindzi went with her. Faced with this statement in court, Morgan claimed that police had tortured him into making it. But the judge, Michael Stegmann, dismissed his assertion as false.

The other piece of evidence about Winnie's whereabouts on 29 December concerned the visit she made with Katiza Cebekhulu to Dr Asvat's surgery. According to Winnie's version, the visit took place on 29 December, before she left for Brandfort. According to Asvat's medical records, Winnie visited him on 30 December. But Asvat's medical records were not produced as evidence during the trial. Nor was his nurse, Albertina Sisulu, asked to testify.

Cebekhulu himself never gave evidence; he was one of the four defendants who disappeared on the eve of the trial. He had previously made a statement to police implicating Winnie in the beating of Stompie and describing Dr Asvat's visit to Winnie's house to examine Stompie shortly before he was taken away to be killed. But the statement was not produced in court. Like Pelo Mekgwe, Cebekhulu subsequently surfaced in Lusaka, under ANC auspices.

Judge Stegmann's judgement, given over six hours on 13 May 1991, contained a devastating indictment of Winnie's character. He described her as 'a calm, composed, deliberate and unblushing liar'. He continued, 'She gave her evidence in a manner which impressed me with her wariness, her unwillingness to commit herself to anything clear-cut or definite, and, in short, with a remarkable absence of candour.' She had gone to extraordinary lengths, he said, to distance herself from the football team bearing her name: 'It is odd to encounter a leader who went to as much trouble as Mrs Mandela to distance herself from the club which adopted her name and many of whose members lived in her own backyard.'

Stegmann was in no doubt that Winnie had masterminded the kidnapping of the four youths. 'To imagine that all those took place without Mrs Mandela as the moving spirit is like trying to imagine *Hamlet* without the prince,' he said. He remained uncertain, however, about her involvement in the beatings. The prosecution had failed to prove that her Brandfort alibis were false, so there remained a reasonable possibility that she had gone there before the assaults began, as she had claimed. Nevertheless, she must have known about the kidnappings and beatings subsequently, but she wilfully ignored the victims' plight. When pressed by Soweto leaders to release the youths, she refused to free them. By continuing to hold them for twenty days and to give accommodation to those who had committed the assault, she had associated herself with the crime. At the very least, Stegmann concluded, Winnie was an accessory after the fact to all that had happened. He found her guilty on four counts of kidnapping and of being an accessory to the assaults.

Sitting listening to this judgement on his wife, Mandela seemed an old and crumpled figure, drained of all dignity. Loyal to the last, after the verdict had been given he embraced Winnie, kissing her on the lips, but even though he managed to control the distress he felt, he was grim-faced and disheartened.

Winnie herself, though shaken by the remarks Stegmann had made about her, quickly recovered her poise. 'As long as you know now that I didn't assault any child,' she declared to journalists gathered around her in the well of the court, 'that is all that matters to me.' She left the court with a clenched-fist salute, maintaining that she had been exonerated.

The following day, Stegmann sentenced her to a prison term of five years on the kidnapping charge and an additional one year for her role as an accessory to the assaults. Winnie, he said, bore the brunt of the moral blame for the criminal actions of those in her immediate circle:

> Your position of leadership was not something which entitled you to play fast and loose with the liberties of others to serve your own purposes. You fundamentally misunderstood or ignored the responsibilities which came with your position as leader. In this case one of the worst features was your complete absence of compassion towards the victims of the assaults, suffering in your own backyard, just outside your window.

Stegmann sentenced her co-defendant, Xoliswa Falati, to six years' imprisonment, and John Morgan, the driver, to one year's imprisonment suspended for five years. George Bizos immediately announced his intention of appealing against Stegmann's verdict and applied for bail.

Mandela was not present in court to hear sentence passed on Winnie, but he continued to protest her innocence. 'My faith in her has been fully vindicated,' he said, after learning of the sentence. 'I also believe that she did not know there was anyone at the back of the house against his will.' The last word in the matter had not yet been spoken, he said: 'We trust that soon her name will be cleared completely.'

Shortly after Mandela's release from prison, photographers taking pictures of Mandela and Winnie at their home in Soweto asked the couple to move closer to one another. Winnie shyly demurred, whereupon Mandela moved his chair closer, put an arm around Winnie and said, 'I am the only man in the world who can control this woman.'

The reality, however, was different. Mandela himself was a victim of Winnie's own manipulation. For twenty-seven years in prison, Winnie had been one of his greatest sources of strength. The sense of guilt he felt for her own plight during those years, he once told her in a letter, ravaged every part of his being. He emerged from prison obdurately loyal to her. It made no difference that she had become a criminal menace or that she was unfaithful to him. Mandela's loyalty was beyond reason and Winnie exploited this fact to the full.

In a plea of mitigation against the sentence Winnie was to be given, George Bizos pointed out to Stegmann that by kidnapping standards her crime had been relatively minor. Indeed, at a time when murders and massacres in South Africa were commonplace, whether carried out by the police, the third force, Inkatha or the ANC, the crimes of which Winnie had been convicted were in themselves of little consequence.

Yet behind the trial lay a larger reality. Winnie had been the head of a criminal gang which had been involved in murder, rape, arson and assault. Her activities had contaminated the reputations of the ANC and of Mandela, upon whom the future of South Africa was seen largely to depend. Mandela compounded the problem by wilfully refusing to come to terms with what had happened. Even after her conviction, he continued to support Winnie's drive for power and office. Time and again she was to become embroiled in scandal, causing one embarrassment after another; and time and again, she was to survive the consequences. But the burden of all this was to be carried by Mandela, making the monumental tasks he already faced that much harder.

CHAPTER 23

Codesa

By mid-1991, eighteen months after de Klerk's bold reforms, South Africa was mired in crisis. The country was afflicted by appalling bouts of violence from which there seemed no escape. In Natal, a small-scale civil war was under way. The government's reputation, as a result of Inkathagate, had been seriously damaged. Distrust was manifest on all sides. Little progress had been made towards even starting negotiations. To make matters worse, economic recession was exacting a heavy toll.

The ANC had considerable trouble putting its own house in order. It found the business of converting itself from an underground liberation movement into a properly constituted political organization – establishing party offices, recruiting members, raising funds, organizing the return of thousands of exiles and ensuring the welfare of returning guerrillas – an immensely difficult process, almost beyond its means. The result, more often than not, was chaos.

Internal disputes overshadowed all else. So great was the furore over the ANC's decision to suspend the armed struggle that the national executive committee decided to postpone the holding of the ANC's first national conference inside South Africa for thirty years until July 1991. At a substitute 'consultative conference' in December 1990, Mandela was the target of sustained criticism over his autocratic style, his failure to consult more frequently about policy issues and his cordial relationship with de Klerk. When he and Tambo put forward a proposal advocating the phased lifting of sanctions against South Africa, ANC militants countered with their own resolution insisting that sanctions should be maintained unchanged and received overwhelming support from cheering delegates. In his concluding remarks, Mandela noted ruefully, 'One of the most disappointing features of the conference was that there was hardly a word of praise.' He acknowledged that he and the national executive committee had been wrong not to keep the party membership informed about their contacts and agreements with the government. He said he accepted the criticism 'without qualification' and promised to make 'radical adjustments' to the ANC's leadership. But he also defended his right to continue with what he called 'confidential' discussions with the government. It was simply not practical, he said, to refer every problem back to a party conference.

Not just Mandela but Winnie too was the target of attack from critics within the ANC intent on curbing her ruthless ambition. In April 1991, Winnie made a determined bid, with Mandela's support, to be elected president of the ANC's Women's League. Two other candidates stood for election, Gertrude Shope, an exiled leader who had been head of the ANC's women's division in Lusaka, and Albertina Sisulu. In order to ensure that Winnie was not elected, Albertina withdrew from the election and publicly called on her supporters to cast their votes for Shope. The result was a crushing defeat for Winnie, who gained less than a third of the vote.

At the ANC's national conference in July 1991, at the age of seventy-two, Mandela was elected president, in place of his ailing friend Oliver Tambo. But many of the same criticisms of his leadership were voiced once more. One former UDF leader, Patrick Lekota, openly denounced Mandela for his tendency to try to impose his will on internal decision-making, and received a huge cheer for doing so. There was strong criticism too of the disorganized state of the ANC, attributed by many delegates to the incompetence of the 'old guard' on the national executive committee. A confidential internal report presented to the conference noted: 'We lack enterprise, creativity and initiative. We appear very happy to remain pigeon-holed within the confines of populist rhetoric and clichés.' Attendance at recent rallies had been low, those rallies were poorly organized, membership recruitment had fallen far below expectations and, the report concluded, 'Clearly we have not utilized our full potential to mobilize millions of our people into effective action.'

445

In the election for party posts, half of the old guard were swept away and replaced by former UDF leaders whom Mandela and Winnie had previously contrived to exclude from influence. Despite Mandela's strenuous efforts, the key post of secretary-general went to Cyril Ramaphosa, whose election brought rapturous applause from delegates. Ramaphosa represented the new generation of political activists. As a student, he had served two prison sentences for political activity. A lawyer by training, he had thrown himself into trade union activity, building up membership of the mineworkers' union from 6,000 to 340,000 and helping to launch the trade union federation, Cosatu. His abilities as a successful organizer and as a skilful negotiator were held in high regard by mining company executives, with whom he was often in conflict. He was familiar with the democratic approach of the UDF and held no particular reverence for old-guard politicians from the Mandela generation who considered length of service the principal qualification for party office. In the months preceding Mandela's release from prison, when speculation about it was rife, he remarked in a magazine interview that Mandela should not expect just to walk out of prison and take over the ANC. His standing, he said, was 'no different from the status of any other member of the ANC'; he was just 'one of those people who may have to be considered for a leadership position'. Ramaphosa was also one of the few individuals in the ANC hierarchy prepared to stand up to the malevolence of Winnie Mandela. As one of the authors of the original report exposing her crimes, he was fully aware not only of her guilt but also of the damage that would be done to the ANC if she was allowed to continue her relentless drive for power. Aged only thirty-eight when he was elected secretary-general, Ramaphosa quickly made his mark both on the ANC and on the whole negotiation process.

Despite these curbs to his personal authority, Mandela was successful in gaining support for his efforts in steering the ANC back towards talks with the government, suspended since May, even though none of the demands it had made at the time had been met. Mandela argued that for the ANC to continue postponing talks because of political violence effectively gave a veto to right-wing factions around de Klerk which did not want negotiations to proceed. They should be seen as 'a victory for the ANC' and 'a defeat' for the government, not the reverse. Negotiations, he said, were 'a theatre of struggle'. Any further delay would play into the hands of the enemy: 'It can never be in our interest that we prolong the agony of the apartheid system. It does not serve the interests of the masses we represent and the country as a whole that we delay . . . the achievement of the objective of the transfer of power to the people.' Mandela also put forward for the first time the idea of a 'transitional government of national unity' in which power would be shared with de Klerk's despised National Party.

Although Mandela regained the initiative for negotiations, revolutionary enthusiasts were hard at work, preaching the virtues of mass action. Their day was yet to come.

The first attempt at negotiation between the three main rivals – Mandela, de Klerk and Buthelezi – was largely a disaster. In September 1991, they were brought together for the first time to attend a national peace conference at the Carlton Hotel in Johannesburg organized by a group of business, church and civic leaders. The atmosphere at the conference was extremely tense. One week before, gunmen, assumed to be Umkhonto members, had ambushed an Inkatha march in Thokoza, a township near Johannesburg, killing twenty-three people and injuring eighteen others. Inkatha gunmen retaliated with an indiscriminate attack on buses, taxis and trains. While delegates to the conference were discussing 'codes of conduct' inside the hotel, on the street outside hundreds of Inkatha supporters, armed with traditional weapons, paraded up and down in front of the hotel in a show of support for Buthelezi. By the time he got round to telling the demonstrators to go home, little sense of accord remained. At a subsequent press conference, when de Klerk sought to play down the incident, saying that the Inkatha demonstrators had committed 'no crime' and had 'apparently enjoyed themselves', Mandela reacted in fury, jumping up from his seat to grab the microphone and asserting that if the demonstrators had belonged to the ANC the police would have used force to disperse them. The press conference, intended to mark agreement on a peace accord, degenerated into an ugly public wrangle. Buthelezi demonstrated his disdain for the process by refusing to participate in a three-way handshake with Mandela and de Klerk, suggested by press photographers. When the photographers persisted, Buthelezi, keeping his hands tightly gripped on his ceremonial fly whisk, snapped that he was not going to 'perform like a clown' for them. In October, South Africa experienced one of its worst months of violence on record.

Merely finding a starting point for negotiations proved highly contentious. Mandela and de Klerk held several meetings during September and October but found little common ground on how a new constitution should be formulated. Mandela insisted that the constitution should be drawn up by an elected assembly, so that each party's influence on the final document would be proportionate to its national support. De Klerk wanted an unelected conference, comprising all political parties 'with a proven basis of support', to deliberate upon two crucial issues: the composition, functioning and decision-making process of the actual constitutional negotiating conference, and the broad principles to be contained in a new constitution. He opposed the idea of a constituent assembly, fearing that it would allow a single party or alliance of parties emerging from an election with a commanding majority virtually to write its own constitution – in effect predetermining constitutional issues which were supposed to be the subject of negotiation. Mandela demanded an interim government; de Klerk said he had no intention of handing over power before the new constitution was in place.

The two men were also locked in a long-standing dispute over the status of Umkhonto we Sizwe. De Klerk demanded that the ANC should disband its guerrilla army and put its arms caches under joint control. He maintained it was a 'private army' no longer permissible under the terms of the national peace accord signed in September 1991. Mandela refused, telling de Klerk that for the ANC to demobilize its armed wing when it was subject to armed attack would be tantamount to suicide.

All that was finally agreed was to hold a multiparty conference, to be known as the Convention for a Democratic South Africa, or Codesa, as it was popularly called, together with a date, an agenda and a venue. It had taken nearly two years to get that far.

On 20 December 1991, in a cavernous and gloomy trade exhibition hall near Johannesburg's international airport, there assembled the widest cross-section of political groups that had ever met in South Africa. The only similar gathering that had ever taken place was a national convention in 1908–9, when representatives from the Transvaal, the Orange Free State, the Cape and Natal agreed to establish the Union of South Africa. On that occasion no Africans were present.

Invitations to Codesa had been sent to twenty-three parties, nineteen of which had accepted. In addition to delegations from the government, the National Party and the ANC, there were representatives from the Inkatha Freedom Party; the Communist Party; the Transvaal and Natal Indian Congresses; four 'independent' homeland governments; four 'self-governing' homeland parties; three parties from the Indian and Coloured parliaments; and the liberal parliamentary opposition party, the Democratic Party. Those who refused invitations included the far-right Conservative Party; the extremist Afrikaner Weerstandsbeweging; and the Pan-Africanist Congress. Four days beforehand, the PAC had held a special conference in Cape Town which had decided to boycott negotiations altogether, with delegates shouting, 'One settler, one bullet.'

One other notable absentee was Buthelezi. Although Inkatha was present, Buthelezi had decided to stay away in protest that his demand for two additional delegations, one headed by the king of the Zulus, Goodwill Zwelethini, the other representing the KwaZulu administration, had been turned down. Five days before Codesa opened, addressing supporters outside Durban, he had warned that Zulus should not be left aggrieved 'lest what happens in this country emerges as so terrible and so destructive that the civil wars [in Angola and Mozambique] are child's play by comparison'. Thereafter Buthelezi's contribution to the negotiations process was to consist largely of a similar mixture of threats and bluster.

Codesa's first plenary session, known as Codesa 1, was intended to be largely a formality. Before handing over to a series of working groups, delegations were asked to sign a Declaration of Intent, consisting mainly of expressions of goodwill, which committed them to an undivided South Africa, a multiparty democracy with universal suffrage, a separation of powers, an independent judiciary and a bill of rights. Inkatha immediately adopted a dissident role, refusing to sign on the grounds that the reference contained to an 'undivided' South Africa implied that the federal system it wanted had been ruled out. Only when an amendment was later inserted, giving an assurance that the offending clause did not preclude a federal system, did Inkatha sign.

One speaker after another stepped up to the podium to express goodwill. The National Party's contribution was memorable for the way in which its chief delegate, Dawie de Villiers, endeavoured to offer an apology for apartheid. His party, he said, had hoped that 'a policy of separation' would bring peace to the country, but apartheid had produced instead conflict, injustice and misery: 'In so far as that occurred, we deeply regret it.'

The last two delegates due to speak were Mandela and de Klerk. What occurred, broadcast live on radio and television, sent a shockwave across the country. Mandela had originally been scheduled to speak last, but the previous evening de Klerk had asked him on the phone if he could speak last instead. Several of Mandela's colleagues had misgivings, but Mandela saw no reason not to accord de Klerk the favour.

Mandela, in his address, duly spoke of the importance of the occasion, as other delegates had done. Then de Klerk went to the podium for the final speech of the day. He too began by citing the historic significance of the gathering. He spoke of the need to overcome mutual distrust and suspicion, and of his support for the idea of 'power-sharing'.

But then he turned his speech into an attack on the ANC. The ANC, he said, had failed to honour an agreement to dismantle Umkhonto, and he went on to question whether the ANC's commitment to agreements reached at the convention would be worth the paper they were written on if it did not abandon the armed struggle. His clear intention was to belittle Mandela and to demonstrate to his own followers his toughness in handling the ANC. He spoke in the manner of a headmaster dealing with an errant child.

Mandela was infuriated, not just by de Klerk's accusations but by his deception in trying to get in the last word. Once again, he had trusted de Klerk against the advice of his own colleagues, only to be proved wrong. Seething with anger, he insisted on the right of reply and strode to the podium to denigrate de Klerk in full public view, his voice manifesting all the contempt and loathing he felt for the man:

I am gravely concerned about the behaviour of Mr de Klerk today. He has launched an attack on the ANC and in doing so he has been less than frank. Even the head of an illegitimate, discredited minority regime, as his is, has certain moral standards to uphold. He has no excuse just because he is the head of such a discredited regime not to uphold moral standards . . .

If a man can come to a conference of this nature and play the type of politics he has played – very few people would like to deal with such a man . . .

The members of the government persuaded us to allow them to speak last. They were very keen to say the last word here. It is now clear why they did so. He has abused his position, because he hoped that I would not respond. He was completely mistaken. I respond now.

The ANC, he said, had shown its commitment to peace by suspending the armed struggle. As de Klerk well knew, it had agreed to turn in its weapons only when it was part of a government collecting those weapons: 'What political organization would hand over its weapons to the same man who is regarded by the people as killing innocent people?' He had warned de Klerk on countless occasions that it served no useful purpose to attack the ANC publicly, yet 'he continues to do exactly that and we're going to stop it'.

He went on to accuse de Klerk of pursuing a double agenda towards the ANC, of talking peace and cooperation while simultaneously 'conducting a war' against it. Even while negotiating, the government was secretly funding covert organizations that committed violence against the ANC. It was all well and good for de Klerk to pretend, as he had done at the time of the Inkathagate scandal, that he knew nothing about the large sums of money being channelled through the police to the ANC's main rival, but, he said, 'if the head of state doesn't know when as much as 7 million rands is spent, then he's not fit to be a head of the government'.

Mandela concluded by saying he was nevertheless willing to continue to work with de Klerk: 'I am prepared to make allowances because he is a product of apartheid. Although he wants these democratic changes, he has sometimes very little idea of what democracy means.'

Caught off guard by Mandela's venomous outburst, de Klerk

began by taking notes. Then he put down his pen and stroked his bald pate, becoming increasingly agitated. By the time Mandela had finished, he was apoplectic. He returned to the podium to make an angry rebuttal of Mandela's accusations.

The two sides, he said, had met innumerable times over the previous ten months to try to resolve the issue of Umkhonto. Both he and Mandela had intervened personally to try to break the deadlock, but to no avail. They had last discussed the matter on 12 December and had agreed that further high-level consultations were needed: 'The friendly exchanges that went on over the past few days resulted in absolute stalemate.' Hence his decision to raise the issue in public. It was an issue that had to be solved before other agreements could be reached. Otherwise, de Klerk said, the government would be faced with an ANC carrying 'a pen in one hand and claiming the right to still have arms in the other hand'.

The spectacle on prime-time television of a white head of state being given a dressing-down by a black politician, accusing him of duplicity, trickery and even collusion in murder, was an altogether new experience for South Africans. Even though the two men made the point of shaking hands afterwards, it was evident that they had lost all mutual respect. Neither of them understood the other's predicament over the issue of armed struggle. Both were under strong pressure from their own constituencies to take a firm stand. But by choosing a ceremonial occasion to bring the dispute into the open, de Klerk not only ruined the display of goodwill it was intended to convey but incurred severe damage to his own reputation as a strong leader. In front of the cameras, a discernible shift in power had taken place.

The relationship between Mandela and de Klerk never recovered from this incident. De Klerk believed that Mandela had neither the authority nor the political will to ensure that the ANC adhered to agreements with the government. Mandela was all the more convinced of de Klerk's double agenda to destroy the ANC. Their lack of trust made the search for a settlement even more complicated, just as negotiations were beginning.

The differences in their objectives were already fundamental. De Klerk entered the negotiations with the purpose not of transferring power but of striking a unique power-sharing deal which would ensure that government in a democratic South Africa was subject to a white veto. His model of majority rule was not the standard version – 'simple majority rule', as he disparagingly referred to it – but a constitution which would entrench the position of minority parties in government and restrain majority parties through an elaborate system of checks.

He had moved on from the idea of group rights to the idea of blocking mechanisms. What he proposed was government through an enforced coalition, with a rotating presidency, in which decisions were taken by consensus, thus giving the white minority an effective veto over the majority. He wanted extra representation for white minorities in an upper house of parliament with veto powers, coupled with the requirement for certain legislation in the lower house to obtain specially high majorities before passage. He also wanted regional authorities to be given autonomous powers to curb the possibility of centralized authoritarian rule. Summing up his position, he said, 'A party that wins 51 per cent of the vote should not get 100 per cent of the power.'

In de Klerk's view, the purpose of Codesa was to settle, in a multiparty forum, as many of these constitutional details as possible before the negotiating circus moved on to an elected assembly, where the influence of minority parties was bound to be reduced. He wanted Codesa first to draw up an 'interim' constitution, setting out principles that would include permanently entrenched power-sharing, the devolution of power, protection for minorities and other checks and balances, before proceeding with elections for a constituent assembly and an interim government that would rule for at least ten years.

He repeatedly insisted that the National Party would never surrender to 'simple majority rule', leaving the fate of the white minority of 12 per cent in the hands of a non-racial electorate. It would demand a guaranteed share in power, whatever the outcome of the popular vote, and it would hold out for as long as was necessary to obtain one. Only when the National Party's future was secure was he prepared to relinquish sole power.

Mandela embarked on the negotiations with the aim of achieving unfettered majority rule in the shortest possible time. He assumed that the government's vulnerability to international pressure, popular unrest and economic disruption, the very factors which he believed had led de Klerk to release him and lift the ban on the

ANC in the first place, would work to his advantage in securing a speedy victory.

His aim was to move on rapidly from Codesa to an interim government and to an elected assembly empowered to determine a new constitution. The ANC wanted a radical rupture with the past. In Mandela's view, Codesa's purpose was merely to decide what measures were needed before an assembly could be elected. He was anxious to achieve quick results. The slow progress so far made on the road to majority rule since 1990 had added to the volume of criticism he faced from within the ANC. Moreover, the ANC's support in the townships was being undermined daily as a result of the level of violence there and its inability to provide protection.

While Codesa's working groups grappled with these issues, there were signs that de Klerk's support within the white community was dwindling. Since the announcement of his reforms in February 1990, the right wing had kept up a barrage of attacks on de Klerk, denouncing him as a traitor and a sell-out – 'the only leader in the Western world who is negotiating himself, his party and his people out of power,' railed the Conservative Party leader, Andries Treurnicht.

Treurnicht's objective became the establishment of an independent white state – an Afrikaner *volkstaat*. He offered no suggestions as to what its borders might be or how it might be brought about. There was not a single magisterial district in South Africa where whites, let alone Afrikaners, actually constituted a majority of inhabitants. But it was an idea with immense appeal to the Conservative Party, as well as to other factions on the far right. 'We in the Conservative Party are adamant that there is a territory which belongs historically and otherwise to the white nation,' said Treurnicht. 'While we accept that there are whites who are prepared to live under an ANC government in a unitary state, there are others – we believe, the majority – who will never submit themselves to a communist terrorist regime . . . Unless any future constitutional dispensation addresses the problems of ethnicity and self-determination, it will be a waste of time and a recipe for discord.' He pledged 'a third freedom struggle' in pursuit of Afrikaner self-determination, alluding to the possibility of resistance similar to that of the Boers in the two wars against British imperial rule in the late nineteenth and early twentieth centuries. 'You do not have enough jails to keep Afrikaner nationalism imprisoned,' he declared. 'We warn: this is an unfair government which no longer represents the *volk*.'

Treurnicht's Conservative Party represented the respectable face of the far right. Other groups advocated outright violence. The most prominent was the Afrikaner Weerstandsbeweging, the Afrikaner Resistance Movement, which used Nazi-style insignia and rituals and paraded with swastika-like banners and guns. Led by Eugene Terre'Blanche, a former policeman who specialized in right-wing oratory and bombast, the AWB was the moving force behind the formation of scores of 'commando' units. 'We refuse to be put under an ANC government,' declared Terre'Blanche. 'That night there will be war in South Africa . . . We will fight, as our forefathers fought, until we have won.' In one town after another, white vigilante groups sprang up 'to protect white property, women and children against blacks'. Along with vigilante action came a spate of bomb attacks and 'drive-by' shootings. In August 1991, hundreds of AWB members, armed with knives, guns and teargas canisters, clashed with police in Ventersdorp in an attempt to prevent de Klerk from addressing a public meeting there.

The first electoral shock for de Klerk came in a parliamentary by-election in the Orange Free State in November 1991, when the National Party lost its seat to the Conservative Party in a spectacular swing against the government. In February 1992, the National Party suffered another stunning defeat in the Afrikaner university town of Potchefstroom. The government's faltering support was of more than usual significance, for de Klerk had repeatedly promised that the white electorate would be allowed the final verdict on any agreement made about South Africa's future constitution. Rising white opposition to the government therefore placed the whole outcome of the negotiations in jeopardy.

Rather than delay the matter any further, within days of the Potchefstroom defeat de Klerk announced the holding of a white referendum on the reform process on 17 March. A clear majority in favour, he said, would obviate the need for the government to return to the white electorate. The risks he took were considerable. A defeat for the government would almost certainly have led to civil war. All the resources of the white establishment were thrown into securing a 'Yes' vote. De Klerk explicitly promised the electorate that he would prevent majority rule. The National Party's advertising campaign was based on the slogan, 'Vote Yes, if you're scared of majority rule'. The Conservative Party campaigned for a 'No' vote, claiming that the choice for Afrikaners was between 'the survival of the Afrikaner *volk* and two cars in the garage'. The ANC did its best to support the 'Yes' campaign, reassuring whites about its good intentions in the negotiating process and promising job security for civil servants.

The result was a triumph for de Klerk. About 85 per cent of the white electorate of 3.3 million turned out to vote and some 68 per cent said 'Yes'. Only one out of fifteen regions recorded a majority 'No' vote – Pietersburg, in the strongly conservative northern Transvaal. Even Pretoria, which had for so long symbolized Afrikanerdom in all its might, produced a 57 per cent 'Yes' vote. 'Today,' said de Klerk, 'we have closed the book on apartheid. It doesn't often happen that in one generation a nation gets an opportunity to rise above itself. The white electorate has risen above itself in this referendum.'

In the euphoria which followed the referendum, there seemed few other obstacles remaining in the way of a settlement. Negotiators in several of the working groups held behind closed doors at Codesa reported making significant progress. Indeed, Codesa was noted for its convivial and cosy atmosphere, where participants, wining and dining at the state's expense, were afforded every opportunity to settle their differences. As the deadline approached for the second plenary session, scheduled for 15 May, public expectations were high.

The reality, however, was that the two main participants – the government and the ANC – had come no closer to agreement on what the real role of Codesa should be, let alone the details of a new constitution. In the working groups dealing with the central issues of power-sharing and majority rule, the differences were as fundamental as ever. The government was prepared to haggle indefinitely, believing that the slower the transition proceeded, the better. Its confidence was bolstered by the result of the referendum, which had finally dispensed with the right-wing threat de Klerk feared so much. The ANC, however, was alarmed not only by the lack of progress being made at Codesa but also by signs that it had begun to lose touch with its constituency as the negotiations dragged on. Radicals within the ANC were highly critical of its handling of the negotiations and demanded a more aggressive approach.

When Codesa 2 reached deadlock on 15 May, Mandela and de Klerk met over coffee late that night in their first encounter since the opening day in December. Though they could not find a way out of the impasse, both were anxious to avoid a public confrontation. 'The whole of South Africa and the world is looking at you and me,' Mandela told de Klerk. 'Let us save the peace process. Let us reach some kind of agreement. Let us at least fix a date for the next round of talks.' They agreed to address the convention the following day in a constructive manner, de Klerk speaking first, Mandela last.

De Klerk reiterated the government's position on the need for 'proper checks and balances' to ensure that 'no majority should ever be able to misuse its power . . . to dominate or to damage the interests of minorities'. He rejected once more the idea of 'simple majoritarianism' of 'a winner-takes-all' electoral system.

Following him, Mandela tried to disperse the gloom which had descended over the convention, stressing the areas of agreement that had been reached there. But there was no disguising the fact that the negotiating process, on which so many hopes were based, had foundered.

The ANC now drew up alternative plans. It was just the opportunity for which revolutionary enthusiasts had been waiting.

CHAPTER 24

Winnie's Downfall

The downfall of Winnie began not as a result of her criminal activities but because of her affair with the young lawyer Dali Mpofu. When they met, Winnie was fifty-five and Mpofu was twenty-five. An articled clerk for the law firm representing members of Mandela United, he was intelligent, charming and had a liking for older women. While a law student at the University of the Witwatersrand, he had struck up a relationship with a white lecturer ten years his senior, Terry Oakley-Smith, the daughter of a retired British diplomat. She became pregnant, but soon after the birth of their son in 1989, Winnie lured Mpofu away. When Oakley-Smith confronted Winnie about their involvement one night outside Mpofu's flat, pointing out that Winnie was a grandmother, she was given a foretaste of the kind of threats Winnie habitually used against her adversaries. 'Winnie's reply was something along the lines of, "Listen, my girl, you'll be sorry for this. You don't know who you're dealing with,"' recalled Oakley-Smith, who then received a barrage of threatening phone calls from Winnie, often late at night when she was drunk, telling her in a slurred voice to keep away from Mpofu. She was so worried by the threats that she made a statement to her lawyers in case she came to harm.

When Mandela learned that Mpofu had moved in with Winnie, he sent her a letter from prison telling her to get 'that boy' out of the house. Mpofu left, but the affair continued. From the moment that Mandela returned home to Johannesburg in February 1990, Winnie showed no interest in sharing his bed. The pain and humiliation for Mandela were some of the worst experiences he had known. They made him, he later recalled, 'the loneliest man'.

While the affair remained relatively discreet, Mandela bore it with fortitude, enjoying what he could of Winnie's company, but Winnie soon began to flaunt her lover in public.

In March 1991, she appointed Mpofu as her deputy in the ANC's department of social welfare, even though he had no qualifications for the job. The department which was responsible for the welfare of thousands of returning exiles, former political prisoners and the victims of political violence became notorious for its chaos under Winnie's rule. When Ramaphosa took over as secretary-general in July 1991, two months after Winnie's conviction for kidnapping and assault, he quickly set about reorganizing the ANC's administration, trying to turn it into a more professional organization and to rid it of embarrassing encumbrances like Winnie. But initially he ran straight into opposition from Mandela, who regarded his plans for reorganization as much a threat to his own authority as to Winnie's position.

Winnie, however, soon overstepped the mark. In October 1991, she took Mpofu with her on a spending spree to the United States. Ostensibly, they went to raise money and recruit artistes for a 'Children of Africa Concert', scheduled to be held in Nigeria later in the year. But they raised no funds, signed up no artistes, and instead drew considerable attention to their extravagant lifestyle. Mandela was outraged when he learned of what had happened. But Winnie ignored him and made plans for another trip to the United States with Mpofu, without informing him.

After two years of forlorn hope of re-establishing a family life, he moved out of Winnie's 'palace' in Soweto. He lived for a time at the opulent mansion of one of South Africa's wealthiest Afrikaners, Douw Steyn, an insurance magnate, in the northern suburbs of Johannesburg, before purchasing a comfortable two-storey house in Houghton which he came to regard as home. He rarely spoke to Winnie after that.

The Winnie saga was still to cause him endless embarrassment though. In March 1992, just weeks before her appeal was due to be heard, she became embroiled in an ugly wrangle with her co-defendant, Xoliswa Falati. Falati, whose appeal was due to be heard at the same time, had been told by her lawyer that there were no funds to pay for the costs of her appeal and that therefore she would have no option but to serve her sentence of six years'

459

imprisonment. The news came as a severe shock to Falati, who had hitherto assumed that the Mandelas would see that she was properly represented. Her lawyer suggested that she contact Mandela and, when she did, Mandela reassured her that he would take care of the problem.

The following day, 28 March, Falati received a telephone call from Winnie telling her to get out of the room at the back of the garage at Mandela's old house in Orlando, where she had been allowed to stay. Falati called Mandela for help again. He told her to ignore Winnie and to stay in the room.

That night, after a few drinks, Winnie burst into Falati's room, brandishing a small pistol and shouting at her to get out. 'She came at me like a mad woman,' Falati said later. 'I saw her pistol and just pushed her and ran.' Winnie's driver stopped her at the gate. 'For a moment I thought I was going to be shot. Winnie was drunk and screaming at me that I was going to prison.' After throwing Falati's clothes out into the street, Winnie locked the room and stormed off.

When she had gone, Falati made two telephone calls, one to Mandela and one to the local newspaper, *The Sowetan*, telling them what had happened. *The Sowetan* immediately sent a reporter and a photographer to the scene. When they arrived, Falati began telling them how she had 'protected' Winnie and how Winnie was 'dumping me now that I have served my purpose'. Shortly afterwards, Mandela arrived, clearly embarrassed by the whole business, asked Falati not to talk to the press and urged the reporter not to write the story. He later telephoned *The Sowetan*'s editor three times to inquire about the paper's intentions. When the editor and the reporter called on Mandela to discuss the incident, he pleaded with them to play it down. It could ruin Winnie's chances of a successful appeal, he said. Mandela's intervention, however, made *The Sowetan* all the more determined to publish the story and it duly appeared on 30 March.

Winnie's petty act of vengeance against Falati reignited the whole controversy over the murders of both Stompie Moeketsi Seipei and Dr Asvat. Fearing for her life, Falati agreed to tell ANC officials all that she knew. Falati now claimed that she had lied at her trial to try to save Winnie from being convicted; that Winnie had been involved in the torture of Stompie and had ordered the murder of

Asvat because he had seen Stompie in her house shortly before his death; that she had ordered other deaths, including the murder of a senior journalist on *The Sowetan* who had been investigating her criminal activities; and that only four months before she had drawn up a list of five other people whom she wanted assassinated, including Cyril Ramaphosa. Falati's allegations duly appeared in the press. She said she was not prepared to go to prison for 'an ungrateful woman'.

Still more damaging evidence against Winnie surfaced. Her driver, John Morgan, who had received a one-year's suspended sentence for his role in the kidnapping, now claimed, like Falati, that he had lied in court to 'protect' Winnie. In a press interview published on 12 April, he said that Winnie was not only present at the house during Stompie's beating but led the assault. He described how, pointing to Stompie's prostrate body, she told him 'to pick up the dog and dump him' – which, he said, he refused to do. 'I knew he was dead because he had already been stabbed and had blood on his neck.' Morgan made the same allegations on national television.

Press investigations now added further details. From Lusaka, the missing witness, Katiza Cebekhulu, told a lawyer acting on behalf of the *Christian Science Monitor* that Winnie had ordered Dr Asvat's murder because he could have given evidence of her part in Stompie's death. In Johannesburg, Dr Asvat's family now demanded that the case of his murder be reopened.

Mandela was left with no option other than to distance himself publicly from Winnie. He still felt personally responsible for what had happened to her, but the extent of the damage both to the ANC and to his own reputation could now be contained only by an announcement of their separation. The media was already critical of his role in trying to suppress *The Sowetan*'s story about Winnie. Ramaphosa and Sisulu went to see him to press him to reach a decision.

For a man as intensely private as Mandela, with such a strong dislike of discussing his personal affairs and difficulties even with friends, the ordeal of having to announce the end of the marriage which he had cherished so deeply before the massed ranks of the world's media required all the discipline he could muster. He accomplished it with great dignity, but with barely disguised anguish. Flanked by his old friends Walter Sisulu and Oliver Tambo, in a room at the ANC's headquarters in Johannesburg, he made a statement to journalists on 13 April notable for its generosity, paying tribute to 'Comrade Nomzamo', as he called Winnie, for her devotion to him and to the anti-apartheid struggle:

> Owing to the pressures of our shared commitment to the ANC and the struggle to end apartheid, we were unable to enjoy a normal family life. Despite these pressures our love for each other and our devotion to our marriage grew and intensified . . .
>
> During the two decades I spent on Robben Island, she was an indispensable pillar of support and comfort to myself personally . . . Comrade Nomzamo accepted the onerous burden of raising our children on her own. She endured the persecution heaped upon her by the government with exemplary fortitude and never wavered from her commitment to the freedom struggle. Her tenacity reinforced my personal respect, love and growing affection. It also attracted the admiration of the world at large. My love for her remains undiminished.
>
> However, in view of the tensions that have arisen owing to differences between ourselves on a number of issues in recent months, we have mutually agreed that a separation would be best for each of us. My action was not prompted by the current allegations being made against her in the media . . . Comrade Nomzamo has and can continue to rely on my unstinting support during these trying moments in her life.
>
> I shall personally never regret the life Comrade Nomzamo and I tried to share together. Circumstances beyond our control, however, dictated it should be otherwise. I part from my wife with no recriminations. I embrace her with all the love and affection I have nursed for her inside and outside prison from the moment I first met her.

Reading the statement had left Mandela drained and exhausted. Rising from his seat, he appealed to the press: 'Ladies and gentlemen, I hope you appreciate the pain I have gone through.' Then, in silence, he walked stiffly from the room.

Behind the scenes, Ramaphosa now went to work to force Winnie's 'retirement from politics'. He wanted her resignation both from her position as head of the social welfare department and from membership of the ANC's national executive committee. But Winnie fought back tenaciously. All that she agreed to do was to resign as head of the social welfare department.

On 15 April, at a press conference announcing her resignation from the department, she remained defiant, protesting her innocence of any crimes and blaming her predicament on those who wished to destroy her and discredit the ANC:

> The step I am taking is not because of the false allegations being made against me but because of the devotion that I have for the ANC and my family. Over the years, many have tried to divide and weaken the ANC. They have failed, and they will fail again. I have taken this step because I consider it to be in the best interest of the ANC, whose cause and policies I will support until the end of my life.

Winnie lost no time strengthening her popularity with radical youth groups and squatter communities, determined to present herself as the champion of the poor and dispossessed, with a powerful constituency of her own. Within days, she appeared at one scene of township violence after another, berating the government and Inkatha and fulminating against the negotiations process. 'We are certainly not going to keep on talking to a government that is killing our people,' she said. On national television, she declared, 'As far as I am concerned, my political career goes on as if nothing had happened.'

She used her position as leader of the ANC's Women's League in the Johannesburg region to instigate a march demanding her reinstatement as head of the social welfare department, an action that created turmoil in the Women's League. One attempt after another was made to dislodge her, but she clung on with a vengeance.

The end, however, was nigh. In May 1992, ANC officials announced that they were conducting an investigation into charges that Winnie and her dismissed deputy, Dali Mpofu, had been responsible for the disappearance of 400,000 rands from the department of social welfare. While the investigation was proceeding, they came into possession of a letter Winnie had written to Mpofu on 17 March 1992, one month before her resignation as head of the department. The letter was leaked to South African newspapers and appeared in print on 6 September 1992, making her position untenable.

It was four pages long, written by hand, mostly in English but with occasional phrases in Xhosa, and blazed with anger and venom about Mpofu's affairs with other women. Winnie admitted that she had agreed to Mpofu having another relationship 'as a cover to defuse our problem', even though she 'shuddered at the thought of you lying and pretending to love this other woman'. But that did not mean Mpofu could go 'running around fucking at the slightest emotional excuse'. She accused him of deceiving her and complained about his 'shabby treatment' of her: 'You have hurt and humiliated me as a woman.' She grumbled about his indifference to how 'the situation is deteriorating at home' – she had not been speaking to Mandela for five months. Yet Mpofu had not bothered because he was out every night satisfying himself with another woman.

Amid this tirade were references to bank accounts which proved fatal. Winnie berated Mpofu over his lack of concern about her financial problems, mentioned how much money she had spent on him and spoke of her fears about the investigation into the accounts of the social welfare department. 'I tell you I'm in trouble with the Simmons Street a/c which reflects over R160,000 drawn over a period for you,' she wrote. 'You don't even bother to check how we can overcome this.' Mandela, she said, had ordered an inquiry into her account. Her secretary at the department of social welfare, Ntombi, was talking to the investigators: 'I tell you Ntombi is gossiping about the cheques we used to ask her to cash for in the name of the Dpt and how I gave you all that money.'

Mandela was shown a copy of the letter before it was published in the press. He recognized the handwriting and the style and knew that certain details, such as Winnie's assertion that they had not spoken for five months, were accurate. He decided to ask George Bizos to take a copy to Winnie to check its authenticity. According to Mandela, 'she broke down and wept'.

Four days later, Winnie resigned from all her remaining posts in the ANC, from the national executive committee and the Women's League, with an emotional outburst against her 'enemies' inside and outside the organization and displaying deep-rooted delusions about her own importance. In a rambling statement to a press conference, she gave no clear explanation of why she had decided to resign other than to say it was 'primarily in the interest of my dear husband and my beloved family'.

Addressing herself to her family 'and to all my people in South

Africa, in our squatter camps, in our villages, in the violence-torn and poverty-stricken areas', she said, 'There is no reason to be overwhelmed by a sense of isolation and abandonment. I have only been a mere servant to you and I will always be.' However, Winnie's ambition was not so easily thwarted.

In October 1992, a glittering wedding reception, attended by 800 guests, was held in the ballroom of the Carlton Hotel in Johannesburg to celebrate the wedding of Zindzi Mandela and Zwelibansi Hlongwane, a shop-owner several years her junior. Zindzi's life had been marked by personal dramas as much as her mother's. She had borne four children from four different fathers, one of whom savagely assaulted her, leaving her for dead, and another of whom, a Mandela United gangster, committed suicide. Beneath the glamour of the occasion, there were turbulent undercurrents. Mandela treated Winnie as if she did not exist, not addressing a word to her. He appeared so grim at times that an old friend, Helen Suzman, passed up a note to him: 'Smile, Nelson! You look like John Vorster used to in parliament!' He read the note, burst into a radiant smile briefly, then lapsed again into a sphinx-like stare.

In his speech to the guests, he reflected on the plight of his family: 'We watched our children growing without our guidance and when we did come out [of prison], my children, for example, said, "We thought we had a father and one day he'd come back. But to our dismay, our father comes back and he leaves us alone almost daily because he has now become the father of the nation."' Mandela said he had often pondered on whether the struggle had been worth the loss of a normal family life but had always concluded, 'It was, it is, the correct decision that we should commit ourselves.'

CHAPTER 25

The Sunset Clause

Soon after the Codesa negotiations reached deadlock, the ANC announced a campaign of mass action: a series of rolling strikes, demonstrations and boycotts across the country, intended to force the government to back down at the negotiating table. The campaign was to be organized with the help of the ANC's allies, the trade union federation, Cosatu, and the South African Communist Party. Its climax would be a general strike.

Most groups within the 'tripartite alliance' regarded mass action as a necessary component of the negotiating process. A show of strength on the streets, bringing industry to a halt, would make the government more amenable, they believed. A radical faction within the Communist Party, however, saw mass action not as a means of gaining compromises but as a way of bringing the government down. These 'insurrectionists', as they were known, pointed to events in Eastern Europe, especially to Leipzig, where street demonstrations had helped topple the East German regime three years before, and believed that the same result could be engineered in South Africa.

Among those favouring the 'Leipzig option' was Ronnie Kasrils, a member of the Communist Party's central committee, a former Umkhonto intelligence chief and a member of the ANC's national executive committee. A middle-aged man driven by boyish enthusiasm for revolutionary exploits and clearly bored by the proceedings at Codesa, which he rarely attended, Kasrils had been agitating for months for mass action. With the failure of Codesa, he was given his chance and put in charge of organizing the ANC's campaign. He dubbed it Operation Exit.

466

The ANC's strategy carried high risks. Mass action was to be launched at a time when many townships were in turmoil. The Reef war continued unabated. All previous experience of strikes, boycotts and demonstrations showed that they led to an upsurge in violence as supporters resorted to coercion to get their way. The risk now was that the turmoil and the violence might become uncontrollable.

The date chosen for the start of the mass action campaign was 16 June, the anniversary of the beginning of the Soweto revolt in 1976. Dressed in a track suit and wearing a baseball cap, Mandela marched at the head of a column of ANC supporters through the streets of Soweto to the Orlando football stadium to launch the campaign. Addressing the huge crowd packing the stands, he explained the need for mass action: 'The National Party wants a system where people can vote but the result is fixed beforehand. All parties, they say, would have veto powers.' So if an ANC majority in government wanted to change apartheid policies on education or housing, they would be able to do so only with the consent of the white minority. Negotiations had not budged de Klerk, he said, so the time had come for a change of strategy. In the face of violence deliberately planned by the security forces and their 'vigilantes', the ANC's codeword for Inkatha, it was imperative, he said, that ANC supporters set about the protests peacefully. It was even more imperative to resist suggestions from within the ANC's ranks to take the violence to white areas. 'This would be a disaster of the first magnitude. We don't want innocent people killed, black or white.'

A mass stay-away the ANC organized for 16 June was judged to be a success. The following night, however, there occurred an incident of such brutality that, just like Sharpeville and Soweto, its name came to be remembered around the world and to represent another grim landmark in the passage of South Africa's violent history. It plunged South Africa into a crisis far worse than anyone had expected.

On 17 June, a group of Inkatha hostel dwellers in Boipatong, a small township in the Vaal Triangle, forty miles south of Johannesburg, attacked a nearby shack settlement, kicking in doors, smashing windows and then hacking, stabbing and shooting residents at random in a killing spree that lasted more than four hours, leaving forty-five residents, mostly woman and children, dead. It was the fourth mass killing that week in a black area near Johannesburg. The police were once again accused of collusion. Two days later, three people died when police opened fire on a crowd which had gathered to protest at the massacre.

The event propelled Mandela into the radical camp. He suspended all talks with the government, saying, 'I can no longer explain to our people why we continue to talk to a regime that is murdering our people and conducting war against us.' His language became increasingly intemperate. He described the activities of the National Party and its Inkatha allies as similar to Nazi attacks on Jews. 'They are killing our people in an effort to stop the ANC getting into power,' he said. The negotiations process was 'completely in tatters'. When hardline members on the ANC national executive committee argued that negotiations had proved useless and should be abandoned altogether, Mandela was inclined to agree. Among rank and file supporters, there was a huge groundswell in favour of reverting to armed struggle. Placards waved at Mandela during a rally to mark the Boipatong massacre read, 'Mandela, we want arms now' and 'Victory through battle not talk'.

Mandela refused to believe that de Klerk did not have the power to curb the violence. In his mind, there were only two possible explanations for why it continued: either the security forces were out of control or de Klerk was conniving with them. 'In my view, he might not be aware of every attack. But generally speaking, the fact that the police and security services are involved, he would know very well,' Mandela said in July. 'A head of state who does not know the things that are happening is not fit to be a head of state.'

Much to de Klerk's embarrassment, there was a continuing trickle of evidence implicating security forces in violent activity. In April 1992, a white police captain and four black 'special constables' were convicted of the killing of eleven people – six women, three men and two children – in a small rural settlement in Natal whom they believed were supporters of the ANC. The 'special constables' were Inkatha men who had been selected and trained by the police. The judge's verdict was that the massacre was part of a security force operation to disrupt the community, oust an established ANC-aligned residents' association and give Inkatha control of the area. The judge said he was convinced that there had been a conspiracy among senior officers reaching up to police headquarters to cover up the crime. In his evidence, the police captain, Brian Mitchell, said he saw himself as a soldier in a civil war in which the enemy were pro-ANC groups. The murders had been carried out in 1988, but Mitchell's views were still common among white police officers.

The military were also implicated. In May 1992, the press published the contents of a military intelligence signal proposing the 'permanent removal' of three prominent black activists in the Eastern Cape. Two weeks after the signal was sent, the killing of two of them took place, along with two other activists. The incident occurred in 1985, but the disclosure seven years later of military involvement not only stirred black anger against the army but reinforced all the fears and suspicions already harboured about the activities of a 'third force'. The man who authorized the signal was Brigadier Christoffel van der Westhuizen, then head of joint operations at the Eastern Cape Province command. In 1992, van der Westhuizen, promoted to the rank of general, was chief of military intelligence.

It was the Department of Military Intelligence that was the main focus of suspicions. For years, the DMI had been in control of special force operations supporting Renamo rebels in Mozambique and Unita rebels in Angola fighting to overthrow Marxist governments. It had also been involved in training Inkatha members. The units which the DMI had run across South Africa's borders – like 32 Battalion, composed mainly of Portuguese-speaking mercenaries – had returned to South Africa once the DMI's campaign of destabilization in neighbouring countries had come to an end and once the war with Swapo guerrillas in Namibia was over. Many senior officers were bitterly resentful of the outcome. In a 1992 message to soldiers who had fought in Angola and Namibia, Colonel Jan Breytenbach, a former commander of the much-feared 32 Battalion, reflected their discontent. 'You did not lose in Angola,' he told them. 'You did not lose in Namibia. You were betrayed by politicians under foreign pressure.' From their bases in South Africa, these special force units provided a ready source of recruits for disgruntled officers intent on organizing covert operations. Other irregular units included Koevoet, a police counter-insurgency force once used in Namibia, many of whose members were now active in the South African police force. All had been trained to hunt down ANC or Swapo cadres in the streets and shebeens of southern Africa and were prone to violent and lawless conduct.

But as well as anti-ANC groups at work in the townships, the ANC's own self-defence units were running amok. SDUs had been set up with the help of Umkhonto with the aim of protecting ANC communities from Inkatha attacks. By mid-1992, about eighty-five SDUs were in operation. But many of them had spun completely out of ANC control and had been taken over by gangsters, warlords and renegade Umkhonto guerrillas. In July 1992, the Communist Party leader, Chris Hani, writing in the party's publication *Umsebenzi*, admitted that they often served as fronts and shelters for criminals. They had brought about, he said, 'an alarming revival of kangaroo courts and kangaroo politics'. Some had been infiltrated by police and army agents intent on subverting them.

The task of sorting out the evidence was given to a judicial commission into public violence and intimidation, headed by Judge Richard Goldstone, which had been set up as a result of the 1991 national peace accord. In May 1992, Goldstone published an interim report which concluded that the primary cause of the violence was not security force activity, as Mandela maintained, but the political battle between supporters of the ANC and Inkatha: 'Both sides resort to violence and intimidation in their attempts to gain control over geographic areas.' There would be no lessening of violence 'unless and until the leaders and supporters' of the two factions agreed to disarm and 'abandon violence and intimidation as political weapons'.

The commission exonerated de Klerk himself and his government from any direct involvement in political violence. It had received no evidence justifying allegations of 'any direct complicity in or planning of current violence', no credible evidence of a 'third force' at work. But it sharply rebuked the government for failing to implement earlier recommendations it had made, including the need to impose security measures at hostels and to ban the carrying of all dangerous weapons. The commission also noted that its previous recommendation regarding the withdrawal from townships of 32 Battalion, whose members had been found responsible for rape and other assaults during 'peace-keeping' operations, had been blocked by the army commander, General George Meiring. The government, said the commission, 'must be able to demonstrate that it has control over its security forces'.

Police actions were also severely criticized. An independent inquiry into the Boipatong massacre, carried out with the help of British experts, concluded in July 1992 that while there was no evidence of police or government complicity, the police were to blame for 'a failure of leadership at all levels'. The inquiry castigated the police for 'serious incompetence' throughout its organization.

For month after month, as the mass action campaign continued, South Africa was convulsed by strikes, protests and boycotts. All that was left publicly of the negotiations process was an angry exchange of memoranda between Mandela and de Klerk. In July, Mandela issued a list of fourteen demands the government would have to meet before talks could be resumed. De Klerk responded with a thirty-one-page memorandum, deriding Mandela as a 'captive' of 'insurrectionists' in the Communist Party and warning of harsh measures to prevent chaos in the country. Mandela answered with a twenty-four-page rebuttal, labelling de Klerk a liar and blatant propagandist suffering from self-delusion. Negotiations to bring about democracy had failed, he said, because 'the ruling National Party keeps looking for ways to exercise power even if it loses a democratic election'. His letter contained lengthy appendices charging the government with responsibility for political violence: 'The acts of omission and commission by government in numerous cases can only be explained in terms of direct complicity in the violence in order to make party political gains at great cost in black lives and economic damage to our country.' Mandela ended with a stern admonition to de Klerk:

> Find a way within yourself to recognize the gravity of the crisis . . .
> Find a way to address the demands we have placed before you
> . . . so that negotiations can become meaningful and be vested with
> the urgency that the situation requires. Failure to respond in
> this way can only exacerbate the crisis. You may succeed in de-
> laying, but never in preventing, the transition of South Africa to
> democracy.

471

In August, the ANC alliance brought the campaign to a climax with a general strike by several million workers. Much of the country's business and industry came to a halt or was forced to reduce output. The strike was followed by mass marches. In Pretoria, Mandela led more than 50,000 supporters through the heart of the city to the seat of white government, Union Buildings. 'Today we are at the door of Union Buildings,' declared Ramaphosa. 'Next time, F. W. de Klerk, we are going to be inside your office.' Mandela hailed the strike as 'unquestionably one of the great events in our history'.

Yet for all the fervour that mass action achieved, it produced nothing in terms of forcing any movement in the government's position. Nor was it a strategy that ANC supporters could afford to continue indefinitely. The ANC was divided over what to do next. Some wanted to seek a way back into negotiation. The initiative, however, lay with Kasrils and his group of insurrectionists. They argued that though mass action might not bring Pretoria to its knees, it would work against weaker governments in the homelands, in KwaZulu, Bophuthatswana and Ciskei, the allies of Pretoria which had so far kept a tight clamp on all ANC activity.

Ciskei was a particularly tempting target. It was ruled by a military dictator, Brigadier Oupa Gqozo, who had only recently seized power and had increasingly resorted to repressive measures to stay there. All the ANC's efforts to engage in political activity in Ciskei had been blocked. Mandela had spoken several times on the phone to Gqozo about the clampdown, and had met him twice in Bisho, the Ciskei capital. 'In one of our meetings, we agreed that we should each lead delegations of ten,' said Mandela. 'His delegation was composed of seven whites and three Africans. All these whites were seconded from South Africa. We got nowhere.'

The insurrectionists believed that a mass march on Bisho from neighbouring King William's Town, a few miles away across the 'border' in white South Africa, would trigger a switch of allegiance by the Ciskei army and public servants, causing the homeland administration to collapse. Kasrils travelled to Ciskei on a reconnaissance mission and pronounced it ripe for popular insurrection. 'I have just spent a week in Ciskei and I have never encountered such hatred for a despot,' Kasrils told a reporter. Once Gqozo was overthrown, the next targets would be Lucas Mangope in Bophuthatswana and Buthelezi in KwaZulu.

On 3 September, the ANC sent a memorandum to de Klerk demanding that Gqozo be removed as ruler of Ciskei and replaced by an interim administration that would permit free political activity. De Klerk refused, pointing out Ciskei's 'independence'. He sent Mandela three letters warning of the dangers of a bloody confrontation and pleading with him to call off the march. Gqozo himself issued a warning that he would meet with force any attempt to march on his capital.

The march was set for 7 September. The night before, Gqozo sought an urgent court order prohibiting the march. A local magistrate granted permission for the march to take place but ordered that it should not proceed beyond Bisho's independence stadium, just over the border from white South Africa but more than a mile from the town. The Ciskei police and military, commanded by white officers seconded from Pretoria, were ordered to stop the marchers there.

In the morning, a column of 70,000 marchers set out from King William's Town along the road to Bisho. Their aim, according to one leading activist, was 'to drive the pig from the barn'. The border was closed by a line of razor wire, with Ciskei troops deployed behind it. But scouting ahead of the column, Kasrils noticed a gap in the outer fence of the independence stadium alongside the road, which seemed to offer a route into the centre of Bisho. Returning back down the hill to colleagues, Kasrils urged that he should lead a breakaway group from the main column, storm through the gap and head on to Bisho. 'It's going to be a cinch,' he was overheard to say.

But Kasrils had failed to spot a detachment of Ciskei troops covering the gap from trench positions. As his breakaway group raced through the gap, the troops opened fire. Kasrils and other ANC leaders survived. But twenty-eight marchers were killed.

The day of the insurrectionists was over.

A mood of deep despondency hung over South Africa during those months in 1992. The cycle of violence seemed endless, destroying all prospect of a political settlement. The economy was sunk in the third year of recession, with no end in sight. A catastrophic

473

drought had laid waste to farming areas. The very institutions of government, it seemed, were rotten: the police proven incompetent and the military contaminated by dirty tricks. A wave of corruption scandals beset the administration. In the case of one government department dealing with the homelands, a judge concluded that 'millions, if not billions' of rands had been pilfered and misspent. Corruption was everywhere in the air. White civil servants and politicians scrambled to top up their pension schemes and fix long-term contracts before the day of reckoning. Security officials insisted on indemnities. The columnist Shaun Johnson wrote in *The Star*, 'If you stand on a street corner in Pretoria late at night, I am sure you can hear the sound of shredders shredding. Of assets being stripped. Of pockets being stuffed.'

The ANC added to the growing list of scandals. An internal inquiry confirmed allegations made by former ANC members that torture and executions had taken place in its camps in Angola during the 1980s. The ANC refused to disclose the names of its torturers, but the press published them, revealing that several were serving in high places in the ANC. One of them was a member of Mandela's own bodyguard. What was worse, ANC leaders like Oliver Tambo and Chris Hani were accused of failing to stop the ill-treatment of its prisoners. Mandela accepted 'collective responsibility' for the incidents, but the overall result was to leave the ANC's leadership discredited.

On top of all this was the crippling stalemate within the political arena. After nearly three years of effort, the politicians had little to show and nothing to offer. Each side denied its own responsibility. While they squabbled in public, the field was left open to insurrectionists like Kasrils to pursue their revolutionary fantasies. Whatever confidence there was about the country's future was rapidly ebbing away, both at home and abroad.

So deep was the crisis that it induced a willingness to compromise that had not existed before. In the wake of Bisho, Mandela reasserted his leadership, called a halt to mass action and severely reprimanded Kasrils. The priority, he said, was to haul South Africa 'out of the quagmire'. Both he and de Klerk bore responsibility to see that it happened. In a gesture of conciliation to de Klerk, only one week after the Bisho shooting, he compressed the ANC's fourteen preconditions for resuming talks to three. 'If Mr de Klerk can just say to me, "You have expressed your three concerns, I give you my undertaking that I will address them," ' Mandela said in a press interview, 'then I will be able to go back to my people and say, "Look, he has met us. Let us meet him." '

Behind the scenes, ever since talks had been broken off two key negotiators, Cyril Ramaphosa from the ANC and Roelf Meyer from the government side, had kept in touch in private, trying to pick up the pieces. Meyer had been appointed the government's chief negotiator in June 1992, a few weeks before the Boipatong massacre. He represented a new generation of Afrikaner leader, anxious to move ahead with the reforms that de Klerk had initiated in 1990. He was less concerned to protect white privileges from the past than to secure an accommodation for whites in the future that would last. With Ramaphosa, he struck up an effective working relationship. Meyer was forty-five; Ramaphosa was forty. Meeting in private in hotel rooms, they managed to establish a measure of trust which survived amid the turmoil and provided the basis for the negotiation process to resume.

Meyer and Ramaphosa became convinced that the way out of the impasse was for the government and the ANC to reach a bilateral understanding before multiparty talks continued. For de Klerk, however, the drawback of this approach was that bilateral talks between the government and the ANC were likely to jeopardize his hopes of forging an electoral alliance with regional black leaders like Buthelezi. Buthelezi's national support was considered to be of minor importance, but his following in KwaZulu-Natal, according to opinion polls, was still substantial. His pro-capitalist policies were far more compatible with National Party ideology than the ANC's plans for 'redistribution'. Moreover, a significant section of the cabinet, the National Party, the military and the police, as well as a coterie of white businessmen in Natal, much preferred Buthelezi as an ally to the prospect of having to do business with the likes of Mandela.

But de Klerk's overriding concern was to get the negotiations under way again. Reciprocating Mandela's gesture of conciliation, he issued a public invitation to him to join him in a summit meeting to find a way of ending the spiral of violence. Mandela responded positively. The harsh rhetoric he had employed against de Klerk for months on end was dropped. In his garden in Houghton late one

475

Sunday afternoon, he mused quietly about de Klerk's difficulties. 'I phoned him two days ago,' he said, 'and I must say he sounded a bit down. He is a very brave chap, you know, very bright and confident, and it was worrying to hear him sounding so down.' In the hurly-burly of South African politics, such moments were rare, however, and soon forgotten.

The date for the summit was set for 26 September, less than three weeks after the Bisho shooting. For ten days beforehand, the two sides, led by Meyer and Ramaphosa, negotiated night and day over the three conditions set by the ANC for resuming talks. All were highly contentious. Two of them required action against Inkatha: the ANC demanded that Inkatha hostels should be fenced and that Inkatha members should be prohibited from carrying traditional weapons in public. These were demands opposed outright by the pro-Buthelezi faction within de Klerk's cabinet. The third demand de Klerk himself opposed. It involved the release of a number of ANC prisoners, three of whom had been sentenced to death for murder, including an Umkhonto member, Robert McBride, who had killed three young white women in a bomb attack outside a bar on Durban's beach-front. In the white community, the idea of releasing such convicted murderers was anathema.

Two days before the summit, the ANC's negotiators reported to Mandela that only one obstacle lay in the way: de Klerk had balked at the release of the three murderers; he had said he would 'never' release them. They proposed a back-down to ensure that the summit went ahead. But Mandela would have none of it. 'De Klerk needed us more than we needed him,' Mandela recalled. 'He desperately needed that summit.' Ramaphosa described Mandela's stubbornness over the issue: 'He has nerves of steel. Once he has decided that a particular issue has to be pursued, everything else matters very little. And he can be very harsh when dealing with an opponent who is unreasonable, very brutal in a calm and collected sort of way.'

Mandela spoke to de Klerk on the phone. Either de Klerk agreed to release the prisoners, he said, or there would be no summit. Mandela advised de Klerk against adopting intransigent positions, against saying he would 'never' release the prisoners: 'Because you know in the end you are going to give in. Because if you don't, we are going to humiliate you. And I will see to it that that happens.'

Ramaphosa feared that Mandela had gone too far and told him so, but Mandela remained relaxed. He laughed and said, 'This chap, I have had enough of him. We hold the line here today.' After several more phone calls, de Klerk agreed to release the three men.

At the summit meeting, Mandela applied the same techniques. Facing strong opposition from members of his cabinet over the Inkatha issues, de Klerk attempted to prevaricate and asked for more time to study the matter. 'Very well, Mr de Klerk, you can have the time,' Mandela replied, 'provided you understand that when we leave here to have a press conference, I shall say that this meeting has been a total failure.' De Klerk hastily convened a 'working committee' led by Meyer to study the issue; it met over the lunch break and duly approved the concession.

The summit ended with Mandela and de Klerk signing what was termed a Record of Understanding, thus breaking the deadlock on constitutional negotiations. But its real significance went even further, for it marked the point at which the government was no longer able on its own to control the transition process, as de Klerk had assumed it always would. Henceforth, government action had to take into account the requirements of the ANC. No deal could be done without it. The summit also marked the point at which Mandela gained a psychological ascendancy over de Klerk which he was never to lose. Another shift in the balance of power had occurred.

Buthelezi reacted to the accord between the government and the ANC with a fit of rage, seeing it as a move to leave him on the sidelines while they constructed their own deal. He denounced de Klerk's 'appeasement' of the ANC and warned that his followers would never give up carrying traditional weapons and would tear down any fences erected around Inkatha hostels 'with their bare hands'. He poured scorn on the ANC's threat to march on his capital, Ulundi, reminding it of the grim fate of a British army column which had invaded Zululand in 1879. Zulus, he said, were ready for 'another washing of the spears'.

Buthelezi now played the tribal card for all it was worth, presenting himself as the defender of all Zulus against external enemies like the ANC and its communist allies bent on their destruction. At mass rallies, he warned Zulus that their very existence was at stake, that their foes planned to wipe KwaZulu 'off the face of the earth'. Claiming that secret deals were being made, he broke off negotiations with the government, determined to wreck the process.

Meanwhile, the search for a settlement between the government and the ANC began in earnest. It received a dramatic boost in October from an unexpected quarter: Joe Slovo. Slovo believed that what the ANC needed at this juncture was some 'shock therapy' about its own negotiating position. Just as he had taken the initiative in arguing for the suspension of the armed struggle in 1990, so now he took the lead in proposing a highly controversial compromise in negotiations. Writing in the Communist Party journal *African Communist*, Slovo suggested that as an alternative to making a bid for total power, it might be necessary for the ANC to offer the government 'a sunset clause' in a new constitution which would entrench power-sharing in a government of national unity for a fixed period. The ANC might also have to give ground by offering guarantees on regional government, by accepting an amnesty for security officials and by honouring the contracts of civil servants, either by retaining them or by compensating them. 'The ANC is not dealing with a defeated enemy; an early seizure of power is not realistic; the capacity of the white civil service, army and police to destabilize a newly born democracy is enormous; and a sunset clause should be inserted in the new constitution to provide for compulsory power-sharing for a fixed number of years.' To emphasize the point, Slovo warned, 'All we will achieve when we have won the election is to gain political office. We would not gain state power in the sense of having a complete transformation on day one of the police, the armed forces, the judiciary and the civil services.' Coming from a figure with such impeccable revolutionary credentials, these ideas carried all the more weight.

Slovo's suggestions created a furore within the ANC and the Communist Party. Hardline communists like Harry Gwala contemptuously dismissed them as 'bourgeois reformism'. Pallo Jordan, an independent Marxist, claimed Slovo was advocating total 'capitulation'. The Slovo scenario, he said, aimed at nothing less than enabling 'the liberation movement and the regime to ride blissfully into the sunset together'. Members of the ANC national executive committee sceptical of the outcome of the negotiations argued that the National Party would never abandon power, no matter what was offered.

But in other quarters in the ANC, the idea of 'sunset' clauses for the white community had gained a certain currency. Mandela himself had long believed that a multiparty coalition might be needed in the early years of democratic rule to help assuage the fears of minorities. 'It may not be enough to work purely on one-person one-vote,' he said in 1991, 'because every national group would like to see that the people of their flesh and blood are in government.'

The ANC's negotiating commission developed Slovo's ideas into a document of its own, entitled 'Negotiations: A Strategic Perspective', which was formally adopted in November. Because of the pressure on the ANC to achieve results and the government's ability to 'endlessly delay', it said, there was a need to make compromises and to pursue a swift negotiation process. This process would have to address questions of job security, retrenchment packages and a general amnesty for 'all armed formations and sections of the civil service'. Of crucial importance, the ANC argued in favour of a government of national unity. The way forward, it suggested, was for the government and the ANC to reach a bilateral agreement on those issues before including other parties in a multiparty forum. Government negotiators were quick to discern the makings of a deal on this basis.

De Klerk was still a long way from accepting the idea of majority rule, even under a government of national unity. His goal remained a constitution which would ensure that blacks could not govern without the agreement of whites. But his authority was steadily being eroded. In November 1992, the Goldstone Commission uncovered a secret operation set up in 1991 by the Department of Military Intelligence to run a dirty-tricks campaign against the ANC, using a covert unit based in Pretoria which employed a network of 'prostitutes, homosexuals, shebeen owners and drug dealers' to compromise ANC and Umkhonto leaders by involving them in criminal activity. The existence of the unit, run by the army's senior intelligence officer, provided the most damning evidence so far of a deliberate strategy at high government level to discredit the ANC.

A subsequent investigation carried out by the army's chief of staff, General Pierre Steyn, uncovered evidence of military intelligence involvement in train massacres, assassination, gun-running, smuggling and other criminal activity. Unable to dismiss the problem any more as a 'few rogue individuals', de Klerk was forced to start cleaning up the military. He sacked or suspended twenty-three officers, including two generals, and ordered a purge of military intelligence staff. Special force units like 32 Battalion and the police counter-insurgency unit, Koevoet, were disbanded. Military personnel and their associates, de Klerk admitted, 'have been involved, and in some cases are still involved, in illegal and unauthorized activities and malpractices. There are indications that some of the activities and some of the individuals might have been motivated by a wish to prevent us from succeeding in our goals'. The overall result was to tarnish de Klerk's reputation and to vindicate Mandela's claims about the existence of a third force.

Bilateral meetings between the government and the ANC, starting in December 1992 with a four-day bush summit or *bosberaad* held in a wildlife resort, now began to make steady progress. By February 1993, the two sides were agreed upon the outline for a new order, which meant de Klerk giving up many of his original negotiating aims. The new order involved an interim five-year government of national unity in which all parties polling over 5 per cent would be represented proportionately in the cabinet. After five years, the government of national unity would become a simple majority-rule government. A transitional executive council, representing all parties accepting the process, would oversee preparations for elections and would assure a 'level playing field' for all the contestants. During the five-year interim, an elected constituent assembly would draw up the final constitution but it would be based on a set of principles agreed to previously at multiparty negotiations which would launch the whole process.

There were critics of this compromise arrangement on both sides, but the most extraordinary attack of all came from Winnie Mandela. Still awaiting the outcome of her appeal against convictions for kidnapping and assault, she was endeavouring to resurrect her political career by adopting hardline positions popular with militants. Her attack was launched not just against the negotiations process but against the role of the ANC's leaders and, by implication, Mandela himself. The negotiations process, she said, was being conducted between 'the élite of the oppressed and the oppressors', ignoring the interests of the masses:

> The NP élite is getting into bed with the ANC in order to preserve its silken sheets. And the leadership of the ANC is getting into bed with the NP to enjoy this new-found luxury. The concern is that this new amalgam of power is promoting its own self-interest and overlooking the plight and needs of the underprivileged masses . . . The quick-fix solution sought by our leaders can only benefit a few and will backfire massively on the country as a whole. The disillusion that will follow when the masses awaken to the fact that they have not been included in the new freedom and in the new wealth enjoyed by their leaders will have worse implications than what we experienced in the 1970s and 1980s, and will plunge the country irrevocably into yet another vortex of mass violence and protest.

A new breed of leadership was needed, she said, truly representative of the aspirations of the 'oppressed'.

Winnie's own lifestyle – a grandiose mansion, an expensive wardrobe, a Mercedes-Benz, a retinue of bodyguards and retainers – was well known for its luxury and extravagance. Senior ANC officials dismissed her as no more than an opportunist. 'Who on earth is she to be speaking of silken sheets?' demanded one official. Yet Winnie's remarks found a ready audience in the shack and squatter settlements she patronized. And it was this mass of impoverished people, she believed, who would carry her back to power within the ANC.

In April 1993, multiparty negotiations resumed. No agreement on what the new negotiating forum should be called had been reached, so it was given no formal name. The number of groups now represented had expanded from nineteen to twenty-six. This time, the Conservative Party was present, forsaking its vow never to sit down with 'terrorists'. So was its offshoot, the Afrikaner Volksunie. The Pan-Africanist Congress also attended, even though it still professed to be committed to the armed struggle and had been involved in recent murders of white farmers to prove it. Places had also been found for traditional leaders like the Zulu king, Goodwill Zwelethini, whose presence had been repeatedly demanded previously by Buthelezi. The participation of so many parties seemed to augur well.

Then, within a matter of days, South Africa was struck by a cataclysmic event. On the morning of Easter Saturday in April

1993, as Chris Hani stepped out of his car in the driveway of his home in Dawn Park, a predominantly white suburb of the gold-mining town of Boksburg on the East Rand, he was assassinated by a lone white gunman who had been waiting for him in a red Ford car parked across the road. As the gunman drove off, an Afrikaner neighbour, who had heard the shots, memorized the registration number and phoned the police. Fifteen minutes later, the gunman was arrested on a highway outside Boksburg.

Hani was a hero to millions of black youths, a legendary guerrilla commander who had risen to become Umkhonto's chief of staff. A lifelong communist, he championed the cause of the poor and dispossessed. He was tough, ruthless and hugely popular, second only to Mandela, according to an independent poll in November 1992. He was also famous for fiery speech-making. Yet, even though he had misgivings, Hani had been converted to the cause of negotiation. When radical activists advocated a break with negotiations, Hani had argued determinedly in favour of pursuing them. He was pragmatic about the need to offer security forces an amnesty. When self-defence units in the townships began degenerating into vigilante gangs, he had been the first to call for their disbanding. He had moved to the white middle-class suburb of Dawn Park in 1991 in an attempt to break down racial barriers, influencing other black political and union officials to do the same. A few days before his death, he had declared, 'I am now a combatant for peace.' His following among the youth remained huge. If anyone was capable of mobilizing this vast, unruly constituency behind the negotiation process, it was Hani. His death at the hands of a white assassin seemed certain to plunge South Africa into an inferno of violence.

Mandela was at his house in Qunu in the Transkei on that Easter Saturday, working on his autobiography with the writer Richard Stengel. After an early-morning walk in the countryside, Mandela had returned to the study to begin a taped interview. He had hardly started when his housekeeper interrupted to let him know that members of the Transkei police rugby team had arrived at the house and wanted to greet him. Mandela rose stiffly from his chair and went outside. While he was in the middle of shaking hands with each member of the team in the driveway, the housekeeper ran out, in tears, telling him of an urgent telephone call. Mandela excused himself and went inside to be told of Hani's assassination. 'Mandela put down the phone and looked off into the distance, his face drawn and concerned,' wrote Stengel, in his own account of the incident. He then stood up, apologized to Stengel for the interruption and returned to the driveway to finish shaking hands with the rugby players.

With remarkable speed, the leadership of the crisis was assumed not by the government but by the ANC and Mandela. On radio and television throughout the day, ANC officials appealed for peace. Mandela rushed back to Johannesburg in time to make a national address on television: 'With all the authority at my command, I appeal to all our people to remain calm and to honour the memory of Chris Hani by remaining a disciplined force for peace.'

The circumstances around Hani's murder grew more ominous. The assassin, Janusw Waluz, a Polish immigrant who had lived in South Africa for twelve years, was a member of the extremist Afrikaner Weerstandsbeweging. The weapon he had used came from a batch of arms stolen from an air force armoury in 1990 by a well-known Afrikaner extremist. One suspect arrested in connection with the murder was a prominent member of the Conservative Party. The possibility of a right-wing conspiracy to wreck the transition aggravated all the tension.

Seeking to harness the tide of outrage, the ANC announced a week-long campaign of mass protest, including a national stay-away and memorial services. The risks of violence breaking out from such action were only too well known. On the eve of a day of mourning declared by the ANC, Mandela again addressed the nation on radio and television, appealing for calm in broadcasts he repeated at 7 p.m., 8 p.m. and 11 p.m.

> Tonight, I am reaching out to every single South African, black and white, from the very depths of my being. A white man, full of prejudice and hate, came to our country and committed a deed so foul that our whole nation now teeters on the brink of disaster. A white woman, of Afrikaner origin [Hani's neighbour], risked her life so that we may know, and bring to justice, this assassin . . . Now is the time for all South Africans to stand together against those who, from any quarter, wish to destroy what Chris Hani gave his life for – the freedom of all of us.

He called for discipline and dignified conduct: 'Chris Hani was a soldier. He believed in iron discipline . . . Any lack of discipline is trampling on the values that Chris Hani stood for. Those who commit such acts serve only the interests of the assassins.'

By the standards to which South Africa had become accustomed, the events in the days following Hani's assassination were relatively orderly. In nearly every urban area, chanting crowds swept through city centres; in several they left streets in chaos, with burnt cars and smashed and looted shops. But mostly the demonstrators heeded Mandela's call for discipline. Some 4 million workers participated in the stay-away, again in relative calm. But the sheer size and intensity of feeling of the protests were something white authority had never before experienced.

Radical factions were active in clamouring for revenge. At a protest rally at a squatter settlement in Cape Town, organized by the ANC's youth leader Peter Mokaba and by Winnie Mandela, Mokaba was captured on television chanting, 'Kill the Boer! Kill the farmers!' Winnie followed by calling on the ANC's youth to oust the ANC's leadership and take the streets by storm. At a memorial service in Soweto, when Mandela referred to a message of sympathy from the National Party, he was jeered. Demonstrators were not just angry about Hani's murder but impatient at the failure of the negotiation process to deliver concrete results. 'Mandela released three years ago: South Africa still not free,' read one placard at Hani's funeral.

The significance of these events, however, went far beyond the question of violence. It was the time when Mandela emerged as a national leader, comprehending at once the magnitude of the crisis, seeking to calm white fears as well as black anger, demanding discipline and receiving it. De Klerk and his government, meanwhile, were hardly to be seen. From his Cape holiday home, de Klerk issued statements, clearly partisan in nature, aimed at white constituents alarmed by the violence. His preoccupation, as one Johannesburg newspaper noted, was 'to assure whites that they were safe from the black hordes'.

In the long struggle between Mandela and de Klerk, no other single event provoked such a dramatic shift in the balance of power, nor revealed so clearly to the white community how important Mandela was to their future security.

CHAPTER 26
The Loneliest Man

Two weeks after Hani's assassination, Oliver Tambo suddenly died after suffering a second stroke. Though his first stroke had left him partly immobilized on his right side, he had remained active as the ANC's national chairman, working three days a week at the party headquarters in central Johannesburg, right up to the day of his death. He was widely revered for his soft-spoken, lucid manner, always seeking compromise and consensus. While Mandela inspired admiration, even awe, Tambo inspired love.

Tambo's death was a colossal blow to Mandela. The trio of Mandela, Sisulu and Tambo had sustained the African nationalist struggle for fifty years. Tambo's friendship, like Sisulu's, had spanned Mandela's entire adult life, starting from their days together at Fort Hare, through the Youth League, their law partnership and the Defiance Campaign, to the treason trial and the formation of Umkhonto we Sizwe. Even during his years in prison, Mandela said in his autobiography, Tambo was never far from his thoughts: 'Though we were separated, I kept up a lifelong conversation with him in my head.' On the day of his release from prison in 1990, Mandela described as 'the most wonderful moment' the occasion late at night when a telephone call came through from Tambo in Sweden, where he was recuperating from his first stroke. Their reunion in Stockholm later in the year was joyous. 'When we met we were like two young boys in the veld who took strength from our love for each other,' Mandela wrote. On the day of Tambo's death, Mandela spoke to journalists. 'I will feel his loss in a unique manner,' he said. 'We are bleeding from the invisible

485

wounds that are so difficult to heal.' To a friend, he remarked that he felt like the loneliest man in the world.

His home life compounded the sense of loneliness he felt. Separated from Winnie, he lived alone in his six-bedroom house in Houghton, frequently with only bodyguards and servants for company. When Zindzi paid him visits, she would often find him on his own, eating supper at the large dining-room table by himself.

In private, with his own children, he remained a stern figure. Zindzi, who knew little of him until his release in 1990, noted how he avoided bodily contact. 'He'll only hold your hand for a moment,' she said. In a magazine interview, she described Mandela as 'a typical African father', demanding strict obedience. 'He thinks very traditionally,' she said. 'He is head of the family . . . His will is law.' With his son, Makgatho, Mandela still insisted he should pursue his studies.

All his affection he concentrated on his grandchildren. He developed a special bond with one of Zindzi's sons, Bambatha, whose father, Sizwe Sithole, had hanged himself in a police cell shortly before Mandela's release. Bambatha was only three months old at the time. For two years, while Zindzi lived with her parents in Soweto, Mandela was able to spend much time with Bambatha. He enjoyed putting him to bed at night. 'He even got up in the middle of the night to change his nappy and give him his bottle, as if Bambatha were his own son,' Zindzi recalled. But with older grandchildren, Mandela could be as stern and demanding as he was with his own children.

In the company of friends, he found it difficult to relax. His circle of friends was wide and varied, but there were few with whom he was on intimate terms. With the death of Oliver Tambo, only Walter Sisulu survived of the group of young firebrands from the 1940s who had played such a central role in his early life. To Sisulu, Mandela remained as he had always been: warm, kind and sociable. 'That type of a nature doesn't really change,' mused Sisulu, after fifty years of friendship. Other old friends included Yusuf Cachalia and his wife, Amina, a strikingly attractive woman for whom Mandela had a particular affection. Mandela and Cachalia had once cooked a pigeon pie to celebrate Amina's twenty-first birthday and she reminded him of the occasion in a letter sent to him on Robben Island. Mandela replied, 'My dear Amina, How dare you torture me by reminding me of that pigeon meal!' He wrote too of his lasting friendship with the Cachalias, citing 'the powerful links that hold us tightly together'. When Amina first saw him in Pollsmoor, after twenty-four years, she was shocked by his thin and emaciated appearance. She noticed that he had become quieter, more gentle, more measured. She realized too the huge adjustments he faced upon his release from prison: 'He had a lot to learn, a whole new lifestyle.'

But outside a handful of close friends, Mandela kept his distance. The aloofness that he had shown before his imprisonment had hardened during the long years he spent there. He evaded intimacy. Even friends like Kathy Kathrada, who had known him on close terms for so many years in prison, still found him to be 'a very cool person – self-contained to an exceptional degree'. Not once during their prison life did Kathrada ever hear Mandela proclaim any personal ambition. 'If he had any inner feelings about what he wanted to be, it was never evident,' said Kathrada. 'In prison we never ever talked even lightly about his being president of the country.' As one of Mandela's key aides upon his release from prison, Kathrada still found it difficult to tell what went on in his mind. 'Take the latest incident involving Winnie,' he said. 'When I would meet him for work or casually, you would never decipher in his attitude towards us what was going on in his mind about this matter. He would not even mention it.'

Mandela was often most at ease in dealing with strangers or acquaintances. He remained courteous and attentive to individuals, whatever their status or their age. His aides sometimes had to chastise him from rising from his chair to greet everyone who approached. Soon after his release from prison, when he attended a friend's birthday party in an affluent white suburb of Johannesburg, he spent most of the evening greeting a constant stream of maids, gardeners and domestic staff from the neighbourhood who came to see him, shaking each one by the hand and conversing at length with all of them. At luncheons and banquets, he always made a point of shaking hands with the staff, showing the same courtesy to them that he would to dignitaries.

He was also attracted to people of wealth and fame. Among his many acquaintances were millionaires only too willing to ingratiate themselves. The insurance magnate Douw Steyn lent him a home after he left Winnie. The casino tycoon Sol Kerzner helped pay for Zindzi's extravagant wedding and provided a honeymoon suite at one of his hotels in Mauritius. He dined regularly with the Oppenheimers and spent holidays with the Menells, another prominent mining family. Mandela might mock his relations with the rich and famous – at the end of one of his sessions with Richard Stengel, he remarked, 'I am having lunch today with the third richest family in South Africa; I will not starve' – but he often seemed to prefer their company. When he approached twenty leading businessmen for at least 1 million rands each to help him with election expenses, all but one complied.

In the absence of any real family life, all Mandela's efforts were concentrated on political work. His daily schedule, for a man of seventy-four, was punishing. He still arose at about 5 a.m. for his exercises. When he first arrived in Houghton, he enjoyed an early-morning jog through its leafy streets, but after the assassination of Chris Hani he confined himself to exercising at home. By 7 a.m. he was at work in his tenth-floor office in ANC headquarters at Shell House in central Johannesburg. The rest of the day was filled with meetings, interviews, speeches, negotiations, conferences, working lunches, fund-raising appearances and banquets. He liked to be back home by 9.30 p.m. to catch up on his reading. His foreign trips were as numerous as before.

With increasing frequency, Mandela suffered from bouts of exhaustion. His doctors pointed out that what was remarkable, in view of his schedule, was not that he was so tired but that he remained so energetic. Dr Louis Gecelter, who examined him regularly, concluded that Mandela possessed the mental and physical attributes of a man of fifty. The explanation, he said, lay partly in the dietary discipline and exercise routine of twenty-seven years in prison. But it was also because Mandela was a man for whom life was only just beginning, for whom the important goals in life still lay ahead.

Within the ANC, Mandela played an elevated role, largely removed from administrative concerns, internal squabbles and the hard grind of negotiations. He usually left detail in the hands of officials like Ramaphosa. He was recognized as being the ANC's greatest asset, its elder statesman, able to achieve for the ANC a degree of international respectability and support that would otherwise be missing. But he was not always sure-footed. His pronouncements, notably on foreign affairs, sometimes left ANC officials aghast. During a telephone conversation with President George Bush, he lectured him on the perils of US policy towards the Iraqi dictator, Saddam Hussein. He also infuriated the Bush administration by taking Colonel Gaddafi's side in the feud over the bombing of Pan Am flight 103. He heaped praise on Cuba as an 'inspiration to all freedom-loving people'. On British television, he spoke of his support for the IRA's 'struggle against colonialism'. At home, his suggestion that the franchise should be extended to fourteen-year-old children became a national joke.

The one subject Mandela would not discuss was Winnie; about her, he maintained a stony silence. In June 1993, two years after her conviction for kidnapping and assault, the verdict on her appeal was finally handed down by the chief justice, Michael Corbett. In reaching its decision, the Appeal Court heard no new evidence. The allegations made by Xoliswa Falati, John Morgan and others while the appeal process was under way were not part of the Appeal Court's purview. All that the Appeal Court was concerned with was evidence given during the original trial.

Justice Corbett ruled that there was no doubt that Stompie Moeketsi Seipei and three other young men had been kidnapped and assaulted in Mrs Mandela's home in December 1988. He found that the trial judge had been correct in finding Winnie guilty of kidnapping them. But he accepted Winnie's claim that she had been far from home during the beatings and consequently found her not guilty of being an accessory to the assaults. He reduced her six-year sentence to a two-year suspended sentence, and ordered her to pay a fine of 15,000 rands and compensation of 5,000 rands to each of the surviving kidnap victims. With the threat of a prison sentence now lifted, Winnie was free to pursue her own political ambitions. Falati, however, lost her appeal and was ordered to serve two years in prison.

Mandela's comment on the outcome was terse: 'I am very happy my estranged wife will not have to go to jail,' he said. A few weeks later, he made his own gesture of contrition to Stompie's mother when, during a political rally at her home town of Parys, he insisted she be given a place of honour on the podium and spoke to her at length, pointedly, for all to see.

On 18 July 1993, at a party to celebrate Mandela's seventy-fifth birthday, some 650 guests were invited, but Winnie was not one of them.

In the wake of Hani's assassination, Mandela was able to force the pace of negotiations, insisting on swift, tangible progress. On 3 June 1993, negotiators at the multiparty forum at the World Trade Centre outside Johannesburg voted to set a date for the first democratic election – 27 April 1994 – even though agreement on an interim constitution was nowhere near being in sight.

As the spectre of majority rule moved closer, a motley collection of the ANC's opponents – homeland leaders and extreme right-wing groups – banded together to thwart the process. The central figure was Buthelezi. Though Inkatha had rejoined the multiparty forum in April 1993, Buthelezi produced proposals of his own for an autonomous region for KwaZulu-Natal and threatened a 'go-it-alone' approach if a referendum in the territory approved the plan. Buthelezi's proposals not only reduced the functions of central government to a minimum, they concentrated enormous power in the hands of the rulers of KwaZulu-Natal, with few checks and balances. The case for a federal South Africa was eminently respectable; it would have suited several minority groups. But Buthelezi, influenced heavily by white advisers, presented his plan on an all-or-nothing basis, believing that he was too important for the process to continue without him. Even his negotiators conceded that Buthelezi's ego was a significant part of the problem. Buthelezi also objected to the two-stage approach of the drafting of the final constitution, insisting that the full text should be drawn up by the present negotiators before an election rather than by an elected constitution-making body in the future. In protest against the setting of the April 1994 date for the elections, Buthelezi withdrew Inkatha from the negotiations process, clearly expecting it to founder in the same way as it had done the previous year when the ANC walked out of Codesa.

Buthelezi found common cause with two other homeland leaders, Lucas Mangope, the autocratic ruler of Bophuthatswana, and Brigadier Gqozo, the military dictator of Ciskei. Both hoped to be able to secure a future for themselves in the kind of federal system proposed by Buthelezi. Mangope had been an ideal partner in the apartheid system and benefited from it substantially. Like Buthelezi, he ran a tight one-party system, with control of parliament, radio and television, and brooked no opposition. At a recent election in October 1992, all his own candidates had been returned – unopposed. Opinion polls suggested that Mangope possessed minimal public support – less than 1 per cent – far less than Buthelezi's following, but this had never troubled him. As far as apartheid's rulers were concerned, Mangope had been far more reliable, more predictable, than Buthelezi. Whereas Buthelezi had refused 'independence', Mangope had taken it. When Mangope was threatened by a military coup in 1988, the South Africans had duly come to the rescue. 'Oh! I never knew how friends could be so loyal!' Mangope told the white minister who arrived on the scene to help him. Despite Mangope's evident lack of popularity, de Klerk had always considered him a potential ally for the National Party in an anti-ANC coalition. Like Brigadier Gqozo in Ciskei, he had refused to allow the ANC to conduct any political activity in his territory.

Mandela had by now lost all patience with Buthelezi. 'He reached a point where he was very, very angry,' Sisulu recalled. 'In fact, so angry that when the whole executive took a lighter line, saying that Buthelezi should be spoken to, he said no.' Senior ANC officials, examining Buthelezi's constitutional proposals, were convinced that his real objective was secession from South Africa altogether. They argued that no matter what concessions Buthelezi was offered, he would still continue to boycott the transition process because he feared the consequences of an election. They also took the view that though Buthelezi's participation in the election was preferable, to ensure a wider legitimacy, it was not essential. He could therefore be ignored. A hardcore of militants, led by Harry Gwala, still advocated using force to oust both him and his allies.

In his dealings with Mangope, Mandela found him to be equally obdurate. He travelled to Mangope's capital, Mmabatho, near the Botswanan border, to see if they could come to terms, suggesting that they both address a rally in Bophuthatswana to make clear their commitment to a peaceful resolution. Mangope at first agreed, but then changed his mind. 'The discussions broke down,' said Mandela. 'I have phoned him since on numerous occasions and he has avoided me.' As with Buthelezi and Gqozo, Mandela believed that Mangope posed no serious threat to the transition process.

The real threat, as Mandela and others in the ANC saw it, came from extreme right-wing organizations. On their own, they were known more for weekend parades and for fierce rhetoric than for action. They were divided into a host of splinter groups, constantly squabbling with each other. But what worried Mandela was the extent of support they had from within the security forces and from army and police reserve units stationed across the country. 'The ultra-right is powerful in the proper sense of the word,' said Mandela. Their support within the public service, the army, the police and other strategic institutions was significant: 'They are trained and experienced and they know the country better than we do . . . They can derail any democratic government in this country.'

The common aim of many extreme right-wing groups was to establish an Afrikaner homeland, a *volkstaat*. At the entrance to many *platteland* towns, road signs decorated with the flags of the old Boer republics already declared their allegiance. Demands for a *volkstaat* were frequently accompanied by threats of violence. 'Mandela, give us a *volkstaat* or you'll have total war in South Africa,' the AWB leader, Eugene Terre'Blanche, told supporters at Lichtenburg. A spate of bomb explosions on railway tracks, power pylons and ANC property in the Transvaal and the Orange Free State underlined the message.

Yet after nearly four years of talks about a *volkstaat*, far-right parties still failed to make clear where it would be located or how it would work. No explanation was forthcoming about the rights of non-Afrikaners living in an area declared a *volkstaat*, or how their opinions would be taken into account. De Klerk described the idea as 'a hopeless illusion'.

In May 1993, in an attempt to present a united demand for a *volkstaat*, a 'committee of generals', consisting of retired army and police commanders from the 'total strategy' era, formed an Afrikaner Volksfront, an umbrella group bringing together twenty-one organizations including the Conservative Party, the neo-Nazi AWB, the Transvaal Municipal Associations, white trade unions and farmers' unions from the Transvaal and the Orange Free State. The AVF's leader, General Constant Viljoen, a former chief of the defence staff, hoped to provide the right wing with a more pragmatic leadership. His own experience of warfare in Angola, Mozambique and Namibia had led him to conclude that violence was the worst possible option. He also wanted to establish a respectable image for the AVF. But he had to contend with the inane antics of the AWB.

On 25 June, at a demonstration organized by the AVF outside the World Trade Centre, intended to promote its demand for a *volkstaat*, a group of AWB supporters led by Terre'Blanche, brandishing shotguns and revolvers, broke through a police cordon, drove an armoured security vehicle through the glass front of the building and stormed into the conference chamber, screaming abuse and assaulting delegates, officials and journalists along the way. They then occupied delegates' seats, scrawled slogans on walls and urinated on the floor. Viljoen's efforts to restrain the mob were ignored.

Despite such acts of hooliganism and violence, Mandela was determined to seek a dialogue with the far right to avert what he feared might become a concerted effort to sabotage the transition to majority rule. In August, at a secret meeting in a private house in Houghton, Mandela met three of the AVF's generals, including Viljoen. He was blunt in presenting his appraisal of the situation:

> If you want to go to war, I must be honest and admit that we cannot stand up to you on the battlefield. We don't have the resources. It will be a long and bitter struggle, many people will die and the country may be reduced to ashes. But you must remember two things. You cannot win because of our numbers: you cannot kill us all. And you cannot win because of the international community. They will rally to our support and they will stand with us.

The meeting achieved an unexpected result. Mandela believed, just as much as de Klerk, that the idea of a *volkstaat* was a hopeless illusion. His aim was to engage the AVF in talks for as long as possible in the hope that right-wing fears about their future security under majority rule might in time begin to diminish. He found the generals amenable to further talks. A committee of ANC officials was set up to meet the AVF generals on a regular basis. What was unexpected was that Mandela and Viljoen developed an immediate liking for each other. Mandela felt a genuine sympathy for Viljoen's concerns about Afrikaner culture, religion and language, which were in marked contrast to de Klerk's preoccupations with pensions and privileges. The degree of trust that Mandela and Viljoen shared from their first meeting was to have important consequences in crises that lay ahead.

Meanwhile, negotiators at the World Trade Centre ploughed on, doggedly assembling a new constitution. The most contentious issue was federalism – the balance of power between central government and the provinces. The ANC wanted a strong central government with powers to override the provinces. The National Party advocated a measure of devolution, but made only a half-hearted effort to fight for it. The liberal opposition Democratic Party favoured devolution, but possessed too little weight in the negotiations process to secure it. Buthelezi was the most insistent on the need for maximum devolution, but he threw away what chances there were of obtaining greater federal powers by choosing to boycott the negotiations. Consequently, the first drafts of the new constitution to emerge from the World Trade Centre in July and August contained only minor elements of federalism.

Buthelezi denounced the result and, with a warning of civil war 'or worse', threatened to boycott the 1994 elections unless his demands for autonomy were met. Right-wing parties took the same line. The Conservative Party described the draft constitution as 'hostile to Afrikaner interests' and 'a recipe for civil war, further economic deterioration and a spiral of violence'. Its new leader, Ferdi Hartzenberg, said the Conservative Party would participate in further talks only when Afrikaner self-determination was 'unequivocally accepted'.

A new alliance of opposition groups was launched to fight for a federal or confederal state. Called the Freedom Alliance, it consisted of Buthelezi from KwaZulu, Mangope from Bophuthatswana, Gqozo from Ciskei, Hartzenberg from the Conservative Party and General Viljoen from the Afrikaner Volksfront – a motley crew, but one that possessed a high potential for disruption.

On the Witwatersrand, the Reef war burst out with renewed ferocity. Townships on the East Rand such as Thokoza and Katlehong became war zones, their streets lined with deserted, burnt-out houses, wrecked vehicles, barricades and boulders, as Inkatha hostel dwellers and ANC comrades fought for territorial possession. Many hostel dwellers found themselves virtually under

494

armed siege; food and other supplies had to be delivered under paramilitary police protection. Hit-and-run raids continued relentlessly. In the first ten months of 1993, some 1,300 people died in political violence in the East Rand townships. Similar strife, though on an even greater scale, occurred in the killing fields of Natal.

Mandela, now that he was close to inheriting the problem of township violence, no longer saw fit to blame it solely on de Klerk. He still castigated the government for its failure to deal effectively with the violence, but accepted that the ANC had an equal responsibility for trying to bring it to an end. However, the message of peace and reconciliation he tried to convey was often drowned out.

Arriving in Katlehong to address a rally at a football stadium, Mandela found a message awaiting him, scribbled on the table next to his microphone. It read, 'No peace. Do not talk about peace. We've had enough. Please, Mr Mandela, no peace. Give us weapons. No peace.'

After criticizing the government, Mandela scolded his own supporters, undeterred by the angry murmuring in the crowd of some 10,000 people: 'There are times now when our people participate in the killing of innocent people. It is difficult for us to say when people are angry that they must be non-violent . . . But the solution *is* peace; it *is* reconciliation; it *is* political tolerance.'

Some in the crowd jeered, but Mandela continued:

> We must accept blacks are fighting each other in our townships. So the task of the ANC is to unite black people as well ... We must accept that responsibility for ending violence is not just the government's, the police's, the army's. It is also our responsibility ... We should put our own house in order. If you have no discipline, you are not freedom fighters. If you are going to kill innocent people, you don't belong to the ANC. Your task is reconciliation. You must go to your area and ask a member of Inkatha: why are we fighting?

The crowd shouted back. 'Listen to me! Listen to me!' he cried above the din. 'I am your leader. As long as I am your leader, I am going to give leadership. Do you want me to remain your leader?' Chastened, the crowd roared back, 'Yes!' Mandela went on, 'Well, as long as I am your leader, I will tell you, always, when you are wrong.'

Back at the World Trade Centre, after seven months of haggling, drafting and redrafting, deadlocks and deadlines, negotiators struggled through to the last remaining points of dispute. The most difficult of all – how cabinet decisions were to be taken in the government of national unity – had deliberately been left to the end. De Klerk insisted that cabinet decisions should require a two-thirds majority, potentially a means of minority veto. The ANC's negotiators wanted an ordinary majority, but were privately prepared to agree to a 60 per cent majority if necessary to break the deadlock. Hours before the final plenary session was due to sit on 17 November, the issue still had not been resolved.

In a final encounter late at night on 17 November, Mandela and de Klerk confronted each other over the last remaining clause. Mandela was adamant. The majority in cabinet would decide, he said; he could not run a cabinet in any other way. There would be no minority veto. Power would be shared voluntarily or not at all.

As the remains of his power drained away, de Klerk surrendered even on this point. All that he managed to salvage was an agreement that the cabinet would function in accordance with a 'consensus-seeking spirit'. At the very last minute, de Klerk had been obliged to accept majority rule.

In the early hours of 18 November, the interim constitution was approved by the plenary session, signalling the end of 341 years of white rule that had begun when the Dutchman Jan van Riebeeck first set foot on the Cape of Good Hope in 1652. Mandela used the occasion to urge South Africans 'to join hands and march into the future'.

After such a marathon endeavour, there was a sense of euphoria about the outcome. The scent of power was particularly heady for the ANC. Its chief negotiator, Cyril Ramaphosa, crowed about how the National Party's negotiating position at the last hour had 'collapsed'. Joe Slovo, writing in the *African Communist*, proclaimed 'a famous victory', adding, 'We got pretty much what we wanted.' Widespread protests at the way the ANC had blocked the use of a double ballot paper for the election of national and provincial legislatures, which would have enhanced the chances of smaller regionally based parties, were dismissed with contempt. The issue, said the ANC, was not negotiable. There would be no further concessions made to demands for greater regional powers.

Ramaphosa curtly rejected proposals that the name of KwaZulu should be retained by incorporating it into a province renamed KwaZulu-Natal. The name KwaZulu, he said, was a creation of apartheid and would not feature on maps of post-apartheid South Africa. The province would be known henceforth simply as Natal. At early meetings of the transitional executive council, the ANC was quick to start throwing its weight about. Any sign of trouble from the provinces, a senior ANC official warned, and they would 'let the tanks roll in'. As the ANC celebrated its triumph, whatever prospects there were of broadening the settlement to include Inkatha and other members of the Freedom Alliance rapidly degenerated, pushing South Africa towards civil war.

What had been achieved, nevertheless, was remarkable. Four years previously, South Africa had been in the hands of a ruthless, authoritarian government, determined to protect white power and privilege, buttressed by formidable security forces and a vast administrative apparatus, and with access to huge state revenues. De Klerk had embarked upon his reforms assuming that his government enjoyed such a preponderance of power that it could set the terms of any settlement. He scorned all notion of majority rule, holding firm to the need for group rights. Indeed, even after the new constitutional agreement was reached, he still argued that separate development for different ethnic groups as a constitutional option was morally justified. What de Klerk expected to emerge from the negotiations process was a government coalition of moderate parties which the National Party would dominate.

Yet stage by stage, he had been forced into compromise. From group rights he had moved on to the idea of power-sharing through a permanently enforced coalition, repeatedly insisting that he would never surrender to 'simple majority rule'. Whatever the outcome of a popular vote, he said, he would demand a guaranteed share in power and he would hold out as long as necessary to obtain one. At the very least there would have to be a white veto in cabinet.

The compromises that de Klerk had been induced to accept came about in part through skilful negotiation, in part by force of circumstance, like the Hani assassination, which led to de Klerk's irreversible commitment to an election date. But they also reflected changes in the government's thinking about white interests and ways of protecting them. Apartheid had brought the whites unprecedented prosperity. For much of the white community, prosperity rather than power had become their preoccupation. Like other white communities in Africa, they had come to accept the old adage: give them parliament and keep the banks. As Joe Slovo had foreseen when putting forward his 'sunset clause', guarantees about employment, pensions and property were sufficient to break the log jam in negotiations. But what de Klerk also came to realize was that the indispensable role played by whites in the civil service, the security forces and the economy would give them far greater leverage over a new government than mere constitutional clauses. Even when making his last stand against Mandela over the issue of the cabinet veto, de Klerk acknowledged that a voluntary agreement on the need for 'consensus-seeking' was likely to give the whites more influence in cabinet than an entrenched clause in the constitution which an ANC majority would seek to thwart.

Underpinning the settlement was the extraordinary stature that Mandela had attained in the four years since his release from prison. His exemplary lack of bitterness, his insistence on national reconciliation and his willingness to compromise had earned him enduring respect among his white adversaries. The white community would not vote for him, but they would accept a government under his presidency.

On a personal basis, the relationship between Mandela and de Klerk never recovered from the long war of attrition they had fought. In public and private, their dealings over who was to blame for the violence remained abrasive. Mandela was infuriated by what he claimed was de Klerk's indifference to the loss of black lives. He was also irked by de Klerk's refusal to condemn the principle of apartheid. While de Klerk was willing to admit that the apartheid system had led to injustice and hardship, for which he apologized, he still continued to speak approvingly of the idea of ethnic separation, provided it was voluntary.

Even on the occasion when the two men were jointly awarded the Nobel Peace Prize in Oslo in December 1993, the friction was still evident. In interviews, Mandela spoke of his 'disappointment' with de Klerk's conduct in the negotiations and once more accused the government of involvement in township violence. De Klerk, for his part, appeared to resent being upstaged by Mandela, believing that his own efforts had been overlooked. In choosing them as 'Men of the Year' for 1993, *Time* magazine noted that 'the mutual bitterness and resentments between de Klerk and Mandela are palpable', and it asked rhetorically, 'How could these two have agreed on anything – lunch, for instance, much less the remaking of a nation?'

At a political level, however, Mandela recognized how important de Klerk was to the whole settlement. 'My worst nightmare is that I wake up and de Klerk isn't there,' Mandela told guests at a private dinner party. 'I need him. Whether I like him or not is irrelevant. I need him.'

CHAPTER 27
The Election Roller-coaster

In the election campaign, Mandela was the star attraction. Everywhere he went, from one township to another, from one stadium to the next, he was greeted by huge exuberant crowds eager to catch a glimpse of him. For many, he was a messianic figure bringing them the promise of freedom. Long before the election took place, he was regarded as the victor. Seeing Mandela was an event in itself. He made the most of his appearances, standing in open vehicles, smiling and waving in obvious pleasure, punching his fist in the air, ignoring the concerns of his bodyguards in order to stretch out and shake hands, while cheerful pandemonium erupted all around.

He proved to be a natural campaigner, as much at ease with crowds as with small gatherings and bystanders, tailoring his speeches and his attire for each audience. For white businessmen, he chose elegant striped suits; for the townships, flamboyant shirts. Appearing at a mineworkers' meeting in a suit, he apologized, saying that he had not had time to change into something more casual, then delighted his audience by donning a miner's helmet. Colourful silk shirts, buttoned at the neck, soon became his trademark.

The manifesto he launched in January 1994 was thick with promises. Using the slogan 'A better life for all', Mandela undertook to introduce what he described as a 'gigantic' programme of public works, providing houses, essential services, electrification, better schools, roads, clinics and formal employment for millions of people. The specific targets laid out in the manifesto were ambitious: jobs and training for 2.5 million people over ten years; 1 million houses to be built over five years; electrification for 2.5 million rural and urban homes; running water and flush lavatories for over 1 million families over five years; ten years of free and compulsory education for all children; free school textbooks to be doubled in number within one year; affordable access to telecommunications; and basic health care for all. Other items included land reform, affirmative action programmes, small business development, lower food taxes and income tax reductions for low-paid workers.

No explanation was forthcoming in the manifesto about how all these undertakings would be financed. Like the Freedom Charter of 1955, the manifesto contained a large number of utopian notions. The objectives themselves were laudable enough, but amounted to little more than a wish list.

As well as the manifesto, the ANC produced a 'reconstruction and development programme' in an endeavour to provide a policy framework for the future. But its list of promises and moral imperatives was even longer than that contained in the manifesto and included everything from paid maternity leave to a reduction in traffic accidents. Once again, no costs were given, no suggestion of a funding strategy was made, no priorities were set and policy options were left wide open.

Finding an agreed economic policy proved to be a difficult business for the ANC. It re-emerged in South Africa in 1990, a revolutionary organization laden with a great deal of ideological baggage, proclaiming the virtues of socialism and state control despite the collapse of socialist regimes in Eastern Europe. The Freedom Charter, with its commitment to nationalization of the banks and 'monopoly' industry, was regarded as sacrosanct. When Mandela first came out of prison in 1990, he was asked whether he had changed his view in any way about the need for a radical redistribution of wealth in South Africa. 'No,' he replied, without a moment's hesitation. 'My views are identical to those of the ANC. The question of the nationalization of the mines and similar important sectors of the community is a fundamental policy of the ANC and I believe that the ANC is quite correct in this attitude.' His remarks caused a wave of panic among businessmen and sent share prices on the Johannesburg stock exchange plummeting.

Under pressure from the business community, foreign investors and international financial institutions like the International

Monetary Fund and the World Bank, the ANC modified its views but still held firm to the ideals of the Freedom Charter. Time and again, Mandela spoke of the need for a redistribution of wealth and property. Addressing a panel at the World Economic Forum in Davos, Switzerland, in 1992, Mandela declared, 'Taking some key enterprises into public ownership will itself be a major step towards overcoming the huge inequality in the ownership of our country's wealth.' He was mortified to find, however, that both de Klerk and Buthelezi, addressing the same meeting but promising a vigorous free-enterprise system, were given a far more enthusiastic reception from the world's top businessmen.

Yet Mandela's subsequent efforts to shift the direction of ANC policy encountered strong resistance. At an ANC economic policy conference in 1992, held after the Davos meeting, when Mandela warned that the ANC would alienate the business community worldwide if it persisted with its nationalization programme, Ben Turok, the Marxist economist who had helped draft the Freedom Charter's economic clause nearly forty years before, rose to ask how Mandela could now turn his back on the Charter. Facing outright opposition, Mandela withdrew his proposal to drop nationalization as an option.

The battle continued throughout 1993. Determined to ensure that the ANC did not lose sight of its socialist principles once it was involved in a government of national unity, a group of trade unionists, communists and ANC officials initiated the idea of a 'reconstruction' programme setting out a string of radical pro-posals. The reconstruction and development programme, as it was eventually called, went through six drafts before the final version was approved. In the end, the ANC emerged committed to fiscal and monetary discipline and stressing the importance of the private sector and the need to develop a favourable investment climate. Privatization, as well as nationalization, was cited as a policy option. No mention was made of the word 'socialism'.

On the campaign trail, Mandela went through a routine of explaining how the reconstruction and development programme would bring more jobs, more houses, better education and health services. His speeches tended to be dull and didactic, delivered in a stiff and wooden manner, something of an anticlimax after the frenzy and excitement surrounding his arrival. While promising a better future, he spent much time trying to damp down black expectations. Change, he warned, must be gradual and there must be no dislocation: 'Do not expect to be driving a Mercedes the day after the elections. You must have patience. You might have to wait for five years for results to show.' Narrowing the gap in income, employment and education between white and black would not be easy. Black demands for land and better living standards would have to be addressed without taking white assets.

Mandela was equally forthright in upbraiding his audience for bad habits: 'If you want to continue living in unbridled poverty, without clothes and food, then go and drink in shebeens. But if you want better things you must work hard. We cannot do it all for you; you must do it yourselves.' Mandela also took men to task for failing to undertake more domestic chores. 'I make my own bed. I can cook a decent meal. I can polish a floor,' he said. 'Why can't you do it?'

White audiences sometimes received the same stern treatment. When a white businessman in Potchefstroom expressed concern about the number of communists active within the ANC, Mandela responded by admonishing his audience for being selfish, hypocritical and racist, in the manner of a Dutch Reformed *predikant* railing against a congregation of sinners. The Communist Party and the ANC had fought the brutal system of apartheid together, he said. Together, members of both organizations had suffered harassment, arrest and imprisonment: 'Homes were broken up by a government professing to be Christian.' The Communist Party had done none of these things, but rather, 'You Christians have done them. Why should we listen to you about our comrades in the Communist Party?' Mandela continued. 'Is this not a sign of selfishness on your part? You have the temerity to come to me . . . [expecting that] I will say to an ally with whom we have fought and suffered that we will now abandon them, on the verge of victory − on your instructions. You, who have no concern for me.' Apartheid, he said, had been inflicted on masses of people by 'a community which claimed to be committed to religious values . . . You must stand ashamed. Your community used the word of God to justify [apartheid].'

At the behest of his campaign managers, Mandela and a group

of other elderly inmates, including Sisulu, Mbeki and Kathrada, returned to Robben Island in February 1994, accompanied by a horde of television crews and journalists. The event was full of good humour, rarely affording a glimpse of the anguish that prisoners there suffered. In the cramped space of cell number seven, Mandela demonstrated how, by standing at an angle, he had been able to wave his arms about for exercise. Looking through the barred window of the cell, he grinned broadly at the photographers outside. 'Could we have one serious one, please?' pleaded a photographer.

'My advisers tell me that on this occasion, I should talk about myself and not be shy,' he said. He spoke at length of the hardship of working in the lime quarry, of the isolation of his prison cell, of the stimulation of political discussions with his colleagues. Only once did he mention personal grief, in recalling the death of his mother and his oldest son. His favourite topic was the comradeship of his fellow prisoners. Taking a stroll in the lime quarry, he recalled, 'Quarry work was hard at first, but we sang freedom songs as we worked.' A television journalist asked, 'Could you sing a freedom song for us now, Mr Mandela?' and he duly obliged. When their duty to the media was done, Sisulu remarked, 'It's nice to know that I'll be going home at the end of the day.'

Mandela enjoyed a good working relationship with journalists. He was attentive to their needs and invariably courteous, apologizing whenever he was late. When a British journalist died in a car accident during the campaign, Mandela found time in the middle of a hectic schedule to phone his wife, speaking to her for nearly half an hour. He particularly enjoyed the company of women journalists, befriending two or three of them, with whom he used to flirt when the occasion permitted. One was Deborah Patta, a reporter for Johannesburg's Radio 702. During the visit to Robben Island, seeing her struggle with a heavy bag loaded with radio equipment, Mandela asked if he could carry it for her. Once, at the end of a summit meeting when journalists had been waiting for six hours, he spotted his friend: 'Deborah, I am most concerned. Have you had an opportunity to have any food today?'

Occasionally, amid the constant stream of promises about jobs and housing, the election campaign was enlivened by an exchange of insults. Mandela derided de Klerk's efforts to woo black voters for the National Party: 'They are a pathetic collection of weaklings unable to reconcile themselves with the fate of extinction that stares them in the face.' The National Party had never served the mass of South Africans: 'They only know how to serve the white community.'

De Klerk, for his part, avoided personal attacks on Mandela, but branded the ANC as 'a dangerous party', with no experience, no proven ability and addicted to policies of nationalization, communism and socialism which had failed everywhere else in the world: 'The ANC would cast us back into the Dark Ages. It is secretly controlled by communists, militants and extremists. They are quiet now but they will shout loudly if the ANC wins control.'

There was also controversy about a number of unsavoury characters standing as candidates, in particular Winnie Mandela. In December 1993, Winnie managed to claw her way back to election as president of the ANC's Women's League which entitled her to a place on the national executive committee. Despite her criminal conviction, she was then chosen as a candidate for the party list for parliament, in effect ensuring her a seat. The return of Winnie came as a nasty surprise to prominent figures in the ANC hierarchy who had assumed that her forced resignation from all ANC posts the year before had settled her fate. When Mandela was asked how he could justify having a convicted criminal on his list of candidates, he replied glibly that Winnie had been the choice of the people, a matter with which the ANC could not interfere.

The National Party was quick to take advantage of the event. Full-page newspaper advertisements appeared containing a large photograph of Winnie Mandela, her right arm raised in a clenched-fist salute, with a three-paragraph commentary beneath which said:

> On 10 July 1993 Winnie Mandela was convicted of kidnapping a child who later died from his wounds. On 8 December 1993 she was elected to be the most powerful woman in the ANC, the president of the ANC Women's League. After 27 April 1994, Mrs Mandela could be your new Minister of Law and Order, or even the Minister of Child Welfare . . . Only your vote can stop this.

The climax of the campaign was a televised debate between Mandela and de Klerk before a panel of journalists. The questions they were asked and the ground over which they skirmished, after weeks of campaigning, were largely familiar to viewers. What counted as much as content was style. De Klerk, more comfortable on television than Mandela, maintained a conciliatory countenance, admitting past wrongs, promising reconciliation, focusing on policy issues. Mandela was grim-faced, more aggressive, resorting to personal attacks on de Klerk's character and credibility, tending to dwell on the past evils of apartheid and sharply critical of the National Party's record.

But towards the end of the debate, thinking that he had been too harsh on de Klerk, Mandela made a dramatic gesture. 'The exchanges between Mr de Klerk and I should not obscure one important fact,' he said. 'I think we are a shining example to the entire world of people drawn from different racial groups who have a common loyalty, a common love, to their common country . . . In spite of my criticism of Mr de Klerk,' he went on, looking across to de Klerk, 'sir, you are one of those I rely upon . . . We are going to face the problems of this country together.' Then, reaching over to de Klerk, he said, 'I am proud to hold your hand for us to go forward.'

De Klerk clasped his hand and smiled wanly.

Throughout the election campaign, the threat of conflict edged ever closer. Buthelezi's answer to the ANC's refusal to countenance any further constitutional concessions was to reject Inkatha's participation in the election. His rhetoric became increasingly belligerent. 'It is impossible for me to lie to you and reassure you that the IFP's opposition to fighting the election under the present constitution will not bring casualties and even death,' he told a special Inkatha congress in Ulundi in January 1994. 'But we must resist the ANC and their communist surrogates. We are the only thing that stands in the way of their quest for power.' He urged followers to 'fight back', telling them, 'This is a region where we dominate. No foreign forces shall come into it to rule over us.'

To shore up his position, Buthelezi drew the Zulu king, Goodwill Zwelethini, into the confrontation. A weak, pusillanimous figure, Zwelethini had been pushed around for years by Buthelezi, who once spent a whole afternoon in the KwaZulu legislative assembly heaping abuse on the king, causing him such distress that he jumped from his seat and ran out of the chamber. Nevertheless, allegiance to the king was far more widespread among Zulus than any loyalty to Inkatha. His influence was much greater than Buthelezi's on his own.

The issue which helped galvanize Zwelethini was the ANC's insistence on removing the name of KwaZulu from the map of South Africa. In a memorandum sent to de Klerk in January, Zwelethini said that this rendered the new constitution 'so alien' that he felt obliged to reject it: 'It amounts to the expunging of the very name of my kingdom from the constitution of South Africa. We cannot, therefore, be expected to regard it as our constitution. This has sent shock waves throughout the psyche of every one of our Zulu subjects.'

Goaded on by Buthelezi, by February the king had become more ambitious. He now demanded a sovereign Zulu kingdom encompassing the whole of Natal, restoring what he claimed were its 1830s boundaries, before the era of white conquest. 'I am asking for something that belongs to me and my people – no one else,' he said. In public speeches, he began to use the same kind of rhetoric as Buthelezi: 'I will die rather than insult the memory of my great ancestral kings by handing over the land of their people to our political enemies.' He duly rejected the interim constitution and declared he would not abide by the election results.

Mandela was soon forced to concede that the threat to the election was far more serious than he had anticipated during the first flush of excitement about the prospect of majority rule. By the time the official deadline for the registration of parties had been reached on 12 February, the four key members of the Freedom Alliance – Inkatha, the AVF, the Conservative Party and Bophuthatswana – were all standing firm against participation in the election. Only Ciskei, whose military dictator, Brigadier Gqozo, had succumbed to pressure from his own troops worried about their career prospects, had thrown in its hand. Security briefings given to Mandela warned that right-wing groups were making serious preparations for resistance, stockpiling weapons, ammunition and medical supplies and organizing training. The briefings also warned of doubts about the loyalty of security force elements that might be required to deal with right-wing threats at the behest of an ANC-dominated government. The assessment of the government was that everything possible had to be done to avoid any kind of confrontation that would enable the alliance to make a common stand, drawing large numbers of their followers into the fray.

The possibility of active resistance to the election was reinforced by reports from the Goldstone commission investigating 'third force' activity. In February, Judge Goldstone acquired what he later described as 'convincing evidence' of 'a horrible network of criminal activity' involving high-ranking police officers in Pretoria, Inkatha and the KwaZulu police. This activity, according to Goldstone, included assassination, train massacres, hostel violence, gunrunning and the subversion of justice. Factories in the Transvaal had been used by a police covert unit to manufacture home-made guns which, along with large quantities of other weapons, had been smuggled to Inkatha and used in attacks in Natal and on the Reef. Goldstone emphasized that only a small group within the police force was involved, but he added, 'The whole illegal, criminal and oppressive system is still in place and its architects are in control of the South African police.' Among the officials whom Goldstone named were the head of police counter-intelligence and the police second-in-command. Goldstone recommended that the police commissioner himself should be removed from office forthwith.

In an attempt to draw the Freedom Alliance into the constitutional process, Mandela announced on 16 February a series of concessions he had previously spurned. These included the use of a double ballot for provincial and national elections; guarantees of wider powers for provincial government; and the renaming of Natal province to KwaZulu-Natal. Mandela also approved the inclusion in the constitution of a principle of 'internal' self-determination for groups sharing a common culture and language, intended to meet the anxieties of both Zulu and Afrikaner nationalists. He proposed that the issue of a *volkstaat* should be dealt with by authorizing the establishment of a twenty-member council, to be elected by MPs who supported the establishment of a *volkstaat*, enabling the idea to be pursued by constitutional means.

Mandela's concessions went a long way towards meeting the demands the Freedom Alliance had made in December. General Viljoen for one was ready to accept the inclusion of a principle of self-determination and a *volkstaat* council as a reasonable basis for agreeing to participate in the election.

But Buthelezi was determined to get more, believing that the election could not take place without Inkatha. Within hours, without waiting to consult his colleagues in the Freedom Alliance, he dismissed the concessions as nothing more than 'cheap politicking', adding, 'Mr Mandela's supposed concessions do not even begin to address our demands.'

To keep the electoral process on course, the Independent Electoral Commission imposed a final deadline for political parties to register of 4 March. A further short period was to be allowed after that date for political parties to present their list of candidates, thereby effectively confirming their participation in the election. The deadline set for that, eventually, was 11 March.

In a final effort to bring Inkatha into the election, Mandela arranged to meet Buthelezi in Durban on 1 March. Addressing a political rally beforehand, Mandela declared, 'I will go down on my knees to beg those who want to drag our country into bloodshed and to persuade them not to do so.' The meeting was only their fourth encounter in the four years since Mandela's release from prison. It brought no movement in the dispute over the constitution, but what it did produce was a deal of minor significance which was to have profound repercussions. In exchange for Mandela's agreement to submit their differences on the constitution to international mediation – a device which Buthelezi hoped would postpone the election altogether – Buthelezi agreed to register Inkatha for the election 'provisionally'.

Buthelezi's sudden turnabout on the election threw his allies in the Freedom Alliance into turmoil. Rival groups within each party argued over which course to take. General Viljoen and his fellow retired generals decided to keep open the possibility of right-wing participation in the election by registering a new party, the Freedom Front, arriving at the registration office with only minutes to spare before the deadline of midnight on 4 March. But their action was immediately denounced by other Volksfront leaders. The Conservative Party rejected participation in the election, as did Bophuthatswana's president, Lucas Mangope.

Mangope's refusal to take part in the election plunged Bophuthatswana into crisis. Accustomed to ruling with an iron rod and relying on the police to silence opponents, Mangope had little respect for the groundswell of public discontent building up. Technically, under South African law, Bophuthatswana was still an independent state. Nevertheless, the adult population of 2 million had been given the right to vote in the April election. Bophuthatswana's fate, once the election had taken place, was to be reincorporated into South Africa as part of North West Province. Civil servants and other public-sector workers, worried about their pensions and their future after the election, launched a wave of strikes. ANC supporters, resentful of Mangope's curbs on political activity, joined the fray.

Mangope's response to the disturbances was to ignore them. 'I love him dearly, but he is living in a different world,' reported South Africa's 'ambassador' to Bophuthatswana, Tjaart van der Walt. 'I failed to convey a sense of reality to him.' Mandela, in his conversations with Mangope, urging him to let the people of Bophuthatswana decide their future, also admitted failure: 'It seems I am talking to a stone. I think we have now given him enough time. I have tried to reason with him but it is clear he has no vision. Further pressures will be used and I have no doubt he will not be able to withstand them.'

Aided and abetted by ANC activists, the strikes spread through Bophuthatswana, crippling civil service departments, schools, telecommunications, health services, electricity supplies, transport and industry. Radio and television broadcasts went off the air. Running battles broke out between police and striking workers and students. Looters began to raid shopping centres. Policemen started to defect. The demands of the strikers no longer centred just on pension payments but included demands for Bophuthatswana's immediate reincorporation into South Africa, for free and fair elections and for Mangope's removal.

Facing popular revolt, Mangope took action with such potential for disaster that it suggested he had lost all touch with reason. On 9 March, he contacted General Viljoen, his Freedom Alliance partner, pleading for help from armed white paramilitary groups in the extremist Afrikaner Volksfront. Mangope's only stipulation was that Viljoen was not to include any AWB men, notorious for their lawless conduct and racist attacks on blacks. Viljoen agreed to cooperate. On 10 March, he mobilized 4,000 men and dispatched some 1,500 of them to Mangope's capital, Mmabatho, carrying only side-arms. The plan was for the AVF force to rendezvous at the town's airport with units from the Bophuthatswana Defence Force, which was commanded by white officers who would provide them with weapons. As they headed for Mmabatho, many right-wingers believed that they might be on the verge of establishing a *volkstaat*.

The plan went awry from the start. The AWB leader, Terre'-Blanche, learning of the instruction to mobilize, issued a call, broadcast on a right-wing radio station near Pretoria, for his supporters to join in. On the night of 10 March, hundreds of AWB members, armed with an assortment of shotguns and hunting rifles, crossed into Bophuthatswana in convoys of pick-up trucks. Their arrival provoked immediate dissension. White officers in the BDF ordered them out, but they refused to leave and went on what was described as 'a kaffir-shooting' expedition in the streets of Mmabatho, firing at random at bystanders and terrorizing local inhabitants. BDF troops mutinied, leaving Viljoen's men without weapons. The operation swiftly collapsed. As the AWB pulled out, one of its vehicles, carrying three men, was caught in a gunfight with troops manning a roadblock. One man was killed outright; his two companions survived but were executed by a policeman as they lay on the ground, in full view of television cameras. The scene was replayed on South African television again and again.

As the South African army moved into Mmabatho to restore a semblance of order, the fate of Mangope remained undecided. De Klerk was willing to allow him to stay in office, provided he agreed to participate in the election and allowed free political activity, but Mandela would have none of it, saying that Mangope had obstructed the electoral process, precipitated the crisis and should be removed from office immediately. On 12 March, the transitional executive council duly resolved that Mangope should be deposed. A deputation was sent to his luxurious house near Zeerust to tell him. Mangope tried to argue, but to no avail.

These events in Bophuthatswana produced dramatic changes across the political landscape. The threat of organized right-wing resistance to the election effectively collapsed. The AWB had been shown up to be nothing more than a murderous rabble. Fear of the extreme right gave way to ridicule. While Terre'Blanche tried to claim his men had scored a 'brilliant victory' in Bophuthatswana, many Afrikaners were disgusted by this farcical boasting carried out in the name of the Afrikaner people.

The Freedom Alliance also collapsed. Appalled by the fiasco of armed intervention in Bophuthatswana, Viljoen broke with the AVF and, with only minutes to spare before the deadline at midnight on 11 March, lodged a list of Freedom Front candidates ready to participate in the election, providing a vital route for the far-right to remain in the political process. Several prominent members of the Conservative Party announced they would join him.

Buthelezi's position became increasingly isolated. Unlike Viljoen, he failed to register a list of candidates, effectively eliminating himself and Inkatha from the election. But his options were limited. The only way he could prevent the ANC from winning control of KwaZulu-Natal at the polls was to stop the election taking place and force a postponement in the hope that a more favourable deal might be obtained at a later stage, possibly through international mediation. The only way of doing this was to threaten violence or to use it. Yet the events in Bophuthatswana had shown that Mandela and de Klerk were determined to protect the election process from obstruction and that the South African military were ready to support them. They were equally adamant that the election would not be postponed.

Ten days after Mangope's downfall, Buthelezi's last remaining ally, Brigadier Gqozo, capitulated. Faced with striking civil servants and rebellious police, Gqozo asked Pretoria to take over Ciskei's administration. Once again, South African troops moved in to secure control. 'Two down,' commented Joe Slovo gleefully, 'one more to go.'

In the wake of Bophuthatswana and Ciskei, ANC officials, sensing that another victory was within their reach, became increasingly arrogant. Slovo predicted that Buthelezi would be 'merely a smell in history' after the election, boasting that he himself, a non-Zulu, could get more votes in KwaZulu-Natal than Buthelezi. Ramaphosa spoke recklessly of the need for a military solution, having no concept of what it involved. For those in Ulundi, the message was all too clear: the ANC wanted to smash KwaZulu by force.

Yet Buthelezi's power base was far stronger than the glib pronouncements of ANC politicians suggested. In the rural backwaters of KwaZulu-Natal lived several million Zulus ready to obey the command of their traditional chiefs, the *amakhosi*, who remained loyal to Buthelezi. Moreover, Buthelezi had the support of the king. Talk of a military solution in these circumstances was nothing more than a dangerous fantasy. The military had neither the capacity to take control of Buthelezi's administration in Ulundi without precipitating a revolt nor the means to suppress the insurgency that was bound to follow.

The scale of violence was already immense. Some 10,000 people had died in KwaZulu-Natal over the previous six years. As the election approached, the conflict became ever more deadly. A group of fifteen ANC election workers, after putting up election posters, were shot and hacked to death. Election activity of any kind became a dangerous business in many areas. The level of intimidation from both sides soared by the day. 'Vote?' said a retired teacher in Port Shepstone. 'Why vote? Inkatha is killing us, the ANC is killing us. We are all going to die.'

After a visit to KwaZulu in March, vainly seeking local assistance for staging the election, the head of the Independent Electoral Commission, Judge Kriegler, warned Mandela and de Klerk that without a sufficient degree of stability and cooperation, free and fair elections in KwaZulu-Natal would be frustrated. Kriegler spoke of his determination to mount an election. KwaZulu alone possessed some 2.5 million potential voters, about 60 per cent of Natal's black electorate and some 12 per cent of the national electorate. Without its involvement, the overall election result would be seriously impaired. What was required, said Kriegler, was a political initiative.

Both sides meanwhile resorted to shows of strength. On 25 March, the ANC organized a march through the city centre of Durban. Despite fears of violence, the event passed off relatively peacefully. Inkatha then decided to respond in kind in Johannesburg, but with calamitous results.

On 28 March, thousands of Zulus, brandishing spears, clubs and cowhide shields, marched through the streets of the city's main business district to a rally at Library Gardens. The demonstration turned into a bloodbath when snipers opened fire from nearby buildings. For several hours, as Zulus went on the rampage, the streets in the city were scenes of chaos. At the ANC's headquarters at Shell House, ANC security guards shot and killed eight protesters who they claimed were trying to storm the building; eyewitnesses disputed their account. By the end of the day, fifty-three people were dead, most of them demonstrators.

The spectacle of central Johannesburg being turned into a war zone set off a wave of alarm throughout South Africa and far beyond its borders. The prospect of a peaceful election seemed increasingly remote. Public confidence in the transition and in the ability of South Africa's politicians to manage it successfully rapidly waned at home and abroad. In anticipation of further violence, a surge of stockpiling began – canned food, candles, batteries, Primus stoves, toilet paper, guns and ammunition. Foreign investors too lost faith, withdrawing funds and shelving plans.

The event also tarnished Mandela's reputation. He was not present when Zulu demonstrators arrived outside Shell House, but the following day, when police wanted to search the premises for weapons and for forensic evidence, he personally refused to allow them entry. Asked later at a press conference if, in a new government, his law and order minister would allow political opponents to set conditions for police probes into criminal activity, he replied, 'Let's face that when we are the government. I am entitled to negotiate with law and order officials.' The Johannesburg *Sunday Times* observed caustically, 'What a rare achievement for the ANC. It has succeeded in putting itself above the law *before* taking power. In most banana republics it happens the other way around.' A year later, Mandela admitted that he had instructed ANC security guards on the phone that day to shoot to kill demonstrators if necessary to protect the building.

The carnage in Johannesburg set Buthelezi off on another round of wild rhetoric. 'The Shell House massacre shows that we have now entered a final struggle to the finish between the ANC and the Zulu nation,' he said. The only way this could be prevented, he claimed, was to postpone the election.

With less than three weeks to go before the polls were due to open, Mandela, de Klerk, Buthelezi and Zwelethini finally agreed to meet to see if they could hammer out terms for Inkatha's participation in the election and decide about the king's future status. Mandela believed that the key to defusing the crisis was to prise Zwelethini away from Buthelezi. He drew up a proposal offering to entrench the Zulu monarchy with constitutional powers in the new constitution of KwaZulu-Natal and to provide it with a royal constabulary and a budget, giving the king a status not even accorded him under the KwaZulu constitution. The only condition Mandela wanted for all this was Zwelethini's support for the election. He hoped to be able to speak to Zwelethini in private in advance of formal discussions.

The meeting, held on 8 April at Skukuza, a lodge in the Kruger National Park, was ill-tempered. Mandela found no opportunity to talk to Zwelethini in private. Surrounded by Buthelezi's aides, the king appeared as obdurate and uncooperative as Buthelezi himself. For his part, Buthelezi rejected the idea that the king's requirements could be separated from Inkatha's demands and insisted that the election be postponed. Mandela refused: 'That day is sacrosanct.' The meeting ended in deadlock. The only matter they could agree on was to allow international mediation to proceed.

But even this ended in farce. A mediation team, including the former US secretary of state, Henry Kissinger, and the former British foreign secretary, Lord Carrington, arrived in Johannesburg only to find that the ANC and Inkatha could not agree its terms of reference. Buthelezi wanted mediation to include the election date; the ANC did not. The mediators promptly left.

With the failure of international mediation, Buthelezi had exhausted viable options. His strategy of obstruction had left him completely isolated. Out of reach of Buthelezi, King Zwelethini sent an emissary to Mandela telling him that he wanted to accept his offer on the Zulu monarchy. Inkatha was rumbling with discontent at the prospect of being denied a legitimate place in the new dispensation; civil servants in Ulundi were deeply worried about the risk to their salaries and pensions. Buthelezi himself faced nothing more than a future in the wilderness.

On 19 April, with only seven days remaining, Buthelezi capitulated, accepting the offer of a constitutional role for the Zulu monarchy and abandoning all his other demands.

In the early morning, as the sun rose over the green rolling hills of Natal, Nelson Mandela stood beside a grave in the grounds of a small rural school in Inanda, thinking of old friends like Oliver Tambo, Bram Fischer and Albert Luthuli who would not be voting that day. Mandela had chosen to come to Inanda, near Durban, to cast his vote, for it was there that the founding president of the ANC, John Dube, was buried, and it was the school that he had founded which was to serve as a polling station during the election. After laying a wreath on Dube's grave, he walked down the slope towards the school. 'I did not go into that voting station alone,' he said. 'I was casting my vote with all of them.'

He emerged from the polling station, his face wreathed in smiles, and spoke of a bright future. 'This is for all South Africans an unforgettable occasion,' he said. 'We are moving from an era of resistance, division, oppression, turmoil and conflict and starting a new era of hope, reconciliation and nation-building.'

In their millions, South Africans made their way to the polls, black and white citizens alike sharing a common determination to make the election a success. Many walked miles to reach a polling station. Some arrived on crutches and some in wheelchairs; some dressed in their Sunday-best clothes and some wore outfits they had made specially for the occasion.

Long queues formed outside polling stations, circling around city blocks and winding back along dirt roads and across fields. Many arriving in the early morning were still waiting to vote late in the afternoon, tired and hungry; some in rural areas had to vote by candlelight. Yet, hour after hour, they remained patient. And when they finally returned home, having voted, it was with a sense of profound fulfilment, not just from participating in the election of a new government, but from exercising a right which had been denied to most South Africans for so long. Time and again, voters leaving polling stations spoke of how their dignity had been restored.

On each of the four polling days, South Africa was more peaceful than it had been for many years. The fever of violence suddenly abated. Even the killing fields of KwaZulu-Natal fell silent. On the Witwatersrand, members of rival factions found themselves joining the same queue in townships, swapping complaints about the long delays.

For many whites, the experience of the election was as moving as it was for blacks. Standing side by side with blacks, waiting to vote, they felt a sense of their own liberation. The feelings of relief that the curse of apartheid had finally been lifted were as strong among the white community which had imposed it as among the blacks who suffered under it.

There were many incidents which marred the election. Afrikaner extremists staged a series of bomb attacks, one in the centre of Johannesburg's business district, another at its international airport, killing twenty-one civilians and injuring nearly 200 others. But the effect was to increase the resolve of voters not to be deterred.

The performance of the Independent Electoral Commission was woefully defective and at times so incompetent that it threatened the whole electoral process. Shortages of ballot papers, ballot boxes and other equipment created chaos at many polling stations. The counting process was equally flawed. Opportunities for electoral fraud proliferated. Serious disputes arose over the conduct of the election in KwaZulu-Natal.

But rising above all the muddle and confusion was the clear verdict of the people. By voting in their millions, free from intimidation and from violence and with great dignity, South Africans ensured that the birth of their democracy was a triumph.

The results, moreover, were broadly acceptable to all sides. The vast bulk of the black electorate provided the ANC with a handsome victory: the ANC obtained 62.6 per cent of the vote, taking 12.2 million of the 19.5 million valid votes cast, gaining 252 seats in the 400-seat National Assembly and winning control of seven of nine provincial assemblies. But the ANC failed to gain the two-thirds majority which would have given it the power to write the final constitution on its own, thereby helping to still the fears of minority groups that it would be tempted to ride roughshod over their interests. Some ANC officials were disappointed, but Mandela was not one of them. He wanted the final constitution to achieve a broader measure of support. A majority of the white, Coloured and Indian communities held fast to the National Party, giving it 20.4 per cent of the vote and control of the Western Cape province. Zulu nationalists voted for Inkatha, giving it only 10.4 per cent of the national poll but 50 per cent of the KwaZulu-Natal provincial vote and therefore control of the provincial assembly – a key factor in defusing the potential for another round of political warfare. Afrikaner nationalists, hoping for a *volkstaat*, put their trust in the Freedom Front, but in smaller numbers than General Viljoen had hoped: the Freedom Front obtained 425,000 votes, less than half the target Viljoen had set and only 2.17 per cent of the national poll. A diminished band of white liberals voted for the Democratic Party, giving it 1.7 per cent of the national poll. Finally, an insignificant rump of black radicals voted for the Pan-Africanist Congress, which won only 1.2 per cent of the vote.

The victory of the ANC at the polls was as much a personal tribute to Mandela as it was to the movement he led. His ordeal of imprisonment had never been forgotten by the people for whom he spoke and was duly acknowledged when the time came for them to vote. Time and again, it was said, 'He went to prison for us.' For blacks, the election was, above all, about liberation – a celebration of their freedom from white rule – and it was to Mandela's leadership that many attributed that liberation.

The transfer of power was accomplished in an atmosphere of much goodwill. Closing the book on three centuries of white rule, de Klerk chose words of encouragement fitting for such a historic moment: 'Mr Mandela has walked a long road and now stands at the top of a hill. A man of destiny knows that beyond this hill lies another and another. The journey is never complete. As he contemplates the next hill, I hold out my hand to Mr Mandela in friendship and cooperation.'

In his victory speech, Mandela was equally gracious. After congratulating de Klerk for the strong showing the National Party had made in the election, he continued: 'I also want to congratulate him for the . . . four years that we have worked together, quarrelled, addressed sensitive problems and at the end of our heated exchanges were able to shake hands and to drink coffee.'

At a victory celebration in the ballroom of the Carlton Hotel in Johannesburg, which he attended despite a heavy dose of flu, Mandela took to the floor with a slow, dignified solo dance before an exuberant crowd of ANC luminaries. The dance was quickly copied in the townships and became known as 'The President's Jive', performed to much merriment in a stiff, wooden manner with a fixed smile.

At every opportunity, Mandela sought to calm the apprehensions of whites and other minorities about the coming of majority rule.

The liberation struggle, he said, had not been a fight against any one group but against a system of oppression. 'Nothing we can say can fully describe the misery of our people as a result of the apartheid repression,' he told a multidenominational thanksgiving service in Soweto. 'But the day we have been fighting for has come. Let us forget the past.' He made an emotional plea for people of all races to 'hold hands' and unite: 'The time has come for men and women, Africans, Coloureds, Indians, whites, Afrikaners and English-speaking, to say: we are one country; we are one people.'

On the occasion of Mandela's election as president in parliament in Cape Town on 9 May, the same spirit of reconciliation prevailed. To thunderous applause, Mandela and de Klerk entered the chamber together. They walked down the central aisle, shook hands, then went their separate ways, Mandela to the government side, de Klerk to the opposition benches. Before the swearing-in ceremony, Mandela left his seat and crossed the floor several times to greet other opposition leaders, first embracing and shaking hands with Buthelezi, then General Viljoen and finally Clarence Makwetu of the Pan-Africanist Congress. Mandela's nomination as president was proposed by Albertina Sisulu and went unopposed. The chief justice, Michael Corbett, announced, 'I accordingly declare Mr Nelson Rolihlahla Mandela duly elected as the President of the Republic of South Africa.' The house erupted in cheering.

Only one note of discord was apparent. After Winnie Mandela had been sworn in as a member of parliament alongside her husband, she sat next to him briefly. But Mandela stared straight ahead, ignoring her, according her not the slightest sign of recognition, his face grim and cold. There was to be no reconciliation with Winnie.

The day of Mandela's inauguration, 10 May 1994, was marked by the greatest celebrations ever seen in South Africa. From all over the world, visiting dignitaries – heads of state, royalty and government leaders representing some 170 countries – gathered in Pretoria, as much in tribute to Mandela as to mark South Africa's rite of passage. The acclaim he received that day from around the world was unique: no other world leader could match the stature he had achieved in fighting for the cause of democracy. But even more important was the acclaim he was accorded by South Africans, both black and white. That too was unique. For in fighting for so long for national reconciliation in such a divided country, Mandela had earned measures of trust and admiration that were his alone.

In a glittering array, the guests assembled in the amphitheatre in front of Union Buildings, the monumental sandstone edifice designed by Herbert Baker, built during the years of British rule after the Anglo-Boer War and regarded ever since as the bastion of white power. Among the guests whom Mandela personally invited were three of his former prison warders.

Inevitably, there were family dramas beneath the surface. Winnie was among the first of the luminaries to arrive, resplendent in a long green silk dress. Initially she was shown to a seat among lesser dignitaries, sitting there in fury until she was allowed on to the main podium with a seat next to Zindzi. Mandela's son, Makgatho, remained in Durban, where he was busy with law exams. His daughter Makaziwe, an academic at the University of the Witwatersrand, attended, but she had previously made it known that she voted for the Democratic Party. Mandela's first wife, Evelyn, stayed at home in Cofimvaba. For his escort, Mandela chose Zenani, who sat alongside him on the podium, wearing an outsize top hat.

With all duly assembled, the new national flag was slowly raised to the accompaniment of two national anthems. One was 'Nkosi Sikelel' iAfrika', 'God Bless Africa', the song composed by the Xhosa teacher Enoch Sontonga at Johannesburg's Nancefield location in 1897 and first performed in 1899. It had made a strong impression at the inaugural meeting of the ANC in 1912 and was officially adopted as its anthem in 1925. The other was 'Die Stem van Suid Afrika', 'The Voice of South Africa', a poem written in 1918 by the Afrikaner nationalist writer C. J. Langenhoven and set to music in 1921. It had become South Africa's national anthem after the National Party victory in 1948. Neither group was familiar with the other's anthem, but for Mandela, standing to attention with his hand across his heart in a mark of respect, the playing of the two national anthems symbolized the true importance of the day's events.

In his inaugural address as president, Mandela emphasized the need for South Africans to build a new society from the legacy of apartheid: 'Out of the experience of an extraordinary human disaster that lasted too long must be born a society of which all humanity will be proud.'

He went on:

> The time for the healing of the wounds has come. The moment to
> bridge the chasms that divide us has come. The time to build is
> upon us.
>
> We have, at last, achieved our political emancipation. We pledge
> ourselves to liberate all our people from the continuing bondage of
> poverty, deprivation, suffering, gender and other discriminations . . .
>
> We enter into a covenant that we shall build the society in which
> all South Africans, both black and white, will be able to walk tall,
> without any fear in their hearts, assured of their inalienable right
> to human dignity – a rainbow nation at peace with itself and the
> world.

Towards the end of his speech, the 4,000 guests rose spon-
taneously to their feet for an ovation, in a moment of genuine
emotion, as he declared, 'Never, never and never again shall it be
that this beautiful land will again experience the oppression of one
by another and suffer the indignity of being the skunk of the world.'

As the cheering died down, from a distance, across the hills of
the Muckleneuk Ridge, came the roar of formations of jet fighters
and helicopters trailing the national flag. And as the squadrons
passed overhead in a final affirmation of white loyalty to black
rule, saluting their new commander-in-chief, the crowds below
erupted with an outpouring of enthusiasm. Many who witnessed
that moment of national catharsis were moved to tears.

CHAPTER 28

Reinventing South Africa

No sooner had one struggle ended than the next began. At the age of seventy-five, after fifty years as a political activist, Mandela embarked on a campaign for economic advancement. In the aftermath of his election victory, the mood of expectation was high. The electorate was impatient for change. Mandela's pledges – more jobs, more housing, better education and health services – still reverberated across the country. Yet the reality was that this second struggle was going to be even more difficult than the one for political rights.

Mandela's achievement in securing a negotiated revolution in South Africa in collaboration with its white rulers meant that he inherited an administration both powerful enough and sufficiently amenable to begin undertaking the ambitious targets he had set for his government. The old white establishment, comforted by de Klerk's presence in the cabinet as a deputy president, by Mandela's constant efforts to reassure whites about their security and by the guarantee on jobs and pensions given them under the constitution, adapted to the new government with remarkably few qualms. So peaceful was the transfer of power that it brought about a swift resurgence of confidence in the future among the white community, on whose skills, expertise and capital the fortunes of South Africa still largely depended, as Mandela publicly acknowledged.

Yet the system he inherited had been designed largely to promote white interests. Other than parliament, all the main institutions – the civil service, the security forces, the business community, the universities, the media, the stock exchange, the banks – were dominated by whites. All required eventual transformation, but some changes were particularly urgent. South Africa needed not only a new administration capable of undertaking major programmes of economic and social development but also a whole new structure of provincial and local government as well, involving the incorporation of former homeland territories into nine new provinces and the redesign of some 800 segregated local authorities into 300 new multiracial municipal governments. The police service required an overhaul to make it more acceptable to local communities. The new national defence force required reorganization to absorb units from Umkhonto we Sizwe and former homeland armies. In short, Mandela's task was to reinvent South Africa.

South Africa possessed considerable assets with which to fashion its future. These included one of the world's richest stores of minerals, with 44 per cent of world diamond reserves, 82 per cent of manganese reserves and 64 per cent of platinum-group metal reserves. It was the world's largest producer of gold, mining a third of world production. Its financial, banking and legal systems were well established and efficient; the Johannesburg stock exchange was the tenth largest in the world. Its manufacturing base, though overprotected and uncompetitive by world standards, was capable of considerable expansion. The infrastructure of roads, railways, ports and airports was well developed. Telephone and electricity services were reliable. Universities and technical colleges turned out a ready supply of competent graduates. In statistical terms, South Africa, with a gross domestic product of $120 billion, ranked as one of the world's twenty-five largest economies. In Africa, it stood out as a giant, with an economic hinterland stretching as far north as Zaïre.

Beneath such promising statistics, however, lay a massive disparity in wealth. According to the 1994 United Nations Human Development Report, if white South Africa was treated as a separate country, its standard of living would rank twenty-fourth in the world, just below Spain's; black South Africa on the same basis would rank one hundred and twenty-third, below Lesotho and Vietnam. The average white income was eight times greater than the average black income. Whites, comprising 13 per cent of the population, earned 61 per cent of total income. Although the black middle class was growing apace, its share of total income was still comparatively small. Barely 2 per cent of all private-sector assets were black-owned. On an overall basis, South Africa ranked only ninety-third in the world of terms of human development. Out of a population of 40 million, 22 million lacked adequate sanitation, including 7.5 million in urban areas; 12 million lacked clean water supply; 7.8 million lived in shacks; more than 1 million were homeless; 23 million had no access to electricity; and some 2 million children were without schools. Almost half of all households in South Africa lived below the poverty line; a quarter lived on an income of less than half of the poverty-line income; some 8 million were estimated to be 'completely destitute'. A third of the population was illiterate.

The economic legacy bequeathed to Mandela's administration was also none too healthy. South Africa was emerging from the longest recession in its history. For twenty years it had suffered from double-digit inflation. The government's domestic debt was huge. The cost of debt service and current expenditure consumed 92 per cent of government revenue, leaving only 8 per cent for capital spending on development.

The unemployment figures were daunting. Only about half of the economically active population held formal-sector jobs. Several million more earned a living in the informal sector – hawkers, small traders, domestics, backyard businesses. Even so, the official unemployment rate was calculated as 33 per cent. A high proportion of the estimated 5 million unemployed possessed no skills or training and had little prospect of ever finding a job. Of the 450,000 new entrants to the labour market in 1994, only 27,000 were expected to be able to find a job. On average, the formal sector of the economy could absorb no more than 6 per cent of new entrants to the labour market. When the new government advertised civil service vacancies for 11,000 managers, clerks and cleaners, more than 1.5 million people applied.

Mandela's approach to tackling this economic mountain was cautious and conservative. He was determined to convince foreign and local investors about the government's commitment to fiscal discipline and sound economic management. South Africa's future prospects depended heavily on attracting foreign capital. Local resources were not sufficient to raise the annual growth rate much above 3 per cent. Merely to absorb the annual number of new entrants into the labour market required an annual growth rate of

6 per cent. To make any inroads into the rate of unemployment required a growth rate of between 8 and 10 per cent. Without foreign investment, none of Mandela's ambitious targets for social and economic development could be achieved. Yet foreign investors were reluctant to commit themselves until they could see something of the new government's track record.

The slow pace of change led to increasing restlessness. Apart from two measures that Mandela swiftly introduced – free health care for young children and pregnant mothers and primary school feeding schemes – there was little tangible evidence of his government delivering the improvements it had promised. Fewer houses were built on government initiatives in Mandela's first year in office than in de Klerk's last year. Labour unions, which had helped put the ANC in power, began to flex their muscles, wanting rewards for their endeavours. A spate of strikes and threatened strikes suggested that industrial stability would be difficult to achieve.

Mandela also had to contend with the legacy of protest politics from the apartheid era. The culture of protest ran deep. Township residents accustomed to years of boycotting rent and service charge payments in protest against apartheid policies showed little inclination to start paying their dues even though a new government was in power. Outbreaks of lawlessness were commonplace. Students seized teaching staff as hostages, vandalized buildings and looted shops. Striking policemen set up roadblocks. Nurses deliberately spread viruses among their patients. Prison warders allowed dangerous criminals to escape. Former MK guerrillas in the defence force absconded without leave. Taxi drivers blockaded central Johannesburg. Squatters invaded vacant houses. Shop workers went on a looting rampage. Added to all this was an epidemic of violent crime. Some 200 policemen were killed during 1994.

The scale of disorder was serious enough to prompt Mandela to read the riot act. Opening the second session of parliament in February 1995, he launched into a tirade against workers and students who resorted to acts of anarchy and disruption to secure their demands. 'Let it be clear to all that the battle against the forces of anarchy and chaos has been joined. Let no one say that they have not been warned,' he said. 'I speak of those who engage in such totally unacceptable practices as the murder of police officers, the taking of hostages, riots, looting, the forcible occupation of public highways, vandalization of public and private property and so on.' He went on, 'Some have misread freedom to mean licence . . . popular participation to mean the ability to impose chaos.' But, he warned, 'let me make abundantly clear that the small minority in our midst which wears the mask of anarchy will meet its match in the government we lead.'

Mandela was equally blunt about those who demanded immediate benefits from his government:

> The government literally does not have the money to meet the demands that are being advanced. Mass action of any kind will not create resources that the government does not have. All of us must rid ourselves of the wrong notion that the government has a big bag full of money. The government does not have such riches. We must rid ourselves of the culture of entitlement which leads to the expectation that the government must promptly deliver whatever it is that we demand.

It was a sober message to deliver after so much euphoria over the coming of majority rule. What Mandela was demanding was discipline and belt-tightening from a population which had been led to expect something different.

Reflecting on the results of his first year in office, Mandela said he was satisfied with the pace of change. 'People must be patient,' he said. 'They must give us time.' Yet there was a noticeable lack of decisiveness about Mandela's administration, a lack of urgency in determining priorities and tackling them, a tendency to let government business drift. It was as though the sheer size of the agenda it faced was too daunting. For those hoping for faster results, there was a growing sense of disillusionment.

The advances that Mandela made in pursuing national reconciliation were far more immediate. National reconciliation became his personal crusade. From the moment of his inauguration as president, he strove to establish a new racial accord, constantly reassuring the white minority of their well-being under majority rule. Addressing a huge crowd on the lawns below Union Buildings on inauguration day, he urged a spirit of forgiveness. '*Wat is verby is verby,*' he said in Afrikaans. 'What is past is past.'

Towards his old political adversaries, he remained magnanimous. He described de Klerk as 'one of the greatest sons of Africa', praising him for his contribution to establishing democracy. He had kind words for P. W. Botha, 'a first-class gentleman', he said, 'the real forerunner, paving the way for eventual negotiations'. Every year, Mandela made the point of phoning Botha on his birthday, to wish him many happy returns. When asked by a television interviewer who his hero was, he nominated the former prisons minister, Kobie Coetsee, explaining that Coetsee had chosen to meet him at a time when government enmity towards the ANC was at a peak. Coetsee was duly rewarded under the new dispensation by being named president of the senate.

He was assiduous in cultivating right-wing politicians, determined to avert the risk of right-wing resistance. He developed his warm relationship with General Viljoen, grateful for the role he had played in helping to keep right-wing extremists inside the political process in the run-up to the election. In parliament, Viljoen's small band of Freedom Front members duly became Mandela's most loyal opposition. Viljoen spoke of 'the great mutual trust and regard' between himself and Mandela. Mandela also made approaches to the recalcitrant white Conservative Party, which had boycotted the election, inviting its leader, Ferdi Hartzenberg, for a series of talks. Even the extremist Afrikaner Weerstandsbeweging was included in discussions with government ministers. When the Volkstaat Council began its deliberations soon after the election in 1994, it was accorded due recognition.

The gestures of goodwill he made were manifold. In his opening address to the new parliament in Cape Town, he recited a moving poem by an Afrikaner poet, Ingrid Jonker, who had committed suicide in 1965, noting how her dream of emancipation had now been fulfilled. He spoke again in Afrikaans when appealing to civil servants to support the reforms in government policy. In changing the name of his official residence in Cape Town from Westbrook, he chose an Afrikaans name, Genadendal, meaning 'Valley of Mercy'. He made the point of attending a service at the Nederduitse Gereformeerde Kerk in Pretoria, the church to which Verwoerd and Vorster, Strijdom and Malan had belonged, surprised by the warmth of his reception from the congregation: 'If I had gone there four years ago the security would have had to protect me against assault, against people who would want to kill me. This time they were there to protect me from being killed out of love.'

In one particularly memorable event, he organized what he called 'a reconciliation lunch', bringing together the wives and widows of former apartheid leaders and leading black activists. To his presidential residence in Pretoria, Mahlamba' Ndlopfu, came the widows of John Vorster and Hans Strijdom, of Steve Biko and Moses Kotane. 'These are the wives of the heroes of both sides,' said Mandela, introducing his seventeen guests to the press on the lawn before lunch. 'We have fought our fights in the past. We have forgotten it now. We must build a new South Africa. By attending this occasion, each one is putting an important brick in that new building we are putting up.'

One of the widows he invited, Betsie Verwoerd, replied that at the age of ninety-four she was too infirm to travel to Pretoria for the occasion, so Mandela made arrangements instead to pay a courtesy call on her two weeks later at her home in Orania, a town on the banks of the Orange River in the Northern Cape province which Afrikaner *bittereinders* had preserved as a small whites-only colony.

The *burgemeesters* of Orania gathered in their Sunday best to greet Mandela as he arrived in an air force helicopter and conducted him to the nearby community hall where Betsie Verwoerd, a frail, diminutive figure, was waiting for him with tea and traditional *koeksusters*. After tea, she emerged with Mandela to meet the press, clutching a two-page speech she had written to thank him for coming. But when she tried to read it without her spectacles, she became distressed. Peering over her shoulder, Mandela began softly prompting her in Afrikaans, a half-smile on his lips: '. . . I ask the president to consider the *volkstaat* with sympathy and also to decide the fate of Afrikaners with wisdom.' When she had finished, she looked up to him towering above her with a radiant smile of thanks.

Even more remarkable was the invitation to lunch he sent to Percy Yutar, the prosecutor in the Rivonia trial who had argued for Mandela to be given the death sentence and expressed regret when this did not happen. Yutar's name was still reviled by liberal lawyers for his conduct of the trial. But Mandela took the view that Yutar had played only a 'small part' in a grand system driven by politicians. Like others who witnessed Mandela's efforts at reconciliation, Yutar was struck by awe at the occasion: 'I wonder in what other country in the world you would have the head of the government inviting someone to lunch who prosecuted him thirty years ago. It shows the great humility of this saintly man.'

So much attention did Mandela devote to reassuring whites that black critics claimed he was making greater efforts on their behalf than on addressing black grievances. Mandela brushed aside such criticism: 'We had to allay the fears of whites to ensure the transition process took place smoothly. If we had not done so, the civil war that was threatening would have broken out.' Reassuring whites, he said, involved no cost. He pointed to opinion polls which showed that his support among the white community had risen from about 1 per cent before the election to more than 50 per cent, thus helping to ensure political stability.

The climax to Mandela's efforts came during the 1995 Rugby World Cup tournament, which South Africa hosted – the largest sporting event in its history. Rugby was a sport embraced with almost religious fervour by Afrikaners. During the apartheid era, when South Africa was expelled from world rugby, the blow to Afrikaner morale was far greater than any economic sanction or oil embargo. The black population generally ignored rugby, their passion being soccer. Rugby was regarded as a 'Boer game', a symbol of white supremacy. On Robben Island, Mandela used to infuriate warders by supporting any team that was playing against South Africa's national team, the Springboks.

When South Africa won approval to hold the 1995 World Cup, Mandela began to take a personal interest in the event. Although there was strong pressure within the ANC to give a new name to the national team, Mandela decided against any change. He developed a warm relationship with François Pienaar, the newly appointed Springbok captain, whom he met in Union Buildings in Pretoria in June 1994. Pienaar confessed to reporters beforehand that he was nervous about meeting a man of such standing. But he emerged with Mandela smiling and readily adapted to the role of ambassador for the 'new South Africa' that Mandela hoped he would be. He promised to instruct all members of his team to learn and sing the words of 'Nkosi Sikelel' iAfrika'.

For their team song, the Springboks adopted an old miners' song in Xhosa, 'Tshotsholoza', which was popular with soccer fans and which Mandela and his fellow prisoners on Robben Island used to sing when working in the lime quarry. As part of their preparations for the World Cup, team members spent an hour a day with a black coach teaching them the correct pronunciation of the Xhosa words. 'Tshotsholoza' soon became a hit in the white community.

White enthusiasm for the rugby festival was overwhelming. But it was Mandela who turned it into a national event. He arrived at the Springbok training ground near Cape Town, gave his personal blessing to the squad, all but one of them white, and urged blacks to rally behind them: 'We have adopted these young men as our boys, as our own children, as our own stars. This country is fully behind them. I have never been so proud of our boys as I am now and I hope that that pride we all share.'

In the week leading up to the final match between South Africa and New Zealand on 24 June, Mandela took to wearing a green rugby supporter's cap, adorned with the Springbok emblem. 'This cap does honour to our boys,' he told a black crowd. 'I ask you to stand by them, because they are our kind.' With boyish enthusiasm, he visited the team at their practice fields and in their dressing rooms. Pienaar responded by saying he would 'play his heart out' for the president.

As the team took to the field at Ellis Park, Mandela emerged on to the pitch wearing the green and gold number 6 jersey of the team captain, Pienaar, and a Springbok cap, sending the overwhelmingly white crowd into a frenzy of enthusiasm and excitement. The stadium reverberated with chants of 'Nel-son! Nel-son!'

The match produced one of the most intense afternoons of physical endeavour and emotion that any of those present were ever likely to witness. At full time, the two teams were locked at 9–9, so extra time was necessary. Seven minutes from the end, a drop goal gave South Africa victory. The crowd went wild. Presenting Pienaar with the trophy, Mandela said, 'Thanks for what you have done for South Africa.' Pienaar replied, 'Thanks for what *you* have done to South Africa.'

The whole of South Africa erupted in celebration, blacks as joyful as whites. Johannesburg became a giant street party. In the northern suburbs, domestic workers rushed out on the streets shouting, 'We've done it! We've done it!' Never before had blacks had cause to show such pride in the efforts of their white countrymen. It was a moment of national fusion that Mandela had done much to inspire.

In selecting ministers for his new government, Mandela made one decision which he swiftly came to regret. The appointment of Winnie Mandela as deputy minister for arts, culture, science and technology caused immediate controversy. Her record as a common criminal, her involvement in the criminal activities of the Mandela Football Club, her reputation as 'a deliberate and unblushing liar', as confirmed by a high court judge, and the allegations of fraud made against her by an internal ANC commission of inquiry all served to make her a perverse choice for a government anxious to establish its international credentials for probity. Mandela's reasoning was that at a time of reconciliation, when South Africans were being urged to move on from the past, there was no reason why Winnie should be excluded. The new coalition government, he said, with its mixture of ANC, National Party and Inkatha representatives, contained a number of people 'whose hands were dripping with blood'. Moreover, so the reasoning went, Winnie was likely to do less damage inside the government than outside it. This was a serious error of judgement.

Winnie's link to the murder of Stompie Moeketsi Seipei would not go away. Within days of assuming office, she was obliged to take legal action to silence her fellow convict, Xoliswa Falati, who emerged from prison, after serving eight months of her two-year sentence, seeking revenge and announcing she would reveal details of 'atrocities' she claimed Winnie had perpetrated. In parliament, the liberal opposition Democratic Party launched a ferocious attack on Winnie, producing a list of 'unsolved crimes' with which it alleged Winnie was associated.

Winnie's response was to blame the apartheid regime and to exonerate herself. She had been 'criminalized' by an apartheid court, she said, 'a court which studiously ignored the black perspective, black culture, black values and judged everyone by white standards'.

She denied any personal responsibility for what had happened to Stompie:

My deepest regret is that I failed Stompie, that I was unable to protect him from the anarchy of those times and he was taken from my house and killed, adding his life to hundreds, perhaps thousands, who fell victim to the terror of intolerance and the injustice of the kangaroo courts . . .

I lived in the terror of those times and was repeatedly burnt by its fires. I did not flinch. I did not run away . . . And there are men in this gathering who, in the calm safety of their Houghtons, literally fiddled and mounted the steps of power, while our townships burned, who today dare to question my membership of this august House. I say to them, examine your lives and compare it with mine and then tell me, in all sincerity, who is more fit for this House.

As well as old scandals, new ones surfaced. Hoping to make money out of a diamond deal, Winnie hired an executive jet and dispatched her son-in-law Prince Musi Dhlamini, Zenani's husband, to Angola, to collect a package of diamonds from President Eduardo dos Santos. In court, Prince Dhlamini testified that he took orders from 'Mummy' unquestioningly. The deal fell through when dos Santos said he knew nothing of it, leaving Winnie with a bill for a charter flight which she refused to pay until ordered by a court to do so.

Winnie's other money-making activities also aroused controversy. Using the name of the ANC's Women's League, she linked up with a foreign film star, Omar Sharif, to establish a tourist venture called Road to Freedom Tours, aimed at encouraging black Americans to visit South Africa's 'sites of struggle', like Mandela's birthplace and his prison cell on Robben Island. Other officials of the Women's League were furious when they learned of what had happened without their knowledge. Eleven of them, including the treasurer, Adelaide Tambo, the widow of Oliver Tambo, resigned in February 1995 in protest against Winnie's 'bad leadership, undemocratic practices and unaccountability'. They presented a memorandum to the ANC listing her 'offences' and accusing her of 'using her position as president of the Women's League to further her own financial and political aims'.

Another public row resulted from Winnie's blatant use of her office as an arts minister to promote a private business venture between her daughter Zindzi and American concert promoters. When faced with criticism from the local entertainment industry,

Winnie responded by accusing both the media and the local entertainment industry of being racist. Her ministry, she said, took a
'dim view' of the pop group the Rolling Stones for using a white
promoter for a forthcoming tour of South Africa rather than
a black one, suggesting that they too were motivated by racial
prejudice.

Winnie also used her ministerial position in an attempt to influence the outcome of a legal dispute between a local government
agency, the Pretoria regional services council, and an electrical
contractor, Costa Livanos, who was claiming 22 million rands in
damages for breach of contract. Writing on ministerial notepaper,
she criticized the regional services council, reminded its chairman
that she was 'a minister in the government that employs you' and
suggested that he should settle the matter out of court. In arbitration
proceedings, the regional services council won its case.

Other scandals involved a charitable agency called Coordinated
Anti-Poverty Programmes (Capp), which Winnie had set up in 1992
after being forced to resign from her ANC posts. Ostensibly Capp's
purpose was to help destitute communities, but critics claimed it
was no more than a vehicle for Winnie's self-promotion. Capp
obtained contributions from local businesses and foreign embassies,
but was lax about keeping proper accounts. The focus of its
attention was several squatter communities near Johannesburg, in
particular Phola Park, a fractious and often violent camp on the
eastern outskirts of the city. Winnie's style was to pay regular visits
to Phola Park, gaining huge popularity as the result of the promises
she made. When improvements in Phola Park occurred – a new
school, a larger clinic, a sewerage system – Winnie took the credit
for them. But local leaders and developers claimed her role was a
sham. The improvements there were due not to Winnie, they said,
but to the efforts of other organizers. 'The only thing she has
brought to Phola Park is promises,' said one local leader. According
to one of its employees, the only project Capp actually undertook
was to distribute tents donated by local businesses to residents of
Phola Park.

In February 1995, Capp was cited by the Registrar of Companies
for failing to file financial statements as required by law. A
subsequent examination of the accounts showed that Winnie, as
chief executive officer, had made huge expense claims on the

organization, including an item of 67,200 rands for repairs and maintenance for six cars.

Even though Mandela had pledged 'to put the country on a new moral footing', he seemed paralysed by Winnie's antics. One by one, the news items mounted up: a controversy over huge expense claims she made for her bodyguards; a questionable friendship with a convicted illegal diamond trader who lent her a house in Cape Town; a raid she made on the offices of a traditional leaders' organization, seizing furniture and equipment; reports of her disruptive conduct in the ministry of arts, culture, science and technology. When the Canadian government refused her permission to enter Canada because of her criminal record, she resorted to publicly attacking it. Through it all, Mandela dithered. 'He seemed to be so tired of the issue,' said a member of a Women's League deputation who went to see him to complain about Winnie's activities.

Only when Winnie turned to criticizing his government was Mandela provoked into action. Addressing a crowd at a funeral for a black police officer in Soweto on 5 February, Winnie accused the government of doing more to appease whites than to redress the racial iniquities of apartheid. She described the ANC's 'over-indulgence' in reconciliation as a weakness and she challenged ANC leaders to demonstrate whether 'we are in power or just in government'. Stung by the criticism, Mandela ordered her to retract her remarks or face dismissal.

Winnie's initial response was to issue not so much an apology as an explanation. In a letter submitted to Mandela on 13 February, she wrote:

> In this note I will try to clarify my motives and intentions in making the said comments. First and foremost, I must make it abundantly clear that it was not my intention to insult the President or to embarrass the Government of National Unity. I was merely trying to assure the masses that the Government and the ANC were aware of and concerned about the flaws that the Government must deal with.
>
> The impression of the people is that we neither care nor know about these things. I was trying to correct that perception. If in doing so I created a different impression, that was not my intention.
>
> I have always been an honest and forthright member of the ANC.

I have tried to be equally faithful to the Government, and I mean to remain so.

Mandela swiftly rejected Winnie's 'explanation' and demanded a proper apology. Another letter was drafted that day, which she was then obliged to sign:

> I would like to apologize most sincerely for the impression the speech caused that I sought to condemn the Government of National Unity.
>
> If such criticism of the Government were intended, I could not have excluded myself as a member of the Government.
>
> Indeed, I am aware that the GNU is concerned to end racism in our society, is determined to address this matter vigorously and has instituted programmes in pursuit of this objective.
>
> I would also like to reaffirm my commitment to the concept and practice of collective responsibility on the part of Cabinet ministers and deputy ministers and, on this basis, am prepared to serve the Government loyally, working with all the members of the Government.
>
> I sincerely regret any embarrassment that the speech might have caused the President and the Government as a whole and therefore accept this censure which the delivery of the speech at the funeral occasioned.

But having signed the apology, Winnie then made her real feelings clear in another letter to Mandela written on 15 February, in which she objected to being 'made to sign, under duress':

> As you will know, when you were forcibly prevented from exercising your inalienable right to free speech, I and the children, with others, spoke up for humanity.
>
> Circumstances forced me into becoming a political activist. The children and I suffered for refusing to succumb to the oppression of the apartheid regime. We were banned and banished and were also jailed and physically manhandled.
>
> I continue the long tradition of speaking without fear on matters that are vital to all the people of South Africa.
>
> As it happened, in a recent speech, I did not realize – as I have since been advised – that in certain respects I no longer have the right of free speech. I have made amends for not fully appreciating the consequences of that, and realize that in some respects, my public statements must be limited.

She then stated her objections to signing the apology: 'I fail to see how I am supposed to tolerate such continuing violation of my constitutional and fundamental rights.'

One week later, defying Mandela's specific instructions that she should not travel abroad, Winnie set off for a tour of West Africa. While she was away, yet another scandal broke.

On 1 March, fraud squad officers, backed up by armed police, raided Winnie's mansion in Soweto and the offices of Capp in Johannesburg, seizing documents, letters and bank statements. Winnie was accused of accepting payments of 72,000 rands from a private building firm in exchange for using her influence to secure housing contracts. Returning from West Africa the following day, Winnie immediately launched into legal action, challenging the validity of the police search warrants. She claimed she was the victim of a 'diabolical' vendetta by 'charlatans and cowards' and 'the forces of reaction'. The police, she said, merely wanted to discredit her:

> I feel betrayed. This has been the ultimate humiliation by my own people. This is not the South Africa I ruined my life for ... I am embittered and annoyed by the secret manoeuvrings in our movement. The last three weeks have been the most traumatic period of my political life. As a family, we have never felt so helpless, so unprotected.

The range of charges against Winnie was extraordinary. They included open defiance of the president; using her public office for personal advantage; misappropriation of funds; and receiving kickbacks. Yet still Mandela prevaricated. When a court ruled on 22 March that the police search warrants used to raid her house were defective and ordered the return of Winnie's documents, she returned to the fray with a vengeance, openly challenging Mandela: 'I owe my allegiance to the people of South Africa. It is only they who will determine my political future. No man has the capacity to undermine that will – no matter who that individual might be.'

Addressing a meeting of the ANC's Women's League in Port Elizabeth on 25 March, she resumed her attack on Mandela's government, accusing it of being indifferent to the plight of the poor: 'Nothing has changed. In fact, your struggle seems much worse than before, when the fight was against the Boers.' She also criticized government expenditure in connection with a state visit by Britain's Queen Elizabeth, an event in which Mandela took particular pride.

On 27 March, Mandela finally sacked his estranged wife from the government. He gave no reason other than to say that the decision had been taken 'in the interests of good government and to ensure the highest standards of discipline'. He suggested, politely, that Winnie might like 'to review, and to seek to improve on, her own conduct in positions of responsibility'.

But Winnie was not yet finished. In a final act of revenge, she challenged her dismissal in the courts, claiming that proper procedures had not been followed and enlisting the support of Chief Buthelezi, the minister of home affairs, a man only too willing to help embarrass the ANC. Rather than face legal proceedings, Mandela was obliged to reinstate her briefly, before sacking her for a second time.

It was an episode which left Mandela's government looking weak, indecisive and incompetent.

Mandela now proceeded with plans to divorce Winnie, hoping that the matter could be settled in private. He sent several emissaries to her. 'I asked her to settle it amicably and not to wash our dirty linen in public,' he said. But Winnie fought on relentlessly, opposing divorce to the last. Mandela's case was that his marriage had irretrievably broken down as a result of Winnie's 'brazen public conduct and infidelity'. Winnie argued that reconciliation was still possible.

The hearing came before the Rand Supreme Court in Johannesburg in March 1996. Mandela arrived there, grim-faced, wearing a grey three-piece suit, ready to take the witness stand for the first time since the Rivonia trial in 1964. Winnie, elegantly attired in a gold and black dress, still attractive at the age of sixty-one, sat at a long wooden table only ten feet away. Apart from a curt handshake, they avoided looking at each other.

Called as the first witness, Mandela confirmed that when announcing his separation from Winnie in 1992, he had issued a statement expressing affection and respect for his wife. He explained: 'This is my wife, with whom I had in the past shared some of the happiest moments in our lives. I wanted to make the parting as painless as possible, especially because of the children. I knew it would be a terrible experience for them and therefore I expressed affection for her. And respect, because I respect her very highly.'

Later that year, amid gossip about Winnie's affair with the lawyer Dali Mpofu, a local newspaper editor had brought him a copy of a love letter written by her to Mpofu which the paper was about to publish. 'The contents of the letter, My Lord, were incompatible with a marriage relationship and even if there was a possibility of reconciliation, it confirmed my decision never to reconcile with the defendant.'

They had not talked to each other 'for years', except for 'the exchange of pleasantries'. Winnie's avowals of affection for him at political rallies were 'cosmetic and hypocritical'. The marriage existed 'only on paper'.

He said he had delayed divorce proceedings because he did not want it to be thought that they were connected with Winnie's trial over the Stompie affair, in which he believed she was innocent.

He was asked by his lawyer, Wim Trengove, about an affidavit Winnie had obtained as part of her defence from his kinsman Kaizer Matanzima, the former ruler of the Transkei, who had been his close friend for many years and who had once tried to woo Winnie. According to Matanzima, writing in his capacity as paramount chief of Western Thembuland, under customary law the divorce could not proceed until mediation had been attempted by tribal elders. Members of the Thembu royal house had tried to intervene, but Mandela had refused to meet them and had failed to accord them 'proper respect'.

Trengove told the court that it was 'inappropriate' for Matanzima to 'meddle' in the Mandela relationship. His status as paramount chief had been accorded him by the apartheid regime. Mandela regarded him 'as a sell-out – in the proper sense of the word', said Trengove. Moreover, Matanzima had once competed for Winnie's affections before her marriage, 'but lost out to the plaintiff'. Trengove nevertheless wanted to ascertain Mandela's view on the issue of tribal mediation in matrimonial disputes.

'I respect custom but I am not a tribalist,' said Mandela. 'I fought as an African nationalist and I have no commitment to the custom of any particular tribe.' Custom was not 'moribund', he added:

It is a social phenomenon which develops and changes. For example, my father was a polygamist. In Thembu custom, you normally have a customary marriage and one of the methods of observing them is for a man who wants to get married to waylay a girl as she goes to the river to fetch water and take her home. And the parents will follow. I am not committed to that kind of custom.

He expressed 'shock' at Winnie's action in obtaining an affidavit from Matanzima: 'Several times he wanted to visit me in jail and I refused, because I did not want to be tainted by his reputation.'

'Is there any way that an intervention by him would save your relationship?' asked Trengove.

'Can I put it simply, My Lord? If the entire universe tried to persuade me to reconcile with the defendant, I would not. And least of all from Matanzima . . . I am determined to get rid of this marriage.'

Mandela continued:

Ever since I came back from jail, not once has the defendant ever entered the bedroom whilst I was awake. I kept on saying to her: 'Look, men and wives usually discuss the most intimate problems in the bedroom. I have been in jail a long time. There are so many issues, almost all of them very sensitive, I would like to have the opportunity to discuss with you.' Not once has she ever responded . . .

I was the loneliest man during the period I stayed with her.

Listening to Mandela's testimony, Winnie never looked up, but stared into her lap or scribbled notes.

In his cross-examination, Winnie's lawyer, Ismail Semenya, sought to portray Winnie as a woman who had suffered greatly at the hands of the apartheid authorities and sacrificed everything for their marriage. Mandela conceded that Winnie had suffered 'gross persecution' and 'brutal treatment' at the hands of the security police, but added that she was not alone. 'There were many women who suffered more than she did,' he said, citing as an example Albertina Sisulu. 'I am saying this not to underestimate the role she played. Just so long as this does not create the impression that she was all alone in the struggle . . . She was no exception.'

When Semenya continued to blame apartheid, Mandela became irritated, declaring that there were 'even more serious reasons why

I left home'. Three times he begged Semenya not to force him to divulge any more painful details: 'I would like you to know I am not keen to wash our dirty linen in public. I appeal to you not to put any questions which might compel me to reveal facts which could damage the image of the defendant and bring a great deal of pain to our children and grandchildren.'

Having finished his cross-examination, Semenya then asked the court for an adjournment for several days to allow him time to assemble witnesses. When the judge, Frikkie Eloff, rejected his request, Winnie intervened with a last melodramatic flourish, fired her lawyer and asked the court for an adjournment while she found another. Trengove sprang to his feet to denounce 'the oldest trick in the book'. Mrs Mandela, he said, 'should not be allowed to get away with a ploy as obvious as that'. Judge Eloff asked Winnie either to call witnesses or to take the stand herself. With tears in her eyes and a shaky voice, she said she could not take the stand and needed legal guidance: 'I am an ordinary person, a layman. I do not want to be heard. I do not know what to do. I am assuring Your Lordship that it is not a ploy on my part.' The judge was unmoved and, after a further offer to Winnie to take the stand, he declared the defence case closed.

While waiting for Eloff's verdict during a final adjournment, Mandela sat slumped in his chair, gazing into the middle distance, his face etched with misery. The judge returned to grant Mandela a divorce. It was the end of thirty-eight years of marriage – a marriage which, during his long years of imprisonment, he had cherished above all else.

As president, Mandela maintained a frugal lifestyle. He had the use of two grand state mansions, Genadendal in Cape Town and Mahlamba' Ndlopfu, formerly Libertas, in Pretoria, but whenever possible he preferred to stay at his comfortable suburban house in Houghton, where three of his grandchildren and a young relative lived with him. He liked to get away from the formality of official residences; at home, he could relax. His income as president was substantial. He had an annual salary of 552,000 rands with large additional allowances, but he donated a third of his salary to a children's charity he set up. Much of his other income – royalties from his autobiography, money from the Nobel Peace Prize – was also given to charity or to the ANC. Accustomed to a life of austerity, Mandela wanted to set a new style of leadership, free from the greed and corruption for which National Party rule had been renowned. The political 'gravy train', he had said during the election campaign, would come to an end: 'We are not going to live as fat cats.'

The new dispensation, however, offered opportunities for the black élite which they seized with alacrity. One of the first acts of the new parliament was to vote for huge increases in the salaries and allowances of ministers, members of parliament and the president. Ministers' salaries were raised to a level which meant that their monthly pay was three times more than the average worker earned in a year. The increases had been recommended by a commission set up by the apartheid government, enabling ministers to claim they were not responsible for them. Even with the recommended increases, members of parliament continued to argue in favour of yet higher allowances, insisting that they found it difficult to make ends meet.

The public reaction was distinctly sour. The black Sunday newspaper *City Press* published a cartoon showing two senior ministers in the dining car of the Gravy Train, with one telling the other, 'That's enough gravy. Bring on the champagne.'

The most damning comment came from the Anglican leader, Archbishop Desmond Tutu. After raising the issue of government salaries with Mandela in private, Tutu decided to make his concern public. 'The government stopped the gravy train only long enough to get on it,' he remarked.

The public row that broke out between Mandela and Tutu showed Mandela at his most evasive. Instead of confronting the issue, he chose to make a personal attack on Tutu. Addressing an audience in Stellenbosch, he criticized Tutu for siding with his populist critics. 'A respected leader was unable to resist the temptation to jump on the bandwagon,' said Mandela. 'I considered it an act of irresponsibility on his part.' He went on to chastise him for failing to raise the issue before going public.

Tutu's response was first to rebuke Mandela for failing to observe the Ninth Commandment, Thou shalt not bear false witness. 'What is . . . distressing,' he said, 'is the impression the president gives that I did not speak to him personally about the issue.' Then he added, 'But it is very distressing that the president should behave like an ordinary politician, by not answering whether a particular argument or criticism is true but instead impugning my integrity. It is beneath his stature.'

When asked why he thought Mandela had reacted so intemperately, Tutu replied, 'Yes, it was so unlike him. At no point does he normally denigrate anybody, which is why this attack on me is so odd. Why? I don't know . . . but, well, it's good to know he's human.'

Mandela's belated reaction, several months later, was to announce a cut in the pay of ministers and of the president. But by then the damage to parliament's reputation was permanent. MPs found themselves the constant butt of remarks about their 'gravy-train mentality'. Mandela's reputation too suffered from his handling of the salary issue and also of a number of other incidents. Despite his stern pronouncements about the need for belt-tightening and a new moral footing, he was seen to be 'soft' on greed, as lenient with his colleagues as he had been with Winnie, showing them the same kind of perverse loyalty.

One notorious example concerned the Reverend Allan Boesak, an anti-apartheid activist from the Western Cape who had helped found the UDF in the 1980s. Once a leader of the Coloured branch of the Dutch Reformed Church and head of the World Council of Reformed Churches, Boesak had fallen into disgrace by 1990 as the result of affairs which led to the break-up of his marriage and his resignation from all his church posts. Despite local opposition, Mandela intervened to appoint Boesak as the ANC's leader in the Western Cape in the hope that he would bring in the Coloured vote. The Western Cape subsequently was the only province won by the National Party in the election. Boesak was replaced as party leader there, but Mandela compensated him with an appointment as ambassador to the United Nations in Geneva.

A few weeks before he was due to leave for Geneva, the first hint of corruption surfaced. Investigations into the use of aid money donated by foreign organizations to a charity known as the Foundation for Peace and Justice which Boesak had set up in Cape Town to assist the poor and destitute suggested that nearly 3 million rands had gone astray. Determined to establish what had happened to its funds, the Danish agency, Danchurch Aid, asked a Johannesburg law firm to make a thorough inquiry. For six weeks Boesak held out while the scandal was aired in the press. Only when the Office for Serious Economic Offences began its own investigation was he finally persuaded to resign from the foreign ministry.

A further complaint was made by Archbishop Tutu, who called in police to investigate what had happened to a donation of 423,000 rands made by the American singer Paul Simon which he had passed on to Boesak's foundation. 'We are distressed and angry,' he said in a statement, 'that money . . . set aside for child victims of apartheid cannot be accounted for immediately.'

After a three-month investigation, the Johannesburg law firm issued a 600-page report damning of Boesak's conduct. Boesak, their report said, had 'enriched himself substantially' by diverting funds to buy a luxury house and to pay for an inflated salary, vacations, his second wedding and his new wife's business debts. Only a quarter of the foundation's income had gone to projects intended by Scandinavian donors to help apartheid victims. Boesak's response was to deny all responsibility, to blame his staff and to claim that he was a victim of racism. 'I have spent most of my life fighting for the liberation of the people,' he said. 'I have found that the justice I have fought for is not for me.'

The government, meanwhile, had asked one of its own legal advisers to investigate. The adviser produced a three-page report which attempted to pick holes in the law firm's report and went on to clear Boesak of misconduct. The response of the Johannesburg law firm was to describe the government report as 'preposterous' and 'absurd' and to issue an eighteen-page rebuttal, rejecting it point by point.

But Mandela, without waiting to weigh up the evidence and ignoring the work in progress by the Office for Serious Economic Offences, duly proclaimed Boesak innocent. 'The government has investigated the allegations against Dr Boesak and found they were baseless,' he declared. He went on to praise Boesak as 'one of the most gifted young men in the country' who deserved a 'high diplomatic post'. Boesak pronounced himself vindicated, demanded a public apology from Danchurch Aid and offered his services to the government.

In the resulting public furore, Mandela and the government were accused of covering up corruption, of political cronyism and of undermining the course of justice. The outcry eventually died down and Boesak did not get a government job, but the episode showed Mandela capable of gross misjudgement in handling public business.

Mandela rode to the rescue of other colleagues caught in dubious circumstances. When the health minister, Dr Nkosazana Zuma, was pilloried for using 14 million rands of European Union funds to sponsor an anti-AIDS drama by a local playwright, neglecting to inform European Union officials, Mandela used his influence with parliament's health committee, which was set for a showdown over the issue, to stifle its criticisms. 'The result,' noted one parliamentary reporter, 'was a demonstration of pliant foot-shuffling that astounded observers.' Though the public protector found that Zuma had misled parliament, Mandela continued to support her. When journalists pursued the matter, he accused 'the white-owned media' of victimizing her, making a racial issue of it for good measure.

Another colleague whom Mandela protected was the public enterprises minister, Stella Sigcau, who became ensnared in a controversy over bribery started by a fellow minister, Bantu Holomisa. The two ministers were old rivals: Sigcau, a former premier of the 'independent' Transkei, had been overthrown in 1987 by a military coup led by Holomisa. In May 1996, Holomisa caused a storm when he claimed that, ten years previously, Sigcau had received a cut from a substantial bribe paid by casino tycoon Sol Kerzner to Transkei ministers to help him secure exclusive gambling rights in the Transkei. Kerzner had subsequently been charged with bribery by the Transkei authorities but insisted the payment was extortion; Sigcau admitted receiving the money but said it was a gift.

Mandela's wrath at these exposures was directed not at Sigcau but at Holomisa, for washing the party's dirty linen in public. Dismissed from the government, Holomisa retaliated by making ever more sweeping allegations of corruption within the ANC hierarchy, going so far as to claim that Mandela himself had agreed to consider ways to have the Transkei bribery charges against Kerzner dropped in return for a 2-million-rand donation to ANC party funds. The ANC denounced that as 'blatant lies', but to everyone's astonishment Mandela then admitted having received the money, on behalf of the ANC. Both he and Kerzner denied that it had anything to do with the bribery charges, describing it as merely a private contribution to party funds. Holomisa was later expelled for bringing the party into disrepute.

The whole affair suggested that Mandela and the ANC were far less interested in accountability and open government than they professed. What counted more was party loyalty. Press criticism of Mandela reached unprecedented levels. He was accused of stifling dissent, of dictatorial habits, of fostering a personality cult. 'He makes much of his commitment to collective leadership but rules his organization with an iron fist, with people who do not agree with him falling out of favour,' wrote Kaizer Nyatsumba in the Johannesburg *Star*. 'There is all-pervasive fear among ANC office-bearers at the moment, with nobody wanting to be seen to be holding heretical views or differing from the omniscient leadership.'

Mandela reacted with a display of just the kind of intolerance his critics accused him of. He singled out black journalists for abuse, claiming that they were doing the 'dirty work' of white newspaper owners. He summoned one newspaper editor, Khulu Sibiya, of Johannesburg's *City Press*, who had criticized his interference with the selection of a new chief justice, for a dressing-down. 'I have never seen him so furious,' said Sibiya. 'The handling of recent political controversies and the hostility to the press do not augur well.' The final outcome of the Kerzner case was that in April 1997 charges against him were dropped by the Transkei authorities.

However much Mandela tried to focus attention on the poorer sections of society, the immediate beneficiaries of the new South Africa were the black middle class. In the civil service and parastatal corporations, blacks rapidly gained positions of status and responsibility from which they had been barred for so long. The business sector followed suit, anxious to be seen to be redressing the legacy of inequality. Only 10 per cent of managerial posts were held by blacks, despite years of talk about the need for black advancement. The opportunities for those with skills and qualifications were vast. Yet the reservoir of trained and experienced blacks was all too small. Out of a total of 14,000 chartered accountants, for example, only sixty-five were black. A consequence of this was that in one business deal after another, as white-owned corporations sought to promote the development of black capitalism, a small group of successful black entrepreneurs made all the running, enriching themselves hugely in the process.

Even so, the new élite were vociferous in grumbling about the slow pace of black advancement and clamoured for a faster overhaul of the old, white institutions. They pointed to how the National Party, after its 1948 election victory, had ensured the rapid promotion of Afrikaners across the board, transforming a whole range of institutions from broadcasting to the army and the railways into Afrikaner preserves, and demanded that the ANC should take similar action. Some wanted to establish an African version of the Afrikaner Broederbond to promote black interests.

What the Mandela years witnessed, in fact, was a significant widening of the income gap within the black community. The gap had been growing since the late 1970s. During the 1980s, while the poorest half of the population slid ever deeper into poverty, the black middle class fared well, their rising incomes making them the most upwardly mobile group in the country. During the 1990s, the black élite – politicians, bureaucrats, entrepreneurs, managers, businessmen – prospered as never before, many acquiring the lifestyle and status symbols so prized in South Africa – executive cars, swimming pools, domestic staff, private school education, golf handicaps and foreign holidays. Perhaps 5 per cent of the black community reached middle-class status. But for the majority, the same struggle against poverty continued. This new inequality, an inevitable consequence of the apartheid era, was a legacy that would be passed on far beyond Mandela's time.

The honeymoon period between Mandela and his partners in the government of national unity, de Klerk and Buthelezi, was memorable but brief. From the outset, they made strange bedfellows, brought together not so much by common interest as by a quirk of fate. The antagonisms of the past were too close to allow for an easy relationship. De Klerk at first loyally played the part allotted to him as a deputy president, travelling the world, extolling the virtues of the new South Africa, dutifully maintaining a low profile. But it was a role with which he became increasingly disgruntled.

Expecting to make a considerable impact on government policy, he found he had influence but no real power. All his hopes about power-sharing, of making important decisions in concert with Mandela, were soon confounded. Mandela listened, but pursued his own agenda. Nor did de Klerk acquire the leverage he expected to command by acting as the guardian of white interests in the civil service, the police and the business community. White civil servants rapidly switched their allegiance to Mandela, accepting him as the guarantor of their interests rather than de Klerk. The police hierarchy, swiftly reshuffled, followed suit. With the business community, Mandela opened his own direct lines of communications. As an intermediary representing white interests, de Klerk was soon redundant.

He also found himself at odds with Mandela in dealing with the past. Mandela was determined that human rights violations during the apartheid era should be investigated, not for the purpose of exacting retribution but to provide some form of public accounting and to help purge the injustices of the past. Unless past crimes were addressed, he said, they would 'live with us like a festering sore'. He proposed to establish a truth and reconciliation commission, empowered to subpoena witnesses and to grant amnesties. Those who came forward to make a full admission of their crimes would receive pardons. Otherwise they risked the possibility of prosecution in the courts. The commission would then make 'recommendations on steps to be taken to ensure that such violations never take place again'. De Klerk said the proposal would result in 'a witch-hunt', focusing attention upon past government abuses while ignoring ANC crimes. It was likely to 'tear out the stitches of wounds that are beginning to heal'. But his rearguard action against it achieved nothing.

Ghosts from the past continued to haunt the new government. A former policeman testified that the bombing of the Johannesburg headquarters of the South African Council of Churches in 1988 had been carried out not by the ANC, as the government had claimed at the time, but by government agents who were subsequently congratulated by the minister of law and order, Adriaan Vlok. Under pressure to prosecute, the police commissioner was obliged to disclose in January 1995 that two former ministers, Adriaan Vlok, and the former defence minister, Magnus Malan, together with 3,500 policemen, had secretly been granted indemnities by de Klerk's government in its last days in power before the general election in April 1994.

The disclosure caused outrage. At a cabinet meeting at Union Buildings on 21 January, de Klerk attempted to deny all knowledge of the matter. After a protracted discussion, the cabinet decided to declare the indemnities invalid. But just when agreement on the issue appeared to have been reached, Mandela, who had been sitting quietly listening to the proceedings, launched a ferocious personal attack on de Klerk, all the old animosity he had felt towards him resurfacing. What particularly incensed him was not just the covert nature of the indemnity deal but the manner in which de Klerk disclaimed any responsibility for it, just as he had always done with Mandela in past disputes over government complicity in violence. He came close to calling de Klerk a liar, rejecting the denial he made, and went on to criticize his conduct in cabinet, comparing it unfavourably to that of other National Party ministers. In cabinet, said Mandela, de Klerk spoke in a manner in which 'white men used to speak to blacks'. As Mandela continued his attack, de Klerk gathered up his papers, preparing to walk out, saying he would have to reconsider his position. Mandela retorted that if de Klerk did withdraw, it 'would not cause a ripple'. After the meeting had adjourned, ministers from both sides rallied round, hoping to find a way to achieve *rapprochement*. De Klerk declared he had been 'viciously insulted'. He accused the ANC of becoming increasingly intolerant of opposition and criticism; its members, he said, 'tend more and more to become impatient and to adopt a bully attitude when they are opposed and questioned'. But he was nevertheless willing to compromise. When Mandela suggested that they should make 'a fresh start', de Klerk accepted. It seemed unlikely, however, that the coalition would survive its full term. De Klerk was no longer indispensable.

There were other sources of friction, notably over the conduct of South Africa's foreign policy. Despite the overwhelming need to attract Western investment, Mandela persisted with an approach which emphasized friendship with countries like Libya, Cuba and Iran that was likely to deter Western interest. Foreign policy was frequently an area of confusion and muddle, determined as much by which governments had made contributions to the ANC treasury as by other factors. 'Our foreign policy is largely for hire,' complained the opposition Democratic Party. 'If you make a substantial donation to the ANC, you get special foreign policy consideration.' The foreign minister, Alfred Nzo, an old friend of Mandela, became a figure of public ridicule, universally criticized for incompetence. Blunders were commonplace. Mandela added to the toll, describing US aid of $100 million in 1995 as 'peanuts'. The result was to squander much of the goodwill for South Africa retained in Western capitals and to exacerbate tensions with de Klerk.

The final rift with de Klerk came during negotiations over the drafting of the new constitution in 1996. De Klerk fought hard to secure a clause enshrining the principle of a forced coalition on a permanent basis. When he failed to get his way, he decided to withdraw from the government altogether, giving vent to his frustration at the minor role he had been obliged to play. 'We felt for some time now that our influence in the government of national unity has been declining,' he said in May 1996, after the new constitution had been finalized. 'The ANC was acting more and more as if they no longer needed a multiparty government.' He spoke of the need to provide 'a strong and vigilant opposition'. Mandela made it clear that he would have preferred the National Party to remain in the coalition, but otherwise he accepted de Klerk's departure with equanimity. As he had predicted, it caused barely a ripple.

Mandela's relationship with Buthelezi was far more fractious. Appointed minister of home affairs in 1994, Buthelezi was constantly at loggerheads with Mandela over his continuing campaign for greater regional autonomy for KwaZulu-Natal. The dispute was made more complex by the role of the Zulu king, Goodwill Zwelethini, whose decision to switch his support to Mandela just before the election earned him Buthelezi's lasting enmity. In a spectacular display of wild behaviour in September 1994, Buthelezi and his bodyguards barged into a television studio in Johannesburg and during a live discussion programme began abusing and threatening a Zulu prince speaking on the king's behalf.

In the ensuing uproar, rather than force his resignation, Mandela subjected Buthelezi to public humiliation, requiring him to apologize to the cabinet and the nation. As Buthelezi sat alongside him, looking penitent, Mandela read out a statement he had drawn up after a special session of the cabinet:

> The cabinet resolved that this action constituted a serious violation of the right to freedom of speech and freedom of the press. It also posed a threat to the safety and security of citizens. It was therefore a direct challenge to the very constitution which all ministers of the government are sworn to protect and respect. Accordingly, the cabinet passed a motion of severe censure on Dr Buthelezi for conduct inimical to good government and the protection of fundamental human rights.

Buthelezi duly apologized, after explaining that he had not realized the programme was being broadcast live: 'I am not such a bumbling fool that I would go into a live studio and interfere with a programme deliberately.'

For months on end, a row simmered between Mandela and Buthelezi over the question of international mediation on Inkatha's demands for greater regional autonomy in KwaZulu-Natal. Although Mandela had given a commitment agreeing to international mediation in April 1994 in order to get Buthelezi to participate in the election, once in power he failed to honour it, making a variety of excuses. Hoping to embarrass Mandela over this 'breach of trust', Buthelezi reverted to his favourite tactic of boycott, announcing Inkatha's withdrawal from parliament and the constitutional assembly in February 1995. The boycott had little impact and two weeks later Buthelezi ended it on the pretext of allowing more time for negotiation. A month later, when no further progress had been made in resolving the dispute, he suspended Inkatha's participation in the constitutional assembly.

On both sides, the war of words became increasingly reckless, threatening to reignite large-scale violence. In April, Buthelezi called on KwaZulu-Natal to 'rise and resist' the central government over its refusal to negotiate greater regional autonomy. People should be prepared to lay down their lives to safeguard self-determination against the ANC's 'arrogance' over the issue of international mediation and the constitution. 'Let the new struggle for freedom begin. Let our friends and foes be warned that our march to freedom has begun,' he said. 'No amount of intimidation, prevarication and violence can bend into submission the strength of Inkatha, or undermine our determination to defend our self-determination, freedom and pluralism.'

Mandela responded in kind, throwing all caution to the wind. At a rally near Durban, he accused Inkatha of using government funds for KwaZulu-Natal to foment rebellion there and threatened to cut them off. His remarks were denounced by opposition groups as being irresponsible, inflammatory and unconstitutional. When Mandela's advisers sought to defuse the crisis by stressing the president would take no action that was unconstitutional, Mandela weighed in further by saying that if he did not possess the power to cut off funds, he would acquire it if necessary by amending the constitution.

The crisis blew over a day later when Mandela and Buthelezi met and agreed to settle their differences in an orderly manner. Appearing in front of the media afterwards, they smiled and joked for the benefit of the cameras. Mandela described Buthelezi as 'my traditional leader, my chief, and my prince'. Buthelezi declared himself 'a loyal member of the president's cabinet'. He remained in Mandela's cabinet long after de Klerk had departed.

But the episode raised questions once again about Mandela's judgement. By refusing to fulfil his commitment to international mediation, he provided Buthelezi with a legitimate grievance that he was bound to exploit. The verdict of the press on the issue was overwhelmingly hostile to Mandela. By then resorting to the same kind of threats and bluster that Buthelezi habitually used to further his aims, Mandela risked setting off renewed violence in KwaZulu-Natal and undermining South Africa's political stability, upon which so much else depended. It was an example of impetuous brinkmanship which South Africa could ill afford.

From an early stage in his presidency, Mandela began to prepare South Africa for the post-Mandela era. So much confidence, so much trust, had come to be placed in Mandela that there was deep apprehension about the prospect of his departure from government. He was seen as not only the founding father of democracy but also the guarantor of its stability. Whatever the muddles and mistakes of his administration, his presidency had provided South Africa with greater peace than the country had known for years.

Rumours of his ill-health were enough to send the stock exchange and the currency into a tailspin. For a man in his late seventies, he suffered from relatively few ailments – an eye affliction, a slight loss of hearing, swollen ankles. His schedule remained as punishing as ever – early starts, late nights, meetings, speeches, travel abroad. But any sign of exhaustion or fatigue was greeted with alarm. In an attempt to quell speculation about his health, Mandela submitted himself to a three-day 'executive check-up' in March 1996 and passed without difficulty. 'He has the energy of a man half his age,' a specialist consultant remarked. In a letter to a Johannesburg newspaper, Mandela wrote, 'Let me restate the obvious: I have long passed my teens; and the distance to my final destination is shorter than the road I have trudged over the years. What nature has decreed should not generate undue insecurity.' But public concern about a future without him remained high.

While remaining confident that he would serve his five-year term as president in full, Mandela stressed that he had no intention of staying in office for a second term after 1999, regardless of popular demand. 'At the end of my term, I'll be eighty-one,' he said. 'I don't think it's wise that a robust country like South Africa should be led by an octogenarian. You need younger men who can shake and move this country.' He minimized his own importance in government, emphasizing the talent and ability of his cabinet colleagues. 'Many of my colleagues are head and shoulders above me in almost every respect. Rather than being an asset, I'm more of a decoration.'

Much of the government's routine business Mandela left in the hands of his key aide, Thabo Mbeki, whom he selected in 1994 to serve as deputy president and whom he favoured to succeed him as president. The son of Govan Mbeki, he had left South Africa in 1962 at the age of nineteen, not returning until 1990. In his years in exile, he had studied economics in England at the University of Sussex, undergone military training in the Soviet Union and represented the ANC in a series of foreign postings, before joining the staff of Oliver Tambo and then taking over as head of the party's international affairs department in 1989. A soft-spoken, urbane and articulate figure, possessing considerable charm, he came to be seen in the West, during the ANC's years as a revolutionary movement, as its acceptable face, holding firm to the belief that a negotiated settlement was possible. He was particularly skilful in handling contacts with the stream of white South Africans – businessmen, academics and churchmen – who travelled from South Africa in the 1980s to talk to the ANC in defiance of the government, seeking a way through the impasse. Dressed in a tweed jacket and puffing his ubiquitous pipe, Mbeki spoke more the language of the middle class than the rhetoric they expected of revolutionaries. Once back in South Africa from exile, he performed much the same task, pacifying businessmen alarmed by talk of nationalization and right-wing Afrikaners demanding a *volkstaat*. 'He can be diplomatic to the point where many people regard him as weak,' Mandela once observed.

Mbeki possessed no natural constituency within the ANC, but relied heavily on his backroom skills to build political support, making alliances with all and sundry. He was as adept at aligning himself with populist factions when the occasion arose as with the pragmatic wing of the party. While Mandela placed the need for reconciliation above all else, Mbeki put greater emphasis on the need to transform South African society. 'You cannot find reconciliation between blacks and whites in a situation in which poverty and prosperity continue to be defined in racial terms,' he said. 'If you want reconciliation between black and white, you need to transform society. If we have an economy that is geared to benefit the whites and disadvantage the black majority, and you do not address that, you will not have reconciliation.'

Mbeki's record as Mandela's chief executive was none too impressive. He acquired a reputation for announcing grand plans – for privatization of parastatal corporations, for example – but dithering over their implementation. He was responsible for mishandling a number of assignments Mandela gave to him – concerning Winnie Mandela's resignation; the Boesak scandal; Buthelezi's demand for international mediation; and foreign policy initiatives, including a bungled attempt to prevent Nigeria's military rulers from executing a prominent dissident, Ken Saro Wiwa. His critics pointed to other faults, such as his reputation for missing appointments, for enjoying the good life and for hobnobbing with populists.

Mandela, however, pronounced himself well satisfied with

Mbeki's performance and provided him with a personal endorsement. 'Thabo Mbeki is a very talented and very influential man,' he said in 1996. 'And if the party were to elect him when I step down, then I would take the view that they had made the correct decision.'

Mandela himself enjoyed the tasks of nation-building, but kept the prospect of retirement firmly in view. 'I am nearing my end,' he told Afrikaner students. 'I want to be able to sleep till eternity with a broad smile on my face, knowing that the youth, opinion-makers and everybody is stretching across the divide, trying to unite the nation.'

What would he do in retirement?

> Do all the things that I've missed: to be with my children and grandchildren and with my family; the ability to sit down and read what I would like to read. You know, in prison – although it was a tragedy to spend twenty-seven years in prison – one of the advantages was the ability to sit down and think. This is one of the things I miss most.

EPILOGUE

In a letter from prison to his friend Amina Cachalia, Mandela once wrote, 'I have spent all my life dreaming of a golden age in which all problems will be solved and our wildest hopes fulfilled.'

The golden age of which Mandela dreamed remains a distant prospect. Nevertheless, the transformation of South Africa from a country riven by racial division and violence to a fledgeling democracy stands as one of the supreme triumphs of the late twentieth century.

Mandela's role in that transformation was vital to its success. He understood from an early stage the extent to which white fear lay at the core of the conflict. No matter what personal hardships he had to endure, he never lost sight of the goal of non-racial democracy in South Africa, believing that white fear of it could eventually be overcome. The generosity of spirit he showed after his prison ordeal had a profound impact on his white adversaries, earning him measures of trust and confidence which made a political settlement attainable.

As president, he has pursued the cause of national reconciliation with the same tenacity, personifying the values which he wants the new South Africa to represent, using his years in office to foster a climate of tolerance in the hope that it might take root permanently, but knowing of the difficult times that lie ahead.

South Africa faces many hazards. Its crime rate is among the highest in the world, unemployment and poverty are widespread and racial tensions are never far below the surface. But the foundations for a new society which Mandela has helped to lay enable

South Africa to face the future with more hope than once seemed possible. His legacy is a country which has experienced greater harmony than at any previous time in its history.

NOTES ON SOURCES

The published work on Mandela is extensive. His autobiography, *Long Walk to Freedom*, published in 1994, provides a wealth of material. Several collections of his articles and speeches have been produced. The first collection, *No Easy Walk to Freedom*, which appeared in 1965, contains an introduction written by Oliver Tambo and many of the articles Mandela wrote for Michael Harmel's journal, *Liberation*, during the 1950s. A second collection, *The Struggle is My Life*, was published in 1978 to mark his sixtieth birthday. A documentary survey of the struggle against apartheid from 1948 to 1990, *Mandela, Tambo and the African National Congress*, published in 1991, covers the same ground with much additional material. All three collections include extracts from Mandela's testimony in the treason trial and his court statements in 1962 and 1964. A fourth collection, *Nelson Mandela Speaks*, published in 1993, includes speeches and statements he made between 1990 and 1993. Further documentary material on Mandela is contained in the four-volume work on African politics compiled by Thomas Karis, Gwendolen Carter and Gail M. Gerhart, *From Protest to Challenge*. Records of the treason trial and the Rivonia trial are held by the William Cullen Library at the University of the Witwatersrand. In the years after his release from prison in 1990, Mandela gave scores of interviews and press conferences which are located in various newspaper archives.

Two previous biographies have been published. The biography by Mary Benson, a friend of Mandela from the 1950s who interviewed him while he was underground in the early 1960s, first appeared in 1986 and was updated and republished in 1994. The biography by Fatima Meer, another friend, was first published in 1988 and includes a collection of letters and interviews with members of Mandela's family.

Recent overviews of South Africa's history include Leonard Thompson's masterly account, *A History of South Africa* (1994), William Beinart's *Twentieth Century South Africa* (1994), T. R. H. Davenport's *South Africa: A*

Modern History (fourth edition, 1991) and *The Reader's Digest Illustrated History of South Africa* (1994).

The following chapter notes include references to some of the books which I found to be of particular interest and value. A more complete list can be found in the Select Bibliography.

Chapter 1

Mandela's early years are recalled evocatively in his autobiography. The plight of the Xhosa-speaking peoples of the Eastern Cape region in the nineteenth century is described in J. B. Peires's two works, *The House of Phalo* and *The Dead Will Arise*, an account of the Xhosa cattle-killing of 1856–7. Makana's fate is described by Thomas Pringle, Edward Roux and J. B. Peires. Maqoma's life is covered by Timothy Stapleton. Paul Maylam provides a useful overview of African societies. Missionary activity is covered by B. A. Pauw, André Odendaal, Paul Maylam and Michael Ashley. Life at Fort Hare is depicted by Alexander Kerr and by Z. K. Matthews, who spent twenty-four years on the staff there. Tambo's early life is portrayed by Father Trevor Huddleston. Matanzima's account of his student days and his subsequent career is included in *Independence My Way*.

Chapter 2

Johannesburg's early years are brought vividly to life in Charles van Onselen's two-volume work on the Witwatersrand. Nigel Mandy provides a useful account of the city's development. Alan Paton's famous novel *Cry, the Beloved Country* is based on his own experiences of life in Johannesburg in the 1940s. Mandela kept in touch with both Sidelsky and Bregman after his release from prison in 1990. Radebe joined the Pan-Africanist Congress in the 1950s and went into exile after Sharpeville. According to Roux, he was used by the police as an *agent provocateur* and a spy during the 1930s. A profile of Meer appears in Anthony Sampson's *Treason Cage*.

The rise of African nationalism is covered extensively by André Odendaal, Peter Walshe, Tom Lodge, Edward Roux, Mary Benson, Thomas Karis, Gwendolen Carter and Gail M. Gerhart. Sol T. Plaatje's account of *Native Life in South Africa* was first published in 1916. Alfred Stadler describes bus boycotts in Alexandra in his seminar paper 'A Long Way to Walk' and squatter movements in Johannesburg in his article 'Birds in the Cornfield'. Another account of the 1943 bus boycott is given by Miriam Basner. Michael Scott gives his version of the Tobruk episode in his autobiography, *A Time to Speak*, but makes no mention there of Mandela's help. Gail Gerhart examines the development of Africanist politics.

Chapter 3

Indian politics during Gandhi's twenty-year stay in South Africa are covered by Maureen Swan. Michael Scott's description of the Durban 'Resistance Camp' comes from his autobiography. Ahmed Kathrada was born in 1929 in Schweizer-Reineke in the western Transvaal, where his parents owned a retail shop. As a young boy, he was sent to Johannesburg for his education. He joined the Young Communist League at the age of twelve and the Communist Party at the age of fourteen, participated in the passive resistance campaign and distributed pamphlets in the mineworkers' strike. He shared Flat 13 in Kholvad House with Meer and Singh.

Accounts of the Communist Party's early activities are provided by Edward Roux, H. J. and R. E. Simons and Joshua N. Lazerson. A biography of Moses Kotane by Brian Bunting, a prominent party official and son of Sidney Bunting, one of the founding members of the party in South Africa, adds further detail. Dan O'Meara analyses the impact of the mineworkers' strike. Another account of the strike, *A Distant Clap of Thunder*, written by Rusty Bernstein, was published by the South African Communist Party in 1986 to commemorate its fortieth anniversary. Simons and Simons record that the public prosecutor involved in the sedition trial was Dr Percy Yutar, later to gain notoriety in Mandela's Rivonia trial. Yutar claimed the strike was part of a plot by communist revolutionaries to overthrow the government.

The activities of the Congress Youth League are covered by Peter Walshe, Tom Lodge, Gail M. Gerhart and Thomas Karis, Gwendolen Carter and Gail M. Gerhart. Sisulu recalled that he had two major disagreements with Mandela. One occurred over the 'Votes for All' issue, the other during their imprisonment on Robben Island over a strike issue.

Chapter 4

The rise of Afrikaner nationalism is dealt with by Heribert Adam and Hermann Giliomee, W. A. de Klerk, André du Toit, T. Dunbar Moodie, Leonard M. Thompson and F. A. van Jaarsveld. Thomas Pakenham's account of the Anglo-Boer War deserves special mention.

Joe Slovo's autobiography proves a vivid account of his days as a young communist activist in Johannesburg, his marriage to Ruth First and his career as a radical lawyer. Ruth First gives glimpses of her early life in her account of her imprisonment, *One Hundred and Seventeen Days*. A contemporary profile of First appears in Anthony Sampson's *Treason Cage*. Gillian Slovo writes memorably about her parents in *Every Secret Thing*. Fischer described his early life, his political commitment and his underground work during his trial in 1966. Other accounts of Fischer's life come from his daughter, Ruth Fischer, Mandela, Sisulu, Mary Benson, Joel Joffe, Rusty and Hilda Bernstein, Hugh Lewin, and Paul and Adelaide Joseph. Mandela's explanation about the Defiance Campaign was given during the treason trial. Tom Lodge gives a general account of the Defiance Campaign.

Chapter 5

Betty Shein's recollection is recorded by Heidi Holland. The records of Mandela's confrontation with Dormehl were kindly provided by George Bizos. Evelyn Mandela was interviewed by Fred Bridgland in Cofimvaba in the Transkei; his account appeared in the London *Sunday Telegraph* on 25 February 1990 (also used in Chapter 7). Profiles of Lilian Ngoyi are given in Anthony Sampson's *Treason Cage*, in Helen Joseph's books and in Maggie Resha's autobiography.

The anecdote about Dirker is taken from Joe Slovo's autobiography. James Kantor, in his autobiography, said that Dirker came to be 'the most hated person on the entire staff'. Luthuli's career is charted in his autobiography, *Let My People Go*, and by Mary Benson and Anthony Sampson.

Life in Sophiatown in the 1940s and 1950s is covered by a host of authors, including Bloke Modisane, Michael Dingake, Maggie Resha, Trevor Huddleston, Anthony Sampson, André Proctor, Tom Lodge and Edward Feit. David Coplan writes memorably about Sophiatown's musical milieu. The jazz trumpeter Hugh Masekela was given his first trumpet by Huddleston, who received it as a gift from Louis Armstrong. Mike Nicol takes a wider look at township life.

Hendrik Verwoerd was born in 1901 in a small village near Amsterdam to Dutch parents who emigrated to the Cape when he was two years old; his family thus bore none of the scars of the Anglo-Boer War which afflicted so much of the Afrikaner population. Alexander Hepple and Henry Kenney have produced two useful biographies of Verwoerd. Aspects of Bantu education are covered by Trevor Huddleston, Albert Luthuli, Z. K. Matthews, Tom Lodge and Anthony Sampson.

Chapters 6, 8

Janet Robertson looks at the role of traditional liberals; Joshua N. Lazerson concentrates on more radical whites. Helen Joseph was one of the few prominent members of the Congress of Democrats who was not a member of the Communist Party. Mandela's explanation of his attitude towards communists was given at the Rivonia trial.

Matthews's proposal formed part of the charge of treason made by state prosecutors. His references to 'action' and 'going over into the offensive' were regarded as having subversive intent.

A useful guide to the treason trial is provided by Thomas Karis. Other valuable accounts include Lionel Forman and E. S. Sachs's *The South African Treason Trial*, Helen Joseph's *If This be Treason*, Hilda Bernstein's *The*

World That Was Ours and Anthony Sampson's *Treason Cage*. Sampson's account also provides a series of contemporary profiles of the accused, but not one of Mandela. The Treason Trial Defence Fund eventually developed into the International Defence and Aid Fund, with headquarters in London, which provided funds to pay for the defence costs of political activists like Mandela and to help support their families. Funds came mainly from Britain and Scandinavia.

Chapter 7

The most comprehensive account of Winnie Mandela's life is provided by Emma Gilbey in *The Lady*, first published in 1993. Winnie's autobiography, *Part of My Soul*, first published in 1985, is based largely on a series of interviews conducted by Anne Benjamin which provide a wealth of detail about her life with Mandela before and after his imprisonment. Nancy Harrison's authorized biography, *Winnie Mandela: Mother of a Nation*, also published in 1985, provides additional material. Robert Matji's recollection of the Mandela household is recorded by Heidi Holland.

Matanzima's career is covered by Patrick Laurence, Newell M. Stultz, Roger Southall, and Barry Streek and Richard Wicksteed. Several attempts were made to assassinate Matanzima. Winnie's father, Columbus Madikizela, was also the target of assassination. Winnie recalled an incident at home in Orlando when a Pondo man employed by her father as a bus driver, who had arrived with other Pondos to talk to Mandela, walked through to the kitchen, where she was preparing food, and remarked casually how lucky her father had been to escape. 'We shall get him yet,' he said. 'He won't be so lucky next time.'

Lewis Nkosi's essay on the 1950s appears in *Home and Exile*. The assault on Luthuli was described by Hannah Stanton in *Go Well, Stay Well*.

Chapter 8

Benjamin Pogrund writes sympathetically about Sobukwe, whom he came to know as a friend. Bishop Ambrose Reeves gives an independent account of the Sharpeville shooting. Tom Lodge provides a wider view of the crisis. Tambo's journey into exile was organized with the help of Ronald Segal.

Chapter 9

Joe Slovo's essay 'South Africa: No Middle Road' served as a standard guide for all would-be revolutionaries for many years. He adds further detail of the move towards violence in his autobiography. His account of his attempt to blow up the Johannesburg Drill Hall was published in a special edition of a magazine called *Dawn*, produced by the ANC in 1986 to mark the twenty-fifth anniversary of the formation of Umkhonto we Sizwe. Ben Turok published a critical analysis of the armed struggle in 1974. Howard Barrell gives a useful overview of MK from its formation. Mary Benson met Mandela on several occasions while he was underground, as her autobiography records. Details of Mandela's journey abroad in 1962 emerged during the Rivonia trial. Mary Benson described his London visit in her autobiography.

Chapter 10

Millard Shirley retired from the CIA in 1973. According to Gerard Ludi, a police agent who successfully infiltrated the Communist Party and knew him well, Shirley 'had friends in high and low places on both sides of the fence', including a well-informed Indian communist based in Durban. In 1986, the *National Reporter*, a left-wing monitor of US covert activity, identified Don Rickard as the American diplomat who had boasted about his role in Mandela's arrest (Vol. 10, No. 2, August/Winter 1986). In 1990, Joseph Albright reported on Eckel's remarks just as Mandela was making his first visit to the United States.

Several personal accounts describe the perilous existence of the conspirators. As well as producing *The World That Was Ours*, Hilda Bernstein wrote a novel about the early 1960s entitled *Death is Part of the Process*. Other valuable accounts include those by Helen Joseph and AnnMarie Wolpe. Gerard Ludi adds further detail. The government minister speaking on the need for censorship, Jan de Klerk, was F. W. de Klerk's father.

Poqo's activities are covered by Tom Lodge. While Umkhonto operated as an élite group, Poqo took on the form of a mass movement, reaching a peak of influence in 1963. Swanepoel is portrayed in accounts by Joel Carlson, James Kantor and Ruth First, among others. Carlson wrote, 'I saw the essence of the man in his eyes: they were cold, oily and frightening.' Winnie Mandela was later interrogated by Swanepoel.

Chapter 11

The full text of Operation Mayibuye and Sisulu's radio broadcast are reproduced in Thomas Karis et al., Vol. 3. AnnMarie Wolpe described a dinner with the Slovos at a restaurant near Zoo Lake shortly before Joe Slovo's departure. Slovo discusses Operation Mayibuye in 'South Africa: No Middle Road' and in his autobiography. Govan Mbeki, in an interview with the author in 1995, still insisted that it had been given full approval. Michael Dingake describes the circumstances surrounding the arrests of Hlapane, Mthembu and Brian Somana.

Chapter 12

Several accounts of the Rivonia trial have been produced. They include H. H. W. de Villiers's *Rivonia: Operation Mayibuye* and Lauritz Strydom's *Rivonia Unmasked*. Joel Joffe's valuable account was written in 1965 but not published until 1995. Bruno Mtolo gave his version in *Umkonto we Sizwe: The Road to the Left*. James Kantor writes of his experiences in *A Healthy Grave*. Other memorable accounts are provided by AnnMarie Wolpe's *The Long Way Home* and Hilda Bernstein's *The World That Was Ours*. Hlapane, who had been recruited to the Communist Party by Slovo in 1955, was assassinated by an Umkhonto unit in 1982. The activities of the African Resistance Movement are covered by Miles Brokensha and Robert Knowles in *The Fourth of July Raids*. Hugh Lewin, sentenced to seven years' imprisonment for his part in the African Resistance Movement, writes of his experiences in *Bandiet*. Mary Benson, in her autobiography, describes her encounters with Bram Fischer during his underground existence. Lewin records how Fischer, a fellow inmate in Pretoria, was singled out for persecution by prison warders. An Afrikaans newspaper commented on Fischer, *'Die appel het ver van die boom geval'* – 'The apple has fallen far from the tree.'

Chapters 13, 14

Robben Island's history is best dealt with by Nigel Penn and Harriet Deacon in *The Island*, a series of essays compiled by Deacon; Fran Buntman, in the same volume, writes about the life of political prisoners after 1963. Barbara Hutton's *Robben Island* includes maps, diagrams and photographs. Neville Alexander's *Robben Island Prison Dossier, 1964–1974* and his lecture 'Robben Island: A Site of Struggle' provide much valuable material. Personal accounts by Indres Naidoo and Michael Dingake deserve special mention. Jurgen Schadeberg's *Voices from Robben Island* is based on a series of interviews with former prisoners. Ebrahim Ismail Ebrahim was interviewed at length about Robben Island by Heidi Holland. Moses Dlamini, a PAC prisoner, spent two years on Robben Island, arriving there in December 1963. Benjamin Pogrund writes about Sobukwe's time on Robben Island. The visitor to whom Sobukwe complained about forgetting how to speak was Helen Suzman. Suzman writes about her encounters with Mandela and Sobukwe in prison in *In No Uncertain Terms*. James Gregory writes about his growing friendship with Mandela in *Goodbye Bafana*.

Winnie Mandela's account of her life during Mandela's imprisonment is told in *Part of My Soul*. Her book also includes letters from Mandela and interviews conducted by Anne Benjamin with Zindzi and Zenani. Fatima Meer's biography of Mandela includes many of Mandela's letters from prison to family and friends. Emma Gilbey deals with Winnie's involvement with Somana and Mahanyele, and her subsequent trial and imprisonment. Nancy

Harrison provides additional material on Somana, Katzellenbogen and other suspect characters whom Winnie befriended. Joel Carlson gives a graphic account of his battles with security police in *No Neutral Ground*.

Chapter 15

The impact of forced removals is covered by Cosmas Desmond, Laurine Platzky and Cherryl Walker, and the Surplus People Project. In all, more than 3 million people are estimated to have been uprooted from their homes during the apartheid era. The rise of black consciousness is dealt with by Gail M. Gerhart, Millard Arnold, Steve Biko and Donald Woods; and the Soweto revolt by John Kane-Berman, Alan Brooks and Jeremy Brickhill, and Baruch Hirson.

Mac Maharaj gave an extended interview about Robben Island after his release in 1976, which is reproduced in Mandela, *The Struggle is My Life*, and by Sheridan Johns and R. Hunt Davis Jr, who also include accounts by Eddie Daniels (released in 1979), and by Sisulu, Kathrada and Motsoaledi (released in 1989).

Anne Benjamin describes her visits to Brandfort to interview Winnie in *Part of My Soul*. Emma Gilbey recounts the tensions Winnie aroused there in *The Lady*.

Chapters 16, 17, 19

Accounts of the visits by Healey and MacNicoll to Mandela in prison are reproduced in Sheridan Johns and R. Hunt Davis Jr. Buthelezi's early career is dealt with by Gerhard Maré and Georgina Hamilton. The full texts of Mandela's reply to Botha's offer of freedom and his 1989 memorandum to Botha are reproduced in Johns. The accounts of the visits to Mandela by Nicholas Bethell and Samuel Dash are also reproduced there. The Commonwealth Group of Eminent Persons published an account of their endeavours in *Mission to South Africa*. The series of secret negotiations between Mandela and the government, and Mandela's secret excursions from Pollsmoor, are described in Allister Sparks's *Tomorrow is Another Country*, in Patti Waldmeir's *Anatomy of a Miracle* and in James Gregory's *Goodbye Bafana*.

Chapters 18, 22

The most detailed account of Mandela United and its aftermath is provided by Emma Gilbey in *The Lady*. Much of the evidence comes from the trials at the Rand Supreme Court of Jerry Richardson in May 1990 (Case no. 184/89) and Winnie Mandela in April 1991 (Case no. 167/90). Investigations by John Carlin published in the *Independent*, London, and by David Beresford published in the *Guardian*, London, and the *Weekly Mail*,

Johannesburg, deserve special mention. Kenny Kgase's account of Stompie Moeketsi's fate was published in the *Sunday Telegraph*, London, on 22 July 1990.

Chapters 20–26

Willem de Klerk's biography of his brother, *F. W. de Klerk: The Man in His Time*, provides intriguing insights into his character. Other valuable accounts of the de Klerk era and the tortuous negotiations between de Klerk and Mandela are given by Allister Sparks in *Tomorrow is Another Country*, by Patti Waldmeir in *Anatomy of a Miracle* and by David Ottaway in *Chained Together*. Ronnie Kasrils gives his version of the Bisho episode in *'Armed and Dangerous'*. Richard Stengel's account of working with Mandela on his autobiography was published in *The Spectator*, London, on 19 November 1994. Zindzi Mandela gave a frank interview about her family in the March 1995 issue of *Thandi*, Johannesburg.

Chapter 27

The 1994 election is examined in detail by R. W. Johnson and Lawrence Schlemmer. Other accounts include those by Martin Meredith and by Andrew Reynolds.

Chapter 28

The account of Mandela's years in office has made extensive use of South Africa's press and publications of the time, including *The Star*, *Business Day*, *The Citizen*, *The Sowetan*, *Sunday Times*, *Sunday Independent*, *Weekly Mail and Guardian*, *Financial Mail* and *Finance Week*.

SELECT BIBLIOGRAPHY

Abrahams, Peter, *Return to Egoli*, Faber, London, 1953

Adam, Heribert, and Giliomee, Hermann, *Ethnic Power Mobilized: Can South Africa Change?*, Yale University Press, New Haven, 1979

Alexander, Neville, *Robben Island Prison Dossier, 1964–1974*, UCT Press, Cape Town, 1994

— 'Robben Island: A Site of Struggle', in Neville Alexander, Nigel Penn and Harriet Deacon (eds.), *The Politics of Rock and Sand*, UCT Press, Cape Town, 1992

Alexander, Peter, *Alan Paton*, Oxford University Press, Cape Town, 1994

Arnold, Millard (ed.), *The Testimony of Steve Biko*, Maurice Temple Smith, London, 1978

Ashley, Michael, 'African Education and Society in the Nineteenth Century Eastern Cape', in C. Saunders and R. Derricourt (eds.), *Beyond the Cape Frontier: Studies in the History of Transkei and Ciskei*, Longman, London, 1974

Barrell, Howard, *MK: the ANC's Armed Struggle*, Penguin, Harmondsworth, 1990

— *Conscripts to Their Age: ANC Operational Strategy, 1976–86*, doctoral dissertation, Oxford University, 1993

Basner, Miriam, *Am I an African? The Political Memoirs of H. M. Basner*, Witwatersrand University Press, Johannesburg, 1993

Beinart, William, *Twentieth Century South Africa*, Oxford University Press, Oxford, 1994

Benson, Mary, *The African Patriots: The Story of the African National Congress of South Africa*, Faber, London, 1963; republished as *South Africa: The Struggle for a Birthright*, Penguin, Harmondsworth, 1966

— *Chief Albert Luthuli of South Africa*, Oxford University Press, Oxford, 1963

— *Nelson Mandela: The Man and the Movement*, Penguin, Harmondsworth, 1994

— *A Far Cry: The Making of a South African*, Ravan Press, Johannesburg, 1996

Bernstein, Hilda, *The World That Was Ours*, Heinemann, London, 1967

— *Death is Part of the Process*, Grafton, London, 1986

— *The Rift: The Exile Experience of South Africans*, Cape, London, 1994

Bethell, Nicholas, 'An Interview with Nelson Mandela,' in Mark A. Uhlig (ed.), *Apartheid in Crisis*, Penguin, Harmondsworth, 1986

Biko, Steve, *I Write What I Like*, Bowerdean Press, London, 1986

Bozzoli, Belinda (ed.), *Labour, Townships and Protest*, Ravan Press, Johannesburg, 1979

Brokensha, Miles, and Knowles, Robert, *The Fourth of July Raids*, Simondium, Cape Town, 1965

Brooks, Alan, and Brickhill, Jeremy, *Whirlwind Before the Storm*, International Defence and Aid Fund for Southern Africa, London, 1980

Bundy, Colin, *The Rise and Fall of the South African Peasantry*, University of California Press, Berkeley, 1979

Bunting, Brian, *Moses Kotane: South African Revolutionary*, Inkululeko Publications, London, 1975

Cammack, Diana, *The Rand at War, 1899–1902*, James Currey, London, 1990

Carlson, Joel, *No Neutral Ground*, Davis-Poynter, London, 1973

Carter, Gwendolen M., Karis, Thomas, and Stultz, Newell M., *South Africa's Transkei: The Politics of Domestic Colonialism*, Northwestern University Press, Evanston, 1967

Commonwealth Group of Eminent Persons, *Mission to South Africa*, Penguin, Harmondsworth, 1986

Coplan, David, *In Township Tonight: South Africa's Black City Music and Theatre*, Ravan Press, Johannesburg, 1985

— 'The African Performer and the Johannesburg Entertainment Industry: The Struggle for African Culture on the Witwatersrand', in Belinda Bozzoli (ed.), *Labour, Townships and Protest*, Ravan Press, Johannesburg, 1979

Crocker, Chester, *High Noon in Southern Africa: Making Peace in a Rough Neighbourhood*, Jonathan Ball, Johannesburg, 1992

Davenport, T. R. H., *South Africa: A Modern History*, fourth edition, Macmillan, London, 1991

Davis, Stephen M., *Apartheid's Rebels: Inside South Africa's Hidden War*, Yale University Press, New Haven, 1987

Deacon, Harriet (ed.), *The Island: A History of Robben Island, 1488–1990*, David Philip, Cape Town, 1992

de Kiewiet, C. W., *A History of South Africa: Social and Economic*, Oxford University Press, Oxford, 1941

de Klerk, W. A., *The Puritans in Africa: The Story of Afrikanerdom*, Rex Collings, London, 1975 de Klerk, Willem, *F. W. Klerk: The Man in His Time*, Jonathan Ball, Johannesburg, 1991

Desmond, Cosmas, *The Discarded People: An Account of African Resettlement in South Africa*, Penguin, Harmondsworth, 1971

de Villiers, Dirk, and de Villiers, Johanna, *PW*, Tafelberg, Cape Town, 1984

de Villiers, H. H. W., *Rivonia: Operation Mayibuye*, Afrikaanse Pers-Boekhandel, Johannesburg, 1964

Dingake, Michael, *My Fight Against Apartheid*, Kliptown Books, London, 1987

d'Oliveira, John, *Vorster – the Man*, Stanton, Johannesburg, 1977

Dlamini, Moses, *Robben Island: Hell-Hole*, Spokesman, Nottingham, 1984

Driver, C. J., *Patrick Duncan: South African and Pan-African*, Heinemann, London, 1980

du Toit, André, 'No Chosen People: The Myth of the Calvinist Origins of Afrikaner Nationalism and Racial Ideology', *American Historical Review*, 88, October 1983

Elphick, Richard, and Giliomee, Hermann (eds.), *The Shaping of South African Society, 1652–1820*, Longman, London, 1979

Feit, Edward, *African Opposition in South Africa: The Failure of Passive Resistance*, Hoover Institution, Stanford, 1967

— *Urban Revolt in South Africa, 1960–1964*, Northwestern University Press, Evanston, 1971

First, Ruth, *One Hundred and Seventeen Days: An Account of Confinement and Interrogation under the South African Ninety-day Detention Law*, Penguin, Harmondsworth, 1965

Forman, Lionel, and Sachs, E. S., *The South African Treason Trial*, Calder, London, 1957

Gerhart, Gail M., *Black Power in South Africa: The Evolution of an Ideology*, University of California Press, Berkeley, 1978

Gevisser, Mark, *Portraits of Power: Profiles in a Changing South Africa*, David Philip, Cape Town, 1996

Gilbey, Emma, *The Lady: The Life and Times of Winnie Mandela*, Cape, London, 1993

Gregory, James, *Goodbye Bafana: Nelson Mandela, My Prisoner, My Friend*, Headline, London, 1995

Harington, A. L., *Sir Harry Smith: Bungling Hero*, Tafelberg, Cape Town, 1980

Harrison, Nancy, *Winnie Mandela: Mother of a Nation*, Grafton, London, 1986

Hepple, Alexander, *Verwoerd*, Penguin, Harmondsworth, 1967

Hirson, Baruch, *Year of Fire, Year of Ash: The Soweto Revolt, Roots of a Revolution?*, Zed Press, London, 1979

— *Revolutions in My Life*, Witwatersrand University Press, Johannesburg, 1995

Holland, Heidi, *The Struggle: A History of the African National Congress*, Grafton, London, 1989

Huddleston, Father Trevor, C. R., *Naught for Your Comfort*, Collins, London, 1956

Hutchinson, Alfred, *Road to Ghana*, Gollancz, London, 1960

Hutton, Barbara, *Robben Island: Symbol of Resistance*, Mayibuye Books, Bellville, 1994

Joffe, Joel, *The Rivonia Story*, Mayibuye Books, Bellville, 1995

Johns, Sheridan, and Davis Jr, R. Hunt, *Mandela, Tambo and the ANC: The Struggle Against Apartheid, 1948–1990 – a Documentary Survey*, Oxford University Press, New York, 1991

Johnson, R. W., and Schlemmer, Lawrence, *Launching Democracy in South Africa: The First Open Election, April 1994*, Yale University Press, New Haven, 1996

Johnson, Shaun, *Strange Days Indeed*, Bantam, Johannesburg, 1993

Joseph, Helen, *If This be Treason*, Deutsch, London, 1963

— *Tomorrow's Sun*, Hutchinson, London, 1966

— *Side by Side: The Autobiography of Helen Joseph*, Zed Books, London, 1986

Kane-Berman, John, *Soweto: Black Revolt, White Reaction*, Ravan Press, Johannesburg, 1978

Kantor, James, *A Healthy Grave*, Hamish Hamilton, London, 1967

Karis, Thomas, *The Treason Trial in South Africa*, Hoover Institution Bibliographical Series, XXIII, Hoover Institution on War, Revolution and Peace, Stanford University, 1965

Karis, Thomas, Carter, Gwendolen, and Gerhart, Gail M. (eds.), *From Protest to Challenge: A Documentary History of African Politics in South Africa*, 4 vols., Hoover Institution Press, Stanford, 1972–7

Kasrils, Ronnie, *'Armed and Dangerous': My Undercover Struggle Against Apartheid*, Heinemann, Oxford, 1993

Keane, Fergal, *The Bondage of Fear: A Journey Through the Last White Empire*, Viking, London, 1994

Kenney, Henry, *Architect of Apartheid: H. F. Verwoerd – an Appraisal*, Jonathan Ball, Johannesburg, 1980

Kerr, Alexander, *Fort Hare, 1915–48: The Evolution of an African College*, C. Hurst, London, 1968

Koch, Eddie, 'Without Visible Means of Subsistence. Slumyard Culture in Johannesburg, 1918–1940', in Belinda Bozzoli (ed.), *Town and Countryside in the Transvaal*, Ravan Press, Johannesburg, 1983

Kuper, Leo, *Passive Resistance in South Africa*, Cape, London, 1956

Kuzwayo, Ellen, *Call Me Woman*, The Women's Press, London, 1985

Laurence, Patrick, *The Transkei: South Africa's Politics of Partition*, Ravan Press, Johannesburg, 1976

Lazerson, Joshua N., *Against the Tide: Whites in the Struggle Against Apartheid*, Mayibuye Books, Bellville, 1994

Lelyveld, Joseph, *Move Your Shadow: South Africa, Black and White*, Michael Joseph, London, 1986

Lerumo, A., *Fifty Fighting Years: The Communist Party of South Africa, 1921–71*, Inkululeko Publications, London, 1971

Lewin, Hugh, *Bandiet: Seven Years in a South African Prison*, Barrie and Jenkins, London, 1974

Lipton, Merle, *Capitalism and Apartheid: South Africa, 1910–1984*, Gower, Maurice Temple Smith, Aldershot, 1985

Lodge, Tom, *Black Politics in South Africa Since 1945*, Longman, London, 1983

Ludi, Gerard, *Operation Q-018*, Nasionale Boekhandel, Cape Town, 1969

Luthuli, Albert, *Let My People Go*, Fount, London, 1982

Macmillan, Harold, *Pointing the Way, 1959–61*, Macmillan, London, 1972

Mandela, Nelson, *No Easy Walk to Freedom*, Heinemann, London, 1965

— *Nelson Mandela Speaks: Forging a Democratic, Nonracial South Africa*, Pathfinder, New York, 1993

— *Long Walk to Freedom*, Little, Brown & Co., London, 1994

Mandela, Winnie, *Part of My Soul*, Penguin, Harmondsworth, 1985

Mandy, Nigel, *A City Divided: Johannesburg and Soweto*, Macmillan, London, 1984

Maré, Gerhard, and Hamilton, Georgina, *An Appetite for Power: Buthelezi's Inkatha and the Politics of Legal Resistance*, Ravan Press, Johannesburg, 1987

Marks, Shula, and Trapido, Stanley (eds.), *Industrialization and Social Change in South Africa: African Class Formation, Culture and Consciousness, 1870–1930*, Longman, London, 1982

Matanzima, Kaizer D., *Independence My Way*, Foreign Affairs Association, Pretoria, 1976

Matthews, Z. K., *Freedom for My People*, Rex Collings, London, 1981

Maylam, Paul, *A History of the African People of South Africa*, David Philip, Cape Town, 1986

Mbeki, Govan, *South Africa: The Peasant's Revolt*, Penguin, Harmondsworth, 1964

— *Learning from Robben Island: The Prison Writings of Govan Mbeki*, David Philip, Cape Town, 1991

— *The Struggle for Liberation in South Africa*, David Philip, Cape Town, 1992

Meer, Fatima, *Higher Than Hope: The Authorized Biography of Nelson Mandela*, Penguin, Harmondsworth, 1988

Meredith, Martin, *In the Name of Apartheid: South Africa in the Post-war Era*, Hamish Hamilton, London, 1988

— *South Africa's New Era: The 1994 Election*, Mandarin, London, 1994

Minnaar, Anthony, Liebenberg, Ian, and Schutte, Charl, *The Hidden Hand: Covert Operations in South Africa*, HSRC Publications, Johannesburg, 1994

Modisane, Bloke, *Blame Me on History*, Thames and Hudson, London, 1963

Moodie, T. Dunbar, *The Rise of Afrikanerdom: Power, Apartheid and the Afrikaner Civil Religion*, University of California Press, Berkeley, 1975

Mphahlele, Ezekiel, *Down Second Avenue*, Faber, London, 1959

Mtolo, Bruno, *Umkonto we Sizwe: The Road to the Left*, Drakensberg Press, Durban, 1966

Naidoo, Indres, *Island in Chains*, Penguin, Harmondsworth, 1982

Ngubane, Jordan, *An African Explains Apartheid*, Pall Mall Press, London, 1963

Nicol, Mike, *A Good-looking Corpse: The World of Drum – Jazz and Gangsters, Hope and Defiance in the Townships of South Africa*, Secker and Warburg, London, 1991

Nkosi, Lewis, *Home and Exile*, Longman, London, 1983

Odendaal, André, *Vukani Bantu! The Beginnings of Black Protest Politics in South Africa to 1912*, David Philip, Cape Town, 1984

O'Meara, Dan, 'The 1946 African Mineworkers Strike', *Journal of Commonwealth and Comparative Politics*, XIII, 2, 1975

— *Volkscapitalisme: Class, Capital and Ideology in the Development of Afrikaner Nationalism, 1934–1948*, Cambridge University Press, Cambridge, 1983

Ottaway, David, *Chained Together: Mandela, De Klerk and the Struggle to Remake South Africa*, Times Books, New York, 1993

Pakenham, Thomas, *The Boer War*, Weidenfeld and Nicolson, London, 1979

Paton, Alan, *Cry, the Beloved Country*, Penguin, Harmondsworth, 1988

Pauw, B. A., *Christianity and Xhosa Tradition*, Oxford University Press, Cape Town, 1975

Peires, J. B., *The House of Phalo: A History of the Xhosa People in the Days of Their Independence*, Ravan Press, Johannesburg, 1981

— *The Dead Will Arise: Nongqawuse and the Great Xhosa Cattle-killing Movement of 1856–7*, Ravan Press, Johannesburg, 1989

Plaatje, Sol T., *Native Life in South Africa*, Ravan Press, Johannesburg, 1982

Platzky, Laurine, and Walker, Cherryl, *The Surplus People: Forced Removals in South Africa*, Ravan Press, Johannesburg, 1985

Pogrund, Benjamin, *Sobukwe and Apartheid*, Jonathan Bell, Johannesburg, 1990

Price, Robert M., *The Apartheid State in Crisis*, Oxford University Press, New York, 1991

Pringle, Thomas, *Narrative of a Residence in South Africa*, Struik, Cape Town, 1966

Proctor, André, 'Class Struggle, Segregation and the City: A History of Sophiatown, 1905–1940', in Belinda Bozzoli (ed.), *Labour, Townships and Protest*, Ravan Press, Johannesburg, 1979

The Reader's Digest Illustrated History of South Africa, Reader's Digest, Cape Town, 1994

Reeves, Ambrose, *Shooting at Sharpeville*, Gollancz, London, 1960

— *South Africa: Yesterday and Tomorrow*, Gollancz, London, 1962

Resha, Maggie, *My Life in the Struggle*, Congress of South African Writers, Johannesburg, 1991

Reynolds, Andrew (ed.), *Election '94, South Africa*, David Philip, Cape Town, 1994

Robertson, Janet, *Liberalism in South Africa, 1948–1963*, Clarendon Press, Oxford, 1971

Roux, Eddie, and Win, *Rebel Pity: The Life of Eddie Roux*, Rex Collings, London, 1970

Roux, Edward, *Time Longer Than Rope*, second edition, University of Wisconsin Press, Madison, 1964

Russell, Diana E. H., *Lives of Courage: Women for a New South Africa*, Basic Books, New York, 1989

Sachs, E. S., *Rebel's Daughters*, MacGibbon and Kee, London, 1961

Sampson, Anthony, *Drum: A Venture into the New Africa*, Collins, London, 1956

— *The Treason Cage: The Opposition on Trial in South Africa*, Heinemann, London, 1958

— *Black and Gold: Tycoons, Revolutionaries and Apartheid*, Hodder and Stoughton, London, 1987

Schadeberg, Jurgen, *Voices from Robben Island*, Ravan Press, Johannesburg, 1994

Scott, Michael, *A Time to Speak*, Faber, London, 1958

Segal, Ronald, *Into Exile*, Cape, London, 1963

Simons, H. J., and Simons, R. E., *Class and Colour in South Africa, 1850–1950*, Penguin, Harmondsworth, 1969

Slovo, Gillian, *Every Secret Thing*, Little, Brown & Co., London, 1997

Slovo, Joe, 'South Africa: No Middle Road', in Basil Davidson, Joe Slovo and Anthony Wilkinson, *Southern Africa: The New Politics of Revolution*, Penguin, Harmondsworth, 1976

— *The Unfinished Autobiography*, Ravan Press, Johannesburg, 1995

Southall, Roger, *South Africa's Transkei: The Political Economy of an 'Independent' Bantustan*, Heinemann, London, 1982

Sparks, Allister, *Tomorrow is Another Country*, Struik, Johannesburg, 1994

Stadler, Alfred, 'Birds in the Cornfield: Squatter Movements in Johannesburg, 1944–1947', in Belinda Bozzoli (ed.), *Labour, Townships and Protest*, Ravan Press, Johannesburg, 1979

— 'A Long Way to Walk', University of the Witwatersrand African Studies Institute seminar paper, 1979

Stanton, Hannah, *Go Well, Stay Well*, Hodder, London, 1961

Stapleton, Timothy J., *Maqoma: Xhosa Resistance to Colonial Advance*, Jonathan Ball, Johannesburg, 1994

Streek, Barry, and Wicksteed, Richard, *Render Unto Kaizer: A Transkei Dossier*, Ravan Press, Johannesburg, 1981

Strydom, Lauritz, *Rivonia Unmasked*, Voortrekkerpers, Johannesburg, 1964

Stultz, Newell M., *Transkei's Half Loaf: Race Separation in South Africa*, Yale University Press, New Haven, 1979

Surplus People Project, *Forced Removals in South Africa*, 5 vols., Surplus People Project, Cape Town, 1983

Suzman, Helen, *In No Uncertain Terms*, Jonathan Bell, Johannesburg, 1993

Swan, Maureen, *Gandhi: The South African Experience*, Ravan Press, Johannesburg, 1985

— 'Ideology in Organized Indian Politics, 1891–1948', in Shula Marks and Stanley Trapido (eds.), *The Politics of Race, Class and Nationalism in Twentieth Century South Africa*, Longman, London, 1987

Taylor, Rev. J., *Christianity and the Natives of South Africa*, Lovedale Institution Press, 1928

Thompson, Leonard M., *A History of South Africa*, Yale University Press, New Haven, 1994

Turok, Ben, *Strategic Problems in South Africa's Liberation Struggle*, LSM Press, Richmond, Canada, 1974

Van Jaarsveld, F. A., *The Awakening of Afrikaner Nationalism, 1868–1881*, Human and Rousseau, Cape Town, 1961

— *The Afrikaner's Interpretation of South African History*, Simondium Publishers, Cape Town, 1964

Van Onselen, Charles, *Studies in the Social and Economic History of the Witwatersrand, 1886–1914: Vol. 1, New Babylon; Vol. 2, New Nineveh*, Longman, Harlow, 1982

Villa-Vicencio, Charles, *The Spirit of Freedom: South African Leaders on Religion and Politics*, University of California Press, Berkeley, 1996

Waldmeir, Patti, *Anatomy of a Miracle: The End of Apartheid and the Birth of a New South Africa*, Viking, London, 1997

Walshe, Peter, *The Rise of African Nationalism in South Africa: The African National Congress, 1912–1952*, C. Hurst, London, 1970

Willan, Brian, *Sol Plaatje: South African Nationalist*, Heinemann, London, 1984

Wilson, Monica, and Thompson, Leonard (eds.), *The Oxford History of South Africa*, 2 vols., Clarendon Press, Oxford, 1969, 1971

Wolpe, AnnMarie, *The Long Way Home*, David Philip, Cape Town, 1994

Woods, Donald, *Biko*, Paddington Press, London, 1978

INDEX

'M' indicates Nelson Mandela and 'SA' South Africa.

Journal of Psychiatric

10/30/81   Oct 1980   Vol. 53